Current Readings on Money, Banking, and Financial Markets

1987 Edition

Current Readings on Money, Banking, and Financial Markets

1987 Edition

Edited by

James A. Wilcox
School of Business Administration
University of California, Berkeley

Frederic S. Mishkin
Consulting Editor
Columbia University

 Little, Brown and Company   Boston   Toronto

Library of Congress Cataloging-in-Publication Data

Current readings on money, banking, and financial markets.

1. Finance. 2. Money. 3. Banks and banking. 4. International finance.
I. Wilcox, James Allen, 1952-   . II. Mishkin, Frederic S.
HG175.C87   1987   332   87-4116
ISBN 0-316-94020-8

Library of Congress Catalog Card No. 87–4116

ISBN 0-316-94020-8

9 8 7 6 5 4 3 2 1

MV

Published simultaneously in Canada
by Little, Brown & Company (Canada) Limited

Printed in the United States of America

Preface

Keeping abreast of developments in money, banking, and financial markets is challenging and exciting. In the past few years these developments have been rapid and important: A vast array of new financial instruments has appeared; deregulation of financial institutions has dramatically increased managerial latitude and blurred traditional distinctions between institutions; record-breaking numbers of banks and thrift institutions have failed; the thrust of monetary policy and even its basic underpinnings have shifted in the last decade; and financial markets have become increasingly internationalized. The readings in this book explore the driving forces behind these changes, document their extent, explain why these developments have altered the basic operation of many institutions and markets, and discuss the likely evolution of financial instruments and institutions in the future.

The material in this book is appropriate for courses both on money and banking and on financial markets and institutions and is designed to be accessible to students in undergraduate economics departments and business schools as well as in MBA programs. Used in conjunction with a textbook, this reader provides students with the necessary exposure to modern principles, the current institutional environment, and up-to-date facts.

Three features of this collection of readings make it a genuine complement to the primary textbook used in such courses: its currency, its coverage, and its conciseness. Students and instructors alike will value the book's currency: Almost half the readings were published in 1986. This means that the most recent data, regulations, issues, and opinions are here. No textbook can match that. Our plan to update the book every year ensures that the need for this type of currency will always be met. The readings also cover institutions, markets, instruments, and operations in more detail than textbooks normally do, and the scope of topics included is broader than that in many readers. Finally, the book is concise. Succinct treatments of each topic have been chosen, making the reader about half as long as such anthologies typically are and allowing the entire range of topics addressed to be handled, if desired, in a single course. This conciseness also makes the reader less expensive than others. For many, the purchase price will be less than the cost of having the same collection photocopied, while the hassle and uncertainty of copyright regulations are avoided.

The collection aims for both flexibility and readability. The six sections roughly parallel the most widely used textbooks in money and banking, financial institutions, and financial markets courses. Readings within sections, or even entire sections, can be reordered or omitted if necessary to follow more closely the order of treatment in the textbook or the interests of the instructor.

To make the anthology more readable, most of the articles selected presume little or no familiarity with the jargon of the field but instead strive to teach some of that jargon within the reading. (Some of the readings even have a short glossary at the end.)

Half the book's material is contained in the first two sections, which together cover financial markets, instruments, and institutions as well as the determination of interest rates. The continuing, dramatic changes in these areas dictate that a large share of the book be devoted to them. Section One, Financial Markets and Interest Rates, leads off with an article that clearly develops the principles of diversification and of risk-return trade-offs. The next three readings describe the workings of the long-running government securities market, the features of more recently developed securities in the secondary mortgage market, and the emergence of "securitization" of all sorts of assets. Next, attention turns to the recognition, measurement, and avoidance of interest rate risk in financial institutions. The last two articles attempt to identify the sources of high real interest rates in the 1980s.

Section Two, Financial Institutions, covers the evolution and recent deregulation of the financial institution industry. These readings present the facts and arguments about interstate banking, individual and aggregate bank and thrift failures, and the effects of deposit insurance and the problems the deposit insurance funds now face.

Section Three, The Money Supply, shows the inroads new accounts have made at depository institutions and how, in practice, their existence makes the Federal Reserve's job more difficult. The last article in this section documents the relatively slow penetration of electronic funds transfers (EFT) at the retail level, but also makes a case for their eventual importance due to cost advantages.

Sections Four and Five address the short-run and long-run aspects of monetary policy. Central Banking and Monetary Policy illustrates how the Federal Reserve actually operates. The first two readings here describe, with numerous examples, how and why open market operations are conducted daily and the purposes and operation of the Fed's discount window. The last two selections explain, respectively, why and to what extent monetary policy tries to adapt to changes in the money-income, or velocity, relationship.

Section Five, Monetary Theory, has a decidedly long-run focus. Milton Friedman argues that only institutional redesign will lead to consistently superior performance by the Fed. Robert Lucas and Thomas Sargent argue that the conventional models of the macroeconomy used by the Fed and other policymakers have led, and will lead in the future, to serious policy failures. Nobel Laureate James Buchanan then outlines his position that current institutional arrangements consistently lead to short-run policies that are ultimately judged to be failures in the long run.

The final section, International Finance, provides the international analogue to earlier sections. The workings of both the foreign exchange and Eurodollar markets are described. The current short-run pressures and long-run implications of the international debt crisis are probed. Finally, the difficulty and necessity of applying the portfolio approach to international lending are discussed.

In putting together this book, I have had the benefit of working with an especially talented group of people. Special thanks go to the following for their insightful comments on early drafts: Zena Seldon, University of Wisconsin, La Crosse; Morgan Lynge, University of Illinois; Beverly Lapham, University of Minnesota; John Knudsen, University of Idaho; Steve Davis, University of Chicago; Beverly Hadaway, University of Texas, Austin; James Wible, University of New Hampshire; Robert Schweitzer, University of Delaware; Ron Balvers, University of Notre Dame; Scott Bloom, North Dakota State University; Larry Kruse, Franklin and Marshall; and Yoktone Benjauthrit, Washington State University. Thanks also go to Virginia Shine, Paul Santoro, Carolyn Woznick, and Elizabeth Hunt at Little, Brown for their help with production of the book; to Stephanie Lee for her all-round help; to Rick Mishkin for his ever-ebullient encouragement and good sense; and especially to Denise Clinton at Little, Brown for her grace under pressure.

James A. Wilcox

Acknowledgments

Article 1: "Modern Financial Theory," Richard R. Simonds, *MSU Business Topics*, Winter 1978, pp. 54–63. Reprinted by permission of the College of Business, Michigan State University.

Article 2: "The Government Securities Market: Playing Field for Repos," Richard Syron and Sheila L. Tschinkel, Federal Reserve Bank of Atlanta *Economic Review*, September 1985, pp. 10–19.

Article 3: "A Primer on Mortgage-Backed Securities," John R. Brick, *Bankers Magazine*, January/February 1984, pp. 44–52. Copyright 1984 John R. Brick. All rights reserved. Reproduced with permission.

Article 4: "Securitization and Banking," Randall J. Pozdena, Federal Reserve Bank of San Francisco *Weekly Letter*, July 4, 1986, pp. 1–3.

Article 5: "Measuring Interest Rate Risk: What Do We Really Know?" James E. McNulty. Reprinted from the *Journal of Retail Banking*, Spring/Summer 1986, Vol. VIII, Nos. 1 and 2, pp. 49–58. © Copyright 1986 Lafferty Publications, 3945 Holcomb Bridge Rd., Suite 301, Norcross, GA 30092. By permission.

Article 6: "Hedging Interest Rate Risk with Financial Futures: Some Basic Principles," Michael T. Belongia and G.J. Santoni, Federal Reserve Bank of St. Louis *Review*, October 1984, pp. 15–25.

Article 7: "Interest Rates Swaps: a New Tool for Managing Risk," Jan G. Loeys, Federal Reserve Bank of Philadelphia *Business Review*, May/June 1985, pp. 17–25.

Article 8: "Real Interest Rates: What Accounts for Their Recent Rise," A. Steven Holland, Federal Reserve Bank of St. Louis *Review*, December 1984, pp. 18–29.

Article 9: "Three Views of Real Interest," Adrian W. Throop, Federal Reserve Bank of San Francisco *Weekly Letter*, November 7, 1986, pp. 1–3.

Article 10: "Technological and Regulatory Forces in the Developing Fusion of Financial Services Competition," Edward J. Kane, *Journal of Finance*, July 1984, pp. 759–772. Reprinted by permission.

Article 11: "The Impact of Geographic Expansion in Banking: Some Axioms to Grind," Douglas D. Evanoff and Diana Fortier, Federal Reserve Bank of Chicago *Economic Perspectives*, May/June 1986, pp. 24–38.

Article 12: "Recent Bank Failures," Anthony W. Cyrnak, Federal Reserve Bank of San Francisco *Weekly Letter*, April 11, 1986, pp. 1–3.

Article 13: "Deposit Insurance and Bank Failures," George J. Benston, Federal Reserve Bank of Atlanta *Economic Review*, March 1983, pp. 4–17.

Article 14: "Alternative Methods for Assessing Risk-Based Deposit Insurance Premiums," James B. Thomson, Federal Reserve Bank of Cleveland *Economic Commentary*, September 15, 1986, pp. 1–4.

Article 15: "Regulation of Banks' Equity Capital," Larry D. Wall, Federal Reserve Bank of Atlanta *Economic Review*, November 1985, pp. 4–18.

Article 16: "The Thrift Industry's Rough Road Ahead," James R. Barth, Donald J. Bisenius, R. Dan Brumbaugh, Jr., and Daniel Sauerhaft. Reprinted with permission of publisher, M. E. Sharpe, Inc., 80 Business Park Drive, Armonk, New York 10504, USA, from the September/October 1986 issue of *Challenge*.

Article 17: " 'Recapitalizing' the FSLIC," Frederick T. Furlong, Federal Reserve Bank of San Francisco *Weekly Letter*, October 24, 1986, pp. 1–3.

Article 18: "Examining the Recent Surge in M1," Bharat Trehan and Carl Walsh, Federal Reserve Bank of San Francisco *Weekly Letter*, November 15, 1985, pp. 1–3.

Article 19: "Should Money Be Redefined?," Brian Motley, Federal Reserve Bank of San Francisco *Weekly Letter*, September 5, 1986, pp. 1–3.

The views expressed in the articles from Federal Reserve Bank publications are those of the authors and not necessarily those of the Federal Reserve Bank or the Federal Reserve System.

Article 20: "Interest Checking," Gary C. Zimmerman and Michael C. Keeley, Federal Reserve Bank of San Francisco *Weekly Letter*, November 14, 1986, pp. 1–3.

Article 21: "The Evolution of Retail EFT Networks," Steven D. Felgran and R. Edward Ferguson, Federal Reserve Bank of Boston *New England Economic Review*, July/August 1986, pp. 42–56.

Article 22: "Federal Reserve Open Market Techniques," Howard L. Roth, Federal Reserve Bank of Kansas City *Economic Review*, March 1986, pp. 3–15.

Article 23: "The Discount Window," David L. Mengle, Federal Reserve Bank of Richmond *Economic Review*, May/June 1986, pp. 2–10.

Article 24: " 'Financial Crises' and the Role of the Lender of Last Resort," James R. Barth and Robert E. Keleher, Federal Reserve Bank of Atlanta *Economic Review*, January 1984, pp. 58–67.

Article 25: "Why Does Velocity Matter?," Daniel Thornton, Federal Reserve Bank of St. Louis *Review*, December 1983, pp. 5–13.

Article 26: "What Has Happened to M1?," Herb Taylor, Federal Reserve Bank of Philadelphia *Business Review*, September/October 1986, pp. 3–14.

Article 27: "The Case for Overhauling the Federal Reserve," Milton Friedman, *Challenge*, July/August 1985, pp. 4–12. Reprinted by permission of Hoover Press.

Article 28: "After Keynesian Macroeconomics," Robert E. Lucas, Jr., and Thomas J. Sargent, Federal Reserve Bank of Minneapolis *Quarterly Review*, Spring 1979, pp. 1–16.

Article 29: "Can Policy Activism Succeed? A Public Choice Perspective," James M. Buchanan, from R. W. Hafer, ed., *The Monetary versus Fiscal Policy Debate* (Totowa, NJ: Rowman & Allenheld, 1986), pp. 139–149. Reprinted by permission.

Article 30: "Central Bank Behavior and Credibility: Some Recent Theoretical Developments," Alex Cukierman, Federal Reserve Bank of St. Louis *Review*, May 1986, pp. 5–17.

Article 31: "Higher Deficit Policies Lead to Higher Inflation," Preston J. Miller, Federal Reserve Bank of Minneapolis *Quarterly Review*, Winter 1983, pp. 8–19.

Article 32: "A Guide to Foreign Exchange Markets," Alec Chrystal, Federal Reserve Bank of St. Louis *Review*, March 1984, pp. 5–18. Table 1 (left): Reprinted by permission of *The Wall Street Journal*, © Dow Jones & Company, Inc. 1983. All rights reserved. Table 1 (right): Reprinted by permission from the *Financial Times*, 8 September 1983. Table 3: Reprinted by permission of *The Wall Street Journal*, © Dow Jones & Company, Inc. 1984. All rights reserved.

Article 33: "Current Illusions about the International Debt Crisis," Lawrence J. Brainard, *The World Economy*, March 1985, Vol. 8, No. 1, pp. 1–9. Reprinted by permission of the Trade Policy Research Centre.

Article 34: "Eurodollars," Marvin Goodfriend, *Instruments of the Money Market*, Federal Bank of Richmond 1986, pp. 53–64.

Article 35: "Country Risk, Portfolio Decisions, and Regulation in International Bank Lending," Ingo Walter, *Journal of Banking and Finance*, March 1981, Vo. 5:1, pp. 77–92. Reprinted by permission of North-Holland Information & Business Division, a branch of Elsevier Science Publishers B.V.

Contents

Section One

Financial Markets and Interest Rates

Most financial institutions face interest rate risk in that the maturity dates of their assets and liabilities differ. They hold long-term assets whose yields may change slowly, partially, or not at all over the life of the asset. Typically these assets are funded with short-term liabilities whose yields may change frequently and by large amounts. The readings in this section demonstrate how various financial instruments can be used to lessen interest rate risk and how the markets for these instruments operate.

In the first article, "Modern Financial Theory," Richard R. Simonds introduces the concepts that underlie the diversification of portfolios, the relation between returns and risks, and market efficiency. He begins by demonstrating simply why portfolio risk can be reduced through diversification and showing the optimal amount of diversification. The implications of these results are then used to demonstrate why the return on an asset rises not with its own riskiness, but with the amount of extra risk that the asset imparts to the entire portfolio. Next, Simonds defines various concepts of market efficiency and briefly notes some of the evidence for their relevance. The article concludes by describing applications of each of the results developed here.

The second article, "The Government Securities Market: Playing Field for Repos" by Richard Syron and Sheila L. Tschinkel, delves into the workings of the market for government securities. The features of Treasury bills, notes, and bonds are first presented. Next, the authors describe the auction process the Federal Reserve uses, on behalf of the Treasury, to sell new Treasury issues. The article also demonstrates how yields on various Treasury issues are calculated from their prices. The various roles that government securities dealers play in this market are detailed. Finally, the article shows how the "book-entry" system of electronic bookkeeping works.

Over the last few years, the secondary mortgage market has grown extraordinarily. In "A Primer on Mortgage-Backed Securities," John R. Brick explains the differences between the three major classes of mortgage-backed securities: pass-through certificates, mortgage-backed bonds, and pay-through bonds (including the recently developed CMO, collateralized mortgage obligation). For each class, he identifies the types of mortgages it is backed by, the legal and accounting status of its underlying mortgages, its credit rating, and its advantages and disadvantages for the managers of financial institutions.

In the mid-1980s, not only mortgages but also car loans, credit card balances, and a number of other, previously nonmarketed financial assets have come to be either sold en masse or used as collateral for marketable debt. In the fourth article, "Securitization and Banking," Randall J. Pozdena documents the enormous increase in the range and the dollar value of assets that are now being "securitized." He then points to the forces propelling this phenomenon. Noteworthy are the development of information processing, the explicit government subsidies provided to the mortgage market, and the implicit subsidies that may arise through deposit insurance.

Before interest rate risk can be managed, it must be measured. In "Measuring Interest Rate Risk: What Do We Really Know?" James E. McNulty illustrates how to measure risk with each of the two major techniques that sophisticated managers currently use: gap analysis and duration analysis. He then assesses the relative virtues and vices of each method, arguing that since the strengths of one tend to be the weaknesses of the other, both should be used. In effect, the manager chooses a portfolio of methods to use.

The article by Michael T. Belongia and G. J. Santoni, "Hedging Interest Rate Risk with Financial Futures: Some Basic Principles," works through examples to show how maturity mismatches between assets and liabilities expose a financial institution's net worth to interest rate risk. The authors then discuss the principles of hedging and demonstrate how Treasury bill futures contracts can be used to insulate a firm from such risk. They also make two distinctions that are often forgotten in practice. The first is between the commonly used tactic that hedges cash flows and the tactic that hedges the value of the firm. The second distinction is between futures positions that reduce and those that increase interest rate risk.

Though financial futures are often helpful in reducing interest rate risk, they are not perfect. One problem is that contracts that specify delivery a year or more in the future are either expensive or simply not available. Another difficulty encountered is that the specific interest rate whose risk the institution is trying to hedge will not move perfectly with the Treasury bill rate. These are some of the shortcomings that led to the explosive growth of the interest rate swaps market. The article by Jan G. Loeys, "Interest Rate Swaps: A New Tool for Managing Risk," uses a detailed example to illustrate how a typical swap of fixed for floating interest payments works and why such a deal can be advantageous to both parties.

A. Steven Holland holds that, by historical standards, interest rates during the first half of the 1980s were very high. In "Real Interest Rates: What Accounts for Their Recent Rise?" he shows that this is true for interest rates short or long, nominal or real, before-tax or after-tax. Holland points to erratic monetary policy as the primary source of these high real rates. By increasing economic uncertainty, such policy has generated larger risk premiums and concomitantly higher after-tax real interest rates. He also contends that real rates were driven up and down in the 1980s by ups and downs in aggregate economic activity. At the same time, Holland contends that there is less evidence that either increases in deficits or declines in business taxes were responsible for the higher interest rates.

In the final article in this section, "Three Views of Real Interest," Adrian W. Throop provides a different explanation. He argues that higher federal budget deficits were the most important reason for high real rates after 1982.

Throop states that the reason for the high real rates through 1982 was not that Federal Reserve policy was erratic but that it became steadily more restrictive. Coupled with short-run operating procedures that no longer attempted to stabilize interest rates, this policy led to high and volatile rates. The less erratic behavior of interest rates since 1982 is attributed to the Fed's having reverted to less rigid control of bank reserves. Throop also dismisses financial deregulation as an important source of increased volatility of open-market interest rates.

Article One

Richard R. Simonds

Modern Financial Theory

Developments in the past twenty-five years have application to public utility regulation, to investor portfolio selection, and to corporate capital budgeting.

The most significant academic developments in finance in the past twenty-five years have been portfolio theory, capital market theory, and efficient market theory. Portfolio theory is concerned with how a risk-averse investor should go about selecting an optimal portfolio of investment assets. Capital market theory extends portfolio theory and attempts to describe the way in which the equilibrium market price or expected return of an individual investment asset is related to the asset's risk of return. Efficient market theory deals with the relationship between information and security prices and the resulting implications for investors.

This article attempts to present the major theoretical concepts in these areas in as nontechnical a manner as possible. Several statistical terms are used along the way but only after the meaning of each is sufficiently developed. Second, empirical support for these theories is briefly summarized. Third, three applications of these theories are illustrated. Although the applications presented are by no means exhaustive, they indicate the scope of the impact of recent academic developments on financial analysis.

Portfolio theory

The one-period return on an individual invest-

ment asset during a specified time is equal to the change in the market value of the asset plus any cash distributions received divided by the initial market value.[1] The return for the ith asset, $\tilde{R}_i$, is given by

$$\tilde{R}_i = \frac{\tilde{V}_{i1} - V_{i0} + \tilde{D}_{i1}}{V_{i0}}, \qquad (1)$$

where

$\tilde{V}_{i1} = i^{th}$ asset market value at the end of the period;

$V_{i0} = i^{th}$ asset market value at the beginning of the period; and

$\tilde{D}_{i1} = i^{th}$ asset cash distribution during the period.[2]

The return on a portfolio, $\tilde{R}_p$, is a weighted average of the returns on the individual assets in the portfolio. That is, for n assets,

$$\tilde{R}_p = A_1\tilde{R}_1 + A_2\tilde{R}_2 + \ldots + A_n\tilde{R}_n, \qquad (2)$$

where A_i equals the proportion of the initial investment committed to the ith asset, and the sum of the A_i's is one.

Expected return. Each return, $\tilde{R}_i$, is uncertain at the beginning of the period. A useful way to deal with this uncertainty is to assign subjective probabilities to possible return outcomes. Having done

Richard R. Simonds is a member of the faculty of the Graduate School of Business Administration at Michigan State University.

so, the expected return may be computed. The expected return is the weighted average of all possible returns where the weights are equal to the probabilities or relative chances of each level of return occurring. The probability of R_{ij}, where R_{ij} represents the jth level of return for the ith asset, is designated P_{ij}, and the sum of the probabilities, P_{i1}, P_{i2}, . . . , P_{im}, for m possible return levels must equal one. The expected value of $\tilde{R}_i$, $E(\tilde{R}_i)$, given the m possible outcomes shown in Exhibit 1, is

$$E(\tilde{R}_i) = \sum_{j=1}^{m} R_{ij}P_{ij}$$

$$= .1(.05) + .2(.06) + .4(.07)$$
$$+ .2(.08) + .1(.09)$$
$$= .07 \text{ or } 7\%. \qquad (3)$$

EXHIBIT 1

SYMMETRIC PROBABILITY DISTRIBUTION OF RETURN
FOR THE ith ASSET IN PORTFOLIO p

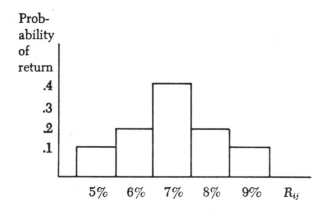

In accordance with expression (2), the expected value of the portfolio return, $E(\tilde{R}_p)$, is equal to a weighted average of the n individual assets' expected returns,

$$E(\tilde{R}_p) = A_1(\tilde{R}_1) + A_2E(\tilde{R}_2) + \ldots$$
$$+ A_nE(\tilde{R}_n),$$
$$= \sum_{i=1}^{n} A_iE(\tilde{R}_i). \qquad (4)$$

Therefore, the contribution of each asset to the expected portfolio return is its own expected return.

Risk of return. The risk of the portfolio return might be stated in terms of a dispersion measure which takes into account both the likelihood of $\tilde{R}_p$ being less than $E(\tilde{R}_p)$ and the size of the downside deviations. However, if the distribution for $\tilde{R}_p$ is symmetric, a measure of dispersion based on both the upside and downside deviations from the expected return level may be used even though it is only the downside deviations which leave the investor less well off than if the outcome had been the expected value. Since security returns and hence portfolio returns appear to be approximately symmetric, it is this two-sided measure of dispersion that is generally used.[3] The variance of return is just such a two-sided measure and is defined as the weighted average of squared deviations from the expected return. The variance of the portfolio single-period return, designated $\sigma^2(\tilde{R}_p)$, is given by

$$\sigma^2(\tilde{R}_p) = \sum_{j=1}^{m} [R_{pj} - E(\tilde{R}_p)]^2 P_{pj}. \qquad (5)$$

Correspondingly, for a single asset the variance is

$$\sigma^2(\tilde{R}_i) = \sum_{j=1}^{m} [R_{ij} - E(\tilde{R}_i)]^2 P_{ij}, \qquad (6)$$

and for the security depicted in Exhibit 1
$$\sigma^2(\tilde{R}_i) = (-.02)^2 (.1) + (-.01)^2 (.2)$$
$$+ (0)^2 (.4) + (.01)^2 (.2) + (.02)^2 (.1)$$
$$= .00012.$$

The variance of the return on an n-asset portfolio with asset weights A_i, $i = 1, \ldots, n$, is also expressible as

$$\sigma^2(\tilde{R}_p) = \sum_{i=1}^{n} A_i \text{ covariance } (\tilde{R}_i, \tilde{R}_p), \qquad (7)$$

where the covariance $(\tilde{R}_i, \tilde{R}_p)$ measures the magnitude of the comovement of the returns on the ith asset and the returns on the portfolio, p, of which asset i is a member.[4] The covariance $(\tilde{R}_i, \tilde{R}_p)$ is expressible as

covariance $(\tilde{R}_i, \tilde{R}_p)$ = (correlation between $\tilde{R}_i$ and $\tilde{R}_p$)
$$\times \sqrt{\sigma^2(\tilde{R}_i) \ \sigma^2(\tilde{R}_p)}. \qquad (8)$$

Expression (7) is significant because it indicates that the contribution of the ith asset to the risk of portfolio p is the covariance $(\tilde{R}_i, \tilde{R}_p)$, and the relative risk of security i in portfolio p is

$$\frac{\text{covariance } (\tilde{R}_i, \tilde{R}_p)}{\sigma^2(\tilde{R}_p)} = \beta_{ip}. \qquad (9)$$

Alternatively, if one considers a portfolio of n assets in which $A_i = 1/n$, $i = 1, \ldots, n$, then $\sigma^2(\tilde{R}_p)$ may be expressed as

$$\sigma^2(\tilde{R}_p) = \frac{\text{average security return variance}}{n}$$

$$+ \left(\frac{n-1}{n}\right)$$

$$\times \begin{pmatrix} \text{average covariance between} \\ \text{returns for pairs of securities} \\ \text{comprising portfolio } p \end{pmatrix}.(10)$$

Two of the most important results of portfolio theory are presented in expressions (7) and (10). Expression (7) shows that the risk contribution of asset i to portfolio p is measured by the covariance $(\tilde{R}_i, \tilde{R}_p)$ and *not* the variance of its own return, $\sigma^2(\tilde{R}_i)$. Expression (10) shows that as a portfolio is expanded to include large numbers of assets, the portfolio variance may not be reduced beyond the average covariance of returns for pairs of securities comprising the portfolio.[6] Consequently, simple diversification in risky assets can be only partially effective in reducing risk.

Two-Parameter Model. Employing expressions (4) and (7), one may calculate $E(\tilde{R}_p)$ and $\sigma^2(\tilde{R}_p)$ for an n-asset portfolio with given weights, A_i. Specifically, if $n = 2$, the possible combinations of expected return and risk for different levels of A_1 and A_2, with the restriction that $A_1 + A_2 = 1$, are indicated by the curved line in Exhibit 2.

Note that it is customary to represent the risk of the portfolio as the standard deviation of the return, which is the square-root of the return variance. The less the returns for assets 1 and 2 are positively correlated, the greater is the curvature of the line representing the locations attainable by combining the two assets.

Next assume that the investor has assigned subjective probability distributions to the returns for all risky investment assets. The set of possible portfolio risk-return pairs resulting from different combinations of these assets would appear as the shaded area shown in Exhibit 3. (Momentarily disregard the straight line shown.) Only the darkened border

EXHIBIT 3

TWO-PARAMETER PORTFOLIO
MODEL WITH n ASSETS

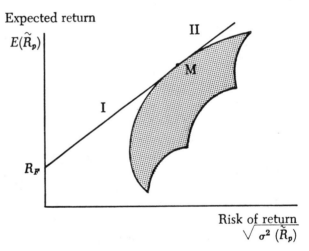

EXHIBIT 2

TWO-PARAMETER PORTFOLIO MODEL
WITH TWO ASSETS

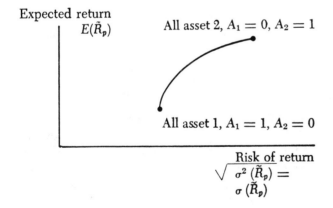

of this set will be of interest to an investor, however. This so-called efficient set offers the highest expected return for a given risk level.[7] Which point on the efficient set of risky assets is best depends on the investor's willingness to accept additional risk in order to increase the level of expected portfolio returns.

Capital market theory

Equilibrium Models. Capital market theory seeks to explain the relationship between the expected equilibrium returns on investment assets and their risk of return. Although several slightly different capital market equilibrium models are derivable from two-parameter portfolio theory, depending on the assumptions imposed, only the best-known model, the Sharpe-Lintner Capital Asset Pricing Model, is discussed here.[8]

If a risk-free asset is available with a return R_F, where R_F is a certain rate at which investors may borrow or lend, the new efficient set becomes the straight line emanating from R_F tangent to the original efficient set of risky assets at point M. Anywhere along the straight line is attainable given the proper allocation of funds to the portfolio M and the risk-free asset. If the investor desires to be in region I, funds are invested in the riskless asset, whereas in region II funds are borrowed at the riskless rate and invested in the portfolio M. The combination of riskless asset and portfolio M selected depends on the investor's level of desired risk exposure. Furthermore, all locations along the straight line offer returns that are perfectly positively correlated with the returns on portfolio M since R_F is a certain rate of return.

If investors' expectations regarding uncertain future returns for investment assets are homogeneous, that is, all investors perceive the same set of risk-return pairs, all investors will choose to hold the portfolio M in combination with the riskless asset.[9] Consequently, M is the market portfolio itself, which is the portfolio of all investment assets.

By referring back to expression (7) and replacing portfolio p with the market portfolio M the variance of the return on the market portfolio is seen to be

$$\sigma^2(\tilde{R}_m) = \sum_{i=1}^{n} A_i \text{ covariance } (\tilde{R}_i, \tilde{R}_m). \quad (11)$$

The relative risk of the ith asset in the market portfolio, which is referred to as the ith asset's beta co-

efficient, is, from expression (9), seen to be equal to

$$\beta_{im} = \frac{\text{covariance } (\tilde{R}_i, \tilde{R}_m)}{\sigma^2(\tilde{R}_m)}. \quad (12)$$

Next consider a fractional investment of A_1 in the market portfolio and $(1 - A_1)$ in the riskless asset; then the portfolio return, $\tilde{R}_p$, is

$$\tilde{R}_p = A_1 \tilde{R}_m + (1 - A_1) \tilde{R}_F, \quad (13)$$

and the expected portfolio return is

$$E(\tilde{R}_p) = A_1 E(\tilde{R}_m) + (1 - A_1) R_F. \quad (14)$$

Beta for the portfolio is

$$\beta_{pm} = \frac{\text{covariance } (\tilde{R}_p, \tilde{R}_m)}{\sigma^2(\tilde{R}_m)}, \quad (15)$$

which, using equation (13), may be expressed as

$$\beta_{pm} = \frac{\text{covariance } (A_1 \tilde{R}_m + (1 - A_1) R_F, \tilde{R}_m)}{\sigma^2(\tilde{R}_m)}$$

or

$$= \frac{A_1 \text{ covariance } (\tilde{R}_m, \tilde{R}_m) + (1 - A_1) \text{ covariance } (R_F, \tilde{R}_m)}{\sigma^2(\tilde{R}_m)}. \quad (16)$$

Since R_F is a certain rate of return, then expression (16) for β_{pm} reduces to

$$\beta_{pm} = \frac{A_1 \sigma^2(\tilde{R}_m) + (1 - A_1)(0)}{\sigma^2(\tilde{R}_m)} = A_1. \quad (17)$$

Using this result for β_{pm} in expression (14) we arrive at

$$E(\tilde{R}_p) = \beta_{pm} E(\tilde{R}_m) + (1 - \beta_{pm}) R_F. \quad (18)$$

Equation (18) is the Capital Asset Pricing Model (CAPM) developed simultaneously by William F. Sharpe and John Lintner. Although it was developed here for portfolios on the efficient set, it can be shown to hold for *each* risky asset in the market portfolio.[10] For each risky asset the relationship between expected return and risk is

$$E(\tilde{R}_i) = R_F(1 - \beta_{im}) + \beta_{im} E(\tilde{R}_m),$$

or

$$E(\tilde{R}_i) = R_F + [E(\tilde{R}_m) - R_F]\beta_{im}. \quad (19)$$

Note that it is the relative risk contribution, β_{im}, of the security to the market portfolio risk that establishes the expected return on the asset and not the total variability of asset return, $\sigma^2(\tilde{R}_i)$. This perspective of risk has dramatic consequences, as will be seen when applications of the CAPM are discussed below.

Beta Coefficients. It is common practice to use

past realized data for security and market returns to estimate beta coefficients for individual securities or portfolios.[11] Employing the market-model regression equation

$$\tilde{R}_i = a_i + b_i\tilde{R}_m + \tilde{e}_i, \qquad (20)$$

estimates are obtained for b_i using standard statistical techniques. Exhibit 4 shows a regression line fitted to monthly observations on $\tilde{R}_i$ and $\tilde{R}_m$.

EXHIBIT 4

MARKET-MODEL REGRESSION EQUATION

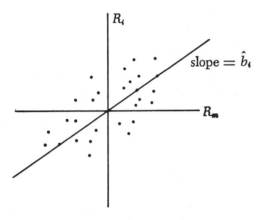

When the error term $\tilde{e}_i$ is assumed independent of $\tilde{R}_m$, the b_i term is equal to covariance $(\tilde{R}_i\tilde{R}_m)/\sigma^2(\tilde{R}_m)$, which is β_{im}. Therefore the estimates of b_i, denoted $\hat{b}_i$, are used as estimates of β_{im}.[12] Equation (20) also provides another description of beta. Beta reflects the sensitivity of the ith asset's returns to the returns on the market as a whole. Beta coefficients over one are deemed more risky than the market, and beta coefficients under one less risky than the market, since the market portfolio itself must have a beta coefficient of one.

If one were to consider equation (20) written separately for many individual securities it becomes clear that the return on a portfolio of n equally weighted securities may be expressed as

$$\tilde{R}_p = \frac{1}{n}\sum_{i=1}^{n} a_i + \frac{1}{n}\sum_{i=1}^{n} b_i(\tilde{R}_m) + \frac{1}{n}\sum_{i=1}^{n} \tilde{e}_i. \quad (21)$$

Alternatively, equation (21) may be expressed as

$$\tilde{R}_p = \bar{a}_i + \bar{b}_i(R_m) + \frac{1}{n}\sum_{i=1}^{n} \tilde{e}_i, \qquad (22)$$

or using notation to reflect that R_p is the return on a portfolio,

$$\tilde{R}_p = a_p + b_p(\tilde{R}_m) + \tilde{e}_p, \qquad (23)$$

where $\bar{a}_i = a_p$ and $\bar{b}_i = b_p$ are averages for the n securities. If the $\tilde{e}_i$ terms are independent of each other, then

$$\sigma^2(\tilde{R}_p) = (b_p)^2\sigma^2(\tilde{R}_m)$$
$$+ \frac{1}{n}(\text{average variance of the } \tilde{e}_i\text{'s}). \qquad (24)$$

Consequently, as n gets very large the risk of the portfolio can be reduced to that resulting from the comovement of the portfolio returns with the market returns. Variations independent of general market returns can be diversified away, but risk cannot be completely eliminated through diversification. This is the same conclusion we arrive at in expression (10). The standard deviation of the $\tilde{e}_p$ term has come to be called the unsystematic risk and the standard deviation of the $b_p\tilde{R}_m$ term the systematic risk. Diversification can effectively eliminate the unsystematic risk but has no such effect on the systematic risk.

Empirical Evidence. The Sharpe-Lintner CAPM was developed based on the normative idea that risk-averse investors should make portfolio choices based on the expected level and standard deviation of portfolio returns, assumed homogeneous expectations, and on the assumed presence of a risk-free rate for borrowing and lending.[13] Therefore, the model is referred to as a two-parameter market equilibrium model. Since expression (19) is stated in terms of expected returns which are unobservable, it may not be tested directly. Various researchers have, however, conducted indirect tests by using data on realized returns for New York Stock Exchange securities. Most notable of these tests are the studies by Eugene Fama and James MacBeth and by Fischer Black, Michael Jensen, and Myron Scholes.[14] Their empirical evidence suggests that the relationship between expected security returns and betas, β_{im}'s, is linear and that beta is the only required factor to explain the differences in levels of expected returns among securities. These findings are consistent with the Sharpe-Lintner CAPM.[15]

Furthermore, these findings support the proposition that securities are priced consistent with a two-parameter portfolio model used to describe how investors should select investment portfolios.

Efficient capital market theory

In an efficient capital market, individual security prices fully reflect all available information. Prices adjust completely and instantaneously to new information. Current security prices represent "correct" or unbiased assessments of all information available at the moment.

Academic researchers have attempted to test the extent to which security markets appear to behave as efficient markets.[16] Three classes of testable propositions derivable from the efficient market theory have been examined.[17] First, do current security prices fully reflect all information available in the sequences of past security prices and return data? This proposition is often referred to as the random walk hypothesis, which implies that successive security returns are not statistically associated. To examine this proposition, researchers have tested complicated buying and selling rules based on securities' past price performances. Such rules have not generated returns sufficiently greater than those available through buy-and-hold strategies to warrant investors behaving in a manner not consistent with the notion that this first efficient market proposition is correct.

"Portfolio theory and capital market theory may be used to estimate both the risk of the equity and the level of expected equity return."

A second testable proposition is that security prices adjust fully and instantaneously to *new* publicly available information. The empirical research regarding this proposition is preponderantly supportive. Studies conducted concerning earnings announcements, announced changes in accounting practices, mergers, stock splits, newly filed SEC documents, and so forth, have all supported this second proposition. It should be kept in mind, however, that even though the evidence reported would not lead one to reject this second proposition, any real market is surely not completely consistent with it either. The important point is that the evidence suggests that individual investors are best off conducting their affairs as if the proposition were correct. Finally, if this second proposition concerning publicly available information is correct, it is only because individual investors are trying to identify securities whose current prices do not reflect their intrinsic values and are making investment decisions based on these assessments. This activity is the driving force behind market efficiency. By so behaving, investors are causing the market to behave in accordance with this second proposition.

A third testable proposition is that no sector can, through superior analysis of publicly available information or through access to nonpublicly available information, realize superior investment performance. Research by Michael Jensen in which he examined mutual fund performance strongly suggests that once returns are adjusted for risk these managers have been unable to outperform other investors.[18] On the other hand, evidence from other studies of stock trading by insiders (managers and directors) and New York Stock Exchange specialists suggests that these individuals are privy to information not reflected in current stock prices which may be used to achieve superior returns.[19] This last bit of evidence against the idea of complete market efficiency does not appear to affect the general conclusion that if investors only have access to publicly available information they are wise to act as if the market were efficient.

Applications

Almost every facet of financial analysis has been affected by the theories described above. This pervasiveness is illustrated here by examining the impact of modern financial theory on public utility regulation, investor portfolio selection, and corporate capital budgeting. Although this examination must necessarily be brief, an effort has been made to point out several practical problems encountered when trying to apply these theories. This effort is important lest the reader get the false impression that modern financial theory has reduced many areas of financial analysis to mechanical formula manipulation.

Public Utility Regulation. Public utility rate of return regulation is based on the legal principle that "the return to the equity owner should be commensurate with returns on investments in other enterprises having corresponding risk."[20] One concept of commensurate return is the market rate of return which investors expect when they purchase other equity shares of comparable risk. If estimates of the risk and associated expected rate of return alluded to in the legal principle above can be obtained for a utility's stock, these estimates may be used along with debt costs to determine a "fair" company rate of return on assets. This company rate of return may be applied to a rate base such as the book value of capital investment to determine utility service rates.

Portfolio theory and capital market theory may be used to estimate both the risk of the equity and the level of expected equity return. As seen in expression (12), for a well-diversified investor the relevant risk measure of a security is its beta coefficient. Expression (19) specifies the level of expected return for a security with known beta, and it also shows all securities with the same beta have the same expected return. Modern financial theory offers a conceptually sound approach to the implementation of the legal principle of "fair" return in regulatory cases and in fact has been used for this purpose.

Testimony has been offered in regulatory cases such as those involving Communications Satellite Corporation, in which experts were requested to prepare an analysis of Comsat's risk in a portfolio context and to estimate Comsat's expected return on equity capital.[21] Two major problems arise in such an analysis. First, a firm's true equity beta coefficient can only be estimated (see expression [20] for the standard statistical approach), and therefore a firm's inherent risk level may not be known exactly. Furthermore, since the "real" or inherent beta coefficient is determined by a firm's operating and financial characteristics, only if these remain constant over time will the theoretical beta remain constant. Consequently, errors may arise from two sources in predicting the future riskiness of a utility's equity shares.

Second, a major problem arises in using expression (19) to estimate the expected return on the utility's equity since values for the expected market return, $E(\tilde{R}_m)$, and risk-free rate, R_F, must be specified. These can only be specified subjectively, which, of course, means that $E(\tilde{R}_j)$, the expected equity return, is a subjective estimate. One meaningful way to proceed, however, is not to generate one estimate but to explore the range of estimates that result when different combinations of $E(\tilde{R}_m)$ and R_F are inserted. Given the limitations cited here it would not appear sensible to consider the CAPM alone a sufficient basis for regulatory decisions but rather one approach to determining the utility's required equity return which should be considered in regulatory proceedings.

Index Funds. An index fund is an investment fund constructed so that its rate of return behavior is approximately the same as that of a major index, such as the Standard & Poor's 500. Therefore, except for transaction costs and compositional differences, these funds offer the same return as the indices they attempt to imitate. The motivation for such funds arises from efficient market theory and portfolio theory.[22]

"It follows that product diversification by a firm for the sole purpose of reducing the variability of the firm's return is not beneficial to investors since they can achieve the same or better diversification within their own investment portfolios."

First, in an efficient market, investors are not able to use publicly available information to identify undervalued or overvalued securities; therefore, market prices reflect intrinsic values. Second, we have shown that the efficient set of portfolios (greatest expected return for a given risk level) is the locus of points on the straight line extending from the risk-free rate through and beyond the market portfolio. All investors should be somewhere on the straight line of efficient portfolios. By combining an investment in the market portfolio with an investment in the risk-free asset one may obtain efficient portfolios less risky than the market portfolio. An efficient portfolio riskier than the market portfolio is achieved by borrowing at the risk-free rate and investing in the market portfolio.

If the Standard & Poor's 500 index is a good surrogate for the market portfolio, investors may approximate the market portfolio by holding the index fund. If less risk is desired part of the investor's wealth can be diverted to short-term Treasury Bills, which serve as a substitute for a risk-free asset. Positions riskier than the market may also be achievable by buying on margin.[23] However, since actual margin loan rates are greater than the risk-free rate, the leveraging process is not as effective as that shown for region II in Exhibit 3. The slope of the efficient set is diminished for points past the market portfolio M.

Capital Budgeting. The two-parameter portfolio model has been applied in the capital budgeting area to develop a new market portfolio concept of project risk. This perspective suggests that the management of a publicly held firm should not be concerned with the impact a project has on the firm's total variability of return but rather with the project's relative risk. The relative risk is the incremental effect of the project on the variability of returns on a portfolio of investment assets held by a well-diversified investor holding the firm's stock. This is the same concept of risk we developed earlier for investment assets held in a portfolio and was represented by the asset's beta coefficient. It follows that product diversification by a firm for the sole purpose of reducing the variability of the firm's return is not beneficial to investors since they can achieve the same or better diversification within their own investment portfolio. The market portfolio concept of project risk shifts the emphasis away from measuring risk in the narrow context of the firm to measuring it in the context of the entire market of investment assets.

Associated with a project's relative risk measure is a required rate of return on the investment project. This rate of return is estimable using expression (19) for the Sharpe-Lintner CAPM. If the pre-

EXHIBIT 5

PROJECT SELECTION CRITERION

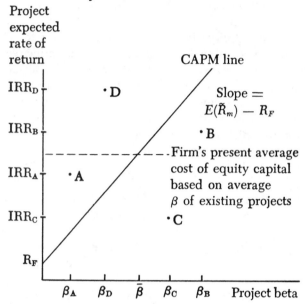

dicted internal rate of return (IRR) on the equity financed portion of a capital investment project does not exceed the project's required rate of return, the project is not acceptable. This required return is represented by the straight line of slope $E(\tilde{R}_m) - R_F$ in Exhibit 5 for a firm with a fixed capital structure.[24]

The project's expected rate of return is interpreted to be the expected return on the equity financed portion of the project. Or, stated differently, we now wish to consider the return of the project based on the generated cash flows adjusted for debt charges and the amount of the investment in the project reduced by the portion financed through debt. The project beta is considered to be the covariance between the return on the equity financed portion and the market return. Projects are positioned in Exhibit 5 by their estimated internal rates of return on the equity financed portion and their estimated betas. If a project lies above the CAPM line of slope $E(\tilde{R}_m) - R_F$ it is acceptable; otherwise it is not. Consequently, projects A and D are acceptable while C and B are not. Note that project A is acceptable even though its expected equity return is below the firm's average cost of equity capital. Apparently project A is sufficiently less risky than the firm's average project to warrant its acceptance.

Estimating betas for capital investment projects is especially difficult, much more so than for publicly traded securities. Several approaches are available, however. First, it may be possible to identify an existing firm, whose stock is publicly traded, which is involved in activities that approximate the project the firm is considering.[25] If such is the case, statistically estimated betas using historical stock return data for this firm may provide an adequate estimate of the project's beta.

Second, if the project is similar to one with which the firm has had prior experience, it may be possible to construct historical rates of return on the equity financed portion for different time periods and combine these with the corresponding market returns (actually a surrogate such as the Standard & Poor's 500) to estimate a beta coefficient using expression (20).[26] Third, the firm might resort to constructing a simulation model of the project under consideration to help in estimating its beta.

Summary

Modern financial theory and empirical evidence suggest that investors are well advised to make investment decisions assuming that security prices fully and instantaneously reflect all publicly available information. Furthermore, investors should hold efficient portfolios. Efficient portfolios offer the highest possible level of expected return for a given level of risk and represent combinations of a risk-free asset and the market portfolio.

When investors hold efficient portfolios, the risk of an individual asset is measured in terms of how much it contributes to the efficient portfolio's risk of return. This contribution is not adequately represented by the individual asset's total variability of return since a portion of this variation may be diversified away. The proper measure of the asset's risk contribution is its beta coefficient, which is based on the covariation between the asset's returns and returns on the market portfolio. The higher this covariation, the more the asset contributes to the risk of an efficient portfolio.

The Sharpe-Lintner capital asset pricing model (CAPM) expresses the equilibrium relationship between the expected return on an individual investment asset and its risk stated as a beta coefficient. The CAPM has been used extensively to analyze theoretical and practical problems in finance. Applications of the model in public utility regulation and corporate capital budgeting were illustrated here. A particularly striking conclusion is that the risk of a capital investment project and its associated required level of return should not be judged on the basis of the project's total variability returns. The proper basis of evaluation is to examine how the project's returns are estimated to covary with the returns on the market portfolio.

1. Although the theory is properly presented in terms of all investment assets, most applications have focused on financial assets.

2. The tilde, $\sim$, on $\tilde{R}_i$, $\tilde{V}_{i1}$, and $\tilde{D}_{i1}$ indicates that these quantities are uncertain at the beginning of the period and hence are random variables.

3. In fact, return distributions on individual securities and portfolios are approximately normal, with monthly returns better described by the normal distribution than daily returns. See Eugene Fama, *Foundations of Finance* (New York: Basic Books, 1976), chapter 1.

4. $$\sigma^2 (\tilde{R}_p) = \sum_{i=1}^{n} \sum_{k=1}^{n} A_i A_k \text{ covariance } (\tilde{R}_i, \tilde{R}_k),$$

therefore,

$$\sigma^2 (\tilde{R}_p) = \sum_{i=1}^{n} A_i [\sum_{k=1}^{n} \text{ covariance } (\tilde{R}_i, A_k \tilde{R}_k)],$$

and since

$$\tilde{R}_p = \sum_{k=1}^{n} A_k \tilde{R}_k, \text{ and } \sum_{k=1}^{n} A_i = 1,$$

$$\sigma^2 (\tilde{R}_p) = \sum_{i=1}^{n} A_i \text{ covariance } (\tilde{R}_i \tilde{R}_p).$$

5. See Fama, *Foundations of Finance*, p. 252. It should be emphasized that the notion that the effects of single-period risk of return tend to cancel out in the longer run is incorrect. The relationship between the future value of a security and the sequence of its n single-period returns is

Future Value $= [(1 + \tilde{R}_1) (1 + \tilde{R}_2) (1 + \tilde{R}_3) \ldots$
$\quad (1 + \tilde{R}_n)]$ (Current Value),

where the subscript refers to the time period. For commonly encountered levels of security returns,

Future Value $\backsimeq [1 + \tilde{R}_1 + \tilde{R}_2 + \tilde{R}_3 + \ldots$
$\quad + \tilde{R}_n]$ (Current Value).

If the returns, $\tilde{R}_i$, are independent and of constant variance, σ^2, then the variance of the future security value after n periods is equal to $\sigma^2 \times$ (current value) $\times$ (n), or n times the variance of the security value one period hence. Single-period risk effects do not cancel out in the longer run.

6. Almost all security returns appear to be positively cor-

related with one another, implying positive covariances between asset returns. The average covariance of returns discussed here can therefore be presumed to be positive. See Fama, *Foundations of Finance*, pp. 251–54.

7. The use of the word *efficient* here is not to be confused with its usage in describing capital markets.

8. See Michael Jensen, "Capital Markets: Theory and Evidence," *Bell Journal of Economics and Management Science* 3 (Autumn 1972):357–98, for an excellent presentation of other models.

9. This result is frequently referred to as the separation theorem.

10. The best presentation of the complete derivation of the Sharpe-Lintner CAPM is found in Fama, *Foundations of Finance*, chapter 8.

11. A surrogate for the market return, such as the return on the Standard & Poor's 500 index, is usually employed in this process.

12. An alternative market model specification is stated in terms of excess returns, namely,

$$\tilde{R}_i - R_F = a_i + b_i(\tilde{R}_m - R_F) + \tilde{e}_i.$$

This form is also used by some investigators to obtain estimates of β_{im}.

13. It is also assumed that investors do not incur transaction costs and are indifferent to capital gains or dividends.

14. Eugene Fama and James MacBeth, "Risk, Return and Equilibrium: Empirical Tests," *Journal of Political Economy* 71 (May-June 1971): 607–36, and Fischer Black, Michael Jensen, and Myron Scholes, "The Capital Asset Pricing Model: Some Empirical Tests," in Michael Jensen, ed., *Studies in the Theory of Capital Markets* (New York: Praeger, 1972), pp. 79–121.

15. It must be stated that although these findings are consistent with the Sharpe-Lintner CAPM other evidence suggests that a slightly different version of a two-parameter capital market equilibrium model which does not presume the presence of a risk-free asset is superior. Black has presented such a model in which the expected return on a riskless portfolio ($\beta_{pm} = 0$) replaces the risk-free rate in equation (19). The linearity of the relationship between $E(R_i)$ and β_{im} and the singular importance of β_{im} is not altered in any way, however. See Fama, *Foundations of Finance*,

chapter 8, for an excellent discussion of the differences between the various two-parameter capital market equilibrium models which have been developed.

16. Most of this testing has been conducted using securities traded on the New York Stock Exchange. Caution should be exercised in generalizing these test results to all security markets.

17. Most of the studies of market efficiency are also implicitly testing a market equilibrium model. See Fama, *Foundations of Finance*, chapter 5, for a discussion of this point.

18. Michael Jensen, "The Performance of Mutual Funds in the Period 1945–1964," *Journal of Finance* 23 (May 1968: 389–416.

19. Jeffrey Jaffe, "Special Information and Insider Trading," *Journal of Business* 47 (July 1974): 410–28.

20. Supreme Court Decision in *Federal Power Commission et al. v. Hope Natural Gas Company*, 320 U.S. 591 (1949) at 603.

21. Federal Communications Commission, Communications Satellite Corporation. Prepared Testimony, S. J. Meyers. F.C.C. Docket 16070; 1972.

22. The appeal of index funds stems from efficient market and efficient portfolio considerations. However, if a majority of investors were to invest in a few index funds the market would no longer be efficient. This would destroy the underlying basis for index funds.

23. Most institutions are legally precluded from buying on margin, however.

24. Questions concerning the optimal capital structure are not considered here. See Mark Rubinstein, "Mean-Variance Synthesis," *Journal of Finance* 28 (March 1973): 167–81, and Robert Hamada, "The Effect of the Firm's Capital Structure on the Systematic Risk of Common Stocks," *Journal of Finance* 27 (May 1972): 435–52, for applications of the CAPM model to questions relating to capital structure.

25. One should in this process adjust the beta coefficient for differences in capital structure that may exist. See Rubinstein, "Mean-Variance Synthesis."

26. See James Van Horne, *Financial Management and Policy*, 4th ed. (Englewood Cliffs: Prentice-Hall, 1977), pp. 175–78.

Article Two

11 3/4	4/30/1986-N	102.12	16	-3	7.76
7 7/8	5/15/1986-N	99.31	3	-2	7.73
9 3/8	5/15/1986-N	100.29	1	-1	7.82
13 3/4	5/15/1986-N	103.26	30	-3	7.82
12 5/8	5/31/1986-N	103.06	10	-1	7.91
13	6/30/1986-N	104.00	4	-1	7.71
14 7/8	6/30/1986-N	106.03	7	-3	6.94
12 5/8	7/31/1986-N	103.28	0	-2	7.95
8	8/15/1986-N	100.01	5	+1	7.83
11 3/8	8/15/1986-N	102.29	1	0	7.98
12 3/8	8/31/1986-N	103.27	31	-1	8.11
11 7/8	9/30/1986-N	103.20	24	-1	8.14
12 1/4	9/30/1986-N	104.00	4	0	8.14
11 5/8	10/31/1986-N	103.18	22	-1	8.21
6 1/8	11/15/1986	97.30	30	+1	7.07
11	11/15/1986-N	102.27	31	-2	8.34
13 7/8	11/15/1986-N	106.02	6	-3	8.33
16 1/8	11/15/1986-N	109.05	9	-1	7.84
10 3/8	11/30/1986-N	102.07	11	-1	8.34
9 7/8	12/31/1986-N	101.22	26	-1	8.40
10	12/31/1986-N	101.28	0	-2	8.37
9 3/4	1/31/1987-N	101.16	20	-1	8.50
9	2/15/1987-N	100.19	23	0	8.46
10 7/8	2/15/1987-N	103.00	4	-2	8.53
12 3/4	2/15/1987-N	105.17	21	-1	8.50
10	2/28/1987-N	101.28	0	-2	8.54
10 1/4	3/31/1987-N	102.09	13	+1	8.58
10 3/4	3/31/1987-N	103.00	4	+1	8.58
9 3/4	4/30/1987-N	101.16	20	-1	8.67
12	5/15/1987-N	105.00	4	-1	8.68
12 1/2	5/15/1987-N	105.24	28	0	8.70
14	5/15/1987-N	108.02	6	0	8.70
9 1/8	5/31/1987-N	100.16	20	+1	8.73
8 1/2	6/30/1987-N	99.14	18	+1	8.77
10 1/2	6/30/1987-N	102.25	29	+1	8.74
8 7/8	7/31/1987-N	99.30	0	+1	8.88
12 3/8	8/15/1987-N	105.29	1	+1	8.93
13 3/4	8/15/1987-N	108.11	15	0	8.91
8 7/8	8/31/1987-N	99.28	30	+1	8.91
11 1/8	9/30/1987-N	104.01	5	+2	8.88
7 5/8	11/15/1987-N	97.28	4	+2	8.58
11	11/15/1987-N	103.30	2	+2	8.92
12 5/8	11/15/1987-N	107.00	4	+1	8.98
11 1/4	12/31/1987-N	104.17	21	+1	8.98
12 3/8	1/15/1988-N	106.26	30	+2	9.05
10 1/8	2/15/1988-N	102.03	7	+2	9.09
10 3/8	2/15/1988-N	102.20	24	+1	9.09
12	3/31/1988-N	106.07	11	+2	9.17
13 1/4	4/15/1988-N	109.01	5	+1	9.22
8 1/4	5/15/1988-N	98.06	14	+2	8.91
9 7/8	5/15/1988-N	101.12	16	+2	9.23
10	5/15/1988-N	101.21	25	+1	9.24
13 5/8	6/30/1988-N	110.09	13	0	9.34
14	7/15/1988-N	111.11	19	+1	9.29
9 1/2	8/15/1988-N	100.16	20	+1	9.25
10 1/2	8/15/1988-N	102.30	2	+3	9.29
11 3/8	9/30/1988-N	105.06	10	+3	9.34
15 3/8	10/15/1988-N	115.13	21	+2	9.45
8 3/4	11/15/1988-N	98.21	29	+5	9.15
11 3/4	11/15/1988-N	106.04	8	+2	9.44
10 5/8	12/31/1988-N	103.06	10	+2	9.44

The Government Securities Market: Playing Field for Repos

Richard Syron and
Sheila L. Tschinkel

Our nation's government securities market is characterized by its huge volume, its efficiency, and its lack of comprehensive regulation. Here is a look at how the market operates and why it has grown so rapidly.

Repurchase agreements are important transactions in the U.S. government securities market, the world's largest and most liquid capital market—having absorbed over $1 trillion in gross new issues in 1984 to raise close to $200 billion in new funds and to refinance maturing debt.

The market has grown substantially in recent years because of the rapid expansion of Treasury debt. Trading in the secondary market has grown at an even faster pace. One salient characteristic of this market is its lack of comprehensive regulation. This freedom has encouraged rapid entry into the market by many types of firms, keen competition, and extraordinary innovation.

Understanding the market's structure and functions is essential to gaining a sound understanding of repurchase agreements, including recent problems involving their use and the procedures necessary to avoid loss. This article describes the market's structure, the organization and operations of major participants, and its performance.

The Market's Structure

The government securities market consists of five broad categories of participants: the

The authors are senior vice president and advisor at the Federal Reserve Bank of Boston and senior vice president and director of research at the Federal Reserve Bank of Atlanta, respectively.[1]

U.S. Treasury Department, the Federal Reserve System, primary securities dealers, other dealers, and a wide array of investors. The fount of this market is the Treasury Department, the pre-eminent issuer of short- and long-term debt securities on a regular basis. The Treasury auctions bills, notes, and bonds to finance new U.S. government debt as well as maturing securities (see Box 1). Several government-sponsored agencies also issue securities. Government and agency securities have a wide variety of maturities, and this along with particular characteristics and the level of interest rates determines their market values.

The Treasury does not market its securities directly but relies on the Federal Reserve to serve as its fiscal agent. The Fed's fiscal agency role has several aspects. The Fed issues most new securities on behalf of the Treasury through a computerized book-entry system (see Box 2). Most Treasury securities no longer are issued in a tangible form as engraved certificates that can be kept in a vault, technically referred to as "definitive securities," and the issuance of definitive securities soon will be discontinued altogether. The Fed transfers most securities between depository institutions over its own wire system, called the Fedwire, in much the same way money is transferred electronically among depository institutions. The Fed not only maintains and transfers securities but also handles the initial sale of the securities. The Fed conducts auctions of new Treasury securities by collecting and processing competitive and noncompetitive bids from dealers, banks, individuals, and others.

Although the Fed serves as fiscal agent for the Treasury, it does not buy securities directly from the Treasury (except to roll over maturing holdings). Rather, if the System wishes to change its own holdings of Treasury securities for monetary policy reasons, it does so by transactions in the open secondary market. Thus, the Federal Reserve has a key interest in the government securities market because of its responsibility for implementing monetary policy as well as executing investments for foreign central banks. The New York Fed's trading desk purchases and sells government securities to implement the directives of the Federal Open Market Committee.[2] The Fed's open market operations—or transactions in government securities—influence the pace of monetary expansion. The New York Fed often uses repos and a transaction similar to reverse repos to provide or absorb bank reserves on a temporary basis. Last year the aggregate gross volume of open market transactions including repurchase agreements and transactions similar to reverse repos exceeded $200 billion in addition to Fed market transactions on behalf of 150 foreign central banks and other foreign official institutions.

In its market operations the Fed transacts only with certain dealers, known as primary dealers. Among these primary dealers currently are banks or bank subsidiaries, diversified investment houses, and specialty firms. There are now about 36 of these so-called primary dealers. Ten years ago there were about 25. No formal limit governs their number.

Primary dealers serve two crucial functions in the market: they help distribute the Treasury debt and they stand ready to "make markets," or buy and sell securities for customers. Their selection by the Fed as counterparties revolves around their ability to fulfill these two functions. Besides their ability to meet the needs of the Fed, criteria for being a primary dealer include volume of activity and participation in Treasury auctions, breadth of customer base, ability and commitment to buy and sell securities for customers even when market conditions are unfavorable, financial strength, depth of experience of management, and commitment to fulfilling this role over the long term.

In addition to primary dealers, many other firms routinely trade in U.S. government securities. These also include a mix of depository institutions, diversified securities firms, and specialty firms. Some participating firms are as large as primary dealers but have elected not to seek designation as such. Others service clients in a particular region. Still others may specialize in small transactions or odd lots.

This diversity is advantageous to investors because it provides them a greater choice of firms and services. Of course, these investors in government securities make up the largest sector of the market, and they include individuals; insurance, financial, and other corporations; pension funds; state and local governments and authorities; banks and savings institutions; and foreign investors.

Treasury Securities
Lisa Rockoff

The market for Treasury securities has grown rapidly in recent years largely in response to the federal government's expanding financial requirements. In addition to the growth in new issue activity, trading in the secondary market also has increased even more rapidly, attracting new dealers and greater customer participation.

What Are Treasury Securities?

The U.S. Treasury provides for the federal government's financial needs. In this capacity the Treasury is responsible for debt management, which includes borrowing funds to cover any shortfall between outlays and revenues and arranging for the refinancing, servicing, and repayment of maturing debt.[1] To meet this responsibility the Treasury issues debt securities in a wide variety of initial maturities. The best-known Treasury securities are bills, notes, and bonds. Bills are short-term, one year or less; notes are medium-term, one to 10 years; and bonds are long-term issues, greater than 10 years. Currently, the Treasury issues three-month, six-month, and one-year bills in minimum denominations of $10,000, with multiples of $5,000; two- through 10-year notes; and 20- and 30-year bonds in denominations of $1,000, $5,000, $10,000, $100,000, and $1 million. Occasionally, the Treasury issues very short-term cash management bills, with minimum denominations of $1 million, to bridge gaps when its cash balances are temporarily low.

The increasing size of the federal budget deficit in recent years has enlarged the volume of debt that the Treasury needs to sell. Because the timing and amount of its offerings can have a substantial impact on the financial markets, the Treasury has adopted a practice of issuing specific maturities on a regular schedule in order to facilitate absorption of its marketable debt with minimal disturbance. Quarterly Treasury announcements of the major mid-quarter refundings provide information on the exact amounts of each maturity to be offered, the amount of new cash to be raised by the operation, and the amount being refinanced. It also indicates the total amount of financing remaining to be done in that quarter and a range of financing likely to be done in the following quarter. Other auctions generally are announced about a week before they are held. The public can determine when an issue is forthcoming by consulting the financial sections of major daily newspapers or the 24-hour information lines on scheduled auctions at all 12 Federal Reserve Banks. In addition, customers may request that their names be added to any Federal Reserve Bank's mailing list for note and bond circulars.

How Are Treasury Securities Marketed?

Aside from nonmarketable securities, such as savings bonds, most Treasury securities can be bought in two ways—at Treasury auctions when they initially are offered or in the secondary market through a dealer.

Initial interest rates on marketable, or negotiable, Treasury securities (and the coupons on coupon-bearing notes and bonds) are established at auction.

Bids are made on both a competitive and a noncompetitive basis. A competitive bidder submits a tender for the amount of securities he or she wishes to purchase at a specified rate carried out to two decimal places. The Treasury generally limits competitive tenders to 35 percent of the amount offered to the public in each auction per single bidder. A noncompetitive bidder specifies the amount of securities he wishes to purchase but agrees to accept the average rate (and price) established through competitive bidding. The Treasury limits noncompetitive tenders, except those of the Federal Reserve System and its customers, to $1 million per bidder. Therefore, most noncompetitive bids come from smaller investors.

On the day of the auction, all Federal Reserve Banks receive tenders until a specified time, usually 1 p.m. Eastern time. Subsequently, these are wired to the Treasury. After all timely bids have been received, the volume of noncompetitive tenders is subtracted from the total amount to be issued. Allowable noncompetitive tenders are accepted in full. The remainder of the issue is allocated to competitive bidders, beginning with those who bid the lowest rate. After filling the bids at the lowest rate, the Treasury awards issues at the next higher rate and so on until all of the issue has been awarded. A partial award may be made at the highest accepted rate (the stop-out rate) in order to come as close as possible to the exact amount the Treasury plans to sell. Once the stop-out bid is reached, a weighted average rate is computed from all accepted competitive bids. Noncompetitive bidders are awarded their securities at a price based on the established average rate. Competitive bidders whose tenders have been accepted pay the price equivalent to the rate they specified. Auction results can be found in the financial sections of many major daily newspapers on the day following the auction.

In most respects, auctions for bills are conducted in a manner similar to those for notes and bonds. There are a few key differences, though, largely due to differences in the way the two types of Treasury securities are priced, discussed below.[2]

How Are Prices and Rates of Return on Treasury Securities Determined?

Treasury Bills. Treasury bills, or T-bills, are non-interest bearing securities issued at a discount. That is, Treasury sells the bills at a price that is below their face value—or at a discount—and redeems them at face value. Thus, the return to the investor is determined by the discount at which the securities are bought and the length of time until maturity. The Treasury computes the price per $100 face value of discount securities using the following formula:

$$P = \left(1 - \frac{r_d \times D}{360}\right) \times 100$$

where

P = price per \$100 face amount,

r_d = interest rate on a discount basis decimalized (e.g. 7.36% = 0.736),

D = days to maturity.

For example, assume six-month (182-day) bills are purchased at a 7 percent discount rate. The price of the bill is calculated as follows:

$$P = \left(1 - \frac{0.07 \times 182}{360}\right) \times 100$$
$$= 96.4611112$$

The Treasury rounds the price to three decimal places, so \$96.461 is the price per \$100 face value of securities. Thus, the purchase price of \$1 million of these bills would be \$964,610.00.

Rates quoted on a discount basis do not reflect the fact that the amount invested is less than the face value of the securities. In addition, Treasury bill rates are calculated on a 360-day basis, whereas interest on longer-maturity Treasury securities is computed on a 365-day basis. To allow rate comparisons, bill rates are often converted into bond-equivalent yields (BEY). The BEY on a discount instrument with a maturity of six months or less is derived as follows:

$$BEY = 100 \times \left[\frac{(100 - P) \times 365}{P \times D}\right]$$

Using our earlier example, the bond-equivalent yield on a six-month bill with a 7 percent discount rate is found as follows:

$$BEY = 100 \times \left[\frac{(100 - 96.461) \times 365}{96.461 \times 182}\right]$$
$$= 7.36\%$$

For a bill with a maturity of six months or more, the BEY calculation must reflect the approximate return that would have been obtained if interest had been paid at the end of six months (since interest payments on securities with interest coupons are made every six months). The formula is complex but similar in principle to deriving the yield on coupon securities in the case where the coupon is set at zero.

Treasury notes and bonds. Unlike bills, notes and bonds pay separate interest every six months. They carry a fixed interest payment, the coupon rate, and, hence, are also called coupon securities. The coupon rate is established at auction.[4] Bidding on coupon issues is based on yields, not prices. After an issue has been awarded at auction, the Treasury establishes a fixed coupon, rounded down to the nearest eighth of one percent, based on the weighted average of the accepted competitive yields.

The price charged to competitive bidders is set at or rounded down to slightly below par. At the time of issue, prices are expressed as a percentage of par, par equaling 100.

In the secondary market, fractional prices are expressed in 32nds. Securities that trade below par are said to be at a discount, while those trading above par are said to be at a premium. For example, the price of a coupon security trading below par might be expressed as 99 12/32, often shown as 99.12. This figure represents a price of \$993.75 for a \$1,000 bond. A bond trading above par might be quoted at 102 5/32, or 102.5, implying a price of \$1,021.56 for a \$1,000 bond.

The coupon rate established on any note or bond represents the simple annual interest rate the Treasury pays to the investor on the face value. Since the Treasury pays interest semiannually, the interest payment each six months is represented by the formula:

$$i = \frac{\text{Coupon Rate} \times \text{Face Value}}{2}$$

The rate of return on notes and bonds held to maturity when both the present value of the future interest payments and the redemption value of the security are taken into account is called the yield to maturity. The present value may be viewed as the amount one is willing to pay now for the stream of coupon payments plus the face value received at maturity. The higher (or lower) the yield, the less (or more) one is willing to pay to receive any specified payment in the future. Thus, price varies inversely with yield.

The longer the maturity of the security, the greater the number of payments. Also, the further away a payment is in time, the more its present value changes in response to any change in yield. Thus, for any given yield change the size of the resulting price change—or volatility—varies directly with maturity.

Finally, price changes depend on the coupon. The lower the coupon, the larger the share that the present value of the final payment represents in the calculation of present value or price. Since that payment is furthest in the future—and so is most sensitive to a yield change—the more the price of the entire security will change to reflect a given change in yield. Thus, price volatility varies inversely with the coupon rate. Some investors use a measure known as duration in figuring yield. While the computation of this measure is too complex to describe succinctly, duration essentially recognizes both the relative importance of coupons and the final maturity of a bond or note. Therefore, the price volatility of debt securities varies directly with both their duration and the volatility of interest rates.

In calculating yield to maturity one assumes coupon payments are reinvested every six months at the same yield, specifically the yield to maturity. Although using a current interest rate as a proxy for future rates is somewhat arbitrary, alternative methods involve estimating expected rates in the future, an extremely complex and equally unrealistic process.

After-tax yield calculations need to take into account any capital gain or loss arising from the difference between a security's purchase price and its face value at redemption. For example, if an investor purchases notes and bonds at slightly below par, say, at 99.120 (or $993.75 for a $1,000 bond) and redeems it at face value (or $1,000), the investor receives a capital gain of $6.25.

Most outstanding 30-year bonds have 25-year call provisions, which allow the Treasury to redeem the bonds at par after 25 years. Technically, the Treasury might exercise this option if interest rates 25 years after issue are below the coupon on the bond. Valuation of callable bonds can be complex, but they typically behave as if they have a 25-year maturity when interest rates are significantly below their coupons and a 30-year maturity when the opposite holds.

———————

The author is an analyst in the Research Department of the Federal Reserve Bank of Atlanta.

NOTES

[1] Treasury borrowing constitutes only one part—albeit the largest—of total government-related borrowing. Federally sponsored agencies set up by Congress to make credit available to specific sectors of the economy also borrow. Agencies financing in the open market include the Federal National Mortgage Association (FNMA), the Farm Credit Banks, the Federal Home Loan Banks, and the Government National Mortgage Association (GNMA). There are differences between Treasury and agency borrowing. First, whereas the Treasury borrows to finance the federal deficit, agencies act more as financial intermediaries. Second, while some agency debt is guaranteed as to principal and interest by the U.S. government or has the full faith backing of the U.S. government, other agency debt does not have this backing.

[2] Another difference pertains to tenders by the Fed. Fed tenders typically are noncompetitive. On three- and six-month T-bills the amount tendered by the Fed is subtracted from the total. In contrast, the amount tendered by the Fed on one-year T-bills, notes, and bonds is not subtracted from the total since the Fed is issued securities in addition to the amount offered to the public.

[3] The bill price formula illustrates that price varies inversely with interest rate. It also reflects the fact that, for any given rate change, the size of price movements varies directly with the maturity of the bill. That is, the farther away in time a customer receives the face amount, the less he is willing to pay now for the bill.

[4] Under the public debt statutes there is a 4 1/4 percent interest-rate limit on bonds. When interest rates were low, the Treasury had no problem issuing bonds under this constraint. As interest rates rose, though, this limit forced the Treasury to concentrate debt issuance in short- to intermediate-term issues. Therefore, in the early 1970s Congress granted a partial exemption from this ceiling for a specified dollar amount (face) of bonds and has since raised these amounts several times. Congress also responded to the problem by extending the maturity of notes (which are not subject to the rate ceiling) from a maximum of five years to seven and later to ten years.

How Government Securities Dealers Operate

Government securities dealers perform three interrelated activities. First, they make markets for customers and provide information, analysis, and advice to encourage transactions and customer loyalty. Second, to meet customer needs, they generally maintain an inventory of securities. The composition of this inventory is structured to allow dealers to sell securities at a higher price than they bought them. Third, they manage their positions, speculating on market trends with a view to profiting from swings in interest rates.

When a dealer makes a bid or an offer to a customer, the dealer is buying or selling securities for its position. That is, the dealer is acting as principal and not as agent. When a dealer finances his holdings of securities, he is also acting as a principal. Thus, dealers are distinct from brokers. The latter earn a profit by acting as go-betweens, matching parties with complementary needs and charging a commission for their services.

Securities dealers absorb and distribute a large share of the U.S. government debt when it is sold at auction. They also buy and sell existing securities in the secondary market. The price at which a dealer is willing to buy a security is called a "bid"; the price at which he is willing to sell is an "offer." A dealer firm tries to earn the spread between the bid and offer prices on customer transactions.

Dealers also position securities to reflect their assessment of likely changes in interest rates. If a dealer expects interest rates to fall and hence prices of debt securities to rise, he will typically "take a long position" in these issues. If he expects rates to rise, he will "go short," selling securities he does not own in the expectation of buying the securities back later at a lower price. Long and short positions generally are highly leveraged, or supported with borrowed funds, at times to over 99 percent. Thus, position management is a major source of variation in profit and capital in either direction.

As explained earlier, in a repo the dealer agrees to sell a security at a specified price for a specified period after which he agrees to repurchase the security, usually at the agreed-upon price. In return for the security, the dealer receives funds to finance its positions in government securities. Since the dealer has use of the

The Book-Entry System for Treasury Securities[1]
A. E. Martin III

An important aspect of the government securities market is understanding how a book-entry system for recording ownership of and interests in securities operates. In contrast to "definitive" securities (those represented by a physical certificate), an interest in book-entry securities is reflected by an entry, often computerized, in the accounts of a book-entry custodian indicating the party for whom it holds the securities. The following discussion provides a brief overview of the book-entry system for U.S. Treasury securities. U.S. Treasury bills are issued exclusively in book-entry form; Treasury notes and bonds, although available in definitive form as well, are held mainly in book-entry. Moreover, the Treasury Department has announced its plans to offer new issues of Treasury notes and bonds exclusively in book-entry form beginning some time in 1986.

The book-entry system for Treasury securities is governed by Treasury regulations, which facilitate the establishment of a "tiered" custodial system whereby the ownership of securities is represented by entries on the books of a series of custodians. This system extends from the Treasury itself through the Federal Reserve Banks, depository institutions, and brokers

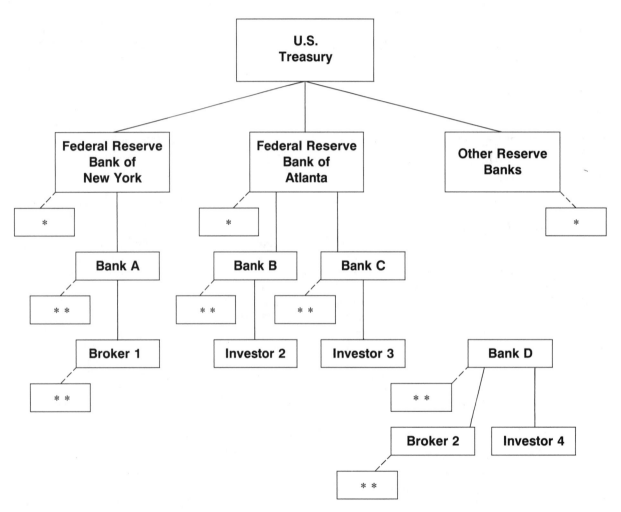

*Other depository institutions.
**Other custodians (depository institutions, brokers/dealers, etc.) or ultimate investors.

or dealers to the ultimate owner or party in interest.[2] The Treasury's records reflect the total amount of an issue of securities outstanding and the portion held by each Federal Reserve Bank. In turn, each Reserve Bank's entries establish how much of the issue is held by the depository institutions in its district that maintain book-entry accounts with it.[3]

A depository institution's records further divide the amount it holds at its Reserve Bank, reflecting how much it holds for itself, for other depository institutions (including those that do not maintain accounts at the Federal Reserve), for brokers and dealers, and for the ultimate investors. Thus, the custodial chain may include only the Treasury, a Reserve Bank, and a depository institution, or additional custodians such as other depository institutions and broker/dealers. Payments of principal at maturity as well as interest payments on Treasury notes and bonds are made through the crediting of funds by the Treasury down through the custodial tiers.

Under Treasury regulations and the operating circulars of the Reserve Banks, only depository institutions may have book-entry accounts at a Reserve Bank.[4] Other parties must have their holdings reflected on the books of a depository institution or other "depositary" that in turn holds through a depository institution.[5] In certain limited instances, such as the pledge of securities by a depository institution to secure the deposits of state or local government funds, a third party's interest in book-entry securities may be noted at the Reserve Bank level. However, securities acquired under a repurchase agreement are not held to secure deposits and are not eligible for such treatment.

Transfers and pledges of book-entry securities are effected by making appropriate entries, according to the instructions of the parties involved in the transaction, on the records of the custodian(s) involved. Under Treasury regulations, making such an entry renders the custodian a "bailee," or legal custodian, with respect to the party for whom it holds.[6] Referring to the chart, a transfer from Broker 1 to Investor 2 would involve not only the ultimate making of an entry on Bank B's books, reflecting the transfer to Investor 2, and on Broker 1's books, decreasing its own holdings, but also entries on the books of Banks A and B, both Federal Reserve Banks, and the Treasury. A transfer

from Investor 2 to Investor 3 would entail entries on the books of Banks B and C and the Atlanta Reserve Bank but not the Treasury. At the other extreme, a transfer from Broker 2 to Investor 4 would involve only an entry on the books of Bank D, reallocating a portion of the amount it held through its Reserve Bank between Broker 2 and Investor 4. No revision of entries on the books of the Reserve Bank or the Treasury would be involved.

Under Treasury regulations, a transfer or pledge of book-entry securities is accomplished by means that would be effective under applicable law a transfer or perfect a pledge of definitive securities in bearer form. No filing or recording with a public recording office or officer is required. A transferee, or pledgee, may obtain from its custodian acknowledgment that securities are held for it. A Reserve Bank, however, deals exclusively with the depository institutions for which it holds book-entry accounts and does not accept notices or instructions from remote parties holding through depository institutions regarding their interests in securities.

Procedurally, transactions are effected by instructions transmitted by and through the parties and custodians involved. If a transaction involves entries on the books of a Reserve Bank or several Reserve Banks (and the Treasury), then the Fedwire (the Federal Reserve's wire transfer system) is used to transmit instructions electronically.[7] For transactions that do not reach the Reserve Bank level in the custodial chain, no specific mode of communication is required for the transfer. This distinction has implications for repurchase transactions of small amounts or short duration.

Don Ringsmuth's article in this issue discusses several types of delivery and custodial arrangements that can be used in a repo transaction. The foregoing summary of the mechanics of the book-entry system for Treasury securities is designed to provide only a brief structural overview of the system. There are additional issues and factors that require expertise or the advice of experienced counsel to engage in repo transactions.

The author is an attorney in the Legal Department of the Federal Reserve Bank of Atlanta.

NOTES

[1] This box discusses only the book-entry system for Treasury securities, although similar systems exist for other types of securities that are also used in repo transactions, including some securities issued by federal agencies and handled by the Federal Reserve.

[2] Subpart O of 31 C.F.R. Part 306 - The General Regulations Governing United States Securities ("Treasury regulations") governs the book-entry system for Treasury securities. Virtually identical rules with respect to Treasury bills held in book-entry through the Federal Reserve are contained in Subpart D of 31 C.F.R. Part 350. Subpart C of these Treasury bill regulations also establishes a system whereby Treasury bills may be held in book-entry accounts maintained by the Treasury itself. Transactions in bills so held, however, require that the bills be transferred into the tiered system described in this article.

[3] Prior to the Monetary Control Act of 1980, only member banks of the Federal Reserve System could maintain book-entry accounts with the Federal Reserve. Now any depository institution may do so.

[4] Section 306.117 of the Treasury regulations; each of the Federal Reserve Banks has issued an operating circular, letter, or bulletin containing additional provisions governing the maintenance of book-entry securities accounts at the Federal Reserve. See, e.g., Operating Circular No. 21 of the Federal Reserve Bank of Atlanta.

[5] Under the Treasury's regulations (section 306.118(b)), a "depositary" is defined as a bank, banking institution, financial firm, or similar party, which regularly accepts in the course of its business Treasury securities as a custodial service for customers and maintains accounts in the names of such customers reflecting ownership of or interest in such securities. In this box, the term "custodian" is used rather than "depositary" to avoid confusion with the term "depository institution," which is one type of depositary.

[6] Section 306.118(b) of the Treasury regulations.

[7] Each of the Federal Reserve Banks also has issued an operating letter or circular regarding the wire transfer of book-entry securities, such as Operating Circular No. 20 of the Federal Reserve Bank of Atlanta.

Chart 1. Common Holding Company Structure

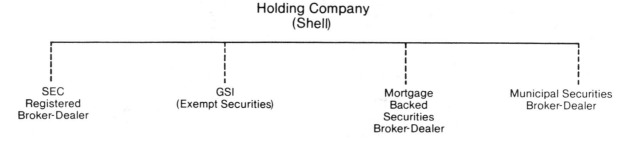

Holding Company
(Shell)

| SEC Registered Broker-Dealer | GSI (Exempt Securities) | Mortgage Backed Securities Broker-Dealer | Municipal Securities Broker-Dealer |

customer's money while the repurchase agreement is outstanding, the dealer agrees to pay interest to the customer.

Dealers often use reverse repos, whereby they provide money and take in customer securities, to obtain the securities they have sold short—those they have sold without owning and need to deliver. When one party is executing a repo, the counterparty must be executing a reverse repo.

Some dealers also arrange repos and reverse repos at the same time, operating what is called a "matched book," to earn income from the spreads between what they receive from one type of transaction and pay for the other. Such dealers are acting as a principal and are intermediating, or raising funds from one customer and providing funds to another.

Matched books also may be used to speculate on the direction of short-term interest rates. If a dealer expects short-term rates to rise, he will arrange repos with a longer maturity than the reverse repos in his matched book. That is, he will raise funds for a longer period than he provides them, expecting that rates on the rollover of the reverse repo will rise relative to the rate set on the repo.

Types of Dealer Organization

The way that a government securities operation fits into a firm's overall organizational structure determines whether the operation is subject to the oversight and capital rules of the SEC. Four forms of organization are widely used by government securities dealers. The simplest is a single firm where the government securities dealer is a department in the overall securities firm or bank. In two cases the dealer operation is a separate subsidiary in a holding company; in the other, the dealer is a commonly owned affiliate. Securities firms of all sizes use the holding company structure. In many instances, the holding company is a shell with activity transacted through its subsidiaries (see Chart 1).

Government securities may be traded in the same entity which also trades nonexempt securities. In this case, the whole entity, including its government securities operations, is subject to SEC rules. However, many organizations using a holding company structure conduct regulated activities through their principal subsidiary, a broker-dealer registered with the Securities and Exchange Commission (SEC), while government and other exempt security activity is transacted through another subsidiary known as a Government Securities, Incorporated (GSI). The GSI is not constrained by the SEC's capital or custodial rules.

The separation of exempt and nonexempt securities activities increases the firm's overall flexibility. For example, less capital must be devoted to the GSI than would be the case if the business were SEC regulated. Similarly, an organization may use other subsidiaries to separate management authority or legal liability for other activities, such as mortgage-backed or municipal bond trading.

Using another organizational structure, many smaller specialty firms concentrate their government and other exempt securities trading in the parent company while setting up a small SEC-registered broker-dealer subsidiary to trade in regulated markets (see Chart 2). A fourth form of organization involves affiliation of multiple firms through common ownership (see Chart 3).

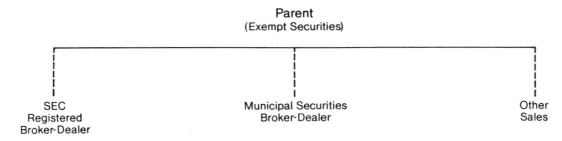

Chart 2. Common Specialty Firm Structure

Parent
(Exempt Securities)

SEC
Registered
Broker-Dealer

Municipal Securities
Broker-Dealer

Other
Sales

Customers should be careful to review financial statements for the specific subsidiary with which they are dealing. In some cases financial statements for holding companies with multiple subsidiaries are prepared for the consolidated firm only. In these consolidated holding company financial statements, the footnotes concerning "excess capital" under the SEC's rules refer only to the SEC-regulated affiliates. Furthermore, common ownership or affiliation may or may not be reported in financial statements or disclosed by the firm. If there are substantial transactions with affiliates, customers should ask for financial statements on any such affiliated entities.

Regulatory Framework

Whether a particular dealer firm is subject to official oversight depends on the markets in which the firm participates and on its individual characteristics and organization. Most diversified securities houses, for example, deal in corporate issues and municipal securities as well as U.S. government securities. Since the Securities and Exchange Commission regulates corporate issues, these firms are subject to SEC regulation. The SEC in turn delegates some of its supervisory responsibilities to the various stock exchanges, the National Association of Securities Dealers, and the Municipal Securities Rule-Making Board. Some small government securities dealers that participate in the financial futures exchanges are regulated by the Commodities Futures Trading Commission (CFTC). Because of their corporate affiliation, dealer departments of banks are subject to examination by federal and state bank regulatory authorities such as the Fed, the Office of the

Comptroller of the Currency (OCC), and the Federal Deposit Insurance Corporation (FDIC). Primary dealers also are subject to oversight by the Fed. The New York Fed scrutinizes the primary dealers with which it transacts as part of its business relationship with them and its concern for the health of the markets. The Fed, however, has no statutory authority to regulate these firms.

Some government securities dealers are free from any form of federal supervision or regulation. Dealers in this group trade only exempt securities—U.S. government and agency securities, certificates of deposit, bankers' acceptances, and commercial paper—and are not subject to examination by the SEC, the Fed, or any federal banking regulator. Furthermore, there is no federal regulation of GSI subsidiaries or affiliates of seemingly "regulated" firms.

Advantages and Disadvantages of Unrestricted Entry

The government securities market, in many respects, exemplifies the free markets described in classical economics. No formal barriers restrict entry. Dealers must meet no licensing requirements, for example. Anyone can become a government securities dealer, and the diversity among secondary dealers demonstrates that many different kinds of businesses enter the market. Once a firm is in the market, no uniform capital requirements or standards for custodial control or sales practices apply. Furthermore, there are no margin requirements; dealers can and often do finance over 99 percent of the purchase cost of most Treasury securities.

The resultant structure of the securities market has produced competition, efficiency, and in-

Chart 3. Common Holding Company Structure

Common Ownership

| SEC Registered Broker-Dealer | Municipal Securities Broker-Dealer | GSI (Exempt Securities) | Other Entities |

novation. The profusion of competitors helps narrow the spread between the prices at which a dealer buys securities from a customer and the prices at which a dealer sells securities to a customer. This clearly is advantageous to customers. Customers also benefit by being able to compare the prices offered by several dealers over the telephone or through dedicated telecommunications services that report such information continually. The availability of information enables customers to transact at the best price. The market's intense competitiveness also reduces the Treasury's cost of issuing debt. Finally, free entry has enabled all kinds and sizes of customers to obtain service from the myriad firms in the market.

However, the lack of uniform supervision has permitted abuses to go undetected longer than they probably would have under a more regulated regime. The wide scope of these problems became apparent earlier this year when defaults by several government securities dealers resulted in costly losses for a number of local governments and thrift institutions. Given the problems that have appeared in the repo market, many people, including members of Congress, have questioned whether the government securities market should remain under its current incomplete and diverse regulatory framework. Several bills have been introduced in Congress to address this issue.

The Federal Reserve favors some form of minimum regulation involving registration, capital and operating standards, and inspection. To help protect investors in the interim or in the absence of full-scale regulation, the Federal Reserve has developed a voluntary capital adequacy guideline for government securities dealers not already subject to some regulation.[3] The guideline, along with the Fed's efforts to educate investors regarding proper procedures to use with repurchase agreements, is designed to help guard against abuses while minimizing inefficiencies and additional costs and preserving the strength and dynamism of the market.

Conclusion

The government securities market enjoys a favorable record characterized by efficiency, competitiveness, and innovation. While the recent spate of losses involving investors in repurchase agreements is disturbing, failures and defaults have been rare exceptions. The liquidity and other positive characteristics provided by the market have contributed to its growth and attractiveness to a broad array of investors and made the market a vital part of our nation's financial markets.

NOTES

[1]This article also draws from work done by Edward Geng, senior vice president of the Federal Reserve Bank of New York.

[2]The FOMC consists of the seven members of the Board of Governors, including the chairman, the president of the Federal Reserve Bank of New York, and presidents of the other II District banks, serving on a rotating basis.

[3]This is discussed in this issue by Gary Haberman and Catherine Piche in "Controlling Credit Risk Associated with Repos: Know Your Counterparty."

Article Three

A Primer on
Mortgage-Backed Securities

JOHN R. BRICK

*The new instruments
may be worth playing.*

UNTIL THE MID-1970s, the major sources of capital for the residential mortgage market were savings and loans associations, mutual savings banks, and commercial banks. Financial institutions such as life insurance companies, pension funds, endowments, and trust funds tended to avoid direct investments in residential mortgages because of the cumbersome nature of the instrument and its high cost. Much paper work is required for each mortgage loan; moreover, physical facilities and a trained staff are needed to administer a mortgage loan portfolio. Compounding the problem is the fact that residential loans are usually made in relatively small denominations. The result is that residential mortgages have a high administrative cost per dollar of investment. In contrast, bonds require considerably less administrative effort and have low transaction costs. The costs related to a bond portfolio may be spead over large denominations, so the administrative cost per dollar invested is quite low.

A related impediment that affected the flow of capital to the mortgage market was simply the inaccessibil-

John R. Brick is Associate Professor of Finance, School of Business, Michigan State University. This article is adapted from a chapter in *Commercial Banking: Text and Readings*, copyright © 1984 by John R. Brick, published by Systems Publications, Inc., Haslett, Michigan, all rights reserved.

ity of large institutions such as insurance companies and pension funds to borrowers, and vice versa. Unless such an institution had a decentralized investment operation with geographically dispersed outlets, it was virtually impossible for these types of institutions to channel a significant amount of funds into the residential mortgage market.

In recent years, however, the growing acceptance of mortgage-backed securities in the financial markets has led to dramatic changes in both the mortgage market and financial practices of many financial institutions. Three such instruments underlie these changes and dominate the markets. Some of the characteristics of two of these, *the pass-through certificate* and the *mortgage-backed bond,* are relatively well known. At this time, though, there is confusion surrounding the *pay-through bond.* This confusion stems from the fact that the pay-through bond combines important features of the pass-through certificate and the mortgage-backed bond.

PASS-THROUGH CERTIFICATES

The pass-through certificate represents direct ownership of a portfolio of mortgage loans. The portfolio is created when a mortgage lender assembles a pool of mortgage loans that are alike in their term, interest rate, and quality. The portfolio is then placed in trust with a bank and certificates of ownership are sold to investors. Ownership of loans in the pool lies with the holders of the certificates and not the original lender. Since the pass-through arises through the sale of the issuer's assets, pass-through certificates are not debt obligations of the issuer; they do not show up on the issuer's financial statement.

Although the holders of pass-through certificates own the mortgage loans, the loan originator "services" the mortgage pool. The originator collects monthly payments, handles the accounting, and disburses the principal and interest payments to the pool owners. All interest, principal, and prepayments on the underlying mortgage loans, less the servicing fee, are passed through monthly and in a single payment to the owners—hence the name "pass-throughs." The payment is accompanied by an itemized statement showing the proportions of principal and interest. The holder of a certificate owns a portion of a mortgage portfolio by holding an instrument with convenient, bond-like characteristics.

Ginnie Mae Pass-Throughs

The pass-through concept was developed in 1970 by the Government National Mortgage Association (GNMA), a direct agency of the federal government.

The most important characteristic of these GNMA issues, commonly referred to as "Ginnie Mae pass-throughs," is that they are riskless with respect to default. This stems from three sources of financial backing:

- The securities are collateralized by mortgage loans held in trust for the holders of the certificates.
- The mortgage loan portfolio underlying the Ginnie Mae pass-through is comprised entirely of government-backed FHA and VA loans.
- The GNMA, an arm of the federal government, guarantees the prompt monthly payment of both principal and interest—*regardless of whether or not it has been collected.*

The guarantee of the monthly payments has the effect of "modifying" the actual stream of mortgage payments. If a mortgage loan is in a nonpaying or even a foreclosure status, it is irrelevant to the holder of the pass-through certificate since principal and interest are paid by Ginnie Mae. If a foreclosure results and the loan is repaid by the FHA or VA, this constitutes a prepayment and it is passed through to the owners of the pool.

In light of the collateral, FHA and VA backing, and the Ginnie Mae guarantee, it is difficult to imagine a security with more financial backing than a Ginnie Mae pass-through. Because of this backing, the securities are considered direct obligations of the U.S. Government. They may be held in any amount by regulated financial institutions such as banks, S&Ls, and credit unions.

Loans in the pool should be similar in their quality, interest rate, and term. This facilitates the pricing process since the entire portfolio may be viewed as a single loan. When offering a new pass-through security made up of new thirty-year loans, the yield is estimated (or the price determined) by assuming that the cash flows stem only from the scheduled amortization payments for twelve years; at the end of this period all loans are fully prepaid. This assumption is used because on new pools of new loans, there is no prepayment experience available. Since it is known that most mortgage loans will be prepaid, some prepayment assumption must be made. The yield produced by the twelfth-year prepayment assumption corresponds to the yields historically generated by pools of FHA-insured loans. However, specific pools may prepay at a much faster or slower rate than the general FHA experience. If the certificate was bought at a discount from or premium over par value, as is usually the case, the rate of repayment and changes in the rate affect the buyer's yield. After a Ginnie Mae pass-through has been outstanding, information is published regarding the speed at which the specific issue is being prepaid. This speed determines the average life of the portfolio. The information can then be used to obtain a better estimate of the yield.[1]

New issues of Ginnie-Mae pass-throughs are available in minimum donominations of $25,000 and with terms of twenty-eight to thirty years. Because of the loan reduction through amortization and prepayments, older issues are available in smaller denominations and with shorter terms. The interest income is taxable at federal, state, and local levels. Although lacking liquidity because of their price sensitivity resulting from changes in interest rates, an active and well-developed secondary market provides a high degree of marketability for these securities.

Freddie Mac Pass-Throughs

The success of Ginnie Mae pass-throughs prompted the Federal Home Loan Mortgage Corporation (FHLMC)—known as "Freddie Mac"—to develop its own version of the pass-through. This indirect federal agency was chartered by Congress in 1970 for the purpose of increasing the flow of capital to the mortgage market. Unlike Ginnie Mae, which only purchases FHA-VA loans primarily from mortgage bankers,

---

[1] For a numerical example of the pricing process of pass-throughs, see *Pass-Through Yield and Value Tables*, Pub. No. 175 (latest ed.) (Boston: Financial Publishing Co.).

Freddie Mac purchases uninsured and privately insured mortgage loans, primarily from S&Ls and banks. To finance this activity and support an active secondary market for such loans, the agency issues several types of securities. The most important of these is a pass-through security called a "participation certificate" (PC).

PCs are similar in concept to the Ginnie Mae pass-through. The PC represents ownership of a portion of a mortgage portfolio. However, there are some important differences. The mortgage loans underlying the PCs are either uninsured loans with L/V ratios of 80 percent or less, or privately insured loans if the L/V ratio exceeds 80 percent. The loans are not government-backed so PC mortgage pools are geographically diversified and considerably larger than the Ginnie Mae mortgage pools. Each pool usually contains between 2,000 and 5,000 loans.

As with the Ginnie Mae pass-throughs, mortgage loans constitute the source of repayment and back the PC. The financial risk of these loans is minimized by the owner's equity or private mortgage insurance. In addition, the PCs are guaranteed by Freddie Mac as to the "timely payment of interest and the full return of principal." This means that the monthly interest is guaranteed but the principal is passed through as collected. Although the full repayment of principal is guaranteed, there may be slight delays in the event of default by borrowers. Since the loans are high quality, there are few such defaults and delays are relatively few. When such delays do occur, the effect on the total monthly payment is small because of the large number of loans in each pool.

Although Freddie Mac's guarantee does not constitute formal backing by the federal government, the guarantee coupled with well-secured loans results in a security of exceptionally high quality. In fact, PCs are like Ginnie Mae pass-throughs in that they are exempt from any "percent of asset" limitations imposed by regulators of banks, S&Ls, and credit unions. This means that PCs may be held in unlimited amounts.

Although the pricing of PCs is similar to that of Ginnie Maes, there is a tendency for conventional and privately insured mortgages to repay at faster rates than FHA loans. The result is a shorter average life of about seven to nine years for the PCs, rather than ten to twelve years for Ginnie Maes. The experience of individual pools, however, may differ considerably.

Because of a large minimum denomination, $100,000, the market for PCs is dominated by financial institutions. An active secondary market provides reasonably good marketability. Generally, the yields on PCs are about 15 to 25 basis points higher than yields on comparable term Ginnie Mae pass-throughs. The spread varies depending on market conditions.

Private Sector Pass-Throughs

In September 1977, the Bank of America successfully issued the first private sector pass-through security. This offering was backed solely by conventional mortgages. There were no government or agency guarantees and, as pass-throughs, the securities were *not* debt obligations of the BofA. However, the imaginative use of private mortgage insurance on the entire pool (rather than on each individual loan) and special hazard insurance substantially reduced the risk of loss to the holders of the pass-throughs. This landmark financing became a model for private sector pass-throughs. It also had an immediate and widespread impact on both the mortgage market and the management policies of many financial institutions.

☐ *Quality Rating.* The key to a private sector pass-through offering by a financial institution is the quality of the security as measured by bond rating services such as Standard & Poor's and Moody's. The rating plays a role in several ways. From the standpoint of many regulated financial institutions as buyers of such securities, the purchase of an unrated issue must be justified to examiners. As a result, most institutions simply avoid buying unrated issues or issues with ratings lower than BBB or Baa. From the issuer's standpoint, the sale of pass-throughs constitutes a sale of assets. The price received by the selling institution depends on the rating. In fact, the entire pass-through concept depends on the quality rating.

If the BofA pass-through issue cited above were rated BBB rather than AA, the required yield to investors may have been 10 percent, which was greater than the average interest rate on the pool. The mortgages would have to be sold at a discount and the capital loss absorbed by the bank. This would inhibit the use of the pass-through as a financing device. As it was, the BofA issue was sold at a profit because the default risk related to each loan was minimized by careful underwriting, special hazard insurance, and mortgage insurance.

To obtain a high rating on a pass-through security, several criteria must be satisfied. Loans underlying the pass-through must be secured by first mortgages on single-family, owner-occupied, primary residences. The loan-to-value ratio must be no greater than 80 per-

cent. The pool's mortgage insurance and special hazard policies must provide ample protection. The financial strength of the loan servicer, trustee, and insurance companies are other important elements in the rating process.[2] Although most pass-through issues involve fixed-rate mortgage loans, this need not always be the case. Adjustable-rate pass-through certificates rated AA have been sold in the public debt markets.

☐ *Some Variations.* In an attempt to further reduce both the cost and default risk of pass-throughs, and at the same time increase the price at which they may be sold, some commercial banks back their issues with an irrevocable letter of credit (LOC). The LOC replaces the mortgage insurance and special hazard insurance policies. When there is a delinquency on any loans in the pool, the trustee calls on the bank to make payments under provisions of the LOC. Since the issuing bank has a binding obligation to make such advances, the bank has parted with the assets but retains some of the risk. To limit this risk and comply with legal restrictions on borrowings, the Comptroller of the Currency, the regulator of national banks, has ruled that the amount of LOC backing is limited to 7 percent of the principal balance in the pool.

Another innovative approach to the risk-reduction problem is to divide the mortgage pool into senior and subordinated certificates. The senior certificates have a priority claim on the principal and interest payments made on mortgage loans in the pool. The holders of subordinated certificates receive no payments until the holders of senior certificates have been completely satisfied for a specified period. Because of the added backing of the loans underlying the subordinated certificates, the senior certificates usually obtain a very high rating. The rating of the subordinated certificates is lower unless some other form of protection is provided.

☐ *Managerial Implications.* The ability to package and sell conventional and alternative mortgage loans in a convenient, bond-like form enables mortgage lenders to obtain capital from nontraditional sources such as pension funds, life insurance companies, trust funds, and endowments. The ready acceptance of pass-throughs by financial institutions carries over to the private placement market where large, complex transactions can be negotiated quickly between a small number of financial institutions.

---

[2] For a discussion of the rating process for mortgage-related securities, see *Credit Overview: Corporate and International Ratings* (New York: Standard & Poor's Corporation, 1982), pp. 64-70.

Existence of an active private placement market for pass-throughs has important implications for smaller mortgage lenders. Since the minimum size for a public offering is about $20 million, many smaller institutions are unable to package a sufficiently large portfolio. A logical alternative is to place smaller issues privately with other financial institutions. Issues as small as $5 million have been placed in this manner. Another approach for smaller institutions is to sell their individual mortgage loans to so-called conduits. Several private mortgage insurance companies, for example, act as an intermediary and buy small blocks of mortgage loans from lenders and then pool the loans for resale as a pass-through security in the national markets.

The pass-through concept has enhanced the financial flexibility of mortgage lenders and is accomplished without incurring additional liabilities. The capital structure, and thus the financial risk of the lender, is unchanged when pass-through securities are sold. This is not the case with mortgage-backed bonds.

MORTGAGE-BACKED BONDS

The mortgage-backed bond (MBB) is a debt obligation of a mortgage lending institution and is collateralized by mortgage loans. Unlike pass-throughs, the issuer retains ownership of the loans. From the investor's standpoint, these instruments are like other bonds in that they have a stated maturity with the interest usually paid seminannually. Typically, bonds in the private sector have a maturity ranging from five to twelve years. This maturity range corresponds to the average life of a portfolio of fixed-rate conventional mortgage loans. Since these bonds do not have long maturities, they are usually not callable. However, bonds with maturities toward the longer end of the spectrum may have a sinking fund to provide for an orderly repayment schedule.

Although federal agencies issue mortgage-backed bonds, the focus of this section is on private-sector issues. Since these bonds lack direct federal or agency guarantees, the indenture provisions and certain aspects of the collateral mortgage loan portfolio assume added importance.

Despite the lack of any direct government backing, the private sector mortgage-backed bond is an unusually high-quality instrument. This is a result of three sources of financial strength. First, the bonds are direct liabilities of the issuer and, as such, the bonds are backed by the creditworthiness of the issuing mortgage lender. The second source of financial strength is the quality of the underlying mortgage loans that are held in trust as collateral for the bondholders. If the loans are FHA- or VA-backed, the collateral is riskless from a credit standpoint. Although not riskless in this respect, uninsured and privately insured mortgages represent high-quality collateral. Third, the quality of a bond hinges on a key indenture provision—the required collateral level.

Collateral Level

When structuring a mortgage-backed bond, a collateral level is specified in the indenture. To obtain the highest possible bond rating, AAA or Aaa, the collateral must be at least 180 percent of the par value. Thus, a $50 million offering would require that mortgage loans with a market value of at least $90 million be placed in trust to collateralize the bonds. The market value of the collateral pool is the present value of the loans discounted at the prevailing mortgage loan rate. The pool is valued quarterly. If the value falls below 180 percent of the bonds outstanding, the issuer must add additional mortgage loans or other securities to the pool to bring the collateral up to the required amount. If the amount of bonds outstanding declines because of debt retirement, the amount of collateral may decline subject to the 180 percent constraint.

Why is so much collateral required? There are three reasons. First, since the outstanding balance of any mortgage pool declines over time and the cash flows go to the issuer, the pool must have excess collateral that is "used up" between valuation dates. The second is to provide additional credit protection for the bondholders. Since uninsured and privately insured mortgage loans are not riskless, foreclosures could result in losses and reduce the value of the collateral. Finally, the high collateral level protects the bondholders against declines in the market value of the collateral resulting from rising interest rates.

Although held in trust for the bondholders, the mortgage loans continue to be owned by the issuer of the bonds. In the event of a default, the trustee can sell the mortgage loans in the secondary market in order to redeem the bonds with full interest. For this reason, only high-quality, marketable loans are acceptable as collateral.

Quality Rating of MBBs

Like pass-throughs, the quality rating of MBBs is a major factor in the feasibility of such financing. Most publicly offered MBBs are rated AAA by Standard and

Poor's because of the "overcollateralization" feature. The key factors involved in the rating process are the quantity of collateral as evaluated by the collateral level, the quality of the collateral, and the creditworthiness of the issuer. Because of the need for marketability, certain types of loans such as balloon loans, second mortgage loans, and loans underlying non-owner-occupied properties are excluded in order to get the higher bond rating. Usually loans in the collateral pool are written in conformance with standards required by the secondary mortgage market, especially the Federal Home Loan Mortgage Corporation and the Federal National Mortgage Association.

Because of the high collateral requirements underlying these bonds, an issue of MBBs may have a rating of AAA, even though unsecured debt of the same issuer may be rated only BBB. If the general creditworthiness of an issuer is a concern, the collateral level may be increased to offset the added risk.

Managerial Implications

The MBB is an important financing device for S&Ls and mutual savings banks. However, it is unclear whether federally chartered banks and some state-chartered banks have the authority to issue collateralized bonds.[3] With the exception of public deposits, federally chartered banks are prohibited from collateralizing deposits and thus giving preferred status to any depositors. The Federal Reserve Bank defines "deposit" as "any member bank's liability on a note, acknowledgment of advance, due bill, or similar obligation (written or oral) that is issued or undertaken by a member bank primarily as a means of obtaining funds to be used in its banking business."[4] This definition is sufficiently broad to cast doubt on the ability of national banks to issue MBBs. The uncertainty has inhibited their use. Similarly, with the exception of public deposits, the laws of some states prohibit state-chartered banks from pledging assets to secure any depositors or creditors. However, a bank may be actively involved in this market as a trustee for the bondholders.

---

[3] This and a subsequent discussion of the legality of collateralized bonds draws from Richard B. Foster, Jr., "Pay-Through Bonds—How Financial Institutions Can Increase Their Profits on Long-Term, Low-Yielding. Real Estate Mortgages," a paper presented at the Midwest Finance Association Meeting. St. Louis, Missouri, April 8, 1983.

[4] Reg. Q, 12 C.F.R. § 217.1(f).

MBBs enable a medium-grade issuer to obtain low-cost, triple-A money. Raising funds in the national capital markets also avoids or minimizes adverse effects on the issuer's cost of local deposit-related funds. For example, a savings and loan association may decide to raise funds by increasing the rate paid on a certain type of deposit from, say, 9 percent to 10 percent. This may seem preferable to offering MBBs at 11 percent. However, the marginal cost of obtaining the incremental funds by raising the deposit rate may exceed the cost of MBBs. This occurs because the S&L will have to pay the higher deposit rate on both new and old deposits. Thus, "old" 9 percent money may now cost 10 percent, so the increase in interest costs might be much greater proportionally than the increase in deposits. An offering of MBBs would leave the existing deposit cost structure unaffected. The marginal cost of the new funds would be the MBB offering rate.

The use of MBBs has two opposite effects on the financial risk of the issuer. Since these bonds are direct obligations of the issuer, their use increases leverage and thus the financial risk of the firm. (Increasing the deposit level has the same effect.) On the other hand, MBBs have a risk-reducing impact in that they allow the mortgage lender to lengthen the maturity of a portion of its liability structure. These bonds represent one of the few sources of longer-term, fixed-rate funds available to mortgage lenders. Financing mortgage loans with MBBs enables financial institutions to reduce the adverse effects of financing a long-term, fixed-rate loan portfolio with short-term funds during a period of rising interest rates.

PAY-THROUGH BONDS

The *pay-through* bond combines features of both the mortgage-backed bond and the pass-through security. Like the MBB, the pay-through is a bond collateralized by mortgage loans, so it appears on the issuer's financial statement as debt. The cash flow from the mortgage loan pool is "dedicated" to servicing the bonds in a manner quite similar to that of pass-throughs. Unlike the pass-through, however, an issuer can "liquify" low-yielding mortgage loans without selling the loans and realizing substantial losses.

A Numerical Example

In Table 1, a numerical example of a pay-through bond is shown. A $25 million pay-through issue is fully amortized over a twelve-year period at 12 percent with monthly payments of $328,355. To generate these payments and support the pay-through bond, the issuer assembles a large pool of mortgage loans that have a combined, remaining loan balance of $35 million, a

TABLE 1

EXAMPLE OF FULLY AMORTIZING PAY-THROUGH BOND

Bond characteristics:

Par value	$25 million
Coupon rate	12%
Amortization term	12 years
Monthly bond payments	$328,355
Cash reserve requirement	10% of outstanding bonds

Mortgage collateral characteristics:

Remaining loan balance	$35 million
Average loan rate	8%
Average remaining term	14 years
Monthly cash flow	$346,961
Monthly contribution to cash reserve	$18,606[a]
Present value of cash flows	$28,175,465[b]
Overcollateralization	$3,175,465[c]

[a] The monthly contribution to the cash reserve fund is the difference between the monthly bond payments and the cash flow from the collateral pool. When the reserve requirement is reached, 10 percent of the outstanding bonds in this example, the excess cash flow reverts to the bond issuer.
[b] The present value is found by discounting the collateral cash flows at the pay-through rate, 12 percent in this example.
[c] Overcollateralization is the difference between the par value of the bonds and the present value of the collateral cash flows.

remaining average term of fourteen years, and an average interest rate of 8 percent. This collateral pool generates a monthly cash flow of $346,961, which is sufficient to cover the monthly debt service requirements of $328,355. Each month the balance of $18,606 is added to a reserve fund until it reaches an amount equal to 10 percent of the outstanding bonds. When the reserve reaches this level, excess cash flows and interest income earned on the funds revert to the issuer. The nature of this reserve is discussed below.

Using the pay-through bond rate as the discount factor, the present value of the cash flow from the collateral pool is about $28.2 million. Since it is unlikely that any of the loans could be sold at the pay-through bond rate, this present value is somewhat overstated and thus it is only an approximation. This is sufficient because the emphasis of a pay-through bond is on the cash flow rather than the liquidation value. The main point is that the amount of collateral necessary for a pay-through bond is considerably less than that required for a mortgage-backed bond. Assuming a collateral requirement of 180 percent, a $25 million issue of MBBs would require collateral with a present value of $45 million rather than $28.2 million.

It is unlikely that the cash flow pattern of a collateral pool will precisely coincide with the bond's payout requirements. Prepayments are passed through to the bondholders in the form of additional principal. Temporary cash shortfalls or permanent losses may result from delinquencies and foreclosure proceedings. However, the timely payment of principal and interest pay-

ments by the trustee can be assured by drawing on the reserve fund. To the extent that permanent losses are incurred in the collateral portfolio, the excess cash flow that reverts to the issuer is reduced. As owner of the loans, the issuer absorbs credit-related losses. Mortgage insurance and bank letters of credit are other approaches that may be used along with, or in lieu of, the cash reserve to reduce the risk of loss to the pay-through bondholders.

Collateralized Mortgage Obligation

In June 1983, Freddie Mac offered a pay-through bond known as a collateralized mortgage obligation (CMO). Under this arrangement, a pay-through issue is divided into three classes. Each class of bonds receives semiannual interest payments according to the coupon rate on the bonds. However, all monthly principal payments and any prepayments from the collateral pool are paid first to the so-called Class 1 bondholders. These monthly payments are accumulated and paid semiannually. The principal payments are such that the Class 1 bonds will be completely repaid no later than five years after the offering date. After repayment of the Class 1 bonds, the collateral pool's principal payments are then allocated to the Class 2 bondholders. These bonds are completely repaid after about twelve years. Then the pool's principal payments are allocated to the Class 3 bondholders with an expected payoff of about twenty years. Although all three classes of bonds could be paid off somewhat sooner than expected because of an increase in the payoff speed of the pool, full payoff by a specified date is contractually required.

A pay-through bond structured in this manner has broad market appeal. The structure enables institutional investors to more closely match the terms of their asset and liability structures. Banks and thrift institutions are the primary buyers of the short-term bonds, while life insurance companies and pension funds are the main buyers of the intermediate- and long-term bonds. Structuring bonds in this manner eliminates much of the uncertainty associated with the actual term of a mortgage pool. Buyers of the intermediate- and long-term issues have a form of call protection that is not otherwise possible with the dedicated cash flow that characterizes both pass-throughs and the standard version of the pay-through discussed.

Advantages of Pay-Throughs

Since a pay-through bond is the functional equivalent of a pass-through security, it has all the advantages of a pass-through. However, since the mortgage loans are not actually sold, low-rate mortgage loans may be used without realizing capital losses. Unlike pass-throughs, lower-quality mortgage loans may also be used, provided the added credit risk is offset with a combination of additional collateral, a larger cash reserve, a letter of credit, or mortgage insurance.

A pay-through bond is the functional equivalent of a pass-through security. . . .

When forming a pass-through pool, all loans must be similar with respect to their interest rate, term, and quality for pricing purposes. Depending on the size of the issue and the issuer, up to several months may be needed to form a sufficiently large pool of similar loans. In a volatile interest rate environment, changing market conditions could disrupt the formation process and possibly result in the sale of loans at a loss. This problem does not arise with pay-through bonds.

The pay-through also has a number of important advantages over mortgage-backed bonds. Since the emphasis is on the collateral's cash flow rather than its marketability, an issuer's less marketable, nonhomogeneous loans may be used effectively to reduce borrowing costs rather than lying dormant. Less marketable loans might include those with high L/V ratios, large loan balances, low interest rates, or a junior lien position. Again, to the extent that these loans increase the credit risk of the pool, additional collateral can be pledged or other arrangements made. This flexibility greatly expands the list of loans that may be used as collateral.

Since the collateral pool of a pay-through is fixed at the time of the offering, the pool need not be "marked-to-market" on a quarterly basis like the collateral of the MBB. The pool is self-supporting, so it does not have to be replenished for any reason, even defaults.

Quality Rating of Pay-Throughs

Like pass-throughs and MBBs, the quality rating of a pay-through is crucial because it determines the issuer's cost of funds. Because of their flexibility in the way they may be structured to reduce the bondholder's risk, pay-through bonds are usually rated AA or AAA by Standard & Poor's. Credit risk of the collateral pool, cash flow coverage of scheduled bond payments, the extent of overcollateralization, and external sources of protection such as mortgage insurance or a bank letter of credit are among the factors evaluated.

Because the pay-through bond is self-supporting, the financial strength of the issuer is not a major factor in the rating analysis. However, the issuer's servicing and loan underwriting capabilities are evaluated. Since federally insured S&Ls, savings banks, and commercial banks are not subject to bankruptcy laws, pay-throughs issued by these institutions are considered "bankruptcy-proof." That is, the failure of these types of institutions would not disrupt the collateral pool and its cash flow. Other issuers, such as mortgage bankers and home builders, can achieve the same result by forming a single-purpose financing subsidiary to own the collateral and issue the bonds.

Legality of Pay-Throughs

Regulators and governing statutes allow most savings and loan associations and savings banks to pledge their assets and issue pay-through bonds. However, many commercial banks are restricted by the same regulations limiting their use of MBBs. Recall that some states prohibit state-chartered banks from pledging assets to secure deposits of any other borrowings except public deposits. Federally chartered banks are not allowed to pledge collateral to secure "deposits." As pointed out earlier, the Federal Reserve's definition of the term "deposit" is so broad that sufficient doubt is raised regarding the ability of a national bank to pledge collateral and issue pay-throughs, at least directly.

A bank could issue such bonds indirectly through a wholly owned subsidiary. The mortgage loans would be transferred to the subsidiary in return for all of the capital stock of the subsidiary. The subsidiary, as owner of the loans, then pledges the loans to secure pay-throughs without recourse to the subsidiary or the bank. The proceeds of the financing are then loaned to the bank by the subsidiary. Using this approach, the bank has not pledged its assets, and neither the subsidiary nor the bank have any further financial obligation.

CONCLUSION

The ability to convert cumbersome financial instruments into a convenient, high-quality, pass-through securities with bond-like characteristics provides opportunity for mortgage lenders to sell mortgage loans at a profit. The underlying funds may be recycled and used to generate an ongoing stream of front-end points and servicing income on new loans. The use of marketable mortgage loans to collateralize MBBs enables mortgage lenders to obtain low-cost triple-A-rated money and, at the same time, lengthen their liability structures. Similar results can be achieved by developing a pay-through bond and the "pseudosale" of less marketable loans. Even low-yielding "deadwood" loans may be liquified without incurring book losses.

In light of these advantages, a thorough working knowledge of mortgage-backed securities is essential in the management of mortgage loan portfolios.   □

THE TEN WORST

Here are the largest U.S. commercial bank failures ranked by asset size according to the Federal Deposit Insurance Corp:

1. Franklin National Bank, New York, N.Y. (National) Closed Oct. 8, 1974. Deposit assumption by European American Bank & Trust Co., New York.

2. First National Bank of Midland, Midland, Tex. (National) Closed Oct. 14, 1983. Deposits and other liabilities approximately $620 million. Assets $1.4 billion. Deposit assumption by Republic Bank First National Midland, Midland, Tex.

3. United States National Bank, San Diego, Cal. (National) Closed Oct. 18, 1973. Deposits $932 million. Assets $1.266 billion. Deposit assumption by Crocker National Bank, San Francisco, Cal.

4. United American Bank, Knoxville, Tenn. (Nonmember) Sold to First Tennessee Bank, Knoxville, Feb. 15, 1983. Deposits $794 million. Assets $838 million.

5. Banco Credito y Ahorro Ponceno, Ponce, Puerto Rico. (Nonmember) Closed March 22, 1978. Deposits $608 million. Assets $713 million. Deposit assumption by Banco Popular de Puerto Rico and Banco de Santander-Puerto Rico, both of San Juan, Puerto Rico.

6. Penn Square Bank NA, Oklahoma City, Okla. (National) Closed July 5, 1982. Deposits $470 million. Assetts $517 million. Insured deposits assumed by Deposit Insurance Bank of Oklahoma City.

7. Abilene National Bank, Abilene, Tex. (National) Merged into Mercantile 10.9Texas Corp., Dallas, Tex., on Aug. 6, 1982. Deposits $310 million. Assets $446 million.

8. Hamilton National Bank of Chattanooga, Chattanooga, Tenn. (National) Closed Feb. 16, 1976. Deposits $336 million. Assets $412 million. Deposit assumption by First Tennessee National Corp., Chattanooga, Tenn.

9. American City Bank, Los Angeles, Cal. (Nonmember) Closed Feb. 27, 1983. Deposits $253 million. Assets $272 million. Deposit assumption by a consortium of five banks headed by Central Bank, Oakland, Cal.

10. Metropolitan Bank and Trust Co., Tampa, Fla. (State member) Closed Feb. 12, 1982. Deposits $172 million. Assets $261 million. Deposit assumption by Great American Bank of Tampa, Tampa, Fla.

Securitization and Banking

Securitization is not a word that can be found in the dictionary but is heard with increasing frequency in financial markets. Securitization is the process of turning an otherwise illiquid financial asset into a marketable piece of paper. The securitization of mortgages, automobile loans, accounts receivable, credit card receivables and a variety of other financial assets is a growing practice in both U.S. and international financial markets.

This *Letter* examines the causes of rapid growth in securitization and evaluates the implications. As we shall see, securitization increases the efficiency of financial markets but also brings a special type of risk and has important implications for the structure of the banking system in particular.

Securitization

Securitization refers to the practice of creating marketable debt instruments that are backed by specifically designated assets. A mortgage-backed security, such as those guaranteed by the Government National Mortgage Association (GNMA) for example, is backed by specific mortgages on specific parcels of real estate. The payments of interest and principal to holders of such securities are supported by the payments on the underlying loans. (Indeed, in the case of GNMA "pass-through" securities, the payments on the underlying mortgages are simply passed through to the holders of the GNMA securities.)

Although securitization of an asset is, in some sense, tantamount to selling the asset, the original holder of the asset usually retains some responsibilities related to the asset. For example, the responsibility for servicing securitized loans (that is, collecting interest and principal payments) may remain with the originator of the loan. The issuer of a loan-backed security may even *guarantee* interest and principal payment, thereby retaining the responsibility to manage default risk. In such a case, creation of a loan-backed security involves "transfer [of the loan] with recourse." Unlike a true sale of a loan out of portfolio, transactions with recourse relieve the issuer (such as a bank) of the securitized

asset of interest rate risk (the risk that changes in interest rates will affect the loan's value) but leave him with credit risk (default risk).

Securitization and financial intermediation

To understand better the causes and implications of securitization, it is helpful to relate securitization to the process of financial intermediation as it has traditionally been performed by commercial banks and others. In general, financial intermediaries facilitate the flow of funds from savers to borrowers. They do this by creating liability and asset instruments that simultaneously satisfy the diverse needs of lenders and borrowers, respectively.

Individual savers, for example, may wish to loan out their funds in smaller denominations and for shorter periods of time than borrowers may wish to borrow. Among the services financial intermediaries provide is the matching of small denomination savers with large denomination borrowers ("denomination intermediation") and making long-term loans to borrowers using funds provided by the short-term deposits of savers ("interest rate intermediation"). In addition, because financial intermediaries loan out deposited funds in a diversified manner, savers implicitly enjoy some reduction in the credit or default risk to which they would otherwise be exposed.

Securitization, in contrast, involves savers directly in the process of lending to borrowers. Although financial intermediaries may originate the securitized assets (such as mortgage loans), in the end, securitization creates a direct obligation between specific borrowers and specific lenders and is more nearly like direct placement of debt. The extent to which securitization occurs depends, in part, on how economically the goals of savers and borrowers can be achieved in this manner rather than through financial intermediaries.

With modern electronic transactions technology and with the growth of certain specialized financial markets, it has become increasingly easy to synthesize the services of the financial intermediary in an "unbundled fashion," leading to increased demand for securitized debt by savers. Until recently, for example, it was difficult for savers to avoid the interest rate risk associated with making long-term loans directly.Today, active financial futures and options markets permit individual savers to buy directly the desired degree of protection from interest rate risk in specialized markets. Similarly, mutual funds permit an individual saver to acquire relatively small-denomination, diversified interest in debt securities. Such developments make it possible for savers and borrowers to satisfy their diverse needs without employing a financial intermediary in the traditional sense.

Government protection and securitization

Various government policies also intentionally or unintentionally encourage securitization. Certain securities backed by residential mortgages, for example, are guaranteed against loss of principal or interest by the federal government. These guarantees make such securities — notably those issued by GNMA — easier to market. They also promote an active secondary market for residential mortgages that helps mortgage lenders adjust the composition of their asset portfolios.

Securitization also is stimulated, perhaps inadvertently, by the implicit and explicit protection of bank liabilities that results from the reluctance of policymakers to let banks fail. This encourages banks to sell guarantees or recourse services for securitized assets. These guarantees —in the form of Standby Letters of Credit (SLCs) or Recourse Notes — are essentially liabilities of the bank and may therefore be perceived by the marketplace as enjoying some of the protection explicitly afforded insured deposit liabilities. The result is that banks may be able to offer credible guarantees more competitively than noninsured institutions. (Indeed, it was only very recently that the Supreme Court ruled that SLCs are *not* to be treated as insured liabilities.)

Deposit protection only encourages securitization in general, but when combined with other regulatory policies, it also encourages insured financial intermediaries to sell their own assets with recourse. The reason is that, under current regulation, removing the asset from their portfolios makes it easier for financial intermediaries to comply with capital/asset ratios and, at the

same time, profitably increase their effective degree of leverage.

Growth of securitization

Securitization is thus one manifestation of how financial innovation — driven by technological and other changes — is moving some parts of financing activity away from financial intermediaries. Even venerable securitized instruments such as "pass-throughs" backed by residential mortgages grew 40 percent between 1983 and 1985 versus only 20 percent and 17 percent, respectively, for mortgages and commercial and industrial loans (C&I) held in the portfolios of financial intermediaries. The growth trend is even more pronounced for the newer asset-backed securities such as collateralized mortgage obligations (CMOs), and securitized automobile loans, commercial mortgages and credit card receivables. Public offerings of securities backed by automobile loans, for example, reached approximately $1.5 billion in the first half of 1986 — twice the volume in all of 1985, and CMOs (a more complicated variant of the mortgage pass-through) grew by over 300 percent between 1983 and 1985.

It is interesting to note that the vast majority of this securitization activity involves assets that are directly or indirectly guaranteed by government agencies or depository institutions. This is consistent with the notion discussed above that securitization to some extent is "subsidized" by government policies or is the result of tighter capital requirements on banks.

Such is not universally the case, however. Recently, over $1 billion in bonds backed by commercial mortgages were privately sold with a guarantee issued by an insurance company. In addition, Standard and Poor's recently introduced a system of rating the credit quality of commercial mortgage-backed bonds.Thus, the existence of direct or indirect government guarantees is an important but not exclusive contributor to the trend toward more securitization.

Pros and cons

Whether or not a particular class of assets is securitized depends upon whether a sufficiently large and homogeneous population of assets exists. Only when the market can "understand" those assets can they be securitized economically and then sold.

Although many assets are potentially securitiz-able, the virtues of continued rapid growth in securitization are actively debated. One of the benefits of securitization clearly is that it permits more economical transfer of loanable funds from savers to borrowers. If this were not so, then it would not be competitive with the other major means of bringing borrowers and lenders together, namely, direct placement of general debt obligations and financial intermediation. For securitization to exist and grow so rapidly, it must offer lenders higher rates of return and bor-rowers lower costs of borrowing, everything else being equal, than the alternatives.

Because securitization of assets requires rela-tively homogeneous — and therefore standardiz-able — assets, some also believe securitization enhances competition in the underlying assets. For example, the standardization of residential mortgage loan features that is stimulated by securitization presumably makes it easier for mortgage borrowers to compare the mortgage loan instruments available to them. The result, some claim, is that the standardization also enhances competition among mortgage lenders. Others, however, see such standardization as working to the detriment of at least some market participants with needs not met by the standard-ized securitizable asset.

A more important criticism is that securitization, by separating the origination and servicing of the asset from its ownership, may create an incen-tive to perform slipshod analysis of the asset when it is first originated or acquired. The orig-inator of a loan that will be securitized (without recourse), for example, has less incentive to per-form a careful credit evaluation than the origina-tor who holds the loan in portfolio. Although the development of appropriate standardization or rating procedures can help avoid this problem, this potential for "adverse selection" must be recognized by market participants, and is a source of risk attending the trend toward securi-tization.

Securitization and banking

The "unbundling" of intermediation services also has implications for the structure of finan-cial markets. In particular, the role and clientele of commercial banks is likely to change as securitization progresses. Increasingly, bank assets will consist of loans to borrowers who are unable to issue their own liabilities econom-ically, whose creditworthiness is difficult for the marketplace to assess, or whose liabilities are sufficiently "nonstandard" as to be difficult to securitize. In general, these are likely to be indi-viduals and smaller corporations and businesses.

The ability of banks to participate in providing components of the "unbundled" intermediation services will depend upon a number of factors. Because loan origination requires familiarity with local market conditions and companies, and loan servicing requires continued contact with borrowers, banks are likely to retain a com-parative advantage over most other organiza-tions in those functions. Their ability to provide guarantee or recourse services competitively, however, flows in part from the combination of government guarantees and capital regulation as currently implemented. Similarly, their ability to provide interest rate risk management for bor-rowers and lenders will depend upon how eco-nomically these services can be provided by banks versus their competitors in the brokerage and underwriting industries, which also depends on the extent of regulation.

In conclusion, the trend toward securitization is a natural consequence of markets evolving to provide fundamental financial services in the most economical manner. Although the pace of its development is contingent on an expanded scale of certain financial markets and the pace of financial innovation, securitization will con-tinue to have an important impact on the rela-tive role of traditional financial intermediaries in our economy.

Randall J. Pozdena

Article Five

*Both gap analysis and duration analysis have their
limitations in measuring rate risk; however, each
provides information that the other does not.*

Measuring Interest Rate Risk:
What Do We Really Know?

JAMES E. MCNULTY

With bankers exhorted from all sides to reduce interest rate risk, increasing attention is
directed to how that risk can best be measured.
Without the ability to measure interest rate risk,
proper management is impossible.

Gap analysis, the method most commonly used
for measuring interest rate risk, has come under
significant criticism in the past few years from advocates of an alternative approach, duration analysis.
George Kaufman, for example, states that "duration
analysis has substantial advantages over alternative
techniques for measuring interest rate risk," such as
asset-liability gap analysis.[1] Both Kaufman and
Alden Toevs argue that the standard asset-liability
gap analysis (henceforth referred to as gap analysis)
provides an arbitrary set of numbers that fails to
measure accurately a financial institution's interest
rate risk. This, says Toevs, may provide false signals that net interest income is protected from rate
changes. Additional shortcomings, according to
Toevs, include the "inability to generate a simple
and reliable index of interest rate risk exposure" and

"unnecessary restrictions imposed on the bank's
choice of assets and liabilities," which may fail to
meet the needs of bank customers for certain maturities of deposits and loans.[2]

The purpose of this article is to evaluate gap
analysis in light of four major criticisms that have
been advanced in the literature. Part of the process
will be to compare the two approaches to interest
rate risk measurement—gap analysis and duration
analysis. How well do these two approaches measure interest rate risk? What are the primary
strengths and weaknesses of each? What are the
assumptions and how valid are they? What is the
relationship between the two approaches? Are they
really in conflict with one another, or are they
complementary?

Gap Analysis

Most readers are familiar with gap analysis, so only
a brief summary is presented here.[3] Table 1 illustrates the technique: A hypothetical financial institution's balance sheet has been segmented by
maturity. The individual assets and liabilities of
this institution are placed in separate columns or

James E. McNulty is vice president-economist at the Federal
Home Loan Bank of Atlanta and adjunct professor of finance
at Emory University, Atlanta.

Table 1. Gap Analysis — An Example
(in $ Millions)

| | Maturity or Time to Re-pricing | | | |
	1 Year	2 Years	3 Years	Total
Assets	$ 50	$ 50	$200	$300
Liabilities and Net Worth	100	100	100	300
Gap	− 50	− 50	100	0
Cumulative Gap	− 50	−100	0	0

Assumptions

1. Interest rates increase by 500 basis points at all maturity levels at the beginning of year one.

2. All assets and liabilities are re-priced at the beginning of the year in which they mature.

3. Changes in spreads, rate volatility, prepayments, and all other factors affecting income are ignored.

4. The fact that no explicit interest is paid on net worth is ignored to simplify the arithmetic. Thus, net worth is treated the same as a liability item.

Effect of a 500-Basis-Point Increase in Rates

Effect in Year One
  Income Change:
    Assets x Rate Change
    50 x .05 = +2.50
  Expense Change:
    Liabilities x Rate Change
    100 x .05 = +5.00

  Net Income: −2.50
  Net Income Calculated from Cumulative Gap Formula:
    CUMGAP x CHRATES
    −50 x .05 = −2.50

Effect in Year Two
  Income Change:
    Assets* x Rate Change
    100 x .05 = +5.00
  Expense Change:
    Liabilities* x Rate Change
    200 x .05 = +10.00

  Net Income: −5.00
  Net Income Calculated from Cumulative Gap Formula:
    CUMGAP x CHRATES
    −100 x .05 = −5.00

Effect in Year Three
  No change — Net income returns to the level of the base year since all assets and liabilities have been repriced.

---

* Includes all assets or liabilities that are re-priced either in or before the given year.

"maturity buckets" designating when they mature or when they can be re-priced. This institution has $300 million in total assets, of which $200 million will mature at the beginning of year three. For ease of exposition, assume that the longest maturity of any asset or liability is three years. Gap analysis can be extended to as many maturity buckets as the user wants. The choice depends entirely on the personal preferences of the user and the balance sheet of the financial institution.

One measure of interest rate risk used in this approach is the gap—the difference between assets and liabilities in a certain maturity category. If liabilities exceed assets, as they do in the one- and two-year maturity categories, the gap is negative. The cumulative gap can be derived by simply summing up the individual gaps. For the first maturity bucket, the individual and cumulative gaps are the same, −$50 million. For the second maturity bucket, the cumulative gap is −$100 million, reflecting a −$50 million gap in each of the first two buckets.

The cumulative gap is a direct measure of interest rate sensitivity. This can be seen from the following formula:

$$\text{CHINCOME}(t) = \text{CUMGAP}(t) \times \text{CHRATES}$$

Where:

CHINCOME(t) = the change in a financial institution's net income in period t which results from a given change in interest rates. (The change is measured from some base year, rather than as a year-to-year change.)

CUMGAP(t) = the cumulative gap at the end of that period of time.

CHRATES = a permanent once and for all change in all interest rates at all maturity levels.

The use of this formula can be seen in the examples in Table 1, which examine the effect of a 500-basis-point increase in interest rates on net income. The institution has $100 million in liabilities, which will re-price at the higher interest rates at the beginning of year one. This will raise interest expense by $5 million, which will be partially offset by the increased income from the $50 million in assets, which will re-price at the same time. The difference, which is the cumulative gap of $50 million, indicates the excess amount of liabilities.

The decline in net income of $2.5 million can be calculated two ways, as shown on the table. The second method, which is a direct application of the previously stated formula, highlights the significance of the cumulative gap. The reader can follow the arithmetic for years two and three in the same fashion.

As shown, the cumulative gap tells you how many more liabilities (assets) re-price than assets (liabilities) at the end of a certain period of time. If interest rates go up, institutions with negative cumulative gaps will be hurt. If rates go down, these institutions will experience a gain in net income.

In the example, if rates go down by 300 basis points, net income will go up by $1.5 million, which equals the cumulative gap (−$50 million) times the change in rates (−0.03). The cumulative gap, therefore, shows how much of a "bet" an institution is making on interest rates. The institution in the example has a negative cumulative gap in the shorter maturities and will lose its bet if rates go up and gain if rates come down. An institution that has a positive gap will lose if rates go down and gain if rates rise. Again, these relationships follow directly from the formula.

Most of the proposed strategies for reducing interest rate risk can be looked at in gap analysis terms. Sales of longer term fixed-rate loans, with the proceeds reinvested in shorter term assets, reduce the short-term gaps by adding assets to these maturity buckets. Shifting new lending from fixed-rate to adjustable-rate consumer or mortgage loans does the same thing. For institutions with too many long-term assets, other strategies work by moving liabilities from the near-term maturity buckets to those with longer maturities. These include interest rate swaps, financial futures (which can also be used on the asset side), and extension of the maturity of deposit liabilities.

Limitations of Gap

Criticism One. The first criticism leveled at the gap approach is that the individual gap numbers are arbitrary, since they depend on the size of the matu-rity buckets chosen by the person doing the analysis. For example, if the two- and three-year buckets in Table 1 were combined, the analysis would show a gap of + $50 million rather than a − $50 million and + $100 million.

It is also argued that if the buckets are too large there can be significant interest rate risk even within a single maturity bucket.[4] Suppose that the one-year gap is zero, but all the liabilities mature at the

---

In gap analysis, the crucial measure of interest rate risk is the cumulative gap, not the individual gaps.

---

beginning of the period and all the assets mature at the end. If rates were to increase, the institution could suffer a significant loss of income during the year, even though its gap analysis suggested it had no interest rate risk.

This criticism does not invalidate gap analysis; it simply indicates that the size of the maturity buckets has to be determined by someone who has a thorough knowledge of the nature of the interest rate risk facing the institution. For the traditional savings and loan association with large amounts of 20-30 year assets and 0-6 month liabilities, a limited number of maturity buckets may be appropriate because the main source of the interest rate risk is obvious. For a retail bank, a more comprehensive analysis using a larger number of maturity categories would be necessary. The fact that the user has to choose the proper level of disaggregation does not establish that the technique itself is faulty.[5]

A more important "defense" of gap analysis from the criticism of arbitrariness follows from the formula discussed above, which establishes that the crucial measure of interest rate risk is the cumulative gap, not the individual gaps. The cumulative gap at a given point in time is completely independent of the size of the individual maturity buckets because the cumulative gap measures the excess amount of liabilities (assets) that will have re-priced by the end of a given period of time in the future. For example, in Table 1 the gap of − $50 means that $50 million more liabilities will re-price during the second year. The cumulative gap of − $100 means that $100 million more liabilities will have re-priced *by the end* of year two. Since the cumulative gap is measured by summing up the individual gaps, it must be independent of the period of time used to construct the individual gaps. Any item that is omitted from one maturity bucket will be picked up in another.

Criticism Two. A second criticism leveled at gap analysis is that the standards required to "immunize" or to protect the institution from interest rate changes are impossible to achieve. Toevs implicitly argues that complete immunization would require calculating the gaps using daily maturity buckets and setting all the daily gaps equal to zero, which is simply not practical. The institution is thus left without a realistic goal to strive for in managing its interest rate risk.[6]

In actual practice, however, it is relatively easy to develop tolerance levels for key financial ratios such as the cumulative gap to total assets at various maturity levels. For example, one approach might be to let the ratios deviate within a range of, say, $+3\%$ to -3%, or $+5\%$ to -5%, and take action to reduce the gap only when it falls outside that range. This would not provide complete protection against interest rate changes, but the amount of protection it would provide is easily measurable using the standard gap formula above. For instance, a $100-million institution with a -5 million (-5%) cumulative gap at one year would be exposed to a potential decline in net interest income of $100,000, if interest rates rose by 200 basis points ($5 million $\times$ .02 = $100,000). This can be compared with the institution's capital position to determine if this level of risk is acceptable.

The idea that the gaps need to be calculated at one day maturities and set equal to zero assumes that complete avoidance of all interest rate risk is a realistic goal. Interestingly, few gap analysis practitioners advocate anything like zero gap strategy. Assuming some interest rate risk is probably unavoidable in conducting the business of a financial institution, but the amount of risk inherent in the balance sheet should be carefully measured so that the level of risk that the institution does take on becomes a management decision.[7]

Criticism Three. The critics' third point is that gap analysis "unnecessarily constrains the bank's choice of assets and liabilities, which reduces the bank's ability to accommodate customer demands for bank services."[8] For instance, if a bank has six month deposits, it has to have an equal amount of six month loans. If the bank's customers want something other than six month loans, the bank will be left watching as its customers go somewhere else. Several points need to be made in response to this.

First of all, it assumes that financial institutions must follow a pure zero-gap strategy. As indicated above, this is clearly not the case. Second, numerous tools and techniques are available for altering the maturities of assets and liabilities to reduce interest rate risk and still accommodate customer demands. With the development of the interest rate swap market, for example, financial institutions have a way of changing the maturity of their liabilities so that this situation need not arise.[9]

Such maturity transformations can reduce potential profits, however. With an upward sloping yield curve, extending the maturity of a liability by using, for example, interest rate swaps will increase the cost of the liability. This highlights another aspect of the third objection to gap analysis—the impact on profitability. As Stanley Diller expresses it, "The traditional gap approach allows one side of a balance sheet to dictate what will be on the other, at the expense of profits."[10] Diller argues that because of the movement toward matched maturities, spreads between yields on assets and liability costs at the same maturity are being compressed so that institutions that match maturities dollar-for-dollar may earn an unsatisfactory rate of return.

This is simply a reflection of one of the basic principles of finance—the risk-return trade off. The expected rate of return on any project or set of projects depends upon the risk of the project. To earn a higher expected return, you need to take more risk. If you don't take any risk, you only earn the risk-free rate of return, which can be approximated by the three-month U.S. Treasury bill rate, for example.

Table 2 illustrates a common risk-return dilemma facing institutions mixing fixed-rate loans. The purpose of the example is to illustrate that gap analysis provides certain important information about the timing of the impact of various asset and liability management strategies on profitability that duration analysis does not provide. The institution has the opportunity to make fixed-rate loans with an expected life of 12 years at a rate of 12.5 percent. The institution can finance these asset acquisitions with one-year deposits yielding 8 percent and earn a 450-basis-point spread the first year. This spread comes only with enormous risk, however.

The second alternative is to finance the asset acquisition with 10-year liabilities at a cost of 11 percent. While this eliminates much of the interest rate risk, it leaves the institution with a spread of only 150 basis points. For most institutions, this would not be enough to even pay operating costs, let alone produce a profit.

The third alternative would be to finance the acquisition of the 12-year asset with five-year liabilities at a cost of 10 percent. This produces a 250-basis-point spread, but it entails some interest rate risk. The amount of risk involved can be measured by the cumulative gap. For years one through five, profits are completely protected, as reflected in the cumulative gap of zero. The institution's profitability is at risk in year six after the liability matures. If rates remain stable or decline, the institution can extend the maturity of the liability and preserve or increase the spread. If rates rise substantially, the spread will erode, and the institution could suffer a loss on the transaction.

Rightly or wrongly, many institutions today are apparently choosing this third alternative. For example, conversations with interest rate swap dealers indicate a significant interest in five-year swaps by savings institutions as a result of recent rate declines. The same thing has happened to the demand for intermediate-term Federal Home Loan Bank advances.

It should be emphasized that gap analysis provides important information about the interest rate risk inherent in this transaction that duration analysis does not provide. Duration analysis would show that if the institution pursued strategies one or three and interest rates rose, the market value of the institution would decline. It also would show that the decline would be less for strategy three than for strategy two because of the longer liability maturity in strategy three. But duration analysis says nothing about *when* the institution's net interest margin is at risk.

In evaluating the third criticism of gap analysis, it should be clear that gap analysis does not impose artificial constraints on the balance sheet, and it does not require pure matched maturities. In fact, the example shows that it can be a useful tool for analyzing the relative risk of different strategies, each of which involves some degree of maturity mismatch. A case study presented later in this article illustrates one approach to asset and liability management that, through a blending of gap and duration analysis, produces a relatively low level of interest rate risk without pure dollar matching of maturities for each transaction.

Criticism Four. A fourth major criticism of gap analysis is the "inability of the model to generate a simple and reliable index of interest rate risk exposure."[11] Rather than providing a single number that tells management exactly what its risk is, gap analysis produces too many numbers—so many that interpretation becomes muddled, say the critics. Toevs has commented that different people can often look at the same gap report and come to completely different conclusions as to what the risk is and what strategies should be followed to reduce it.

But if interest rate risk management is important —and no one argues that it is not—then a single number may obliterate or distort the effect of a large number of contingencies, options, and other technical and special factors that affect that risk. As

Table 2. Gap Analysis for Alternative Strategies (in $ Millions)

	Maturity or Time to Re-pricing			
	Under 1 Year	1-4 Years	5-9 Years	10 Years + Over
Strategy 1:				
Assets	—	—	—	$100 (12.5%)
Liabilities and Net Worth	$100 (8.0%)	—	—	—
Gap	−100	0	0	100
Cumulative Gap	−100	−100	−100	0
Strategy 2:				
Assets	—	—	—	100 (12.5%)
Liabilities and Net Worth	—	—	—	100 (11.0%)
Gap	0	0	0	0
Cumulative Gap	0	0	0	0
Strategy 3:				
Assets	—	—	—	100 (12.5%)
Liabilities and Net Worth	—	—	100 (10.0)	0
Gap	0	0	−100	100
Cumulative Gap	0	0	−100	0

Table 3. Calculating the Macaulay Duration for a
6-year, $100 Par Value Bond
(Paying a 12% Annual Coupon Rate, Priced to Yield 10%)

(1) Cash Flow Period (years)	(2) Cash Flow	(3) Present Value of Cash Flow (discounted at 10%)	(4) Weights (col. 3 ÷108.71)	(5) Weighted Cash Flow Periods (col. 4 x col. 1)
1	$ 12	$ 10.91	.1004	.10
2	12	9.92	.0913	.18
3	12	9.02	.0830	.25
4	12	8.20	.0754	.30
5	12	7.45	.0685	.34
6	112	63.22	.5815	3.49
Column Sum		$108.71	1.0000	4.67

(Totals of individual figures given may differ from sums because of rounding off.)

Source: Adapted from Robert A. Ott, "Duration Analysis and Minimizing Interest Rate Risk," *Review*, Federal Home Loan Bank of Atlanta (December 1984), p. 2, as corrected.

seen in the previous example, the timing of interest rate exposure is one factor that financial managers will want to be aware of. Another example is the prepayment option provided to the mortgage borrower. This is one-sided since it will be exercised much more frequently if interest rates go down.

Interest rate risk, then, is a multi-dimensional concept; there are so many factors affecting it that to rely on a single number by itself would, no doubt, hide many of them. The economist attempting to forecast the behavior of the economy uses many indicators—gross national product (real and nominal), the money supply, employment and unemployment, retail sales, industrial production, to name only a few. The manager of a financial institution also needs numerous bits of information. For example, what is the cumulative gap at one year, three years, five years? How are the gaps affected by various prepayment assumptions? What is the effect of different assumptions about passbook savings? The manager will also want to know the duration of his assets and liabilities to put this information into perspective and to see the overall degree of risk in the balance sheet.

Duration Analysis: Assumptions

Duration analysis begins with a completely different premise than gap analysis. Gap analysis is concerned only with the net interest margin and its effect on net income, as measured by conventional accounting practices. Duration analysis ignores accounting considerations and concentrates on the market value of the net worth of the firm. As Toevs expresses it, "the current market value of net worth represents the present value of this and all future years' net interest income. If net worth declines, then some or all yearly net interest incomes must decline. That is, market value of net worth is a leading indicator of the stream of net interest incomes."[12]

Duration had its origins in the area of bond portfolio management. In fact, duration is a measure of the average life of a stream of payments, such as those that might be produced by a bond. To the bond analyst, duration is often a better measure of the average life of a financial contract than maturity. Maturity only tells you when the final payment is due; it says nothing about the size or timing of either the interest payments or any early repayment of principal. The standard Macaulay duration measure can be calculated as follows:

$$D = \frac{\sum\limits_{t=1}^{n} \frac{P_t}{(1+r)^t} \times (t)}{\sum\limits_{t=1}^{n} \frac{P_t}{(1+r)^t}}$$

Where

D = the Macaulay duration measure

P_t = payment of interest or principal at time t

t = the amount of time before the cash flow (P) is received

n = the final maturity of the financial contract

r = current market interest rates for the security under consideration

Table 3 gives an example of how the Macaulay duration is calculated. Notice that each payment has a weight, the weights sum to 1.00, and each weight is the ratio of the present value of that cash flow to the total present value of all the cash flows ($108.71). Each cash flow is thus weighted by its importance in determining the total present value of the financial contract. Since present value is equal to the price of the bond (because no one would pay more or sell for less than the bond is worth), the weights reflect the importance of each cash flow in determining the price of the financial instrument. Duration, which in this case is 4.67 years, is simply a weighted average measure of maturity.

Duration is also a direct measure of the sensitivity of market value to changes in interest rates. The measurement, however, is only approximate, as the following formula indicates:

$$\Delta P \cong -d \times \Delta i$$

Where:
ΔP = the percent change in price for the asset or liability
d = the duration of that asset or liability
Δi = the change in market yield for the financial instrument under consideration

For instance, if rates increase by 10 basis points and the duration of a bond is 3 years, the percentage change in price will be about -0.3 percent (i.e., $-3 \times .001 = -.003$). For small changes in interest rates, the approximation produced by this formula is reasonably accurate. For large changes, however, this is not the case.

Duration is measured in units of time, since it is a measure of average maturity, but duration is almost always smaller than maturity. The exception would be a zero coupon bond or a discount security such as a Treasury bill. For these instruments, duration and maturity are equal.

Advocates of the duration approach to interest rate risk management, such as Kaufman and Toevs, suggest that the durations of the institution's assets and liabilities be calculated separately. If the duration of assets exceeds the duration of liabilities, as it would, for example, at most savings institutions, the market value of the assets will decline more than the market value of the liabilities when interest rates rise. This means, of course, that the institution sees its profits erode when interest rates rise and experiences a gain when rates fall. Interest rate sensitivity is therefore eliminated when the duration of the assets equals the duration of the liabilities. Duration matching thus replaces asset and liability maturity matching as the key element in this approach to interest rate risk management.

Its advocates contend that duration overcomes the four primary limitations of gap analysis. First, duration is unique—it is not an arbitrary number that depends upon the size of a maturity bucket. Second, it provides a clear and practical goal that will "immunize" the institution from interest rate changes. While setting all daily gaps equal to zero is clearly impossible, approximate duration matching is feasible.

Third, duration allows the institution to offer different maturities for deposits and loans, thus meeting customer needs without taking on undue interest rate risk. This is possible because one of the

---

Duration analysis is a direct measure of the sensitivity of market value to changes in interest rates.

---

mathematical properties of duration is that durations can be averaged. If a customer wants loans that have a duration of three years, these can be funded with equal amounts of one- and five-year (duration) liabilities or two- and four-year liabilities, or any other combination with an average duration of three years. This is extremely important because it allows the financial institution to continue to perform one of the classic functions of financial intermediaries—to "intermediate" between various maturities to meet the needs of both depositors and borrowers. These needs, of course, will not always be for the same maturity. Customers may want short-term deposits, for example, while borrowers may prefer longer term loans.

Since duration provides a single number—the difference between the duration of assets and liabilities—as a convenient summary measure of interest rate risk, it also overcomes the fourth alleged limitation of gap analysis—the lack of any such summary statistic. Nonetheless, it needs to be emphasized that duration also has limitations. [13]

Limitations of Duration Analysis

The limitations of duration follow from the assumptions. Immunization against interest rate changes using the standard Macaulay duration measure requires that the interest rate change be a proportionate, once and for all, change in all interest rates at all maturity levels. In other words, the yield curve moves upward by a constant percentage amount, say 10 percent. If short-term rates were 8

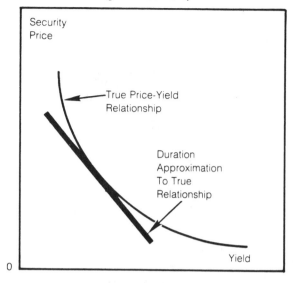

Figure 1. Convexity

Security Price

True Price-Yield Relationship

Duration Approximation To True Relationship

Yield

0

percent, they increase to 8.8 percent. If long-term rates were 10 percent, they increase to 11 percent. If the interest rate change is of any other type, the financial institution will not be immunized against that particular rate change. In the course of an interest rate cycle, however, short-term rates usually go up more than long-term rates.

It is possible to construct different duration measures for different rate change environments. In effect, one needs to know in advance what type of rate change to expect in order to know what duration measure to use. However, the whole idea of interest rate risk mangement is to protect institutions against *unforeseen* rate changes. The savings and loan crisis of 1981-82 occurred because no one thought short-term rates could go as high as they did.

Another limitation of duration analysis stems from the fact that, as noted above, duration is only an approximation. Figure 1 shows a typical price-yield relationship for a U.S. Treasury security. When yields go up, of course, bond prices go down, which accounts for the fact that the curve is downward sloping. However, the relationship is not linear; it is convex and duration provides only a linear approximation to the true relationship. If the asset and liability do not have the same convexity, duration will not match the market value changes on both sides of the balance sheet. If the asset is a mortgage and the liability is a time deposit or interest rate

swap, the "convexities" will not be the same. The reason is that the mortgage amortizes, and it is also likely to be repaid if rates come down, while the liability does not have this feature.[14]

Related to this is the phenomenon of "duration drift." Even if asset and liability durations are matched initially, they will not necessarily remain this way over time. Robert Ott presents a situation in which a package of mortgage loans is financed with a combination of five- and 10-year loans from the Federal Home Loan Bank. Initially the duration of the assets equals that of the liabilities at 5.3 years. After four years, the duration of the assets declines slowly to only five years, but the duration of the liabilities drops to about three years. After eight years, the duration mismatch is even greater. This situation occurs because, while initial durations were matched, initial maturities were not.

A Case Study: Blending Gap and Duration Analysis

The Federal Home Loan Bank of Atlanta uses both gap and duration analysis to measure its interest rate risk, with the primary focus on gap analysis. The following example shows how the two can complement one another. When the Bank participates in an issue of FHLB System debt, it may use a portion of the proceeds to purchase U.S. Treasury securities of comparable maturity. This hedge protects the Bank in the event interest rates fall and loans have to be made at lower rates. For the five-year maturity, the gap report would be affected by this transaction as follows:

Assets	
U.S. Treasury Securities	+50
Liabilities	
FHLB Consolidated Obligations	+50
Gap	No Change

When five-year loans are made, the hedge securities are sold so there is again no change in the gap. The loans would simply replace the hedge securities in the asset account above.

The Bank is required to stand ready to make loans in a full range of maturities out to 10 years. As a practical matter, however, it is impossible to hold hedge securities in all maturity ranges at all times. What is done is to use hedge securities of one maturity to fund loan demand at another maturity on a weighted basis. The weights are derived from duration analysis.

Suppose a hypothetical reduction in interest rates of 10 basis points would raise the price of $1 million of three-year securities by $2,000. An identical change in rates would, of course, have a larger effect on the price of five-year securities; let's say this effect is $3,000. Then it would require the sale of only $0.67 million of five-year securities to hedge a $1 million three-year advance. This hedge would, in effect, protect the market value of the Bank's net worth.

This type of duration-weighted hedge transaction is also used to improve the Bank's gap. For example, in one situation the Bank faced a demand for $75 million of three-year advances. At that time, the Bank had a negative gap (excess of liabilities over assets) at the three-year maturity, so the additional three-year assets were welcome. At the same time, the gap in the five-year area was positive. By selling approximately $50 million of five-year hedge (Treasury) securities to fund this advance and reducing its overnight assets (federal funds sold) by $25 million, the Bank was able to reduce both the three-year and five-year gaps.

Another important aspect of this process is the calculation of overall duration measures for the Bank's balance sheet. By providing a summary risk measure, the duration calculation can tell the Bank which gaps need to be closed. This provides important information when decisions about the maturity of new debt issues are made. Given the importance of interest rate risk management, the two methods—gap and duration—are then compared so as to be sure they both point in the same direction. At the end of June 1985, for example, the durations of assets and liabilities were approximately 12.6 and 13.1 months, respectively. At the same time, the cumulative gap at most maturity levels out to five years was positive, but less than 4 percent of assets. Both the gap and duration measures suggest a very modest, almost negligible, risk exposure to falling interest rates.

Conclusion: Are Gap and Duration in Conflict?

The reader who has followed the discussion to this point may see himself in a dilemma. Interest rate risk management may be crucial to bank performance, and the regulators are now attempting to

measure each institution's risk with double digit precision. Nonetheless, both the two principal tools for measuring this risk have significant limitations. What is one to do?

The advocates of duration analysis have provided a useful service in highlighting the limitations of gap analysis. However, duration is also based on a number of restrictive assumptions so that exclusive reliance on it could lead to significant problems if

---

Gap analysis and duration analysis can be used as complementary approaches to interest rate risk management.

---

these assumptions are invalid. In the opinion of the author, the limitations of gap are not as severe as its critics contend, and gap analysis can continue to be a primary tool of interest rate risk management.

Duration asks a completely different question than gap. By ignoring accounting considerations and the timing of the effect of interest rate changes, it calls the analyst's attention to the effect of interest rate changes on market value. Since the focus of the two approaches is completely different, the limitations should tend to offset one another.

Consider the following example of the interrelationship between gap and duration. A retail bank has a positive gap (excess assets) of $100 million at four years and a negative gap (excess liabilities) of $100 million at seven years. It can add four-year liabilities to correct the first situation; it can add seven-year assets to correct the second. Assume the overall duration on the asset side exceeds the duration on the liability side by a significant amount. Adding four-year liabilities will help correct the duration imbalance while adding seven-year assets will worsen it. (The sources or uses of the funds are ignored for simplicity). While the gaps are equal in dollar amount, closing one will reduce the overall level of interest rate risk, while closing the other would increase it and thus be counterproductive. Duration, then, can tell the financial manager which gaps need to be closed.

At the very least, each approach provides information that the other does not. As indicated in this example and in the case study, it is possible to use the two as complementary rather than competing approaches to interest rate risk management.

Notes

1. George Kaufman, "Measuring and Managing Interest Rate Risk: A Primer," *Economic Perspectives*, Federal Reserve Bank of Chicago (January-February 1984), 16-29.

2. Alden Toevs, "Gap Management: Managing Interest Rate Risk in Banks and Thrifts," *Economic Review*, Federal Reserve Bank of San Francisco (Spring 1983).

3. A more detailed summary of gap analysis is contained in Steven J. Goldstein and Eric I. Hemel, "Gap Analysis: Using Section H of the Quarterly Report," Office of Policy and Economic Research, Federal Home Loan Bank Board, July 1984; and Joseph Sinkey, *Commercial Bank Financial Management* (New York: Macmillan, 1983), 493-509. An extensive bibliography can be found in Sinkey, 512-15.

4. Toevs, "Gap Management," 22-23.

5. An analogy might be useful to reinforce this point. For over 40 years, economists have been using multiple regression analysis to estimate the relationship between the demand for individual commodities and their price. In their analysis, a choice has to be made as to the level of detail at which the analysis should be conducted (e.g., meat in general, or beef, pork and veal separately). The choice clearly depends on what the analysis is to be used for. The fact that a choice has to be made does not establish that multiple regression is a faulty technique.

6. Toevs, "Gap Management," 23-34.

7. See, for example, Goldstein and Hemel, "Gap Analysis," 16-17.

8. Toevs, "Gap Management," 20.

9. An interest rate swap is an "interest-exchange agreement." One party, say a savings institution, has a short-term liability on which it makes variable-rate payments. Another party has a fixed-rate, longer term liability. The two institu-tions enter into an agreement whereby the party with short-term liability agrees to pay the interest expense that would be paid by the party with the long-term obligation, and the other institution does the reverse. In actual practice, no exchange of principal occurs and the short-term payments are tied to an index.

10. Stanley Diller, "Parametric Analysis of Fixed Income Securities: Options, Passthroughs, Convexity, Asset Liability Management" (New York: Goldman Sachs, Financial Strategies Group, June 1984).

11. Toevs, "Gap Management," 31.

12. Alden Toevs and Jeffrey Wernick, "Hedging Interest Rate Risk Inclusive of Prepayment and Credit Risks," in *Identification and Control of Risk in the Thrift Industry*, Proceedings of the Ninth Annual Conference, Federal Home Loan Bank of San Francisco (December 1983), 99. For a more detailed description of the principles of duration and a discussion of the calculation of duration statistics see Kaufman, "Managing Interest Rate Risk," 16-29; Robert A. Ott, "Duration Analysis and Minimizing Interest Rate Risk," *Review*, Federal Home Loan Bank of Atlanta (December 1984) 1-5; or Alan Winger, "Duration in the Analysis of Interest Rate Risk," *Quarterly Review*, Federal Home Loan Bank of Cincinnati (First Quarter 1984).

13. This is discussed more extensively in Ott, "Duration Analysis," 1-5.

14. Methods of dealing with this problem, such as by using strips of FHLB advances or certificates of deposit with different maturities are discussed in Diller, "Parametric Analysis" and Toevs and Wernick, "Hedging Interest Rate Risk." As the number of different liability maturities is increased, the problems created by convexity are reduced, because cash flows are more closely matched. But this is precisely what gap analysis would suggest.

Article Six

Hedging Interest Rate Risk with Financial Futures: Some Basic Principles

Michael T. Belongia and G. J. Santoni

FOR much of the postwar period, stable rates of inflation — accompanied by stable levels of interest rates — created a comforting economic environment for managers of depository institutions. Beginning in the mid-1970s, however, more variable interest rates, brought about in part by more variable inflation, caused a substantial change in the economic conditions facing depository institutions. Offering long-term credit at fixed rates became riskier as larger and more frequent unexpected changes in interest rates introduced more variation into the market value of these assets.[1]

This article describes how variation in interest rates affects the market value of depository institutions. The discussion then demonstrates how financial futures contracts might be used to hedge some of the interest rate risk of a portfolio composed of interest-sensitive deposit accounts and loans of unmatched maturities. Although some regulatory authorities have denied or strictly regulated the use of futures contracts by de-

pository institutions in the belief that futures trading is risky and unduly speculative, we argue that the judicious use of futures can reduce the firm's exposure to interest rate fluctuations.[2]

DURATION GAP AND INTEREST RATE RISK

In the mid-1970s, when large fluctuations in interest rates began to occur, it became increasingly evident that depository institutions needed some measure of the relative risks associated with various portfolio holdings. One approach to the measurement of interest rate risk is called Duration Gap analysis. "Duration" refers to the "average" life of some group of assets or liabilities. "Gap" refers to the difference between the durations of an institution's assets and its liabilities.[3]

Michael T. Belongia is an economist and G. J. Santoni is a senior economist at the Federal Reserve Bank of St. Louis. John G. Schulte provided research assistance.

[1]For a general description of events that have introduced or increased interest rate risk, see Carrington and Hertzberg (1984) and Koch, et al. (1982).

[2]Legal restrictions and guidelines on the use of financial futures by different types of financial institutions are summarized in Lower (1982). A comparison of statutes on the use of futures by insurance companies is made in Gottlieb (1984).

[3]For more detailed discussions of duration analysis and its application to financial institution portfolios, see Kaufman (1984); Bierwag, Kaufman and Toevs (1983); Toevs (1983); Santoni (1984); Samuelson (1944); and Hicks (1939), pp. 184–88.

Table 1

Expected Streams of Receipts and Payments

	Day				
	0	**90**	**180**	**270**	**360**
Panel A: No Change in Interest Rates					
Asset (loan)					
Receipts					$1,000.00
Payments	$909.09				
Liabilities (borrowings)					
Receipts	909.09	$926.75	$944.76	$963.11	
Payments		926.75	944.76	963.11	981.82
Net Receipts	-0-	-0-	-0-	-0-	$ 18.18

Present Value $18.18/1.10 = $16.53

	0	**90**	**180**	**270**	**360**
Panel B: Interest Rates Rise by 200 Basis Points					
Asset (loan)					
Receipts					$1,000.00
Payments	$909.09				
Liabilities (borrowings)					
Receipts	909.09	$926.75	$949.10	$971.98	
Payments		926.75	949.10	971.98	995.42
Net Receipts	-0-	-0-	-0-	-0-	$ 4.58

Present Value = $4.58/1.12 = $4.09

	0	**90**	**180**	**270**	**360**
Panel C: Interest Rates Fall by 200 Basis Points					
Asset (loan)					
Receipts					$1,000.00
Payments	$909.09				
Liabilities (borrowings)					
Receipts	909.09	$926.75	$940.35	$954.15	
Payments		926.75	940.35	954.15	968.15
Net Receipts	-0-	-0-	-0-	-0-	$ 31.85

Present Value = $31.85/1.08 = $29.49

An Example

The risk introduced into a portfolio of assets and liabilities of different duration is illustrated in tables 1 and 2. In this example, for expositional simplicity, the firm's planned life is assumed to be only one year. It has extended a loan with a face value of $1,000 to be repaid in a single payment at the end of the year at an interest rate of 10 percent. The present value of the loan, and, thus, the amount paid out by the firm to the borrower, is $909.09. To finance this loan, the firm borrows $909.09 for 90 days at 8 percent interest. The two percentage-point spread is the return earned by the firm for employing its specialized capital in intermediating between borrowers and lenders.

The amount that the firm will owe in three months' time is $926.75 (= $909.09(1.08)$^{.25}$), which it plans to pay by borrowing this amount for another 90 days. Because the firm's proceeds from the new loan and its payment of the old loan cancel, its net receipts at this time are zero. The firm anticipates being able to roll the loan over every 90 days at the same interest rate. Consequently, at the end of 180 days, the firm expects to owe $944.76 (= $926.75(1.08)$^{.25}$), which it plans to pay with new borrowings. At the end of the year, the firm

Table 2

Interest Rate Changes and the Present Value of a Portfolio of Assets and Liabilities of Different Durations

Panel A: Initial Conditions

Present Values

Asset:		Liability:	
$\dfrac{\$1,000.00}{1.10}$ = $909.09		$\dfrac{\$981.82}{1.10}$ =	$892.56

Equity:

$909.09 − $892.56 = $16.53

Panel B: All Interest Rates Rise by 200 Basis Points

Present Values

Asset:		Liability:	
$\dfrac{\$1,000.00}{1.12}$ = $892.86		$\dfrac{\$995.42}{1.12}$ =	$888.77

Equity:

$892.86 − $888.77 = $4.09

Percentage change in equity = −75.26

anticipates having to pay $981.82 (= $909.09 × 1.08). This amount will be paid out of the $1,000 proceeds from its matured asset. The firm's expected net receipt at year-end is $18.18, as shown in panel A of table 1.

Panel A of table 2 is a balance sheet summary of the present value of this investment plan. The present value of the expected net receipt at year-end is $16.53 and is equal to the difference between the present value of the asset, $909.09 (= $1,000/1.10), and the present value of the expected liability, $892.56 (= $981.82/1.10). Both future values are discounted at 10 percent, the firm's opportunity cost.

The Effects of Changing Interest Rates on Equity

This package of assets and liabilities is subject to considerable interest rate risk because the 10 percent interest rate on the firm's loan is fixed for one year while its borrowings must be refunded every 90 days. In this example, the gap between the durations of the

asset and liability is 270 days (= 360 − 90).[4] As a practical matter, the asset's longer duration implies that a given change in interest rates will change the present value of the asset more than it will affect the present value of the liability. This difference, of course, will change the value of the firm's equity.

Panel B of table 1 shows the effect of an unexpected 200 basis-point rise in interest rates. The increase raises the firm's anticipated refunding costs. As a result, the amount the firm expects to pay at year-end increases to $995.42. Net receipts fall to $4.58 and the present value of the investment plan falls to $4.09.

Panel B of table 2 presents a balance sheet summary of the effect of the change on the present values of the asset, liability and owner equity. The increase in interest rates reduces the present values of both the asset and liability, but the asset value falls by relatively more because its life is fixed for one year, while the liability must be rolled over in 90 days at a higher interest rate. The increase in interest rates causes owner equity to fall by $12.44, or about 75 percent. In contrast, had the interest rate declined by 200 basis points, the net present value of the firm's equity would have risen to $29.49 (see panel C of table 1), an increase of about 78 percent.

This extreme volatility in the firm's equity is due to the mismatch of the durations of the asset and liability that make up the firm's portfolio. Table 3 illustrates this point. The only difference between this and earlier examples is that, in table 3, the duration of the liability has been lengthened to match the duration of the asset. While a 200 basis-point increase in the interest rate still causes the present value of the portfolio to fall, the change, − $0.30 or − 1.8 percent, is much less than before. Clearly, matching the durations of the asset and liability exposes the value of the portfolio to much lower interest rate risk.

COPING WITH THE GAP

Depository institutions, particularly savings and loan associations, maintain portfolios of assets and liabilities that are similar to the one shown in the initial example.[5] That is, the duration of their assets

---

[4]The durations of single-payment financial instruments are equal to the maturities of the instruments. In other cases, calculation of duration is not as straightforward. See footnote 3.

[5]Savings and loan associations are required to maintain a significant share of their portfolios in long-term home mortgages in order to obtain federal insurance of deposits. See Federal Home Loan Bank Act of 1932, sec. 4(a).

Table 3

Interest Rate Changes and the Present Value of a Portfolio of Assets and Liabilities of the Same Duration

Panel A: Initial Conditions

Present Values

Asset:	Liability:
$\dfrac{\$1,000.00}{1.10} = \$909.09$	$\dfrac{\$981.82}{1.10} = \$892.56$
	Equity:
	$\$909.09 - \$892.56 = \$16.53$

Panel B: All Interest Rates Rise by 200 Basis Points

Present Values

Asset:	Liability:
$\dfrac{\$1,000.00}{1.12} = \$892.86$	$\dfrac{\$981.82}{1.12} = \$876.63$
	Equity:
	$\$892.86 - \$876.63 = \$16.23$
	Percentage change in equity = -1.8

typically is longer than the duration of their liabilities. As a result, the market values of these institutions have been particularly sensitive to interest rate fluctuations. This, along with the recent experience of highly variable interest rates, has led these institutions to seek out methods to reduce their exposure to interest rate risk. Among other things, these firms have made greater use of floating rate loans and interest rate swap agreements. Recent regulatory changes have allowed them to allocate more of their loan portfolios to short-term consumer loans. In addition, a number of institutions are using financial futures to reduce their exposure to interest rate risk.[6]

---

[6]See Booth, Smith and Stolz (1984). While a number of financial firms are employing the futures market, it seems that accounting requirements have discouraged the use of futures to hedge interest rate risk. Until recently, regulators and accountants feared that losses from futures transactions could be hidden in financial reports. Therefore, they would not permit a hedge to count as one transaction with spot gains or losses offsetting futures markets losses or gains. Instead, they required futures losses to be marked to the market while spot gains could be deferred. This asymmetric treatment of gains and losses on the two sides of a hedge distorted earnings estimates and, therefore, discouraged the use of futures.

Futures Markets and Risk

It may seem odd that the futures market, which is generally thought of as being very risky, can be used to reduce risk. Futures trading is risky for people who bet on the future price movements of particular commodities or financial instruments by taking long or short positions in futures contracts. Such speculative bets on future price movements, however, are not unique to futures market trading. The nature of most types of businesses requires a speculative bet about the future course of a particular price.

Growing crops, for example, gives farmers long positions in physical commodities during the growing season. These long positions expose the farmer to the risk of price declines — declines that can reduce the profits from efficient farming (the activity that the farmer specializes in). Judicious use of the futures market allows the farmer to offset his long position in the commodity by selling futures contracts. Since the sale reduces his net holdings of the commodity, the farmer's exposure to the risk of future price declines is reduced. Similarly, futures trading presents depository institutions with the opportunity to reduce their exposure to the risk of interest rate changes.

Futures Contracts

A futures contract is an agreement between a seller and a buyer to trade some well-defined item (wheat, corn, Treasury bills) at some specified future date at a price agreed upon *now* but paid in the future at the time of delivery. The futures price is a prediction about what the price of the item will be at the time of delivery.

In the case of commodities, the price of the good today (the spot price), on average, will be equal to the futures price minus the cost of storage, insurance and foregone interest associated with holding the good over the interval of the contract. A similar relationship exists between the spot and futures prices of financial instruments. However, since the storage and insurance cost of holding these instruments is very low, the spread between the spot and futures prices is largely determined by the interest cost.

See Morris (1984) for more detail on changes in accounting standards. Asay, et al. (1981) provide examples of how former accounting standards discouraged the use of futures by banks and thrift institutions.

The Relationship Between Spot and Futures Markets for Treasury Bills: An Illustration

In January 1976, the International Monetary Market (IMM), now part of the Chicago Mercantile Exchange (CME), began trading futures contracts in 13-week Treasury bills.[7] The basic contract is for $1 million with contracts maturing once each quarter in the third week of March, June, September and December. Since there are eight contracts outstanding, the most distant delivery date varies between 21 and 24 months into the future.

Panel A of table 4 presents quotations for Treasury bill futures for the trading day of August 7, 1984. Panel B of table 4 lists spot quotations for Treasury bills for the same trading day.[8]

Panel A of table 4 is interpreted as follows: September Treasury bill futures were trading at a discount of 10.49 percent on August 7, 1984. Any person trading this contract obtained the right to buy (sell) a Treasury bill the third week in September with a remaining maturity of 13 weeks at a discount rate of 10.49 percent. A similar statement holds for the other contracts listed in panel A.

Panel B lists spot market quotations. For example, Treasury bills due to mature August 9, 1984, traded at a discount of 9.91 percent (bid) to 9.79 percent (ask), while those maturing September 20, 1984, traded at a discount of 9.95 (bid) to 9.91 (ask), etc.

We noted earlier that the spot and futures markets must be closely related, and the data in panels A and B can be used to illustrate this point. For example, on August 7, 1984, an investor could purchase a Treasury bill due to mature December 20, 1984 (i.e., 134 days later). If he purchases the bill on the spot market, he obtains the asked discount of 10.39 percent. At this discount rate, the price he pays for the bill is $96.41 per $100 of face value.[9]

Table 4

Market Quotations for U.S. Treasury Bills: August 7, 1984[1]

Panel A: Treasury Bill Futures (IMM)

	Contract	Discount settle
1984	September	10.49
	December	10.85
1985	March	11.13
	June	11.35
	September	11.52
	December	11.66
1986	March	11.79
	June	11.90

Panel B: Treasury Bill Spot

	Discount	
Maturity Date	Bid	Ask
August 9, 1984	9.91	9.79
September 20, 1984	9.95	9.91
December 20, 1984	10.45	10.39
March 21, 1985	10.63	10.56
June 13, 1985	10.72	10.66
July 11, 1985	10.73	10.69

[1]*Wall Street Journal*, August 8, 1984, pp. 38–9.

Alternatively, the investor could purchase a futures contract that gives him the right to buy a Treasury bill in September that will mature the third week in December. This alternative gives him a discount rate of 10.49 percent. Buying the Treasury bill in September at this discount would require a payment of $97.54.[10] This payment will be made 43 days into the future, roughly, September 20, and the present value of the payment on August 7 is $96.44.[11] Notice that this is very near the amount that the investor would pay ($96.41) if he were to purchase a Treasury bill on the spot market that matured during the third week of December.

Of course, other alternatives are open to the investor as well. He could, for example, buy a Treasury bill that matured the third week in March on the spot market.

---

[7]Futures contracts in other types of financial instruments, such as GNMA passthrough certificate contracts, 90-day CDs, Treasury bonds and Treasury notes, also are available at the Chicago Board of Trade.

[8]The information in table 3 is taken from pages 38 and 39 of the August 8, 1984, *Wall Street Journal*. The actual tables in the *Wall Street Journal* contain more information than is presented here. For our purposes, however, the additional information is extraneous.

[9]$96.41 = $100/(1.1039)^{37}$. The discount factor is raised to the power of 134/360 = .37. This calculation is slightly different from the discount calculation used in determining actual trading prices, but

numerical differences between the two formulas are small. See Stigum (1981) for the market's discount formula.

[10]$97.54 = $100/(1.1049)^{25}$.

[11]$96.44 = $97.54/(1.0991)^{12}$. The interest rate used in the calculation is the rate on August 7 for a security maturing on September 20 (43 days in the future).

The present cost of doing this should be near the present cost of buying a futures contract that allows him to purchase a Treasury bill in December maturing the third week in March. Table 5 uses the data in table 4 to compare the present costs of this and other alternatives. In each case, the present costs of employing the spot vs. the futures market are very close.[12] Because a close relationship between these markets exists, the Treasury bill futures market can be used effectively to hedge interest rate risk.[13]

HEDGING THE GAP

The Streams of Receipts and Payments

The example in table 1 can be used to illustrate how futures contracts can be applied to hedge the interest rate risk caused by the mismatch in the lives (durations) of the firm's assets and liabilities. Considerable confusion appears to exist as to what the firm's hedging objective should be and how hedges should be constructed. One possible hedging strategy is to protect the equity of the firm (in the present value sense) from interest rate fluctuations. Another often-cited strategy is to minimize discrepancies between cash flows over time. It seems clear, however, that firm owners will choose a hedge that protects their net wealth (present value of the firm's equity). This focus on net wealth is crucial because, as the examples show, reducing cash flow mismatches to zero does not minimize the exposure of the firm's equity to interest rate changes.

Hedging Net Wealth: An Example

Suppose it is September 15, 1984, and the firm initiates the transactions summarized earlier in panel A of table 1. In addition, to hedge each of its three refunding requirements, the firm sells December, March and June futures contracts at 10 percent discounts.[14] The price of each contract is $1,000/(1.10)^{.25} =

---

[12]Small differences are due to the existence of transaction costs. If the differences were large, profitable arbitrage opportunities would exist. These, of course, would vanish quickly as traders took advantage of the situation.

[13]There is, of course, the problem that the spot instrument being hedged may not be identical to the futures market instrument. If so, the price of one may diverge from the other because of a change in a factor that affects the price of one but not the other. This is called "basis risk" and is ignored in the following examples.

[14]A flat yield curve is assumed for ease of exposition. The examples become more complicated if the yield curve slopes up or down and/ or the spread between borrowing and lending rates changes.

Table 5

The Relationship Between Treasury Bill Spot and Futures Prices: August 7, 1984, Per $100 of Face Value

Case 1: Purchase of a Treasury bill that matures the third week in December 1984

	Present Cost
Spot Market Purchase	$96.41
September Futures Purchase	96.44
Difference	.03

Case 2: Purchase of a Treasury bill that matures the third week in March 1985

	Present Cost
Spot Market Purchase	$93.92
December Futures Purchase	93.94
Difference	.02

Case 3: Purchase of a Treasury bill that matures the third week in June 1985

	Present Cost
Spot Market Purchase	$91.45
March Futures Purchase	91.47
Difference	.02

$976.45. These contracts obligate the firm to deliver a 13-week Treasury bill with a face value of $1,000 during the third week of December, March and June in exchange for $976.45.

Panel A of table 6 presents the firm's expected streams of receipts and payments given the structure of interest rates on September 15. It is identical to panel A of table 1 except that the streams of receipts and payments generated by the futures contract are included. The futures contract generates a certain stream of receipts equal to $976.45 in December, March and June in exchange for delivery of the 90-day Treasury bills. The firm must acquire these bills in order to make delivery and, on September 15, the expected cost of acquiring each of the Treasury bills is $976.45. If interest rates remain unchanged, expected and actual costs will be the same so that the actual receipts and payments generated by the futures contract net out in each period. The net flow of receipts is zero until year-end when the firm receives $18.18. The present value of this amount is $16.53.

In panel B, interest rates are assumed to rise unexpectedly by 200 basis points immediately following

Table 6

Expected Streams of Receipts and Payments

	Day				
	0	**90**	**180**	**270**	**360**
Panel A: No Change in Interest Rates					
Asset (loan)					
Receipts					$1,000.00
Payments	$909.09				
Asset (futures)					
Receipts		$976.45	$976.45	$976.45	
Liabilities (borrowings)					
Receipts	909.09	926.75	944.76	963.11	
Payments		926.75	944.76	963.11	981.82
Liabilities (futures)					
Payments		976.45	976.45	976.45	
Net Receipts	-0-	-0-	-0-	-0-	$ 18.18

Present Value = $18.18/1.10 = $16.53

	0	90	180	270	360
Panel B: Interest Rates Rise by 200 Basis Points					
Asset (loan)					
Receipts					$1,000.00
Payments	$909.09				
Asset (futures)					
Receipts		$976.45	$976.45	$976.45	
Liabilities (borrowings)					
Receipts	909.09	926.75	949.10	971.98	
Payments		926.75	949.10	971.98	995.42
Liabilities (futures)					
Payments		972.07	972.07	972.07	
Net Receipts	-0-	$ 4.38	$ 4.38	$ 4.38	$ 4.58

Present Value = $4.38/(1.12)^{25} + $4.38/(1.12)^{50} + $4.38/(1.12)^{75} + $4.58/(1.12) = $16.50

	0	90	180	270	360
Panel C: Interest Rates Fall by 200 Basis Points					
Asset (loan)					
Receipts					$1,000.00
Payments	$909.09				
Asset (futures)					
Receipts		$976.45	$976.45	$976.45	
Liabilities (borrowings)					
Receipts	909.09	926.75	940.35	954.15	
Payments		926.75	940.35	954.15	968.15
Liabilities (futures)					
Payments		980.94	980.94	980.94	
Net Receipts	-0-	$ -4.49	$ -4.49	$ -4.49	$ 31.85

Present Value = − $4.49/(1.08)^{25} − $4.49/(1.08)^{50} − $4.49/(1.08)^{75} + $31.85/(1.08) = $16.52

the firm's September 15 transactions. As in panel B of table 1, the increase in interest rates raises the firm's refunding cost and reduces the net year-end receipt to $4.58. In addition, however, the increase in interest rates reduces the expected cost of acquiring the Treasury bill to $972.07. Since the firm will receive $976.45 upon delivery of the Treasury bills, the futures contract will generate a net flow of receipts equal to $4.38 in December, March and June. The present value of this flow added to the present value of the net receipt at year-end ($4.58) is $16.50, which is nearly identical to the present value for the case in which interest rates remained unchanged (the small difference is due to rounding errors).

Panel C illustrates the outcome for a 200 basis-point decline in interest rates. In this case, the futures contract generates negative net receipts for the firm in December, March and June. The present value of this negative flow added to the present value of the higher positive net receipt at year-end sum to $16.52. As the examples show, this hedge protects the net wealth of the firm regardless of the direction of the change in interest rates.

While this hedge protects net wealth from changes in interest rates, it does so by allowing net cash receipts to vary. Net cash receipts, both in amount and timing, are considerably different in panels A, B and C. In panel A, net receipts are $18.18 at year-end while in panel B net receipts are spread out over the year and total only $17.72. In panel C, the firm has negative net receipts during the year and a large positive net receipt at year-end for a total of $18.38. However, the present value of the firm is the same in all three cases.

The Balance Sheet

Panel A of table 7 presents the firm's balance sheet position in terms of present values. The futures contracts are entered as both assets and liabilities, leaving equity the same as that shown in panel A of table 2.[15] The futures asset is the present value of the future receipt of a *fixed* amount. The futures liability, on the other hand, is the present value of the *expected* cost of covering the futures contract given the structure of interest rates on September 15. Panels B and C illus-

trate the effect on the present values of the firm's assets, liabilities and equity if, immediately following the above transactions, interest rates rise unexpectedly (panel B) or fall unexpectedly (panel C) by 200 basis points.

An unexpected increase in interest rates causes the present value of the loan to fall relative to the present value of the liability. By itself, this would cause a reduction in the firm's equity. At the same time, however, the increase in interest rates generates a positive expected net cash flow from the futures contracts, which, of course, has a positive net present value. Other things the same, this causes equity to rise. The net effect of both changes is that equity remains unchanged. The reverse occurs if interest rates decline by 200 basis points.

This hedge has eliminated the firm's exposure to interest rate risk. In contrast, recall that a 200 basis-point change in the interest rate causes the equity of the unhedged firm in table 2 to change by about 75 percent.

Hedging as a "Profit Center"

The purpose of hedging is to reduce the variance of a firm owner's wealth. In a textbook example of a perfect hedge, the gain or loss from a short position in the futures market will offset exactly the compensating loss or gain on the spot assets and liabilities held by the firm. A hedge is constructed because — in the presence of an uncertain future — wealth is greater if the institution foregoes a profit stream that is higher on average (if it goes unhedged) in exchange for a profit stream that is lower on average (by the cost of the hedging operations) but more certain.

Some portfolio managers, however, lose sight of this fact and assume speculative positions in the futures market with the objective of earning profits from the position if interest rates change in their favor. While speculative positions in futures (or spot instruments) can increase earnings, they can have the opposite effect as well.

One potentially significant danger in the use of futures contracts to hedge interest rate risk is that the firm may misunderstand the nature of the hedging function. Trading futures for hedging is *not* intended to generate profits from the trading itself. Rather, its purpose is to establish futures positions so that the owner's wealth is held constant; this will occur if the increase (decrease) in the value of the firm's spot holdings of assets and liabilities is offset exactly by the loss (gain) in the futures market.

---

[15]Strictly speaking, futures contracts entered into by member banks of the Federal Reserve System are treated as balance sheet memoranda items. These are reported on Schedule L, Commitments and Contingencies, of the Call Report. Hence, for accounting purposes, futures contracts do not affect the assets and liabilities of the firm until the contracts are exercised.

Table 7

Interest Rate Changes and the Present Value of a Hedged Firm

Panel A: Initial Conditions (9/15/84)

Present Values

Assets:		Liabilities:	
Loan: $1,000.00/1.10 =	$ 909.09	90-day CD: $981.82/1.10 =	$ 892.56
Contracted Future Receipts		Expected Cost of Covering the Futures Contract:	
December Future: $976.45/(1.10)^{25} =	953.46	December Future: $976.45/(1.10)^{25} =	953.46
March Future: $976.45/(1.10)^{50} =	931.01	March Future: $976.45/(1.10)^{50} =	931.01
June Future: $976.45/(1.10)^{75} =	909.09	June Future: $976.45/(1.10)^{75} =	909.09
	3,702.65		3,686.12
		Equity:	16.53
			3,702.65

Panel B: All Interest Rates Rise by 200 Basis Points

Note: The expected cost of covering each contract falls to $1,000/(1.12)^{25} = $972.07 while the contracted future receipt remains unchanged.

Present Values

Assets:		Liabilities:	
Loan: $1,000.00/1.12 =	$ 892.86	90-day CD: $995.42/1.12 =	$ 888.77
Contracted Future Receipts:		Expected Cost of Covering Futures Contract:	
December Future: $976.45/(1.12)^{25} =	949.17	December Future: $972.07/(1.12)^{25} =	944.92
March Future: $976.45/(1.12)^{50} =	922.66	March Future: $972.07/(1.12)^{50} =	918.52
June Future: $976.45/(1.12)^{75} =	896.88	June Future: $972.07/(1.12)^{75} =	892.86
	3,661.57		3,645.07
		Equity:	16.50
			3,661.57

Panel C: All Interest Rates Fall by 200 Basis Points

Note: The expected cost of covering each contract rises to $1,000/(1.08)^{25} = $980.94

Present Values

Assets:		Liabilities:	
Loan: $1,000.00/1.08 =	$ 925.93	90-day CD: $968.15/1.08 =	$ 896.44
Contracted Future Receipts:		Expected Cost of Covering Futures Contract:	
December Future: $976.45/(1.08)^{25} =	957.84	December Future: $980.94/(1.08)^{25} =	962.25
March Future: $976.45/(1.08)^{50} =	939.59	March Future: $980.94/(1.08)^{50} =	943.91
June Future: $976.45/(1.08)^{75} =	921.68	June Future: $980.94/(1.08)^{75} =	925.92
	3,745.04		3,728.52
		Equity:	16.52
			3,745.04

Real World Complications in Hedging

The examples in tables 6 and 7 simplify real world problems to illustrate the basic concepts of interest rate risk and hedging. In practice, a number of complicating factors will make the construction of a hedge considerably more difficult.

The first difficulty to note is that the calculation of present values for a large portfolio composed of many different assets and liabilities will require a great deal of information. Moreover, resources will be needed to estimate interest elasticities (or durations). And, unlike our examples, which are based on single-payment loans and deposits of known durations, firms face the additional problem of loans that are subject to early payment and deposits that are subject to early withdrawal.

Even with a good estimate of its exposure to interest rate risk, firms will face practical problems in implementing a hedge. Typically, liquidity is very thin in futures contracts dated for delivery more than nine months in the future. Firms also are not likely to find futures contracts for the exact dollar amount they wish to hedge or for the specific spot asset or liability being hedged. For example, money market certificates (MMCs) might be hedged with Treasury bill futures. It is possible, however, that interest rates on MMCs and Treasury bill futures will not move by identical amounts or in the same direction, an event that will reduce the effectiveness of a hedge. When the futures contract does not correspond exactly to the spot commodity, as in this case, the firm is exposed to "basis" risk.

Firms also face the possibility of changes in the slope of the yield curve; that is, unlike our examples, short- and long-term rates could change by differing amounts. If, for example, long rates increased 200 basis points but short rates increased only 100 basis points, the change in the difference between the present values of spot assets and spot liabilities would not be completely offset by a change in the difference between the present values of the futures asset and liability. True hedges, however, are implemented under the expectation of no change in the yield curve's slope. It is easy to see, therefore, that hedging does not eliminate this source of risk.

SUMMARY

Higher and more variable interest rates have increased the risk faced by financial institutions associated with attracting deposit funds and extending credit. This article presented some simple examples of techniques that can isolate and quantify sources of a financial institution's exposure to interest rate risk. The discussion also described how financial futures can be used to reduce this risk. A simple hedging example indicated that relatively conservative use of futures markets can have a potentially large impact on reducing risk exposure. The use of futures trading is a threat to the long-run performance of a financial firm only if applied in a manner inconsistent with hedging.

REFERENCES

Asay, Michael R., Gişela A. Gonzalez, and Benjamin Wolkowitz. "Financial Futures, Bank Portfolio Risk, and Accounting," *Journal of Futures Markets* (Winter 1981), pp. 607–18.

Bierwag, G. O., George G. Kaufman and Alden Toevs. "Bond Portfolio Immunization and Stochastic Process Risk," *Journal of Bank Research* (Winter 1983), pp. 282–91.

Booth, James R., Richard L. Smith, and Richard W. Stolz. "Use of Interest Rate Futures by Financial Institutions," *Journal of Bank Research* (Spring 1984), pp. 15–20.

Carrington, Tim, and Daniel Hertzberg. "Financial Institutions Are Showing the Strain of a Decade of Turmoil," *Wall Street Journal* (September 5, 1984).

Federal Home Loan Bank Act of 1932. Public No. 304, 72 Cong., HR 12280.

Gay, G. D., and R. W. Kolb. "The Management of Interest Rate Risk," *Journal of Portfolio Management* (Winter 1983), pp. 65–70.

Gottlieb, Paul M. "New York and Connecticut Permit Insurers to Use Futures and Options: A Comparison," Chicago Mercantile Exchange *Market Perspectives* (May/June 1984), pp. 1–6.

Hicks, J. R. *Value and Capital* (Oxford: Clarendon Press, 1939).

Kaufman, George G. "Measuring and Managing Interest Rate Risk: A Primer," Federal Reserve Bank of Chicago *Economic Perspectives* (January-February 1984), pp. 16–29.

Koch, Donald L., Delores W. Steinhauser and Pamela Whigham. "Financial Futures as a Risk Management Tool for Banks and S&Ls," Federal Reserve Bank of Atlanta *Economic Review* (September 1982), pp. 4–14.

Kolb, R. W. *Interest Rate Futures: A Comprehensive Introduction* (Robert F. Dame, Inc., 1982).

Kolb, Robert W., Stephen G. Timme and Gerald D. Gay. "Macro Versus Micro Futures Hedges at Commercial Banks," *Journal of Futures Markets* (Spring 1984), pp. 47–54.

Lower, Robert C. *Futures Trading and Financial Institutions: The Regulatory Environment* (Chicago Mercantile Exchange, 1982).

Morris, John. "FASB Issues Rules for Futures Accounting," *American Banker* (August 24, 1984).

Olson, Ronald L. and Donald G. Simonson. "Gap Management and Market Rate Sensitivity in Banks," *Journal of Bank Research* (Spring 1982), pp. 53–58.

Samuelson, P. A. "The Effect of Interest Rate Increases on the Banking System," *American Economic Review* (March 1944), pp. 16–27.

Santoni, G. J. "Interest Rate Risk and the Stock Prices of Financial Institutions," this *Review* (August/September 1984).

Simonson, Donald G., and George H. Hempel. "Improving Gap Management for Controlling Interest Rate Risk," *Journal of Bank Research* (Summer 1982), pp. 109–15.

Stigum, Marcia. *Money Market Calculations: Yields, Break-Evens and Arbitrage* (Dow Jones-Irwin, 1981).

Toevs, Alden. "Gap Management: Managing Interest Rate Risk in Banks and Thrifts," Federal Reserve Bank of San Francisco *Economic Review* (Spring 1983), pp. 20–35.

Wardrep, Bruce N. and James F. Buch. "The Efficacy of Hedging with Financial Futures: A Historical Perspective," *Journal of Futures Markets* (Fall 1982), pp. 243–54.

GLOSSARY

Basis	The price or yield difference between a futures contract and the cash instrument being hedged
Basis point	1/100 of 1 percent
Delivery month	A specified month within which delivery may be made under the terms of the futures contract
Discount yield	The ratio of the annualized discount to the par value
Evening up	Buying or selling to offset or liquidate an existing market position
Futures contract	A standardized contract, traded on an organized exchange, to buy or sell a fixed quantity of a defined commodity at a price agreed to now but delivered in the future
Gap analysis	A technique to measure interest rate sensitivity
Hedge	An attempt to reduce risk by taking a futures position opposite to an existing cash position
Interest rate swap	The exchange of two financial assets (liabilities) which have the same present value but which generate different streams of receipts (payments)
Long hedge	A hedge in which the futures contract is bought (long position)
Macro-hedge	A hedge designed to reduce the net portfolio risk of an organization
Micro-hedge	A hedge designed to reduce the risk of holding a particular asset or liability
Open interest	The number of open futures contracts, that is, unliquidated purchases *or* sales of futures contracts
Short hedge	A hedge that involves selling a futures contract (short position)
Spot price	The current market price of the actual physical commodity

Article Seven

Interest Rate Swaps:
A New Tool For Managing Risk

*Jan G. Loeys**

INTRODUCTION

Sharp movements of interest rates in recent years have created serious problems for firms in which the maturity of their assets does not match the maturity of their liabilities. For example, some financial institutions and other corporations have long-term, fixed-rate assets financed with short-term liabilities. Such firms experience an earnings squeeze whenever market interest rates rise unexpectedly, because their cost of borrowing rises faster than the yield on their

assets. As a result, many firms look for ways to reduce the sensitivity—or exposure—of their earnings to interest rate fluctuations. A recent technique that allows firms to hedge (reduce) this exposure is the "interest rate swap." Used first in the Eurobond market during 1981, interest rate swaps have taken the market by storm; and now the volume of interest rate swaps in the United States alone is close to $80 billion.

Why are interest rate swaps so popular? What are the advantages of this instrument over other hedging techniques, such as refinancing the firm's debt or purchasing interest rate futures? The answers to these questions require first an explanation of what interest rate swaps are and how they can be used to reduce interest rate risk.

*Jan Loeys is a Senior Economist in the Macroeconomics Section of the Research Department of the Federal Reserve Bank of Philadelphia. The author is indebted to Charles Gibson for helpful comments.

WHAT ARE INTEREST RATE SWAPS?

An interest rate swap typically involves two firms that want to change their exposure to interest rate fluctuations in opposite directions. For example, one firm has long-term assets that yield a fixed rate of return; but it also has liabilities with interest payments that fluctuate with market rates of interest (that is, floating rate liabilities).[1] This firm loses when interest rates rise unexpectedly, because the interest cost of its liabilities rises but the revenue from its (fixed-rate) assets remains the same. Conversely, this firm gains from an unexpected drop in interest rates. This sensitivity of a firm's net earnings to interest rate fluctuations is the firm's *exposure to interest rate risk*. The other firm involved in the swap faces the opposite situation: its assets yield a return that fluctuates with market rates, but the interest payments on its liabilities are fixed for a longer period of time. A rise in interest rates benefits this firm, because its revenues rise faster than its cost of borrowing; but a drop in market rates reduces its net earnings.

When two firms such as these have opposite interest risk exposures, one has the makings of a swap. In a typical swap the two firms get together—sometimes through an intermediary—and, in effect, exchange some of their interest payments. A firm with floating-rate liabilities essentially takes over some of the interest payments of a firm with fixed-rate liabilities, and in return the firm with the fixed-rate liabilities takes over some of the interest payments of the firm with floating-rate liabilities. For example, a firm that has liabilities on which the interest rate fluctuates with the 3-month Treasury bill (T-bill) rate could agree to pay another firm a fixed rate of 12 percent on an agreed upon dollar amount (principal) in exchange for a floating-rate payment of 50 basis points over the 3-month T-bill rate on the same principal. *In effect*, one firm converts the interest payments on its liabilities from a floating-rate to a fixed-rate basis, and the other converts its liabilities from fixed to floating rate. (For a more detailed discussion of the mechanics of swap arrangements, see HOW A SWAP WORKS.) Parties to a swap agree to make *interest payments* to each other—they do not actually swap liabilities, nor do they lend money to each other. Each firm remains responsible for paying the interest and principal on its own liabilities. Therefore, swaps do not appear on a firm's balance sheet; instead they are used to alter the exposure to interest rate risk implied by the balance sheet.

In just a few years, interest rate swaps have become very popular as a hedging instrument (see FROM ZERO TO $80 BILLION IN THREE YEARS p. 21). But why are firms using swaps rather than other more established hedging techniques, such as purchasing interest rate futures?

SWAPS: LONGER THAN FUTURES, BUT MORE EXPENSIVE

Futures are contracts that generate cash flows that can be used to reduce a firm's interest risk exposure. An interest rate futures contract is an agreement to buy or sell a certain financial asset, such as a T-bill, for a specific price at a specific date in the future. During the life of the futures contract, each time the market value of the asset falls (interest rates rise), the seller in the contract makes a profit, and receives cash, and the buyer takes a loss, and pays cash, and vice versa if the asset's market value rises.[2]

---

[1]There are two types of floating-rate debt: one is a short-term liability that has to be refinanced frequently; the other is a long-term liability on which the interest rate fluctuates with the interest rate of a specific market instrument.

[2]Cash flows are generated because the exchange where the contract is traded requires that both the buyer and seller in a futures contract post a certain margin. If the price of the underlying asset falls, the buyer has to deposit additional funds with the exchange to maintain the margin requirement, and the seller has his account credited by the same funds. Margins may consist of Treasury securities. For more details, see Howard Keen, Jr., "Interest Rate Futures: A Challenge for Bankers," this *Business Review* (November/December, 1980), pp. 13-25; Mark Drabenstott and Anne O'Mara McDonley, "Futures Markets: A Primer for Financial Institutions," Federal Reserve Bank of Kansas City *Economic Review*

HOW A SWAP WORKS

The following example is based on an actual transaction that was arranged by an investment bank between a large thrift institution and a large international bank; it is representative of many swaps that have been arranged since 1982. "Thrift" has a large portfolio of fixed-rate mortgages. "Bank" has most of its dollar-denominated assets yielding a floating-rate return based on LIBOR (the London Interbank Offered Rate).

On May 10, 1983, the "Intermediary," a large investment bank, arranged a $100 million, 7-year interest rate swap between Thrift and Bank. In the swap, Thrift agreed to pay Bank a fixed rate of 11 percent per year on $100 million, every 6 months. This payment covered exactly the interest Bank had to pay on a $100 million bond it issued in the Eurodollar market. Thrift also agreed to pay Bank the 2 percent underwriting spread that Bank itself paid to issue this bond. In exchange, Bank agreed to make floating-rate payments to Thrift at 35 basis points (.35 percent) below LIBOR. Intermediary received a broker's fee of $500,000.

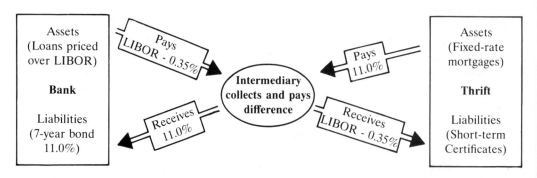

Twice a year, Intermediary (for a fee) calculates Bank's floating-rate payment by taking the average level of LIBOR for that month (Col. 2), deducting 35 basis points, dividing by 2 (because it is for *half* a year), and multiplying by $100 million (Col. 3). If this amount is larger than Thrift's fixed-rate payment (Col. 4), Bank pays Thrift the difference (Col. 5). Otherwise, Thrift pays Bank the difference (Col. 6).

[1] Date	[2] LIBOR	[3] Floating-rate payment 1/2 (LIBOR -0.35%)	[4] Fixed-rate payment 1/2 (11%)	[5] Net Payment from Bank to Thrift	[6] Net Payment from Thrift to Bank
May 1983	8.98%	—	—	—	—
Nov 1983	8.43%	$4,040,000	$5,500,000	0	$1,460,000
May 1984	11.54%	$5,595,000	$5,500,000	$95,000	0
Nov 1984	9.92%	$4,785,000	$5,500,000	0	$ 715,000
May 1985	8.44%	$4,045,000	$5,500,000	0	$1,455,000

The swap allows both Bank and Thrift to reduce their exposure to interest rate risk. Bank can now match its floating-rate assets priced off LIBOR with an interest payment based on LIBOR, while the fixed-rate interest payments on its bond issue are covered by Thrift. At the same time, Thrift can hedge part of its mortgage portfolio, from which it receives fixed interest earnings, with the fixed-rate payment it makes to Bank. However, the floating-rate payment that Thrift receives is linked to LIBOR while its cost of borrowing is more closely linked to the T-bill rate. Since LIBOR and the T-bill rate do not always move in tandem, Thrift is still exposed to fluctuations in the relation between LIBOR and the T-bill rate.

Consider again the case of a thrift institution that has long-term fixed-rate assets, like mortgages, that it funds with short-term liabilities, like certificates of deposit (CDs). If interest rates rise unexpectedly, this thrift will lose—it suffers reduced net earnings. But the thrift could hedge its interest rate risk with a futures contract to deliver (sell) a CD. Then, if interest rates rise, the market value of the CD falls, and the thrift receives a cash flow. This cash inflow offsets the reduced net earnings from the higher interest cost of the thrift's short-term liabilities. When interest rates *drop*, the futures contract produces a cash outflow, but this loss is offset by a lower interest cost on the thrift's short-term liabilities. By buying enough of these futures contracts, the thrift can, in principle, fully hedge its exposure to interest rate fluctuations.

One disadvantage of futures is that they are standardized contracts that exist only with certain specific delivery dates and deliverable types of financial instruments.[3] In particular, futures are available only for delivery dates at 3-month intervals out to about 2-1/2 years. This makes it impossible to hedge interest rate risk beyond 2-1/2 years.[4] Interest rate swaps, in contrast, are private contracts with virtually every aspect of the agreement open to negotiation. Conse-

quently, a swap can be tailor-made to fulfill one firm's particular needs, assuming another firm can be found to fit the other end of the contract. This flexibility allows firms to set up long-term arrangements—most swaps have a final maturity of three to ten years—thereby filling the gap left by futures.

The ability to customize interest rate swaps does not come without its disadvantages. The lack of product standardization makes it more difficult to find another party and to negotiate a mutually agreeable contract. It also costs more to close out a swap contract if the need arises, than a futures contract position, which can be closed out readily. Apart from certain fixed costs of setting up an account with a trader and meeting regulatory requirements, the brokerage costs of initiating and eventually closing out a futures contract are 2 to 5 basis points. This is much lower than the arrangement fee of about 25 basis points that most swap brokers charge (not including additional fees for settling and guaranteeing the agreement).

Because swaps are agreements between private parties, they also have the disadvantage that one of the parties may default and thus be unable to continue the agreement. Although the other party has no principal at risk, it would again be stuck with an interest risk exposure. It could negotiate a new swap arrangement with another firm, but the terms of that agreement would depend on current market interest rates, which may be more or less advantageous to the firm. Default risk can be reduced by requiring collateral, standby letters of credit, or a third-party guarantee—all of which are costly.[5] Fu-

---

(November 1984), pp. 17-23; and Nancy Rothstein (ed.), *The Handbook on Financial Futures*, (New York: McGraw-Hill, 1984).

[3]The four delivery dates are March, June, September, and December. The deliverable assets are Treasury bills, notes, and bonds; Bank and Eurodollar CDs; Sterling CDs and Gilts; and Ginny Maes. However, there are no interest rate futures on the prime rate or on the London Interbank Offered Rate (LIBOR), although many firms have their cost of borrowing tied to either of these two rates. Firms that use, say, a T-bill futures to hedge their LIBOR-based borrowing are still exposed to fluctuations in the relation between the T-bill rate and LIBOR. Swaps, though, frequently have the same problem as it is difficult to find two firms with opposite exposure to the same market rate of interest (see the example in HOW A SWAP WORKS).

[4]As a practical matter, a firm that wants to hedge as closely as possible, say, a 5-year fixed-rate asset when only 2-1/2 year futures contracts are available, has to buy the contract

with the longest available delivery date and then replace it every three months with the new 2-1/2 year contract. In this way, the firm can keep the delivery date of its futures contract as close to 2-1/2 years as possible. The firm will keep doing this until the remaining maturity of the asset reaches 2-1/2 years.

[5]Often the third-party guarantee is provided by the intermediary who would be required to step in and take over the obligation of the defaulting party. So far, there have been no reports of defaults on a swap agreement.

FROM ZERO TO $80 BILLION
IN THREE YEARS

Interest rate swaps first emerged in the Eurobond market in late 1981.[a] Large international banks, which do most of their lending on a floating-rate basis, were involved in the first swaps so that they could use their fixed-rate borrowing capacity to obtain lower-cost floating-rate funds. Initially, the swapping partners consisted mainly of utilities and lower-rated industrial corporations that preferred fixed-rate financing. During 1982, the first domestic interest rate swap occurred between the Student Loan Marketing Association (Sallie Mae) and the ITT Financial Corp., with Sallie Mae making floating-rate payments to ITT. Since then, the market has grown tremendously; in 1984 about $80 billion in swap agreements were concluded.[b] Any large corporation can now use interest rate swaps as an instrument for asset-liability management.

Both investment banks and commercial banks have been active in arranging interest rate swaps. These intermediaries earn fees by bringing the different parties together, by acting as settlement agent (that is, collecting and paying the net difference in the interest payments), and by serving as guarantor of the agreement. Most intermediaries have recently gone beyond their initial role of merely bringing different parties together and function also as dealers. As a dealer, the intermediary is also the counterparty to each swap it "sells." That is, each party has an agreement only with the intermediary and is totally unaware of who might be on the other side of the swap. This arrangement allows the intermediary to sell one leg of the swap before selling the other and to work with an inventory of as yet unmatched swap agreements. The existence of dealers also facilitates an informal secondary market in swaps, where parties to a swap can sell their position to the intermediary or to another party, thereby increasing the liquidity of this instrument.

A typical swap involves a bond issue for $25 to $75 million with a 3 to 10 year maturity on one side, and a floating-rate loan on the other side. Initially, this floating rate loan was priced at a fraction over LIBOR, the London Interbank Offered Rate. Recently floating-rate loans have also been using the prime rate, the T-bill rate, or other indices of the cost of short-term borrowing.

The most common type of swap is the one described above: a dollar fixed-rate loan swapped for a dollar floating-rate loan, otherwise called the "plain-vanilla" swap. However, several variations on this basic swap have emerged in the market. One such variation is a floating-to-floating swap where parties agree to swap floating rates based on different indices. For example, a bank with assets tied to the prime rate and liabilities based on LIBOR may want to swap the interest payments on its liabilities with payments on a prime-tied, floating-rate loan. Another type of arrangement involves currency swaps such as a swap of a sterling floating-rate loan for a dollar fixed-rate loan. For firms whose assets are denominated in a different currency than are its liabilities, this type of swap may be more appropriate. Finally, rather than exchanging interest payments on liabilities, swaps can also be used to exchange yields on *assets* of different maturities or currencies.

The interest rate swap market has proven to be very flexible in adjusting its product to new customer needs. This innovativeness all but guarantees that swaps will remain a permanent feature of international capital markets.

---

[a] For more technical and institutional details on interest rate swaps, see Carl R. Beidleman, *Financial Swaps: New Strategies in Currency and Coupon Risk Management*, (Homewood, Illinois: Dow Jones-Irwin, 1985); and Boris Antl (ed.), *Swap Financing Techniques*, (London: Euromoney Publications Limited, 1983).

[b] Since there are no official reporting requirements on swaps, estimates of the size of this market vary tremendously. The amount of $80 billion, as estimated by Salomon Brothers (see *The Economist*, March 16, 1985, p. 30, Table 16), appears to be somewhere in the middle.

tures, on the other hand, are guaranteed by the exchange in which the contracts are traded and by the funds that both parties to a futures contract must hold on margin with the exchange.

To reduce the costs stemming from the customized nature of swaps, many intermediaries have started to standardize the contract terms of swap agreements, such as the type of floating interest rate, repricing dates, and margin or collateral requirements.[6] As a result, interest rate swaps may become similar to futures contracts, but with longer periods available for hedging.

Given a choice, firms that want to reduce their exposure to interest rate fluctuations for up to 2-1/2 years may be better off with interest rate futures than with swaps because futures are less costly to use than swaps.[7] For longer-term hedges, interest rate swaps are a more appropriate, though relatively more expensive, hedging instrument.

SWAPS: MORE FLEXIBLE
AND CHEAPER THAN REFINANCING

Rather than using complicated instruments such as swaps and futures, it may seem a lot less trouble for a firm to adjust its exposure directly by issuing liabilities (debt) with the pricing characteristics it desires. For example, a firm that has only floating-rate liabilities but now desires more fixed-rate liabilities, could buy back some of its floating-rate liabilities and issue fixed-rate liabilities instead; that is, it could refinance some of its liabilities. However, "sellers" of interest

rate swaps claim that swaps may be less costly than refinancing for several reasons. One is that firms with lower credit ratings may have to pay relatively higher interest rates—that is higher quality spreads—in the fixed-rate market than in the floating-rate market. Thus, they claim, such firms should borrow in the floating-rate market and then swap, if they desire fixed-rate liabilities. Another reason is that swaps circumvent transactions costs associated with refinancing—such as legal fees, advertising, and regulatory restrictions—because swaps do not involve new borrowing; they only involve the exchange of interest payments on existing liabilities. To understand the advantages swaps can have over refinancing requires a closer look at these quality spread differentials and transactions costs.

Quality Spread Differentials. A quality spread is the premium that a borrower with a low credit rating has to pay over a borrower with a high credit rating. For example, during 1982 when interest rate swaps first became popular in the U.S., the quality spread between Aaa and Baa rated firms in the fixed-rate corporate bond market was over 2 percentage points, a post-war high.[8] At the same time, these quality spreads were less than 1 percentage point in the floating-rate market.

To see how interest rate swaps could exploit this apparent difference in quality spreads, consider an example typical of many of the early swaps. "Company" is a manufacturer whose assets yield a fixed rate of return. Company finances a major part of its assets by borrowing at a floating rate of 1 percentage point above the 3-month T-bill rate. Company prefers to finance its assets with a fixed-rate bond issue, but because of its low Baa credit rating it would have to pay, say, 16 percent.

On the other side is "Bank," a large inter-

---

[6]For more details, see "Swaps: Managing the Future," *Euromoney* (October 1984), pp. 201-221; and "Making a Market in Slightly Used Swaps," *Institutional Investor* (November 1984), pp. 77-84.

[7]Firms could also use options in this case. An option is the right (rather than the commitment) to buy or sell an asset before a certain date in the future. Options are not discussed in this paper because a comparison of options with swaps is very similar to a comparison of futures with swaps. Options, like futures, are mostly standardized products, traded mostly on organized exchanges, and available only up to 2 years. However, certain over-the-counter options are increasingly available for longer periods.

[8]Aaa and Baa are credit ratings assessed by Moody's Investors Services, Inc., a major credit-rating agency. This rating system consists of 10 grades, ranging from Aaa (highest quality) to Baa (medium quality) to Caa (poor quality) to D (default).

national bank, with a portfolio of commercial loans on which it charges a rate based on the 3-month T-bill rate. Bank currently finances its portfolio by issuing CDs at 1/2 percentage point above the 3-month T-bill rate. Given its high Aaa credit rating it has the option of borrowing in the bond market at a fixed rate of 14 percent. Table 1 shows the different alternatives for the two firms. Note that the quality spread is 1/2 percentage point in the floating-rate market, and 2 percentage points in the fixed-rate market.

If each simply wanted to match maturities, Bank would borrow in the floating-rate market at 1/2 percentage point above the T-bill rate and Company would borrow in the bond market at 16 percent. But both borrowers could reduce their cost of borrowing if Bank borrows at a fixed rate and Company borrows at a floating rate and they swap interest payments, with Company agreeing to pay Bank, say, an additional 1 percentage point. In effect, this means that Bank borrows at a 14 percent interest rate, pays Company the T-bill rate plus 1 percentage point (Company's borrowing cost), and receives payments from Company at a 15 percent interest rate. On net, Bank makes interest payments at the T-bill rate [14% + (T-bill rate + 1%) - 15%].

On the other side of the transaction, Company in effect borrows at the T-bill rate plus one percentage point, pays Bank a 15 percent interest rate, and receives payments from Bank at the T-bill rate plus one percentage point. On net, then, Company makes interest payments at a 15 percent interest rate [(T-bill rate + 1%) + 15% - (T-bill rate + 1%)].[9] As a result, Bank effectively borrows at the T-bill rate, better than it could do by itself, and Company borrows at a fixed 15 percent, less than the 16 percent it would have to pay if it had entered the bond market on its own. The source of this reduction in borrowing costs is the difference in quality spreads between the fixed-rate and the floating-rate market. By being able to borrow at a fixed rate through Bank, Company saves more than enough over its own fixed-rate cost of borrowing to compensate Bank for Company's higher (than Bank's) cost of borrowing in the floating-rate market (1/2 percentage point).

The reduction in borrowing costs made possible by these quality spread differentials has been a major selling point for swaps. These cost reductions may be more apparent than real, however. There is a lot of evidence that financial markets are efficient, and that pure arbitrage profits are not readily available.[10] Market efficiency suggests that the difference in quality spreads between fixed-rate and floating-rate markets—200 vs. 50 basis points in the example—reflects differences in risk to lenders in these respective markets. Indeed, the quality spread that is typically quoted does not refer to debt of the same maturity. The floating-rate debt that firms use as a basis for swaps is mostly short- to medium-term, while the fixed-rate debt consists

---

TABLE 1
QUALITY SPREAD DIFFERENTIALS

Issued By:	Interest Rate on Liabilities	
	Floating Rate	Fixed Rate
Company (Baa)*	T-bill + 1.0%	16.0%
Bank (Aaa)*	T-bill + 0.5%	14.0%
Quality spread:	0.5%	2.0%

*Credit ratings are in parentheses. Baa is the lower rating.

---

[9]As explained in HOW A SWAP WORKS, only the *difference* between these two flows of payment actually changes hands. Unless the T-bill rate is above 14 percent, company pays the difference between 14 percent and the T-bill rate.

[10]For a survey of the evidence, see Thomas E. Copeland and J. Fred Weston, *Financial Theory and Corporate Policy*, Second Edition, (Reading: Addison-Wesley, 1983).

of long-term bonds.[11] Debt-holders consider *short-term* debt less risky than long-term debt because they have the option not to renew the debt if the firm looks shakier than anticipated. Therefore, debt-holders require smaller quality spreads on short-term debt than on long-term debt. The possibility that debt will not be renewed, however, makes issuing short-term debt rather than long-term debt more risky to *equity-holders*. Issuing short-term rather than long-term debt therefore merely shifts risk from debt-holders to equity-holders.[12] A firm that considers swapping the floating-rate interest on its short-term debt for a fixed-rate interest payment as an alternative to borrowing directly long term must take into account that the lower cost of borrowing produced by the swap comes at the cost of increased risk to the firm's equity-holders.

Quality spread differentials may seem to offer profit opportunities, and they may look like a good reason to use swaps instead of refinancing. But market efficiency suggests that true profit opportunities are likely to be short-lived at best, and that most of the time they are illusory. But there are more solid reasons why refinancing is more costly than interest rate swaps, and they are transactions costs and other non-interest costs (as opposed to interest costs in the form of high quality spreads).

Transactions Costs. Refinancing can take a lot of time, while a swap can be arranged within a few days. To refinance, a firm has to buy back its outstanding liabilities, which can be expensive, or wait until these liabilities mature. Then the firm must try to convince its regular lenders to provide a different type of funds. A thrift, for example, may have to expend much time, effort, and expense to convince its depositors of short-term funds to invest instead in long-term time deposits.

If a firm's regular customers are unwilling to provide, say, fixed-rate funds, the firm can look to alternative markets, such as the domestic or the Eurodollar bond market. Bond markets, however, are costly to use. Domestic bond markets, for one, are highly regulated. To issue a new domestic bond, a firm has to register with the Securities and Exchange Commission (SEC) and meet its disclosure requirements.[13] In addition, a prospective bond issuer is well-advised to obtain a credit rating from the major rating agencies, such as Moody's, or Standard and Poor's, which requires additional expense. The actual selling of a bond issue involves other costs such as advertising, legal fees, and an underwriting spread—that is, the difference between what the firm issuing the debt receives and the (higher) price that ultimate investors pay for the debt. This spread, which runs anywhere from 25 to 500 basis points and which averages about 80 basis points for investment grade debt, serves as payment to the underwriter (or underwriter's syndicate) for distributing the issue to the ultimate investors, and for committing himself to buy that part of the issue that is not bought by the public at a given price.

---

[11]The floating-rate debt that firms use as a basis for a floating-to-fixed interest rate swap consists mostly of bank credit, commercial paper, certificates of deposits (CDs), and floating-rate notes (FRNs). More than 90% of commercial and industrial loans by U.S. banks are short term. Commercial paper usually has a maturity of 3 to 6 months, while most large negotiable CDs of financial institutions are for 6 months or less. Although FRNs have stated maturities of 7 to 15 years, almost all FRNs issued in the U.S. have covenants that give the holder the right to redeem the note at 3-year intervals, thereby reducing the effective maturity of these FRNs to 3 years. Some of the FRNs that do show large quality spreads usually give the issuer the option to exchange the issue for fixed-rate debt before a certain date. Thus, these last FRNs are more like fixed-rate bonds.

[12]For a formal treatment of this issue, see Thomas Ho and Ronald Singer, "Bond Indenture Provisions and the Risk of Corporate Debt," *Journal of Financial Economics* (1982), pp. 375-406.

[13]Under SEC rule 415 firms can shortcut the normally lengthy registration procedure by filing a single registration statement covering securities they expect to sell from time to time within two years. These firms can then sell securities "off the shelf" whenever they choose. However, this procedure is only available to the largest and most creditworthy corporations.

As an alternative to the domestic bond market, a firm also can try the Eurodollar bond market. Eurodollar bonds are dollar-denominated bonds issued by international syndicates anywhere outside the United States. The Eurobond market has the advantage that it is almost totally unregulated (that is, there are almost no registration or disclosure requirements), so that issuing a bond does not take a lot of time. On the negative side, however, underwriting spreads on Eurodollar bonds are three to four times those on domestic bond issues. Also, because there are no disclosure requirements in Eurobond markets, investors are reluctant to lend to firms that do not have an excellent credit rating. Therefore, for relatively unknown firms the Eurodollar bond market is even less accessible than the domestic bond market.

The existence of interest rate swaps makes it possible for firms to borrow in the markets in which they have a comparative advantage rather than refinancing in markets in which they don't. These firms can then swap interest payments with firms that have a comparative advantage in another market to achieve the interest payments characteristics they desire. Comparative advantage can take the form of lower interest costs and lower transactions costs. Such lower costs can be the result of name recognition, an established retail network for issuing liabilities, government subsidies and regulations, or other attributes associated with borrowing or lending in certain markets. For example, international banks have the name recognition that allows them to borrow in the Eurodollar market. Domestic banks and thrifts, on the other hand, have the retail network and deposit insurance that give them a comparative advantage in attracting retail savings-type deposits. Interest rate swaps allow banks and thrifts to protect themselves against interest rate risk without having to give up the retail (short-term) savings market in which most of them specialize.

SUMMARY

The high interest rate volatility of recent years has induced many firms to look for ways to protect their profit margins—to hedge—against interest rate fluctuations. A recent and popular technique is the interest rate swap, in which different parties *in effect* swap the interest rate payments on each other's liabilities. An interest rate swap typically allows a firm with floating-rate liabilities to exchange its floating-rate interest payments with another party for fixed-rate payments, thereby effectively acquiring a fixed-rate cost of borrowing.

In only a few years, interest rate swaps have become very popular hedging instruments because frequently they are better suited or less expensive than other hedging techniques, such as purchasing interest rate futures or refinancing the firm's debt. Because interest rate futures are standardized products traded on an organized market, they are inexpensive to use. But because of their standardization, they do not always meet a firm's specific requirements to hedge its interest rate risk exposure. In particular, futures have delivery dates only out to 2-1/2 years, while there is no such limit for swaps. Swaps are freely negotiated agreements between private parties, and, therefore, they can be tailor-made. But this customization makes swaps more expensive to use than futures.

Interest rate swaps can also be very useful when the high costs of entering a market as a new borrower make it too expensive for a firm to obtain directly the type of financing it needs to achieve its desired interest risk exposure. A firm may find that attracting fixed-rate financing in the bond market, for example, is very costly because of high underwriting fees, disclosure costs, or the high risk premium that relatively unknown borrowers may have to pay. An interest rate swap allows a firm to exchange interest flows in order to achieve the desired characteristics of its interest payments without changing the structure of its balance sheet. Interest rate swaps are thus an indirect way of entering financial markets in situations where firms find it very costly to obtain financing directly.

Real Interest Rates: What Accounts for Their Recent Rise?

A. Steven Holland

NOMINAL interest rates have risen to unprecedented levels in the last five years, and the common perception is that expected real rates of interest — rates minus expected inflation — have risen as well. These higher rates are blamed for a variety of economic ills including reduced capital investment and slowdowns in such interest-sensitive sectors as housing and automobiles.

This paper is concerned, first, with establishing that real interest rates have indeed been higher during the 1980s than in the previous two decades and, second, with examining possible causes of this major shift. Potential causes include changes in the expected rate of inflation, monetary policy, the state of the economy, taxes, federal budget deficits and the declining relative price of energy.

ESTIMATES OF BEFORE- AND AFTER-TAX REAL INTEREST RATES

The real interest rate is not known with certainty at the time a security is purchased, but the purchaser has an expectation of it. The nominal interest rate, i, is the sum of the expected real rate of interest, r, and the expected rate of inflation, $\dot{p}^e$:

$$(1)\ i = r + \dot{p}^e.[1]$$

The expected real rate, thus, can be estimated according to the formula:

$$(2)\ r = i - \dot{p}^e,$$

as long as an estimate of the expected inflation rate is available.

Proxies for the expected rate of inflation frequently are based on weighted averages of past inflation rates or the predicted values from regression equations in which the inflation rate depends on past inflation rates, past rates of money growth and a number of other variables.[2] Because empirical results can be sensitive to assumptions about the way expectations are formed, however, a potentially more fruitful approach is to use "observed" inflation forecasts to estimate expected inflation.[3] In this article, data from surveys of both short- and long-term inflation expectations are used to estimate short- and long-term expected real rates of interest.

This analysis oversimplifies the problem, since it applies only to the expected real *before-tax* yield. Since interest payments are taxable as earned income, the expected real after-tax yield (r^*) is:

$$(3)\ r^* = i - ti - \dot{p}^e$$
$$= (1-t)i - \dot{p}^e,$$

where t is the marginal tax rate. An estimate of the average marginal tax rate on personal income is used below to estimate expected after-tax real interest rates.

The estimates presented in this article are intended to represent the pattern of recent real interest rate *movements*, not to provide completely accurate estimates of real interest rates at any point in time. Potential sources of error in the estimates include (but are not limited to): (a) measurement error in calculating the expected rate of inflation, (b) the effects of different

---

A. Steven Holland is an economist at the Federal Reserve Bank of St. Louis. Jude L. Naes, Jr., provided research assistance.

[1]This equation is a widely used approximation of the "Fisher equation." See Fisher (1965).

[2]As pointed out by Santoni and Stone (1982), however, the difficulty with this procedure is that any change in economic policy or any structural change or "shock" that affects inflation expectations will not be incorporated in the estimate of expected inflation.

[3]For an example of the sensitivity of empirical results to assumptions about expectations formation, see Holland (1984).

Chart 1
Nominal and Real 1-Year Interest Rates

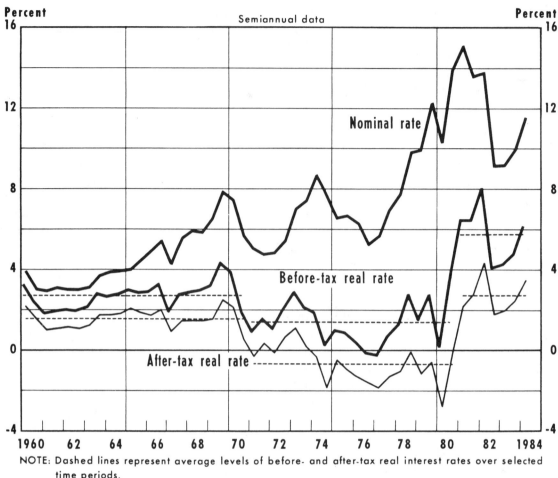

NOTE: Dashed lines represent average levels of before- and after-tax real interest rates over selected time periods.

marginal tax rates across market participants and (c) the difference between the marginal tax rate expected to hold at the time interest payments are received and the current rate.[4] Whenever real interest rates are referred to in the following discussion, it will mean expected real interest rates.

Estimates of Short-Term Real Interest Rates

Chart 1 plots nominal returns and estimates of the before- and after-tax real returns on one-year Treasury securities, based on one-year inflation forecasts from

the Livingston survey from 1960 to the first half of 1984.[5] Between 1960 and 1970, the nominal rate rose from around 3 percent to over 7 percent. Estimates of

[4]In addition, the return that is relevant for decision-making depends on risk and the tax burden on alternative uses of funds. More will be said about risk later in the article. See Ezrati (1982) and Mehra (1984) for discussions of the implications of taxes on alternative uses of funds.

[5]Joseph Livingston of *The Philadelphia Inquirer* conducts a survey of economists each spring and fall, requesting respondents to indicate their predictions of the consumer price index (CPI). Because the survey results published, for example, in June contain predictions for the following December and June, Livingston refers to them as six- and 12-month-ahead forecasts as this article does. Because the respondents to the June survey are thought to know only the April CPI, however, they are actually predicting eight- and 14-month rates of change. For a detailed discussion of the Livingston expectations data, see Carlson (1977). This article uses the data in Carlson's revised form updated to the present. The nominal interest rates used in the charts and table are the quarterly averages of the rates for the quarter in which the Livingston survey was taken. The same calculations were made for six-month Treasury bills based on six-month inflation forecasts. Since the pattern of movements was nearly identical, however, only the one-year rates are reported. The estimate of the average marginal tax rate comes from Chase Econometrics.

Chart 2

Nominal and Real 10-Year Interest Rates

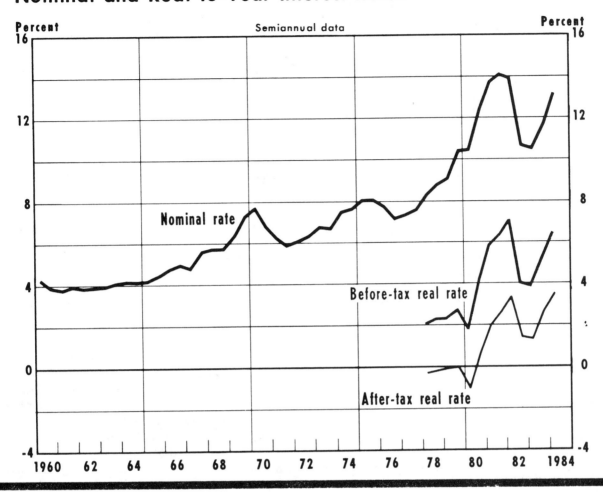

Percent
Semiannual data
Percent

the expected real rate indicate this was due primarily to higher expected inflation, since both the before- and after-tax real rates appear to have risen only slightly, if at all, over the period.

Between 1971 and 1980, short-term nominal interest rates, on average, were much higher than in the 1960s; real rates, for the most part, were lower. In fact, estimated before-tax real rates were below 1 percent from the second half of 1974 to the first half of 1978 and were even negative in late 1976 and early 1977. After-tax real rates were negative for nearly the entire period from 1974 to 1980. Nominal rates increased dramatically after 1977, with increases of about 200 basis points occurring in late 1978 and again in late 1979. These increases, however, served only to bring real rates closer to the levels that had prevailed before 1974.

From late 1979 to early 1982, short-term nominal interest rates were higher than at any time during the

1960s or 1970s. Short-term real interest rates, however, did not break with precedent until 1981 when before-tax real rates climbed above the 6 percent level; they continued to rise through early 1982. After-tax real rates behaved in a similar fashion and, on average, have been higher since 1981 than in the previous two decades. The difference is not as great, however, as it is for before-tax real rates. Both nominal and real rates have declined since early 1982, but they remain at very high levels relative to past history.

Estimates of Long-Term Real Interest Rates

We expect long-term real interest rates to behave in a manner broadly similar to short-term real rates; if short-term rates rise, long-term rates are forced up so that real yields over any holding period are compara-

Table 1

Spreads Between Yields on Ten- and One-Year Treasury Securities

Date	(1) Nominal rate spread	(2) Before-tax real rate spread	(3) After-tax real rate spread
I/1978	0.53	0.97	0.82
II/1978	−1.00	−0.38	−0.09
I/1979	−0.83	0.94	1.15
II/1979	−1.82	0.09	0.57
I/1980	0.20	1.81	1.76
II/1980	−1.42	0.50	0.89
I/1981	−1.38	−0.50	−0.11
II/1981	0.54	−0.02	−0.17
I/1982	0.13	−0.88	−0.91
II/1982	1.54	0.07	−0.30
I/1983	1.36	−0.25	−0.58
II/1983	1.74	0.62	0.23
I/1984	1.65	0.46	0.09

ble whether one holds short- or long-term bonds.[6] Because of data limitations, however, it is much more difficult to get an accurate representation of the market's expectation of inflation over the distant future than over the near future.[7] In fact, it is only since 1978 that a survey of expected inflation over periods substantially longer than a year has been undertaken. The survey, known as the Decision-Makers Poll, provides estimates of expected inflation over the next five and 10 years.[8]

---

[6]This assumes the absence of segmented markets. In other words, there is a high degree of substitutability between short- and long-term securities. This is not meant to imply that the term structure of interest rates does not change over time, only that short- and long-term interest rates behave in a broadly similar fashion.

[7]It is also more difficult to know the appropriate tax rate to use in calculating the after-tax yield, since interest payments are made much farther in the future.

[8]Richard Hoey of Drexel Burnham Lambert, Inc., conducts this survey of institutional portfolio managers. Each respondent predicts the rate of change of consumer prices over the next five years and over the five subsequent years. The average of the two provides the estimate of expected inflation over the next 10 years.

Since 1980, the survey has been conducted at least four times a year. To facilitate comparison with the shorter-term real interest rate estimates, we use data from surveys taken as close as possible to the dates of the Livingston surveys. There is never more than one month's difference in the dates of the surveys of the short- and long-term inflation expectations used in this paper. In 1978 and 1979, there was only one survey in each year (taken near the middle of the year). These two surveys provided data for the estimates of long-term inflation expectations for the first halves of 1978 and 1979. Estimates for the second halves of both years were calculated by interpolation.

Chart 2 plots the nominal yield on 10-year Treasury securities since 1960, as well as estimates of the 10-year, before- and after-tax real rates since 1978 based on the mean inflation forecasts from the survey. As expected, the pattern of movements in long-term nominal rates during the 1960s and 1970s is similar to that in short-term rates. In particular, when short-term nominal rates shot upward in the late 1970s, so did long-term nominal rates. Long-term real rates also reached heights comparable to those of short-term real rates in 1981 and 1982.[9] Thus, it appears that the increase in long-term real rates occurred at roughly the same time and was of roughly equal size as the increase in short-term real rates.

The Term Structure of Real Interest Rates

Nominal long-term rates have been substantially above nominal short-term rates since 1982, reversing the pattern from the late 1970s and early 1980s. This is illustrated in column 1 of table 1, which gives the difference between the yields on 10-year and one-year Treasury securities since 1978. Comparable differences for before- and after-tax real rates, respectively, are presented in columns 2 and 3 of the table.

The estimated real term structure tells an entirely different story than the nominal term structure. There

---

[9]Five-year rates exhibited a similar pattern.

Figure 1
Initial Equilibrium in the Market for Loanable Funds

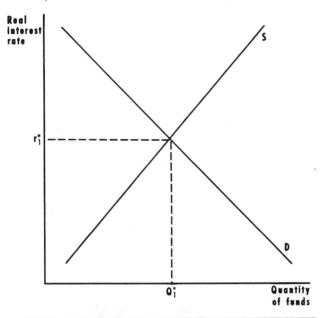

Figure 2
The Effects of an Increase in the Supply of and Reduction
in the Demand for Loanable Funds

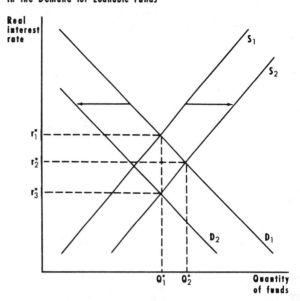

is, for the most part, very little difference between short- and long-term real rates. In other words, the real "yield curve" — the relationship between the term to maturity and the real rate of interest on securities — has been much flatter in recent years than the nominal yield curve. The average absolute difference between the one- and 10-year nominal rates from 1978 to 1984 is 109 basis points; for before-tax real rates, it is 58 basis points, while for after-tax real rates it is 59 basis points. These figures imply that long-term real rates have not differed substantially from short-term real rates in recent years.[10]

WHY DID REAL INTEREST RATES RISE?

The real interest rate is determined by the interaction of the supply of and demand for loanable funds. The quantity of funds available for lending (the quantity supplied) increases as the real rate of interest increases. The quantity that people wish to borrow (the quantity demanded) decreases as the real rate increases. The equilibrium real rate is that for which the quantity demanded and quantity supplied are equal.

[10]Notice that long-term inflation expectations were substantially lower than short-term inflation expectations from 1978 to early 1981, a period of predominantly rising inflation. This pattern has been reversed for late 1981 through early 1984, a period of generally declining inflation.

In figure 1, this occurs at the real rate r_1^*, where S represents the supply curve and D represents the demand curve. Factors that affect the positions of the supply and demand curves determine the equilibrium rate. Potentially, these factors include the expected rate of inflation, monetary policy, the state of the economy, taxes, federal budget deficits and the declining relative price of energy. The potential impact of each of these factors on real interest rates is discussed below.

Expected Inflation

We know that expected inflation affects nominal interest rates. In fact, our real rate estimates are derived by subtracting the expected inflation rate from the nominal interest rate. Changes in expected inflation, however, also have the potential to alter real interest rates. One reason, associated with Mundell (1963), is that higher expected inflation causes people to transfer part of their assets from money to (higher) interest-earning assets, thereby increasing the supply of loanable funds and driving down the real interest rate. This occurs because money provides a very low or negative real return during times of inflation, whereas the return on interest-earning assets generally keeps better pace with expected inflation. A similar notion, associated with Tobin (1965), is that higher expected inflation causes people to shift part of their money balances into real capital. This induces net investment in capital that ultimately depresses the marginal return on capital, reducing the demand for loanable funds and the real interest rate.

An additional argument, based on the effect of expected inflation on the return to capital investment, is associated with Feldstein and Summers (1978): Higher inflation drives up the replacement cost of capital, while current tax law provides for depreciation allowances for businesses based on the historical cost of capital. Therefore, higher expected inflation results in a lower expected real return on capital investment, reducing the demand for loanable funds and, consequently, the real interest rate.

These effects are illustrated in figure 2. The Mundell effect shifts the supply curve from S_1 to S_2 (an increase in supply), resulting in a decline in the equilibrium real rate of interest from r_1^* to r_2^*. Similarly, the Tobin and the Feldstein-Summers effects shift the demand curve from D_1 to D_2 (a reduction in demand), resulting in a decline in r^* (to r_3^* if both shifts occur).

There is, however, a potential positive effect of expected inflation on the real interest rate that works through the personal income tax system.[11] Under the assumption that people try to maintain a constant after-tax real rate, higher expected inflation leads to higher before-tax real interest rates since taxes are assessed on the nominal return.[12] Thus, the higher the nominal return, the greater the spread between the before- and after-tax real rates, all other things equal. The widening of the spread between before- and after-tax real rates as the nominal interest rate increases can be seen in chart 1, where the averages of the before- and after-tax real rates for the periods 1960–70, 1971–80 and 1981–84 are given by the dashed lines.

Therefore, with the combination of the Mundell-Tobin and Feldstein-Summers effects and the income tax effect, it is not possible to say a priori whether an increase in expected inflation leads to higher or lower before-tax real interest rates, although we expect it to

cause lower after-tax real rates.[13] From 1960 to 1980, the correlation between expected inflation and both before- and after-tax real rates on one-year Treasury securities was negative and statistically significant: −0.38 for the before-tax rate and −0.81 for the after-tax rate. This provides support for the Mundell-Tobin and Feldstein-Summers effects. From 1981 to 1984, however, the correlation has actually been positive for the before-tax rate and essentially zero for the after-tax rate. The same is true for the correlation between inflation expectations and long-term real rates over the 1981–84 period.[14] Furthermore, during the period of rapidly rising real rates from 1980 to 1982, long-term inflation expectations were also rising. Thus, though the evidence on the effect of expected inflation on real interest rates from simple correlations is mixed, it does not appear that changes in expected inflation were a major factor in the recent rise in real interest rates.

Monetary Policy

The effect of monetary policy on real rates of interest is a subject of considerable controversy. Textbooks typically describe the impact of an increase in money supply on the real rate as follows: An increase in the money supply relative to money demand creates an excess supply of money; in response, individuals increase their purchases of securities and goods until the interest rate declines by enough to induce them to hold the larger amount of money. Thus, the supply of loanable funds increases, driving down the real interest rate. Furthermore, an expansionary monetary policy leads to short-term increases in real income due to the increased demand for goods, which has two effects that influence real rates in opposite directions: (1) the level of savings increases, putting downward pressure on the real rate, and (2) the demand for money increases, causing the real rate to rise.[15]

One consequence of increasing the growth rate of the money supply, however, is a rise in future rates of inflation and also in *expected* future rates of inflation.

---

[11]See Darby (1975) and Feldstein (1976).

[12]To see this consider that

$$r^* = (1-t)i - \dot{p}^e$$

and that a constant after-tax real return, r^*, implies that

$$\Delta r^* = (1-t)\Delta i - \Delta \dot{p}^e = 0.$$

Therefore,

$$\Delta i = (1/1-t)\Delta \dot{p}^e.$$

With the tax rate, t, between 0 and 1, this implies that the change in the nominal interest rate, Δi, is greater than the change in the expected inflation rate, $\Delta \dot{p}^e$. If the tax structure is progressive, then higher expected inflation results in an even wider spread between before- and after-tax real rates.

---

[13]See Makin and Tanzi (1983).

[14]The correlation coefficients for 1981–84 are: for the one-year before-tax real rate, 0.48; for the one-year after-tax real rate, −0.06; for the 10-year before tax real rate, 0.38; for the 10-year after-tax real rate, −0.04.

[15]For more detail, see Santoni and Stone, and Brown and Santoni (1983). The theory of rational expectations states that a fully anticipated change in the money supply will have no effect on real interest rates. When people forecast money growth and future inflation in an optimal manner — by using all of the information currently available at sufficiently low cost — then the monetary authority is powerless to affect real behavior of any kind unless it is able to fool the public. This implies that only an unanticipated change in money supply affects the real interest rate. See Fischer (1980).

Chart 3
2-Quarter M1 Growth and 1-Year Real Interest Rate

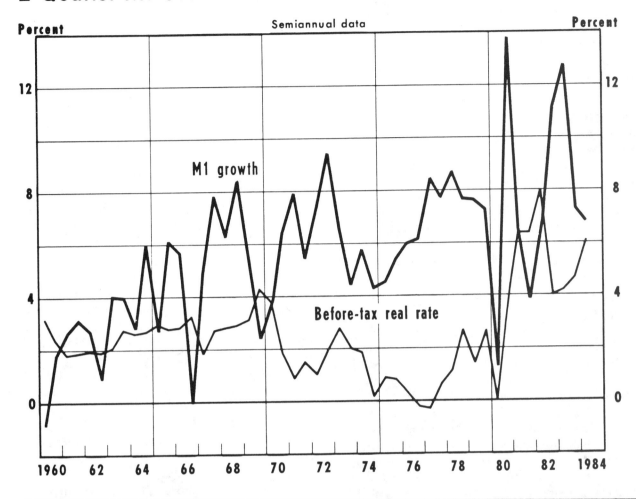

Percent   Semiannual data   Percent

Therefore, the effect of increased growth of the money supply on nominal rates is likely to be positive in the long run even if its immediate effect on real rates is negative.

Empirical evidence suggests that there is little, if any, long-term effect of changes in the money supply on real interest rates. Hafer and Hein (1982) found that an initial negative effect of higher money growth on estimates of real interest rates was completely offset one quarter later. Similarly, Santoni and Stone (1982) found no evidence to link money growth and real rates over the long term.[16]

Chart 3 plots the two-quarter growth rate of M1 along with our estimate of the before-tax real interest rate on one-year Treasury securities. The first point to make is that the correlations between money growth and the real interest rate series are negligible for the sample period used in the chart.[17] It is true, however, that real rates of interest began to rise in 1980 just after a tremendous reduction in two-quarter M1 growth. This reduction was followed by an equally large increase in M1 growth, but real interest rates continued to climb nonetheless.

The data illustrated in the chart suggest another possible role for monetary policy in the determination

---

[16]Carlson (1982) actually finds a weak positive association between money growth and real interest rates.

[17]The correlation coefficient for two-quarter M1 growth and the before-tax real interest rate on one-year Treasury securities for 1960–84 is 0.076. The correlation between money growth and the before-tax real 10-year rate for 1978–84 is –0.071. Correlations with the after-tax yields on the same securities for the same time periods are –0.157 and –0.004, respectively.

of real interest rates: more variable money growth leads to higher real rates. The explanation for this is that the instability created by highly variable money growth makes for increased uncertainty about future returns on both short- and long-term interest-earning assets and capital and raises the demand for money relative to these assets. This is, in effect, a reduction in the supply of loanable funds, which causes an increase in real interest rates.[18]

Another way to state this is: lenders, if they are risk-averse, require that a greater "risk premium" be added to interest rates in order to offset the greater uncertainty associated with the future real return.[19] The effect of monetary variability on real interest rates is not completely unambiguous, however, since risk-averse borrowers reduce their demand for loanable funds as uncertainty increases. A recent empirical study by Mascaro and Meltzer (1983) suggests that the overall effect of monetary variability on nominal interest rates is positive. Since the variability of money growth should not affect expected inflation, it follows that the effect on real interest rates is positive as well.[20]

A casual glance at chart 3 suggests that money growth became substantially more variable in 1980, the same year that real rates of interest began to rise. The standard deviation of two-quarter M1 growth is substantially higher for 1980–84 than for 1960–79, 4.1 percent compared with 2.5 percent. The source of greater monetary variability is an unsettled issue, but many analysts attribute it to the change in Federal Reserve operating procedure that occurred in October 1979.[21] Other events also may have contributed to the rise in monetary variability including the innovation in financial markets (such as the introduction of NOW, Super NOW and money market deposit accounts) and the imposition and removal of credit controls in 1980.[22]

Thus, it appears that an increase in the variability of money growth in 1980 contributed to the increase in

real rates of interest that occurred in 1980 and 1981. Furthermore, there is as yet no indication that the short-run instability of money growth was much affected one way or another by the Federal Reserve's shift to a more judgmental operating procedure in the fall of 1982, and real interest rates have yet to return to their pre-1981 levels.[23]

The State of the Economy

When the economy enters a recession, business firms experience excess capacity, and the need for additional capital is reduced. A reduction in both the demand for loanable funds and the real rate of interest follows. As the economy recovers, some firms begin to push toward their capacity constraints, requiring additional investment and increasing the demand for funds. Thus, higher real interest rates tend to accompany an expansion.

Chart 4 plots a measure of the amount of "slack" in the economy, the GNP gap, along with our estimate of the before-tax real rate on one-year Treasury securities. The evidence suggests that the state of the economy helps to explain movements in real interest rates both before and after the recent upward shift in real rates, but the shift itself appears to have little to do with overall economic conditions. The GNP gap has a correlation of −0.56 with the before-tax real rate for the period 1960–80, and −0.44 for 1981–84.[24]

---

[18]See Friedman and Schwartz (1963).

[19]The analysis assumes that it is not possible to diversify one's holdings in a manner that completely offsets the greater risk associated with monetary variability.

[20]Mascaro and Meltzer estimate the variability of unanticipated money growth, which turns out to be highly correlated with the variability of actual money growth.

[21]The Federal Reserve announced on October 6, 1979, it would place less emphasis on confining variations in the federal funds rate and more emphasis on reserve aggregates as a sign of its commitment to longer-run restraint on money growth.

[22]See Hafer (1984) for a discussion of how financial innovations may have affected the accuracy of M1 as a measure of transaction balances.

[23]As evidence that the money supply continues to be highly variable, consider the behavior of M1 during 1983 and 1984. M1 grew during the first two quarters of 1983 at a 12.8 percent rate and during the second two quarters of 1983 at a 7.3 percent rate. Similarly, in 1984 the growth rate of M1 was 6.8 percent in the first half of the year, compared with −0.4 percent from June to October.

It is generally recognized that the Federal Reserve altered its operating procedure again in late 1982. The post-1982 procedure is not the same as the pre-1979 procedure, however. See Wallich (1984). Another effect of the 1979 change in operating procedure was an increase in the day-to-day variability of nominal interest rates, which adds an additional element of risk in securities markets. This increased variability occurred in late 1979, however, while real interest rates did not begin to rise until late 1980. In addition, the federal override of state usury ceilings effective in March 1980 may have contributed somewhat to higher real interest rates, although there is no reason to think this action would push real rates to levels higher than those during previous periods (such as most of the 1960s and early 1970s) when these ceilings were not binding.

[24]The measure of the GNP gap is the difference between potential and actual GNP as calculated by the Council of Economic Advisers. To get data for 1984, potential GNP was assumed to grow at its average rate for 1960–83, 3.44 percent. For the 10-year before-tax real rate, the correlation for 1981–84 is −0.55. For after-tax real rates, the correlations are −0.62 for the 1960–80 period and −0.13 for the 1981–84 period for the one-year rate and −0.37 for the 1981–84 period for the 10-year rate.

Chart 4
GNP Gap and 1-Year Real Interest Rate

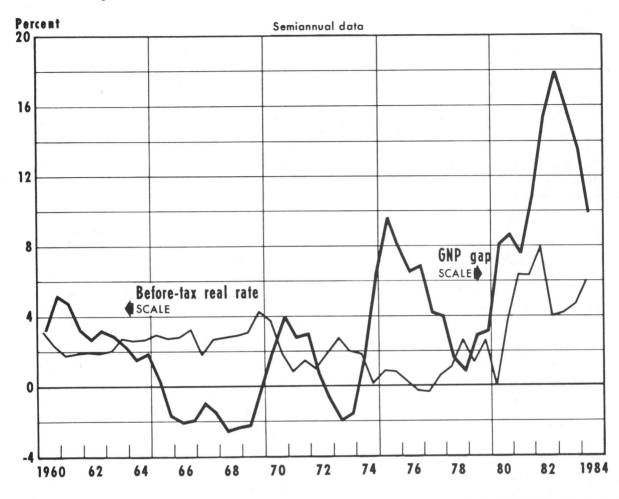

Percent   Semiannual data

Business Taxes

As noted above, the higher the return on investment in physical capital, the greater the demand for loanable funds. A tax on business profits reduces the real return on investment and the demand for loanable funds, thereby lowering real interest rates. A tax on business profits is not the only business tax that affects investment and the real interest rate, however. Businesses often receive tax credits or deductions from taxable income for certain types of investment expenditures. Furthermore, tax deductions to offset the depreciation of capital equipment and structures can affect the investment decision and real rates, since these depreciation allowances may or may not reflect the true depreciation of the capital. If the allowances overstate the depreciation over a period of time, they tend to spur additional investment, driving up the demand for loanable funds and the real rate of interest. If allowances provide for smaller deductions than the actual loss from depreciation, they hinder investment and real rates are reduced.[25]

The Economic Recovery Tax Act of 1981 was designed to spur investment, primarily by altering the way in which depreciation is treated for tax purposes. The magnitude of the effect of the act on investment is a controversial issue, but there is fairly strong evidence

---

[25]See Ott (1984).

that it spurred investment spending. For instance, the growth rate of real nonresidential fixed investment as a percentage of real GNP was 8.7 percent over the expansionary period from the fourth quarter of 1982 to the second quarter of 1984, up from an average of only 1.5 percent over similar periods following the previous six recessions.[26]

One problem, however, with concluding that the new tax legislation is a primary cause of higher interest rates is that the legislation was not passed until August 1981 (although its provisions were retroactive to the beginning of 1981), while the shift in real rates began in 1980 and was mostly complete by August 1981. For this legislation to have been the primary factor in the recent rise in real interest rates, the passage of the legislation must have been predicted and the demand for loanable funds increased many months in advance as the predicted future return on capital investment rose. On the other hand, this legislation could have contributed both to the rise in real rates that occurred in late 1981 and early 1982 in the face of a severe recession and to the maintenance of relatively high real interest rates right up to the present.

Federal Budget Deficits

Government borrowing represents an increase in the total demand for loanable funds. This suggests that real interest rates rise as the size of the government budget deficit increases in real terms. One rarely sees a positive correlation between the size of deficits and the levels of interest rates, however. This is probably because they respond in opposite directions to changes in economic conditions; deficits tend to rise during business recessions and fall during expansions (because tax revenues and outlays for transfer payments are sensitive to the state of the economy), while interest rates typically fall during recessions and rise during expansions.[27]

As for the recent rise in real interest rates, it is clear from chart 5 that the recent dramatic increase in the cyclically adjusted budget deficit did not occur until late 1982, by which time real and nominal interest rates had begun to fall. A closer look at the chart

indicates that two major increases in the size of the cyclically adjusted deficit have occurred in recent years: one in 1975 and the other in 1982. Neither was associated with rising real interest rates.

This does not necessarily imply that deficits have no effect on real interest rates. Since interest rates are based on expectations, expected future deficits could have an impact on today's real interest rates. If one assumes the budget projections of the Congressional Budget Office (CBO) are representative of the market's expectation of future deficits, however, then deficit projections do not appear to have been the major instigator of the recent rise in real interest rates. The CBO report published in July 1981 projected a 1982 deficit of less than $30 billion and *surpluses* in the next four years growing to over $200 billion by 1986.[28] Recall that at the time this report was written, our estimates of both short- and long-term before-tax real interest rates were already far in excess of historical norms and after-tax real rates had risen to near their previous peaks. By February 1982, the CBO had altered its projections and was predicting a deficit of nearly $200 billion in 1983, growing to nearly $300 billion by 1987.[29] Yet 1982 was a year of generally falling real and nominal interest rates.[30] Like the change in the tax laws, however, expectations of future deficits may be helping to keep real interest rates at levels that are quite high relative to past history.

Declining Relative Price of Energy

Finally, it has been suggested that drastic increases in the relative price of energy contributed to the low real interest rates of the 1970s, which would imply that the generally falling relative price of energy of the 1980s has contributed to higher real interest rates.[31] The argument is that the demand for capital fell during the 1970s because of a reduction in the supply of

---

[26]The six previous expansionary periods were IV/1949–II/1951, II/1954–IV/1955, II/1958–IV/1959, I/1961–III/1962, IV/1970–II/1972 and I/1975–III/1976. The difference between the growth of the investment-GNP ratio in the current recovery and the average growth in the six previous recoveries is statistically significant.

[27]See Tatom (1984).

[28]Congressional Budget Office (1981). Carlson (1983) discusses possible sources of bias in the CBO's budget projections.

[29]Congressional Budget Office (1982). In discussing the reasons for the change in the outlook on the deficits between 1981 and 1983, the Congressional Budget Office (1983, p. 18) says that, "Over the entire five-year period, 60 percent of the change in outlook from budget surpluses to budget deficits can be attributed to the failure of the economy to perform as projected two years ago." In addition, it says (p. 20) that, "Legislative actions are the second largest reason for differences between the two baselines, accounting for about 30 percent of the change over the five-year period."

[30]It is possible that higher projected government budget deficits lead to greater expected inflation, in which case higher deficits would cause higher nominal, but not necessarily real, interest rates.

[31]See Wilcox (1983).

Chart 5
Cyclically Adjusted Budget Deficit and 1-Year Real Interest Rate

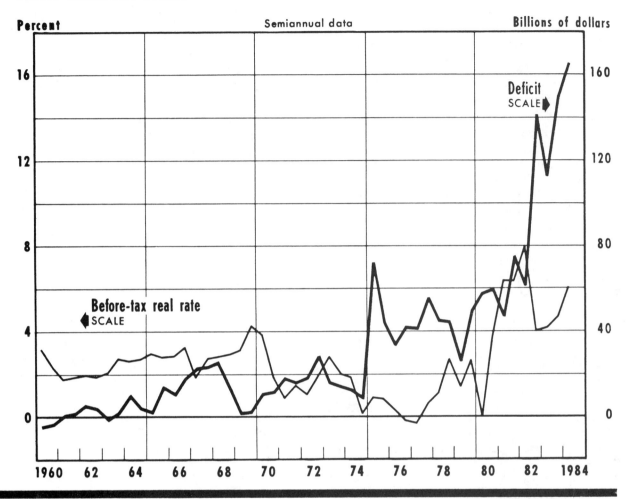

complementary energy inputs, which resulted in reduced demand for loanable funds and lower real interest rates.[32]

Once again, however, the timing of the recent rise in real interest rates fails to lend credence to the theory. During the period of most rapidly rising real interest rates in 1980 and the first half of 1981, the relative price of energy was still rising rapidly as a result of the second oil crisis; the growth rate of the relative price of energy between IV/1979 and II/1981 was 18.3 percent.[33]

Reductions in the relative price of energy did not begin until late 1981, after most of the increase in real interest rates already had occurred.

CONCLUSIONS

The 1980s have seen unprecedented behavior in several key economic variables, the most notable being interest rates. According to estimates of real interest rates based on surveys of expected inflation, both short- and long-term real rates rose to record levels in 1981 and 1982 and, although they have declined somewhat since then, have not returned to the levels of the 1960s and 1970s.

A comparison of estimates of before- and after-tax real interest rates indicates that the overall pattern of

[32]See Tatom (1979) for a discussion of the impact of energy shocks on investment.

[33]The measure of the relative price of energy is the producer price index for "fuels and related products and power" divided by the business sector deflator.

their movements has been similar. The spread between the before- and after-tax real rates increased over much of the sample, however, as nominal interest rates (and expected inflation) increased. Therefore, after-tax real interest rates have not been nearly as high relative to previous experience as before-tax real rates. Nonetheless, they have been higher on average than they were in the 1960s and much higher than in the 1970s.

The phenomenon most closely coincident with the rise in real rates was an increase in the variability of money growth, which increased economic uncertainty and the risk premium on interest rates. Major changes in current and projected government budget deficits and in tax policies happened *after* much of the upward shift in real interest rates already had occurred, but may have contributed to some additional upward movement. Changes in economic conditions have been a major influence on the movement of real interest rates since 1981; periods of slow growth or recession have produced falling real rates, while expansions have pushed real rates upward.

REFERENCES

Brown, W. W., and G. J. Santoni. "Monetary Growth and the Timing of Interest Rate Movements," this *Review* (August/September 1983), pp. 16–25.

Carlson, John A. "A Study of Price Forecasts," *Annals of Economic and Social Measurement* (Winter 1977), pp. 27–56.

Carlson, Keith M. "The Mix of Monetary and Fiscal Policies: Conventional Wisdom Vs. Empirical Reality," this *Review* (October 1982), pp. 7–21.

_____ . "The Critical Role of Economic Assumptions in the Evaluation of Federal Budget Programs," this *Review* (October 1983), pp. 5–14.

Congressional Budget Office. *Baseline Budget Projections: Fiscal Years 1982–1986* (U.S. Government Printing Office, July 1981).

_____ . *Baseline Budget Projections for Fiscal Years 1983–1987* (GPO, February 1982).

_____ . *Baseline Budget Projections for Fiscal Years 1984–1988* (GPO, February 1983).

Darby, Michael R. "The Financial and Tax Effects of Monetary Policy on Interest Rates," *Economic Inquiry* (June 1975), pp. 266–76.

Ezrati, Milton J. "Inflationary Expectations, Economic Activity, Taxes, and Interest Rates: Comment," *American Economic Review* (September 1982), pp. 854–57.

Feldstein, Martin. "Inflation, Income Taxes, and the Rate of Interest: A Theoretical Analysis," *American Economic Review* (December 1976), pp. 809–20.

Feldstein, Martin, and Lawrence Summers. "Inflation, Tax Rules, and the Long-Term Interest Rate," *Brookings Papers on Economic Activity* (1:1978), pp. 61–99.

Fischer, Stanley. "On Activist Monetary Policy with Rational Expectations," in Stanley Fischer, ed., *Rational Expectations and Economic Policy* (The University of Chicago Press, 1980), pp. 211–47.

Fisher, Irving. *Appreciation and Interest* (1896), Reprints of Economic Classics (Augustus M. Kelley, Bookseller, 1965).

Friedman, Milton, and Anna Jacobson Schwartz. *A Monetary History of the United States 1867–1960* (Princeton University Press, 1963).

Hafer, R. W. "The Money-GNP Link: Assessing Alternative Transaction Measures," this *Review* (March 1984), pp. 19–27.

Hafer, R. W., and Scott E. Hein. "Monetary Policy and Short-Term Real Rates of Interest," this *Review* (March 1982), pp. 13–19.

Holland, A. Steven. "Does Higher Inflation Lead to More Uncertain Inflation?" this *Review* (February 1984), pp. 15–26.

Makin, John, and Vito Tanzi. "The Level and Volatility of Interest Rates in the United States: The Role of Expected Inflation, Real Rates, and Taxes," Working Paper No. 1167 (National Bureau of Economic Research, July 1983).

Mascaro, Angelo, and Allan H. Meltzer. "Long- and Short-Term Interest Rates in a Risky World," *Journal of Monetary Economics* (November 1983), pp. 485–518.

Mehra, Yash. "The Tax Effect, and the Recent Behaviour of the After-Tax Real Rate: Is It Too High?" Federal Reserve Bank of Richmond *Economic Review* (July/August 1984), pp. 8–20.

Mundell, Robert. "Inflation and Real Interest," *Journal of Political Economy* (June 1963), pp. 280–83.

Ott, Mack. "Depreciation, Inflation and Investment Incentives: The Effects of the Tax Acts of 1981 and 1982," this *Review* (November 1984), pp. 17–30.

Santoni, G. J., and Courtenay C. Stone. "The Fed and the Real Rate of Interest," this *Review* (December 1982), pp. 8–18.

Tatom, John A. "Energy Prices and Capital Formation: 1972–1977," this *Review* (May 1979), pp. 2–11.

_____ . "A Perspective on the Federal Deficit Problem," this *Review* (June/July 1984), pp. 5–17.

Tobin, James. "Money and Economic Growth," *Econometrica* (October 1965), pp. 671–84.

Wallich, Henry C. "Recent Techniques of Monetary Policy," Federal Reserve Bank of Kansas City *Economic Review* (May 1984), pp. 21–30.

Wilcox, James A. "Why Real Interest Rates Were So Low in the 1970's," *American Economic Review* (March 1983), pp. 44–53.

Article Nine

Three Views of Real Interest

After 1979, interest rates in the U.S. economy became much more volatile. For example, the degree of volatility in short-term interest rates nearly doubled. At the same time, real interest rates (nominal rates adjusted for inflation) fluctuated around much higher levels than before. Since 1982, however, the volatility of short-term real rates has declined. More recently, the general level of real interest rates has tended to diminish as well.

Analysts have proposed three main explanations for these phenomena. First, they point to the lifting of deposit rate ceilings and other types of financial deregulation. Second is the October 1979 shift in the Federal Reserve's operating procedures, which put more emphasis on controlling bank reserves and less on controlling interest rates in the short run. The final explanation relates to the effects of large and growing federal budget deficits in the United States. This *Letter* discusses the theoretical relevance of these explanations and presents some empirical evidence to help discriminate among them.

Financial deregulation
During periods of tight credit prior to 1979, Regulation Q ceilings on deposit rates tended to restrict deposit flows into thrift institutions that specialized in housing finance. Although commercial banks also experienced run-offs in time and savings deposits, they were better able to offset the effects through asset and liability management.

Thrifts had difficulty offsetting the lack of deposit inflows by selling mortgage loans from their portfolios because of a relatively undeveloped secondary market and an unwillingness to show capital losses. They were also slow to develop new sources of funds and, in fact, did not issue significant amounts of large CDs until the late 1970s. In addition, usury ceilings reinforced the short-run tendency of mortgage lenders to ration credit by means other than interest rates. To the

extent that these restrictions in the availability of mortgage credit at thrift institutions could not be offset by other lenders, fluctuations in residential investment were more severe.

Regulation Q ceilings also tended to reduce the extent to which market interest rates on assets other than mortgage loans rose during periods of tight credit. In the extreme case where lenders regard thrift deposits and alternative market instruments as perfect substitutes, these market interest rates would not rise above the level of Regulation Q ceilings on deposit rates unless the level of deposits were driven to zero. On the more realistic assumption that deposits at thrifts are regarded as imperfect substitutes for alternative market instruments by at least some depositors, a positive interest differential would be required to attract funds away from deposits in periods of tight credit. In this more realistic case, market interest rates would rise as credit conditions tightened, but not by as much as they would in a completely unregulated financial environment.

Over the last decade, the market for mortgage credit has become more integrated with other financial markets mainly because of financial deregulation. Greater integration has tended both to reduce credit availability effects on housing and to increase the volatility of market interest rates. A recent study conducted at this Bank found that deposit rate ceilings and related factors did indeed exacerbate the housing cycle *and* reduce the volatility of market interest rates to a small but measurable degree prior to 1979. Financial deregulation was found to lessen the severity of the housing cycle and to increase the volatility of interest rates in a simulation that removed the estimated effects of deposit flows in the 1966-67, 1969-70, and 1974-75 periods of disintermediation and which assumed an unchanged rate of monetary growth. However, the quantitative magnitudes of these effects were estimated to be relatively small.

The simulated effects on interest rates are shown in the chart, which compares the historical path of the real, or inflation-adjusted, 6-month commercial paper rate over the period 1962 to 1985 with that resulting from the simulation where no credit availability effects are allowed to operate through the effects of deposit flows.

The simulation shows that, in the absence of credit availability effects, real interest rates would have risen by somewhat more in periods of tight credit. However, because the effects themselves are estimated to have been quite small, the estimated increase in the overall variability of real interest rates is also small. In the 1966 to 1975 period, the standard deviation of the real commercial paper rate from its average level rises from 131 basis points in the historical observation to 141 basis points in the simulation. This small rise indicates that financial deregulation produced only a 7.6 percent increase in the volatility of real short-term interest rates.

After 1979, the actual variability of real short-term interest rates nearly doubled. Thus, the estimated effects of financial deregulation explain only a very small portion of the increased variability in real interest rates. Deregulation also does not fully explain the rise in the level of real interest rates after 1979. In the simulation, deregulation raised the levels of real interest rates very little, whereas the average level of real short-term rates increased about 400 basis points after 1979.

Monetary policy
One alternative explanation for the increase in the variability and level of real interest rates after 1979 is the effect of the Federal Reserve's switch in operating procedures in October of that year. The Federal Reserve put greater emphasis on controlling bank reserves and less on controlling interest rates in the short run. The new procedure should have increased the short-run volatility of interest rates because it meant that the Fed would no longer tend to accommodate short-run changes in the demand for money.

The Fed directed this new operating procedure at slowing the rate of monetary growth to reduce inflation. Reductions in monetary growth would

have produced temporary increases in the level of real interest rates until the price level had fully adjusted to a reduced stock of money. The slowing in monetary growth, thus, probably contributed to peaks in real interest rates from 1979 through 1982, but it cannot explain the continued high level of real interest rates since then.

In October 1982, when financial deregulation and disinflation were making monetary velocity much more unpredictable, the Federal Reserve shifted back to an operating procedure characterized by less precise short-run control over monetary growth. This shift provides a good explanation for the reduction in the volatility of interest rates that occurred after 1982. But real short-term interest rates were still about 200 basis points higher than in the pre-1979 period.

Large federal deficit
The federal budget deficit is the most important reason for continued high U.S. real interest rates after 1982, and there have been two main facets to its impact. First, larger U.S. budget deficits tend to drive up the international level of real interest rates. Because the world capital market is highly integrated and securities are highly substitutable, real interest rates tend to be equated across countries.

The U.S. structural budget position (including state and local as well as federal governments) shifted from a surplus equal to 1.2 percent of GNP in 1979 to a deficit equal to 2.1 percent of GNP in 1986. At the same time, the budget deficits of other major industrialized countries have shown little long-term trend. Thus, the net effect of larger U.S. budget deficits should have been to increase the world level of real interest rates.

Second, even in a fully integrated world capital market, real interest rates take several years to equalize across countries after a disturbance. The initial effect of larger U.S. budget deficits is to drive up real interest rates at home compared to those abroad. This leads to an increase in *desired* net capital inflows, which generates an appreciation of the dollar. But the interest differential in favor of the U.S. causes the dollar to overshoot its long-run equilibrium. An expected future depreciation of the dollar compensates for the difference in real interest rates.

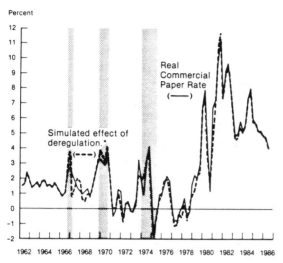

Deregulation Raises Interest Rate Variability Only Slightly

Percent

Real Commercial Paper Rate (——)

Simulated effect of deregulation.* (- - -)

Shaded areas represent periods of estimated credit availability effects.
*Without credit availability effects of regulation.

As the full effect of a dollar appreciation manifests itself in a change in the trade balance, and thus in *actual* capital flows, U.S. real interest rates then tend to fall back toward foreign levels. U.S. short-term real interest rates remained relatively high from 1982 through 1984, but have since dropped close to foreign real rates. This suggests that the equalization process is nearly complete.

The equalization process may be attenuated somewhat by the effects of a growing accumulation of debt to foreigners. As foreigners absorb more and more U.S. debt, they may require a larger differential in the rate of return over investments in their home countries. This would reduce the size of the net capital inflows occurring in response to the U.S. budget deficit and drive a wedge between U.S. and foreign real interest rates. Although the weight of the evidence suggests that such differentials are small and that the world capital market is indeed

highly integrated, the foreign accumulation of U.S. debt is occurring rapidly enough that this factor may be of some importance in holding up U.S. real rates.

Conclusion

The unusually high level and volatility of real interest rates after 1979 are best explained by a combination of factors. An econometric simulation indicates that financial deregulation contributed only slightly. By producing higher peak levels of interest rates in periods of tight credit, financial deregulation tended to raise both the average level and volatility of real rates, but our estimates show these effects to be quite small.

Of greater importance have been the effects of monetary policy. The heightened volatility of interest rates from October 1979 to October 1982 was due basically to the Federal Reserve's shift in operating procedure that aimed at reducing inflation by slowing money growth. This procedure sought greater short-run control over bank reserves. When the Fed again changed its operating procedure in October 1982 toward less emphasis on controlling bank reserves in the short run, the volatility of interest rates fell significantly. Also, the Fed's disinflation policy could have generated higher real interest rates, but not for a prolonged period of time.

Real interest rates have been held at higher levels primarily by larger U.S. budget deficits. In an integrated world capital market, U.S. budget deficits drive up the world level of real interest rates. Since real interest rates take several years to equalize across countries after such a disturbance, U.S. real rates tend to rise by more than foreign rates for a while. Also, U.S. real interest rates may stabilize at a somewhat higher level than foreign rates if foreign investors require a higher relative return for their continued investment.

Adrian W. Throop

Section Two

Financial Institutions

The 1980s are proving to be a turbulent decade for financial institutions and their customers. Interest rates not only reached record highs but also fluctuated dramatically. Businesses and households were subjected to wide swings in the macroeconomy, to sizable changes in the federal tax code, and to boom and bust in major sectors like energy and agriculture. As if this were not enough, various major regulations were either eased, extended, or abandoned entirely. To compound matters, technological advances in information significantly lowered the cost of providing financial services. Equally striking were the repercussions all this turmoil had on deposit insurance agencies. The readings in this section address the causes and effects of these events.

In "Technological and Regulatory Forces in the Developing Fusion of Financial Services Competition," Edward J. Kane analyzes how financial institutions change their organizational form to avoid regulations, to minimize taxes, and to take advantage of economies of scope. This last opportunity is generated partly by flat-rate deposit insurance, which allows any insured institution to raise funds at the risk-free interest rate. These institutional changes lead to regulatory reactions. "Reregulation" more than deregulation describes this process, with tightening of some and loosening of other regulations often proceeding simultaneously. The interplay of these forces is described in the case of "nonbank banks".

Douglas D. Evanoff and Diana Fortier review old and present new evidence on the effects of allowing more bank branching within and across states in "The Impact of Geographic Expansion in Banking: Some Axioms to Grind." Among their findings is that branching leads to greater arrays of and easier access to financial services at unchanged prices without threatening the viability of smaller banks.

"Recent Bank Failures," by Anthony W. Cyrnak, documents the surge in bank failures in the mid-1980s. Cyrnak notes that most of the banks that failed were small and located in farm belt or energy-producing states, a pattern that is likely to persist. The article also explains the choices the FDIC has when one of its insured banks fails and describes the two main options, deposit payoff and purchase-and-assumption. The increased incentive for risk taking that these methods generate for banks are then explored.

George J. Benston, in "Deposit Insurance and Bank Failures," surveys the benefits and costs of current deposit insurance arrangements. The article highlights why banks are special and shows that deposit insurance not only insures against losses but also prevents bank runs, which historically have been the major source of bank failures and depositor losses. Deposit insurance reduces depositors' risks, yet it allows banks to raise funds cheaply and invest them in risky projects. Until the 1980s, this practice was kept in check by regulators' restrictions on bank entry, products, prices, and capital and by regulators' examination and supervision of banks. Many of these regulations have become less desirable and less enforceable in recent years, however. To deal with these difficulties, Benston proposes a number of procedural improvements.

James B. Thomson presents "Alternative Methods for Assessing Risk-Based Deposit-Insurance Premiums." Two broad categories of proposals for modifying the FDIC's current flat-rate premium schedule have surfaced. By the explicit premium adjustment method, premiums would be charged that fully compensate the FDIC for risk. The implicit methods change the exposure of the FDIC, shifting losses back to the bank's owners and creditors. Within each category, three proposals are described and the strengths and weaknesses of each outlined.

Larry D. Wall enumerates various methods for regulating bank capital and assesses their practicality in "Regulation of Banks' Equity Capital." The theory of capital regulation, together with its pros and cons, and empirical evidence for its effects are surveyed, although the data to date are largely inconclusive about its net effects.

"The Thrift Industry's Rough Road Ahead," is by James R. Barth, Donald J. Bisenius, R. Dan Brumbaugh, Jr., and Daniel Sauerhaft, and recounts how the thrift industry was battered by the macroeconomy in the early 1980s. It also points out that, by the middle of the decade, the industry as a whole had become remarkably profitable but that hundreds of thrifts were on the edge of insolvency. The cost to the deposit insurance agency of closing these thrifts is perhaps four times greater than the agency's reserves. The authors argue that wide-spread insolvency is a result of the increased risk taking allowed by the easing of balance-sheet restrictions, coupled with flat-rate deposit insurance.

Frederick T. Furlong discusses the rationale for the savings and loan deposit insurance fund borrowing in " 'Recapitalizing' the FSLIC," the final article in this section. This borrowing will now enable it to pay off insured depositors at insolvent savings and loans. It does not, however, solve the problem of how the FSLIC will pay off both this debt and anything but minimal insurance obligations in the future. If enacted, the plan may shift resources to the present and problems to the future.

Article Ten

Technological and Regulatory Forces in the Developing Fusion of Financial-Services Competition

EDWARD J. KANE*

ABSTRACT

Product lines of traditionally heterogeneous financial institutions are rapidly fusing into a homogeneous blend. Institutions and market structures are reshaping themselves to lower the cost of serving customer demand for financial services. This paper contends that contemporary adaptations exploit scope economies rooted in technological change and deposit-insurance subsidies to innovative forms of risk-bearing.

As they reorient work flows, financial firms are simultaneously restructuring their organizations to lower net burdens from government regulation. Alternative state and federal regulatory and legislative bodies compete vigorously for the regulatory business of developing institutional hybrids. Evolution of Federal Reserve policy toward "nonbank banks" exemplifies the process.

ALTHOUGH THE TERM is applied almost universally to events in the financial-services industry, deregulation has become a misleading catchword for the evolutionary fading away of lines of market cleavage that delimit inherited patterns of competition. Jimmy Durante's signature line, "*Every*body wants to get into the act," sums up the landscape of contemporary financial competition. With and without the explicit blessing of specialized financial regulators, deposit institutions, brokerage firms, and insurance companies are feverishly expanding into one another's traditional bailiwick. Providing opportunities for customers to transact these diverse lines of financial business in a single-statement framework is restructuring front-office and back-office work flows. It is turning a growing number of banking lobbies into pinstriped caricatures of Istanbul's famous covered bazaar and back offices into electronic transactions and communications centers.

* The author is Everett D. Reese Professor of Banking and Monetary Economics, The Ohio State University, and Research Associate, National Bureau of Economic Research. For helpful comments on an earlier draft, the author wishes to thank Richard C. Aspinwall, George G. Kaufman, Edward J. McCarthy, Benson Hart, James Moser, Eli Shapiro, and Richard F. Syron. Opinions expressed are those of the author and do not represent those of the NBER.

1. An Introductory Overview

In at least two ways, deregulation misrepresents the nature of the adjustments taking place. First, it locates the impetus for change in the political arena to the exclusion of the economic one. It intimates that *exogenous* governmental policy decisions are causing nontraditional competitors to enter geographic markets and product lines from which exclusionary laws drafted by clever lawyers had previously shut them out. Such a perspective fails to acknowledge the prior breakdown of the inherited system of exlusionary regulation or to raise the issue of why society might suddenly reveal a preference for abandoning rather than rebuilding legal barriers to entry in the financial-services industry. To analyze these issues, one must focus on scope economies and on opportunities for structural arbitrage. By structural arbitrage, I mean adaptive changes in a firm's organizational form designed to lighten its tax and regulatory burdens. In turn, one must recognize that structural arbitrage creates costs and benefits for government officials that require reactive changes in operative tax codes and regulations. Contemporary realignment of federal and state regulatory frameworks is largely a process of competitive *reregulation*.

The second way that deregulation misleads is in suggesting that the process involves the complete abandonment of regulation rather than its selective and partial relaxation. Talking about deregulation diverts attention from regulations that are being tightened or left unaltered and from reallocations of regulatory authority. Particularly with respect to destabilizing incentives established by deposit-insurance pricing and coverage, unchanged and tightened restrictions play at least as important a role in shaping financial market structures as the particular regulations undergoing relaxation.

Endogeneity of Market Structure. Rationalizations for laws intended to segment interinstitutional competition presume that, while scale economies may be important in finance (so that small firms need to be protected), scope economies are not. Contemporary events and a conjectural reading of cross-section evidence on the jointness and U-shapedness of commercial-bank costs functions (Benston, Berger, Hanweck, and Humphrey, 1983) suggest that both halves of this presumption are wrong. In the financial-services industry scope has always been correlated with firm size, making it hard to isolate the role played by economies of joint production in the growth and profitability of successful firms.

This paper depicts the fusion of financial-services competition as confirming the contestability model of multimarket competition (Baumol, Panzar, and Willig, 1983). Contestability theory maintains that, far from being an exogenous determinant of industry performance, market structure adapts through entry and exit to permit customer demand to be served as minimum cost. The desegmentation of financial markets involves the expansion of low-cost producers at the expense of high-cost ones.

Regulatory interference slows the rate of adaptation by imposing entry restrictions and corresponding avoidance costs on particular firms. But in a free society in which multiple legislatures and regulatory agencies compete—under jurisdictions that overlap—for regulatees, tax receipts, and/or budget funds, authorities can only induce great or long-lasting divergences between the actual and the cost-minimizing market structure when the costs of structural arbitrage are high.

Implications for Deposit Insurance. In the financial-services industry, any act of regulatory avoidance or reregulation sets into motion two interacting processes (Kane, 1981):

1. Adaptive responses by competing state and overlapping federal regulators (and their supporting political coalitions) to reoptimize their spheres of control by adjusting the rules under which the financial-services game is played;
2. Adaptive responses by various types of financial institutions (including foreign ones) to minimize regulatory burdens by arbitraging differences in applicable regulatory structures.

Because the inherited system of deposit insurance is not rationally priced, changes in organizational form and expansions in financial-institution product lines may also arbitrage differences between the price of risk-bearing in capital markets and implicit and explicit premiums imbedded in federal deposit insurance (Buser, Chen, and Kane, 1981). Since at least the late 1970s, structural arbitrage has combined with rising interest volatility to increase FDIC and FSLIC risk exposure faster than these agencies have been able to reset their conceptions of contingent claims on their resources. The expanding subsidy to risk-bearing creates a growing need for fundamental deposit-insurance reform. Although we lack the space to discuss them here, the shifting of these subsidies explains a series of anomalous features in the contemporary pattern of financial-services competition.

2. Exclusionary Rules, Avoidance, and the Cost of Multiproduct Operation

To model the costs of multiproduct operation and of laws meant to enforce product specialization, it is sufficient to posit two goods, X_1 and X_2. (By interpreting X_1 as a vector of $N-1$ outputs, the formulation can easily be generalized to any number of outputs.) Economies of scope exist when the total costs of producing the two goods jointly, $C(X_1,X_2)$, is less than the combined cost, $C_1(X_1) + C_2(X_2)$, of producing the same amounts of each good separately. Economies of scope are economies of joint production. They occur when two outputs share one or more capital or labor inputs in the production process, either directly or through networking. A traditional example concerns unallocable joint costs that occur in constructing and operating a multipurpose dam to produce electricity, flood control, and recreational services. Abstracting from offsetting costs of managerial coordination, a financial intermediary's computer, communications network, and branch-office system should make it cheaper for it to offer standardized deposit, loan, brokerage, and insurance products in combination than a series of specialized producers could produce the same products on a stand-alone basis.

During the last 15 years, technological change (in the form of the computerization of record-keeping and transacting, the robotization of teller functions, and expanding telecommunications links with customers, services, and financial markets) has increased the role of multipurpose capital equipment in producing financial services. The desirability of spreading the costs of operating this "telemation" equipment across additional product lines underlies the rapid progress toward homogenization of function observed for different types of financial intermediaries. It also explains the attraction of nonfinancial firms (particularly those in data-processing and communications) into financial services.

The Generic Financial-Services Firm. Homogenization in the product lines of formerly specialized financial institutions leads to the concept of the all-purpose *financial-services firm*: a generic reconceptualization of financial-industry boundaries broad enough to encompass the range of activities being undertaken by contemporary institutional competitors. The financial-services firm (FSF) produces informational and transactional products for a base of customers with whom it has established relationships. Informational products include advice, data-processing, and communications services. Transactional products include execution of trading and payment orders, bidirectional funds rental, and risk-bearing services.

To deliver any financial service, an FSF must exchange information with its customers. Customers and FSFs exchange information by means of information media, which today include: personal contacts, paper evidences (such as loan agreements, checks, and deposit slips); telephonic messages; magnetic entries on striped plastic cards, tapes, or discs; and keyboard-actuated video displays. These media connect the customers with the particular FSF product he wishes to use.

Increasingly, financial services register on and occur through an electronic transactions and record-keeping system. This system employs three kinds of productive processes: (1) techniques for maintaining and communicating with remote data bases; (2) techniques for executing transactions; and (3) techniques for delivering services to customers. Because the first two types of technology are known as back-office technology, the third type is called front-office technology. Elements of front-office technology confront the customer every day: brick-and-mortal offices, automated teller machines, drive-in teller windows, and home-based electronic equipment such as telephones and computer terminals.

Among the elements that the customer does not see are the complicated interfaces that connect FSFs across the transactions system. Efficient production requires that FSFs belong to networks in which they both compete with and serve one another. With respect to back-office services, competing banks have always shared some resources. Interbank cooperation is exemplified by such developments as regional clearinghouses, check standardization, ATM networks, and loan syndications. At the same time that brokerage firms and correspondent banks act as wholesalers of back-office services to FSF customers, they compete with these customers for front-office business. Federal Reserve Banks play a quadruple role. They not only supply correspondent and communications services to firms they compete against, they are even empowered to regulate their competitors' activities. Moreover, as regulators they compete against other federal agencies and state banking departments.

Costs of Exclusionary Rules. This section states a condition for exclusionary rules to be successful and develops a measure of these rules' social costs. A key component of both equations is $C_{a,r}$, the cost of perfectly circumventing or avoiding a given set of restrictions against multiproduct operation in the most efficient way known at the time. Opportunities for circumvention act as a brake on the welfare burden of regulation, keeping this burden lighter than it would otherwise be.

By construction, $C_{a,r}$ is nonnegative. Avoidance costs may be conceived as the incremental costs of creating an unregulated substitute product or instutional arrangement. Examples include the extra costs of running a zero-balance sweep operation to circumvent the prohibition against paying explicit interest on demand deposits or the extra costs of offering a prohibited product through a subsidiary corporation or holding-company affiliate. Whether X_1 and X_2 are produced jointly or singly depends on which of the following costs is smaller:

$$C(X_1, X_2) + C_{a,r} \text{ versus } C_1(X_1) + C_2(X_2) \qquad (1)$$

This condition confronts only half of the resource waste inherent in effective regulation. The social cost of a regulatory exclusion is the sum of two items: (1) administrative costs of promulgating and enforcing the restriction and (2) the lesser of $C_{a,r}$ and the forfeited economies of scope $[C(X_1) + C(X_2) - C(X_1, X_2)]$.

The Impact of Technological Change. Technological change lowers *both* components of the lefthand side of condition (1). It increases the role of multipurpose "telemation" equipment in financial-services production and makes it easier for management to coordinate unregulated substitute arrangements such as sweep accounts or the activities of an array of subsidiary firms. Hence, it makes product-line homogenization increasingly likely.

Unless regulators increase administrative and avoidance costs to offset technological change, exclusionary rules would tend to lose their effectiveness. However, the social costs of regulation could rise, fall, or remain the same. We look at constraints that regulatory competition places on the behavior of regulators in Section 3.

This paragraph illustrates numerically how technological change might undermine exclusionary rules. Let us suppose that prior to a change in technology $C(X_1, X_2)$ equalled 8 and $C_{a,r}$ was 3, while $C_1(X_1) + C_2(X_2)$ was 10. Because scope economies of 2 fall short of avoidance costs, the exclusionary rule would succeed and specialized producers would be observed. The social cost of regulation would be the sum of forgone economies of scope (2) and administration costs (which we arbitrarily assume to be 3). Next, let us assume that innovation drives the costs of joint production to 7 and avoidance costs to 2, without affecting the costs of specialized operation. This change makes the exclusionary rule unenforceable, because it increases the costs of forgone economies of scope to 3 while reducing avoidance costs to 2. To minimize the burden of regulation, product-line homogenization would develop. If regulatory costs remained unchanged at 3, the social costs of regulation would stay at 5, but avoidance costs would now register in place of forgone scope economies.

Scope Economies Are Partly Rooted in the Mispricing of Deposit-Insurance. Mispricing deposit-insurance guarantees provides an unintended subsidy that reduces an insured institution's exposure to risk in product-line expansions. When brokers and insurers incorporate a deposit institution into their operation and when deposit institutions diversify into brokerage and insurance activities, some of the blessing of deposit insurance extends to these firms' nondepository affiliates. This is because, as a practical matter, it is impossible for deposit-insurance bureaucrats to prevent an insured deposit institution from assisting its troubled affiliates and subsidiaries whenever management perceives such assistance to be in its own best interest (Eisenbeis, 1983a).

Currently federal deposit insurance fully guarantees an institution's deposit accounts up to $100,000 per distinct combination of accountholders, with accounts held singly and jointly and accounts held in different institutions each afforded a separate insurance status. To exploit the opportunity for individuals to multiply their coverage, funds brokers have developed software and communications facilities that distribute multimillion-dollar concentrations of wealth across individual institutions in $100,000 pieces. In recent months, such brokers are said to have played a significant role in funneling deposits to seriously troubled banks and thrifts eager to pay a premium rate on $100,000 CDs.

Deposit-insurance guarantees are supported by *explicit* premiums of 1/12 of one percent of total (insured and uninsured) deposits booked at domestic offices. Currently, this premium is rebatable in part for FDIC clients, but not for FSLIC customers.

Because this pattern of explicit pricing is not sensitive to differences in either interest-rate volatility or an FSF's leverage, asset, or affiliated-institution risk, client risk-taking must be regulated directly. It is instructive to view capital-adequacy requirements and back-up regulatory penalties for excess risk-taking as *implicit* premiums that agency managers vary to control these and other bureaucratically recognized forms of risk-taking.

Three things are wrong with this coverage and pricing system. First, it is *allocationally inefficient*: By underpricing risk, it wastes scarce resources. Second, it is *distributionally unfair*: It overcharges conservatively managed deposit institutions and forces them to stand ready to bail out high-flying competitors. Third, it fosters *financial instability*: It subsidizes deposit-institution risk-taking *most* when markets are most volatile and loads the burden for financing this subsidy onto both conservatively managed deposit institutions that are sure to survive any crisis and taxpayers at large. The implicit liability facing surviving institutions is underscored in the still-unresolved failure of a state-insured institution in Lincoln, Nebraska in late 1983. When the state insurance fund was revealed to have only $2 million to cover $70 million in guarantees, politicians immediately proposed assessing surviving financial institutions and taxpayers for the difference.

FDIC and FSLIC premium structures subsidize *unregulated* forms of risk-bearing. They lead dynamically to a continued search for (and expansion of) such new forms of risk-taking as entry into futures markets, investment banking, or insurance underwriting. They also make bureaucratic conceptions of operative categories of deposit-institution risk-taking play the pivotal role in preventing a system breakdown.

Federal deposit insurers would not end up subsidizing risk-taking if they were quick to adapt their regulatory policies to emerging problems (Bierwag and Kaufman, 1983). But this is merely a counsel of perfection. Unless bureaucratic incentive systems can be made to mimic those of profit-oriented enterprises, this counsel of perfection has no empirical importance. Bureaucrats are inherently slower in responding to changes in interest-rate volatility and other emerging forms of risk than private insurers would be. Politically appointed agency heads typically have short horizons and are sensitive to political constraints that overlay an agency's strictly economic interests in the decisions it makes. This leaves government bureaucracies markedly lower in *adaptive efficiency* than value-maximizing firms. Given this relative weakness and a financial-services environment changing as rapidly as our own, it is poor public policy to require an agency to follow policies that thrust its adaptive efficiency in protecting its economic interest into a pivotal role. Such an agency spends its energy playing catch-up, much like a sprinter who is habitually late out of the starting blocks or a baseball pitcher who slips persistently behind the count.

3. Structural Arbitrage and Competitive Reregulation

Through structural arbitrage and the threat or promise of structural arbitrage, value-maximizing managers of U.S. deposit institutions may to a large extent choose the set of laws and the particular regulatory bodies by which they are governed. This is because the set of restrictions applicable to their business operations and the particular agencies assigned to oversee their behavior vary with how they resolve a series of options concerning the institution's structural form.

Structural Options. The broadest set of options concerns the type of *charter* under which a deposit institution elects to operate. First, it may charter or recharter itself as a commercial bank, a savings-and-loan association (S&L), or a savings bank (MSB). Rechartering may be accomplished by charter conversion or by merging into an institution that already has the desired charter type. Second, each type of charter is available alternately from state or federal authorities. While commercial banks and S&Ls are chartered in all 50 states, MSB charters are available in only 17. Whenever the location of an institution's offices is not predetermined, these options generate a space of as many as 120 (= 2 × 51 + 18) different regulatory "micro-climates."

Most of these micro-climates involve multiple regulators and dimensions of additional choice. For example, federally chartered commercial banks (national banks) have the Comptroller of the Currency as their primary regulator, but are subject to additional oversight from the Federal Reserve and the FDIC. Although under the direct supervision of its state banking department, a state-chartered commercial bank typically subjects itself to federal co-supervision. This occurs whenever it is federally insured, with an even richer regulatory climate coming on line if it chooses to become a member of the Federal Reserve System.[1]

Until 1979, all savings banks were state-chartered and insured either by the FDIC, a state insurance fund, or both. Federal charters have gained in popularity since the Garn-St Germain Depository Institutions ACT (DIA) of 1982, which permits a converting MSB to retain FDIC insurance. Prior to the DIA, federal

---

[1] Only in about three states, may a new bank elect against FDIC insurance and the additional balance-sheet regulation that comes with it. Until universal reserve requirements dictated by the Depository Institutions Deregulation and Monetary Control Act (DIDMCA) of 1980 are fully phased in, member banks face higher reserve requirements than nonmembers do.

savings banks had to be insured by the FSLIC, which meant that a MSB could convert only when the prior insurer(s) and the FSLIC could agree on compensation for shifting the liability associated with the insurance guarantee over to the FSLIC.

Micro-climates for S&Ls are in some respects richer than for MSBs. First, S&Ls have an institutionally specialized federal regulator (the Federal Home Loan Bank Board or FHLBB) and deposit-insurance fund (the FSLIC). In addition, most states have separate agencies regulating banks and S&Ls. Five states also operate insurance funds for state-chartered thrifts (Massachusetts, Maryland, North Carolina, Ohio, Pennsylvania).

A second variety of option concerns the *form* of institutional ownership. For managers who elect against seeking a commercial-bank charter, the opportunity exists to operate under either stockholder or mutual ownership. The outcome of this election affects the incentive structure under which management functions, in that managers of stockholder institutions are subject to SEC disclosure requirements and to possible dismissal in proxy fights and unfriendly takeovers, on the one hand; but are able to work out a rich variety of stock-based compensation schemes or even to participate in leveraged buyouts, on the other. For existing institutions, the conversion option is effectively one-way: from mutual to stock ownership.

For stock firms, the most important option is whether or not to allow the stock to be owned by a holding company (i.e., to interpose a layer of indirect ownership—a corporate stockholder—between the deposit institution and its ultimate owners). Deposit-institution holding companies (HCs) are differentially taxed and regulated as compared to deposit institutions themselves. Deposit-institution HCs are subject in some states to additional state regulation and to federal regulation of permissible activities under the Fed or FHLBB. However, under special provisions of federal law, S&L HCs are currently exempted from the layer of FHLBB regulation as long as the HC chooses to own only one S&L. Deposit-institution HCs are also subject to disclosure regulation by the SEC from which deposit institutions themselves are exempt, but HCs may avoid SEC oversight by keeping the HC's value of equity and number of stockholders within legislated limits. Notwithstanding this exposure to incremental regulation, the HC device provides opportunities to circumvent many restrictions on deposit-institution activities. Nonbank affiliates may undertake activities that deposit institutions cannot. Moreover, tax and regulatory burdens even on permissible activities may be lightened in important ways.

A similar set of options exists even for non-HC institutions. This concerns whether or not to use *subsidiary corporations* (or, in the case of deposit-institution subsidiaries of HCs, affiliated corporations) to operate various lines of deposit-institution business. Spinning off some product lines may lighten the burden of federal capital-adequacy requirements and, not only circumvent interstate and intrastate restrictions on office locations, but allow individual product lines to be produced in the micro-climate in which they can generate the highest after-tax profit.

Competition Among Legislatures and Regulatory Bodies. Markets for regulatory services should be regarded as nearly as contestable as those of regulatees. This contestability makes applicable laws and the regulatory postures of different authorities partly endogenous. Deposit institutions' structural choices have economic consequences for legislatures and for turf-maximizing regulatory agencies. Their desire to influence the outcomes of regulatee choices leads these bodies to compete for the "regulatory business" of potential clients. This competition gives deposit-institution lobbyists political leverage with which to play authorities off against each other to win regulatory forbearance for circumvention activities and to educe favorable changes in legislation or agency rules.

Competition between overlapping federal and state regulators looks in the short run like wasteful duplication, but leads in the long run to better-adapted regulatory rules. When the opportunity cost of an exclusionary rule rises, pressures develop to soften the rule. It is unlikely that laws meant to hold deposit institutions out of brokerage and insurance activities and brokers and insurance companies out of deposit-institution markets can stand up indefinitely against opportunities to reduce product costs created by growing scope economies. While it is natural for lobbyists from an invaded industry to fight a rearguard political action to delay change, American politics and ideology favor innovation over regulation in many ways. In one way or another, low-cost schemes for producing and distributing products are able to push aside high-cost ones. This is partly because reregulation is a competitive process that responds to *economic* as well as political forces.

Banks' recent success in winning favorable product-line regulation in Delaware and South Dakota illustrates the process. Legislatures in these states have given specialized subsidiaries of out-of-state HCs long-desired freedoms and powers, particularly with respect to credit-card and insurance operations. Especially if (as I contend) economies of joint production are increasing over time, scope economies give deposit institutions an incentive to probe nationwide for political weak points in exclusionary policies. At the same time, the tax, budget, and employment benefits of winning regulatory refugees from other jurisdictions give bureaucrats and legislatures an incentive to trade in regulatory relaxation.

Similar pressures are fueling the drive for legislation permitting reciprocal interstate banking at least within collections of neighboring states. Limited-reciprocity laws have already passed the Massachusetts, Connecticut, and Rhode Island legislatures, and are actively being considered by state officials in other regions. Maine and New York permit acquisitions by out-of-state banking organizations from any state that grants reciprocal privileges to banks in their state, while Alaska allows virtually unconditional acquisition of *existing* institutions by out-of-state organizations. Lawsuits have been brought against the limited-reciprocity laws on several grounds, including the claim that the Constitution's interstate-commerce clause precludes states from imposing conditions on interstate entry. But by the time that these suits wend their way fully through the courts, odds are good that either Congress will have already blessed these regional experiments or interstate operation of deposit institutions will prove (as NOW accounts and remote ATMs did in 1980) politically too well-established to be undone.

By realigning its organization structure, a financial firm can not only reorganize its regulatory environment, it can also create pressure on legislatures and regulators to rewrite the regulations under which it has to play. Competitive reregulation occurs not only among officials in different states, but also between state and federal officials and between managers of different federal agencies. Regulators try to forestall changes in organizational form that would transfer some or all of their traditional regulatees' business from their dominion to that of another agency. When an agency suffers a cumulative loss of regulatees, it maneuvers both administratively and in the legislative arena to recapture its clientele, usually by lowering the net burden its regulations place on its clients. Federal Reserve (and eventually Congressional) response to the Fed's membership problem of the 1960s and 1970s and the granting of new powers for state-chartered institutions to state banking departments and legislatures in response to the DIDMCA of 1980 exemplify the typical pattern of defensive reaction.

But it must never be forgotten that some regulatory agencies and legislatures have capacities for a punitive retightening of regulations, with the U.S. Congress having the greatest capacity of all. Congress can vote retaliatory *preemptions* of state laws able to nullify particular legislative and regulatory actions in every state. It can also enact lengthy *moratoria* that suspend the opportunity to effect particular types of organizational change. With the courts, Congress serves as the final arbiter of disputes over alternative agencies' dominion and power.

Such disputes arise frequently at the federal level, especially between the SEC and banking regulators (e.g., over who should be entitled to regulate brokers of $100,000 CDs or discount-brokerage subsidiaries of deposit-institution HCs) and between the Federal Reserve and other federal regulators of deposit institutions. In such contests, the Fed has special clout with Congress. This clout grows out of the Fed's responsibilities for macroeconomic stability and its willingness to be scapegoated for unfavorable macroeconomic events. The Bush Task Group's difficulties in dispersing the Fed's existing regulatory authority among more specialized deposit-institution agencies provides renewed evidence of the Fed's special primacy in the arena of financial regulation.

Distressing, Implications for Financial Stability and Public Policy Toward the Nonbank Bank. Pre-existing conflicts over regulatory turf have been heightened in the 1980s by cross-industry merger activity and product-line expansion by brokerage, insurance, and deposit firms. The ongoing robotization and electronification of systems for producing and delivering financial services is extending the boundaries of regional competition and sweeping the activities of individual deposit institutions into new states and into the orbits of securities and futures-market regulators and state insurance departments. These same forces are simultaneously thrusting the activities of securities, futures, and insurance firms into the orbits of state and federal deposit-institution regulators.

If the scope economies that are driving financial change did not include subsidies to risk-bearing rooted in the mispricing of risk in federal deposit insurance, structural arbitrage and competitive reregulation would shape up as unambiguously resource-saving activities. However, until federal deposit insurers explicitly price such unregulated risks as those associated with borrower default, asset maturity, balance-sheet leverage, affiliated institutions, and technological change, social welfare is served by regulatory action to limit risk-taking by insured firms. Although this concern justifies authorities' search for ways to constrain and supervise a deposit institution's portfolio positions as well as risky activities undertaken by any holding-company affiliates, it in no way proves the optimality of the particular policies actually adopted.[2]

In the short run, bureaucratic competition for jurisdiction is leading various state and federal regulators to facilitate forms of structural arbitrage that undermine the inherited system of federal deposit insurance. Although this arbitrage is vastly increasing the risk exposure of the FDIC and FSLIC, political pressures and competition from other regulators have deflected the deposit-insurance agencies from bringing these new risks under administrative control.

Structural arbitrage is a game that may be played by brokers and insurers, too. The existence of patterns for circumventing regulatory restrictions on deposit-institution activities makes deposit institutions more attractive candidates for takeover by nondepository firms. Just as deposit-institution HCs can acquire nondepository firms, nondepository financial institutions (such as Merrill Lynch, Dreyfus Corp., and Prudential Insurance) and even nonfinancial firms (such as Sears Roebuck, J.C. Penny, National Steel, and the Parker Pen Co.) can acquire a stockholder-owned deposit institution. If the acquired firm is a thrift institution or is converted into one, its parent can avoid specialized federal oversight at the holding-company level as long as it meets the definition of a unitary savings-and-loan company. If the acquired firm is a bank, spinning off either the demand-deposit or the commercial-loan side of the business makes it possible in principle for the parent firm to elude Fed regulation as a bank HC. The hybrid operation that results is known paradoxically as a "nonbank bank." In terms of the operative definitions of the Bank Holding Company Act, the institution becomes a "non-bank," even though as the holder of a bank charter it may continue to gather time and savings deposits and to have these deposits insured by the FDIC. Moreover, it even seems possible to circumvent restrictions on interstate banking (or at least it seemed possible to the management of Dimension Corp.) by operating a network of limited-service banks in different states.

To some deposit-institution regulators and trade associations, the freedom afforded nonbank banks and unitary S&L HCs represents a glaring pair of loopholes in the legislative fabric of exclusionary regulation (Eisenbeis, 1983b). During 1983, Fed Chairman Volcker, citing a growing threat to the traditional separation of banking from commerce and investment banking, repeatedly urged Congress to pass a temporary moratorium on nondepository acquisitions of deposit institutions and on state and federal actions that allow different types of financial-services firms to expand beyond their traditional lines of business.

Volcker's position on the desirability of separation was not supported by other

---

[2] Kane (1983) discusses how deposit-insurance subsidies are shifted to selected borrowers and depositors, and suggests a series of reforms ranging from market-value accounting for insured institutions to changes in FDIC and FSLIC risk management, coverages, and pricing. Any subset of the reforms would allow scope economies to be pursued without surrendering control of the aggregate risk to which the FDIC and FSLIC are exposed.

federal regulators of deposit institutions. Although the Comptroller of the Currency imposed his own moratorium on applications for *de novo* national-bank charters by securities firms and other nonbanking businesses (extending from April 6, 1983 to March 31, 1984), his stated goal was to give Congress time to redraw industry boundaries. His office continued to process pending applications and to permit nondepository firms to acquire *existing* national banks. In even sharper contrast, the FDIC and FHLBB encouraged their regulatees to undertake various forms of securities activities, with the FHLBB asymmetrically delaying action on applications by brokerage firms and insurance companies to acquire thrifts.

Lack of consensus among federal regulators and among financial-industry trade associations left Congress reluctant to legislate. Congress hates to choose sides in contests in which the social costs and benefits of alternative solutions are highly uncertain. For this reason, Congress appeared willing to permit structural arbitrage to set the future parameters of financial-services competition and to accept any resulting strains on the deposit-insurance system.

Unwilling to accept these same strains, on December 14, 1983 the Federal Reserve Board launched a bold reregulatory counterattack whose ultimate legality remains uncertain. Frustrated by Congressional inaction, the Board unilaterally broadened its interpretation of what activities it holds to be "commerical loans" and "demand deposits" under the Bank Holding Company Act. Its definition of commercial loans now includes sales of federal funds, extension of call loans to brokers, and purchases of commercial paper, certificates of deposit and bankers acceptances, while the category of demand deposits now includes NOW and super-NOW accounts.[3] These redefinitions force nonregistered corporate owners of most nonbank banks to confront a pair of nested dilemmas. They must either further narrow the product lines of their nonbank-bank subsidiary (e.g., by focusing on MMDAs and noncheckable deposit accounts, repurchase agreements, and consumer and mortgage loans) or, within two years, either divest themselves of the nonbank bank or register with the Fed as a bank HC and accept Fed dominion over its activities. Sugaring the pill, the Fed simultaneously added five new powers to the list of permissible activities for nonbanking subsidiaries of bank HCs: issuing money orders; arranging equity financing for real estate, underwriting and dealing in government and specified money-market obligations; providing foreign-exchange advisory services; and performing as a futures commission merchant.

In contrast to the customary regulatory practice of exempting or grandfathering all combinations undertaken under the old rules, the new definitions are retroactive. However, the Fed proposed to permit combinations established before December 10, 1982 to apply for exemptions based on hardship and fairness. The cutoff date coincides with a Board ruling that Dreyfus Corp. would have to register as a bank HC before it acquired a New Jersey bank (a ruling Dreyfus later circumvented by acting under state authority).

[3] This act of redefinition recalls the Comptroller's unsuccessful attempt to rule that off-premises ATMs were not legally branch offices whose locations were subject to regulation under existing branch-banking laws.

These actions increase the expected value and the variance both of the Fed's own administrative costs and of costs for unconventional entrants of circumventing Fed regulation of bank holding companies. If Fed officials were truly confident in the Board's authority to close the nonbank-loophole on its own, one must suppose that Chairman Volcker would not have allowed a problem that so obviously distressed him to fester for so long. The most logical way to read the Board's action is as a forcing move designed to make Congress and the federal courts referee the game of HC reregulation. Effectively, the Fed has demanded that Congress and the Courts either sustain or overrule its redefinitions and choice of cutoff date. Unlike Chairman Volcker's polite pleas for legislative action, this public challenge raises constitutional questions that cannot be turned aside. No matter what the referees finally decide, their merely having the issue under advisement and the threat of additional unilateral action by the Fed promise to reduce for the duration prospective net benefits to brokers and insurers from entering the banking business.

4. Summary

On the TV show, *You Bet Your Life*, a minister once thanked Groucho Marx for all the joy his work had brought into the world. Without missing a beat, Groucho in turn thanked the minister for all the joy his work have taken *out* of it. For brokers, insurance companies, and Dimension Corp., Chairman Volcker has taken some of the joy out of the world of finance. The Board's action leaves the opportunity for deposit institutions to enter brokerage and insurance asymmetrically much greater than the opportunity for insurers and brokers to enter banking. If brokers and insurers seek a legislative rebalancing of regulatory subsidies, and come to appreciate the size of deposit-insurance subsidies and their role in lessening the risk of product-line extension by deposit institutions, they may tip the balance of lobbying pressure toward deposit-insurance reform.

As long as scope economies and deposit-insurance subsidies remain substantial, almost "everybody" should still want to get into each other's act. The Fed's redefinition of its regulatory domain temporarily reduces the product-line flexibility of nonbank financial-services firms relative to banks. In raising the costs of interstate and nonbank entry into banking markets and forcing the hand of Congressional and judicial referees, the Fed transformed a routine regulatory price war into a constitutional struggle over the limits of the Fed's power as financial regulator and stabilizer of last result.

REFERENCES

Baumol, William, Panzar, John C., and Willig, Robert D., "On the Theory of Perfectly Contestable Markets," Bell Laboratories Discussion Paper No. 268 (June 1983).

Benston, George J., Berger, Allen N., Hanweck, G. A., and Humphrey, D. B., "Economies of Scale and Scope in Banking," in *Proceedings of Conference on Bank Structure and Competition*, Chicago: Federal Reserve Bank of Chicago, 1983 (forthcoming).

Bierwag, Gerald O. and Kaufman, George G., "A Proposal for Federal Deposit Insurance with Risk-Sensitive Premiums," in Proceedings *of Conference on Bank Structure and Competitors*, Chicago: Federal Reserve Bank of Chicago, 1983 (forthcoming).

Buser, Stephen, Chen, Andrew H., and Kane, Edward J., "Federal Deposit Insurance, Regulatory Policy, and Optimal Bank Capital," *Journal of Finance*, 36 (March 1981), pp. 51–60.

Eisenbeis, Robert A., "Bank Holding Companies and Public Policy," in George J. Benston (ed.), *Financial Services: The Changing Institutions and Government Policy*, Englewood Cliffs, NJ: Prentice-Hall, Inc. for the American Assembly, 1983(a), pp. 127–155.

Eisenbeis, Robert A., "Policy Issues Raised by the Expansion of Nonbank Banks," unpublished manuscript, University of North Carolina, Chapel Hill, 1983(b).

Kane, Edward J., "Accelerating Inflation, Technological Innovation, and the Decreasing Effectiveness of Banking Regulation," *Journal of Finance*, 36 (May 1981), pp. 355–367.

Kane, Edward J., "A Six-Point Program for Deposit-Insurance Reform," *Housing Finance Review*, 2 (July 1983), pp. 269–278.

Article Eleven

The impact of geographic expansion in banking: Some axioms to grind

Douglas D. Evanoff and *Diana Fortier*

In recent years the potential impact of relaxing geographic restrictions on banking organizations has been actively debated. Proponents argue that the ability to expand into new markets will produce efficiencies enabling banks to offer improved services at preferred prices. Opponents counter that expansion will result in increases in concentration and market power leading to higher prices and inferior service, and, eventually, impairing the safety and soundness of the industry. The opposing groups have supported their positions relentlessly with the same unchanging arguments. As a result there have evolved several almost axiomatic statements concerning the impact of relaxed geographic restrictions.

This article provides evidence on the validity of a number of these popular "axioms." Past research on geographic barriers to intrastate expansion is reviewed and new evidence is introduced to determine whether these popular conceptions are sound or are overstated arguments. The findings should aid legislators and may help the industry avoid the continual imposition of inefficient market restrictions aimed at avoiding situations which, in fact, have little probability of occurring.

Among the arguments commonly presented in opposition to geographic expansion in banking are: 1) Geographic expansion will lead to significant increases in market concentration. Over time, a relatively small number of institutions will gain control of the local marketplace. 2) Antitrust legislation is not effective in curtailing concentration increases in banking. 3) Banking organizations which compete with each other in a number of markets will, in effect, collude with one another by avoiding aggressive competition in one market, expecting similar behavior by rival firms in other markets (the mutual forbearance hypothesis). 4) Small banks are not able to compete with large banking organizations. Therefore, if increased geographic expansion is allowed, a significant number of bank failures will occur, and the number of small independent banks will significantly decline. 5) Re-

moving restrictions on geographic expansion will lead to excessive market power resulting in an inferior level of banking services. 6) Allowing expansion will lead to higher bank service prices. 7) Service accessibility will decline if geographic expansion is allowed. Additionally, the number of bank alternatives from which financial services can be obtained will decline. 8) Geographic expansion will not significantly aid, and may actually hinder, rural areas because expansion will take place only in more attractive urban markets.

The recent development of regional banking compacts, modified state laws, interstate stakeout agreements, and limited service banks has heightened the controversy over the validity of the preceding statements. The evidence presented here indicates that some of the arguments posed against geographic expansion have little basis in reality.

Axiom #1: Market structure will become significantly more concentrated.

Perhaps the foremost concern with respect to interstate banking is the potential for increased concentration of banking resources. An aversion to the concentration of financial and economic resources has been a major theme in the history of the United States and was in part the impetus behind the Sherman and Clayton Acts and, with respect to banking, the Bank Holding Company Act (BHC Act). The major goals of the BHC Act are the prevention of an undue concentration of resources and the preservation of competition in banking.

Economic theory holds that increased concentration results in reduced competition. That, in turn, leads to a suboptimal allocation of resources and a distortion in the distribution

Douglas D. Evanoff is a senior financial economist and Diana Fortier is a regulatory economist at the Federal Reserve Bank of Chicago. A more comprehensive discussion of issues related to geographic expansion in banking can be found in *Toward Nationwide Banking*, Federal Reserve Bank of Chicago, 1986.

of income. That is, the probability of non-competitive behavior can be inferred from the number and size distribution of firms in the market.[1] This perceived relationship prompted antitrust legislation to prevent the concentration of markets and the resulting higher prices, higher profits, inferior services, and reduced output. The adverse effects associated with concentration are of particular concern in markets where customers are limited to local service providers. In banking this primarily means the market for retail financial services since the wholesale market (e.g., corporate loans) is already regional or national in scope.[2]

The ultimate impact of geographic barrier removal depends on two opposing forces. First, barriers create an anticompetitive environment by preventing new entry into a market. Lifting them should result in increased potential and actual market entry. Potential entry is important because the mere threat of new entry may be sufficient to induce procompetitive behavior. Markets in which firms continue to behave anti-competitively would soon be serviced by new entrants.

Most bank expansion occurs, however, through acquisition, rather than de novo. This creates a concern that the elimination of entry constraints may lead to extensive acquisition activity, increased concentration, and possibly collusion among large institutions. Although these two opposite considerations pose a dilemma, numerous studies generally support the hypothesis that a relaxation of geographic restrictions has procompetitive effects.[3]

The removal of geographic restrictions is expected to affect concentration of the industry at the national and/or state level differently than that at the local market level. For our analysis, the impact at the local market level is most relevant because measures at broader levels can frequently mask the local situation. For example, the concentration level could, hypothetically, be 100% in all local banking markets (i.e., controlled by one firm) but be relatively low at the state level. To analyze local market conditions, nonmetropolitan county and metropolitan area boundaries were used as approximations of banking markets in the United States.

Between 1970 and 1983 the Herfindahl-Hirschman Index (HHI), a measure of local market concentration, declined significantly; see Table 1. This decline occurred in local markets regardless of branching restrictions. However, the greatest deconcentration occurred in areas allowing relatively liberal branching.[4]

A closer evaluation of the variation in the HHI between areas with different branching laws indicates that the absolute level of concentration was essentially the same in 1983 irrespective of branching status. However, this is a substantial change from earlier years. In 1970, local markets allowing branching were significantly more concentrated than were markets permitting unit banks only. Over the next ten years the decline in concentration in branching markets was much greater than the decline on average. Apparently, increased market entry, a result of the ability to branch, served to generate the current lower levels of concentration.

The data in Table 1 also indicate the absolute level of concentration differed substantially between metro and non-metro markets. The average HHI has historically been approximately 50 percent lower for metro areas because these markets are better able to support a larger number of competitors. The relatively smaller number of competitors in non-metro areas results in a comparatively high HHI. However, regardless of the absolute levels of concentration, both types of markets have experienced a decline in concentration.

The impact of branching has also been different in metropolitan and nonmetropolitan areas. The variation in the average HHI between markets with different branching status is rather minimal in nonmetro areas. However, the index is significantly lower for metro markets in unit banking states than for those in branching states. This difference has declined over time as the metro markets allowing branching have experienced the greatest concentration decline.

The HHI is a comprehensive measure of market concentration in that it takes into account the market shares of all firms in a market. Alternatively, the one-, three-, and five-firm concentration ratios consider only the largest firms in the market. These ratios are, however, the more commonly reported statistic.

An analysis of concentration in local markets using the three-firm concentration ratio, C3, produced results very similar to those found using the HHI. The concentration trend has been downward with the greatest declines

Table 1

Table 1
Local market structure data by branching status

Type of market	Concentration measure & year	All states[1]				States not changing branching status[1]			States changing branching status[1]		
		All states	Statewide	Limited	Unit	All states	Branching	Unit Banking	All states	Limited	Statewide
All markets	HHI 1970	4441	4918*	4387	4267	4594	4693†	4466	3895	3306	5098
	1980	4081	4054	3979*	4226	4224	4223†	4226	3569	3140	4036
	1983	4013	3946	3947	4141	4143	4145†	4140	3546	3132	3995
	C3 1970	88.6%	93.2%*	88.5%*	86.6%	90.0%	91.2†	88.5%	83.4%	78.8%	94.7%
	1980	87.0%	87.4%*	86.6%	87.1%	88.4%	89.4%†	87.1%	81.8%	78.3%	85.6%
	1983	86.6%	86.8%	86.6%	86.6%	88.0%	89.1%†	86.6%	81.7%	78.2%	85.5%
Nonmetropolitan counties	HHI 1970	4706	5257*	4708*	4468	4856	5018†	4659	4153	3402	5213
	1980	4341	4489	4187*	4426	4483	4531†	4426	3818	3238	4535
	1983	4269	4367	4154	4340	4398	4444†	4340	3797	3236	4490
	C3 1970	90.7%	95.3%*	91.1%*	88.4%	92.0%	93.6†	90.1%	85.8%	79.7%	95.3%
	1980	89.5%	91.8%*	88.5%*	89.2%	90.8%	92.2†	89.2%	84.7%	79.4%	91.2%
	1983	89.2%	91.3%	88.5%	88.8%	90.5%	91.9†	88.8%	84.7%	79.4%	91.2%
Metropolitan areas	HHI 1970	2297	2731*	2293*	1973	2368	2514	2035	2081	2038	2837
	1980	1972	2024*	2077*	1711	2024	2161†	1711	1815	1842	1801
	1983	1933	1986*	2065*	1625	1982	2139†	1625	1782	1771	1786
	C3 1970	71.5%	79.2%*	71.0%	66.4%	73.1%	75.5†	67.6%	66.7%	66.9%	81.7%
	1980	66.2%	66.8%*	68.6%*	61.2%	67.6%	70.5†	61.2%	61.7%	63.5%	61.0%
	1983	65.5%	65.7%*	68.8%*	59.6%	67.0%	70.2†	59.6%	61.0%	62.4%	60.4%

[1] States changing branching laws refers to those changing status between 1960 and 1983. (In 1960 there were 16 statewide, 16 limited and 15 unit banking states. In 1970 there were 19 statewide, 16 limited and 16 unit banking states. In 1980 there were 23 statewide, 16 limited and 11 unit banking states. In 1980 and 1983 there were 23 statewide, 16 limited and 11 unit banking states. States changing from unit to limited were Arkansas, Iowa, Minnesota, and Wisconsin. States changing from limited to statewide were New Hampshire, New Jersey, New York, Maine, and Virginia. Florida changed from unit to limited in 1977 and from limited to statewide in 1968.) South Dakota changed from unit to statewide in 1980. Metropolitan areas crossing states with different branching laws in any year were deleted from the sample. The same number of markets were analyzed for each year by branching status in the given year.

*Mean for statewide or limited branching states is signficantly different at the .05 level from the mean for the given year for unit banking states.

†Mean for branching states not changing branching laws is significantly different at the .05 level from the mean for branching states changing status (i.e., status changing from unit to limited or statewide, and from limited to statewide.

SOURCE: FDIC Summary of Deposit data as of June 30, 1970, 1980 and 1983.

in markets with liberalized branching laws. The only apparent difference is the amount of decline in concentration in nonmetropolitan areas. The C3 would not detect entry unless the entrants obtained a significant share of the market. The HHI, however, would account for a new entrant regardless of the market share obtained. This difference between the measures produces a significant decline in the HHI in nonmetropolitan areas over the period examined without a corresponding significant decline in the C3. Given this difference, the HHI may be the preferred measure of market concentration.[5]

Trends toward increased concentration are of prime concern in markets that are already highly concentrated. Separating local markets by level of concentration (based on HHI data not presented in the tables) shows that highly and moderately concentrated markets became less concentrated between 1970 and 1983. This is true regardless of branching status or changes in branching laws. Moreover, the number of highly concentrated local markets has fallen, and, correspondingly, the number of moderately concentrated local markets has increased.

The above analysis of concentration uses the traditional cluster approach in that it includes only commercial banks as purveyors of the relevant line of commerce. As a result of deregulation and technological developments, other depository institutions compete or have the ability to compete with commercial banks along several service lines. The inclusion of these additional organizations in the relevant line of commerce, in particular, thrifts, will alter absolute concentration measures. In most cases it is expected to lower the level of concentration without affecting the general downward trend in local market concentration.[6]

In summary, concentration in banking has decreased over time. Markets in branching states have shown a greater decrease than have unit banking markets. Concentration levels in non-metropolitan markets do not differ significantly with branching status. However, concentration in metropolitan areas is higher when branching is allowed. Yet, it is in these very markets that concentration decreases have been the greatest.

Axiom #2: Antitrust laws are not effective in preventing concentration increases.

The existing evidence does not support the hypothesis that interstate banking necessarily leads to more concentrated local markets. However, for markets in which this could occur, the critical issue is whether antitrust laws can adequately prevent substantial anticompetitive effects. There has been significant disagreement on the effectiveness of antitrust laws. One way of evaluating that impact is to compare concentration levels in states introducing branching before and after the 1960 Bank Merger Act.

Table 1 subdivides bank structure data into markets located in states which enacted branching laws prior to the 1960 Bank Merger Act and those that did not. Mergers occurring in the latter period were subject to approval by the principal federal regulatory agency and, more importantly, were subject to antitrust laws. If antitrust provisions were effective, anticompetitive mergers would occur less frequently in the latter period. The data in Table 1 suggests that markets allowing branching in the earlier period are indeed more concentrated than those introducing it in the latter period. Statistical tests indicate the difference is significant.

Additional analysis accounting for demographic differences indicate that factors determining the business attractiveness of a banking market, e.g., high population and income levels, produce lower concentration levels. Similarly, the more stringent local regulators are in allowing the chartering of new institutions, the higher the resulting HHI. After accounting for these factors, the impact of branching was considered and, again, was found to influence concentration measures positively only if it was allowed prior to the imposition of antitrust laws in 1960. In markets introducing branching after this period, concentration has not been significantly influenced.[7] Thus, in preventing concentration increases resulting from excessive merger activity the evidence suggests antitrust enforcement has had a significant impact.

An alternative means of evaluating the effectiveness of antitrust legislation is to evaluate its impact on the number of banking organizations in local markets. Studies evaluating the change over time in states changing to a more liberal branching status found that the number of organizations did not decline. However, numerous cross-sectional studies have found that significantly fewer organizations exist in areas with more liberal branching.[8]

The cross-sectional studies have been criticized for failing to consider demographic differences and to account for the length of time that branching had been allowed. Additionally, areas allowing branching prior to 1960 can be expected to have fewer organizations than areas in which branching was later introduced.

To evaluate the validity of these criticisms, additional analysis was performed. First, data for the average number of banking organizations in local markets in 1970 and 1980 were obtained. Data presented in Table 2 indicate that the number of organizations (i.e., customer alternatives) was less in states allowing branching. This difference was negligible by 1980. A closer analysis of those areas allowing branching prior to 1960, and those introducing it later reveals substantial differences. The average number of organizations is significantly less in regions where branching was introduced in the earlier period. In fact, areas with the most liberal branching laws introduced after 1960 actually had *more* banking alternatives.

The data in Table 2, while supporting the argument that the branching impact has been different in the pre- and post-Bank Merger Act period, ignore demographic factors. These are probably the most important factors determining the number of banking options. To account for these factors a series of estimates were obtained.[9]

After controlling for demographic factors, the changing imposition of antitrust enforcement over time, and the length of time branching had been allowed, the findings suggest that initially branching does adversely influence the number of organizations in the market. However, branching is shown to have had a much larger impact if allowed prior to the Bank Merger Act. Most important, the variable included to account for the length of time that branching had been allowed indicates that the initial negative impact of branching is essentially offset in approximately three years as organizations branch into new markets.

Table 2
Average number of banking organizations per local market

Totals	Organizations per banking market*	
	1970	1980
All markets	5.32	6.06
Unit banking markets	5.55	6.06
Branching markets	5.15	6.05
Legislated after 1960	5.72	7.96
Legislated before 1960	5.06	5.29
Unlimited branching markets	4.84	7.60
Legislated after 1960	4.30	9.45
Legislated before 1960	5.06	6.57
Per capita (x 1000)		
All markets	.236	.232
Unit banking markets	.327	.342
Branching markets	.167	.171
Legislated after 1960	.258	.227
Legislated before 1960	.152	.150
Unlimited branching markets	.191	.186
Legislated after 1960	.270	.283
Legislated before 1960	.158	.160

*Banking markets are defined as counties.
SOURCE: FDIC Summary of Deposits.

The preceding discussion suggests that antitrust law has had an important impact on the structure of local banking markets. If there is significant concern over potential increases in concentration, existing guidelines can be utilized or new guidelines can be introduced to preclude it.

Axiom #3: Firms competing in several markets will collude to avoid competition.

With interstate banking, more merger cases will likely involve market extensions, i.e., non-horizontal mergers, rather than combinations within the same market. The resulting potential for anticompetitive behavior associated with linked oligopoly or mutual forbearance is a concern. The issue is whether multi-market firms competing with each other in several markets will behave collusively rather than competitively for fear of retaliation in other (weaker) markets. Such collusion could offset any benefits resulting from the elimination of entry barriers. For this behavior to be effective, the rival firms must hold significant market shares and be among relatively few firms in the market. The basic premise is that competitive behavior of rivals is interdependent, i.e., each firm acknowledges that its competitive behavior will adversely affect its rivals, which will react in kind. The optimal behavior, therefore, may be to cooperate with or not compete aggressively against the rival firm.

However, interstate expansion need not lead to collusive behavior. Competition may actually be strengthened as firms try to outguess the strategy of their competitors. Indeed, the majority of empirical studies of the linked oligopoly hypothesis do not support it, but instead findings indicate that multimarket links result in increased market competition.[10] Even if firms were to have multi-market links across the nation, competition would likely increase in these markets. With broader expansion, a substantial number of competitors and geographically dispersed markets would diminish the ability of firms to behave collusively. Since the largest and most attractive markets are likely to be metropolitan areas, it is in these markets that consumers are most likely to gain benefits.

Axiom #4: The viability of small banks and the safety of the industry will be jeopardized.

Bank performance is the final element of the structure-conduct-performance paradigm, and an important factor indirectly affecting the consumer. It is often alleged that a liberalization of branching laws may threaten the viability of the small bank, and, more importantly, the general safety and soundness of the banking system. However, the evidence does not support either of these allegations.

Data summarized in Figure 1 support the contention that small banks can compete effectively with larger organizations. In fact, small banks have generally outperformed or kept pace with the larger banks. Across all branching categories, it is the larger banks that have performed below average and below that of the smallest banks as measured by return on assets (ROA). Additionally, the experience of California and New York, two large states with over ten years of statewide branching experience, suggests that small banks can survive under liberalized branching laws.[11]

Bank performance data by size and branching status*

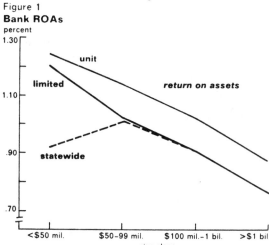

Figure 1
Bank ROAs

Figure 2
Loan behavior

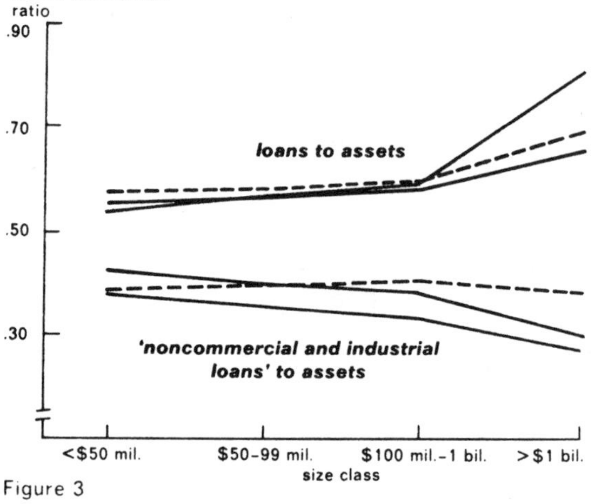

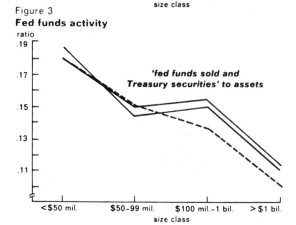

Figure 3
Fed funds activity

*The impact of branching is understated because banks changing status in 1984-85 had little time to adjust.

SOURCE: Data are 6-year averages from *Reports of Condition,* June 30, 1980-1985. ROA data are annualized.

The increased level of competitiveness associated with branching is also evident from the data. Institutions located in branching states have a lower average ROA than do banks in the same size class in unit banking states. Statistical tests indicate the differences are significant. These data reflect more competitive markets in the more liberal branching states wherein potential competition hinders the ability of organizations with significant market shares to reap above-normal profits. The relaxation in branching laws is, therefore, likely to have the greatest impact on bank performance in unit banking states. Banks in these states will no longer be able to use their protected markets to earn higher rates of return.

Bank failure has been shown to be more closely related to management expertise than to the structure of banking laws. Nonetheless, data presented in Table 3 indicate that since 1970 the number of failed banks corresponds directly with the extent of geographic branching restrictions. That is, over this period, 23 percent, 32 percent, and 45 percent of failed banks were in statewide branching, limited branching, and unit banking states, respectively. The majority (74 percent) of failed

banks were unit banks, and the percentage of these failed unit banks corresponds directly with the extent of restrictions on branching. i.e., statewide branching states had the fewest unit bank failures. Additionally, the percentage of unit banks failing between 1970 and 1983 was twice that of branch banks, i.e., 0.1% and 0.05%, respectively. One possible explanation for this disparity is the competitive advantage of branching banks resulting from geographic and customer diversification.

Another concern raised with respect to geographic expansion is the threat to the financial health of expanding banking organizations, and, potentially, the banking system. Some fear that an environment of extensive acquisition activity may cause overly ambitious organizations to pay excessive premiums, over-leverage their capital, spread management too thin, or enter into new types of operations and lending activities in which management is relatively inexperienced. However, bank regulatory agencies already impose controls on bank mergers and acquisitions to prevent such behavior. The Federal Reserve has denied proposed acquisitions on both financial and managerial grounds.[12] Regardless of interstate

Table 3
Number of banks closed because of financial
difficulties by branching status (1970-1983)*

Year	Total	Statewide branching states Unit banks	Statewide branching states Branching banks	Limited branching states Unit banks	Limited branching states Branching banks	Unit banking states Unit banks
1970	6	0	0	4	0	2
1971	6	0	0	1	0	5
1972	3	0	0	1	1	1
1973	6	0	1	1	0	4
1974	4	0	1	2	0	1
1975	10	1	0	1	2	6
1976	13	0	4	1	2	6
1977	4	0	0	1	2	1
1978	5	0	0	3	0	2
1979	10	0	1	2	2	5
1980	9	1	0	1	1	6
1981	9	1	3	2	0	3
1982	41	3	7	10	4	17
1983	47	9	7	6	11	14
Total	173	15	24	36	25	73
(% of total)	100%	8.7%	13.9%	20.8%	14.4%	42.2%

*Excludes banks not in the continental United States, Hawaii or Alaska. Data were not available by branching status for nine banks: one in 1970, 1977, 1980 and 1981; two in 1975; and three in 1976.

SOURCE: FDIC Annual Reports 1970-1983.

banking laws, financial and managerial standards governing acquisitions will continue to protect the financial health of banks and the banking system.

Some small banks will fail or be acquired if geographic expansion is allowed. Some may be perfectly willing to sell to expanding organizations or may simply not be able to compete. However, most of the studies of the profitability and viability of small banks suggest many will continue to thrive. Finally, the empirical evidence suggests that regardless of institution size, branching results in a lower return on assets. This is indicative of a more competitive market for financial services.

Axiom #5: The range and level of financial services will be inferior.

From a social welfare point of view, perhaps the most pertinent factor to be considered with the geographic expansion of banking is the potential impact on consumers concerning service offerings, prices, and availability.[13] One measure of the level of service provided by commercial banks is the range or array of services made available. Perhaps the most important variable influencing service offerings is institution size. Large institutions can justify new services because they generally have a larger customer base and can more readily generate the necessary service volume required for profitability. More services are also offered by larger institutions because they frequently compete by introducing tangential services aimed at acquiring new, or maintaining existing, customers.

Evidence from previous studies tends to support the view that large banks provide a larger array of services.[14] Table 4 summarizes findings from a recent study analyzing bank survey data. The percentage of institutions offering the services increases with institution size. This increase holds true for both consumer and business services.

The available evidence suggests that branching status also affects the array of service offerings. Early studies found trust services, special checking accounts, payroll services, and foreign exchange transactions all to be more commonly offered at small branch banks than at small unit banks. Recent studies have substantiated that finding. Larger institutions tend to offer a more complete banking package,

thus, branching status does not have as significant an impact on their offerings.

Liberalizing geographic expansion could, thus, increase the array of services available to consumers for two reasons. First, smaller institutions would expand their offerings as they branched into new markets, or as they retained their unit bank status and expanded offerings to compete with new branch bank competitors. Secondly, larger institutions, the ones most likely to expand into new regions, would bring with them a larger array of services as they enter new markets. Since unit banking states are characterized by numerous small banking organizations, the benefits would be greatest in these areas.

In addition to leading to a larger array of services, geographic expansion should also influence the supply of bank services. By opening branches or acquiring banks in new markets, banks would be more geographically diversified and less susceptible to deterioration in local economic conditions. Thus, their flow of deposits should be more stable. Similarly, these institutions can be expected to develop new loan customers and, be less susceptible to individual customer failures and resulting loan losses. Both geographic and customer diversification will, therefore, decrease an organization's risk, allowing it to hold fewer highly liquid assets. This will enable it to increase the size of its loan portfolio. Thus, *ceteris paribus*, diversification should enable an institution to better serve its customers' loan needs.

Figure 2 provides data supporting this hypothesis. The loan-to-asset ratio increases with bank size suggesting the banks most likely to branch will tend to offer more loans. The presence of liberalized branching also produces a higher loan-to-asset ratio in all but the very largest size groups. Liberalized branching areas also have the highest non-corporate loan-to-asset ratios indicating that branching leads to improved servicing of consumer loan needs. Figure 3 presents additional information on the liquidity of bank assets. The "fed funds sold plus Treasury securities" -to-asset ratio decreases with institution size, suggesting that liquid assets at smaller institutions are replaced by loans at larger institutions. Branching status is again shown to be important in determining the ability of banks to make loans. In all but one size category, banks located in the most liberal branching areas hold fewer

Table 4
Percentage of sample banks offering special
customer services—arrayed by bank size*

Type of services	Bank deposits in millions				
	Under $10	$10-25	$25-50	$50-100	Over $100
A. Consumer deposit services	53.4	61.3	71.6	74.2	78.6
B. Business deposit services	44.4	53.9	65.4	67.2	81.8
C. Consumer & business services	47.5	48.5	53.5	58.8	67.1
Examples					
Trust services	22.4	40.9	69.6	80.0	97.1
Drive up windows	78.4	92.2	99.1	100.0	98.6
Special no-minimum checking	38.1	40.8	55.4	54.4	66.2
Revolving charge card	24.5	35.2	50.5	68.4	78.3
Special check services for businesses	36.5	50.0	75.2	76.3	95.5
Locked box services	13.9	27.0	42.0	39.4	74.2
Foreign exchange service	41.7	47.6	60.2	64.1	79.7

*Sample data are from Rose, Kolari, and Riener. "A Nationwide Survey Study of Bank Services and Prices Arrayed By Size and Structure," in *Journal of Bank Research* (Summer 1985) pp. 72-85. Percentages presented for business and consumer services are averages of a longer list of services provided in the original article.

liquid assets. Again, this indicates they are making more loans.

Geographically diversified institutions may also be better able to allocate resources, efficiently transferring funds between areas of low demand and excess demand. In fact, this is a major reason for expansion. This ability would be even further enhanced with interstate banking because regions with surplus or deficit funding do not necessarily correspond to state boundaries. While the same transfer could be made between independent unit banks or by way of a correspondent bank relationship, additional costs may be introduced by the middle agent.

This reallocation of resources, however, may not benefit local customers if their loan demands are not met because deposits are skimmed off and directed elsewhere. Additionally, opponents of branching argue, funds may be directed to large borrowers only. Thus, this efficiency could lead to funds being directed toward the main office of the bank. Because these offices are usually located in large metropolitan areas, funds may be drained from rural areas. However, with a sufficient branch network, the funds could as easily shift between rural areas. The transferring to urban areas would only occur if the expected return on investments in these areas was higher than that expected in the rural areas. Although agricul-

tural loans have not performed well in recent years, the evidence does not suggest that rural investments earn an inferior return. The evidence on this skimming phenomenon is somewhat limited, frequently dated, and imposes rather restrictive assumptions, but generally does not support the hypothesis that funds are drained from rural areas.[15] Additionally, one could argue that the tendency for unit and small banks to sell a substantial amount of fed funds is also a means of skimming funds away from the local market.

Whether branching organizations adequately service the needs of smaller businesses that are usually limited to local market alternatives is an additional consideration. Larger institutions tend to have larger loan-to-asset ratios, which makes their availability of loans greater. However, they may also deal almost exclusively in large loans, which could leave small businesses with few options. A number of studies have indicated that small businesses may be adversely affected by bank concentration, and many believe that branching may lead to more concentrated local banking markets, particularly in nonmetropolitan areas.[16] Statistics also suggest that a large portion of the dollar value of large bank loans is provided to larger borrowers, while most small bank loans are to small borrowers. However, the statistics are not very meaningful in determining if the smaller borrowers would be shunned by larger branch organizations. Large banks make large loans because they have the ability to do so, while small banks do not.

A more appropriate way to view this issue is to analyze small loan requests. A recent study surveying small, independent businessmen, after accounting for business type, size, recent growth trends, and demographic factors, indicates that the credit needs of smaller businesses tend to be denied more, or not as adequately met, when liberal branching is allowed.[17] However, when credit needs are met, the terms are generally considered satisfactory. The study may have implications concerning the objectivity of branch bank management in applying credit rating criteria. Smaller businesses may suffer somewhat if branching organizations rely more on financial statements and credit scoring models, and less on the character of the borrower and specific circumstances surrounding the loan request. From an economic viewpoint, these less subjective criteria would be appropriate. Additionally, the argument can still be made that if creditworthy borrowers are not being adequately serviced, a regional institution willing to specialize in this area will enter and profitably service this group.

Axiom #6: Deposit rates will be lower and/or loan rates higher.

If banking markets were perfectly competitive, each facility would sell homogeneous services (e.g., loans, deposit options) at cost-driven prices, and free entry would eliminate any excess profits. These two conditions obviously do not characterize the U.S. banking industry. Significant barriers to entry, non-price competition, market power, and operating efficiencies lead to deviations from purely competitive prices.

Restricted geographic expansion is an obvious impediment to market entry and one reason to expect prices to differ between branching and nonbranching institutions. It has already been shown that relaxation of geographic restrictions eases entry and lowers profitability. It would be logical to assume this lower profitability results from lower loan rates and/or higher rates on deposits.

There are several reasons for expecting branch banks to have lower prices. If cost ef-

ficiencies exist with branching, branch banks could offer better prices than independent banks. While most studies evaluating economies of scale in banking have found them fully exhausted at relatively low output levels, branch banks may have an advantage in that they can keep the size of each branch near the cost efficient level by opening new branches. Studies have, however, found cost advantages as a result of offering an array of services that can efficiently be produced in conjunction with one other (i.e., economies of scope).[18] As shown previously, branch banks tend to offer a wider array of services. Prices could also be affected if the process of shifting funds between geographic areas is more cost efficient between affiliated banks than between independent banks. The geographic and customer diversification discussed earlier could also produce efficiencies resulting in preferred prices.

Most of the empirical work analyzing the impact of organizational structure on service prices is dated and frequently fails to account adequately for non-structural factors. Conflicting results are also found. Service charges on demand deposits were found to be higher with branch than with unit banks. However, more recent studies found little or no difference. Conflicting results also occur when determining if branch banks pay higher interest rates on time and savings accounts. Finally, similar inconsistencies have been found when evaluating the rates charged on loans.[19] The conflicting results suggest that the various assumptions and assertions made in these studies significantly affect the findings. There simply is no conclusive evidence that branching affects service prices.

Axiom #7: Service accessibility will be adversely affected.

Improved customer service may be the most commonly cited advantage associated with branch banking. Branches can be conveniently distributed and provide basic services, while specialized services may be provided only at the head office or at a limited number of offices. The larger array of services provided by branch banks was discussed earlier. An important element of customer service is the level of service accessibility, i.e., the number of offices available to meet customer needs. Branching can be expected to lead to greater service accessibility for a number of reasons. Perhaps the major one is that a particular market may be capable of supporting a branch office, but not a new bank. Additionally, accessibility is a form of non-price competition which only branch banks can practice.

Early studies evaluating the impact of branching on service accessibility found little, or even an inverse, relationship between branching and the population per banking office. However, many of these studies failed to account for demographic and market differences. The results from more recent studies viewing either the number of offices or the number of offices per capita suggest that branching does indeed lead to improved accessibility. One study found that if all states had allowed statewide branching in 1975, the number of bank offices in the United States would have increased by 1275, or 4 percent. However, another recent study found that one of the most commonly acclaimed benefits of branching—improved service accessibility in rural areas—could not be supported.[20]

An alternative way to view accessibility is to analyze the number of offices per square mile in branching and nonbranching states after taking demographic factors into account. Since customer convenience is most accurately measured as the required time and distance to access services, a measure incorporating the geographic area will be more appropriate. For example, in a study based on the number of offices per capita, a decline in the number of offices would imply a deterioration of service adequacy. However, an actual deterioration would occur only in the extreme case wherein offices became more congested, had longer lines, and imposed time-consuming hardships on customers. Utilizing the office-per-area measure and taking demographic differences into account, findings indicate that branching significantly improves accessibility in both metropolitan and nonmetropolitan areas. In fact, while results differ slightly depending on the service area considered (i.e., county, metropolitan areas, etc.), service accessibility has been shown to be over 50 percent greater when branching is allowed.

To evaluate thoroughly the impact of branching on service accessibility, the number of alternative banking organizations should also be considered. While an increase in the number of offices may lead to improved accessibility, variety and competition will be lacking if most of the offices are affiliated. Most studies indicate that the number of organizations in a state decreases with the presence of branching. This could be expected at the state level because most expansion would be accomplished by acquisition of existing banks instead of *de novo*. Thus, although the number of offices may remain relatively constant, the offices would be controlled by fewer organizations. However, we have already shown in the discussion of Axiom #2 that *at the local level* branching may actually increase the number of organizations after an initial adjustment period. This occurs because organizations branch into new markets. It is this local level that is most important in evaluating service accessibility.

Axiom #8: Benefits from branching will not be realized in rural areas.

Stated or implied in many of the arguments against geographic expansion has been a concern about the fate of rural markets. Will local market concentration increase in rural areas, leading to inferior market prices and service levels? Will funds be drained away from rural markets so that local demand for loans is not adequately met? Will funds be reinvested in more lucrative metropolitan markets? Such effects of interstate banking would obviously impair the growth of the local rural economy.

As we have seen, however, local market concentration in rural areas is not related to branching status. Similarly, the improved array of services and level of service accessibility resulting from the presence of branching was not limited to metropolitan areas. Indeed, many of the benefits of branching are realized in rural markets also. In fact, the potential for improvements from geographic expansion is very significant in rural areas. Organizations, whether currently present in the market or not, have greater ability to respond to changing market conditions with liberalized branching laws. Rural areas in which the demand for services is not sufficient to warrant a new unit bank may merit expansion via a branch office. The more vehicles of entry available, the larger the number of potential entrants and the greater the probability that entry will occur.

Given this potential for new entry, and its resulting benefits, whether or not it actually occurs will depend entirely on economic factors. Banking organizations will evaluate the demand for loan and deposit services and, if justified, introduce a new office. It should also be emphasized that market forces cannot be eliminated by regulation. For example, numerous states which have approved or are considering entry by out-of-state banks have "protected" local customers by imposing reinvestment requirements. These requirements however, affect the attractiveness of the new market, and, perhaps more importantly, the entering bank's pricing decisions. If state regulations require a larger reinvestment in the local market than market factors would generate, the entering bank will compensate by charging local customers higher loan rates and offering lower deposit rates. The higher loan rates will be of limited value to the community because existing banks would have similar or lower ones. Lower deposit rates will encourage customers to utilize alternative, perhaps nonlocal institutions, thus, again causing funds to leave the local marketplace. Market forces, not legislated restrictions, determine the viability of banking markets.

That banking organizations do indeed respond to market forces is supported by analysis of market growth data. The absolute and percentage change in the number of banking offices and organizations is positively correlated with population growth in all markets. To the extent that population is an adequate proxy for market attractiveness, market entry appears to have been based on market conditions. In rural areas where branching was allowed there was a somewhat closer association between population growth and entry—measured as new offices.[21] The essence of this analysis is that branching apparently has not negatively affected the entry of banks in rural areas. In fact it may have helped it.

Summary and conclusions.

Over time, a number of arguments against liberalizing geographic expansion in banking have come to be accepted almost as axioms. Several of the statements are shown to be inaccurate and little evidence exists to support the remaining ones.

In evaluating these statements our basic findings suggest:

1) The trend in local banking market concentration has been downward. This deconcentration trend has been greatest in markets allowing liberal branching activity. The absolute level of concentration in nonmetropolitan areas does not significantly differ as a result of branching, although the absolute level is higher in metropolitan areas when liberal branching activity is allowed. However, it is in these metropolitan areas that the decline in concentration has been the greatest.

2) Stringent antitrust laws can be relatively effective in preventing non-competitive behavior in banking. Evidence suggests that concentration and the number of banking organizations in local markets have been significantly influenced by the imposition of antitrust laws on the banking industry in the early 1960s.

3) To date, there is little support for the contention that liberalized branching will lead to collusive behavior by banking organizations as proposed by the linked oligopoly, or mutual forbearance hypothesis.

4) Lower average returns on assets suggest that competition is greater in more liberal branching markets. Additionally, evidence does not support the contention that liberalizing geographic expansion will threaten the viability of smaller banks.

5) Branch banks and larger institutions, those most likely to branch if allowed, provide a wider array of financial services.

6) There is no substantial evidence suggesting that branching results in service prices that differ from those of unit banks. However, branch banks engage in more lending and have lower profit rates. This suggests that branching induces more intense competition.

7) Service accessibility is superior in markets allowing branching activity—including rural areas. Although the number of alternative service providers may initially decline when branching is introduced, this trend will be reversed over time as entry occurs.

8) Rural areas also stand to benefit from branching in the form of increased market entry, a wider array of services, improved accessibility, and increased competition.

Given these findings, some of the standard criticisms of geographic expansion in banking are shown to be of questionable merit. Realistically, attempts to prevent expansion will probably not be effective if bank management perceives the benefits to be substantial. The fact that numerous institutions have gained an interstate presence via regional compacts, emergency mergers, and regulatory loopholes suggest the perceived benefits are indeed significant. The benefits to the customer also appear to be substantial, suggesting further deregulation of geographic restrictions would be warranted.

A final comment should be made concerning the increasing number of state legislatures considering proposals to develop regional compacts allowing expansion across specific state lines. Response at the national level has been slow, suggesting that liberalization will probably continue to result from action by state governments. When proposals are made, the feasibility of including a *trigger* to move to nationwide expansion is often considered. To date, a number of state laws have excluded this provision. It should be emphasized that the benefits of geographic expansion are not limited by state boundaries. Thus, strong consideration should be given to incorporating these triggers in future legislation.

---

[1] Joe S. Bain, *Industrial Organization*, (John Wiley and Sons, 1959), pp. 98-101 and 295. For a review of structure-conduct-performance studies in banking see Stephen A. Rhoades, "Structure-Performance Studies in Banking: An Updated Summary and Evaluation," Staff Studies, 119, Board of Governors of the Federal Reserve System, 1982. These studies conclude that relative to other industries, in banking the importance of structure on performance is small.

[2] That concentration is of particular concern in local markets was stated in *U.S. v. Philadelphia National Bank* 359 U.S. 31(1963), *U.S. v. Phillipsburg National Bank* 399 U.S. 363-4 U.S. 350 (1970). A case study of interstate mergers suggests that the most significant factor influencing such mergers is the desire to acquire an extensive retail distribution network. See Dave Phillis and Christine Pavel, "Interstate Banking Game Plans: Implications for the Midwest," in *Toward Nationwide Banking*, Federal Reserve Bank of Chicago, 1986.

[3] See Alan S. McCall and Manferd O. Peterson, "The Impact of *De Novo* Commercial Bank Entry," *Compendium of Issues Relating to Branching by Financial Institutions*, Subcommittee on Financial Institutions of the Committee on Banking, Housing and Urban Affairs, United States Senate, October

1976, 499-521; and Donald R. Fraser and Peter S. Rose, "Bank Entry and Bank Performance," *Journal of Finance*, March 1972, pp. 65-78. Bernard Shull, "Structural Impact of Multiple-Office Banking in New York and Virginia," *The Antitrust Bulletin* (Fall 1978) pp. 511-50. Samuel H. Talley, "Recent Trends in Local Banking Market Structure," Staff Economic Studies 89 (Board of Governors of the Federal Reserve System, 1977). Arnold A. Heggestad and Stephen A. Rhoades, "An Analysis of Changes in Bank Market Structure;" *Atlantic Economic Journal*, vol. 4 (Fall 1976), pp. 64-69). These studies were conducted based on 1960-70 data and for that reason may be less conclusive than more current studies because antitrust enforcement was more stringent in the 1970s.

[4] A study by Stephen A. Rhoades on local market concentration across states with different branching status also took into account the relative presence of multibank holding companies. The study concluded that the extent of MBHC activity makes little difference in local market concentration except in the case of unit banking states with MBHCs accounting for less than 50 percent of state deposits. See Stephen A. Rhoades, "Concentration in Local and National Markets," *Economic Review*, Federal Reserve Bank of Atlanta, March 1985.

[5] A relatively high C_3 may be of concern if, for example, the dominant firm in the market is able to affect market price through its output decisions.

[6] For a discussion of the 'cluster approach', see "The product market in commercial banking: Cluster's Last Stand?" Harvey Rosenblum, John J. Di Clemente and Kathleen O'Brien, *Economic Perspectives*, January/February 1985, Federal Reserve Bank of Chicago. John J. Di Clemente, "The Inclusion of Thrifts in Bank Merger Analysis," Staff Memoranda 83-7, Federal Reserve Bank of Chicago, 1983.

[7] This discussion was based on the following regression results:

$$CR = 14.32 - .29(\text{Pop}) - .36(\text{Y}) - .18(\text{S}) + .02(\text{B}) + .02(\text{Pre60})$$
$$\quad (43.1) \quad (-44.4) \quad (-9.4) \quad (-5.7) \quad (.91) \quad (10.9)$$

where CR is the HHI, pop = population in the area, Y = per capita income in the area, S = degrees of regulatory stringency measured as the state charter approval rate during the previous three years, B is a branching binary = 1 if branching is allowed in the market, 0 otherwise, and Pre 60 = B if branching was allowed prior to 1960, zero otherwise. Numbers in parentheses below the estimates are t values. Tests for homoskedasticity could not be rejected.

[8] See Board of Governors Staff, "Recent Changes in the Structure of Commercial Banking," *Federal Reserve Bulletin* (March 1970) pp. 195-210; and

Shull, "Structural Impact of Multioffice Banking in New York and Virginia."

[9] First, the number of banking organizations in local markets in 1980 was estimated ignoring any influence from differing degrees of antitrust enforcement over time. The estimates suggest that branching had a significant negative impact on the number of banking organizations. The estimates were arrived at via an ordinary least squares estimate of a double log form equation, i.e.,

$$Orgs = \underset{(-31.3)}{-8.85} + \underset{(6.92)}{.47} (Pop) + \underset{(18.7)}{.62} (Y) + \underset{(6.6)}{.20} (S) - \underset{(-16.0)}{.28} (B)$$

$$R^2 = .72$$
$$F = 1914$$

where Orgs = number of organizations and the remaining variables are as defined in the previous footnote 7. t values indicate that the impact of each individual variable is statistically significant. However, this significant negative impact is overstated if antitrust legislation was not enforced uniformly prior to and after the Bank Merger Act. This was tested by reestimating the same equation for two groups of local markets, i.e., those having 1980 branching laws in place prior to 1960, and those changing after this period. The two sets of estimates were significantly different. For markets with laws in place prior to 1960, branching decreased significantly the number of banking organizations. However, for the second group the branching impact was not important. More precisely, the estimates below are for the subgroup with branching status determined (1) prior to 1960, and (2) after 1960, respectively:

(1) pre-1960 subgroup: Orgs =

$$\underset{(-22.1)}{-7.70} + \underset{(65.2)}{.48} (pop.) + \underset{(11.9)}{.48} (Y) + \underset{(5.0)}{.17} (S) - \underset{(-20.1)}{.38} (B)$$

$$R^2 = .71$$
$$F = 1531$$

(2) post-1960 subgroup: Orgs =

$$\underset{(-12.6)}{-8.05} + \underset{(31.2)}{.45} (pop.) + \underset{(9.1)}{.56} (Y) + \underset{(6.5)}{.48} (S) - \underset{(-1.0)}{.42} (B)$$

$$R^2 = .78$$
$$F = 504$$

Finally, an attempt was made to account for differences in the two time periods and for the length of time branching had been allowed—i.e., an adjustment period. Different degrees of antitrust enforcement were again accounted for with a binary variable, Pre60. Assuming ten years was the maximum time needed for the impact of branching to be realized, the adjustment period was accounted for with Lth = length of time branching had been allowed (0,1,2,...10). The results of OLS estimates are presented below.

$$Orgs = \underset{(-28.6)}{-8.04} + \underset{(71.5)}{.48} (Pop.) + \underset{(15.6)}{.52} (Y) + \underset{(7.2)}{.22} (S)$$

$$\underset{(-4.1)}{-.27} (B) \ \ \underset{(-11.7)}{-.34} (Pre60) + \underset{(2.8)}{.10} (Lth)$$

$$R^2 = .73$$
$$F = 1384$$

Reestimating and varying the maximum value of Lth resulted in similar results.

[10] See David D. Whitehead and Jan Luytjes, "Can Interstate Banking Increase Competitive Market Performance? An Empirical Test," *Economic Review,* Federal Reserve Bank of Atlanta, January 1984; and Donald L. Alexander, "An Empirical Test of the Mutual Forbearance Hypothesis: The Case of Bank Holding Companies," *Southern Economic Journal,* (July 1985), pp.122-140.

[11] Analysis for individual years generally resulted in similar findings. For an analysis of 1984 data see Douglas Evanoff and Diana Fortier, "Geographic Expansion in Commercial Banking: Inferences from Intrastate Activity," in *Towards Nationwide Banking.* See statement by Paul Volcker before the Subcommittee on Financial Institutions, Supervision, Regulation and Insurance of the Committee on Banking, Finance and Urban Affairs; U.S. House of Representatives, April 24, 1985. 71, *Federal Reserve Bulletin* 430 (1985). Additional studies evaluating small banks' ability to compete include Rhoades, Stephen A. and Donald T. Savage, "Can Small Banks Compete?". *Bankers Magazine,* vol. 164 (Jan.-Feb. 1981), pp. 59-65; Leon Korobow, "The Move to Statewide Banking in New York and New Jersey," *The Banker,* September 1974, pp.11-33.

[12] For an example of a denial on financial grounds, see Corporation for International Agricultural Production Limited 70 *Federal Reserve Bulletin* 39 (1984). For an example of commitments made in light of financial concerns see IVB Financial Corp. 70 *Federal Reserve Bulletin* 42 (1984).

[13] See Jack M. Guttentag and Edward S. Herman, *Banking Structure and Performance,* New York University, February 1967; also Robert Weintraub and Paul Jessup, "A Study of Selected Banking Services by Bank Size, Structure, and Location," Subcommittee on Domestic Finance of the House Committee on Banking and Currency, Washington, 1964. For a more recent and comprehensive review of the impact of branching on various aspects of the banking industry see Larry Mote, "The Perennial Issue: Branch Banking," *Business Conditions* (February 1974) pp. 3-23; and Gary Gilbert and William Longbrake, "The Effects of Branching by Financial Institutions on Competition, Productive Efficiency and Stability: An Examination of the Evidence," *Journal of Bank Research* (Part I - Autumn 1973, Part II - Winter 1974) pp. 154-167, 298-307; Larry Frieder, et. al., *Commercial Banking and Interstate Ex-*

pansion - *Issues, Prospects, and Strategies,* Ann Arbor, UMI Press, 1985; and U.S. Department of the Treasury, *Geographic Restrictions on Commercial Banking in the United States,* January 1981. In the present study, the analysis of the potential impact of interstate activity on the customer is based on the activity occurring via branching activity. If geographic expansion proceeds by bank holding company expansion the impact on the customer could differ.

[14] Pete Rose, James Kolari, and Kenneth W. Riener, "A National Survey Study of Bank Services and Prices Arrayed by Size and Structure," *Journal of Bank Research* (Summer 1985) pp. 72-85.

[15] For a discussion and evidence on this issue see Donald Fraser and Pete Rose, "Bank Entry and Bank Performance," *Journal of Finance* (March, 1972) pp. 67-78; also Donald Jacobs, "The Interaction Effects of Restrictions On Branching and Other Regulations," *Journal of Finance* (May 1965) pp. 332-49. Also Verle Johnston, "Comparative Performance of Unit and Branch Banks," in *Proceedings of a Conference on Bank Structure and Competition,* Federal Reserve Bank of Chicago, March 1967. For an analysis which considers both the source and use of funds, see Constance Dunham, "Interstate Banking and the Outflow of Local Funds." *New England Economic Review,* (Federal Reserve Bank of Boston, March/April 1986), pp. 7-19.

[16] See Robert A. Eisenbeis, "Local Banking Markets for Business Loans," *Journal of Bank Research* (Summer 1971) pp. 30-39; and Donald P. Jacobs, *Business Loan Costs and Bank Market Structure.* New York: Columbia University Press, 1971; and also Paul A. Meyer, "Price Discrimination, Regional Loan Rates, and the Structure of the Banking Industry," *Journal of Finance* (March 1967) pp. 37-48.

[17] Peter L. Struck and Lewis Mandell, "The Effect of Bank Deregulation on Small Business: A Note," *Journal of Finance* (June 1983) pp. 1025-1031.

[18] See Thomas Gilligan, Michael Smirlock, and William Marshall, "Scale and Scope Economies in the Multi-Product Banking Firm," *Journal of Monetary Economics* (May 1984) pp. 393-405. For other discussions of economies of scale see Jeffrey A. Clark, "Estimates of Economies of Scale in Banking Using a Generalized Functional Form," *Journal of Money, Credit, and Banking,* (February 1984) pp. 53-68; and George Benston, Gerry Hanweck, and David Humphrey, "Scale Economies in Banking: A Restructuring and Reassessment," *Journal of*

Money, Credit, and Banking (February 1984) pp. 435-56.

[19] See Mote or Gilbert and Longbrake for a review of past studies. See also Rose, Kolari, and Riener; and Donald T. Savage and Stephen A. Rhoades, "The Effects of Branch Banking on Pricing, Profits, and Efficiency of Unit Banks," *Proceedings of a Conference on Bank Structure and Competition,* Federal Reserve Bank of Chicago, 1979, pp. 187-95. Prices could also be impacted by market pre-emptive behavior. Branch banks could "flood" the market with offices aimed at minimizing the potential market for new entrants. This behavior could increase costs that would be passed on to the customer. See Douglas Evanoff, "The Impact of Branch Banking on Service Accessibility," Staff Memoranda 85-9, Federal Reserve Bank of Chicago, 1985.

[20] See Donald Savage and David Humphrey, "Branching Laws and Banking Offices," *Journal of Money, Credit, and Banking* (March 1979) pp. 153-60 and William Seaver and Donald Fraser, "Branch Banking and the Availability of Banking Offices in Nonmetropolitan Areas," *Atlantic Economic Journal* (July 1983) pp. 72-8. Other studies evaluating the impact of branching on service accessibility include Robert F. Lanzillotti and Thomas A. Saving, "State Branching Restrictions and the Availability of Branching Service," *Journal of Money, Credit, and Banking* (November 1969) pp. 778-88; William Seaver and Donald Fraser, "Branch Banking and the Availability of Banking Services in Metropolitan Areas," *Journal of Financial and Quantitative Analysis* (March 1979) pp. 153-60. For a discussion of service accessibility measured in a spatial context see Evanoff, *op. cit.*

[21] The correlation coefficients supporting this are as shown below (* indicates that the correlations are *not* significantly different from zero.)

	Change in population ($\frac{absolute}{percentage}$)	
	Metro	Rural
Change in # of banks ($\frac{absolute}{percentage}$)		
Branching areas		
offices	.26/.41	.53/.26
organizations	.09*/.34	.31/.30
Unit banking areas		
offices	.34/.04*	.34/.31
organizations	.17*/.23	.38/.34

Article Twelve

Recent Bank Failures

The number of bank failures in the U.S. has increased steadily over the past several years. It reached 120 in 1985 — far more than in any other year since the Great Depression. In addition, the Federal Deposit Insurance Corporation continues to rate more than 1100 banks as "problem" banks based on its assessment of their capital, assets, management, earnings, and liquidity (CAMEL rating). These figures seem to indicate that the rise in bank failures that began in 1982 has not yet run its course. This *Letter* examines recent trends in bank failures, their causes, and ways in which failures are resolved by bank regulators.

Recent experiences

Until 1981, bank failures in the post-World War II era averaged about six per year and, except for the occasional failure of a very large bank (e.g., Franklin National in 1974), were not a source of great concern to most observers. Since 1982, however, the number of bank failures has grown rapidly, rising from 10 in 1981 to the post-Depression record level of 120 in 1985 (see chart).

The assets of banks that failed in 1985 amounted to $9.1 billion, or nearly three times the $3.3 billion 1984 level (a figure that excludes the Continental Illinois rescue). More than half of the 1985 total was due to the failure of a single New York savings bank (Bowery Savings Bank, assets of $5.3 billion). Except for the assets of this organization and one other sizable savings bank (also in New York), the total volume of assets in failed banks in 1985 was nearly identical to that in 1984. In all, the assets of failed banks in 1985 represented less than one-half of one percent of total U.S. bank assets.

Banks that failed in 1985 generally were smaller than those that failed in 1984. The smaller average size of failed banks in 1985 mainly reflected the greater concentration of bank failures within farmbelt states, where banks tend to be relatively small. For the year, the average size failed bank held $28 million in assets (ignoring the two large savings bank failures), as compared to $41 million in assets in 1984. The largest commercial

bank to fail in 1985 held assets of $214 million, while the smallest held assets of $2.7 million. All but six of the 120 banks that failed in 1985 had assets of less than $100 million.

Economic factors in recent failures

Empirical research offers somewhat limited insight into the broader causes of bank failures by linking them to such economic variables as the unemployment rate, real interest rates, and the level of corporate debt burden. An analysis of recent failures, however, suggests that more specific economic factors have played an important role.

Certainly, with sharp recessions in 1980 and 1982, commercial bank loan quality has suffered. For a number of banks, the problems have persisted well into the recovery because asset quality has been slow to improve in many lending areas. Specifically, an overall improvement has been hampered by a shift from a high-inflation to a low-inflation environment, a relatively strong dollar, persistently high real interest rates, reduced export demand for commodities, and declining farmland and energy prices. Thus, many banks remain saddled with poor quality agricultural, energy, and real estate loans.

Geographic distribution

The geographic distribution of failed banks supports this view. From 1982 through 1985, there were 289 bank failures in the U.S. Seventy percent (201) of these failures occurred in ten states whose economic fortunes are closely linked to the farming and energy industries. These states include Kansas, Iowa, Nebraska, Illinois, Missouri, Oregon, Oklahoma, and Texas. Two other states — California and Tennessee — also experienced numerous bank failures during this period. Failures in Tennessee during the 1982-85 period (31) were largely the result of a major fraud and insider abuse scandal involving numerous commonly owned banks. Bank failures in California (20) were the result of a diversity of factors including agricultural and real estate lending problems. Foreign loans do not appear to have contributed significantly to bank failures in any state during the 1982-85 period. Furthermore, it is important to note that twenty-seven states experienced only one or no bank failures during the 1982-85 period.

The problems of farm banks — those with more than 25 percent of their loans in agricultural credits — have become most acute in recent years. In 1985, farm bank failures accounted for slightly more than half (62 of 120) of all bank failures. This compares to one-third in 1984 and less than one-fourth in 1983 and 1982. Nebraska (13), Iowa (10), and Kansas (9) led the way in farm bank failures in 1985. Eight other states also recorded a total of thirty farm bank failures in 1985. Depressed farm land prices and commodity prices are expected to persist in 1986 and will likely cause additional farm bank failures.

A substantial number (16) of non-farm bank failures also occurred in Texas and Oklahoma last year. Many of these failures, as well as several failures in Wyoming, can be attributed to energy-related loans exposure. The recent plunge in oil prices will only exacerbate such problems.

A scattering of bank failures occurred among other states during 1985. California recorded seven bank failures, while New York had four and Florida two. The cause of insolvencies in these states is more difficult to pinpoint. The presence of important real estate markets within these states suggests that problems in this lending area may have been responsible for some failures.

Effects of deregulation
In addition to farm, energy, and real estate lending problems, some economists believe that financial deregulation and innovation are contributing to bank failures in the 1980s. Deregulation of deposit interest rates has been accompanied by increased competition from new sources — banking and nonbanking alike. This heightened level of competition has meant that banks now operate in a harsher and less forgiving environment in which poor management, fraud, and insider abuse (a contributing factor in as many as three-fifths of all failures since 1980) exact greater penalties than before.

Deposit deregulation and expanded lending and investment powers have been argued to contribute to instability in banking by fostering increased risk-taking by banks. Many argue that the assumption of additional risk is encouraged by what is generally perceived to be a deposit insurance subsidy that partially insulates banks from the costs of assuming higher levels of risk. Deregulation, they argue, gives banks greater scope to act on the incentives to take risks. Some economists, however, take exception to the view that deregulation is at the core of the current spate of bank failures. They contend that the failures are due simply to deteriorated conditions in the agriculture and energy sectors.

Handling failed banks
When a bank fails, the FDIC — a government-run corporation that insures depositors up to $100,000 against loss — can exercise several options in its role of protecting depositors. Its settlement practices are what some observers believe have encouraged banks — especially large banks — to incur excessive risks in recent years.

When a bank fails, the FDIC usually employs either a deposit payoff or a purchase and assumption ("P&A"). In a deposit payoff, the FDIC pays depositors the value of their accounts (up to $100,000), and sells the failed bank's assets to pay off creditors, including the insurance fund and uninsured depositors. Creditors suffer a loss if the proceeds of the asset sale do not cover creditor claims.

In a P&A, the failed bank is sold to another financial institution that is willing to assume most of the bank's liabilities (including all deposits). In return, the acquiring institution receives the failed bank's good assets (performing loans, securities, physical plant) plus cash from the FDIC for the amount by which the assumed liabilities exceed the purchased assets minus the premium paid by the acquiring bank.

Because of the manner in which the FDIC has handled P&As for bank failures, few uninsured depositors at large institutions have suffered losses. Critics of the FDIC argue that the FDIC's settlement practices and the government's

FDIC-Insured Bank Failures

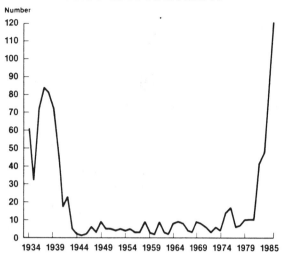

Number

120 110 100 90 80 70 60 50 40 30 20 10 0

1934 1939 1944 1949 1954 1959 1964 1969 1974 1979 1985

pledge never to permit a large bank to fail have created *de facto* deposit insurance for all deposits at large banks, including those that are legally uninsured.

They argue that in the past this has bestowed a deposit-gathering advantage on the largest banks and reduced the crucial role of "market discipline" in restraining risk-taking. Because past guarantees made smaller failed banks more likely to be liquidated at a loss to the uninsured depositor, they may have encouraged large depositors to place funds only in the largest banks.

Without deposit insurance, market discipline would dictate that riskier banks pay more for their funds to compensate depositors for taking greater risks. With *de facto* insurance for all deposits, poorly managed banks or those with low quality assets can raise funds almost as cheaply as much stronger institutions because depositors have little to fear about losing their funds and therefore will not demand as high a risk premium.

Supporters of current settlement practices point to the dangers of moving toward greater market discipline. The present system of formal and informal guarantees, they argue, has worked well to create a sound and stable banking system. Any shift to increased market discipline

could create destabilizing effects by forcing the private sector to speculate on the health of individual banks. The continual prospect of runs precipitated by rumors of troubled banks could jeopardize the entire banking system. In response, many banks would probably become much more conservative in their lending policies and restrict the availability of credit to all but the most creditworthy customers.

Proponents of this view argue in favor of continued reliance on the P&A or, alternatively, a government takeover of large failed banks — an option that, in effect, was exercised in the 1984 Continental Illinois episode. Such takeovers result in losses to shareholders but protect depositors and allow the troubled bank to remain in operation under the regulators' control. Takeovers also give formal recognition to the fact that federal guarantees become the largest asset of the failed bank and that federal guarantors comprise the bank's largest claim holder.

Summary
Last year was a record year for bank failures, with many of them involving relatively small institutions concentrated in a small number of farmbelt and energy-producing states. Banks in those states have been adversely affected by a number of factors including two recessions, persistently high real interest rates, a strong dollar, and declining prices for commodities, farm land, and energy.

A similarly large number of bank failures is expected during 1986 with the failures again to be heavily concentrated within the farmbelt region. Increased failures also could occur among energy banks — particularly in view of the recent and sizable drop in oil prices. However, because the failures will result from specific economic developments whose impacts vary by region and bank portfolio, they do not signal any fundamental weakness in the banking system.

Anthony W. Cyrnak

Deposit Insurance and Bank Failures

While a business failure is painful to those whose dreams and hard work are wiped out, most people recognize failure as a necessary aspect of success. This relationship is well summed up in the aphorism, "nothing ventured, nothing gained and nothing lost." Just as important is the healthy measure of restraint provided by the prospect of failure. The possibility and cost of failure can help avert unprofitable ventures and unfortunate errors by providing a powerful incentive for the decision maker to accept the necessity of making painful choices.

Why, then, is bank failure considered to be so terrible that federal deposit insurance is required? In many important respects, a bank failure is less costly than the failure of many other enterprises. The products provided by one bank are similar to those provided by many other institutions. Checking and savings account services usually are available at scores of institutions, including other banks, savings and loan associations, credit unions and stock brokerage firms—even non-local institutions. Mortgages and consumer loans are available from an even greater number of sources, including depository institutions, mortgage companies, consumer loan companies, merchants, and individuals. Business loans are available from local and, for larger companies, non-local

banks and thrifts, insurance companies, factors, and other businesses.

While a bank's customers lose their business relationship with a bank and its knowledge of them, the loss is less than when most other suppliers fail. For example, the failure of a machinery manufacturer could make spare parts, repair and replacement services unavailable. A distributor's failure might require the development of new channels of supply and sources of information about products and reliability. Often the failed enterprise is unique. In contrast, one bank and its products are very much like another. Only for people in one-bank towns might the failure of the sole bank present a serious problem— and then only until the services are offered by another institution.

Because banks are so similar, their employees' skills are transferrable to other financial institutions. The teller in one bank needs little training to work in another. A lending officer can even benefit from a failure if she can bring her customers with her to another bank. In contrast, employees of many other enterprises often have specialized skills of little value except to their company. The only bank employees who really lose from a failure are the top officers. Not only might they be blamed for the bank's collapse,

With bank troubles again in the news, deposit insurance is receiving its closest scrutiny since the Depression years. This analysis questions whether a new approach to insuring deposits might be in order—with depository institutions able to choose between several public insuring agencies or even turning to private insuring organizations.

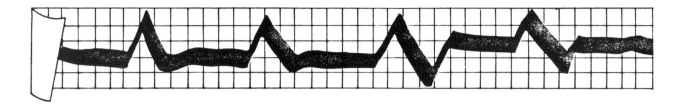

but they will forego the value of the relationships they have established. But, if fear of failure is to be beneficial, this is all to the good.

The shareholders of a failed bank, like its officers, bear costs. But, again, this can prove healthy, for the essence of a private-property, free-enterprise system is that residual owners reap the losses as well as the benefits from their investments. In any event, bank shareholders are in no different position from shareholders of other enterprises. Indeed, when one considers that a bank's fixed assets can be transferred to many other enterprises (including successor banks) at less cost than can the assets of many failed enterprises, a bank's owners face less risk with respect to a failure than most other owners.[1]

This leaves only the creditors, and here is where banks differ importantly from other enterprises. But first the similarities should be mentioned. Creditors are investors with rights over other investors. Debt instruments usually specify the amounts to be paid and the time of payment to their holders, with precedent over the equity holders. But, as with equity holders, creditors accept the risk of non-repayment, which is reflected in their contracts (debt obligations) with the equity holders. Debt holders, like other investors, put up their funds and take their chances. The possibility of failure gives them reason to monitor an enterprise's activities and to insist on a return no worse than they could get for similarly risky investments. In this regard, a bank is a safer investment than many others because its activities are relatively easy to control and comprehend and are subjected to audit. Indeed, losses to creditors (depositors) were not great before the Great Depression. Between 1900 and 1920, deposits in the 1,789 banks that suspended operations averaged 0.10 percent of total deposits each year. Over the 1921-1929 period, 5,712 banks were suspended (an annual percentage of 2.30 of the number active); deposits in these banks averaged 0.42 percent of total

deposits per year. But, after the affairs of the suspended banks were cleared up, the annual losses borne by depositors as a group were only 0.15 percent (Benston (1973), Table II, p. 12).

The Difference Between Banks and Other Enterprises

The important difference is in the demand deposits form of credit. Demand deposits and savings deposits that actually can be withdrawn on demand are much more than investments in banks. These are assets that permit depositors to effect transactions at relatively low cost while providing a means of making investments in the amounts and for the periods desired. Because deposits and withdrawals tend to offset each other, bankers learned hundreds of years ago that they could invest a large proportion of these funds in longer maturity, usually higher yielding assets. This combination of instant possible withdrawal for individual depositors and relative stability of the total of funds invested by depositors as a group gives rise to both profitability and risk in banking.

Unlike bank demand depositors, creditors of other enterprises cannot withdraw their investments when they wish. If a bondholder of an ordinary corporation believes the corporation may be unable to repay the debt as promised, the most that person can do is sell the bond before the purchaser learns the bad news. The bondholder cannot get the corporation to repay the bond until it is legally due. But a depositor who fears a bank failure can withdraw funds in person or by writing a check. A rapid withdrawal of funds by depositors may force the bank to sell assets at distress prices or to borrow at high rates. That may produce losses that exceed the stockholders' investment and have to be absorbed by remaining depositors or other debt holders. Therefore, depositors are well-advised to remove their funds if the probability of loss exceeds the cost of making another banking arrangement plus interest that would be foregone as a consequence of the withdrawal. That is why a run on

---

[1]See Tussig (1967) for a further discussion.

a bank by panicked depositors is very difficult to stop before the bank is forced to suspend withdrawals and possibly fail.

Were it not for three factors, losses from bank runs should not be considered of greater social concern than losses from other business failures. The first factor is the importance of public faith in a safe system for transferring funds. If people feared bank failures, the argument goes, they would be unwilling to accept checks in payment for goods and services, which would increase transactions costs to the detriment of society. But checks are widely and readily accepted despite the risk that the payor may not have funds on deposit when the check is presented to the bank for payment. Though a bank failure represented an additional risk, checks were widely and increasingly used as money before the advent of federal deposit insurance, even in the 1920s when over 600 banks a year suspended operations. Prior to establishment of the Federal Reserve in 1913, notes issued by individual banks were widely used as money, despite the risk that the issuing banks could fail before the notes were redeemed. Consequently, this is not a convincing argument for having a different public policy towards bank failures than towards other business failures.

The second argument for special treatment of banks relates to the depositors' costs of determining and dealing with the riskiness of their investments. Bank deposits, particularly demand deposits, often cannot be diversified efficiently among several banks. If this could be done, depositors could reduce their risk of the expected losses from bank failures generally (which was only 0.15 percent per year even during the 1920s). But such diversification would be costly to many depositors. Rather than having each depositor assessing and monitoring the operations of banks and the riskiness of their portfolios, it seems more cost-effective for a government agency to supervise the banks. But the same argument applies to many (perhaps most) other enterprises. Investors in these enterprises also must assess the risks and returns expected from their investments; in this regard, banks are likely to be easier

to analyze than are other firms. But where small deposits are involved, the depositors' costs in assessing and diversifying risk probably exceed expected benefits. Therefore, social policy could be directed toward making riskless investments and depository services available to people with relatively little to invest. But this protection could be provided by bank-purchased private insurance, rather than a government agency, much as other enterprises and individuals insure their customers and themselves against risks.

Bank Runs

The third argument, preventing multiple bank runs, is the only really strong one for considering bank deposits differently from other investments and services. Demand depositors have a great incentive to remove their funds as soon as they believe a bank **might** fail. Hence, rumors about a bank's financial condition or the failure of similar banks might touch off runs on well-managed banks. Their failures, in turn, reduce the monetary base as people exchange fractional-reserve bank deposits for 100 percent reserve currency, resulting in a multiple contraction of the money supply and the failure of more banks and other businesses. This is what happened, in part, in the 1930s.[2]

While the Federal Reserve can step in to stop this chain-reaction by making reserves available to banks to replace those withdrawn, it did not do so in the 1930s. Between 1930 and 1933, 9,096 commercial banks were suspended, representing an annual average of 11.3 percent of all banks and 4.1 percent of the deposits. The average annual loss to depositors in these banks averaged 0.81 percent. While this was less than a third of the yield on investments (the yield on prime commercial papers ranged from 3.59 percent in 1930 to 1.73 percent in 1933), it probably

---

[2]The Federal Reserve's present policy of reserve-path targeting, however, makes it likely that reserves would not be permitted to decline as they did in the 1930s. Indeed, it makes intervention automatic.

[3]Though these failures no doubt hurt the economy, most scholars agree the banks were primarily the victims rather than the cause of the Great Depression. Warburton (1966) carefully studied the relationship between bank failures by county during the Depression. He concludes: "there was a

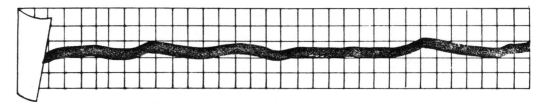

was large for affected depositors who did not hold diversified portfolios.[3]

Bank runs also played an important role in previous financial collapses before the 1930s. "Black Thursday" 1873 saw the failure of Jay Cooke's banking house and the first closing of the New York Stock Exchange. It was followed (perhaps causally) by six years of depression. The failure in 1884 of the Marine National Bank and of former President Ulysses Grant's firm, Grant & Ward, sparked runs and the consequent failure of numerous banks and brokerage houses. The Panic of 1893 was touched off by the 1890 failure of the London banking firm of Baring Brothers, which specialized in financing U.S. enterprises. Baring's European creditors demanded that Americans pay their debts in gold. As a consequence, the base money supply was depleted, a multiple contraction resulted, and 1891 saw a mini-panic. During the following 1893 panic, more than 600 banks and 13 of every 1,000 businesses failed in perhaps the nation's second deepest depression (after the depression of 1837) before 1930. The New York Clearing House suspended convertibility to specie, which ended the run. J. P. Morgan also helped by negotiating a sale in Europe of a $100 million U.S. bond issue. Panic struck again in 1907 when New York City and several corporations were unable to sell high-yielding bond issues. The Knickerbocker Trust Company failed (largely as a consequence of speculation with depositors' funds) and several major banks experienced severe runs. Again, the New York Clearing House suspended convertibility to specie and J. P. Morgan later helped increase reserves with European loans and U.S. Treasury deposits.

Creation of the Federal Reserve in 1913 was supposed to rid the country of these recurring collapses. As the lender of last resort, with great resources and the power of the printing press, it should have been able to better the Clearing House's and Morgan's record. But, when the Bank of the United States collapsed in 1930, the Fed did not prevent the failure of over a third of the banks during the next several years. Establishment of the Federal Deposit Insurance Corporation (FDIC) in 1933, though, appears to have done the job. Though 488 commercial and mutual savings banks were suspended from 1934 through 1942, most of these were leftovers from the pre-FDIC period. From 1943 through 1982, an average of only seven banks a year were closed or merged with FDIC assistance. Most importantly, bank runs appear to be a thing of the past. However, the losses incurred by large depositors when the Penn Square Bank in Oklahoma City was liquidated rather than merged into a solvent bank by the FDIC and the reported shaky condition of some very large banks with loans extended to such borrowers as Brazil, Mexico or International Harvester have provoked some concern about the possibility of runs by uninsured depositors.

Depositors in savings and loan associations, credit unions and a few mutual savings banks also are protected by government insurance agencies—the Federal Savings and Loan Insurance Corporation (FSLIC) and the National Credit Union Share Insurance Fund (NCUSIF). In recent years, unexpectedly increasing interest rates together with the specialization of savings and loans in long-term, fixed-interest assets (mortgages) have resulted in a relatively large number of failures and forced mergers. The increasing number of "troubled institutions" has renewed interest in the present deposit insurance system. This interest is expressed in the Garn-St Germain Depository Institutions Act of 1982, which calls for a study of deposit insurance and a report to the Congress by this April.

The Benefits From Deposit Insurance

Deposit insurance has the salutary effect of obviating bank runs by assuring insured depositors

massive contraction of deposits nationally during the early 1930s relative to the rate of growth during the 1920s, of which less than one-fourth was accounted for by deposits in suspended banks. This indicated that the Depression of the 1930s could not be explained by the impact of balances of payment resulting from adverse conditions in particular industries or areas, but was due to, or at least associated with, some potent force operating on a national scale." (p. 2).

(currently, those with less than $100,000 in an account) that their funds are safe. It also spares most depositors the cost of learning about the operation of banks. But, as a consequence, deposit insurance frees banks from the discipline and cost of those depositors' concerns. Bankers need not pay depositors a premium (in interest, "free" services, or other concessions) to compensate them for the risk of investing in the bank. Thus bank profits are increased if the reduction in their cost of deposits is greater than the cost of the deposit insurance. Such is the case for smaller banks, and was particularly so in the 1930s when the FDIC was established. Initially, FDIC insurance covered depositor accounts up to $2,500. It was raised to $5,000 in 1934, $10,000 in 1950, $15,000 in 1966, $20,000 in 1969, $40,000 in 1974 and $100,000 in 1980.

Federal insurance thus covered most of the depositors (and deposits) of small banks. It was particularly valuable to them because the public had reason to fear for the safety of their funds in small banks; 93 percent of the banks suspended in 1930-1931 had total loans and investments under $2 million, and 70 percent were under $500,000. From the beginning, the FDIC insurance premium has been assessed as a small percentage of **total** deposits, whether or not insured. Thus the large banks, which experienced much lower failure rates and which served many customers with deposit accounts exceeding $5,000 in the 1930s, have subsidized the small banks. But in return they benefited from banking legislation through the prohibition of interest on demand deposits. Golembe has estimated that in the early 1930s, the costs of deposit insurance to the large banks were offset almost exactly by savings from the interest prohibition (Golembe, 1975, p. 7). The small banks also avoided competition

because national banks were denied the right to branch (except as permitted by state law).[4]

Savings and loan associations did not experience the massive number of suspensions that plagued commercial banks in the early 1930s; only 526 of the S&Ls active as of January 1930 (4.4 percent) were suspended from 1930 through 1933. The FSLIC was established by the National Housing Act of 1934 as a means of supporting the housing industry. That purpose dominated government policy towards S&Ls until, perhaps, the last few years when the institutions' survival became an important concern.

Problems With Deposit Insurance

If deposit insurance removes the concern of most depositors for the safety of their funds, it gives bankers an incentive to put the depositors' funds into riskier assets unless the FDIC or FSLIC prevents them from doing so. If a bank encounters trouble, the FDIC and FSLIC pay off the depositors; if profits are made, the shareholders get them. True, in the event of failure the bank's shareholders lose their investments (including the value of the bank charter) first. But they can lose no more. Consequently, unless the FDIC or FSLIC imposes a risk-related insurance premium, an effective minimum capital (stockholders' investment) requirement or other risk-related costs and controls, the banks' expected gains from additional risk-taking will continue to exceed the expected losses.[5]

U. S. history prior to the FDIC bears this out and also provides lessons that should be heeded. Deposit guarantee systems were established in New York (1828), Vermont (1831), Indiana (1834), Ohio (1845) and Iowa (1858).[6] The New York and Vermont systems were state run, the others

---

[4]See Benston (1982) for a description of the offsetting economic advantages garnered by suppliers of financial services from 1930s federal legislation.

[5]This conclusion is demonstrated analytically and rigorously in a number of papers, including Sharpe (1978), Koehn and Santonero (1980) and Hanweck (1982). Also see Flannery (1982) for a clear and concise explication and numerical example.

[6]See Federal Deposit Insurance Corporation (1952, 1953 and 1956) and Edwards (1933) for descriptions from which the following narrative was drawn.

[7]However, it should be noted that the New York State system was phased out as bank charters were granted and renewed under the free (entry) banking law. As banks left the insurance system, the premiums rose considerably.

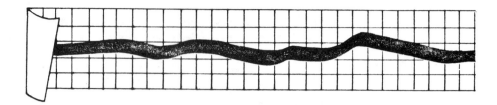

were based on mutual agreements among participating banks. They operated successfully, largely because they empowered system officials to monitor operations of the participating banks and to control excessive risk-taking.[7] Yet a second wave of deposit guarantee plans for state banks proved less successful. With one exception (Mississippi), the plans did not include effective supervision and they failed. These included the compulsory plans of Oklahoma (1908), Nebraska (1909), and South Dakota (1916) and the voluntary plans of Kansas (1909), Texas (1910), and Washington (1917). Since depositors were told that their money was safe, there was a great incentive for unscrupulous operators to take excessive risks; the record shows greater failure rates of guaranteeed banks than among similar non-guaranteed banks operating in the same areas. The Mississippi plan (1915), which included supervision and bank examinations, continued until 1930. Thus, effective supervision appears to be a necessary aspect of deposit insurance.

FSLIC deposit insurance appears intentionally related to risk-taking by insured savings and loan associations. Though technically the mutual associations' liabilities are shares, in actuality they are (except for time certificates) deposits withdrawable on demand by the "shareholders." Hence, were S&L deposits not insured, depositors would have reason to be concerned about the associations' concentration in long-term, local, fixed-interest mortgages. Should the market value of real estate securing the mortgages collapse, or should interest rates unexpectedly surge, the market value of an association's assets could be reduced to less than its liabilities. Fearful depositors would have the same incentive to remove their funds as would depositors in commercial banks. Thus FSLIC insurance prevents

runs on S&Ls and permits them to hold a poorly diversified portfolio, consisting mainly of mortgages.[8]

Past and Present Methods of Coping with the Problems

Restrictions on Entry and Encouragement of Mergers

The FDIC and the other regulatory agencies initially dealt with the problem of bank failures by restricting bank charters. In the 1920s, an average of 361 banks a year was chartered. But from 1935 through 1944, an average of only 53 banks was chartered annually. Understandably, few banks were chartered during World War II. But the expansionary period of 1945 through 1959 saw an annual average of only 94 newly chartered banks. Peltzman (1963, p. 48) estimated that, had the relatively unrepressed chartering policies of the 1920s continued during the 1936 through 1962 period, about 4,500 new banks would have been chartered rather than the 2,272 that were permitted. Partly as a consequence of this restrictive policy, very few banks failed, but fewer banks were established to serve the public.

Not until James Saxon became Comptroller of the Currency was this policy changed. In just four years, 1962 through 1965, he approved charters for 514 national banks, twice the number chartered in the previous 12 years. Contrary to the predictions of Saxon's detractors, neither the newly chartered banks nor their competitors failed in greater proportions than other banks. States also increased the number of bank charters issued to 124 per year over the 1962-65 period—an increase from the annual average of 86 over the previous four years. Though there have been relatively more bank failures in recent years, the number is still small and appears unrelated to the more liberal post-1960s chartering policy.

The regulatory authorities also have encouraged mergers among banks as a means of reducing the probability of failure. Until the Bank Merger Act of 1960 required the regulatory agencies and

[8]Federal authorities also have supported S&Ls' concentration in mortgages by imposing ceilings on deposit interest by giving them greatly reduced taxes based on their investment in mortgages, by developing a national market in mortgages with the Federal Home Loan Mortgage Corporation and by establishing Federal Home Loan Banks that lend money to S&Ls raised with government-guaranteed securities.

> **"[Under previous constraints] the risks banks undertook were relatively easy to monitor and control. [Under deregulation] the possibility that greater risks will result in more failures must be considered...."**

encouraged the Justice Department to evaluate and challenge mergers, their impact on competition was not considered important; safety was the primary concern.

State-enacted legal restrictions on branching have had a negative effect on bank solvency. Almost all of the banks suspended in the 1920s and 1930s were unit banks: only 10 banks with more than two branches outside their home city failed during this period. It is difficult to separate the effects of regional economic depressions and small size from unit banking as causes of the suspension of over 9,000 such banks. Still, it seems clear that the legal prohibition against banks diversifying their locations—and consequently their assets and liabilities—impaired their ability to survive liquidity or local economic crises.

In any event, reducing the number of banks—and thus competition among banks—by controlling entry and encouraging mergers is no longer a viable policy, and not just because of cost to the public. Many unchartered enterprises now offer banking services to the public: these include brokerage firms, money market funds, and specialized lenders including mortgage companies, finance companies, retail stores, factors, and insurance companies. While interstate deposit branching still is prohibited, most large banks maintain loan and customer service offices in cities around the country, as well as affiliates that specialize in such products as mortgage and personal cash loans. Smaller banks can diversify their portfolios by purchasing loans from other banks and by investing in money market instruments, such as U.S. Treasury and state and municipal obligations. Thus, reducing bank failures by controlling entry and exit appears to be neither necessary nor even possible.

The opposite policy has been applied to federal savings and loan associations, with new federal S&Ls encouraged as a means of supporting housing. Between 1933 and 1941, the number of federally chartered associations increased by 162 a year. During World War II, few federal charters were granted. But from 1946 through 1970, federally chartered S&Ls increased by 25 annually.

The recent financial problems of many S&Ls, though, do not appear attributable to excessive chartering. Rather, they are related to traditional restrictions on the portfolios they could hold and services they could offer to the public. The thrift institutions' solvency was never in doubt as long as real estate values increased, interest rates did not surge unexpectedly, and interest rate ceilings on deposits were effective in keeping their costs down but not in encouraging excessive disintermediation. The provisions of the Depository Institutions Deregulation and Monetary Control Act of 1980 and the Garn-St Germain Act of 1982, which permitted thrift institutions to offer most banking services and market rates of interest, came too late for many institutions to diversify their assets and liabilities successfully.

The Federal Home Loan Bank Board's policy change since the late 1970s that removed constraints on branching by federally-chartered S&Ls permitted the institutions to serve the public more effectively. Yet it was timed unfortunately from the standpoint of maintaining solvency. Branching is a means of offering depositors a return on their funds in the form of convenience. But it is often more efficient to offer them direct cash payments through interest and a wider range of services (especially checking and consumer loans). Hence, since the S&Ls can now offer these services to consumers, many branches established earlier are likely to have become financial drains on the associations. Thus, incomplete deregulation inadvertently exacerbated the S&Ls' solvency problems.

Restrictions on Products and Prices

The debacle of the 1930s gave rise to the Banking Act of 1933. This act prohibited commercial banks from underwriting and dealing in corporate securities, prohibited the payment of interest on demand deposits, and imposed a ceiling on savings and time deposits interest rates (Regulation Q). Banks and thrift institutions also were constrained over the years from competing directly and from engaging in non-traditional banking activities. One consequence of these constraints was that the risks banks undertook

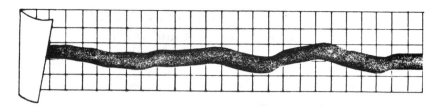

were relatively easy to monitor and control. Another was that, in the 1970s, as nominal interest rates increased and as fund transfer technologies became more efficient, unregulated institutions successfully bid for many of the regulated institutions' depositors. Banks and thrifts also attempted to enter new areas through subsidiaries, one-bank holding company affiliates, and legal expansion of powers. While the result has been greater returns and more choice for consumers, the risks undertaken by depository institutions also are likely to have increased. Nevertheless, re-regulation hardly seems possible or desirable. The possibility that the greater risks will result in more failures, then, must be considered and dealt with.

Equity (Capital) Requirements

Since the stockholders of a bank or S&L absorb losses first, a sufficiently high equity investment would inhibit them strongly from taking risks. Indeed, as long as a deposit insuring agency can step in and liquidate an institution by merger or dissolution before the value of its assets declines to less than its insured deposits, the agency assumes no risk. (Fraud, of course, can create the deceptive appearance of positive equity; therefore audits, for fraud are particularly important.) Consequently, the supervising authorities have viewed capital adequacy requirements as a means of reducing the possibility of failures.

However, the authorities' effectiveness in enforcing edicts is open to question. Mayne (1972) studied 364 randomly sampled Fourth Federal Reserve District banks to determine whether the supervisory agencies had asked them to provide additional capital over the period 1961-1968. Of the 73 percent that replied, 30 percent (81 banks) said that these requests were made, some repeatedly. But of these, only 43 percent fully complied with the authorities' requests, 27 percent partially complied, and 30 percent did

not comply at all. Mayne concluded: "The agencies do differ in their capital prescriptions, but ... these prescriptions have only a limited effect on bank capital positions because of banker resistance to supervisory pressure for more capital" (p. 47). Peltzman (1970, p. 16), who analyzed statewide aggregate data, also found that banks do not "respond to any of the regulators' standards of capital adequacy." But Mingo (1975), who used more recent individual bank data, reports that banks given lower examiner ratings subsequently tend to increase their capital.

These divergent findings may be due to the different periods or samples studied. They also may be the result of uncertainty about how much capital is adequate. Not only are the accounting numbers used to measure capital inadequate estimates of economic values, but there is reason to believe that a balance sheet ratio is not a sufficient indicator of risk.[9] Indeed, an extensive review by Lyon (1969, p. 31) led her to conclude that "the literature is voluminous but consists primarily of the prevailing opinion at any given time stated as a fact by its proponents, without benefit of analytical analysis."

In any event, the data indicate that the ratio of book capital to deposits of smaller (under $100 million in assets) banks has increased 10 percent over the 1970s from 7.6 percent in 1970 to 8.5 percent in 1980. Assuming that these accounting-based numbers reflect economic values consistently over the time period, this increase could have been the result of pressures by the regulatory authorities. Or the banks voluntarily could have increased equity relative to deposits, perhaps because the stockholders (who often are bank officers or relatives) wanted to reduce their personal income taxes by not paying dividends or officers' salaries. However, the equity/deposits percentage for very large (over $5 billion in assets) banks decreased by 13 percent over the 1970s, from 5.3 percent to 4.1 percent.

---

[9]See Vojta (1973), who argues that the present and future expected profitability of a bank should be taken into account. While several studies found lower capital ratios at banks that failed compared to solvent banks of similar sizes, it is unclear whether impending failures reduced their capital

or whether low capital resulted in their failures. (See Cotter (1966) for a study of West Coast banks that failed between 1921 and 1933, and Benston (1975) for an analysis of banks that failed between 1959 and 1971.)

(Over the complete range of bank sizes, the larger banks tended to have lower ratios and, over time, those ratios decreased more for the larger banks.) Again assuming that these numbers are meaningful, it would appear that the authorities have less ability to control the capital investments of large banks. One reason is suggested below.

Until about 1980, when the S&L capital problem became overwhelming, the FHLBB had somewhat greater influence in getting thrifts to maintain their book capital, primarily because many associations' capital/deposit ratios became so low that they feared cancellation of FSLIC insurance. Edward Kane (1981) points out that FSLIC insurance represents a valuable asset to most associations, since it is priced below what would be the market rate. Mutual associations, as a practical matter, cannot raise equity capital except in the form of retained earnings. Hence, Kane shows, "insured S&Ls kept their net worth from falling below the level required to stay eligible for FSLIC insurance...by not realizing capital losses on their mortgage portfolios" (p. 90), even though this would have reduced their tax liability.

Field Examinations and Supervision

Examinations constitute a principal means of reducing failures of banks and thrift institutions. National banks are examined by the Office of the Comptroller of the Currency at least twice every three years. State-chartered Federal Reserve member banks are examined by the Fed at least once a year, and other state-chartered FDIC-insured banks are examined by the FDIC and often also by state banking departments at least once a year. The Federal Home Loan Bank Board examines FSLIC-insured S&Ls annually. State-chartered S&Ls also are examined by some state banking departments.

The examiners look at the documentation and collateral for most large loans and a sample of small loans and they check the institutions' compliance with federal and state laws. Loans are classified into loss, doubtful and substandard categories. The institutions' managers and management procedures and policies also are evaluated.

If an institution is found wanting, it is characterized as a "problem" or "serious problem" and subjected to closer scrutiny and more frequent examinations.

Although it seems clear that examinations of some sort are a necessary aspect of deposit insurance (given its built-in incentive towards risk-taking), there is reason to question the usefulness of examinations for preventing many failures. The examiners' ability to uncover serious problems of fraud and insider dealings appears to be far from perfect, judging from FDIC reports and published research. Among the 56 bank failures that occurred between January 1959 and April 1971, fully 59 percent were rated as "no problem" at the examination just prior to their failures.[10] The principal reasons given for the 56 failures are: fraud and irregularities, 66 percent; brokered funds and loan losses, 27 percent; and inept management, 7 percent.[11]

A more recent study by Sinkey (1977) uses a different set of classifications but draws similar conclusions. He finds that, of 84 failures between 1960 and mid-1976, some 54 percent resulted from improper insider loans or out-of-territory loans involving brokered funds, 30 percent from embezzlement or manipulation, and 17 percent from managerial weakness in loan administration (p. 27). In an earlier failure study by the FDIC, Hill (1975) found similar proportions. It cannot be ascertained, however, whether this record is close to the best possible, in the sense that the cost of preventing more failures would have exceeded the benefit. Also, the more recent record has not been studied.

The effectiveness of the FSLIC's examiners has been studied only with respect to the relatively large number of S&Ls in Illinois that required the FSLIC's financial assistance from 1963 through 1968. These 19 losses represent 75 percent of the total losses suffered by the FSLIC over the period. Bartell (1969, p. 353), stated that he

---

[10]Benston (1975), Table XIII, p. 43.
[11]Benston (1975), Table XI, Table XI, p. 40.

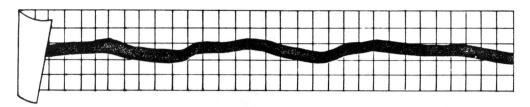

identified nine associations where failure could be attributed primarily to management deficiencies or errors of judgment. In these cases the management apparently believed that the actions which later caused failure were taken in the best interests of the association and its savers. In the second category were 10 associations where fraud, influence, defalcation, or some other criminal intent was the principal cause of failure. In all of these cases, one or more of the officers, directors, and/or major stockholders was indicted for misapplying association funds, and in most cases convictions have been obtained.

With respect to the examinations, Bartell concludes that they were well done; if anything, they were too thorough (p. 418). But, he states, "In contrast with the generally high quality of examinations, supervisory performance in the handling of failed associations leaves much to be desired" (p. 419).

Supervision of financial institutions is functionally related to, though not necessarily dependent on, field examination. To a limited extent the supervisors can specify the portfolios of assets and the nature of the liabilities that insured financial institutions can hold. Supervisors enforce a limitation on loans to any one borrower and they restrict loans to officers, directors and shareholders. They can also restrict the types of loans and investments that can be made. Field examinations to ensure that the regulations are observed would appear to be necessary, particularly where activities conducted at less than arm's length can occur. But the supervisors also can use statistical models and computers to analyze data reported by the institutions for signs of possible problems. Such systems have been used by every federal agency and several state agencies since the mid-1970s.[12] But, as Flannery

and Guttentag (1980) conclude from their analysis of the early warning systems, these systems have not been validated; hence, we do not know how well or even whether they are effective for predicting failure. In fact, the systems appear to be used primarily as a more efficient means for the examiners to look at and structure data for their reports.

The supervisory authorities also must decide when to require an institution to discontinue a criticized practice (such as acquiring brokered deposits or making high-risk loans), dismiss an inept or possibly dishonest officer, obtain more capital from shareholders, terminate insurance,[13] or close or arrange for a merger with another institution. Before the Financial Institutions Supervisory Act of 1966 gave federal supervisors authority to issue cease-and-desist orders, the principal legal sanctions available were cancellation of insurance and seizure of an institution for liquidation or reorganization. Since 1942, the principal procedure used to handle failing banks has been a sale of the bank to an institution that assumes liability for both insured and non-insured deposits.[14] Payoffs limited to insured depositors generally have involved only small institutions located in unit banking states that do not permit another bank to acquire and operate the failed institution as a branch. Recently, in the case of Oklahoma's Penn Square Bank, the poor and questionable condition of the bank's assets precluded its sale. Because they are government agencies, the FDIC, FSLIC, and NCUIF have the power to close an institution before the market value of its assets is less than its insured deposits, which can prevent losses to the insuring agencies except in cases involving rapid deterioration or fraud. But they may also be subjected to political pressure and to the reluctance of a supervisory agency to admit that one of "its" institutions has to be closed.[15]

---

[12] See paper on "Early Warning Systems for Problem Financial Institutions," in Altman and Sametz (1977, pp. 3-68) and Flannery and Guttentag (1980) for descriptions and critiques of these systems.
[13] If insurance is terminated, the institution's existing accounts continue to be insured for two years.

---

[14] See Barnett, Horvitz, and Silverberg 1977, pp. 308-317 for a good discussion of the advantages and disadvantages of the alternative procedures.
[15] Bartell (1969, pp. 419-421) documents the effect of prior congressional criticism of S&L closures on the reluctance of the FHLBB to follow the recommendations of its examiners expeditiously.

"[Since restrictions on entry also reduce competition and service], restricting entry to reduce failures, even if it were desirable, is no longer feasible."

Some critics have argued that divided authority among regulators also has reduced the effectiveness of supervision. While the FDIC and FSLIC have responsibility for insuring the deposits of state-chartered institutions, only the state authorities have the power to close the institutions. (Bartell reports that this was an important problem for the FSLIC with respect to the failing Illinois associations.) Holding companies are regulated by the Federal Reserve but their affiliated banks are chartered by the states and/or the Comptroller of the Currency. Shull (1980) finds in his analysis of holding company failures that, "the extent of actual conflict among federal banking agencies in holding company supervision, while difficult to quantify, is important, time consuming, and diverting in"problem cases" (Vol I, p. 119).

A Changing Environment for Deposit Insurance

Restrictions on entry and the encouragement of mergers have been effective in reducing failures, but at the cost of reduced competition and, therefore, less service to consumers and fewer opportunities for potential bankers. In any event, changes in technology, fueled by inflation-induced high nominal interest rates, have encouraged other, non-regulated suppliers of financial services to enter the market. Their entry no longer can be restricted. Hence, restricting entry to reduce failures, even if it were desirable, is no longer feasible.

Capital adequacy requirements are desirable. But, to be effective, they must be tailored to the asset portfolio and deposit distribution of each institution. If too much equity is required, insured depository institutions will be disadvantaged and resources allocated inefficiently. If too little capital is required, institutions will be encouraged to take greater risks and the costs to the insurance agency are likely to exceed the fees it levies. Furthermore, capital adequacy is a very blunt requirement. It is expensive for financial institutions to raise capital (in addition to retained earnings) in relatively small amounts. Closely

held, usually smaller institutions, are likely to find floating equity quite difficult. Majority shareholders may lack the resources or may not wish to concentrate their wealth further, and outside investors frequently are unwilling to take minority positions except at a considerable discount. Mutual institutions also might find it expensive to market debentures.

Deposit insurance rates that vary with the riskiness of an institution's assets and liabilities have been suggested for years as a preferable means of dealing with the problem. However, the deposit insurance agencies still charge the same percentage to all institutions, partly because it is difficult to set variable premiums. (Indeed, none of those recommending this change have specified how the premiums should be determined.) But the same information is required for an equity requirement. Another reason for the resistance to change is that regulatory agencies believe the present system of field examinations and equity requirements, roughly determined and enforced though they may be, are adequate.

Finally, the present system may be politically desirable, balancing smaller institutions' benefits from having the premiums applied to all (including uninsured) deposits against large banks' benefits from an incomplete control of the risks they take. The residual risk ostensibly is borne by the deposit insurance agencies. But since the government is expected to stand behind the agencies, the general public is accepting the residual risk.

Field examinations have two major shortcomings. One is that they are expensive. Teams of examiners spend days to weeks at each bank, going over records in considerable detail. Not only do the insurance agencies and the institutions they charge for these services incur considerable costs, but the institutions bear such costs as disrupted operations and the expense of preparing and presenting requested data. The second shortcoming is the difficulty of prompt detection of problems precipitated by fraud or changes in an institution's economic environment. These are difficult to detect through periodic inspections of an institution's loan portfolio, management systems, and regulatory compliance.

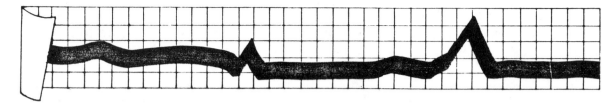

A related problem involves our system of regulation. Supervisors may not be able to control potential problem banks as well when the banks are regulated by several agencies as when they are regulated by a single agency. For many commercial banks, especially the large ones, the chartering agencies (the Comptroller or the states) and the Federal Reserve have regulatory responsibility as well as the FDIC. This divided authority may permit some banks to take greater risks than an insurance agency acting alone would have permitted. But then, the temptation for an insurance agency to reduce risk at the expense of innovation must be recognized.

Proposed Solutions

My analysis has concluded that mandatory deposit insurance is justified because deposits that are withdrawable on demand create the possibility of bank runs, which can visit considerable costs upon banks, their customers and others. The government has been charged with insuring deposits in part as a response to Depression-era political pressures by small banks, the home building industry and some depositors, and in part because the government has the power to enforce its orders on banks and cannot, itself, go bankrupt. Another reason for government intervention in insurance is that the government's control over bank reserves gives it the power to cause and the power to prevent massive numbers of bank failures.

The basic problem with government-provided mandatory deposit insurance is that it provides the insured institutions an incentive to take excessive risks. Consequently, the institutions must be examined and supervised. But there is danger that this process is conducted less efficiently and effectively because the responsible

agencies are monopoly suppliers of the insurance to each group of institutions.

The following changes in current procedures, I believe, would help reduce the costs of achieving the benefits from mandatory deposit insurance.[16]

1. **All** deposits withdrawable on demand, such as checking accounts, NOW accounts, money market deposit accounts, and passbook savings accounts, should be insured by a responsible insurer. The only exceptions would occur where deposited funds are invested in assets that have almost no probability of being worth less than the deposit liability (such as money market funds that are invested in a well-diversified portfolio of short-term government obligations or bank certificates of deposit). All demand-type deposits should be insured for two reasons. One is that runs on uninsured balances can force bank failures or a massive infusion of resources by the authorities to prevent a failure (as was done for the Franklin National Bank in New York). The second reason is that **de jure** deposit insurance is preferable to **de facto** insurance. The public generally believes that large banks will not be permitted to fail, but that smaller banks may fail. Since deposit insurance premiums are imposed on deposits of all insured banks, this **de facto** difference is inequitable.

2. Time-dated deposits (such as CDs, whether negotiable or not) need not be insured, as long as the holder can withdraw funds from the financial institution only at the time stated. (Obligations that permit withdrawal of funds with an interest rate penalty would be classified as funds withdrawable on demand.) Consequently, runs cannot occur with such deposits. In this respect, time deposits are no different from the debt obligations of other companies.[17] Of course, an institution may purchase insurance coverage for these obligations if it wishes. The advantage of this

---

[16] Also see Barnett, Horvitz and Silverberg (1977) and Scott and Mayer (1971) for analyses of suggested changes, some of which mirror the ones presented here.

[17] Though some time-dated obligations are payable almost immediately, institutions (and the insurance agency) have incentives to ensure that the amount due at any time is not excessive.

proposal is that holders of time deposits would monitor the issuing institution. Furthermore, the interest rate paid on the deposits could provide the demand deposit insurance agency with the market's assessment of the riskiness of the institution.

3. Commercial and mutual savings banks are regulated by several agencies, which can lead to conflicting authority and a failure to act in a timely fashion. The agency with the principal interest in supervising financial institutions should be the one that must bear the cost of their failure—the insuring agency.[18] Consequently, it should have the sole authority and responsibility for supervising the financial institutions it insures.

4. The present insurance system suffers from a lack of competition among insuring agencies. As a consequence, examination procedures may be too costly and poorly focused. Because they are monopoly suppliers of deposit insurance, the present agencies have less incentive to adopt more efficient and better directed procedures, such as risk-variable insurance premiums, tests of the predictive ability of statistical models, and research on optimally diversified portfolios. Because the regulatory agencies also are subjected to severe political criticism if "their" banks fail, they may be too restrictive in some instances. They should be faced with equating the marginal costs and benefits from failures and failure-reducing measures as are other insurance providers. Consequently, the following changes should be considered:

a. The Office of the Comptroller of the Currency (OCC) should become a deposit insurance agency, initially providing insurance (and supervision) to national banks. The Federal Reserve's Division of Supervision and Regulation should also provide insurance to the member banks it examines.

These changes would continue the present examination staffs as they are presently constituted, which would minimize the cost of change. The present FDIC insurance fund could be divided among the three agencies in proportion to the total demand deposits held by the banks they insure.

b. Any deposit insured institution should then be allowed to purchase insurance at the OCC, FDIC, Fed, FSLIC or NCUSIF. Thus there would be five potential competitors. Of course, an agency need not accept applications made to it. Each agency could offer its "customers" whatever terms it wished, much as does any insurance company, so long as the terms are offered equally to all clients that present equivalent risk. An agency should, however, give at least one year's public notice before cancelling the insurance on deposit balances. It also could require an insured bank to authorize the agency to seize its assets, given designated circumstances.

c. Any demand depository institution could obtain insurance from non-government insurers, including other banks,[19] if the insurer were accepted by the chartering agency. The non-government insurer could initiate clauses into its contract with the institution that would give the insurer rights similar to (or even greater than) those held by the government agencies. These might include restrictive covenants as to dividends, specified diversification of assets, minimum equity requirements, audits by CPAs or the insurance company's examiners, pre-agreement to cease practices or to remove officers, and seizure and sale of assets after a stated "danger" point is reached.

5. The preceding proposals do not cover the difficulties of insuring deposits in the face of unpredictable problems in the financial system as a whole, problems not controllable by individual institutions. In our fractional reserve banking

---

[18] See Benston (1963) for the analysis on which this conclusion is based.
[19] The agency that insures the deposits of a bank offering deposit insurance to

other banks can adjust its premium accordingly or take other actions to control the risk.

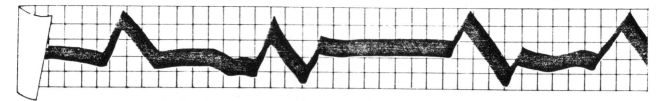

system, a substantial decline in bank reserves for any reason can cause wide-scale banking failures. Such declines in reserves also are very difficult (perhaps impossible) to predict and, thus, deposit insurance premiums cannot be set actuarially. Therefore, to make non-government supplied insurance feasible, the insurers should in some way be relieved of the cost of failures caused by substantial systemwide declines in bank reserves.

—George J. Benston

Professor of Accounting, Economics and Finance, Graduate School of Management, University of Rochester, and Visiting Scholar, Federal Reserve Bank of Atlanta. This article was presented at a Research Seminar at the Federal Reserve Bank of Atlanta on Jan. 6, 1983.

REFERENCES

Altman, Edward E. and Arnold W. Sametz. **Financial Crises: Institutions and Markets in a Fragile Environment,** New York: Wiley-Interscience Publication, 1977.

Barnett, Robert E., Paul N. Horvitz, and Stanley C. Silverberg. "Deposit Insurance: The Present System and Some Alternatives," **Banking Law Journal,** vol. 94, 1977, 304-332.

Bartell, H. Robert, Jr. "An Analysis of Illinois Savings and Loan Associations Which Failed in the Period 1963-68, in Irwin Friend, ed., **Study of the Savings and Loan Industry,** prepared for the Federal Home Loan Bank Board, Washington, D.C., Vol. I, 1969, 345-436.

Benston, George J. "Federal Regulation of Banking: Analysis and Policy Recommendations." **Journal of Bank Research,** Winter, 1983.

Benston, George J. "Why Did Congress Pass New Financial Services Laws in the 1930s? An Alternative View," **Economic Review,** Federal Reserve Bank of Atlanta, April, 1982, 7-10.

Benston, George J. "Bank Examination," **The Bulletin,** (New York University Graduate School of Business Administration, Institute of Finance), 1973, Nos. 89-90.

Edwards, Gurden. **The Guaranty of Bank Deposits,** Economic Policy Commission, American Bankers Association, New York, 1933.

Federal Deposit Insurance Corporation. "State Deposit Insurance Systems, 1908-30," **Annual Report,** 1956, Washington, D.C., 57-73.

Federal Deposit Insurance Corporation. "Bank-Obligation Insurance Systems, 1829 to 1866," **Annual Report,** 1953, Washington, D.C., 45-67.

Federal Deposit Insurance Corporation. "Insurance of Bank Obligations Prior to Federal Deposit Insurance," **Annual Report,** 1952. Washington, D.C., 59-72.

Flannery, Mark J. "Deposit Insurance Creates a Need for Bank Regulation," **Business Review,** Federal Reserve Bank of Philadelphia, January/February, 1982, 17-27.

Flannery, Mark J. and Jack M. Guttentag. "Problem Banks: Examination, Identification, and Supervision," in Leonard Lapidus and Others, **State and Federal Regulation of Commercial Banks,** Federal Deposit Insurance Corporation, Washington, D.C., Vol. II, 1980, 169-226.

Gibson, William E. "Deposit Insurance in the United States: Evaluation and Reform," **Journal of Financial and Quantitative Analysis,** 1972, 1575-1594.

Golembe, Carter. "Memorandum re: Interest on Demand Deposits," Carter H. Golembe Associates, Inc., Volume 1975-10, 1975.

Hanweck, Gerald A. "A Theoretical Comparison of Bank Capital Adequacy Requirements and Risk Related Deposit Insurance Premia," Board of Governors of the Federal Reserve System, manuscript, September 1982.

Hill, George W. **Why 67 Insured Banks Failed—1960-1974,** Federal Deposit Insurance Corporation, Washington, D.C., 1975.

Kane, Edward J. "Reregulation, Savings and Loan Diversification, and the Flow of Housing Finance," in **Savings and Loan Asset Management Under Deregulation,** Sixth Annual Conference, December 1980, Federal Home Loan Bank of San Francisco, 1981, 80-109.

Koehn, Michael and Anthony M. Santomero. "Regulation of Bank Capital and Portfolio Risk," **Journal of Finance,** 35 (December 1980), 1235-1244.

Lyon, Sandra. "History of Bank Capital Adequacy Analysis," Federal Deposit Insurance Corporation, Working Paper No. 69-4, 1969, Banking and Economic Research Section, Division of Research.

Mayne, Lucille S. "Impact of Federal Bank Supervision on Bank Capital," **The Bulletin** (New York University Graduate School of Business Administration, Institute of Finance), 1972, Nos. 85-86.

Mingo, John J. "Regulatory Influence on Bank Capital Investment," **Journal of Finance,** 30 (September), 1111-1121.

Peltzman, Sam. "Entry in Commercial Banking," **Journal of Law and Economics,** 1 (October 1963), pp. 11-50.

Peltzman, Sam. "Capital Investment in Commercial Banking and Its Relationship to Portfolio Regulation," **Journal of Political Economy,** 78 (January-February 1970), 1-26.

Scott, Kenneth E. and Thomas Mayer. "Risk and Regulation in Banking: Some Proposals for Deposit Insurance Reform", **Stanford Law Review,** Vol. 23, 1971, 857-902.

Sharpe, William F. "Bank Capital Adequacy, Deposit Insurance and Security Value," **Journal of Financial and Quantitative Analysis** (Proceedings, November), 701-718.

Shull, Bernard. "Federal and State Supervision of Bank Holding Companies," in Leonard Lapidus and Others, **State and Federal Regulation of Commercial Banks,** Federal Deposit Insurance Corporation, Washington, D.C., Vol. II, 1980, 271-374.

Sinkey, Joseph F. Jr. "Problem and Failed Banks, Bank Examinations and Early Warning Systems: A Summary," in Edward I. Altman and Arnold W. Sametz, **Financial Crises: Institutions and Markets in a Fragile Environment,** New York: Wiley-Interscience Publication, 1977.

Tussig, Aubrey D. "The Case for Bank Failure," **Journal of Law and Economics,** Vol. 10, 1967, 129-147.

Vojta, George J. **Bank Capital Adequacy,** First National City Bank, New York, 1973.

Warburton, Clark. **Depression, Inflation and Monetary Policy, Selected Papers, 1945-1953,** Baltimore: The Johns Hopkins Press, 1952.

Article Fourteen

Alternative Methods for Assessing Risk-Based Deposit-Insurance Premiums

by James B. Thomson

One of the most widely debated topics in the political arena is the proposal to give the Federal Deposit Insurance Corporation (FDIC) the power to vary the cost of deposit-insurance on the basis of risk.[1]

The FDIC was created in 1933 and today is considered an integral part of the federal banking safety net whose purpose is to protect the savings and transactions balances of small savers and to help stabilize the banking system. Federally-insured banks currently pay a flat fee for the FDIC guarantee of the first $100,000 of each deposit account in the bank. Critics do not think this is fair or efficient because banks that take excessive risks with their depositor's money pay exactly the same rate for FDIC insurance as banks that are more conservative in their operations.[2]

As a result, there are currently at least two dozen proposals for adjusting deposit-insurance premia on the basis of risk. Of these, there are at least six different general proposals for reforming the current system by using some form of risk-based pricing. This *Economic Commentary* provides an overview of the various risk-based proposals.

A fragmented approach is used in our discussion in order to highlight the features of each general proposal. With a basic understanding of the intricacies of the basic pricing methods, one can better evaluate and understand the relative advantages and disadvantages of the various reform proposals.

Before discussing any of the pricing system proposals, we should review the system currently used by the FDIC, which features a flat-rate premium levied against the total domestic deposits of the bank. The FDIC charges each insured bank an annual premium equal to a partially rebatable 1/12 of 1 percent of total deposits, regardless of the risk of the bank's portfolio. The size of the rebate returned to the bank is determined by the FDIC's losses and other expenses over the past year. The size of the rebate per dollar of deposits is the same for all banks regardless of risk.[3]

The FDIC attempts to minimize its exposure to risky institutions by increasing regulatory pressure on banks that are thought to be excessively risky. The increased regulatory interference represents an implicit premium adjustment that serves to reduce the value of the bank.[4] However, deregulation and technological innovations have increased the ability of banks to circumvent the current regulatory structure and thereby have decreased the ability of the FDIC to use regulation to adjust the total (explicit plus implicit) deposit-insurance premium on the basis of risk.[5] In contrast to the FDIC's current pricing system, the proposed risk-adjusted systems rely more heavily on the use of incentives other than regulatory interference to force banks to bear more of the costs of the deposit guarantees.

There are two primary ways in which the FDIC could equate the premium it charges with the value of the deposit guarantees received by the bank. The first method is to charge a risk-adjusted deposit-insurance premium that fully compensates the FDIC for the risk-bearing services it provides. This type of premium adjustment is referred to as an explicit premium adjustment. The second method is to alter the value of the guarantee so that its value to the bank equals the deposit-insurance premium. This is known as an implicit premium adjustment. Our discussion in this *Economic Commentary* will examine proposals for implicit and explicit risk-adjusted deposit-insurance premiums.

Implicit Risk-Adjusted Premiums

Implicit risk-adjustment schemes seek to change the underlying risk-reward incentive structure for the insured bank. As we shall see, the majority of implicit risk-adjusted premium proposals are aimed at reestablishing some form of market discipline over the managers of insured banks. In the proposals we discuss, either the stockholders or the subordinated creditors of the bank are relied upon to rein in a bank's risk taking.[6] The second feature of these implicit premium adjustments is that they insulate the FDIC insurance fund from losses on the bank's portfolio.

Increased Capital Requirements. One way of increasing stockholder discipline over a bank's risk-taking is to raise the costs of higher levels of bank risk to bank stockholders through increased capital requirements. Higher levels of capital increase the amount of money that stockholders have at risk in the bank, thus making risky loan and investment strategies pursued by bank managers more costly and less attractive to stockholders. Increased capital requirements thus serve to increase the incentives for bank stockholders to discipline the risk-taking behavior of bank managers.

In addition, increased bank capital requirements protect the FDIC's insurance fund from losses on bank asset portfolios because bank capital is the first line of defense against losses on the bank's assets. The greater the portion of any loss that is absorbed by bank capital, the smaller the loss the FDIC incurs. Higher levels of bank capital also increase the FDIC's ability to alter bank risk-taking behavior through regulatory interference by giving the FDIC more time to detect problems and to take the appropriate regulatory actions.

A major drawback of a uniform increase in bank capital requirements is that it does not discriminate among banks on the basis of risk. Banks that aggressively exploit risky profit opportunities will face the same capital requirement as conservatively managed banks. Although one can argue that increased capital requirements change the risk incentive structure for risky banks more than for conservatively managed banks, it is doubtful that such requirements change incentives enough to remove all significant differences in the risk of their asset portfolios.[8] Furthermore, if the increased bank capital requirements are binding on the conservatively managed banks, the use of this tool to discipline the "high fliers" of the banking industry has the undesired effect of punishing safe banks.

Risk-Adjusted Capital Requirements. Banking regulators are considering risk-based capital requirements as a means of altering risk-taking behavior of banks.[9] A flat-rate deposit-insurance premium, for example, combined with risk-adjusted capital requirements, may have effects equivalent to assessment of a risk-adjusted deposit-insurance premium. With risk-adjusted capital requirements, the level of capital a bank is required to hold is directly related to the riskiness of its portfolio. Under this method, the riskiness of the bank would be reassessed periodically, at least as often as the bank is examined, and if the bank's risk increased since the last reassessment of its capital adequacy, it would be required to increase its level of capital.

Risk-adjusted capital increases, in concept, are a better disciplinary tool than uniform capital increases. First, they change the risk-reward incentive structure for risky banks without punishing conservatively managed banks. Second, they protect the FDIC's insurance fund from risky banks by increasing the amount of potential losses stockholders bear as the risk of the bank increases.

However, there are some practical problems associated with implementing a risk-based capital requirement. The most obvious—and common—problem is the necessity of measuring the risk of the bank's portfolio. (See box.) If the procedures used to evaluate the risk of the bank's portfolio are subject to systematic errors, then adjusting bank capital (deposit-insurance premiums) on the basis of the perceived riskiness of the bank may be less accurate and less effective than uniform capital increases (flat-rate deposit-insurance premiums). In fact, Pyle contends that potential pricing errors associated with risk-adjusted pricing (either risk-adjusted capital or deposit-insurance premiums) may provide banks with perverse risk-taking incentives that make risk-adjusted pricing systems less effective, and potentially less stable, than the current pricing system.[10]

Subordinated Debt. One of the potential flaws in the idea of using stockholders to discipline the bank's risk-taking is the fact that stockholders can profit if the risky strategy pays off. Therefore, raising equity capital to place more of the losses on the stockholders may not always reduce the attractiveness of risky ventures to bank managers. Also, one cannot rely solely on depositors to exert discipline on a bank because of the ability of large uninsured depositors to withdraw or set off their deposits by borrowing (that is, by running) at the first sign of trouble.[11] Uninsured depositors who believe that the FDIC will provide them with 100 percent de facto insurance of their deposits if their bank fails have very little incentive to exert discipline over bank risk taking.

The subordinated debt holder, however, is one class of creditor that does have strong incentives to exert discipline over bank risk-taking—and there are advantages to using subordinated debt as a means of increasing market discipline over banks. Unlike the stockholder, the subordinated debt holder does not receive profits from risky ventures. Unlike the uninsured depositor, the subordinated debt holder can be cut off from any de facto deposit guarantee if the FDIC chooses not to liquidate a bank when it fails, and cannot withdraw his or her funds from the bank at the first sign of trouble. Therefore, the subordinated debt holder's fortunes are inextricably linked to the risk of the bank's portfolio.

Another advantage of forcing banks to issue a significant amount of subordinated debt (Horvitz argues for a 3 percent subordinated debt capital requirement in addition to primary bank capital) is the additional protection that subordinated debt affords the

---

Measuring Risk

Risk is the degree of uncertainty associated with future outcomes of today's decisions. In a financial context, risk refers to the degree of uncertainty of future income. The more uncertain the outcome, the greater the risk. Measuring the risk of the insured banks is the most important ingredient in many of the risk-adjusted deposit-insurance proposals. Unfortunately, measuring the risk of insured banks is very difficult to do.

The risk of an insured bank to the FDIC's insurance fund is typically measured by the variation of its future income streams. Because we do not observe the set of possible future outcomes of decisions made by bank managers today, we do not directly observe the risk of the bank. The most common way of measuring the risk of the bank is to look at its past performance, such as the historical variation of its earnings, and use that as an estimate of the variability of the bank's earnings in the future. In addition, bank regulators periodically examine insured banks and rate the bank's riskiness according to the results of the examination. The rating the bank receives is referred to as its CAMEL rating. CAMEL stands for the criteria on which bank examiners base their risk ratings: Capital, Asset Quality, Management, Earnings, and Liquidity.

FDIC's insurance fund. The FDIC is protected because subordinated debt holders do not have a claim on the assets of the bank until the FDIC, uninsured depositors, and general creditors of the bank are paid.[12]

The practical disadvantage of the subordinated debt proposal is the feasibility of its use for medium-size banks. Large banks with access to capital markets theoretically would not have trouble placing subordinated debt issues. Small community banks probably could sell their issues in their communities. But medium-size banks that are too large to sell an entire issue in their community, but too small to tap national capital markets could have trouble issuing enough subordinated debt to meet mandated standards. This problem is exacerbated by the necessity that the subordinated debt be short-term debt that requires frequent refinancing.

Explicit Risk-Adjusted Premiums

The goal of this major category of pricing system proposals is to charge the bank for the risks it imposes on the FDIC. Unlike implicit risk-adjusted premiums, explicit premiums are a form of direct discipline on insured banks. That is, the FDIC increases the cost of its guarantees to the bank directly, as opposed to relying on third parties (such as stockholders and subordinated creditors), to limit excessive risk-taking. There are three primary types of explicit premiums.

Private Reinsurance of Deposit Guarantees. Private reinsurance of the federal deposit guarantees is a way of using the market's estimate of the value of deposit guarantees to adjust the deposit-insurance premium.[13] The basic concept behind the private reinsurance program is the extension of FDIC guarantees to cover all deposits. The FDIC then would assume direct responsibility for the first $10,000 or so of any deposit liability and private companies would assume direct responsibility for each additional $10,000 layer or tranche of any deposit.[14] This procedure places private capital at risk for any portion of an insured deposit above the base FDIC insurance limit.

The bank's total deposit-insurance premium would be determined by the firms in the private deposit-insurance market. The premiums the bank pays to the private insurers for their guarantees presumably would reflect the risks to the private insurers arising from those guarantees. The FDIC guarantee on the first $10,000 of deposits would be tied to the premiums paid to private insurers for their guarantees.

For the private insurance system to provide the correct premium structure, the government must allow private deposit insurers to fail when they cannot meet their obligations. In such cases, the FDIC would be responsible for guar-

anteeing the deposits previously guaranteed by the defunct private deposit insurer. This approach also requires sharing information on the condition of banks between the private insurance industry and the FDIC. Finally, private insurers would have to be indemnified against losses that would result if public policy allows a bank to continue to operate after it becomes insolvent.

The current lack of interest, and some would argue, lack of resources of the insurance industry in providing deposit guarantees may make private reinsurance infeasible. However, if profit opportunities were available for market participants who provide deposit guarantees, then one would expect a private insurance industry to develop. If a private deposit-insurance industry were to develop, it probably would be necessary to extend some form of capital regulation to the private insurers to ensure that they could reasonably meet their obligations. (Managers of private deposit insurers with little of their stockholders' money at risk may be less likely to correctly price their deposit guarantees.)

Premiums Based on Ex Ante Risk Measures. An alternative method of assessing risk-adjusted premiums is to base the premiums on current expectations as to the performance of the bank over the next rating period. That is, to set up a model that predicts the riskiness of the bank and to use the model to set the criteria upon which the deposit-insurance premiums are assessed.[15] These economic models attempt to estimate the risk exposure of the FDIC to an insured bank. With such estimates, administrative prices could be set to determine the aggregate risk levels for the insured industry. Individual institutions would be allowed to determine the level of risk that is appropriate for their institution, given the administrative price set for the deposit insurance.

The main advantage of an ex ante pricing system is that, like the risk-based capital proposals, it directly affects the risk-taking incentives of insured banks. The primary disadvantage is that we have to be able to measure the riskiness of insured banks. As with risk-based capital guidelines, systematic errors in measuring bank risk can make ex ante risk-adjusted premium systems unstable. In addition, if the model is not flexible and forward-looking, banks may seek to exploit new forms of unregulated risks. The growth of off-balance-sheet risks is an example of how banks can avoid regulations intended to limit risk taking.

Ex Post Premiums. An alternative way of risk-adjusting deposit-insurance premiums is to base them on the actual (ex post) performance of the bank. This would increase the costs of risk-taking by bank managers by charging banks a deposit-insurance premium that is inversely related to the bank's performance. Typically, ex post risk-adjusted pricing proposals would levy a flat-rate deposit-insurance premium on the insured bank at the beginning of the period over which the premium is assessed. The ex post risk adjustment to the insurance premium comes in the form of either a surcharge or a rebate to the insured banks, depending upon the quality of their actual performance.

The size of the premium surcharge or rebate that the bank either pays or receives would be adjusted according to the riskiness of the bank's operations relative to the banking industry as a whole. The total deposit-insurance premium paid by the banking industry would be set to compensate the FDIC for its risk exposure to the banking industry as a whole. The system of rebates and surcharges, however, would allocate the burden of the insurance premium on individual banks on the basis of their performance over the rating period.[16]

The primary advantage of this system is that it could be adopted easily. To implement it would require only slight modifications of the FDIC's existing powers. Ex post pricing schemes based on performance would allow the FDIC to identify and price, after the fact, previously unregulated forms of risk that insured banks may be exploiting. The most severe problem associated with ex post pricing stems from the loose relationship between ex post performance and expected (ex ante) risk.

A bank that performed poorly in the past, for example, might be a conservatively run bank that poses little threat to the FDIC's insurance fund. The profitable bank, on the other hand, might be a risky institution that happened to

bet correctly on oil prices or interest-rate movements. Yet, under the ex post deposit-insurance pricing system, the safe bank would pay higher premiums than the risky bank. However, one would not expect this inconsistency to persist over the long run because the aggregate losses, and therefore the aggregate deposit-insurance premiums paid by the risky bank, should exceed those of the conservatively run bank.

Conclusion

There are at least six general methods for adjusting the cost of the FDIC's deposit guarantees to insured banks. Each method has its advantages and disadvantages and, for simplicity, has been presented here as a competing method for pricing deposit guarantees. However, in practice, many of these methods could be combined to achieve a pricing system that would be superior to any of the separate pricing mechanisms by itself. Indeed, almost all of the current deposit-insurance reform proposals rely on some combination of these methods. The role that we want federal deposit insurance to play in our financial system in the future will be the ultimate deciding factor in determining which combination of the generic methods is adopted.

James B. Thomson is an economist at the Federal Reserve Bank of Cleveland. The author would like to thank William T. Gavin, Gary Whalen, and Walker Todd for helpful comments.

The views stated herein are those of the author and not necessarily those of the Federal Reserve Bank of Cleveland or of the Board of Governors of the Federal Reserve System.

1. See Jay Rosenstein and Bartlett Naylor, "Garn Bill Would Expand Bank Securities Powers," *American Banker*, vol. 151, No. 124, June 25, 1986.

2. See, James B. Thomson. "Equity, Efficiency, and Mispriced Deposit Guarantees." *Economic Commentary*, July 15, 1986, Federal Reserve Bank of Cleveland.

3. After deducting operating expenses and insurance losses from the gross insurance assessment, the FDIC rebates 60 percent of the remaining assessment income back to the banks. See *Federal Deposit Insurance Corporation: The First Fifty Years*. The Federal Deposit Insurance Corporation 1984, Washington, D.C., pp. 60-61.

4. Buser, Chen and Kane refer to this type of implicit premium adjustment as a regulatory tax. The FDIC uses increased regulatory interference to tax away part of the gains the bank receives by holding a riskier portfolio. See, Steven A. Buser, Andrew C. Chen, and Edward J. Kane. "Federal Deposit Insurance, Regulatory Policy, and Optimal Bank Capital." *Journal of Finance* 36 (March 1981), pp. 51-60.

5. The FDIC presents a similar argument in its study of risk-adjusted insurance premiums. See, Federal Deposit Insurance Corporation. *Deposit Insurance in a Changing Environment,* Washington, D.C., April 1983. For a discussion of why the current system of federal deposit guarantees needs to be reformed see, Edward J. Kane. *The Gathering Crisis in Federal Deposit Insurance,* MIT Press, 1985.

6. The subordinated creditors of the bank are investors with a claim on the assets of the bank that is secondary to the claims of depositors, the FDIC, and general creditors. In other words, if the bank fails, and is liquidated ,the subordinated creditors do not have a claim against the bank until the claims of the its uninsured depositors, general creditors, and the FDIC are paid in full.

7. See George J. Benston, Robert A. Eisenbeis, Paul M. Horvitz, Edward J. Kane, and George G. Kaufman. *Perspectives on Safe and Sound Banking: Past, Present, and Future,* MIT Press, Cambridge, MA: 1986.

8. It is possible that increases in capital requirements may have perverse effects on the risk incentives of banks, causing them to increase the risk of their portfolios. See Anthony M. Santomero and Ronald D. Watson, "Determining an Optimal Capital Standard for the Banking Industry." *Journal of Finance,* vol. 32, no. 4 (September 1977), pp. 1267-82.

9. See Robert M. Garson. "Comptroller Says Regulators May Issue One Risk-Based Capital Proposal by Fall." *American Banker,* vol. 151, no. 135 (July 11, 1986).

10. See, David H. Pyle, "Pricing Deposit Insurance: The Effects of Mismeasurement" Federal Reserve Bank of San Francisco, *Working Paper 8305,* October 1983.

11. There is evidence that uninsured depositors exert some discipline over bank risk-taking by charging riskier banks higher premiums for funds. This is evident in the market for large certificates of deposit (CDs) where there appears to be a tiering of CD rates according to the risk of the bank. See, Herbert Baer and Elijah Brewer. "Uninsured Deposits as a Source of Market Discipline: Some New Evidence." *Economic Perspectives,* vol. X, issue 5, September/October 1986, Federal Reserve Bank of Chicago, pp. 23-31.

12. See, Paul M. Horvitz. "The Case Against Risk-Related Deposit Insurance Premiums." *Housing Finance Review,* July 1983, pp. 253-63.

13. See for example Edward J. Kane, "A Six-Point Program for Deposit Insurance-Reform," *Housing Finance Review,* July 1983, pp. 269-278; Edward J. Kane, "Appearance and Reality in Deposit Insurance." *Journal of Banking and Finance* vol. 10, no. 2, June 1986, pp. 175-88, and Herbert Baer, "Private Prices, Public Insurance: The Pricing of Federal Deposit Insurance," *Economic Perspectives,* vol. 9, no. 5 (September/October 1985) Federal Reserve Bank of Chicago, pp. 45-57. For a discussion of the potential problems with private deposit insurance, see Tim S. Campbell and David Glenn. "Deposit Insurance in a Deregulated Environment," Journal of Finance, vol. 39, no. 3, (July 1984) pp. 775-87.

14. There is nothing magical about $10,000. We could easily argue that the federally insured limits should be set at $5,000 or $25,000.

15. See for example, Robert B. Avery, Gerald A. Hanweck, and Myron L. Kwast, "An Analysis of Risk-Based Deposit Insurance for Commercial Banks," *Proceedings of a Conference on Bank Structure and Competition,* Federal Reserve Bank of Chicago, Chicago, Illinois, 1985, pp. 217-250.

16. See for example, David P. Rochester and David A. Walker. "A Risk-Based Deposit Insurance System," Unpublished Manuscript 1985.

Article Fifteen

Regulation of Banks' Equity Capital

Larry D. Wall

Capital requirements appear to augment the buffer protecting the banking system and the FDIC. However, regulating levels of bank capital also may increase banks' risk-taking and hamper their ability to compete with non-banking organizations.

The Depression of the 1930s is often attributed to the failure of the banking system, and many economists believe that another such failure could have equally serious consequences.[1] Beyond its obvious concern over such a banking debacle, the government also worries about the failure of individual banks, because a large institution's collapse could endanger the entire system. Furthermore, the failure of individual banks imposes losses on the Federal Deposit Insurance Corporation (FDIC), whose ultimate guarantor is the United States government.

Among other means, the government tries to limit the risk of bank failures and the magnitude of the FDIC's losses by regulating banking organizations' equity capital. Equity capital, which includes both the owners' investment and the bank's retained earnings, assists a bank in several important ways: during lean times it provides a cushion to absorb losses and ward off insolvency; it protects against illiquidity resulting from deposit runs by helping to maintain depositor confidence;[2] and, should a bank fail, equity capital also reduces the losses the FDIC must bear.

In spite of government regulation, bank capital ratios have fallen dramatically in this century.

The author is an economist in the bank's Research Department.

The ratio of bank equity capital to total assets dropped from 20 percent in 1900 to approximately 7 percent in 1983. Equity to risk assets have fallen even more sharply, from a peak of over 25 percent in the mid-1940s to under 10 percent in recent years.[3] In December 1981 federal regulators renewed their emphasis on bank capital ratios by issuing numerical capital adequacy guidelines that required many institutions to increase their equity capital significantly. Congress demonstrated its support for the regulatory actions by specifying in the International Lending and Supervision Act of 1983 that each "appropriate Federal Banking Agency shall cause banking institutions to achieve and maintain adequate capital by establishing minimum levels of capital." Two years later regulators revised the capital guidelines, imposing a single standard on all banks regardless of size and primary regulator.

The purpose of this study is to review the arguments for and against regulating the equity capital of independent banks and bank holding companies.[4] The current regulatory standards use two definitions of capital: primary capital (the sum of permanent equity capital plus an allowance for possible loan losses and mandatory convertible securities, minus certain intangible assets), and total capital (primary capital plus limited life preferred stock and subordinated debt).[5] Each of the non-equity elements of primary and total capital raises a unique set of issues. For example, equity capital holders (stockholders) can be forced to share in losses without a bank's failing, but subordinated debt holders do not have to share in losses unless the firm is bankrupt.[6]

This study begins with discussion of how capital may protect the banking system and the FDIC. It proceeds to review four arguments against capital regulation: such regulation histcrically has proven ineffective; it will not significantly reduce the riskiness of the banking system; capital regulation carries considerable disadvantages; and other alternatives exist.

Why Regulate Capital?

In a market economy like that of the United States, the presumption is that free-market competition should control individual private sector decisions, except where the market fails to consider important social costs, social benefits, or both. The case for government regulation of capital rests on two such failures: the market does not properly price the effect of bank failure on the stability of the banking system, nor the costs of bank failure to the FDIC.

In the absence of binding government regulation, banks would base capital decisions solely on their competition for customers, investors (in debt and equity), and suppliers (including labor and management). To succeed in this arena, banks must offer potential customers, investors, and suppliers a better deal than other organizations. Banks' capital policies can affect their competitive position; for example, their ability to attract credit and superior management may be enhanced by higher capital ratios, for the additional capital may reduce the risk of failure. The institutions' attraction for equity investors may be reduced by higher capital ratios, however, because more capital can imply a lower return on equity. In theoretical studies of capital ratios, the most simplistic models maintain that the competing demands of creditors and stockholders exactly offset each other, and banks (like other firms) have no optimal capital ratio.[7] A bank's capital ratio is important, however, in more general models that include taxes, the costs of financial distress, and agency costs.[8]

An additional influence on bank capital ratios is the short maturity structure of liabilities. The banking industry differs from almost all other industries in that it issues liabilities that are redeemable on demand, which makes banks more vulnerable to a sudden loss of their creditors' confidence. If creditors of a nonbanking firm lose confidence in its stability, they can do nothing until their debt matures. If depositors begin to doubt the financial condition of their bank, however, they can withdraw demand deposits immediately, without even taking time to determine the institution's actual condition. Sudden deposit runs can be deadly, even to financially strong banks, because most institutions invest part of their demand deposits in illiquid loans.

Few banks can liquidate their loan portfolios on short notice without suffering substantial losses.[9] Capital can reduce the risk of a run on a bank by strengthening customer confidence in the institution's viability.[10]

WHEN LARGE BANKS FAIL

Capital regulation seeks to prevent a collapse of the banking system by reducing the risk of failure of individual banks. One policy question in developing capital guidelines is whether the failure of individual banks is undesirable for the banking system. If individual bank failures are unimportant, then capital guidelines need only prevent the banking system from foundering. If the failure of a small number of banks can cause a systemic problem, however, perhaps the guidelines should be sufficiently stringent to prevent individual banks from failing.

Individual failures become especially significant in the case of large banks. Thomas Mayer (1975) cites four reasons why the demise of a large institution could create runs on the banking system. First, large bank failures receive considerable media attention, while small bank failures may go virtually unnoticed by depositors at other banks.[31] Second, the failure of a large bank probably provides an indication of the asset quality at sizable institutions. Because many small bank failures are due to dishonest or incompetent management or local economic conditions, depositors at other banks may justly conclude that their bank does not suffer from these burdens. Large banks that fail, however, probably have major problems in their loan portfolios. Other depositors may reason that if one large bank failed because of problem loans, their bank also could experience difficulties, since most large banks invest in the same types of loans.[32] Third, large banks have substantially more nondeposit liabilities (many with relatively short maturities) which are not guaranteed protection by the FDIC. Fourth, large banks have more deposits that exceed the coverage guaranteed by the FDIC.

Additional reasons for concern are given by Arnold A. Heggestad and B. Frank King (1982) and Bevis Longstreth (1983). Heggestad and King note that the failure of a large bank could significantly erode the insurance fund, reducing depositors' confidence in its stability. Longstreth points out that most large banks have substantial liabilities due to other banks, and so the demise of one bank could cause many others to fail.

George G. Kaufman (1985) disputes the theory that large bank problems have posed a significant threat to the economy or the banking system since the introduction of the FDIC. Even if a large bank experiences a run, Kaufman contends, funds are unlikely to be withdrawn in the form of currency, which could cause the money supply to contract. Instead, he maintains, they are likely to be re-deposited in banks perceived to be less risky. If institutions that face a run are solvent, the banking system, perhaps with the support of the Federal Reserve, can provide them with liquidity. Admittedly, banks in these straits will have to pay a premium for the recycled money, but this recourse is less serious than a sudden contraction of the money supply. If the bank is insolvent, Kaufman suggests that the FDIC should assume control and write down uninsured liabilities by the excess of losses over the bank's capital.

Without regulation, banks would increase their capital to reduce exposure to deposit runs. The increase would be less than is socially desirable, however, because the benefits to society from a safer banking system play no role in banks' capital decisions. Competitive pressures reflect only private gains to investors and suppliers.

The failure to consider benefits to society is especially important given that the demise of one bank can undermine the confidence of depositors at other banks. This is particularly troubling when a large bank fails (see box). Once a run starts spreading from bank to bank, the suspicion of instability can become a self-fulfilling prophecy with the potential to rock the banking system. Thus, one reason for regulating capital is to improve the banking system's stability by reducing the risk of individual bank failures.

A second argument for regulating capital is that government actions designed to protect banks already interfere with the competitive process that otherwise would determine bank capital. The government lessens the risk of bank runs through deposit insurance from the FDIC and access to the Federal Reserve's discount window. An unintended side effect of lowering depositor risk is that insurance also reduces depositors' insistence on adequate bank capital. According to several studies, banks respond by lowering their capital ratios, which in turn exposes the FDIC to greater potential losses.[11]

These two reasons for regulating bank capital partly offset each other. Increased government protection of banks implies a reduced danger of bank runs. For example, 100 percent insurance would virtually eliminate the risk of runs but would saddle the government with more of the risk of failure. The current insurance system contains elements of risk for the government and depositors alike. The government bears risk because it guarantees insurance up to the first $100,000 per depositor and generally absorbs additional losses. Yet some depositors also are vulnerable because the FDIC guarantees deposit insurance only on the first $100,000 per depositor per bank. The agency has provided protection to larger deposits, but only on a case-by-case basis. Under the current system, large depositors who do not remove their funds from a failing bank quickly enough risk losing part of their deposits.

Influencing Bank Capital

For capital regulations to reduce the risk of bank failure and FDIC losses, the regulations must have some influence over bank behavior. An important question is whether the regulators or the markets are dominant in determining

capital ratios. Indications that market influence is strong and regulatory influence weak have been found by studies in three separate areas: market willingness to supply capital, market control of bank risk-taking, and regulatory effectiveness in enforcing capital adequacy controls.

Ronald D. Watson (1975) and James G. Ehlen, Jr. (1983) emphasize the market's role in allocating capital. Watson argues that banks' problems in raising capital are not due to "a *shortage* of capital but an *unwillingness or inability to pay the 'going rate'*" (emphasis in original). Ehlen notes that large banks' profitability between 1964 and 1974 was too low to support asset growth, and so their equity capital ratios dropped. Gerald P. Dwyer, Jr. (1981) and Adrian W. Throop (1975) both claim empirical support for the market's primacy in allocating capital. They hypothesize that capital inflows into an industry are directly related to its profitability and that investors are willing to invest more in industries with high earnings. Both studies find that changes in bank capital are closely related to earnings. Dwyer's and Throop's studies may overstate the market's role, however, since most increases in bank capital result from retained earnings.[12] Thus, their results may show only that banks retain more income when they have more to retain.

The evidence on the market's role in controlling bank risk, including capital adequacy, is mixed. On the basis of his personal experience as a consultant in this area, David C. Cates (1985a) claims that creditors are monitoring and disciplining high-risk banking organizations. In surveying the literature on market discipline, Robert A. Eisenbeis and Gary G. Gilbert (1985) find evidence that the markets react to differential risk exposure in the pricing of debt and equity issues. One limitation of that body of literature is that it looks only at the market's evaluation of banks with assets in excess of $1 billion. Another limitation is that relatively little research has focused on whether market forces are strong enough to influence bank behavior. That is, even if the market charges higher premiums to riskier banks, those premiums may be too small to affect bank operations.

Evidence prior to imposition of the December 1981 regulatory guidelines suggests that the regulators were ineffective but later evidence implies the guidelines are influencing banking organizations. Sam Peltzman (1970), John H. Mingo (1975), and J. Kimball Dietrich and Christopher James (1983) use similar models to test the regulators' effectiveness in controlling bank capital during the 1960s and early 1970s. Using aggregate bank data from 1963 to 1965, Peltzman suggests that regulators have been ineffective;

Mingo, using a sample of 323 banks in 1970, concludes that regulators influence capital. Dietrich and James contend that Mingo confuses supervisory influence with market influences. Their results, based on the actions of more than 10,000 banks during the 1971 to 1974 period, support their argument that no supervisory influence exists. Alan J. Marcus (1983), who examines a sample of large bank holding companies over a 20-year period ending in 1977, contends that the supervisors evaluated a bank's capital relative to capital levels of its peers and that no absolute standards existed.

The regulators wielded considerable influence over large bank holding companies (over $1 billion in assets) after the capital adequacy guidelines were announced in 1981, according to Larry D. Wall and David R. Peterson (1985). Their study develops two separate models of the determination of bank holding company capital: one is relevant if the process is dominated by the regulatory guidelines, and the other if dominated by the financial markets. They estimate both models using a procedure that assigns each bank a probability of coming from the regulatory regime. From their finding that approximately 90 percent of the institutions are classified in the regulatory regime, the authors conclude that the regulatory guidelines dominate bank capital planning.

Thus, while available evidence suggests that the market may have significantly affected bank capital ratios at one time, one empirical study conducted since the guidelines were adopted indicates that the regulators are currently the dominant influence.

Capital Regulations and Bank Risk

Banks are subject to the risks of insolvency (which occurs when the value of liabilities exceeds the value of assets) and illiquidity (an inability to repay creditors on a timely basis). Increased capital can protect banks from insolvency by providing a cushion to absorb losses; it can shield banks from illiquidity by reinforcing depositors' confidence in their institutions. Indeed, if a bank's capital equals the sum of its risky assets plus its contingent liabilities, only fraud can cause it to fail. However, since banks must compete with other firms for capital, there are limits on the amount of new capital they can raise. Most proposals for increasing banks' equity capital focus on raising the equity capital to assets ratios somewhere between a fraction of a percentage point and a few percentage points. Would an increase of a few percentage points or less significantly reduce banks' risks of insolvency and illiquidity?

Capital's Effect on Insolvency Risk. Some argue against capital regulation on the grounds that management is far more important to bank solvency than is capital. They maintain that no amount of capital can prevent the failure of a mismanaged bank, and that a strong, well-managed bank can operate with little capital.

Empirical evidence that increased bank capital will not significantly reduce banks' risk of failure comes from Anthony M. Santomero and Joseph D. Vinso (1977). Using historical data on the volatility of changes in banks' capital, they estimate the risk that a sample of banks would exhaust their capital base. The evidence from their 1965 to 1974 sample period suggests that the probability of bank failure was small and that reasonable variations in the capital level would not have an economically significant effect on the risk of failure.[13]

Additional support for this hypothesis can be found in some reviews of bank failures. Cates Consulting Analysts, Inc. (1985), examining bank failures in 1984, concludes that capital risk was not a "significant factor in failure." The study notes that failed banks typically had lower capital ratios than their peers but points out that 70 percent of the failed banks had book capital ratios in 1982 that exceed the 1985 guidelines by 35 basis points or more. George Vojta (1973) concludes: "The weight of scholarly research is overwhelming to the effect that the level of bank capital has not been a material factor in preventing bank insolvency, and that ratio tests for capital adequacy have not been useful in assessing or predicting the capability of a bank to remain solvent."

On the other hand, James G. Ehlen, Jr. (1983) suggests that capital "plays a critical, although passive role, in maintaining the financial strength and credibility of a financial institution in the marketplace, a vital role for any institution that must rely on continuing access to funds from a wide variety of sources." While acknowledging that earnings are more important than capital, he remarks that a relatively high return on assets is usually associated with a relatively well-capitalized bank. He also points out that adversity suggests some sort of earnings problems, and that, to the extent earning power is reduced, the focus necessarily shifts to capital.

A study by Leon Korobow and David P. Stuhr (1983), which finds that regulators' evaluations of banks are significantly influenced by capital ratios, lends empirical support to the role of capital in maintaining bank safety. Furthermore, the conclusions Vojta drew in 1973 about scholarly research on bank failures must be reconsidered in the light of recent work. Studies by John F. Bovenzi, James A. Marino, and Frank E. McFadden (1983), Robert B. Avery and Gerald A. Hanweck

(1984), and Eugenie D. Short, Gerald P. O'Driscoll, Jr., and Franklin D. Berger (1985) all show a statistically significant relationship between a bank's capital ratio and its probability of failure.

Recent studies thus indicate that higher levels of capital are associated with a bank's chance of eluding failure. If a bank's losses are sufficiently great, then nothing short of 100 percent capital can prevent failure. But in many cases, greater capital can provide the time necessary for a bank to solve its problems. Empirical evidence suggests that observed variations in existing bank capital structures can have a statistically significant effect on institutions' probability of failure.

Responding to Capital Regulation. The finding that increased capital reduces a bank's risk of failure does not necessarily imply that regulatory mandated increases will reduce this risk. Augmenting capital reduces the risk of failure only if other factors, such as the riskiness of bank assets, are held constant. The same market forces that led banks to shrink their capital ratios prior to regulatory pressure could lead banks to assume other types of risk in response to capital regulation.

Banks can raise their capital ratios but leave their operations otherwise unchanged, accepting a reduced return as the cost of lower risk. The risk aversion of some closely held banks with undiversified portfolios may be such that the difference between the original risk/return relationship and that after capital standards are imposed barely affects management.

Some banks may be forced to innovate in response to capital regulation, however, if their stockholders are unwilling to accept the lower returns accompanying reduced risk. For instance, a bank can try to raise returns by passing the capital regulation costs on to customers. This maneuver will slow a bank's growth to the extent that consumer demand for its products responds to price: the more responsive the demand, the greater the loss. Demand is likely to be most responsive where banks face significant competition from other banks and from nonbank providers. Spared the banks' increased costs, nonbank providers may decline to go along with a price increase. Banks may have more success raising prices on services when contending only with other banks, which also have been forced by regulation to increase their capital. In this case, all banks may choose to raise their prices.

Banks also could increase their income by finding new sources that will not trigger regulatory demands for increased capital. Edward J. Kane (1977) suggests this possibility in his "regulatory dialectic theory," which states that imposing regulation limits banks' ability to serve their customers, and creates opportunities for profitable innovations that circumvent the regulation while meeting its formal requirements.[14] Regulators often respond to such innovations, but generally not until they identify the innovations' various effects. Following this delay, banks resume the process of identifying and exploiting loopholes.

Accepting more risks is an innovation that can raise bank earnings without requiring additional capital under the current guidelines. Increased risk can involve substituting assets with high risk and return for low-risk, low-return assets.[15] Additionally, increased risk can take the form of receiving fee income for risks that are assumed but not placed on the balance sheet, such as writing stand-by letters of credit. Banks that enhance their income in this fashion can maintain their prior return on equity and restore the value of the FDIC subsidy to its original value.

Koehn and Santomero (1980) note that the banks with the weakest capital adequacy (in the sense of capital per unit of risk) are those most likely to respond to higher capital standards by investing in more risky assets. This suggests that imposing binding regulations on all banks would increase rather than decrease the dispersion of bank risk exposure. A further implication is that capital regulations targeted at high-risk banks may be ineffective in reducing their risk of failure.

All the studies suggesting that banks will take more risks in the face of capital regulation are limited in two ways. First, they assume the capital standards are set independently of the particular bank's risk exposure. Risk-based capital standards (discussed in the accompanying box) may discourage banks from offsetting greater capital with riskier assets. Second, the empirical underpinning for the hypothesis is meager. Anecdotal evidence suggests banks are reducing their lower risk, more liquid assets in response to the regulation.[16] G. D. Koppenhaver (1985) examined the off-balance sheet activities of banks in the Seventh Federal Reserve District for September 1984. (These bank commitments may entail some risk but do not require immediate creation of an asset, and thus they are not recorded on bank balance sheets.[17]) Koppenhaver found that loan commitments, stand-by letters of credit, and commercial letters of credit all are inversely related to the bank's equity capital to assets ratio. Fredricka P. Santos (1985) found that changes in multinational banks' primary capital to assets ratio had a statistically significant effect on their off-balance sheet activities (as reported on Schedule L of the Reports of Condition that banks file with federal regulators).

Capital's Effect on Illiquidity Risk. If capital regulation reduces the risk of bank failure due to insolvency, it may in turn strengthen depositors' confidence in an institution, hence decreasing

ALTERNATIVE METHODS OF CAPITAL REGULATION

Studies showing that regulatory mandated increases in equity capital can lead banks to higher risk assume that the standards are risk-independent; that is, that regulators require both risky and safe banks to meet the same capital standards. Perhaps the standards would be more effective if they called for risky banks to maintain higher capital levels. Such variable capital guidelines could be based on preannounced standards or on the discretion of each bank's supervisor.

Measures Incorporating Risk

Regulators can impose variable capital guidelines based on ex ante, or forward-looking, measures of banks' risk exposure. Such measures would examine the risk that a bank could suffer significant losses in the future and would require institutions subject to greater risk to hold more capital. Ex ante measures could be based on the regulators' evaluation of the riskiness of a bank's balance sheet (and possibly its off-balance activities) or they could be derived from financial market pricing of bank securities. By contrast, if ex post measures were used, the regulators would base their current capital requirements for individual banks on the results of recent operations. Banks with a history of greater losses and weaker earnings would be required to hold more capital.

Measures Distinct from Financial Market Measures. U.S. bank regulators have used variable capital guidelines based on ex ante risk measure before. Shortly after World War II, regulators gauged capital adequacy on the basis of capital to risk assets, with risk assets defined as total assets less cash and U.S. government securities. In the 1950s the New York Federal Reserve Bank developed a risk-based system that divided assets into six categories, each assigned a specific percentage of required capital. Later in that decade the staff of the Federal Reserve Board of Governors developed a "Form for Analyzing Bank Capital" (ABC formula) that was used to help identify undercapitalized banks. The Board's formula was based on both the liquidation values that could be obtained for a bank's assets and on its liquidity.[33]

An advantage of using ex ante risk measures is that they provide for a larger capital cushion before a bank begins to experience problems. Thus, some high-risk banks that might otherwise be forced to close during difficult times would have the extra capital needed to survive. A further advantage is that such guidelines limit banks' ability to offset the effects of capital regulation by increasing their risk exposure. Under an ideal system, any benefit a bank obtained by raising its risks would be balanced fully by higher capital requirements.

A potential disadvantage of ex ante measures is that weighing risk can be subject to significant error. Banks could find themselves with artificial incentives to engage in some activities and artificial disincentives to engage in others—a similar drawback to risk-independent capital

guidelines. The major difference is that capital guidelines based on ex ante risk may encourage banks to seek out new ventures that have not been properly rated under the guidelines. In ferreting out opportunities whose dangers are underestimated by the regulators, banks may shoulder more risks than they intended.

Ex ante risk measures have been developed through "early warning studies," research whose purpose was to provide regulators with a system to signal future bank failures.[34] The relationship between capital adequacy and bank failure is more rigorously examined by Sherman J. Maisel (1981), who reviews capital adequacy and the risks that can cause insolvency.[35] Eli Talmor's (1980) work provides a complete theoretical model for determining the optimal capital standard. Using an ex ante risk measure, Talmor's model allows banks to fail due to insolvency or illiquidity.

Market Data. Bank regulators could rely on the financial markets for estimates of bank risk rather than attempting to calculate it themselves. The financial markets already evaluate the riskiness of bank certificates of deposit, subordinated debt, stock, and stock options. If the markets' risk premiums could be determined, these would provide an independent evaluation of a bank's risk.

Use of market risk premiums would necessarily be limited to banking organizations with publicly traded securities. The number of such organizations is relatively small, but they control a majority of the banking system's assets.

Perhaps the most significant objection to relying on market-based rather than regulator-determined measures is that the regulators possess better—or at least different—information than the markets. The regulators can examine individual bank assets and internal documents. Yet this advantage is countered by two advantages of the market. First, the market can make use of all the information it has available, while the regulators face political constraints.

Second, the number of market participants far exceeds the number of regulators. If an investor errs, he can at most have only a minuscule effect on the price of a bank security. If a regulator makes a mistake, it can be corrected by a bank only through a costly appeal to Congress or the courts. Furthermore, Jack Guttentag and Richard Herring (1984) point out that market participants who make systematic mistakes in evaluating what they call "project-specific" risk eventually will be driven out of business.[36]

A variant of the ex ante risk measure that relies on the market for bank stocks comes from George E. Morgan (1984). Morgan states that a bank's risk should be measured by its stock's Beta coefficient from the capital asset pricing model (CAPM). His results suggest that optimal regulation could lead to the regulators' requiring all banking organizations to have the same Beta.

(continued on next page)

A potentially significant problem with Morgan's approach to capital regulation is the weakness in available models of stock returns. The CAPM has been questioned on several points, including its assertion that all stock market returns can be explained by a single factor. An alternative model of stock returns that incorporates multiple factors is the arbitrage pricing model. Morgan notes that the capital regulation model also could be applied if the arbitrage pricing theory (APT) model of stock returns is used. Unfortunately, while APT does not suffer the same problems as the CAPM, the use of APT by the regulators is not feasible until some general agreement can be reached as to which factors belong in the model.[37]

Even if the CAPM and APT models had no theoretical and empirical flaws in explaining stock returns, both measures capture only part of a banking organization's risk exposure. Morgan notes that since Beta measures only the systematic risk of a stock, banks could try to increase their non-systematic risk. One way to capture systematic and non-systematic risk would be to use the implied standard deviations from stock options. Alan J. Marcus and Israel Shaked (1984) and J. Huston McCulloch (1985) recently used this approach to estimate the value of FDIC deposit insurance. Regrettably, the number of stocks with publicly traded options is far fewer than the number of publicly traded stocks and some unresolved empirical issues cloud the estimation of implied standard deviations.[38] Another way is to use the risk premium on bank deposits, as James B. Thomson (1985) has done, to estimate the value of deposit insurance. A minor difficulty in using Beta, implied standard deviations, and deposit risk premiums to establish risk based capital standards is that the financial markets should recognize that short-run increases in bank risk eventually will be offset by regulatory actions. Thus, market measures of risk may be biased toward the regulatory standards.

Ex Post Risk Measures. Ex post risk measures entail less measurement error than ex ante measures, as the results of a bank's past risk-taking are evident in its income statement. One disadvantage is that ex post measures lag behind changes in actual risk exposure. This lag could permit one-time gains to banks that increase their holdings of high-risk, high-return assets in that they would gain the additional income for a period without having to increase their capital ratios immediately. Similarly, banks that decrease their risk exposure would pay a one-time penalty because they would have to maintain the higher capital ratios until their income stream reflected the decrease. Another possible drawback is that ex post capital requirements force banks to raise capital at a time when it is likely to be most difficult. Furthermore, an ex post request for additional capital may come too late to prevent some troubled banks from failing.

An example of an ex post measure of risk is volatility of a bank's capital account, used by Santomero and Vinso (1977). Santomero (1983) points out that the empirical application of this method could be limited by the frequency with which the economic environment changes.

However, he claims this approach has better theoretical justification than many of the early warning studies of bank failure. Another recent study, by Terrence M. Belton (1985), demonstrates how capital standards could be tied to one aspect of bank risk: the risk of loan losses. He finds that such a risk-related standard could have reduced substantially the number of banks for which loan losses exceeded capital in 1983 and 1984.

Supervision without Numerical Guidelines

Capital supervision without preannounced standards was attempted in the period immediately preceding adoption of the current system of capital regulation. This approach theoretically allows regulators to evaluate a variety of factors in determining what constitutes adequate capital for individual banks. Under numerical guidelines, regulators are more likely to focus only on those factors that appear in their formula. For example, the riskiness of a bank loan depends not only on the type of loan (for instance, commercial versus consumer) but also on how the process is managed. Loans that are relatively safe when made by banks with prudent, competent management and sound procedures may be excessively risky when extended by banks with imprudent or incompetent management and weak procedures.[39] The regulators may have more difficulty incorporating their information about a bank's management under numerical guidelines than under an informal system of capital supervision.

The obvious disadvantage of supervision without numerical guidelines is that it has proven ineffective. During the 1970s the regulators supervised bank capital without announcing quantitative standards that individual banks were expected to meet. The result of this type of regulation, according to Marcus (1983), was that regulators could prevent any bank from operating with much less capital than its peers but they were unable to prevent capital ratios from declining throughout the industry.

An inherent reason for this ineffectiveness is the difficulty regulators have defending their judgment in Congress and the courts without some objective standard. An additional reason for guidelines based on a preannounced formula is that the guidelines aid banks in planning for the future.

Summary

Various methods exist for setting regulatory standards for individual banks' capital. The standard may or may not depend on the specific banks' risk. When it does, the risk measure can be calculated from current accounting information, recent market information, or historical accounting results. Furthermore, regulators may choose to announce publicly their formula for determining optimal capital or they may elect to disclose the guidelines only to bank management. The appropriate method for regulating capital depends on such issues as the goals of capital regulation and the workability and enforceability of the various approaches.

their incentive to participate in a bank run. However, an increase in capital of only a few percentage points can do no more than reduce the likelihood of deposit runs—it will not eliminate the risk.[18] Deposit runs are always possible so long as any group of depositors is at risk should a bank fail. The only way to eliminate this risk would be for banks to maintain capital equal to 100 percent of risky assets plus contingent liabilities, or for the FDIC to insure all deposits.

Mingo (1985) argues that capital regulation will increase rather than reduce the risk of bank illiquidity. If an institution falls below the regulatory capital guidelines because of a one-time loss, then the public may believe the bank is undercapitalized and will be subject to regulatory action or perhaps even failure. The result could be a run on the bank by uninsured depositors. Mingo further points out that this risk is independent of the capital standard set by the regulators; it could as easily happen if the standard were 8.5 percent of assets as if it were 5.5 percent.

Mingo's concern should be addressed in the development of capital adequacy standards but it does not necessarily preclude establishment of numerical capital guidelines. The guidelines are intended to create a buffer for losses without resulting in bank failure. To undercut the risk of illiquidity occasioned by a bank run, the agencies could announce that unanticipated losses occasionally will push some banks below the guidelines. In such cases, banks whose capital remains above some other target (for example, whose capital is equal to zero percent of assets) will be subject to special regulatory attention but will not be closed.[19]

Drawbacks to Regulating Capital

Capital regulation can impose a variety of costs on society. For example, while increased capital may protect the banking system by reducing the risk of bank failure, it also shields mismanaged firms. As A. Dale Tussing (1967) points out, banks are disproportionately important to the development of their communities because they control the allocation of credit. Therefore, protecting banks from failure can impose costs as well as provide benefits.

Another potential disadvantage of regulating capital is that it may render banks less competitive by raising their cost of funds. The FDIC deposit insurance guarantee lowers the price banks must pay to attract deposits. Furthermore, the cost of uninsured debt is generally less than that of equity, judging from at least some theoretical models of capital structure.[20]

Two dangers of reducing banks' competitive position are that it could lessen the efficiency of the financial system as well as the proportion of the money supply deposited at banks. A weakened competitive position implies that banks will forgo some share of the market for various financial services. Such a loss may be desirable to the extent that banks' current share is attributable to a deposit insurance subsidy. But where banks' market share owes to their greater efficiency, the loss they suffer ultimately may exact a toll from society, which may be deprived of the efficient competitor.

The market for transaction accounts, where most of the money supply resides, are of special concern because of society's strong interest in protecting the money supply. Currently the safety of transaction accounts at most depositories is assured both by deposit insurance and the institutions' ability to borrow through the Federal Reserve discount window.[21] If insured institutions were to lose a substantial share of the transactions account market, then the government's ability to protect the money supply could be undermined. Thus, capital regulation designed to protect the safety of banks and other insured depositories would be counterproductive if it substantially reduced the depositories' share of the market for transactions accounts.

Two additional disadvantages could arise if banks offset capital regulation by undertaking additional risks. First, the FDIC's losses actually could grow if banks increase their risks by more than they expand their capital. Furthermore, even if banks seek to offset the increased capital only partly, they may inadvertently take on more risks than they intended. The second problem is that as banks attempt to raise their return on equity, they may invest in risky projects that could not otherwise receive funding. Society might find it less costly to allow banks to exploit deposit insurance through inadequate capital than through high-risk investments.

Alternatives to Capital Regulation

Neither of the principal potential advantages—the reduced risk of a banking system collapse and increased protection of the FDIC—is necessarily unique to higher equity capital ratios. Thus, before we adopt capital regulation as a solution to these problems, we should examine the alternatives.

Protecting the Banking System. The banking system is vulnerable to collapse because of its dependence on depositor confidence. Increased equity capital can enhance depositors' confidence in the long-run stability of their banks, thus reducing the risk of deposit runs. However, increasing equity capital is not sufficient to maintain depositor confidence, for depositors remain exposed to some risk. Nor is capital regulation necessary for promoting depositor confidence. The government can lower the risk of deposit runs through deposit insurance, which serves as a substitute for equity capital by curtailing the risk borne by depositors. The FDIC has effectively prevented bank runs from spreading since its creation in 1933. Benjamin M. Friedman and Peter Formuzis (1975) suggest that insurance is such a potent substitute that it virtually eliminates depositors' incentive to demand higher capital ratios.

An alternative to extending FDIC insurance is to rely on the Federal Reserve as the protective "lender of last resort." In this role the Federal Reserve can ensure that the banking system does not collapse by providing liquidity so that banks can meet depositor demands for withdrawals. Eventually, as depositors see that their banks are not going to fail due to illiquidity, they stop withdrawing deposits.[22] One problem is that relying on the Federal Reserve may permit occasional bank runs when depositors temporarily lose confidence in some institutions.

Protecting the FDIC. In addition to protecting society, increased equity capital could reduce the losses to uninsured creditors and the FDIC when banks do fail. Capital regulation may not be appropriate protection for uninsured creditors, who should be able to demand adequate compensation for the risks they take without government help. Capital regulation may be desirable, however, if it reduces losses experienced by the FDIC.

The FDIC generally requires that a troubled bank's losses be borne first by its stockholders and subordinated debtholders before the agency contributes to protect depositors. Losses shouldered by the FDIC should be paid out of banks' accumulated insurance premiums, but if losses exceed the insurance fund the agency would turn to Congress and the Treasury for support.[23]

The FDIC must insist that banks maintain positive economic net worth (the market value of assets less market value of liabilities) if it wishes to prevent banks from operating with negative net worth. As the experience of many savings and loans demonstrates, the market will not necessarily close federally insured depositories even if their economic net worth turns negative.[24]

Additional equity capital may be required to give the FDIC time to identify problem banks and to absorb substantial losses should an institution fail. However, if the FDIC could close banks before their economic net worth turns negative or if it required banks to issue a substantial amount of uninsured, subordinated debt, the agency would have less need for equity capital regulation. The FDIC could even choose to absorb the greater losses that might result from weaker capital standards, but require that banks pay sufficiently higher premiums to cover the expected rise in losses.

Closing Banks. The FDIC would face several problems if it relied solely on closing banks before their economic net worth turned negative. First, failure currently is defined in terms of accounting net worth rather than economic net worth. Banks can show positive book value even when their economic net worth is negative, because they are not required to recognize changes in the market values of their assets and liabilities in their accounting records.[25] Thus, under present procedures the FDIC would be exposed to substantial losses even if it held complete control over the timing of bank closings. Moreover, managements of banks with positive book value but negative net economic worth realize that unless they can increase their earnings by more than their deficit, they face future closure as the economic losses are recognized in the accounting records. This provides a strong incentive to take on assets with high returns even if they also carry high risks. If the assets are good, the bank may continue in operation; if not, the bank management sacrifices nothing since it was headed for failure anyway. The real loser when a bank invests in high risk/high return assets is the FDIC, which must absorb significantly greater losses if the assets prove to be bad.

A possible solution to the net worth problem is to use market values rather than values based on the current generally accepted accounting principles.[26] One difficulty, though, is that the market value of a bank's assets depends partly on whether they are assessed at liquidation value or at their value to the bank if it is a going concern. In the latter case, the assets' value generally exceeds their liquidation value. Recognizing this problem, George G. Kaufman (1985) suggests that large failed banks be run by the FDIC rather than liquidated.

Another obstacle to this approach is that the market value of an asset or liability sometimes is hard to determine. While the effect of interest rate changes can be measured using discounted cash flow techniques, establishing the change in value due to changes in credit risk is much more difficult.[27] Edward J. Kane (1985) recommends that the FDIC's liquidation division arrange periodic auctions of assets as a way of providing some measure of value for assets hard to estimate. Such auctions would not eliminate the problem of valuing assets but might help set reasonable parameters for the process. A further drawback of market value accounting is that the FDIC may find it politically difficult to force banks to reduce the value of some assets even though the agency and the banks know they are overvalued.

Problems with obtaining the market value of many assets and liabilities almost guarantee that their estimated value will differ from their true economic value. Estimated values need not be perfect, however, to represent an improvement over current practice. To the extent that market value accounting yields better estimates of economic net worth than does current accounting practices, this approach may help the FDIC to protect itself better.

A second reason the FDIC might be unable to shield itself from losses is that a bank's value may be subject to discontinuous drops.[28] In theory, the FDIC need not suffer losses if a bank's value drops at a continuous rate. Suppose, however, that a bank loses a substantial portion of its asset value because of management fraud or a sudden change in the market value of its assets. The FDIC would not have ample time to defend itself against such a sudden drop even if it closed banks as soon as it knew their economic net worth had plunged to zero.

The questionable cost-effectiveness of monitoring all banks closely enough to recognize those whose net worth is turning negative is a related problem. Bank examinations are costly to both the government and the banks. The costs of capital regulation must be weighed against those of bank examination to determine the minimum amount of capital required to protect the FDIC.

If the FDIC could close banks before their economic net worth turned negative, then the agency might protect itself from losses even when banks held virtually no equity capital. To justify capital regulation on the grounds of safeguarding the FDIC implies that the agency often is unable to close banks before their economic value turns negative. The problems in using accounting values rather than economic values and in measuring the latter accurately, the risk of discontinuous drops in asset values, and the costs of bank examination all make it difficult for the FDIC to avoid losses. These impediments suggest that some minimal level of capital regulation might be appropriate to give the FDIC time to identify problem banks.

Subordinated Debt. Aside from its role in affording the FDIC time to recognize problems, capital also might be required to absorb substantial losses should a bank fail. If capital guidelines are to be set sufficiently high to protect the FDIC, should the regulations apply to equity capital alone or to the sum of equity capital and subordinated debt? Since subordinated debtholders absorb losses only when a firm is bankrupt, the principal advantage of regulating only equity capital is that banks can charge losses to their capital account without failing. The effectiveness of equity capital in preventing bank failures may be important in reducing FDIC losses if, as Stanley C. Silverberg (1985) suggests, the value of a big institution drops when the market believes it is going to fail.

An advantage to regulating the sum of equity capital plus subordinated debt is that it may reduce regulatory costs by allowing banks to issue subordinated debt rather than equity if debt is less expensive. Furthermore, buyers of subordinated debt wish to invest in low-risk institutions while equity buyers may prefer to invest in riskier banks if expected returns also are higher. Thus, banks that issue subordinated debt are less likely to try to work around capital regulation by taking higher risks.

Insurance Premiums. The argument that the FDIC might reduce its losses through capital regulation does not necessarily imply that such regulation is the best way to protect the fund. An alternative would be for the agency to substitute higher insurance premiums in return for allowing lower capital standards. A potential advantage is that banks might find higher premiums less costly than higher capital standards. The current fixed-rate deposit insurance structure could accommodate such premiums, or they could be part of a risk-rated premium system.[29]

Summary

The theoretical case against relying on the market to control bank equity capital positions is strong. Market determined capital ratios tend to ignore the impact of one bank's failure on other banks. Additionally, it seems clear that banks will exploit the protection offered by deposit insurance to reduce their capital ratios. The importance of both these effects is less clear. Since its creation in the 1930s, FDIC deposit insurance has acted as a potent substitute for bank capital in maintaining depositor confidence: not one bank failure has sparked runs at other banks. Evidence to indicate that the risk of deposit runs would be reduced substantially by capital regulation is sparse. Furthermore, the quantitative effect of insurance on bank capital ratios has yet to be established.[30]

The theoretical case against using equity capital regulation to correct for market failure is strong as well, but it, too, lacks crucial empirical evidence. The primary arguments against such regulation are that the market—rather than the regulators—controls bank capital ratios; that regulation would be ineffective in reducing bank risk exposure; that regulation has significant disadvantages; and that better alternatives exist.

The contention that the market controls bank capital ratios is the least persuasive. Some studies from the period prior to capital guidelines indeed suggest that the market controlled banking organizations' capital; however, evidence from the current policy regime points to the regulators' effectiveness in requiring specified capital levels.

While equity capital has a statistically significant effect on a bank's risk of failure, the benefits of increased capital may be offset by an increase in the riskiness of bank assets and off-balance sheet activities. The theoretical evidence is clear that some banks will respond to capital regulation by assuming additional risk, yet the empirical support for this hypothesis is weak.

The empirical evidence on capital regulation's effect on bank competitiveness and on resource allocation is also weak. However, theoretical evidence implies that capital regulation reduces banks' ability to compete with nonbanking organizations and that it might result in a misallocation of society's resources.

If increased equity capital reduces banks' risk of insolvency, it also could reduce their risk of illiquidity by increasing depositor confidence. However, increased equity capital is neither necessary nor sufficient for preventing bank failures due to illiquidity. The FDIC has effectively shrunk the risk of deposit runs and the danger could be eliminated if the agency provided 100 percent deposit insurance. Alternatively, the Federal Reserve could prevent banks from failing due to illiquidity by acting as a lender of last resort.

Capital regulation could lessen FDIC losses by providing a cushion to absorb losses. Potential substitutes for shielding the FDIC include closing banks before they exhaust their economic net worth, requiring banks to issue additional subordinated debt, and raising FDIC premiums. However, these measures may be inadequate to protect the FDIC fully. The experience of economically failed savings and loans shows the market will not necessarily close bankrupt institutions that are federally insured. This suggests that some minimal equity capital standards may help reduce FDIC losses.

NOTES

[1] Ben S. Bernake (1983) argues that the collapse of the banking system led to a sharp reduction in bank loans to small business and that this caused a sharper drop in economic activity. Milton Friedman and Anna Schwartz (1963) suggest that the collapse of the banking system led to a steep decline in the money supply, which both deepened and prolonged the Depression.

[2] Banks must maintain depositor confidence if they are to remain liquid since a large portion of bank deposits can be withdrawn with little or no notice should depositors lose faith. A significant portion of bank assets are invested in longer term loans, which cannot be liquidated on short notice.

[3] See Karlyn Mitchell (1984) for a discussion of why capital ratios have fallen.

[4] The issues in regulating the capital of banks owned by holding companies are reviewed by Larry D. Wall (1985).

[5] The current regulatory guidelines and some of their effects on banks are discussed by R. Alton Gilbert, Courtenay C. Stone, and Michael E. Trebing (1985).

[6] See David C. Cates (1985a) for a discussion of some of the issues in determining the adequacy of the loan loss allowance. John J. Mingo (1985) argues against reducing primary capital by intangibles. The case for increasing required levels of subordinated debt is given by Paul M Horvitz (1984) and Larry D. Wall (1984). Stanley C. Silverberg (1985) discusses the issues involved in requiring banks to meet a nine percent capital to assets ratio where capital is defined to include subordinated debt.

[7] The proposition that there is no optimal capital ratio was first developed for corporations in general by Franco Modigliani and Merton H. Miller (1958).

[8] See Stewart C. Myers (1984) for a survey of the literature on factors influencing corporate capital ratios. Yair E. Orgler and Robert A Taggart, Jr. (1983) provide a recent discussion of the factors influencing bank capital positions.

[9] See George J. Benston (1983) for a further discussion of banks' vulnerability.

[10] See also John J. Pringle (1974) for a discussion of the influence of maturity structure of liabilities on bank capital.

[11] Among the theoretical studies that have examined this issue are Orgler and Taggart (1983), Stephen A. Buser, Andrew H. Chen, and Edward J. Kane (1981), John H. Kareken and Neil Wallace (1978), William F. Sharpe (1978), and Robert A. Taggart, Jr. and Stuart I. Greenbaum (1978).

[12] Reliance on retained earnings for increased capital is one element of the pecking order theory of capital structure discussed by Myers (1984).

[13] Santomero (1983) points out that the reliability of their estimates depends on the nature of the process generating changes in bank capital. If the stochastic process changes over time, then the estimates of risk or failure must also change.

[14] See also Robert A. Eisenbeis (1980).

[15] See Yehuda Kahane (1977), Michael Koehn and Anthony M. Santomero (1980), and Chun H. Lam and Andrew H. Chen (1985) for theoretical models of the effect of capital regulation on a bank's asset portfolio allocation.

[16] For example, see Eamonn Fingleton (1985).

[17] Not all off-balance sheet activities increase bank risk; some activities can be risk reducing. For example, interest rate options can be used to hedge mismatches in the maturity structure of bank assets and liabilities.

[18] Benjamin M. Friedman and Peter Formuzis (1975) suggest that increased bank capital will provide little additional protection to depositors.

[19] The agencies may choose to close banks with inadequate but non-zero capital if they place a higher priority on protecting the FDIC than on preventing bank failures. See the discussion below on the use of capital standards to protect the FDIC fund.

[20] See Myers (1984).

[21] Among the uninsured alternatives to bank transactions accounts are accounts offered by money market mutual funds. Most money market funds already allow check withdrawals (although they often require that checks at least equal some minimum amount) and the potential exists for them to expand their share of transactions accounts if banks become sufficiently uncompetitive.

[22] See Thomas M. Humphrey and Robert E. Keleher (1984) for a historical perspective on the role of a lender of last resort.

[23] Generally, though, the resources of the FDIC would not be expected to suffice for loss coverage from extraordinarily adverse economic conditions caused by bad macroeconomic policies or unanticipated exogenous shocks to the economy.

[24] See Edward J. Kane (1982) for a discussion of the role of deposit insurance in maintaining failed thrifts.

[25] Kane (1982) discusses the ability of savings and loans to remain in business in spite of very substantial declines in the market value of their mortgage portfolio due to increases in interest rates. He points out that savings and loans, like banks, need not recognize declines in market values and that public confidence in the institutions is maintained by FSLIC insurance.

[26] Both Kane (1985) and George G. Kaufman (1985) have recently advocated this.

[27] One of the biggest problems in applying discounted cash flow techniques would be determining the effective maturity of some types of assets and deposits or valuing the options with which they are associated.

[28]The effect of a discontinuous change in bank operations is developed by Thomas Ho and Anthony Saunders (1981) for the case of depositors' reactions to bank risk taking.

[29]For example, Robert B. Avery, Gerald A. Hanweck, and Myron L. Kwast (1985) develop a variable-rate insurance scheme based on historic FDIC costs. The scheme includes a factor for a bank's equity capital to assets ratio.

[30]Estimation of the effect of insurance on bank capital ratios by comparing insured and uninsured banks is impossible because virtually all banks are insured.

[31]Horvitz (1975) points out that reports of large bank problems do not appear to be causing runs at other banks.

[32]Mayer perhaps anticipated the future in 1975 when he used loans to foreign countries as an example of the type of problem loans that could lead to a systemic problem.

[33]See Sandra L. Ryon for a history of bank capital adequacy standards in the United States.

[34]Recent examples include John F. Bovenzi, James A. Marino, and Frank E. McFadden (1983), Robert B. Avery and Gerald Hanweck (1984), and Eugene D. Short, Gerald O'Driscoll, and Franklin D. Berger (1985).

[35]See Chapters 2 (prepared by Laurie Goodman), 3 and 4 of Sherman J. Maisel's *Risk and Capital Adequacy in Commercial Banks*.

[36]Guttentag and Herring (1984) also point out that the market will systematically underestimate the risk of economy-wide shocks. This could provide a rationale allowing the regulators to evaluate bank risk if it could be shown that they have better estimates of the risk of major macroeconomic shocks.

[37]Richard Roll and Stephen A. Ross (1984) describe the arbitrage pricing model and give the four factors they believe influence stock returns. Not all analysts agree with their factor choices.

[38]See Richard Schmalensee and Robert R. Trippi (1978) for a discussion of some of the empirical questions surrounding the use of the standard deviation implied by stock options.

[39]For example, most banks that made major loans to energy firms did not suffer Penn Square's fate.

REFERENCES

Andrews, Suzanna. "Accounting for LDC Debt." *Institutional Investor*, vol. 18 (August 1984), pp. 189-194.

Avery, Robert B. and Gerald A. Hanweck. "A Dynamic Analysis of Bank Failures." *Proceedings of a Conference on Bank Structure and Competition*, Federal Reserve Bank of Chicago, 1984.

Avery, Robert B., Gerald A. Hanweck, and Myron L. Kwast. "An Analysis of Risk-Based Deposit Insurance for Commercial Banks." *Proceedings of a Conference on Bank Structure and Competition*, Federal Reserve Bank of Chicago, 1985, forthcoming.

Belton, Terrence M. "Risk-Based Capital Standards for Commercial Banks." presented to the Federal Reserve System Conference on Banking and Financial Structure, New Orleans, September 1985.

Benston, George J. "Deposit Insurance and Bank Failures." *Economic Review*, Federal Reserve Bank of Atlanta, vol. 68 (March 1983), pp. 4-17.

Bernake, Ben S. "Nonmonetary Effects of the Financial Crisis in the Propagation of the Great Depression," *American Economic Review*, vol. 73 (June 1983), pp. 257-276.

Bovenzi, John F., James A. Marino and Frank E. McFadden "Commercial Bank Failure Prediction Models." *Economic Review*, Federal Reserve Bank of Atlanta, vol. 68 (November 1983), pp. 14-26.

Buser, Stephen A., Andrew H. Chen, and Edward J. Kane. "Federal Deposit Insurance, Regulatory Policy, and 'Optimal Bank Capital.'" *Journal of Finance*, vol. 36 (March 1981), pp. 51-60.

Cates, David C. "Management Discipline: The True Bulwark Against Banking Crisis," *Issues in Bank Regulation*, vol 3 (Winter 1985a), pp. 4-11.

Cates, David C. "What's an Adequate Loan-Loss Reserve?" *ABA Banking Journal*, vol 77 (March 1985b), pp. 41-43.

Cates Consulting Analysts, Inc. "Analysis of 1984 Commercial Bank and Savings and Loan Failures," mimeo, January 28, 1985.

Dietrich, J. Kimball and Christopher James. "Regulation and the Determination of Bank Capital Changes: A Note," *Journal of Finance*, vol. 38 (December 1983), pp. 1651-1658.

Dwyer, Gerald P., Jr. "The Effects of the Banking Acts of 1933 and 1935 on Capital Investment in Commercial Banking," *Journal of Money, Credit and Banking*, vol. 13 (May 1981), pp. 192-204.

Ehlen, James G. "A Review of Bank Capital and Its Adequacy," *Economic Review*, Federal Reserve Bank of Atlanta, vol. 68 (November 1983), pp. 54-60.

Eisenbeis, Robert A. "Financial Innovation and the Role of Regulation: Implications for Banking Organization, Structure and Regulations." Board of Governors of the Federal Reserve, February 1980.

Eisenbeis, Robert A. and Gary G. Gilbert. "Market Discipline and the Prevention of Bank Problems and Failures." *Issues in Bank Regulation*, vol. 3 (Winter 1985), pp. 16-23.

Fingleton, Eamonn. "Why Capital Ratios Are a Cause for Concern." *Euromoney* (June 1985), pp. 98-99 and 103-104.

Friedman, Benjamin M. and Peter Formuzis. "Bank Capital: The Deposit-Protection Incentive," *Journal of Bank Research*, vol 6 (Autumn 1975), pp. 208-218.

Friedman, Milton and Anna J. Schwartz. *A Monetary History of the United States 1867-1960*. National Bureau of Economic Research, Studies in Business Cycles, no. 12. Princeton: Princeton University Press, 1963.

Gilbert, R. Alton, Courtenay C. Stone, and Michael E. Trebing. "The New Bank Capital Adequacy Standards," *Review*, Federal Reserve Bank of St. Louis, vol. 67 (May 1985), pp. 12-20.

Guttentag, Jack and Richard Herring. "Credit Rationing and Financial Disorder," *Journal of Finance*, vol. 39 (December 1984), pp. 1359-1382.

Heggestad, Arnold A. and B. Frank King. "Regulation of Bank Capital: An Evaluation," *Economic Review*, Federal Reserve Bank of Atlanta, vol. 67 (March 1982), pp. 35-43.

Ho, Thomas and Anthony Saunders. "A Catastrophe Model of Bank Failure." *Journal of Finance*, vol 35 (December 1980), pp. 1189-1207.

Horvitz, Paul M. "Failures of Large Banks: Implications for Bank Supervision and Deposit Insurance." *Journal of Financial and Quantitative Analysis*, vol. 10 (November 1975), pp. 589-601.

Horvitz, Paul M. "Market Discipline Is Best Provided by Subordinated Creditors," *American Banker* (July 15, 1984), pp. 4 and 8.

Humphrey, Thomas M. and Robert E. Keleher. "Lender of Last Resort: A Historical Perspective." Federal Reserve Bank of Richmond Working Paper No. 84-3.

Kane, Edward J. "Good Intentions and Unintended Evil: The Case Against Selective Credit Allocation." *Journal of Money, Credit and Banking*, vol. 9 (February 1977), pp. 55-69.

Kane, Edward J. "S&Ls and Interest-Rate Regulation: The FSLIC as an In-Place Bailout Program," *Housing Finance Review*, vol. 1 (July 1982), pp. 219-243.

Kane, Edward J. "Proposals to Reduce FDIC and FSLIC Subsidies to Deposit-Institution Risk-Taking." *Issues in Bank Regulation*, vol. 8 (Winter 1985), pp. 24-34.

Kahane, Yehuda. "Capital Adequacy and the Regulation of Financial Intermediaries," *Journal of Banking and Finance*, vol. 1 (1977), pp. 207-218.

Kareken, John H. and Neil Wallace. "Deposit Insurance and Bank Regulation: A Partial-Equilibrium Exposition." *Journal of Business*, vol. 51 (July 1978), pp. 413-438.

Kaufman, George G. "Implications of Large Bank Problems and Insolvencies for the Banking Industry and Economic Policy." *Issues in Bank Regulation*, vol. 8 (Winter 1985), pp. 35-42.

Koehn, Michael and Anthony M. Santomero. "Regulation of Bank Capital and Portfolio Risk," *Journal of Finance*, vol. 35 (December 1980), pp. 1235-1244.

Koppenhaver, G. D. "Predicting the Off-Balance Sheet Behavior of Seventh District Commercial Banks." *Proceedings of a Conference on Bank Structure and Competition*, Federal Reserve Bank of Chicago, 1985, forthcoming.

Korobow, Leon and David P. Stuhr. "The Relevance of Peer Groups in Early Warning Analysis." *Economic Review*, Federal Reserve Bank of Atlanta, vol. 68 (November 1983), pp. 27-34.

Lam, Chun H. and Andrew H. Chen. "Joint Effects of Interest Rate Deregulation and Capital Requirements on Optimal Bank Portfolio Adjustments," *Journal of Finance*, vol. 40 (June 1985), pp. 563-575.

Longstreth, Bevis. "In Search of a Safety Net for the Financial Services Industry." *Bankers Magazine*, vol. 166 (July-August 1983), pp. 27-34.

Maisel, Sherman J., ed. *Risk and Capital Adequacy in Commercial Banks*. Chicago: University of Chicago Press, 1981.

Marcus, Alan J. "The Bank Capital Decision: A Time Series-Cross Section Analysis." *Journal of Finance*, vol. 38 (September 1983), pp. 1217-1232.

Marcus, Alan J., and Israel Shaked. "The Valuation of FDIC Deposit Insurance Using Option-pricing Estimates," *Journal of Money, Credit and Banking*, vol. 16 (Nov. 1984), pp. 446-60.

Mayer, Thomas. "Should Large Banks Be Allowed to Fail?" *Journal of Financial and Quantitative Analysis*, vol. 10 (November 1975), pp. 603-610.

McCulloch, J. Huston. "Interest Risk Sensitive Deposit Insurance Premia: Stable ACH Estimates," *Journal of Banking and Finance*, vol. 9 (March 1985), pp. 137-56.

Mingo, John J. "Capital Ratios: The Reg Q Fiasco of the Future," *Bank Expansion Reporter*, vol. 4 (January 21, 1985), pp. 1, 9-14.

Mingo, John J. "Regulatory Influence on Bank Capital Investment," *Journal of Finance*, vol. 30 (September 1975), pp. 1111-1121.

Mitchell, Karlyn. "Capital Adequacy at Commercial Banks," *Economic Review*, Federal Reserve Bank of Kansas City (September/October 1984), pp. 17-30.

Modigliani, Franco and Merton H. Miller. "The Cost of Capital, Corporation Finance, and the Theory of Investment," *American Economic Review*, vol. 48 (June 1958), pp. 261-297.

Morgan, George E. "On the Adequacy of Bank Capital Regulation." *Journal of Financial and Quantitative Analysis*, vol. 19 (June 1984), pp. 141-162.

Myers, Stewart C. "The Capital Structure Puzzle." *Journal of Finance*, vol. 39 (July 1984), pp. 575-592.

Orgler, Yair E. and Robert A. Taggart, Jr. "Implications of Corporate Capital Structure Theory for Banking Institutions," *Journal of Money, Credit and Banking*, rd. 15 (May 1983), pp. 212-221.

Peltzman, Sam. "Capital Investment in Commercial Banking and Its Relationship to Portfolio Regulation." *Journal of Political Economy*, vol. 78 (January 1970), pp. 1-26.

Pringle, John J. "The Capital Decision in Commercial Banks." *Journal of Finance*. vol. 29 (June 1974), pp. 779-795.

Roll, Richard and Stephen A. Ross. "The Arbitrage Pricing Theory Approach to Strategic Portfolio Planning." *Financial Analysts Journal*, vol. 40 (May/June 1984), pp. 14-26.

Ryon, Sandra L. "History of Bank Capital Adequacy Analysis." Unpublished Working Paper No. 69-4, Federal Deposit Insurance Corporation.

Santomero, Anthony M. "Current Views of the Bank Capital Issue." A study prepared for the Trustees of the Banking Research Fund of the Association of Reserve City Bankers. January 1983.

Santomero, Anthony M. and Joseph D. Vinso. "Estimating the Probability of Failure for Commercial Banks and the Banking System." *Journal of Banking and Finance*, vol. 1 (1977), pp. 185-205.

Santomero, Anthony M. and Ronald D. Watson. "Determining an Optimal Capital Standard for the Banking Industry." *Journal of Finance*. vol. 32 (September 1977), pp. 1267-1281.

Santomero, Anthony M. and Joseph D. Vinso. "Estimating the Probability of Failure for Commercial Banks and the Banking System." *Journal of Banking and Finance*, vol. 1 (1977), pp. 185-205.

Santos, Fredricka P. "Capital Requirements and the Growth of Schedule L Off Balance Sheet Activities Among 16 Multinational Banks," presented to the Federal Reserve System Conference on Banking and Financial Structure, New Orleans, September 1985.

Schmalensee, Richard and Robert R. Trippi. "Common Stock Volatility Expectations Implied by Option Premia." *Journal of Finance*. vol. 33 (March 1978), pp. 129-147.

Sharpe, William F. "Bank Capital Adequacy, Deposit Insurance, and Security Values." *Journal of Financial and Quantitative Analysis*, vol. 13 (November 1978), pp. 701-718.

Short, Eugene D., Gerald P. O'Driscoll Jr., and Franklin D. Berger. "Recent Bank Failures: Determinants and Consequences." *Proceedings of a Conference on Bank Structure and Competition*, Federal Reserve Bank of Chicago, 1985, forthcoming.

Silverberg, Stanley C. "Resolving Large Bank Problems and Failures." *Issues in Bank Regulation*, vol. 8 (Winter 1985), pp. 12-15.

Taggart, Robert A., Jr. and Stuart I. Greenbaum. "Bank Capital and Public Regulation." *Journal of Money, Credit and Banking*, vol. 10 (May 1978), pp. 158-169.

Talmor, Eli. "A Normative Approach to Bank Capital Adequacy." *Journal of Financial and Quantitative Analysis*, vol. 15 (November 1980), pp. 785-811.

Throop, Adrian W. "Capital Investment and Entry in Commercial Banking: A Complete Model." *Journal of Money, Credit and Banking*, vol. 7 (May 1975), pp. 193-214.

Tussing, A. Dale. "The Case for Bank Failure." *Journal of Law and Economics*, vol. 10 (1967), pp. 129-147.

Vojta, George J. *Capital Adequacy*. New York: First National City Bank, 1973.

Wall, Larry D. "Affiliated Bank Capital." *Economic Review*, Federal Reserve Bank of Atlanta, vol. 70 (April 1985), pp. 12-19.

Wall, Larry D. "The Future of Deposit Insurance: An Analysis of the Insuring Agencies' Proposals." *Economic Review*, Federal Reserve Bank of Atlanta, vol. 69 (March 1984), pp. 26-39.

Wall, Larry D. and David R. Peterson. "Are the Capital Adequacy Guidelines Influencing Large Bank Holding Companies?" Federal Reserve Bank of Atlanta, Working Paper 85-3 (1985).

Watson, Ronald D. "Banking's Capital Shortage: The Malaise and the Myth." *Business Review*, Federal Reserve Bank of Philadelphia, (September 1975), pp. 3-13.

Article Sixteen

JAMES R. BARTH, DONALD J. BISENIUS,
R. DAN BRUMBAUGH, JR., AND
DANIEL SAUERHAFT

The Thrift Industry's Rough Road Ahead

Insolvent S&Ls are still doing business, taking even greater risks, and straining the resources of regulators. The crisis that emerged in the early '80s could become far worse, if interest rates should rise unexpectedly.

The United States began a period of unprecedented stability among depository institutions with the establishment of federal deposit insurance after the Great Depression. This stability ended abruptly in the early 1980s when thrift institutions (savings and loan institutions and savings banks) and commercial banks began experiencing financial distress that led to record failures. Eighty percent of the 711 thrift failures since the founding of the Federal Savings and Loan Insurance Corporation (FSLIC) in 1934 have occurred in the last six years. Although the number of federally insured thrift failures has declined from a peak in 1982, several hundred thrifts began 1986 at or near insolvency. Despite the recent general profitability of the thrift industry, the prospect for continuing positive economic developments that will resolve the problems of the seriously troubled institutions is dim. The cost of closing these insolvent institutions is estimated to be as much as $22.5 billion, with the cost growing at a rate of $1 billion per year. At the same time, the FSLIC has only $4.6 billion in reserves to cope with the troubled institutions.

What caused the abrupt end to stability in 1980 and what has led to the prolonged thrift crisis? We seek the answer by examining the causes of the recent thrift failures and insolvencies and by analyzing regulatory and legislative responses to them.

The beginnings

Much has been written about how the initial financial distress of thrift institutions in the early 1980s was caused by macroeconomic factors that led to unexpectedly high interest rates. That the crisis is being prolonged due to increased risk-taking by insolvent institutions that remain open is less closely examined. Because of the limited resources of the FSLIC and an absence of market discipline in the presence of deposit

JAMES R. BARTH is Professor of Economics at George Washington University. DONALD J. BISENIUS and DANIEL SAUER-HAFT are financial economists. R. DAN BRUMBAUGH, JR. was until recently Deputy Chief Economist at the Federal Home Loan Bank Board and is now President and Chief Executive Officer of Independence Savings and Loan in California.

insurance, insolvent thrifts remain open. These institutions, especially when paying a flat-rate insurance premium regardless of the risks they take, have incentives to gamble for resurrection. When insurance creates incentives to take the risks against which insurance provides protection, the problem is called *moral hazard*. The deregulation of interest rates that thrifts could pay and other regulatory and legislative changes that were designed to allow the thrift industry to adjust to the high interest rates of the early 1980s now augment numerous opportunities for increased risk-taking by insolvent institutions. The proliferation of these opportunities, in combination with the strained resources of the FSLIC, has encouraged more risk-prone individuals to enter the thrift industry. This phenomenon, by which insurance encourages those most likely to produce the outcome insured against to purchase insurance, is called *adverse selection*.

To understand the changing crisis, it is necessary to recount the difficulties that surfaced in 1980. Between 1980 and 1985, 581 federally insured thrifts failed. Only 130 thrifts failed during the previous 48 years. As Figure 1 shows, failures peaked in 1982 when 252 thrifts failed. Since then, the number of failures has sharply declined. One cannot be too sanguine about this decline, however, because the number of thrifts still operating but insolvent by generally accepted accounting principles (GAAP) has grown from 17 in 1980 to 450 at year-end 1985.

Against this backdrop, Figure 1 illustrates that the initial problem facing thrift institutions was the rise in interest rates. Although interest rates had been rising since 1965, the imposition of interest-rate ceilings on thrift deposits in 1966 had protected the spread thrifts could earn on their portfolio. As market rates rose, however, the potential also increased for massive disintermediation, a process in which thrift depositors withdraw their funds to purchase other market instruments with higher yields.

In light of this potential, federal regulators relaxed interest-rate restrictions in 1978 by allowing institutions to offer money-market accounts at market-related interest rates. By the following year, these money market accounts represented 20 percent of total deposits. While this reduced the threat of disintermediation, it also reduced thrifts' earnings. As Figure 1 shows, the average cost of funds for all federally insured thrifts in 1980 was rising faster than returns from their primary asset—mortgages—and this trend continued until 1982. More important, in 1981 and 1982 the average cost of funds exceeded the average

return on mortgages, causing substantial operating losses.

Congressional and regulatory responses

In response to the unexpected increases in interest rates, Congress passed the Depository Institutions Deregulation and Monetary Control Act in 1980. This act, among other things, established a committee to phase out interest-rate ceilings on deposits. Thrifts were also given additional powers to diversify assets. In an attempt to permit thrifts to adjust to rising interest rates without having to diversify away from housing finance, the Federal Home Loan Bank Board (Bank Board) in April 1981 also authorized federally chartered thrifts to offer adjustable-rate mortgages to their customers.

Thrift institutions, nonetheless, continued to suffer. Unexpectedly high market interest rates had depressed the market value of their assets, and many institutions were reluctant to sell their assets because to do so they would have to realize losses and perhaps become insolvent based on their book value. In response, the Bank Board altered regulatory accounting principles (RAP) in October 1981 by allowing thrifts to amortize the losses on any asset sold over the remaining contractual life of the asset. Thus, thrifts were able to spread capital losses over a number of years. Over time, the loss-amortization provision dramatically raised RAP net worth above GAAP net worth. By year-end 1985, only 123 institutions were insolvent according to RAP, whereas 450 institutions were insolvent according to GAAP. By substantially reducing the number of institutions considered to be RAP insolvent, the number of candidates for closure by the FSLIC also fell.

Despite deregulation and the accounting changes, the deterioration of the thrift industry continued. In response, Congress passed the Garn-St Germain Depository Institutions Act in 1982. The act further relaxed the restrictions on commercial real estate lending and on the combined holdings of consumer loans, commercial paper, and debt securities. In addition, thrifts were given the power to make commercial loans and to offer a money market deposit account.

Simultaneously, some state-chartered, federally insured thrifts were granted powers by their state regulators that far exceeded the powers of federally chartered thrifts. Most notably, California in 1983 substantially removed asset restrictions for state-chartered, federally insured thrifts. This was preceded by similar actions in Florida in 1980 and Texas in 1972. By the end of 1984, more than one-third of the states had granted state-chartered thrifts investment powers that enabled thrifts to invest in assets heretofore severely restricted or prohibited.

The inundation of the FSLIC

Despite declining interest rates, greater diversification powers, the phasing out of deposit-rate ceilings, adjustable-rate mortgages, and accounting modifications, the FSLIC confronted a record number of financially distressed thrifts in 1982. In the thrift industry, the decision about when a distressed institution is closed is a regulatory one rather than one solely determined by market forces. This fact is reflected in Figure 1 by the widening gap between the number of closed and insolvent thrifts. Three factors explain this phenomenon: the procedures and limited reserves of the FSLIC, the

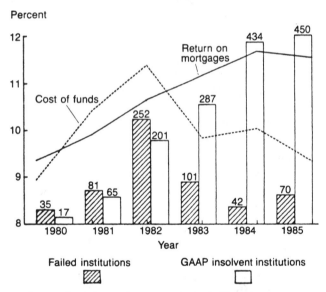

Figure 1   **Thrift Spreads and the Number of Failures and Insolvencies for All FSLIC-insured Thrift Institutions: 1980-1985**

Source: Based on publicly available data from the Federal Home Loan Bank Board.

limited number of employees available to handle the distressed institutions, and the declining economic incentive for financial institutions to acquire distressed thrifts.

To the extent that thrifts can be closed exactly at the time their market-value net worth becomes zero, the FSLIC would incur only administrative costs. Such

timing is difficult because examinations occur at uneven intervals, sometimes exceeding a year, and financial reports are filed only quarterly. Thus, changes in economic events can undermine the financial position of an institution between examinations or reports. Furthermore, even examination and analysis of reports may fail to uncover problems, especially because the reported accounting measures of net worth vary from market measures. The desire not to close an institution with positive market net worth creates a hesitancy by the Bank Board and FSLIC to close an institution until there are clear signs of market-value insolvency.

When the Bank Board does close an institution, the FSLIC frequently bears a cost. The cost results from either the need to cover insured deposits exceeding a thrift's liquidation value or the need to provide financial assistance to the acquiror in the case of a merger. As Table 1 shows, the FSLIC fund fell from nearly $6.5 billion in 1980 to just under $4.6 billion in 1985. RAP net worth as a percent of total assets declined from 5.26 percent in 1980 to 4.38 percent in 1985. The decline was even greater for GAAP net worth. The Bank Board estimated in March 1986 that it will cost as much as $22.5 billion to resolve the problems of insolvent thrifts. Thus, it is no surprise that the FSLIC has moved cautiously in closing insolvent institutions.

As Table 1 also shows, both RAP and GAAP net worth for the industry improved in 1985. The improvement was due to net income of over $1 billion in each of the last three quarters of 1985. This overall increase was achieved despite a negative net income of $561 million in the last quarter of 1985 alone for the 655 institutions with RAP net worth less than or equal to 3 percent. This suggests that a dichotomy exists where the condition of the increasing number of insolvent institutions is deteriorating even though the majority of institutions are solvent and currently profitable.

The limited financial resources of the FSLIC are only a partial explanation for the widening gap between the number of failed and insolvent thrift institutions. There is also a limited staff available to deal with the unprecedented number of troubled institutions. In 1980, there were 34 FSLIC employees to handle 297 troubled institutions. By 1985, the FSLIC staff had grown to 159 but the number of troubled institutions had risen to 655. Over half of the staff had less than two years experience in 1985. Over the same period, the number of field examiners actually declined. Thus, even if FSLIC's reserves had been adequate, the lim-

Table 1   **Profile of the Thrift Industry and its Insurer: 1980–1985**

Year	Number of insured institutions	Assets of insured institutions ($ billions)	FSLIC primary and secondary reserves ($ millions)	FSLIC reserves as a percentage of total assets	RAP net worth as a percentage of total assets	GAAP net worth as a percentage of total assets
1980	4,002	618	6,462	1.04	5.26	5.26
1981	3,779	651	6,302	0.97	4.27	4.15
1982	3,343	693	6,331	0.91	3.69	2.95
1983	3,040	819	6,425	0.78	4.02	3.14
1984	3,167	979	5,605	0.57	3.86	2.87
1985	3,246	1,070	4,557	0.43	4.38	3.39

Source: Based on publicly available data from the Federal Home Loan Bank Board.

ited number of personnel and their relative inexperience made it more difficult to resolve the growing pool of insolvent institutions in a timely manner.

Finally, the FSLIC must choose the least costly way to resolve an insolvent thrift institution. In most cases, a merger results. Since the establishment of the FSLIC in 1934, there have been only 40 liquidations. Arranging a merger in recent years has become more difficult, however, due to the advent of nonbank banks that have been able to expand geographically without mergers. To the extent that geographical expansion is more accessible without mergers, the FSLIC must devote more time to arrange a merger. This can lengthen the time between when an institution becomes insolvent and when it is closed, potentially resulting in a higher cost to the FSLIC.

Seeking the appropriate regulatory response

Even when economic conditions do not threaten thrift institutions, deposit insurance priced without regard to risk encourages greater risk-taking. The flat-rate premium that has been levied since 1934 thus creates moral hazard. Furthermore, once institutions are in trouble they have an even greater incentive to increase their risk-taking activities because, with federally insured thrift institutions, it's "heads the institutions win and tails the FSLIC loses." Insured depositors, moreover, have no economic interest in monitoring a federally insured thrift. Basically, the major creditor of an insolvent thrift is the FSLIC to whom falls the responsibility to close insolvent thrifts. To the extent that the FSLIC's limited resources constrain the FSLIC's ability to close insolvent thrifts, overall risk-taking undoubtedly increases.

This increased risk-taking by insolvent institutions,

moreover, may stimulate risk-taking among solvent institutions. To increase profitability, some insolvent institutions will attempt to attract additional deposits to acquire assets that promise higher returns. If competing solvent institutions fail to match the higher rates, depositors may shift to the higher-yield institutions. To maintain their expected profitability while paying higher rates, both insolvent and solvent institutions who meet the higher rates will need to select a portfolio with greater expected return, and hence, greater risk. It is also possible that, due to the large number of insolvent thrifts, uninsured depositors and other creditors are demanding a risk premium when they lend to thrifts. In 1980, thrifts' cost of funds was on average 35 basis points above what commercial banks paid. (One percent equals 100 basis points.) At year-end 1985, thrifts paid 105 basis points more than banks for funds. This may reflect a risk premium because thrifts are perceived to be generally more risky than banks. To the extent that solvent institutions met the rising rates paid by insolvent thrifts, rates paid by solvent institutions may have risen due to the direct contamination of insolvent thrifts.

In addition to moral hazard, adverse selection can also arise. Overburdened insurance funds and inadequate examination and supervision are clearly attractive to high-risk-takers and those willing to engage in fraud. The larger the number of insolvent federally insured thrifts that continue operating and the more it appears that the FSLIC and other regulatory resources are limited, the more attractive federally insured thrifts become to the same types of individuals. These individuals are also attracted by the unusually large leverage afforded thrifts due to their relatively small required net worth. The net-worth requirements were lowered from 5 to 3 percent from 1980 to 1982, increasing the maximum amount most institutions could invest per dollar of net worth from $20 to $33. Certain phase-in and averaging techniques theoretically allowed some institutions as much as $666 of investment per dollar of net worth. At a time when an increasing number of institutions were in distress and when the capacity constraints of the FSLIC were obvious, the opportunities to take risks were thus increasing.

Although problems arising from moral hazard and adverse selection are not new, they were kept in closer check in the past by various balance-sheet restrictions. Recent federal and state deregulation has substantially eroded this check. Thus, while the recent decline in interest rates reduced losses due to interest-rate risk, moral hazard and adverse selection now have greater opportunity to surface in the form of increased credit risk since institutions can now shift to riskier portfolios. In 1982, approximately 80 percent of the FSLIC's caseload of failed institutions was primarily attributed to interest-rate risk problems. By 1984 that ratio had more than reversed itself so that credit risk is now cited as the predominant problem.

In response, the Bank Board adopted three regulations in 1985 that limit the investment powers of federally insured thrifts on the grounds that certain activities increased the overall risk to the FSLIC. The Bank Board passed a regulation limiting thrifts' direct investments without supervisory approval to 10 percent of assets or twice net worth, whichever is greater. With supervisory approval, an institution can devote more of its assets to direct investment. The Bank Board also adopted a regulation that requires additional net worth for thrifts growing over 15 percent per year. In addition, the Board began to eliminate the phase-in and averaging techniques for calculating minimum required net worth. The Bank Board has also supported legislation that would impose a higher deposit-insurance premium on state-chartered thrifts engaging in activities not allowed federally chartered institutions.

Regulations limiting investment activities of thrift institutions are part of a long-standing balancing act between government subsidies and restrictions. Thrifts were separated from commercial banks and provided federal deposit insurance as well as tax subsidies to promote housing finance. Congress determined that housing finance was a merit good whose consumption should be enhanced by federal subsidies that provide thrifts with a competitive advantage over other lenders. Until the 1980s revealed the risks of asset portfolios dominated by long-term, fixed-rate mortgages, the assets of thrifts were narrowly proscribed.

The relaxation of asset restrictions in 1980 and 1982 was intended to provide thrifts with the potential benefits of portfolio diversification that in turn could strengthen their position in providing housing finance. Through regulatory action, the government is attempting to mimic the outcome that the market would produce if the moral-hazard and adverse-selection problems did not exist.

Unresolved policy issues

Although moral hazard and adverse selection arise with a flat-rate deposit-insurance premium even in the best of times, allowing hundreds of insolvent institutions to remain open greatly exacerbates the problem. The continuing deterioration of these institutions poses a great enough threat that finding ways to close them must be a top, if not the top, priority. The Congress in mid 1986 was considering legislation that would allow the Bank Board to create a "Financing Corporation" that would initially be capitalized with $3 billion from the Federal Home Loan Banks. The Financing Corporation could sell an estimated $15 billion or more in bonds, the proceeds of which would be made available to the FSLIC to handle the costs of closing insolvent institutions.

Several unresolved issues nonetheless exist. Even if additional funds become available, a pressing issue remains about what to do with the operating insolvent institutions that cannot be closed immediately because of the time it will take to establish and fully implement the Financing Corporation's borrowing capability and the time it will take the FSLIC to spend the money. Furthermore, there is the issue of whether the funds legislated will be adequate or whether more funds will have to be requested in the future. Finally, and most important, it is not clear that the healthy thrift institutions will be able to bear the full burden of repaying the borrowings of the Financing Corporations.

The substantial cost of resolution suggests that up until 1985 existing monitoring and supervision was inadequate to the task of ensuring prudent behavior by operating insolvent institutions. In response, the number of examiners was significantly increased in 1985. In addition, the Management Consignment Program (MCP) was created and involves hiring outside management to manage insolvent institutions until a resolution can be arranged. Currently, there are 40 MCP institutions. Whether these efforts will provide sufficient restraint on insolvent institutions is uncertain. It would be useful to consider developing an expanded program, based on the MCP theme, to gain tighter control of perhaps hundreds of insolvent institutions.

For the rest of the thrifts, finding the appropriate combination of improved accounting, net-worth requirements, monitoring, portfolio regulations and, perhaps, risk-sensitive deposit insurance premia or risk-sensitive net-worth requirements is also important. The Bank Board has responded in April 1986 by proposing regulations that would require all thrifts to report on the basis of GAAP, to raise their regulatory net worth to 6 percent over six years, and to hold additional net worth against direct investments, land loans, and other selected assets—in essence an attempt to construct a risk-sensitive net-worth requirement. Moreover, the bolstered examination staff was empowered in 1985 to classify assets—including direct investments—as substandard, doubtful, and loss with corresponding required reserves.

Unresolved issues regarding appropriate portfolio regulation exist. The existing direct-investment regulation is due to sunset at the end of 1986. The current direct-investment regulation, in conjunction with the substantial proposed incremental net-worth requirements on direct investments regardless of an institution's overall net worth, would impose extremely tight restrictions on even well-capitalized institutions seeking greater asset diversification. At issue is whether well-capitalized thrifts, which therefore have strong economic incentives to diversify their portfolio risk with nonmortgage assets, will become too constrained. The broader issue is whether in trying to deal with the problems of insolvent institutions through portfolio restrictions, solvent institutions suffer unduly. It may be that regulators cannot mimic the market

in ways that place appropriate restraints on insolvent institutions without harming solvent institutions.

Several longer-term unresolved issues also deserve attention. The ability to close an institution before it imposes excessive cost on the insurer depends on the ability to monitor market-value net worth and to set a minimum market-value net worth at a level with which the monitoring system allows the insurer to control its loss exposure. Such a cost-containment system depends on developing market-value accounting and improving monitoring techniques. The closer the regulator can get to such a system, the less regulation is needed to protect the insurer against losses. Thus, the long-range goal may not be to perfect the regulator's ability to mimic the market with better regulations and more finely tuned pricing of deposit insurance, but to rely more directly on the market itself.

The thrift-industry crisis also raises the issue of the appropriate government-induced separation of activities among financial institutions. In large part, the restriction of portfolios to mortgage lending, mandated by law, made thrifts vulnerable to the interest-rate spiral of the late 1970s and early 1980s. If the Congress wishes to maintain housing finance as a merit good, it may be appropriate to seek a more efficient method than portfolio restriction.

In summary, the dramatically increasing cost to the FSLIC to dispose of failed institutions' assets ought in itself to be enough to motivate substantial regulatory and congressional action on these unresolved policy issues. The cost, after all, has risen during a period of remarkable overall thrift profitability. A sense of urgency is also justifiable, because the crisis could quickly become far more severe if interest rates rise unexpectedly any time in the next few years.

Article Seventeen

"Recapitalizing" the FSLIC

For 50 years, the direct expenses of the federal deposit insurance agencies were more than adequately covered by the premiums levied on insured banks and thrifts. In the past few years, however, the premium income of the Federal Savings and Loan Insurance Corporation (FSLIC) has not been sufficient to absorb the expenses sustained by the agency in dealing with failing thrifts. As a result, the reserves of the FSLIC have shrunk considerably and are now viewed by the Federal Home Loan Bank Board (FHLBB), which oversees the insurance agency, as inadequate for dealing with the large number of problem thrift cases still outstanding.

To help relieve the FSLIC of its current funding squeeze, the Treasury, in conjunction with the FHLBB, has developed a plan for "recapitalizing" the thrift insurance fund. This plan, which is incorporated into House and Senate bills HR4907 and S2752, respectively, may be the most practical alternative, considering current conditions, for giving the FSLIC the needed boost to its current reserves.

The recapitalization plan, however, provides only short-term relief because of its inability, over the long run, to increase the overall resources available to the FSLIC. The proposal mainly reshuffles future resources to meet current outlays. Without a true recapitalization, a lasting solution to the problem of financial stress on the FSLIC would require a significant reduction in the insurance corporation's future exposure to losses.

The problem and the plan
With its current reserves, the FSLIC reportedly does not have enough resources to recognize the loss it would sustain if all problem thrifts were liquidated or merged with financial assistance from the insurance corporation. In addition, the FSLIC is quite restricted in its ability to raise additional funds to bolster its reserves. For example, the insurance agency cannot issue its own debt or raise its maximum insurance premium, which is set by the Congress.

To give the thrift insurance fund the needed addition to current reserves, the Treasury and the FHLBB have proposed a new funding option that does not involve direct Treasury assistance or a hike in the insurance premium rate. As shown in the chart, the heart of the plan is a newly created federally sponsored agency, referred to as the Financing Corporation, that would be authorized to borrow funds in the capital market and to pass the proceeds on to the FSLIC. While it is not certain, borrowing by the Financing Corporation could amount to about $12 to $15 billion over the next few years.

Under the plan, the 12 regional Federal Home Loan Banks (FHLBs) would advance the Financing Corporation up to $3 billion, for which they would receive nonvoting capital stock in the Financing Corporation. Most of the FHLBs' investment (up to $2.2 billion) would be used by the Financing Corporation to purchase zero coupon bonds whose maturities would match those of the Financing Corporation's own debt. In that way, the principal amount due on the Financing Corporation's bonds could be paid off with the proceeds from the zero coupon bonds.

The interest payments on the Financing Corporation's debt, however, would come primarily from what otherwise would have been the FSLIC's premium income.

Under the plan, the Financing Corporation would be authorized to receive payments directly from FSLIC-insured thrift institutions. Insurance premiums paid by thrifts to the FSLIC then would be reduced by the amount the thrifts had to pay to the Financing Corporation. (If necessary, some of the FHLBs' investment also could be used to make interest payments on the Financing Corporation's debt.)

In exchange for forwarding the borrowed funds to the FSLIC, the Financing Corporation would be given equity in the insurance agency. If $15 billion were borrowed and passed on to the FSLIC, the insurance agency would issue $3 billion in redeemable stock and $12 billion in non-redeemable certificates to the Financing Corporation.

While the $3 billion in stock, which essentially represents the FHLBs' original investment, would be redeemable, the amount eventually repaid would remain uncertain. To provide for repayment to the Federal Home Loan Banks, the FSLIC would make contributions to an "equity return account" beginning in 1997. These contributions would vary with the reserve-to-deposit ratio of the FSLIC. When all of the Financing Corporation's debt matures, which would be no later than 2026, the FHLBs would receive the funds in the equity return account. The repayment realized might be zero or perhaps the original investment plus some return.

Budget issue

A major debate over this recapitalization plan centered on the implications for the federal budget deficit. At issue was whether the funds from the Financing Corporation really would represent equity in the FSLIC or debt obligations of the insurance agency.

Equity contributions received by the FSLIC can be used to offset the insurance agency's expenditures (which are treated as spending in the federal budget), in part, because the insurance agency would have discretion over the distribution of dividends. The Congressional Budget Office (CBO), however, maintained that, under the plan as first proposed, the Financing Corporation's borrowings represented debt obligations of the FSLIC since the FSLIC was directly responsible for the interest costs. As a practical matter, this meant that the FSLIC would have no option but to make those payments, which would not be the case if it were in fact dealing with dividend payments on stock it had issued.

This initial controversy was resolved by giving the Financing Corporation direct access to the insurance premiums paid by thrifts, as discussed earlier. As important as this might be in satisfying the technical aspects of the law, the change is not substantive.

Beyond the budget

In particular, the change in the plan does not alter the fact that only a small portion of the increase in the FSLIC's current reserves would consist of an injection of *new* resources (the investment of the FHLBs). Most of the boost to reserves would come from borrowings, and a large portion of what would have been the FSLIC's future income stream (that is, payments from thrifts to the Financing Corporation) would be committed to paying the interest on that debt. Such a commitment would greatly reduce the resources available to absorb future FSLIC expenses.

At current market rates, the annual interest cost on federally sponsored agency debt of $12 to $15 billion would be on the order of $1 billion. In 1985, regular premium income to the FSLIC totaled only $700 million (1/12th of one percent of thrift deposits). A special assessment raised another $1 billion (1/8th of one percent of thrift deposits) in premiums last year. The special assessment, however, has raised some questions concerning competitive imbalance since thrifts have had to pay more than commercial banks for deposit insurance. Indeed, the thrift industry has been pushing hard to get the special assessment phased out by 1991 as part of the recapitalization plan.

The thrift industry has argued that the special assessment could be eliminated because regular premium income would increase as the thrift deposit base expands. A broader deposit base by itself is not the answer, however. Deposit growth would mean not only higher gross income but also greater risk exposure for the FSLIC, everything else the same. Therefore, even if the higher income generated from the growth in deposits were enough to meet the interest on the Financing Corporation's debt, the FSLIC could need additional resources to cover its other expenses in the future.

Reducing risk

The only way the FSLIC can meet its expenses over time, without access to more resources, is to reduce its exposure to losses. The Federal

The FSLIC Recapitalization Plan

A. Funding

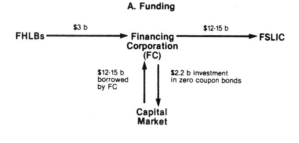

B. Repayments

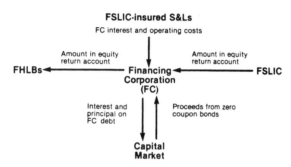

Home Loan Bank Board already has adopted higher capital requirements for insured thrifts to help protect the FSLIC. Currently, the minimum capital requirement for FSLIC-insured institutions is 3 percent of deposits, or about half the required ratio for banks. The FHLBB has announced a new minimum requirement for thrifts of 6 percent of deposits. (The requirement for an individual institution could be higher depending on the composition of its assets and liabilities.) The new standard, which takes effect in 1987, will be phased in over a period of 6 to 12 years. In addition, the FHLBB has *proposed* doing away with the use of regulatory capital (such as net worth certificates issued to thrifts by the FSLIC) to meet the new capital requirements.

These types of policy changes are important to the long-run financial integrity of the FSLIC. But the new capital standards have to be enforced if they are to make a difference. To limit the FSLIC's losses, poorly performing thrifts with "low" capital ratios have to be closed promptly. Such a closure policy is more important to the

FSLIC's ability to remain "self-sufficient" than are innovations such as risk-related insurance premiums.

Even with strictly enforced new capital requirements, capital regulation that is based on book value rather than market value measures of capital could continue to present problems for the FSLIC. This is particularly true if there should be an unexpectedly sharp rise in interest rates. Despite deregulation, exposure to interest rate risk will continue to be a source of potential losses to the thrift industry. As in the past, unexpected increases in interest rates will mean immediate declines in the market value of thrift net worth, with book value net worth adjusting only with a long lag.

Continued reliance on book value could perpetuate the tendency to close institutions too late — that is, when market net worth is already below zero. The degree to which the reliance on book value accounting will result in misleading signals regarding the financial health of thrifts will depend in part on the stability of market interest rates.

Conclusion

It is important for the FSLIC to have the resources needed to deal with the backlog of problem thrift cases. In this regard, the "recapitalization" plan proposed by the Treasury and the Federal Home Loan Bank Board would significantly boost the insurance corporation's current reserves. However, the net addition to the resources available to the FSLIC over time would be limited. Under the plan, the bulk of the funds would come from the Financing Corporation's borrowings, the interest on which must be paid out of the FSLIC's future income stream.

With much of the future income of the FSLIC earmarked to meet the cost of borrowing funds to pay off its current obligations, the insurance fund would be able to meet its future liabilities without still more resources only if those liabilities were quite small. Failure to realize less than minimal exposure to risk would mean that in the future the FSLIC would have to be truly recapitalized, most likely with resources from outside the thrift industry.

Frederick T. Furlong

Section Three

The Money Supply

The value of the typical textbook treatment of the money supply process is its simplicity. Conceptually simple formulas, analogous to those for the Keynesian income multiplier, use readily grasped ratios (excess reserves to deposits, checkable to time deposits, required reserve ratios, and so on) to explain the size of the money supply. The disadvantage of this approach is that most students lack an appreciation of how variable such "constants" can be. The readings in this section document that variability over the past few years and discuss the reasons for it.

In "Examining the Recent Surge in M1," Bharat Trehan and Carl Walsh show how growth rates of different measures of the money supply have diverged dramatically in recent years; when Ml growth rose, for example, M3 growth fell. The authors suggest weak demand for bank loans as the cause. Banks in turn responded to the lack of demand by offering lower interest rates on time deposits, leading the public to shift out of this component of M3 and into components of M1, like NOW and Super NOW accounts, whose interest rates fell much less. Such movements render any single measure of the money stock unreliable as a guide to the stance of monetary policy. In the example at hand, using M1 might mislead one to mistake weaker credit demand for stronger credit supply.

In the next article, "Should Money Be Redefined?" Brian Motley investigates whether a narrower measure of the money supply bears a more consistent relation to GNP than does the M1 measure. If it does, the Fed would be more successful in achieving its goals by targeting that narrower measure rather than M1. The argument in favor of targeting a money supply measure that consists solely of currency and demand deposits (M1A), and that therefore excludes the interest-bearing checking accounts contained in M1, is that M1A consists only of transaction accounts whereas M1 may consist of an ever-shifting mixture of transaction and savings accounts. Arguing against targeting M1A, however, is the empirical evidence, which suggests that M1A is less reliably related to the economy than is M1. Unfortunately, neither measure has been reliably related to the economy over the past two years. Perhaps money should be redefined, but how it should be redefined is still not clear.

Gary C. Zimmerman and Michael C. Keeley detail the extent to which the public's deposits have moved into interest-bearing checking accounts in the third reading in this section, "Interest Checking." The authors argue that a large portion of the funds moved into M1 checkable deposits came from savings-type accounts. These nontransaction balances readily move back and forth between checking accounts and non-M1 savings-type accounts when their relative interest rates change, producing the divergent growth rates across M1, M2, and M3 and making it difficult to interpret the stance of monetary policy. The authors also suggest that the asymmetry in taxing the interest income but not allowing the tax-deductibility of the service charges associated with these accounts leads customers with different average balances to use accounts with different combinations of interest rates, service charges, and minimum balance requirements.

In the last article in this section, "The Evolution of Retail EFT Networks," Steven D. Felgran and R. Edward Ferguson describe the current status of electronic funds transfer at the retail level. Although acceptance has been slow, the authors contend that eventually the lower costs of transferring funds electronically will shift customers away from the long-standing practice of using paper checks.

Examining the Recent Surge in M1

In recent months, many market analysts have questioned whether monetary policy is once again on an inflationary course. This concern has arisen in light of the recent rapid growth in the M1 monetary aggregate (currency plus all checkable deposits). Against a background of generally declining interest rates, M1 grew at an 11 percent annual rate from September 1984 to September 1985. This relatively high average rate of growth, however, masks two distinct episodes: M1 grew at a 7½ percent annual rate from September 1984 to April 1985, but then, in the five succeeding months ending in September, it grew at a substantially higher 16 percent annual rate. Naturally, this latter surge has attracted considerable attention, and led many observers to ask whether it is a sign of an overly expansionary monetary policy.

By some measures, it is not obvious that monetary policy has eased significantly since April. The Fed did reduce the discount rate by half a percentage point in May, but the resulting decline in the federal funds rate — which is often taken as an important indicator of the stance of monetary policy — by itself does not appear sufficient to explain the large increase in the M1 growth rate.

Several other explanations for the rapid growth in M1 have been offered. For example, some analysts have pointed to the recent problems at savings and loan associations and savings banks to argue that increased financial uncertainty has led to an increase in the public's holdings of liquid assets, such as demand deposits, that are part of M1. However, this and other explanations do not seem capable of accounting for all the growth in M1, especially from April onwards. In this *Letter,* we present evidence for a somewhat different explanation of the surge in M1.

We believe part of the explanation can be seen in the movements of the broader monetary aggregates. While M1 growth has picked up since April, the growth rate of M3 (which includes M1 plus MMDAs, money market funds, savings and time deposits, RPs and Eurodollar deposits) has actually slowed. In fact, the term components of M3, i.e.,

components that are not available on demand but that are investments that lock in funds for a fixed term to maturity — such as small and large CDs, term repurchase agreements (RPs), and term Eurodollar deposits — declined from May to August.

The behavior of these components resulted in part from sluggish growth in the demand for bank loans. In response, banks lowered the rates they offered on CDs and other term accounts. They changed the rates on Super NOWs and MMDAs much more slowly and kept the rates on NOW accounts at their regulatory maximum. The disparity in rate adjustments made it more attractive than before to hold funds in M1 and the nonterm component of M3 such as Super NOWs, NOWs, and MMDAs. The rapid growth in M1 relative to M3 thus appears to be a portfolio shift by the public out of term accounts into, among other things, M1 balances. This explanation of the recent rapid M1 growth implies that the surge does not indicate stimulative monetary policy. By the same token, if the portfolio shift should reverse itself in subsequent months, M1 growth could slow markedly (as it seems to have done through mid-October), but the slowdown would not indicate that monetary policy had turned restrictive.

The recent behavior of the monetary aggregates
While M1 growth accelerated after April, M3 growth actually slowed. M3 grew at a 9.4 percent rate from September 1984 to April 1985, but at only a 7.8 percent annual rate from May to August 1985. This deceleration was due mainly to the behavior of those components in M3 that are not in M1 or M2 (large CDs, term Eurodollars and term RPs). The level of these components was actually lower in August than in April, having *declined* at nearly a 3½ percent annual rate over the period.

The divergent growth patterns of the monetary aggregates are illustrated in Chart 1, which shows the monthly growth rates of M1 and those components of M3 that are not in M2 (M2 consists of M1 plus MMDAs, savings and small time deposits, non-institutional money market funds, and overnight

RPs and Eurodollars). Over the past year, the two growth rates have generally tended to move in opposite directions.

The major difference between the two aggregates shown in the chart is that the components of M3 minus M2 are generally term accounts, while none of the components of M1 has a term element. This suggests it may be useful to examine the components of M3 by splitting M3 into purely term and nonterm components. The term components of M3 consist of large and small time deposits, term RPs and term Eurodollars, while all other deposits are included in the nonterm component — this contains M1 (currency, demand deposits, other checkable deposits), savings accounts, MMDAs, etc. The dollar values of these two aggregates are shown in Chart 2. The divergence in their recent behavior is striking. The term component actually declined from June to August, while the nonterm component accelerated. In September, the term component picked up, but it is still below its June 1985 level.

An explanation for the portfolio shift

To understand the causes of this divergence in the components of M3, it is useful to begin by examining the banking sector. Chart 3 shows the rate of bank loan growth since September 1984. Notice that loan growth slowed in December 1984, fell sharply in January 1985, then picked up, but has been slowing again since May. This slowdown in loan growth is due to a reduction in loan *demand* rather than loan *supply*. The fall in the prime rate from 13 percent in August 1984 to 9½ percent in August 1985 supports this view. Bankers react to a slowdown in loan demand by reducing the rates they offer on their term deposits as their need for funds falls. Consequently, during the recent period of low loan demand, CD rates have declined relative to a very short-term rate such as the federal funds rate.

Chart 3 shows that the rate of growth of bank loans has changed in the same direction as the spread between CD and federal funds rates since December. In fact, from May through August, the 3-month CD rate was below the rate on federal funds suggesting that banks were not interested in tying up funds for a short term of around 3 months. This probably reflects expectations that loan demand will remain weak over the next few months.

The downward pressure on CD rates and rates on other term deposits has been reinforced by the reduction in the discount rate in May 1985. Rates on transaction balances — demand deposits, NOWs, and Super NOWs — have not fallen commensurately, so the rate reductions on term accounts lower the opportunity cost of holding highly liquid short-term assets such as M1.

The current rapid growth of M1 relative to M3 can be explained, then, as a portfolio shift by the public in response to the lower spread between the rates on term and nonterm accounts. In addition, the even faster growth in NOWs, Super-Nows, and MMDAs relative to demand deposits also seems to be a response to the fall in CD rates relative to rates on the interest-bearing components of M1 and M2.

Thus, the phenomenon of fast M1 growth from May to August reflected a shift out of term accounts. M3 was not greatly affected since the shift occurred within its components. Within M2, two opposing effects were at work: small time deposits declined because of the decline in rates, but MMDAs and savings accounts both grew extremely quickly. On balance, M2 grew much more slowly than M1. Of course, the effect of the portfolio shift toward nonterm accounts was most pronounced in M1 since that aggregate contains only nonterm deposits.

The near future and policy implications

In the near future, the shift out of term accounts is likely to slow and perhaps reverse for two reasons. First, if the economy picks up, the resulting increase in loan demand will lead to a rise in CD rates as banks scramble for additional funding. As the spread between the rates on term and non-term accounts widens, funds should shift back into the former.

Second, if the economy does not pick up, we expect that banks will bring the yields on Super NOWs and MMDAs into line with other yields since they tend to adjust the rates on these accounts only with a lag of some months. This should lead to a slowdown in M1 growth relative to M2 and M3.

This reversal may have begun already. Chart 3 shows that the CD rate has risen relative to the funds rate, and Chart 2 shows that the term com-

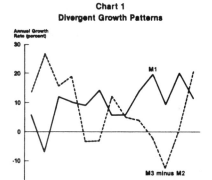

Chart 1
Divergent Growth Patterns

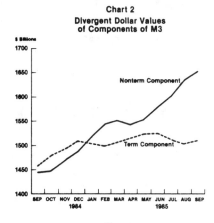

Chart 2
**Divergent Dollar Values
of Components of M3**

Chart 3
**Bank Loan Growth Has Moved
With Interest Rate Spread
Since December 1984**

ponents of M3 have started to rise as the return on these accounts has become more attractive. Also, the rate of growth of nonterm accounts has fallen. Although developments in September do not provide conclusive evidence that the portfolio shift has reversed itself, they do seem to be consistent with the basic hypothesis of this *Letter*.

For policy purposes, it is important to realize that a large part of the recent surge in M1 represents purely a financial "disturbance" — in other words, a rearrangement of the public's portfolio that is not directly linked to spending, production, and employment outcomes in the economy.

Since such disturbances do not signal any change in real spending, the rapid M1 growth does not, by itself, indicate that monetary policy has become more expansionary. Nor does it indicate that monetary policy should be tightened to bring M1 into line with the Federal Reserve's target growth ranges. Conversely, a future reverse portfolio shift out of M1 that produces a large reduction in M1 growth would not signal a major contraction in monetary policy.

More generally, this analysis suggests one must be cautious in using M1 as a measure of the stance of monetary policy. Policy can only influence the funds rate directly, while the demand for M1 does not depend directly on the funds rate. The demand for M1 depends instead upon the difference between the return on M1 and the return on alternative assets, and these returns are likely to be generated by business conditions, loan demands, etc.

If, as this recent episode suggests, money holders are highly sensitive to small changes in the relative returns on different assets, substitution among the

different monetary aggregates is likely to be an important determinant of their relative growth rates, particularly over short periods. Therefore, for any level of very short-term interest rates, the quantity of M1 can vary significantly depending upon the state of the economy, expectations and other factors. Under these conditions, growth in M1 is not likely to provide a reliable signal of future spending plans.

Our analysis implies that while overall movements in interest rates continue to affect the demand for M1, movements in relative interest rates, such as have occurred recently, can lead to wide variation in the growth rate of M1 relative to the broader aggregates. During such periods, it may be difficult to interpret the meaning of any change in a particular monetary aggregate such as M1. However, as the general level of aggregate demand rises or falls, we would expect that all the monetary aggregates will tend to move together.

Bharat Trehan and Carl Walsh,
Economist and Senior Economist

Article Nineteen

Should Money Be Redefined?

Since 1981, the rate at which money changes hands in the purchase of goods and services has trended downward in contrast to its steady growth over the previous two decades. Economists describe this rate as the *velocity* of money and measure it by the ratio of the value of the nation's output (or GNP) to the stock of money. For example, during the 1960s and 1970s, the velocity of M1, which consists of currency and fully checkable deposits, increased quite steadily at an average annual rate of around three percent, but since mid-1981, M1's velocity has *declined* at an average annual rate of more than two percent. Also, as shown in Chart 1, M1's velocity has been more variable in the 1980s than in earlier years.

The unexpected decline and greater variability of velocity have made it more difficult for the Federal Reserve to set targets for monetary growth that are consistent with acceptable rates of growth of GNP. Partly in response, the Federal Reserve has permitted quite rapid M1 growth in recent years. Compared to the 1979-82 period, however, it also has de-emphasized the role of the monetary aggregates, especially M1, in setting policy, and has paid more attention to other indicators of economic activity.

Some economists have argued that the unusual behavior of M1 velocity has been due to a change in the *nature* of this monetary aggregate since the nationwide introduction of interest-bearing checkable deposits (or NOW accounts) in 1981 and the subsequent deregulation of rates on these deposits in 1983 and 1986. According to this argument, balances in M1 prior to the changes were held primarily for transactions purposes, whereas NOW accounts may contain a mixture of transactions and savings balances and hence may not be closely related to spending on goods and services.

Some proponents of this view that the nature of M1 has changed recently suggested that M1 be redefined to include only currency and demand deposits which, because they bear no explicit

interest, are more likely to contain only transactions funds. This narrower definition of money was termed M1A prior to 1983. As shown in Chart 1, the trend of M1A velocity has changed less in recent years than that of M1. This *Letter*, however, will argue that other evidence indicates that the narrower aggregate would not be a superior indicator for monetary policy in the future.

Are NOW accounts spent less often?
In 1985, the annual turnover rate of demand deposits at banks outside New York City was about 300 times. That is, each dollar in these deposits was transferred about 25 times each *month*. In contrast, NOW accounts were transferred less than 17 times per *year*. These numbers suggest that moneyholders treat demand deposits differently from NOW accounts and that the latter may contain a large volume of nontransactions funds.

Much of this apparent difference in activity between the two types of accounts, however, is due to the composition of their holders. NOW accounts are held only by households, who use their money holdings less intensively than businesses. Although there are no separate direct measures of the turnover rates of deposits owned by individuals and corporations, indirect estimates made in the early 1970s (before NOW accounts existed) suggested that, at that time, corporations turned over their accounts three to five times more rapidly than did households. In addition, evidence on the number of payments from various types of accounts suggests that households use NOW accounts about as intensively as they do personal demand deposits. Thus, the lower turnover rates of NOW accounts compared to demand deposits appear to be due to differences in the *holders* of these accounts rather than differences in the nature of the accounts.

Moreover, a majority of transfers of business demand deposits represent either financial transactions or purchases of intermediate products, which do not enter into the demand for GNP and hence do not affect money's measured velocity. Of course, households also engage in financial transactions, but they do so to a smaller extent. Paul Spindt of the Federal Reserve staff has estimated that, in 1982, the annual turnover rates of demand deposits and NOW accounts in the purchase of *final products* only were 7½ and 4 times, respectively. The difference between these rates clearly is much smaller than that between the 300 and 17 times for demand deposits and NOW accounts, respectively, mentioned earlier. It is these "final demand" turnover rates that determine average velocity.

NOW accounts and M1 demand
More importantly, the lower turnover rate of NOW accounts compared to demand deposits does not necessarily imply that M1 is somehow "contaminated" by the inclusion of NOW accounts, or that M1A would consequently be a "purer" and more reliable indicator of monetary policy.

For the nature of M1 to have changed, today's NOW accounts must contain a significant volume of funds that previously were outside M1. But since Money Market Deposit Accounts (MMDAs) and other liquid accounts that are outside M1 provide higher yields than NOW accounts, and have grown rapidly since 1982, it does not seem likely that households have switched a large volume of savings funds into NOW accounts. Moreover, since it is likely that M1A included a certain amount of low-turnover funds before 1981 that have since been shifted into interest-bearing NOW accounts, M1A today probably is not the same aggregate that it was before 1981.

Thus, the relationship between the quantity of M1 that the public desires to hold and the levels of income, prices and interest rates that they face is less likely to have been affected by deregulation since 1981 than the corresponding relationship for M1A. Economists describe this relationship as the *demand function* for a monetary aggregate.

Empirical evidence supports the idea that the demand function has been much more stable for M1 than for M1A. Chart 2 compares actual M1 and M1A with values from simulating a statistical M1A demand equation estimated at this Bank using pre-1981 data — before NOW accounts were widely available. Up to the end of 1984, this equation tracks M1 (including NOWs) quite closely, but it seriously overesti-

mates both the level *and* the growth rate of M1A. This result suggests that the introduction of NOW accounts did not affect the relation of M1 demand to its principal determinants but that it did reduce the demand for M1A as households switched transactions funds from demand deposits into NOW accounts. Had M1 been "contaminated" by an inflow of nontransactions funds from other sources, this equation would have *under*stated the growth of M1 after 1981.

Velocity and money demand
In setting annual targets for growth in the monetary aggregates, the Federal Reserve must make three principal judgments. First, it must judge what rates of growth of real output and inflation are feasible and acceptable for the year ahead. Second, the central bank must estimate the levels of interest rates consistent with these economic projections. Finally, given projections of economic activity and interest rates, the Federal Reserve must estimate how much money the public will want to hold and set money growth targets accordingly.

Clearly, if the demand for an aggregate becomes more difficult to forecast, the third stage would become more difficult as well. For example, if the demand to hold M1 were to increase more rapidly than suggested by its historical relationship with income, prices and interest rates, the aggregate would tend to exceed the Fed's target even though economic activity was evolving as the Fed had projected. These developments would show up as a decline in M1 velocity. If the central bank were to attempt to keep the supply of M1 within its target range despite the increase in demand, interest rates would be driven up and economic activity would tend to slow.

Although an increase in the demand to hold money will, other things equal, lead to a decline in its velocity, unexpected movements in velocity do not necessarily mean that the demand for money has shifted. Between the middle of 1981 and the middle of 1983, for example, M1's velocity declined seven percent, but the public's demand to hold money — given the levels of interest rates, income and prices prevailing — appears to have remained stable. As Chart 2 shows, our money demand equation was able to explain the behavior of M1 during 1982-83 reasonably accurately. Thus, this episode of declining M1 velocity apparently reflected the sharp and unexpected drop in interest rates resulting from the slowing in the

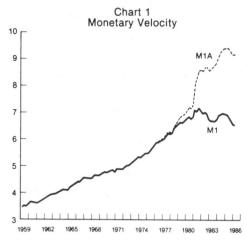

Chart 1
Monetary Velocity

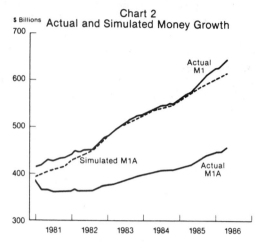

Chart 2
Actual and Simulated Money Growth

inflation rate in 1982 rather than a shift in M1 demand.

The situation with respect to M1A since 1981 has been the opposite of that for M1. Although the velocity of M1A has behaved much as it did in the preceding decades, the demand for this aggregate has not been related in a stable way to income, prices and interest rates. In fact, the lesser variability of MIA's velocity appears to have been largely fortuitous. For example, the failure of M1A velocity to decline in 1982-83 in response to the fall in interest rates apparently was caused by the simultaneous reduction in the demand for M1A as the public continued to move funds into higher-yielding NOWs. Hence, the stability of M1A velocity in that episode does not provide grounds for believing that M1A would be a useful monetary policy indicator in the future.

The 1985-86 experience
Chart 2 suggests that the demand for M1 *has* changed since early 1985 since the simulation underpredicts its growth since then. The reasons for this shift in the demand for M1 are not well understood.

It appears likely that deposit rate deregulation has played a role in shifting M1 demand by effectively raising the return that depository institutions pay on their checkable deposits and thus making the public willing to hold more of their financial wealth in the form of these deposits. A disproportionate amount of the recent increase in M1 has been in NOW accounts.

But it is unclear why this effect was felt in 1985 and not in earlier years since there were no regulatory changes in that year. If deposit rate deregulation were to cause a major shift in M1 demand, one would have expected this to occur in 1983 when Super-NOW accounts bearing fully deregulated interest rates were authorized, or in 1986 when rate ceilings on regular NOW accounts were removed.

The greater-than-expected increase in M1 growth since early 1985 has coincided with a decline in market interest rates. As a result, the differential between the returns available on other highly liquid deposits, such as MMDAs, and that on fully checkable NOW accounts has become extremely narrow. This small spread may explain why the public apparently has taken to holding larger NOW account balances relative to their incomes.

In the future, the impact of changes in interest rates on M1 demand may become more difficult to predict because it will depend on the speed and extent to which banks alter the deposit rates they pay on both NOW accounts and other liquid deposits. As a result, it seems likely that the central bank will find it necessary to continue its recent practice of monitoring other economic indicators as well as the monetary aggregates when setting policy. It also seems likely that M1A will not offer a solution to the problems created by the unusual behavior of M1 that began last year.

Brian Motley

Article Twenty

Interest Checking

On January 1, 1986, all regulatory deposit rate ceilings and minimum balance requirements were removed from personal checking accounts (although the prohibition against paying interest on business checking accounts remains). This completed a process of deposit rate deregulation of personal checking accounts that began in earnest with the nationwide authorization of NOW (Negotiable Order of Withdrawal) accounts on December 31, 1980 and Super NOW accounts on January 5, 1983. The NOW account originally had a maximum deposit rate of 5¼ percent (until January 1, 1986 when the ceiling was removed), while the Super NOW deposit rate was unrestricted. Today, there is no longer any regulatory distinction between the two accounts.

Both the NOW and Super NOW accounts have been extremely popular and have caused major changes in the composition of consumer checking accounts and in the narrowly defined M1 monetary aggregate. Most consumer checking balances and a large part of M1 now bear interest.

In this *Letter* we analyze why these new accounts so dramatically altered both depositors' and banks' portfolios, and examine the sources of the funds deposited in them. In next week's *Letter*, we assess the implications for the behavior of the M1 monetary aggregate, which includes balances in these accounts plus currency, travelers checks, and demand deposits.

Effects of the ceilings
The effects of lifting or removing interest rate ceilings on checking accounts depend to a large extent on how easy it was for depository institutions to circumvent the ceilings through nonprice competition in the first place. Nonprice competition is the practice of providing free or underpriced services in lieu of explicit interest payments.

Depository institutions expend resources on attracting and holding various kinds of deposits with the goal of equating the marginal costs of different types of deposits, including transactions deposits. However, when the payment of interest was prohibited, depositors' returns generally

were less than banks' marginal costs of attracting deposits because nonpriced services are not perfect substitutes for cash interest payments. Since depositors, in general, would have preferred the cash equivalent of nonpriced services, they valued nonpriced services at less than their cost. Thus, by imposing the inefficiency of nonprice competition, deposit rate ceilings drove a wedge between depositories' marginal costs of deposits and depositors' marginal returns.

The inherent inefficiency of nonprice competition implies that lifting or removing a deposit rate ceiling would, in effect, increase depositors' returns without affecting depositories' marginal costs. Undoubtedly then, a major reason for the popularity of interest-bearing checking accounts is the interest they yield. Even at current low interest rate levels, these interest-bearing checking accounts will yield $10 to $11 billion in interest this year. Just a few years ago, checking account balances would have earned no explicit interest. Thus, although interest earnings are taxable, interest payments have provided a powerful incentive to shift zero-interest checking balances and perhaps some savings balances as well into the new interest-bearing accounts.

Strong evidence supporting the view that explicit interest (even after taxes) on the new accounts exceeded the implicit interest previously available on demand deposits is presented in Chart 1. The chart indicates that a sharp drop in demand deposits coincided with the dramatic increase in NOW balances when they were first authorized nationwide on December 31, 1980 (they had been available previously on a limited basis) and, similarly, that NOW deposits fell sharply when Super NOWs were introduced.

These declines suggest that NOWs were successful in attracting large quantities of funds previously held in demand deposits (which paid no explicit interest), and that Super NOWs attracted funds from NOWs (which paid limited interest). These shifts would not have occurred if nonprice competition had circumvented deposit rate ceilings completely so that depositors valued the nonpriced services fully. Thus, in the aggregate, depositors' net returns on Super NOW accounts likely exceeded returns on NOWs, and the returns on NOWs likely exceeded the returns on demand deposits.

These shifts of funds from more regulated to less regulated checking accounts are similar to shifts that occurred from savings and time deposits with interest ceilings into the ceiling-free money market deposit account (MMDA) when it was authorized on December 14, 1982. Depositors moved several hundred billion dollars from lower-return regulated accounts into MMDAs. Just as with transaction balances, there were powerful incentives for depositors to move non-transaction funds into higher-yielding savings accounts.

As Chart 2 shows, the lifting of deposit rate ceilings has dramatically raised the proportion of personal checking account balances that earn explicit interest. At the beginning of 1977, less than 5 percent of the funds in consumer checking accounts were interest-bearing compared to over 70 percent today. In only ten years, these accounts have grown from $1 billion to over $200 billion.

Tax effects
Not all personal demand deposits have shifted into NOWs, nor have all NOW deposits shifted into Super NOWs even though depositors might be expected to prefer the highest yielding account. The explanation for this lies largely in our tax system, which creates incentives for banks to provide a wide variety of checking accounts with different deposit rates, minimum balances, and service charges.

Checking accounts are somewhat unusual in that banks simultaneously "borrow" deposits and "sell" transaction services associated with these deposits. The result of this arrangement is a net payment from either the bank to the customer or vice versa, depending on whether the yield on deposits exceeds the cost of transaction services provided.

The tax system provides an incentive for banks to reduce the deposit rates they pay on personal transaction accounts by enough to cover the cost of the transaction services they provide. Currently, this incentive works through individual (but not business) depositors, who must pay income taxes on explicit interest payments but cannot deduct charges for transaction services.

These depositors can lower their taxes by selecting an account in which the banks' service charges have been netted out of the interest paid. For example, some depositors prefer accounts that pay no interest and have no service charges to accounts that pay taxable interest and charge for services. A bank would be willing to provide such a "free" account as long as its profits on balances in the account equalled or exceeded the costs of providing the associated transaction services.

The tax system also explains why zero-interest checking accounts co-exist with higher yielding checking accounts. Such accounts typically have lower minimum balance requirements than higher yielding checking accounts. Banks use minimum balance requirements to ensure that their net earnings on the deposits cover the cost of the transaction services they provide.

For example, according to a 1985 survey by Sheshunoff and Company, Super NOWs, which paid the highest interest among personal checking accounts, had an average minimum balance requirement of $3,300 to avoid service charges. This compared with a $1,073 requirement for NOWs (which paid lower interest) and a $431 minimum balance requirement for demand deposit accounts, which paid no interest. Depositors who maintained only small balances would have been better off with a zero-interest demand deposit account even though a Super NOW yielded more interest because the interest it yielded would have been more than offset by service charges, especially on an after-tax basis. In contrast, depositors who maintained medium or large balances would have been better off with higher yielding NOW or Super NOW accounts.

In sum, even though deregulation eliminated the inefficiency of nonprice competition, the tax system will continue to ensure that a wide variety of checking accounts co-exist.

Sources of interest-bearing checkable deposits
The sources of funds placed in interest-bearing checkable deposits may be an indicator of how those balances will behave. For example, if NOWs and Super NOWs attracted balances from passbook savings accounts or maturing time certificates, NOW and Super NOW balances might behave more like savings balances than transaction balances. Both NOWs and

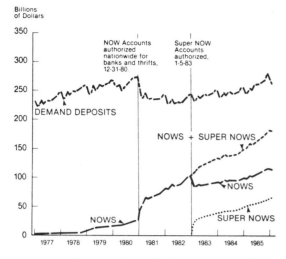

Chart 1
Deposits Shift into NOWS and Super NOWS

Billions of Dollars

NOW Accounts authorized nationwide for banks and thrifts, 12-31-80.

Super NOW Accounts authorized, 1-5-83

DEMAND DEPOSITS

NOWS + SUPER NOWS

NOWS

NOWS

SUPER NOWS

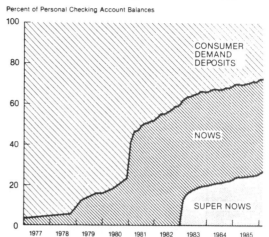

Chart 2
The Changing Composition of
Personal Checking Account Balances

Percent of Personal Checking Account Balances

CONSUMER DEMAND DEPOSITS

NOWS

SUPER NOWS

Super NOWs are believed to have attracted a significant amount of funds from savings and maturing time certificates.

Surveys as well as our own statistical estimates suggest that about one-quarter of the new money that shifted into NOWs during the introductory NOW period came from nontransaction sources. These funds, which probably came from passbook savings and maturing time certificates, are likely to be more interest-sensitive than demand deposits. Super NOWs probably also attracted the same types of nontransaction balances. However, because the MMDA was introduced at about the same time and attracted the same types of funds, it is difficult to measure the magnitude of the transfers.

Another indication of shifts of nontransaction balances into NOWs and Super NOWs is their large average balances — approximately $5,000 in NOWs and $13,000 in Super NOWs. These average balances are much closer to those of traditional savings deposits than to those of personal noninterest checking accounts, which are approximately $1,500.

Conclusion
Deposit rate deregulation has caused a major change in the composition of consumer transaction deposits by raising to 70 percent the propor-

tion of these balances in interest-bearing checking accounts. In contrast, as recently as 1977, virtually no checking balances paid explicit interest. Moreover, since their nationwide introduction on December 31, 1980, interest-bearing checking deposits have been by far the most rapidly growing component of consumer transaction balances.

This dramatic change is due to the inability of nonprice competition to compensate most depositors fully. The $10 billion or more that consumers will earn this year apparently exceeds (even on an after-tax basis) the free or underpriced services that they would have received if regulation continued to prohibit the accounts from paying interest.

The shift in the composition of consumer checking from noninterest-bearing to interest-bearing has also had a significant impact on M1. Interest-bearing transaction balances in M1, including some formerly classified as savings, have grown from virtually nothing before deregulation to over 30 percent by mid-1986. In next week's *Letter*, we present evidence that these effects of deregulation have caused a major change in the relationship between M1 and the economy.

Gary C. Zimmerman and Michael C. Keeley

Article Twenty-One

The Evolution of Retail EFT Networks

The retail payment system consists of cash, checks, credit cards, and other forms of nonelectronic payments, and a relatively small amount of electronic funds transfer (EFT). Though the role of EFT in the payment system has gradually increased over the past decade, consumer use has been largely limited to automated teller machine (ATM) operations, and a growing number of skeptics claim that the "electronics revolution" in payments will "never" arrive. They believe that the importance of EFT has been blown out of proportion by industry interests and by the trade press and that EFT cannot, in reality, displace paper-based payments at the retail level. Though complaints about the media hype are well-founded, EFT is already here and it is growing, albeit slowly.

The slow growth of EFT is due to the evolutionary nature of change in the payment system. Every new payment instrument, regardless of its technological superiority, must contend with relatively high initial costs and a lack of observable demand by the public. The emergence of EFT is an especially long, drawn-out process because its forms and their prices must be able to accommodate an unusually large number of diverse needs and conflicting interests. That EFT will proceed is guaranteed because it uses fewer resources than the paper-based transactions now predominantly used.

The first part of this paper examines recent retail payments in general as they evolve through a product life cycle of introduction, growth, maturity, and decline. The forms of retail EFT have been stuck in the introductory stage for some time because their prices to the public have been set above their long-run costs while charges for nonelectronic payments are largely below costs. Given this price structure and a lack of promotion, retail EFT does not appear to be sufficiently valuable to justify its use. However, if financial institutions and other participants priced retail EFT in line with its long-run costs, certain EFT forms would progress into the growth stage.

*Steven D. Felgran and
R. Edward Ferguson*

*Economist and Research Associate,
respectively, at the Federal Reserve
Bank of Boston.*

One component of retail EFT that has begun to take off recently is ATM use. The second part of this paper reviews the various phases in the evolution of ATMs from proprietary to widely shared networks. This evolution has proven to be a function of changing cost structures and marketing strategies over time. Networks of ATMs will continue to progress towards greater public access unless hampered by regulatory contraints.

Retail EFT also encompasses point-of-sale (POS) transactions and home banking, discussed in the third part of this paper. Retailers are largely skeptical of electronic POS transactions, due mainly to the lack of demand and uniform standards and to security and pricing disputes with financial institutions. The major stumbling block to electronic POS payment is the low price and widespread acceptance of the check form of payment.

The fourth part of this paper examines recent international EFT developments. The evolution of international EFT networks has closely followed the U.S. pattern. Many of the same opportunities and problems have arisen overseas.

I. EFT and Product Life Cycles

The payment system is always evolving towards more technologically sophisticated products and processes. The speed of this evolution depends upon both technological progress and demand for the various means of payment, a function of relative costs and convenience. The mix of payment instruments constituting the system continually changes as each payment instrument evolves through a product life cycle.

Product life cycle theory holds that a product experiences a series of distinct stages over time, each corresponding to particular marketing opportunities and revenue/cost levels. In the introductory stage, a producer is involved with new product testing and the creation of consumer awareness of the new product. Sometimes both producers and consumers are hesitant to try a new technology, though every product area has its "innovators" or early adopters. Progressing beyond the introductory stage is often the biggest hurdle and may require both a long period of time and a change in industry practices. In the growth stage, the producer capitalizes on consumer awareness to increase sales and maximize market share. Increasing numbers of consumers adopt the product after its value has been determined by pre-

vious buyers. In the mature stage, the producer attempts to defend market share and maximize profits. The number of potential buyers falls and the growth rate of sales slows, leveling out at the replacement purchase rate. In the decline stage, the producer relies on the reputation of the product to generate sales. Ultimately, sales decrease as improved brands and new products emerge. The product life cycle and the pattern of consumer acceptance are illustrated in the accompanying diagram.

This framework helps to explain the relative positions of different payment instruments and changes in the forms of payment over time. The mix of payments is now such that most paper-based instruments are in the mature stage, while the retail EFT instruments are progressing through a long introduc-

---

New forms of payment have difficulty attracting both producers and consumers, even if their technological superiority is obvious.

---

tory stage. Paper-based payments including cash, checks, credit cards, money orders, and travelers checks now constitute over 99 percent of the total transaction volume. Electronic payments constitute 78 percent of the value of total payments but this is almost wholly due to the value of wire transfers, which are not retail transactions.[1]

Retail EFT has been in the introductory stage for some time; such extended introductions are standard for payment innovations. New forms of payment have difficulty attracting both producers and consumers, even if their technological superiority is obvious. For example, checks were first introduced in the United States in the late 17th century and achieved a low level of use in the 1830s, but they did not become an important part of the payment system until spurred by banking legislation in the 1860s. Retail EFT would also benefit from a change in the legal or institutional environment that would aid progress to the growth stage.

The acceptance of retail EFT by both producers and consumers has been slow. This prolonged, con-

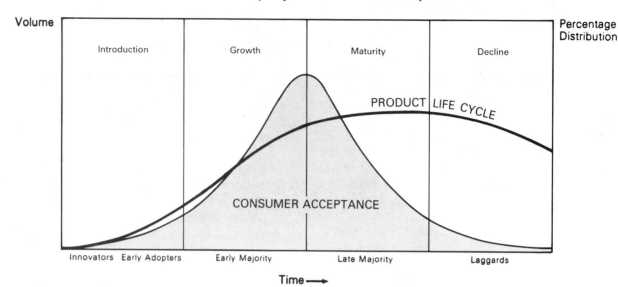

The Product Life Cycle and Consumer Acceptance

current process has led to a "catch-22" kind of dilemma over prices and output: financial institutions will not price EFT products in accordance with the low unit costs that large volumes would produce, yet consumers will not buy these products in large volumes unless they are priced attractively. Financial institutions have largely failed to view EFT as a long-run investment requiring extensive marketing and promotion, concerning themselves instead with short-run cost displacement and profitability. The uncertain demand for EFT and its high start-up costs and long payback period make EFT investment difficult to justify from a short-run perspective. However, if financial institutions were willing to sacrifice short-run for long-run profits, they would set relatively low prices and wait for high volumes to drive down unit costs.

The lack of marketing and promotion by financial institutions has caused the public to be unclear about the advantages and use of retail EFT. Only in the case of ATM use have financial institutions begun to convince consumers of the convenience, reliability, and value of an EFT instrument. The majority of consumers have no knowledge or interest in computer and telecommunications technologies and feel more comfortable with live tellers and traditional banking practices. Under these circumstances, financial institutions must actively market and promote retail EFT, in addition to providing pricing incentives, in order to stimulate demand and build transaction volumes.

Competition from checks and credit cards has been a major factor in the slow growth of retail EFT. Many of the advances in computer and telecommunications technologies that have made EFT possible have also improved the efficiency of these paper-based payment instruments. Since the processing cost gap has narrowed, financial institutions have found it even more difficult to justify EFT investment as a means of cost displacement. Retail EFT has also had to contend with user charges for checks and credit cards that are below their costs due to the value of float. In essence, financial institutions pay customers to use checks and credit cards because customers can earn interest until the funds are collected. As long as float exists, the public is unlikely to substitute electronic payments without compensating benefits.

Table 1 shows that average user charges for retail EFT transactions exceed those for the major paper-based alternatives. For example, an ATM transaction costs 64 cents on average, while a cash payment costs 18 cents and a check payment costs −15 cents. The negative charge for checks is due to the float transfer payment, which in this case produces a subsidy for users. Though average user charges favor cash and checks, average "real resource costs" or costs to society favor retail EFT over noncash payments.[2] For example, the real resource cost of a check payment at 68 cents is double that of an automated clearinghouse (ACH) payment[3] and slightly more than an ATM or POS payment. The real resource costs of EFT payments are lower than paper-based transactions be-

Table 1
Value, Costs, and Prices of Payment Instruments, 1983
Dollars

Type of Payment Instrument	Average Dollar Value[a]	Average Real Resource Cost[b]	Float Transfer Payment[c]	Average User Charge[d]
Paper-Based				
Cash	25	.07	.12	.18
Checks	910	.68	−.83	−.15
Credit Cards	42	.88	−.44	.44
Money Orders	67	1.77	.28	2.05
Travelers Checks	35	1.33	0	1.33
Electronic				
ACH	1800	.34	−.02	.33
ATM	70	.60	.04	.64
POS	30	.60	0	.60
Wire Transfers	2,500,000	5.21	.09	5.30

[a] Estimated value of transactions divided by estimated volume.
[b] Total real resource costs of production and processing divided by estimated volume. Production costs include unit costs of labor, capital, and intermediate inputs or services, and a markup factor to account for normal profits. These costs are adjusted to capture scale effects, scope effects or complementaries in production, and technological change not already embodied in the unit cost of capital. Processing costs include merchant handling and float charges to the payor, such as a premium for using a credit card at gas stations.
[c] Float transfer payment is the interest earned by the payor from the time of payment until the collection of the funds. It is calculated by multiplying the average daily value outstanding of the payment instrument by the average number of days until the collection of funds and the daily market interest rate (90-day Treasury bill rate) and dividing by the estimated volume. Float transfer payment is positive for cost and negative for benefit.
[d] Sum of total real resource cost and total float transfer payment divided by estimated volume.
Source: Allen N. Berger and David B. Humphrey, "The Role of Interstate Banking in the Diffusion of Electronic Payments Technology," in Colin Lawrence and Robert Shay, eds., *Technological Innovation, Regulation, and the Monetary Economy* (Cambridge, Mass.: Ballinger, 1986), pp. 18–19, 28–31.

cause electronic transmissions are relatively inexpensive even with low volumes. The real resource costs would be even lower in the long run due to economies of scale. Though the prices of EFT payments closely reflect their costs, the prices of paper-based payments are sufficiently lower than their relatively high costs to undercut EFT prices.

II. ATM Diffusion and Constraints

Growth and Evolution

The diffusion of ATMs, especially those shared by two or more financial institutions, continues. Shared ATM networks allow the cardholders of one institution to carry out financial transactions at the terminal of another. Transactions that can be accomplished at an ATM include cash withdrawals, deposits, transfers, cash advances, and payments.

As shown in table 2, the number of ATMs grew modestly to 60,000 in 1985, of which over 35,000 were shared. This marks the first time that more ATMs have been shared than not. Total monthly transactions leveled off at 300 million, though transactions at shared machines continued to grow significantly. The number of debit cards increased to 130 million, three-quarters of which can access shared terminals.

The evolution of ATMs has progressed through different phases of the introductory stage of the product life cycle. This progression has been characterized by continuous changes in network organization. Each phase has begun with a new set of network linkages to achieve a marketing advantage, and has ended with that advantage being exhausted. The different phases are motivated by changing marketing strategies and network costs as financial institutions increasingly cooperate to share ATMs. The evolution illustrates the tradeoffs between competition and cooperation as ATM access widens.

The evolution of ATM networks appears to consist of five phases: proprietary, shared, multiple memberships, direct links, and universal (or global) sharing. Initially, a bank may be content to have its own proprietary ATM network. This network gives the bank a competitive advantage that can be used to increase, or at least stabilize, the bank's share of deposits in its market. At the same time, the network may provide savings through reduced teller and check processing costs. Unless threatened by competition, a bank may see no reason to expand ATM services beyond access to its proprietary machines. This situation persists in California, where the five largest banks have each developed extensive proprietary systems.

Eventually, as more banks establish their own networks, the mere possession of proprietary machines is no longer an advantage. Financial institutions enter the second phase of ATM evolution when they begin to share ATMs. Through membership in a shared ATM network, the institution can both in-

Table 2
ATM Trends

	1982	1983	1984	1985	Percent Change		
					1982–83	1983–84	1984–85
Number of ATMs							
Shared ATMs	11,000	16,000	25,000	35,500	+45	+56	+42
All ATMs	31,000	40,000	55,000	60,000	+29	+38	+9
Shared as percent of total	35	40	45	59			
Total Monthly ATM Transactions (Millions)							
Shared ATMs	45	60	115	164	+33	+92	+43
All ATMs	180	240	300	300	+33	+25	0
Shared as percent of total	25	25	38	55			
Monthly Transactions Per ATM							
Shared ATMs	4,100	3,800	4,600	4,620	−7	+21	0
All ATMs	5,800	6,000	5,500	5,000	+3	−8	−9
Shared as percent of total	71	63	84	92			
Number of Debit Cards (Millions)							
Shared	29	50	65	100	+72	+30	+54
Total	60	75	100	130	+25	+33	+30
Shared as percent of total	48	67	65	77			

Note: Yearly data as of July/August of each year. Figures for shared ATMs refer to ATMs on-line to regional shared networks. Figures for totals refer to all ATMs on-line to both shared and proprietary networks. Transaction volumes include both on-us and on-other transactions. All numbers are approximations.
Source: Compiled from *Bank Network News*, "Bank Network News Top 50," October 22, 1982; "Bank Network News Top 100," September 10, 1983; "1985 EFT Network Data Book," September 25, 1984, and "1986 EFT Network Data Book," September 26, 1985.

crease customer convenience by offering access to more machines and lower the unit costs at its own machines through higher transaction volumes. In addition, the institution may generate income by earning transaction fees when other banks' customers use its machines.

Shared ATM networks often start out with policies designed to protect member institutions from having to share ATMs with local competitors. By joining with institutions in neighboring areas through franchising agreements, a bank can achieve economies of scale while retaining the proprietary aspects of its local network. The BayBanks X-PRESS 24 network in Massachusetts has engaged in franchising of this kind. Sharing has also been restricted under exclusive dealer/exclusive territory agreements that formally protect member institutions from their local rivals. CIRRUS and PLUS, the two leading national ATM networks, used to have such restrictions but dropped them in 1985.

As the proportion of shared ATMs in an area increases, the marketing benefits of exclusive sharing begin to be outweighed by the economies of scale gained by sharing more fully. At a more advanced stage, the added convenience to depositors produces additional marketing benefits. Over time, the advantages of increased sharing cause new, larger shared networks to be formed that bypass the restricted sharing phase. For example, AVAIL in Georgia, LYNX in New Mexico, GULFNET in Louisiana, and NYCE in New York were all organized on a statewide or regional basis.

Over time, networks tend to expand to include more and more institutions. Though sets of competing network alignments often appear, sharing can still expand through memberships in multiple networks, the third phase of ATM evolution. An increasing number of institutions have entered into multiple sharing arrangements due to changes in the competitive environment and to more liberal shared network bylaws. Multiple memberships exist in markets where shared ATM coverage is high, and where the marketing advantages of exclusive memberships have eroded.

The continued spread of multiple sharing agreements would eventually produce universal cardholder access to all machines. However, universal service could be achieved more efficiently through the consolidation of ATM networks or by direct links among networks. This fourth phase in the ATM evolution enables financial institutions in different networks to be connected through direct interchange

---

Comparisons between marketing benefits and cost savings determine the extent to which financial institutions share their EFT operations.

---

arrangements that avoid multiple switches and conflicting network procedures. Consolidation will occur as the efficiency of direct linkage outweighs the marketing advantages of memberships in multiple unconnected networks.

Consolidation has already occurred through mergers and joint ventures among some regional ATM networks. In New England, for example, the CASH network has been formed out of the VEC, TX, POCKETBANK, and ACTION networks, though they are retaining their individual logos. In the greater New York region, the NYCE and TREASURER networks have established direct links. In addition, eight major regional networks in the Boston-to-Washington corridor are studying interchange arrangements and central switching systems. The Shared Network Executives Association, which represents many regional networks across the country, is developing guidelines for interregional direct links. Much of this activity is in anticipation of direct debit POS transactions and the realization that multiple networks with their own communications systems are redundant.

In this evolution of shared ATM networks, comparisons are constantly made between marketing benefits and cost savings. These comparisons determine the extent to which financial institutions share their EFT operations. As consolidation continues, the provision of EFT services will become increasingly common while institutions compete over the nature and pricing of these services. In the final phase of evolution, sharing will be universal as all institutions will be connected through "backroom" switching and

clearing operations. Universal sharing will eventually come about unless deterred by government regulation.

Regulatory Initiatives

The successful evolution of ATM networks has been aided by freedom from legislative or judicial interference. However, some believe that the ATM industry should be regulated as a public utility with utility-type access and pricing policies. The public utility approach is supposed to protect small from large institutions and state-chartered from national institutions by guaranteeing equal access to all interested parties.

Among the bills introduced in Congress that seek to control network development is one offered by Senator William Proxmire that is intended to restrict the collection of deposits by national banks across state lines using ATMs.[4] The bill would make universal sharing of all EFT terminals a mandatory condition before a national bank could use such ATMs or other EFT terminals for interstate transactions. The bill could require competitive ATM networks such as CIRRUS and PLUS to become nondiscriminatory utilities or go out of business. Senator Proxmire has indicated that his bill is necessary to preserve competitive equality between state and national banks and to respect the dual banking system in light of a recent court case (discussed below).

The Proxmire bill provides that any EFT terminal used by a bank's customers is a branch of that bank unless the terminal "may be utilized by any bank wishing to do so on a nondiscriminatory basis," in which case it is called "shared electronic banking equipment." Moreover, even if a terminal is "shared electronic banking equipment," it will be deemed to be a branch by virtue of being "rented" by the bank whose customer uses it unless the transaction fee that the bank pays is "assessed in accordance with a uniform fee schedule upon all banks which share, or permit their customers to use" that terminal. In other words, this legislation would preclude an ATM owner from negotiating interchange fees with other financial institutions, and it would require that ATM interchange fees be identical in all interstate systems to which that ATM might be connected.

If the EFT terminal of another entity is "shared electronic banking equipment" and if it is not "owned or rented" by the national bank that wishes to share in its use, then that national bank could be connected to it subject to any state laws or regulations in the state where the terminal is located. National banks could collect deposits at ATMs across state lines only if the ATMs were "shared electronic banking equipment" and if such interstate deposit-taking at these ATMs were expressly authorized by state statute in the state where the ATMs were located.

The public utility approach of the Proxmire bill (and a similar bill in the House) is not appropriate given the structure and behavior of the ATM market.

The evolution of ATM networks has rendered mandatory sharing unnecessary because networks have adopted more liberal access policies and sharing has become increasingly widespread.

In particular, some of the ideas are in fundamental conflict with long-established federal antitrust policies by mandating universal sharing as a condition for interstate ATM interchange by national banks. Mandatory sharing, or involuntary open access, is not in the public interest because it discourages independent initiative and risk-taking by allowing so-called "free riders" to gain access at less than fully allocated costs. Moreover, the evolution of ATM networks has rendered mandatory sharing unnecessary because networks have adopted more liberal access policies and sharing has become increasingly widespread. If an institution has been unfairly denied access to a shared ATM network, it has recourse to the antitrust laws. Antitrust is a much better remedy than mandatory sharing because it considers individual cases on their merits instead of restricting business behavior in general.

The Proxmire bill was first introduced in response to a decision in the so-called Wegmans ATM case.[5] This case is a crucial part of the ongoing discussion over whether ATMs are functionally or legally equivalent to bank branches. The prevailing view, confirmed on appeal in the Wegmans case, is that ATMs not established (that is, owned or rented) by a national bank but available to the bank's customers are not branches of the bank. The appeals court cor-

rectly noted that the definition of "branch" is ambiguous in a world of electronic transfers. In particular, brick-and-mortar branch banking, with a single physical locus of bank-customer transactions, has been supplemented by many other forms of communication that could not have been contemplated in 1927 when the McFadden Act was passed. These forms of communication include not only ATMs but also POS terminals and home computers. In this environment of EFT, the word "branch" loses its meaning.

The evolution of shared ATM networks to date confirms this view of branching. As sharing has increased, the competitive attributes of ATMs have changed. Only in the early stage of proprietary networks does the mere provision of ATM services produce a competitive advantage. As the market evolves and more institutions share an ATM, it no longer has a competitive identity in and of itself. The ATM then is no different from a POS terminal or home computer as far as its identification with a particular bank is concerned. This situation is, of course, very different from brick-and-mortar branch banking.

Furthermore, ownership of the ATM should not determine its branch status. Regardless of whether an ATM is owned by a bank, the ATM should not qualify as a branch of that bank if it has no competitive identity. In the future, when ATMs are universally shared, they will have no competitive attributes and the branch question will be moot. What will matter then will be the relationship between the bank and the customer that the terminal makes possible. Though his decision was later modified, the Comptroller of the Currency in 1974 authorized national banks to establish off-premises customer-bank communication terminals (CBCTs) without regard to McFadden Act branching restrictions.[6] The Comptroller has continued to view ATMs used but not established by national banks as means of communication, not places where banks transact business and, therefore, not branches. The current distinction between ATMs owned and ATMs used is an inappropriate way to determine whether an ATM is a branch of a national bank.

The U.S. Supreme Court in June 1986 decided not to hear the Wegmans ATM case. By letting the appeals court decision stand, the Supreme Court allowed national banks to continue sharing the use of ATMs without violating state branching restrictions. In this climate, it is likely that the Proxmire bill will receive renewed attention. Legislation has also been proposed that would in effect codify the appeals court decision.[7]

III. Potential Developments: Point-of-Sale Transactions and Home Banking

Point of Sale

In addition to the positive trends in ATM sharing, more advanced retail payment systems are emerging. Specifically, direct debit at the point of sale (POS) is widely expected to be the next retail EFT system to be developed. In a POS transaction, the customer uses a debit card to pay retailers for goods or services. In order for POS to work, EFT networks must link customers' banks to merchants' banks.

Several factors suggest that POS is the new frontier in retail EFT. As noted above, the number of debit cards issued and used continues to increase. As more networks are hooked up, access to bank accounts via debit cards will reach the high levels needed to attract retailers. In addition, the growing practice of installing ATMs in retail settings helps to introduce retail EFT to consumers. Finally, many retailers are installing credit card authorization terminals, which can be employed in direct debit POS transactions.

The number of direct debit POS terminals in commercial use grew from 1,900 in 1984 to 7,500 in 1985, of which 6,000 were connected to about 24 shared ATM networks.[8] Many more shared ATM networks are currently testing POS systems, and about 17,000 direct debit POS terminals were on-line in May 1986.[9] About 1.2 million POS transactions took place per month in 1985.[10] Nevertheless, several more years must pass before POS enters the growth phase of its life cycle. As it grows, POS will generate transaction volumes that will significantly exceed ATM volumes.

Table 3 compares selected POS systems over the

Table 3

A Comparison of Selected POS Systems, 1985 to 1986

Market	Network Operator	Number of Terminals		Average Monthly Transactions (thousands)		Significant Merchants	Merchants' Locations	
		3/85	3/86	3/85	3/86		3/85	3/86
California	First Interstate Bank[a]	729	729	102	160	Mobil Oil	700	700
	Crocker National Bank					Arco	29	29
Florida	HONOR	988	2,800	14	95	Mobil Oil	230	275
						7-Eleven	375	375
						Publix Super Markets	10	200
Iowa	ITS, Inc.	308	425	73	83	Hy-Vee Food Stores	17	22
						Dahl's Foods	9	9
Ohio	INSTANET/Ameritrust	275	400	4	5	Gas Town	25	14
						Gray's Drug Stores	17	0
						Shell Service Stations	0	12
Pennsylvania	CASHSTREAM	52	450	16	45	Amoco	6	6
						Gulf	15	15
						PA State liquor stores	29	44
						Mobil Oil	0	300
	MAC	50	75	8	8	Sunoco	50	55
Texas	MPACT	322	2,242	4	30	Mobil Oil	230	287
						Exxon	0	815
						The Shoe Box	13	0
Washington, D.C. and suburbs	MOST CASH FLOW/Sovran	60	106	17	28	Mobil Oil	60	106
Wisconsin	TYME	49	260	20	70	Pick-n-Save Foods	3	24

[a] First Interstate Bank was only participating with Mobil Oil in March 1986.
Source. Surveys conducted by the authors, March 1985 and March 1986.

one-year period between March 1985 and March 1986. While POS did not take off as some authorities had predicted, several networks, including HONOR in Florida and TYME in Wisconsin, experienced a large increase in both the number of merchant locations and terminals, and nearly all the systems experienced significant increases in transaction volumes. In addition, several major POS networks became operational during the year. INTERLINK, a network organized by California's five largest banks, has about 750 locations on line, and the CACTUS SWITCH, a network organized by the Arizona ACH, is handling approximately 370,000 transactions per month.[11] Oil companies, particularly Mobil, continue to be the major participating retailers to date, and supermarkets are next. These are precisely the kinds of high-volume, low-margin retailers for whom POS appears to be most attractive. It will be difficult to design a POS setup that is equally attractive to other kinds of retailers.

The pricing dispute is essentially over which party receives the benefits of POS and should therefore pay for its development.

In general, retailers have remained skeptical of direct debit POS transactions for three reasons. First, consumer demand for direct debit POS has been decidedly lacking. Banks and networks have not actively marketed this service or priced it attractively relative to other forms of payment. In turn, merchants see little incentive to commit to POS payment systems. Second, the standards for debit cards and POS terminals are not uniform, though the American Bankers Association is developing guidelines.[12] Until uniform standards are agreed upon, retailers will have to equip their systems to handle the variety of formats that exist today. Finally and most importantly, merchants and bankers disagree over security and pricing issues.

Most banks have insisted that proper security requires that retailers install POS terminals with personal identification number (PIN) pads and encryption, the scrambling of the numbers during transmission. Many retailers, especially those with large numbers of cash registers, are reluctant to add PIN systems due to their high installation costs. Apparently, they feel that security is sufficient with existing systems such as lists of bad check risks. In addition, many retailers are concerned about such problems as computer failures and delays due to customers who have forgotten their numbers.

The pricing dispute is essentially over which party receives the benefits of POS and should therefore pay for its development. This problem did not exist when ATM networks were developed because they benefited card-issuing banks, which were willing to pay transaction fees to the switch and to the ATM owner. However, card-issuing banks believe that retailers are the ultimate beneficiaries of POS because they profit from instant guaranteed funds, elimination of check cashing services and bad check risks, reduced checkout time, increased customer convenience, and lower processing costs compared with checks or credit cards. Retailers counter that these benefits do not justify investment in POS terminals without fee payments from banks or customers, and that banks benefit from both reduced check processing costs and the value added to their debit cards due to POS access.

The disagreement over pricing is responsible for a confusing set of practices that vary across regions. In general, the card-issuing institution pays a switch fee to the network but the terminal owner does not receive a payment. The network rarely deals directly with the merchant but deals instead with the sponsoring financial institution, which negotiates fees with the merchant. Fees between the merchant and the sponsoring institution vary depending on the ownership of the terminal and business relationships. The variety of pricing arrangements that have emerged include both the payment and receipt of fees by merchants. For example, merchants in the AVAIL network may pay transaction fees up to 14 cents, while merchants in the HONOR network may receive transaction fees up to 15 cents (though this practice is to be phased out later this year).[13] Fees paid by customers tend to be tied to minimum balance requirements, though a major merchant, Atlantic Richfield, plans to directly charge customers 10 cents per transaction.[14] The lack of a consistent pricing structure has resulted in uncertainty about future pricing arrangements, and this has hardened the reluctance of retailers to pay for a service that currently provides marginal benefits.

The pricing uncertainty shows some signs of

abating. A number of banks and EFT networks are beginning to price POS favorably relative to other payment forms, particularly check, to attract retailers. For example, four of the leading networks involved in POS—TYME, HONOR, MPACT in Texas, and ITS in Iowa—are subsidizing POS switch fees using income earned from ATM transactions.[15] Their attempts to bolster POS stem from their assessment of its long-run profitability.

In order for POS to continue expanding, the number of POS logos must be kept relatively low and separate from credit cards. The promotion of POS by regional networks using numerous ATM logos could cause marketing problems for national merchants and for those in overlapping regions. A few national POS logos would be attractive to retailers and lead to a better, more efficient direct debit system. MasterCard and Visa have agreed to jointly sponsor a common national debit card logo solely for POS. The major credit card companies were previously unsuccessful in attempts to launch independent POS logos either de novo or by acquisition of CIRRUS and PLUS. Since regional networks are unlikely to sacrifice their identities in the near term, progress towards national POS logos will occur as the marketing advantages of regional ATM logos decline. This evolution may be similar to the emergence of the two major credit card companies.

The use of ATM logos to promote POS may require that debit cards be kept separate from credit cards in the near term to avoid confusion over the nature of transactions. Approximately one-third of Visa and MasterCard credit cards now have regional or national ATM logos,[16] which could cause misunderstandings about the payment instrument being used at the point of sale. Bankers are concerned that debit/credit cards would cause them to lose credit card discount revenues, because retailers would benefit by processing transactions as lower-cost debits. At the same time, consumers might have unintentional overdrafts. On the other hand, some ATM networks such as TYME are successfully employing multi-function debit/credit cards. Such cards make economic sense by avoiding redundant cards and systems, and may become prevalent should changes in the retail payment system cause debit transactions to become more common. Such changes would include the education of the public about debit card use and the elimination or pricing of float.

Instead of using a debit card, electronic POS transactions could be accomplished using a "smart card" or integrated circuit card. The smart card is the size of a traditional credit card but contains an embedded micro processor or computer chip giving it computing power and memory capability. The smart card

---

In order for POS to continue expanding, the number of POS logos must be kept relatively low and separate from credit cards.

---

can be used to confirm the cardholder's identity, thus avoiding the need for expensive on-line authorization and encryption. It can also contain a record of the cardholder's available funds. Proponents of the smart card predict that its built-in recordkeeping features will lead to a repackaging of existing deposit and credit services, and enable banks to join with nonfinancial institutions in offering many new services. For example, memory chips containing medical histories and insurance information would greatly simplify hospital admissions and payment procedures.[17]

The smart card was invented in France and developed by the French government as part of a planned nationwide cashless payment system. The card was initially rejected in the United States as being too expensive to produce and incompatible with existing systems. Recently, interest in smart card technology has revived due to the increasing telecommunications costs of on-line authorization and the increasing vulnerability of magnetic stripe cards to counterfeiting and theft. Mastercard and Visa have both announced plans to develop smart cards for commercial use. Mastercard is currently testing the cardholder identification capability and plans to examine more sophisticated applications such as storing a monetary value that would be depleted as purchases were made. Visa will first develop an "enhanced magnetic stripe" card, then a conventional smart card, and ultimately a "super smart card," a chip card with a keyboard and display screen. Visa intends to permit member banks to select versions of the card appropriate to their own markets and preferences.

Several obstacles must be overcome before the smart card can become an important payment instrument. First, the smart card is more costly to produce than the magnetic stripe card, and modification of existing ATMs to accept smart cards would be expensive. Some industry observers question whether these costs would be outweighed by the reduced authorization expenses and savings in fraud and credit losses. They contend that new, revenue-generating services must be added to make the smart card viable. Second, the benefits to POS of the smart card would be negated if all POS transactions had to be authorized through on-line, real-time systems and the PIN encrypted at the terminal (as proposed by the American Bankers Association). Finally, no international standards exist for smart cards and the major developers, France and Japan, are taking very different approaches.

Home Banking

Home banking is another component of retail EFT that may move beyond the introductory stage as financial institutions continue to automate their delivery systems. Home banking can either be offered alone or as part of a videotex system, which can exchange information with a central computer. Information usually travels over telephone lines connecting the computer with the user's videotex terminal, personal computer, or adapted television set. Services available include bill paying, securities brokerage, news and financial information, home shopping, electronic mail, and entertainment and educational programs. Of course, home banking cannot provide customers with cash withdrawals, the most popular retail EFT service.

As table 4 shows, home banking is clearly in its infancy. Thirty-eight financial institutions currently have commercial home banking services or tests underway, and an additional 21 institutions intend to enter this business. Though the total number of institutions with home banking operations fell from June 1985 (largely due to the completion of one large pilot test), the number of commercial operations has steadily increased since May 1984. The number of users has also steadily increased and is now estimated at 70,000 to 75,000, about two-thirds of whom subscribe to programs offered by Bank of America or Chemical Bank.[18]

To enter the growth stage, home banking must overcome the skepticism with which it is viewed by most of the public and the banks. Its real benefits to the public are obscured by its complexity, its high equipment costs, subscription fees, and on-line charges, and the lack of receipts or any printed record

Table 4

Home Banking Trends

Date	Number of Institutions On-Line	Commercial Operations	Pilot Test	Intend to Enter	Number of Users
May 1984	26	16	10	26	17,000
January 1985	47	22	25	15	44,000
June 1985	48	25	23	13	58,000
January 1986	38	30	8	21	70,000–75,000

Source: Periodic surveys reported in the American Banker, May 14, 1984, p. 23; January 21, 1985, p. 1; June 4, 1985, pp. 1, 31; and February 10, 1986, pp. 1, 22.

of banking transactions. Most financial institutions find the $1.5 million to $5 million cost of developing home banking systems to be prohibitively high given the uncertain demand for the service.[19]

Despite the slow adoption of videotex to date, and two recent failures of videotex concerns,[20] several factors suggest that development will continue. First, a number of important financial and communications companies have joined forces to develop national videotex systems. The Covidea system, already operating nationally, is a joint venture of Bank of America,[21] Chemical Bank, AT&T, and Time, Inc. The Trintex system, which will begin operations around 1987, is a joint venture of IBM, Sears Roebuck & Co., and CBS. In addition, Citicorp, Nynex Corp., and RCA Corp. have formed a joint venture to engage in research and development of videotex services. The commitment of these organizations to home information services demonstrates that they are willing to build a market. Through joint ventures, they can combine their resources and technical expertise to create new services, and use their financial resources to subsidize equipment and usage costs for subscribers, as has been successfully done in France.

Second, by contracting with existing vendors of home information services, banks can save the high costs of development and more easily offer home banking. The videotex vendors now emerging have set themselves up nationally to accommodate widely dispersed customers and achieve sufficient volumes. Local and regional services will eventually be added to national videotex to appeal to more customers. The national vendors that currently provide access to home banking are Covidea, CompuServe, and Video-Financial Services. The emergence of national videotex companies contrasts with ATM/POS development, which began locally and expanded to regional and national coverage.

Third, shared ATM networks have begun to negotiate licensing agreements for home banking. In addition to lowering the costs to banks, shared ATM networks may be able to provide additional local and regional services to videotex. At present, two regional shared ATM networks, MAC in Pennsylvania and MONEY STATION in Ohio, have licensing agreements in place. As such agreements become widespread, competitive pressures could accelerate the growth of home banking.

Fourth, banks and network operators are now offering an array of financial services to attract additional individual and business customers. These services include checkbook balancing, budgeting, and tax planning, in which customers use the network to obtain the required data and process it off-line. Other services offered to attract small businesses include access to current funds availability, control over cash management, and current information on loan and interest rates. Selling EFT services to businesses may be more profitable than individual sales because businesses have a more immediate need and often have the equipment needed to access these services.

Finally, less expensive terminals are within sight. AT&T recently began marketing a terminal for under $100.[22] Citibank has developed a pocket-size terminal that can be connected to a telephone to access its home banking system. This service is free to customers who have met minimum balance requirements, otherwise it is $5 per month.[23] Some networks are offering incentives such as free modems or hardware discounts to home banking subscribers.

IV. International Developments[24]

Approximately 134,000 ATMs and cash dispensers were installed worldwide as of year-end 1984.[25] The countries with the greatest numbers of installations are the United States and Japan, with 59,300 and 38,366 terminals, respectively. France and the United Kingdom each have approximately 7,000 terminals installed, and Canada, Spain, West Germany, Italy, Australia, South Africa, Sweden, and Hong Kong each have over 1,000 machines in place. These 12 countries account for 95 percent of the terminals installed worldwide, with the remaining machines distributed over approximately 40 countries.[26] The number of ATMs per million people is greatest in the United States and Japan, and Singapore, Hong Kong, Israel and Sweden also have high ATM densities. Table 5 shows selected data for the 10 leading countries.

While not as widespread as ATMs, more sophisticated forms of EFT such as POS and home banking are being planned or tested in many countries. As in

---

The evolution of EFT systems worldwide has followed a path similar to that in the United States.

---

the United States, POS systems are operating largely in gas stations and face many of the same merchant/bank disputes over access and pricing. France and Belgium have the two most well developed POS systems, and Denmark and Norway have national networks in place. Other countries involved in POS testing include Australia, Japan, Hong Kong, New Zealand, Singapore, and South Africa. France is the leader in home banking development, and Japan, West Germany, Sweden, Belgium, Switzerland, Italy, and the United Kingdom are testing or operating home banking systems.

While retail EFT has developed at different rates throughout the world, the evolution of EFT systems worldwide has followed a path similar to that in the United States. In general, ATM deployment begins with competing proprietary systems and, over time, gradually moves to increased sharing. With this increased sharing, POS systems emerge that "piggyback" on the existing ATM networks.

Despite the similarities in development, some differences do exist between foreign and domestic EFT systems. First, the ATMs worldwide generally perform a more limited range of functions, offering primarily cash withdrawals and balance inquiries. They also offer some features, however, that are not available in the United States. For example, approximately 40 percent of the terminals in Western Europe provide a statement and checkbook ordering function, and in Japan, many terminals accept passbooks and "recycle" cash deposits so that the notes can be withdrawn by subsequent customers.[27] Second, rela-

Table 5

The 10 Leading Countries in ATM Development, January 1985

Country	Number of ATMs	ATMs per Million People	Number of Cards Issued (millions)	Percent of Population with a Card	Estimated Annual Volume of Transactions (millions)	Number of Total Networks	Number of Shared Networks
United States	59,300	255	120.0	52	3,600[a]	1,600	560
Japan	38,366	323	99.8	84	1,200[b]	23[c]	5
France	7,172	132	16.1	30	216	4	4
United Kingdom	6,886	122	16.0	28	369	17	2
Canada	3,000	122	9.5	39	180	11	4
Spain	2,772	73	6.9	18	54	3	3
West Germany	2,000	32	18.1	29	72	1	1
Italy	1,798	32	2.9	5	37	1	1
Australia	1,642	110	7.2	48	92	15	3
South Africa	1,597	62	2.5	10	50	12	0

Note: ATM refers to any machine that provides services in addition to dispensing cash.
[a] Data from *Bank Network News*, "1986 EFT Network Data Book," September 26, 1985, p. 1. The transaction volume is as of July/August 1985.
[b] Estimate based on 1979 volumes. Data from *Banking System in Japan*, Federation of Bankers Association of Japan (1979), pp. 63 and 65.
[c] Data from *The Nilson Report*.
Source: "ATMs and Cash Dispensers: An International Survey and Analysis 1985," Battelle London, August 1985, except as noted.

tively few EFT systems are in operation in these foreign countries and they are dominated by large financial institutions. This contrasts with the many competing systems in the United States that often involve third parties such as supermarkets, oil companies, and credit card companies. The overseas structure may lead to relatively fast POS development because fewer parties must be brought together. Finally, overseas ATMs are more likely to be located within bank offices, though increasing numbers of ATMs are being installed elsewhere.

International EFT links have developed as networks have attempted to increase access in a process similar to ATM evolution. The Visa system provides its cardholders with access to about 7,800 ATMs in 13 countries. American Express also provides its cardholders in 13 countries with access to ATMs and travelers check dispensers. The CIRRUS and PLUS networks are connected to major Canadian systems, PLUS will soon provide access to holders of Japan's leading credit card, and MasterCard plans to establish links in three countries later this year. The Euro-

cheque organization, a system that enables cardholders to obtain local currency by check throughout Western Europe, is formulating guidelines for using the Eurocheque card in ATM/POS systems. Currently, cardholders from about five European countries can access ATMs in West Germany and Spain. Finally, individual banks in different countries are establishing links as exemplified by Chemical Bank's agreement to provide the customers of Saitama Bank of Japan with access to NYCE and MASTERTELLER.

The growth of international links has been impeded by several problems concerning standards, reliability, and security. Standardization is necessary but very difficult to achieve because most countries have developed unique approaches to EFT. Unreliable telephone systems are an impediment to EFT links in many countries, and establishing separate communications systems is very costly. Finally, with widespread international EFT links, security risks and the potential for fraudulent activities could increase. Future international links require solutions in all these areas.

V. Conclusion

Retail electronic funds transfer constitutes a small but significant part of the payment system. EFT growth has been slow largely because both producers and consumers have resisted adopting the new technologies. Producers must contend with high initial costs not clearly justified by current demand, while existing payment instruments such as checks have reached mature volumes and provide consumers with free float. Consumers will not demand EFT unless it is inexpensive and believed to be safe and reliable. Though consumers could be induced to substitute EFT for existing payment instruments, producers have been unwilling to adopt the long-run pricing and promotion strategies needed to stimulate demand and drive down unit costs.

The slow adoption of EFT is not unusual given the history of payment innovations. All new payment instruments have lengthy introductions during which producers and consumers become interested and conflicting needs are resolved. The number of conflicts surrounding EFT development has been greater than usual, as shown by the bank/merchant disputes over point-of-sale transactions. Since these conflicts have not yet been resolved, EFT will remain in the introductory stage for at least several more years. However, the continued growth and development of EFT is guaranteed by its many benefits, especially its relatively low costs and its convenience.

[1] Allen N. Berger and David B. Humphrey, "The Role of Interstate Banking in the Diffusion of Electronic Payments Technology," in Colin Lawrence and Robert Shay, eds., *Technological Innovation, Regulation, and the Monetary Economy* (Cambridge, Mass.: Ballinger Books, 1986), p. 17.

[2] Berger and Humphrey define "real resource costs" as the sum of unit production and processing costs to the payor, payee, bank, and Federal Reserve, equivalent to prices paid by users less costs of float transfer payments.

[3] For an extensive discussion of the automated clearinghouse, see *Economic Review*, Federal Reserve Bank of Atlanta, "The ACH in a New Light," March 1986, and "The Automated Clearinghouse Alternative: How Do We Get There From Here?" April 1986.

[4] *Electronic Banking Competitive Equality Act of 1985*, S.1148, 99 Cong. 1 Sess.

[5] *Independent Bankers Association of New York State, Inc. v. Marine Midland Bank, N.A.*, 757 F.2d 453 (2nd Cir.), petition for cert. filed, June 27, 1985 (No. 84-2023). This case is discussed in detail in Steven D. Felgran, "From ATM to POS Networks: Branching, Access, and Pricing," *New England Economic Review*, May/June 1985.

[6] 39 Fed. Reg. 44,416 (Dec. 24, 1974); 12 C.F.R. Section 7.7491 (1975). The Comptroller's 1974 decision was held to be invalid in *Independent Bankers Association of America v. Smith*, 534 F.2d 921 (D.C. Cir.), cert. denied, 429 U.S. 862 (1976). The Comptroller has since ruled that an ATM is not a branch of a national bank unless the bank owns or rents it. 12 C.F.R. Section 5.31(b)(1984).

[7] *Banking Convenience Act of 1985*, S.206, 99 Cong. 1 Sess. See also *Status of ATM's under State Branching Laws*, Hearings before the Senate Committee on Banking, Housing, and Urban Affairs, 98 Cong. 2 Sess. (GPO, 1984).

[8] *Bank Network News*, "1985 EFT Network Data Book," September 25, 1984, and "1986 EFT Network Data Book," September 26, 1985.

[9] American Bankers Association, May 14, 1986.

[10] *Bank Network News*, "1986 EFT Network Data Book," September 26, 1985.

[11] Survey conducted by the authors, March 1986.

[12] Representatives of MasterCard, Visa, CIRRUS, and PLUS have been meeting under the auspices of the American Bankers Association to interpret existing American National Standards Institute (ANSI) and International Standards Organization (ISO) standards for application to the POS/debit card environment and recommend standard guidelines for terminals, cards, processing, and liability issues. The final draft of the recommended guidelines will be released by year-end 1986.

[13] Survey conducted by the authors, March 1986.

[14] Robert Luke, "600 Arco Outlets to Let Customers Pay Via ATM Cards," *American Banker*, March 19, 1986, pp. 2, 11.

[15] Survey conducted by the authors, March 1986.

[16] *Bank Network News*, "A Credit—Debit Mix is Making a Mess," November 11, 1985.

[17] Other possible uses for smart cards include: driver's license, train/subway/bus card, telephone booth card, and a variety of identification cards. For a number of potential applications, see Arlen R. Lessin, "Smart Card Technology and How it Can be Used," *American Banker*, May 20, 1982, pp. 8, 9.

[18] *Bank Network News*, "Video Banking: Guarded Optimism for 1986," December 11, 1985.

[19] William S. Harris, "In Video Banking, the Future Belongs to the Brave and the Early," *American Banker*, February 10, 1986, p. 21.

[20] Viewtron, one of the nation's first videotex systems, and Gateway folded in March 1986.

[21] Bank of America's equity position is pending regulatory approval.

[22] David O. Tyson, "Chemical Bank, BofA Begin Marketing Long-Awaited AT&T Videotex Terminal," *American Banker*, May 9, 1986, pp. 6, 11.

[23] Michael Weinstein, "Citibank's Pocket Terminal: The Next Wave in Banking?" *American Banker*, November 4, 1985, pp. 3, 47.

[24] This section benefited especially from discussions with executives of Inter-Innovation, a Swedish-based ATM manufacturer, and also from information provided by American Express, Bank Network News, CIRRUS, Diebold, MasterCard, NCR, Omron, PLUS, and Visa.

[25] All data in this paragraph from "ATMs and Cash Dispensers: An International Survey and Analysis 1985," Battelle London, August 1985, unless otherwise noted.

[26] 54 countries had major ATM networks at the end of 1984. *The Nilson Report*, June 1985, p. 3.

[27] Battelle, pp. A40 and B284.

Selected Bibliography

Arthur D. Little, Inc. *Report on the Payments System*. Association of Reserve City Bankers, Washington, D. C., 1982.

Baker, Donald I. "Creating and Operating Shared Electronic Funds Transfer Networks: Competitive Issues under Antitrust and Corporate Law," in Practising Law Institute, *Third Annual Financial Services Institute*. New York, April 18-19, 1985, pp. 829-882.

Bank for International Settlements. *Payment Systems in Eleven Developed Countries*. Bank Administration Institute, Chicago, 1985.

Baxter, William F., Paul H. Cootner, and Kenneth E. Scott. *Retail Banking in the Electronic Age: The Law and Economics of Electronic Funds Transfer*. Montclair, N.J.: Allanheld, Osmun & Co., 1977.

Berger, Allen N. and David B. Humphrey. "The Role of Interstate Banking in the Diffusion of Electronic Payments Technology," in Colin Lawrence and Robert Shay, eds., *Technological Innovation, Regulation, and the Monetary Economy*. Cambridge, Mass.: Ballinger Books, 1986, pp. 13-52.

Comprehensive Reform in The Financial Services Industry. Hearings before the Senate Committee on Banking, Housing, and Urban Affairs. 99 Cong. 1 Sess. (GPO, 1985).

Cox, William and Paul Metzker. "Displacing the Check," *Economic Review*, Federal Reserve Bank of Atlanta, August 1983.

Einhorn, Theresa A. and Robert C. Zimmer. *The Law of Electronic Funds Transfer*. Card Services, Inc., Washington, D. C., 1978.

Federal Reserve Bank of Boston. *The Economics of a National Electronic Funds Transfer System*. Conference Series No. 13, October 1974.

Felgran, Steven D. "Shared ATM Networks: Market Structure and Public Policy," *New England Economic Review*, January/February 1984

————. "From ATM to POS Networks: Branching, Access, and Pricing," *New England Economic Review*, May/June 1985.

Flannery, Mark J. and Dwight M. Jaffee. *The Economic Implications of an Electronic Monetary Transfer System*. Lexington, Mass.: Lexington Books, 1973.

Hannan, Timothy H. and John M. McDowell. "The Determinants of Technology Adoption: The Case of the Banking Firm," *Rand Journal of Economics*, vol. 15, no. 31 (Autumn 1984), pp. 328-35.

Humphrey, David B. *The U.S. Payments System: Costs, Pricing, Competition and Risk*. Salomon Brothers and New York University, Monograph 1984-1/2.

King, Mary L. *The Great American Banking Snafu*. Lexington, Mass.: Lexington Books, 1985.

Lipis, Allen H., Thomas R. Marschall, and Jan H. Linker. *Electronic Banking*. New York: John Wiley & Sons, 1985.

National Commission on Electronic Fund Transfers. *EFT in the United States: Policy Recommendations and the Public Interest*. Washington, D. C., 1977.

Penney, Norman and Donald I. Baker. *The Law of Electronic Fund Transfer Systems*. Boston: Warren, Gorham & Lamont, 1980, and supplements.

Solomon, Elinor H. "The Dynamics of Banking Antitrust: The New Technology, the Product Realignment," *Antitrust Bulletin*, vol. 30, no. 3 (Fall 1985), pp. 537-81.

Status of ATM's under State Branching Laws. Hearings before the Senate Committee on Banking, Housing, and Urban Affairs. 98 Cong. 2 Sess. (GPO, 1984).

Walker, David A. "Electronic Funds Transfer Cost Models and Pricing Strategies," *Journal of Economics and Business*, vol. 33 (Fall 1980), pp. 61-65.

Section Four

Central Banking
and Monetary Policy

The readings in this section address various aspects of conducting monetary policy in the short run. Among the topics covered are how the Fed actually operates its open market desk and discount window to counteract typical and atypical variations in the relation between the monetary base and the money supply. This is followed by discussion of the policy implications of variations in the relation between the money supply and income.

Open market operations are the Federal Reserve System's primary method of implementing monetary policy. The lead article in this section, Howard L. Roth's "Federal Reserve Open Market Techniques," shows how the Fed uses open market operations to produce changes in the supply of reserves and to prevent factors beyond its direct control from producing undesired changes in the supply of reserves available to banks and other depository institutions. These latter, defensive operations may be required to offset either temporary or permanent changes in the sources and uses of reserves. The vast majority of the Fed's activity attempts to offset temporary fluctuations in the reserves market. The author describes how repurchase agreements are used to reduce this variability of reserves available to depository institutions.

In "The Discount Window," David L. Mengle gives several examples of why and how financial institutions come to the Fed to borrow reserves. These examples highlight the conditions under which the Fed approves borrowing at the discount window. The Fed does not look kindly on all requests for discount borrowing, however, and it rations loans to prevent inappropriate use of the window. Also discussed is the differential access to the window small and large institutions are granted.

" 'Financial Crises' and the Role of the Lender of Last Resort," by James R. Barth and Robert E. Kelcher, analyzes the nature of financial crises and the similarities and differences between domestic and international crises. The authors discuss how domestic financial crises can be ameliorated by the open market and discount window policies of the Fed. They also discuss how such crises and consequent ameliorating action could often be avoided altogether by assuring markets that action would be taken if a crisis did develop. However, the lack of a world monetary authority that can create reserves means that there really is no "lender of last resort" to provide the liquidity necessary to abort international crises.

In the next reading Daniel L. Thornton answers the question "Why Does Velocity Matter?" He begins by explaining that velocity by definition links money, which the Fed can control, to income, which it hopes to influence indirectly. This task is complicated by the fact that velocity is not only variable but, to an important extent, unpredictable. Among the factors that affect velocity either temporarily or permanently are interest rates, financial innovation, and business conditions. Since the connection between these factors and velocity is not always reliable, and since these factors are themselves difficult to predict, monetary policy is often forced to react to rather than anticipate velocity shifts.

"What Has Happened to M1?" by Herb Taylor concludes the section on the conduct of short-run monetary policy. Taylor documents the breakdown during the 1980s of the historical relationship between the money supply and income. He finds little evidence that changes in taxes or in international trade contributed to this breakdown. On the other hand, there is some support for the money-income relation's having been altered by financial deregulation and by the unusually sharp decline in inflation. As both of these factors stabilize, Taylor expects the traditional relation to reemerge.

Article Twenty-Two

Federal Reserve
Open Market Techniques

By Howard L. Roth

Open market operations are the Federal Reserve's primary monetary policy instrument for promoting noninflationary economic growth and other policy goals. Through open market operations—the buying and selling of U.S. government securities—the Federal Reserve influences interest rates and the supply of money and credit. Changes in financial conditions lead in turn to movements in economic activity and the general level of prices in the economy.

In conducting open market operations, the Federal Reserve uses a number of different techniques, ranging from outright transactions with U.S. government security dealers to self-reversing transactions with foreign central banks. The particular technique used depends, among other things, on the Federal Reserve's operating procedures and changes in factors other than open market operations that affect reserve availability.

Howard Roth is an economist at the Federal Reserve Bank of Kansas City. Richard Roberts, a research associate at the bank, assisted in the preparation of the article.

This article describes the different techniques that are used in conducting open market operations and identifies some changes that have occurred in recent years in their relative importance. The first section provides background material on the role open market operations play in the conduct of monetary policy. The open market operating techniques are described in the second section, while the third section examines the changes that have occurred in the usage of these techniques in recent years.

Open market operations and monetary policy

Open market operations by the Federal Reserve lead initially to changes in the supply of reserves that depository financial institutions have available to meet their reserve requirements. Changes in reserves—which are held either as deposits at Federal Reserve banks or as vault cash—lead in turn to changes in interest rates and the supply of money and credit. For example, when reserves increase, depository institutions are able to increase their loans and investments, and thereby increase the deposit accounts held by borrowers. The attendant rise in the supply of money and credit tends, in turn, to be accompanied by a decline in interest rates. Alternatively, a reduction in reserves leads to a decline in money and credit and upward pressure on interest rates.

The linkage between open market operations and reserves is made clear by the accounting transaction that occurs when the Federal Reserve pays for the securities it buys or is paid for securities it sells. When the Federal Reserve buys securities, it pays for them by crediting the reserve accounts held at the Federal Reserve by the sellers' depository institutions.[1] The sellers' accounts at depository institutions, in turn, are credited. Conversely, sales of securities by the Federal Reserve are handled through debits to depository institutions' reserve accounts at the Federal Reserve. Thus, when the Federal Reserve purchases securities, reserves increase; and when the Federal Reserve sells securities, reserves decline.

The Federal Reserve's portfolio of securities is one of several sources of reserves, as shown in Table 1. Other sources include Federal Reserve loans to depository institutions and Federal Reserve float. Table 1 also shows how the total source of reserves can be used. In general, sources of reserves can be used three ways: they can be used as reserves, be used by the public as currency, or be used to increase other nonreserve liabilities of the Federal Reserve.[2]

As indicated in Table 1, total sources of reserves equal total uses of reserves.[3] Also, as the table shows, reserves equal total sources minus the uses other than reserves. The following reserve equation is similarly constructed and provides a breakdown of sources and nonreserve uses of reserves along the lines of Table 1.

Reserves = Securities + Loans
+ Float + Other Sources
− Currency in Circulation
− Treasury Deposits
− Foreign and Other Deposits
− Other Uses.

The sources and uses on the right hand side of the equation are more generally referred to as factors affecting reserves. The most important factor is the Federal Reserve's portfolio of securities. Loans to depository institutions are also a factor affecting reserves because reserves increase when the Federal Reserve credits the accounts of borrowing institutions for the amounts of their loans. Float—cash items in the process of collection minus deferred availability cash items—arises when the scheduled credit-deferral period on a check presented to the Federal Reserve for collection elapses before the Federal Reserve can collect

[1] The Federal Reserve engages in security transactions with about three dozen large securities dealers. About a third of the dealers are departments in large money center banks. To buy or sell securities from a bank, the Federal Reserve simply credits or debits the bank's reserve account.

[2] The Federal Reserve capital accounts and the Treasury's monetary net worth make up the remaining uses.

[3] Table 1 is a condensed version of a table published weekly in Federal Reserve publication H.4.1, "Factors Affecting Reserve Balances of Depository Institutions and Condition Statement of Federal Reserve Banks," and monthly as Table 1.11 in the *Federal Reserve Bulletin*. The consolidated balance sheet of the 12 Federal Reserve banks is published in the *Federal Reserve Bulletin* every month as Table 1.18. Information about the Treasury's monetary accounts is printed in the *Treasury Bulletin*.

For a description of the items appearing in these tables, see *The Federal Reserve System: Purposes and Functions*, Board of Governors of the Federal Reserve System, Washington, D.C., 1984, *Statfacts: Understanding Federal Reserve Statistical Reports*, Federal Reserve Bank of New York, November 1981, or any of a number of undergraduate money and banking textbooks.

TABLE 1
Sources and uses of reserves
November 20, 1985
(millions of dollars)*

Sources

Federal Reserve portfolio of securities	180,341
Loans to depository institutions from the Federal Reserve	1,178
Float†	1,483
Other sources	47,122
Total sources	230,124

Uses

Currency in circulation	191,471	
Minus vault cash used to satisfy reserve requirements	20,117	171,354
Treasury deposits		3,036
Foreign and other deposits held with Federal Reserve banks		800
Other uses		8,575
Total nonreserve uses		183,765
Reserves		46,359
Total uses		230,124

Source: *Federal Reserve Bulletin*, Tables 1.11 and 1.12, February 1986

*Biweekly averages of daily averages for two-week period ended November 20, 1985

†Cash items in the process of collection minus deferred availability cash items

from the depository institution on which the check was drawn. When this happens, both the presenting institution and the paying institution have credit for the funds, a development that adds reserves to the financial system until the Federal Reserve collects.

Another factor affecting reserves is currency in circulation, which consists of paper currency and coin held outside the Treasury and Federal Reserve banks. As the negative sign in the equation indicates, when currency in circulation increases, reserves of depository institutions decline. Deposits held with the Federal Reserve banks, other than reserve deposits, also affect reserves. These deposits include accounts that the Treasury, foreign central banks, and international institutions hold at

Federal Reserve banks. The Treasury uses its account for depositing tax revenues and other receipts and for making expenditures. Foreign central banks and international institutions hold accounts at the Federal Reserve Bank of New York to facilitate international settlements. When the Treasury, foreign central banks, or international institutions transfer funds from domestic depository institutions to accounts at the Federal Reserve, reserves of depository institutions decline. Increases in these deposits are associated with decreases in reserves.

The factors affecting reserves can be divided into two categories—controllable and uncontrollable—according to whether the Federal Reserve has close control over them. The only factor the Federal Reserve can control closely is its portfolio of securities. All of the other factors cannot be closely controlled.

Within this framework of factors affecting reserves, the Federal Reserve follows a three-step procedure in conducting monetary policy. The first step is to determine a target level of reserves consistent with the objectives of monetary policy.[4] The second step is to estimate the net change in reserves that will occur due to movements in uncontrollable factors. The third step is to undertake open market operations that increase or decrease security holdings enough to bring about the targeted level of reserves. Reserves are targeted over two-week maintenance periods that correspond to periods during which depository institutions are required to hold specified average levels of reserves.

A simplified example helps illustrate the three-step reserve-targeting procedure. Suppose the Federal Reserve determines that the target level of reserves for a reserve maintenance period is $41 billion. Also, suppose reserve projections show that when estimated developments of uncontrollable factors are taken into account, reserves would average $40 billion if the Federal Reserve took no action. In this case, therefore, the Federal Reserve would seek to supply depository institutions with an average of $1 billion in reserves by increasing its holdings of securities through open market operations. If, on the other hand, reserve projections showed reserves would exceed the targeted level, the Federal Reserve would absorb reserves by reducing its holdings of securities.

Open market techniques

Open market operations are carried out by a unit in the Securities Department of the Federal Reserve Bank of New York.[5] This unit, known as the Desk, operates according to directives from the Federal Open Market Committee (FOMC).

The operations available to the Desk for managing reserves fall into two broad categories—outright or permanent transactions and temporary or self-reversing transactions. Buying, selling, or redeeming securities are outright transactions, while engaging in repurchase agreements (RP's) or engaging in matched sale purchase agreements (MSP's) are temporary transactions. With RP's, the Federal Reserve buys securities but agrees to sell them at a specified future date at a specified price.[6] Under MSP's, it sells securities but agrees to buy other securities at specified future dates and terms.

Outright transactions

The Desk uses outright transactions when it wants to provide or absorb reserves over relatively long time spans. Outright transactions typically are used when projections show a shortage or excess that is likely to persist longer than a single two-week maintenance period.

---

[4] More precisely, reserve targets are formulated in terms of nonborrowed reserves—reserves net of adjustment and seasonal borrowing by depository institutions.

[5] Lucid descriptions of these operations are provided by Paul Meek, *U.S. Monetary Policy and Financial Markets*, Federal Reserve Bank of New York, 1982, and in *Open Market Operations*, Federal Reserve Bank of New York, 1985. See also William Melton, *Inside the Fed: Making Monetary Policy*, Dow Jones-Irwin, Homewood, Ill., 1985.

[6] The Federal Reserve's use of "RP" is opposite that of securities dealers. When the Federal Reserve says it is undertaking RP's, it is putting out money and taking in securities, thereby increasing reserves. When securities dealers undertake RP's, they are effectively borrowing money. The conventional definition of an RP, then, is a sale of securities with an agreement to repurchase the securities on a fixed date.

Long-lasting needs to add or drain reserves arise for a variety of reasons—to meet the needs of a growing economy, to offset long-lasting seasonal movements in uncontrolled factors, and to accommodate permanent changes in the demand for reserves.

A growing economy requires a growing money supply. Depository institutions must hold additional reserves to support growth in checkable and nonpersonal time deposits. And growth in currency in circulation must also be supported by additional reserves if reserve availability is to be maintained. Outright purchases supply the reserves needed for monetary expansion.

Seasonal movements in factors affecting reserves for more than a two-week maintenance period also may call for outright transactions. For example, currency in circulation rises before holidays as consumers prepare to make additional purchases, and then returns to more normal levels after the holidays. If not offset, the rise and fall of currency in circulation would first drain reserves from the financial system and then supply reserves. The seasonal pattern for the Christmas holiday season spans several weeks. By purchasing securities outright before Christmas and selling securities outright after Christmas, the Desk can offset much of the seasonal effect of currency in circulation on reserves.[7]

The Desk engages in outright transactions with U.S. government security dealers and with foreign central banks and other institutions that maintain accounts at the Federal Reserve Bank of New York. The Desk acts either as an intermediary between the foreign accounts and the securities market or deals directly with the foreign accounts in buying securities from them or selling securities to them. Foreign central banks and international institutions maintaining accounts at the Federal Reserve Bank of New York usually also hold accounts at domestic depository institutions. When the deposits of foreign institutions rise above the levels needed for ordinary transactions purposes, the surplus funds are normally invested in interest-earning assets. In many instances, foreign institutions ask a depository institution or a securities dealer to invest the funds in the securities market. In other instances, the institutions ask the Desk to invest the surplus funds. Depending on its perception of the need to add or drain reserves from the financial system, the Desk either invests the funds in the market or sells securities from its own account to absorb the funds.

The effects of outright transactions on reserves are illustrated in Table 2. Entry 1 shows the effect of an outright purchase of $1 billion in securities from a security dealer. The Federal Reserve's security portfolio (an asset of the Federal Reserve) is increased by $1 billion. The reserve account of the securities dealer's depository institution (a liability of the Federal Reserve and an asset of the depository institution) is correspondingly increased. The securities dealer's demand deposit at the financial institution (an asset of the securities dealer and a liability of the

---

[7] Recent changes in the long-run demand for reserves by depository institutions have been met with outright transactions. The Depository Institutions Deregulation and Monetary Control Act of 1980 mandated reserve requirements for nonmember banks and thrift institutions. The reserve requirement of these institutions has been phased in over six years. Demand for reserves by these institutions increases on the dates that their reserve requirements increase. The act also provided a schedule for reducing the reserve requirements of member banks. The phasing down, completed in 1984, reduced member banks' demand for reserves. Because they affected the demand for reserves, the phase-ups and phase-downs had to be accounted for in implementing policy. Since a phase-down permanently reduces demand for reserves, its effect on reserves is offset by an outright transaction

reducing the supply of reserves. Similarly, a phase-up is offset by an outright purchase of securities.

TABLE 2

Reserve accounting
(billions of dollars)

	Federal Reserve			Depository Institutions	
(1)	Securities	+1	Reserves +1	Reserves +1	Demand deposits +1
(2)			Reserves −1 Foreign deposits +1	Reserves −1	Demand deposits −1
(3)	Securities	−1	Foreign deposits −1		
(4)			Reserves +1 Foreign deposits −1	Reserves +1	Demand deposits +1
(5)	Securities	+1	Reserves +1	Reserves +1	Demand deposits +1
(6)	Securities	−1	Foreign deposits −1		
(7)			Reserves +1 Foreign deposits −1	Reserves +1	Demand deposits +1
(8)	Securities	−1	Reserves −1	Reserves −1	Demand deposits −1

	Public			Foreign	
(1)	Demand deposits +1 Securities −1				
(2)				Demand deposits −1 Deposit at FRB +1	
(3)				Securities +1 Deposit at FRB −1	
(4)	Securities −1 Demand deposits +1			Securities +1 Deposit at FRB −1	
(5)	Demand deposits +1	RP's +1			
(6)				RRP's +1 Deposit at FRB −1	
(7)	Demand deposits +1	RP's +1		RRP's +1 Deposit at FRB −1	
(8)	Demand deposits −1 RRP's +1				

depository institution) is increased. And the securities dealer's portfolio of securities (an asset of the securities dealer) is reduced. Thus, the outright purchase injects reserves into the financial system. Conversely, an outright sale drains reserves from the financial system, and the associated accounting entries are the reverse of those for an outright purchase.

The effects of outright transactions with foreign accounts are illustrated by entries 2 and 3 in Table 2. The illustration assumes that the Desk sells securities to a foreign account. To see the effect on reserves, it is useful to break the transaction into two components. One is the transfer of excess funds by the foreign institution from its account at a domestic depository institution to its account at the Federal Reserve Bank of New York. The other is the subsequent investment of these funds in securities from the Federal Reserve's portfolio. In entry 2 of Table 2, the foreign institution transfers funds from its account at a depository institution account to its account at the Federal Reserve, a transfer that drains reserves from the financial system. In entry 3, the Federal Reserve sells securities from its own account to the foreign account. The net effect of entries 2 and 3 is that securities are transferred from the Federal Reserve to foreign institutions, demand deposits of foreign institutions are reduced, and reserves are drained from the financial system. Conversely, when the Federal Reserve purchases securities offered for sale by foreign accounts, reserves are injected into the financial system.

When the Desk acts as agent for a foreign account in the securities markets, the level of total reserves in the financial system is not affected. When the Desk buys securities in the market for a foreign account, entry 2 is still appropriate but entry 3 is not. Instead, entry 4 records the investment of the funds in the market by the Federal Reserve acting as agent. When the seller of the securities deposits the check drawn on the foreign institution's account at the Federal Reserve Bank of New York, reserves (and demand deposits) increase to their original level. The net result of the two transactions shown in entries 2 and 4 is that the public has fewer securities and higher demand deposits while foreign institutions have lower demand deposits and fewer securities. Reserves are unchanged.

When the Federal Reserve redeems maturing securities held in its portfolio, the effect is to drain reserves in a similar manner as an outright sale of securities. The Desk redeems maturing securities by subscribing for a smaller amount of the issues offered in a Treasury or federal agency refunding than the Federal Reserve's current holdings of maturing issues. The accounting entries for a redemption are not shown in Table 2.

Temporary transactions

The Desk uses temporary transactions when it wants to provide or absorb reserves for relatively short time periods. Temporary transactions typically will be used when projections show a shortage or excess that is likely to persist no longer than a single two-week maintenance period.

Short-run needs to add or drain reserves typically arise from changes in uncontrollable factors. Temporary transactions are arranged to limit the effects on reserves of anticipated changes in uncontrollable factors and to offset the effects on reserves of unanticipated changes in these factors.

The Desk engages in two kinds of repurchase agreements and two kinds of matched sale-purchase transactions. System RP's are arranged for the account of the Federal Reserve Bank of New York. Customer-related

RP's are arranged for foreign and international institutions holding accounts at the Federal Reserve. MSP's in the market are between the Federal Reserve and securities dealers. The other kind of MSP is between the Federal Reserve and official foreign and international accounts.

The Desk makes available a daily investment facility in which foreign account funds are pooled. This arrangement allows the Desk either to invest the entire pool in the market in one transaction (customer-related RP's), to meet these investment needs from its own portfolio of securities (MSP's with the foreign investment pool), or to engage in a combination of the two. This pooling of foreign funds simplifies Desk operations and enables the Desk to serve the investment needs of more foreign accounts than it could otherwise.

The reserve effects of temporary transactions are also shown in Table 2. As entry 5 shows, the accounting for a System RP is similar to that for an outright purchase. One difference is that the securities dealer considers the transaction as having increased one of its liabilities, repurchase agreements. The securities dealer has borrowed funds from the Federal Reserve with an agreement to repay with interest on an agreed-on date, at most 15 days later. The other difference from an outright purchase is that the transaction is later reversed. Most often, the funds are loaned only overnight. In that case, reserves are increased for only one day. When the transaction is reversed, the accounting entries are reversed and reserves return to their original level.

Customer-related RP's and MSP's with the pool are alternative ways of investing the pool. The Desk does not consider MSP's with the pool a reserve management technique even though the MSP's drain reserves. Instead, when the Federal Reserve forecasts the level of reserves that will be available in the financial system, it assumes that the funds in the pool will be invested with the system as MSP's. That is, the pool is treated as an uncontrolled factor that regularly absorbs reserves, like currency in circulation.

The accounting entries for doing MSP's with the foreign pool are shown in entry 6 of

---

The use of temporary transactions has changed signicantly in the past few years.

Table 2. Making MSP's with the pool does not offset the initial reserve drain when foreign and international accounts transfer their excess funds from depository institutions to the Federal Reserve Bank of New York. The net effect on reserves from lines 2 and 6 is a drain of reserves.

Because the prospective drain on reserves from doing MSP's with the pool is factored into reserve projections, customer-related RP's reduce the drain and increase reserves relative to the level that was projected. In this respect, both customer-related RP's and System RP's supply reserves to the financial system. However, like the outright purchase of securities for foreign or international account illustrated in entries 2 and 4, customer-related RP's have no net effect on reserves when the initial buildup of funds in foreign institutions' accounts at the Federal Reserve is taken into account. The accounting entries recording the investment of funds in the market are shown in entry 7. The foreign institution invests in reverse repurchase agreements (RRP's), an asset. The public, most likely a securities dealer, incurs an increase in RP's, a liability. There is no net effect on reserves when entries 2 and 7 are combined. The entries are reversed as the RP unwinds the next day.

Both System RP's and customer-related RP's increase reserves relative to reserve projections. The choice between the two depends largely on the magnitude of the reserve need that the Desk wants to meet. Customer-related RP's are limited by the amount of funds in the pool. System RP's can be used to meet larger reserve needs. Another consideration can be the duration of the reserve need. Reserve needs extending more than one day can be easily handled with multi-day System RP's. Designing a customer-related RP for this task would be difficult because the future size of the pool cannot be known precisely.

The accounting entries for a MSP in the market are given in entry 8 of Table 2. From the securities dealer's point of view, it has made a short-term loan to the Federal Reserve. The loan is recorded on the dealer's books as a debit to RRP's and a credit to demand deposits, another asset. When the MSP matures, the accounting entries are reversed. Thus, reserves are lower for the duration of the MSP and then return to their original level.

Use of the techniques

In conducting open market operations, the Desk relies more on temporary transactions than on outright transactions. The use of temporary transactions has changed significantly in the past few years. Their use declined sharply in 1980 and 1981, but has increased somewhat since 1981.

The dollar volume of total temporary transactions typically has been ten times the volume of total outright transactions. For example, temporary transactions totaled $310 billion in 1985, compared with $34 billion for outright transactions (Table 3). [8]

The reason for the much heavier use of temporary transactions is that uncontrolled factors are highly volatile in the short run. For example, while total reserves showed a net change of around $80 million a week in 1985, absolute week-to-week changes in uncontrolled factors averaged $1.4 billion during the year. To prevent this short-run variability in uncontrolled factors from leading to weekly variability in reserves, the Desk provided and absorbed reserves through temporary transactions.

The dollar volume of total temporary transactions dropped $63 billion in 1980, fell another $101 billion in 1981, and then increased $41 billion in 1982. From 1983 to 1985, total temporary transactions averaged

---

Changes in operating procedures contributed to the sharp drops in temporary transactions in 1980 and 1981.

---

almost precisely their 1982 level. Much of the pattern since 1979 can be attributed to changes in day-to-day operating procedures and changes in the variability of uncontrolled factors.

Changes in operating procedures contributed to the sharp drops in temporary transactions in 1980 and 1981. Until October 1979, the Desk had used its reserve management techniques in day-to-day operations to hold the federal funds rate to a narrow band around a level thought to be consistent with the desired growth of money and credit. Heavy use of temporary transactions was required. Under the operating procedures instituted in October 1979, the Desk targeted nonborrowed reserves—reserves net of adjustment plus seasonal borrowing by

---

[8] The source of most of the dollar figures in Table 3 is a series of articles published yearly by the staff of the Federal Reserve Bank of New York, "Monetary Policy and Open Market Operations," *Quarterly Review*, Federal Reserve Bank of New York.

TABLE 3
Volume of open market operations
(billions of dollars)

	1978	1979	1980	1981	1982	1983	1984	1985
Outright transactions								
Purchases								
In market	15.0	7.1	8.5	8.8	10.5	10.7	14.1	17.1
From foreign accounts	9.9	14.1	4.4	8.4	9.4	11.8	9.7	9.4
Sales								
In market	0.2	2.3	2.8	2.6	1.5	0	1.1	1.5
To foreign accounts	13.7	5.6	4.5	4.1	7.1	3.4	7.6	2.7
Redemptions	2.3	3.0	3.5	1.9	3.2	2.8	8.0	3.7
Total outright	41.1	32.1	23.7	25.8	31.7	28.7	40.5	34.4
Temporary transactions								
Repurchase agreements								
System	221.5	185.5	167.2	110.9	179.1	124.0	144.8	156.4
Customer-related	47.3	53.0	64.3	79.5	89.1	159.9	126.7	116.7
Matched sale purchases								
in market	140.2	194.6	138.6	78.4	42.0	11.9	55.0	36.6
Total temporary	409.0	433.1	370.1	268.8	310.2	295.8	326.5	309.7

depository institutions from the Federal Reserve. Because the federal funds rate was allowed to vary over a much wider range, fewer temporary transactions were needed.[9]

Another change in operating procedures occurring in the fall of 1982 is consistent with the increased use of temporary transactions after 1981. The nonborrowed reserves operating procedure was modified in late 1982 when a breakdown in the relationship between M1 and economic activity forced the Federal Reserve to rely more on judgments of mone-

tary and economic developments in deciding on the appropriate level of reserves in the financial system. The new procedure has been described as being between a nonborrowed reserves operating procedure and a federal funds operating procedure. As such, the use of temporary transactions might be expected to be more frequent than under the nonborrowed reserves procedure used from late 1979 to late 1982 but less frequent than under the federal funds rate procedure used until late 1979.

A decline in the variability of uncontrollable factors also contributed to the decline in the use of temporary transactions in 1980 and 1981. Chart 1 plots the dollar volume of total temporary transactions and the variability of total uncontrolled market factors for 1978 through 1985. Variability is measured by the average absolute week-to-week change in total uncontrolled market factors. Chart 1 shows that uncontrolled factors became less variable during the years that the use of temporary

---

[9] A study of the new operating procedures revealed that the number of market entries to conduct temporary transactions in the first year under the new operating procedures was about a third less than in the preceding year. See Fred J. Levin and Paul Meek, "Implementing the New Operating Procedures: The View from the Trading Desk," *New Monetary Control Procedures*, Federal Resere Staff Study, Vol. I, Board of Governors of the Federal Reserve System, February 1981. See also Neil G. Berkman, "Open Market Operations Under the New Monetary Policy," *New England Economic Review*, Federal Reserve Bank of Boston, March/April 1981, pp. 5-20.

CHART 1
Relationship between temporary transactions and the variability of uncontrolled factors

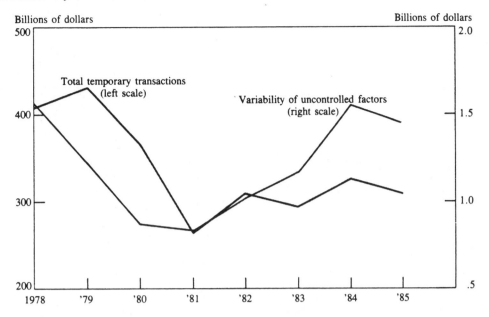

transactions was declining. The average absolute change declined from $1,202 million in 1979 to $850 million in 1981.

An upward movement in the variability of uncontrolled factors appears to be in part responsible for the increased use of temporary transactions after 1981. As shown by Chart 1, the variability of uncontrolled factors reached

---

An upward movement in the variability of uncontrolled factors appears to be in part responsible for the increased use of temporary transactions after 1981.

---

a low in 1981, then rose steadily from 1982 through 1984 before declining slightly in 1985.

The factor contributing most to changes in variability in recent years has been Treasury deposits with the Federal Reserve. The variability of these deposits and their average level fell dramatically in 1979, remained low for three years, and then rose sharply in 1982 (Table 4). Since 1982, these deposits have been quite variable, although not as variable as they were in 1978.

The 1979-81 decline in the variability of Treasury deposits was due to changes in Treasury cash management techniques. In 1978, Congress authorized commercial banks to pay interest on tax and loan (T&L) accounts and charge the Treasury for services. The Treasury returned to a practice followed before 1967 of transferring funds from T&L accounts to Federal Reserve accounts only in anticipation of expenditures. In this way, the Treasury could maintain a fairly constant balance at the Federal Reserve, and the Treasury account at the

TABLE 4
Variability of uncontrolled factors
affecting reserves held at Federal Reserve banks
(millions of dollars)

	Period							
	1978	1979	1980	1981	1982	1983	1984	1985
Uncontrolled factors providing reserves								
Loans	278	305	339	333	246	319	579	511
	(867)	(1,338)	(1,441)	(1,358)	(1,046)	(1,039)	(3,721)	(1,313)
Float	972	1,155	948	722	556	438	465	357
	(5,430)	(6,616)	(4,685)	(3,337)	(2,540)	(1,787)	(830)	(801)
Other sources*	226	284	248	286	283	235	347	323
Uncontrolled factors absorbing reserves								
Currency in circulation	471	522	573	649	737	741	818	828
Treasury deposits with the Federal Reserve	1,665	410	559	365	807	937	1,214	1,097
	(8,034)	(3,238)	(3,018)	(3,163)	(3,800)	(2,164)	(4,399)	(4,071)
Foreign and other deposits with the Federal Reserve	100	156	114	115	128	79	78	155
Other uses†	232	238	110	180	151	101	241	166

Note: Variability is measured as the mean absolute week-to-week change in the weekly averages of daily data for each factor indicated. The yearly average of weekly averages of daily data is shown in parentheses for selected factors.

*Includes other Federal Reserve assets, gold stock, the special drawing rights certificate account, and Treasury currency outstanding (lines 11 through 14 of Table 1.11 in the *Federal Reserve Bulletin*). For a description of these items, see "Statfacts: Understanding Federal Reserve Statistical Reports," Federal Reserve Bank of New York, November 1981.

†Includes other Federal Reserve liabilities and capital, service-related balances and adjustments, and Treasury cash (lines 21, 19, and 16, respectively, of Table 1.11 in the *Federal Reserve Bulletin*).

Federal Reserve became a much less variable factor affecting reserves.

The rise in the variability of Treasury deposits after 1981 has been due to a shortage of collateral to back T&L accounts. Funds in T&L accounts must be backed by U.S. securities owned by the commercial bank. When available collateral is depleted, additional receipts must be transferred to the Federal Reserve.

Float has also contributed to changes in the variability of uncontrolled factors. The variability of float declined substantially, beginning in 1980. The Federal Reserve has taken sev-

eral steps to reduce float in recent years. The most significant step was to begin charging depository institutions for float in 1983. Float is, in effect, an extension of credit to depository institutions presenting checks. This credit was interest-free until 1985. Pricing of float and improvements in transporting and processing checks have led to the reduction of float indicated by the averages appearing in parentheses in Table 4.[10]

---

[10] The Federal Reserve has designed its credit deferral schedule so that presenting institutions generally receive credit no later than when the check clears. Thus, float is seldom negative, on

The variabilities of other uncontrolled factors have not changed dramatically. The variability of currency in circulation grew steadily over the period, about in line with growth in currency.[11] The variability of loans nearly doubled in 1984, primarily because of Continental Illinois' need to borrow heavily on an extended basis. Extended borrowing resulted in more variability of loans than normal again in 1985, although to a less extent than in 1984. The higher variability of loans is most likely temporary.

---

average, during a week. Because of this, the decline in the weekly average of float since 1978 has been accompanied by a decline in the variability of float.

[11] The variability of currency in circulation is partially predictable, making it less troublesome in formulating policy than if it were totally unpredictable.

Summary and conclusions

The Federal Reserve uses a number of techniques when conducting open market operations to control the supply of reserves available in the financial system. Open market operating techniques include outright and temporary transactions with U.S. government security dealers and foreign official institutions. Due to the need to prevent undue short-run variability in reserve availability, temporary transactions are used more heavily than outright transactions. In recent years, though, the use of temporary transactions has declined somewhat, due in part to a change in the Federal Reserve's operating procedures. Changes in the variability of factors affecting reserves other than open market operations have also affected the relative usage of temporary transactions.

Article Twenty-Three

THE DISCOUNT WINDOW*

David L. Mengle

The discount window refers to lending by each of the twelve regional Federal Reserve Banks to depository institutions. Discount window loans generally fund only a small part of bank reserves. For example, at the end of 1985 discount window loans were less than three percent of total reserves. Nevertheless, the window is perceived as an important tool both for reserve adjustment and as part of current Federal Reserve monetary control procedures.

Mechanics of a Discount Window Transaction

Discount window lending takes place through the reserve accounts depository institutions are required to maintain at their Federal Reserve Banks. In other words, banks borrow reserves at the discount window. This is illustrated in balance sheet form in Figure 1. Suppose the funding officer at Ralph's Bank finds it has an unanticipated reserve deficiency of $1,000,000 and decides to go to the discount window for an overnight loan in order to cover it. Once the loan is approved, the Ralph's Bank reserve account is credited with $1,000,000. This shows up on the asset side of Ralph's balance sheet as an increase in "Reserves with Federal Reserve Bank," and on the liability side as an increase in "Borrowings from Federal Reserve Bank." The transaction also shows up on the Federal Reserve Bank's balance sheet as an increase in "Discounts and Advances" on the asset side and an increase in "Bank Reserve

Accounts" on the liability side. This set of balance sheet entries takes place in all the examples given in the Box.

The next day, Ralph's Bank could raise the funds to repay the loan by, for example, increasing deposits by $1,000,000 or by selling $1,000,000 of securities. In either case, the proceeds initially increase reserves. Actual repayment occurs when Ralph's Bank's reserve account is debited for $1,000,000, which erases the corresponding entries on Ralph's liability side and on the Reserve Bank's asset side.

Discount window loans, which are granted to institutions by their district Federal Reserve Banks, can be either advances or discounts. Virtually all loans today are advances, meaning they are simply loans secured by approved collateral and paid back with interest at maturity. When the Federal Reserve System was established in 1914, however, the only loans authorized at the window were discounts, also known as rediscounts. Discounts involve a borrower selling "eligible paper," such as a commercial or agricultural loan made by a bank to one of its customers, to its Federal Reserve Bank. In return, the borrower's reserve account is credited for the discounted value of the paper. Upon repayment, the borrower gets the paper back, while its reserve account is debited for the value of the paper. In the case of either advances or discounts, the price of borrowing is determined by the level of the discount rate prevailing at the time of the loan.

Although discount window borrowing was originally limited to Federal Reserve System member banks, the Monetary Control Act of 1980 opened the

---

* An abbreviated version of this article will appear as a chapter in **Instruments of the Money Market**, 6th edition, Federal Reserve Bank of Richmond, 1986 (forthcoming December 1986).

Figure 1
BORROWING FROM THE DISCOUNT WINDOW

Ralph's Bank		Federal Reserve Bank	
Assets	Liabilities	Assets	Liabilities
Reserves with Federal Reserve	Borrowings from Federal Reserve Bank	Discounts and Advances	Bank Reserve Accounts
+ $1,000,000	+ $1,000,000	+ $1,000,000	+ $1,000,000

Examples of Discount Window Transactions

Example 1 — It is Wednesday afternoon at a regional bank, and the bank is required to have enough funds in its reserve account at its Federal Reserve Bank to meet its reserve requirement over the previous two weeks. The bank finds that it must borrow in order to make up its reserve deficiency, but the money center (that is, the major New York, Chicago, and California) banks have apparently been borrowing heavily in the federal funds market. As a result, the rate on fed funds on this particular Wednesday afternoon has soared far above its level earlier that day. As far as the funding officer of the regional bank is concerned, the market for funds at a price she considers acceptable has "dried up." She calls the Federal Reserve Bank for a discount window loan.

Example 2 — A West Coast regional bank, which generally avoids borrowing at the discount window, expects to receive a wire transfer of $300 million from a New York bank, but by late afternoon the money has not yet shown up. It turns out that the sending bank had due to an error accidentally sent only $3,000 instead of the $300 million. Although the New York bank is legally liable for the correct amount, it is closed by the time the error is discovered. In order to make up the deficiency in its reserve position, the West Coast bank calls the discount window for a loan.

Example 3 — It is Wednesday reserve account settlement at another bank, and the funding officer notes that the spread between the discount rate and fed funds rate has widened slightly. Since his bank is buying fed funds to make up a reserve deficiency, he decides to borrow part of the reserve deficiency from the discount window in order to take advantage of the spread. Over the next few months, this repeats itself until the bank receives an "informational" call from the discount officer at the Federal Reserve Bank, inquiring as to the reason for the apparent pattern in discount window borrowing. Taking the hint, the bank refrains from continuing the practice on subsequent Wednesday settlements.

Example 4 — A money center bank acts as a clearing agent for the government securities market. This means that the bank maintains book-entry securities accounts for market participants, and that it also maintains a reserve account and a book-entry securities account at its Federal Reserve Bank, so that securities transactions can be cleared through this system. One day, an internal computer problem arises that allows the bank to accept securities but not to process them for delivery to dealers, brokers, and other market participants. The bank's reserve account is debited for the amount of these securities, but it is unable to pass them on and collect payment for them, resulting in a growing overdraft in the reserve account. As close of business approaches, it becomes increasingly clear that the problem will not be fixed in time to collect the required payments from the securities buyers. In order to avoid a negative reserve balance at the end of the day, the bank estimates its anticipated reserve account deficiency and goes to the Federal Reserve Bank discount window for a loan for that amount. The computer problem is fixed and the loan is repaid the following day.

Example 5 — Due to mismanagement, a privately insured savings and loan association fails. Out of concern about the condition of other privately insured thrift institutions in the state, depositors begin to withdraw their deposits, leading to a run. Because they are not federally insured, some otherwise sound thrifts are not able to borrow from the Federal Home Loan Bank Board in order to meet the demands of the depositors. As a result, the regional Federal Reserve Bank is called upon to lend to these thrifts. After an extensive examination of the collateral the thrifts could offer, the Reserve Bank makes loans to them until they are able to get federal insurance and attract back enough deposits to pay back the discount window loans.

window to all depository institutions, except bankers' banks, that maintain transaction accounts (such as checking and NOW accounts) or nonpersonal time deposits. In addition, the Fed may lend to the United States branches and agencies of foreign banks if they hold deposits against which reserves must be kept.

Finally, subject to determination by the Board of Governors of the Federal Reserve System that "unusual and exigent circumstances" exist, discount window loans may be made to individuals, partnerships, and corporations that are not depository institutions. Such lending would only take place if the

Board and the Reserve Bank were to find that credit from other sources is not available and that failure to lend may have adverse effects on the economy. This last authority has not been used since the 1930s.

Discount window lending takes place under two main programs, adjustment credit and extended credit.[1] Under normal circumstances adjustment credit, which consists of short-term loans extended to cover temporary needs for funds, should account for the larger part of discount window credit. Loans to large banks under this program are generally overnight loans, while small banks may take as long as two weeks to repay. Extended credit provides funds to meet longer term requirements in one of three forms. First, seasonal credit can be extended to small institutions that depend on seasonal activities such as farming or tourism, and that also lack ready access to national money markets. Second, extended credit can be granted to an institution facing special difficulties if it is believed that the circumstances warrant such aid. Finally, extended credit can go to groups of institutions facing deposit outflows due to changes in the financial system, natural disasters, or other problems common to the group (see Box, Example 5). The second and third categories of extended credit may involve a higher rate than the basic discount rate as the term of borrowing grows longer.

In order to borrow from the discount window, the directors of a depository institution first must pass a borrowing resolution authorizing certain officers to borrow from their Federal Reserve Bank. Next, a lending agreement is drawn up between the institution and the Reserve Bank. These two preliminaries out of the way, the bank requests a discount window loan by calling the discount officer of the Reserve Bank and telling the amount desired, the reason for borrowing, and the collateral pledged against the loan. It is then up to the discount officer whether or not to approve it.

Collateral, which consists of securities which could be sold by the Reserve Bank if the borrower fails to pay back the loan, limits the Fed's (and therefore the taxpaying public's) risk exposure. Acceptable collateral includes, among other things, U. S. Treasury securities and government agency securities, municipal securities, mortgages on one-to-four family dwellings, and short-term commercial notes. Usually, collateral is kept at the Reserve Bank, although some Reserve Banks allow institutions with adequate internal controls to retain custody.

The discount rate is established by the Boards of Directors of the Federal Reserve Banks, subject to review and final determination by the Board of Governors. If the discount rate were always set well above the prevailing fed funds rate, there would be little incentive to borrow from the discount window except in emergencies or if the funds rate for a particular institution were well above that for the rest of the market. Since the 1960s, however, the discount rate has more often than not been set below the funds rate. Figure 2, which portrays both adjustment credit borrowing levels and the spread between the two rates from 1955 to 1985, shows how borrowing tends to rise when the rate spread rises.

The major nonprice tool for rationing discount window credit is the judgment of the Reserve Bank discount officer, whose job is to verify that lending is made only for "appropriate" reasons. Appropriate uses of discount window credit include meeting demands for funds due to unexpected withdrawals of deposits, avoiding overdrafts in reserve accounts, and providing liquidity in case of computer failures (see Box, Example 4), natural disasters, and other forces beyond an institution's control.[2]

An inappropriate use of the discount window would be borrowing to take advantage of a favorable spread between the fed funds rate and the discount rate (Example 3). Borrowing to fund a sudden, unexpected surge of demand for bank loans may be considered appropriate, but borrowing to fund a deliberate program of actively seeking to increase loan volume would not. Continuous borrowing at the window is inappropriate. Finally, an institution that is a net seller (lender) of federal funds should not at the same time borrow at the window, nor should one that is conducting reverse repurchase agreements (that is, buying securities) with the Fed for its own account.

The discount officer's judgment first comes into play when a borrower calls for a loan and states the reason. The monitoring does not end when (and if)

---

[1] For more detailed information on discount window administration policies, see Board of Governors of the Federal Reserve System, **The Federal Reserve Discount Window** (Board of Governors, 1980). The federal regulation governing the discount window is Regulation A, 12 C.F.R. 201.

[2] In order to encourage depository institutions to take measures to reduce the probability of operating problems causing overdrafts, the Board of Governors announced in May 1986 that a surcharge would be added to the discount rate for large borrowings caused by operating problems unless the problems are "clearly beyond the reasonable control of the institution." See "Fed to Assess 2-Point Penalty on Loans for Computer Snafus," **American Banker**, May 21, 1986.

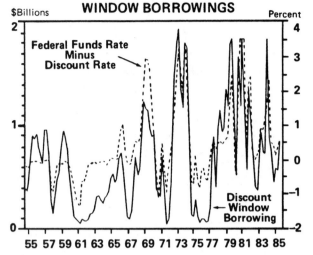

Figure 2

THE SPREAD BETWEEN THE FEDERAL
FUNDS RATE AND DISCOUNT RATE
COMPARED WITH DISCOUNT
WINDOW BORROWINGS

the loan is approved, however. The discount officer watches for patterns in borrowing and may look at such summary measures as discount window loans as a percentage of deposits and of reserves, and duration and frequency of past borrowing. In addition, special circumstances and efforts to obtain credit elsewhere receive attention. Finally, discount window borrowings are compared with fed funds market activity to make sure banks are not borrowing from the Fed simply to lend at a higher rate in the fed funds market.

If the discount officer suspects that borrowing by an institution has possibly gone beyond what is appropriate, he or she makes an "informational" call in order to find out the particular problems and circumstances of the case (Example 3), as well as how the institution plans to reduce its reliance on the discount window. If little or nothing changes, it may be time for counseling as well as a more direct effort to help the borrower find new sources of credit. It is conceivable that an institution's credit could be terminated if counseling were to fail, but this is rarely if ever necessary.

The Borrowing Decision

When deciding whether and how much to borrow from the discount window, a bank's funding officer can be expected to compare the benefit of using the discount window with the cost. The benefit of an additional dollar of discount window credit is the savings of the rate on federal funds, which is normally the next best alternative to the window. The marginal cost contains two elements. The first is the price of discount window credit, that is, the discount rate. The second is the cost imposed by nonprice measures used by the Fed to limit the amount of borrowing. An equilibrium level of borrowing would be reached when the marginal benefit of savings of the fed funds rate is balanced by the marginal cost including both the discount rate and the cost imposed by nonprice measures.[8]

Antecedents

In the United States in the late nineteenth and early twentieth centuries, establishment of a central bank was urged in order to provide an "elastic" currency. The central bank's task would be to expand discount window loans as production (and demand for money) expanded over the business cycle. The loans would then be repaid as goods finally went to market. Such a view of the central bank's role was based on the "real bills" or "commercial loan" school, which asserted that expansion of the money supply would not be inflationary so long as it was done to meet the "needs of trade." In other words, loans made by rediscounting commercial loans (which were considered to be made for "productive" purposes) would be self-liquidating since they would be paid back as the goods produced were sold on the market. The money supply increase would consequently be extinguished.[4] Reflecting the influence of the real bills doctrine, the Preamble to the Federal Reserve Act of 1913 included as a stated purpose "to furnish an elastic currency." Accordingly, the Act contained provisions for the rediscounting of bank loans "arising out of actual commercial transactions" and defining what paper was eligible for rediscount.

Although the real bills doctrine had the most practical influence on the development of central bank lending, some nineteenth century writers argued that the most important function of a central bank was to act as lender of last resort to the financial system. The first major writer to detail the role of a lender of last resort was Henry Thornton at the beginning of the nineteenth century.[5] In today's terms, Thornton described a lender acting as a "cir-

---

[8] See Marvin Goodfriend (1983).

[4] For a demonstration of the fallaciousness of this doctrine, see Thomas M. Humphrey (1982).

[5] For a more detailed treatment of the material in this and the following paragraph, see Thomas M. Humphrey and Robert E. Keleher (1984).

cuit breaker," pumping liquidity into the market in order to prevent problems with particular institutions from spreading to the banking system as a whole. He emphasized that the lender of last resort's role in a panic is precisely opposite that of a private banker in that the former should expand lending in a panic while the latter contracts it. At the same time, Thornton did not advocate lending in order to rescue unsound banks, since that would send the wrong message to bankers, namely, that imprudent management would be rewarded with a bailout. Rather, he urged that loans be made only to banks experiencing liquidity problems due to the panic. In other words, the central bank has a responsibility to protect the banking system as a whole, but not to protect individual banks from their own mistakes.

The other important architect of the lender of last resort idea was Walter Bagehot, who detailed his beliefs in *Lombard Street* in 1873. Generally, Bagehot agreed with Thornton, but developed the lender's role in far greater detail. His contribution is best summed up in the venerable Bagehot Rule: Lend freely at a high rate. This implies three points. First, the public should be confident that lending will take place in a panic, so that there is no question as to the central bank's commitment. Second, lending should go to anyone, not just banks, who presents "good" collateral. In addition, collateral should be judged on what it would be worth in normal times, and not on the basis of its temporarily reduced value due to a panic. Finally, borrowers should be charged a rate higher than prevailing market rates. The justifications for a high rate are several, namely, ensuring that central bank credit goes to those who value it highest, encouraging borrowers to look first to other sources of credit, giving borrowers incentives to pay back such credit as early as possible, and compensating the lender for affording borrowers the insurance provided by a lender of last resort.

The ideas set forth by both Thornton and Bagehot emphasized emergency lending rather than adjustment credit. In actual practice, the Bank of England did act as lender of last resort several times during the late nineteenth century, but such lending was done in addition to its normal practice of providing adjustment credit at the "bank rate." In the United States, the real bills doctrine was more influential in shaping the central bank than were the ideas of Thornton or Bagehot.[6]

---

[6] The lender of last resort idea did surface in the practice of some American clearinghouses acting as emergency lenders during panics. See Gary Gorton (1984).

Evolution of Discount Window Practices

The only type of lending allowed Federal Reserve Banks by the Federal Reserve Act of 1913 was discounting. In 1916 the Act was amended to add the authority for Federal Reserve Banks to make advances, secured by eligible paper or by Treasury securities, to member banks. Advances replaced discounts in practice during 1932 and 1933, when the volume of banks' eligible paper fell precipitously due to the general banking contraction taking place at the time. Emphasis on lending on the basis of "productive" loans gave way to concern with whether or not collateral offered to secure an advance, be it commercial or government securities, was sound enough to minimize risk to the Fed. Since then, advances have been the predominant form of discount window lending.

Nonprice rationing of Federal Reserve credit became firmly established as a matter of practice during the late 1920s. Use of the discount window to finance "speculative" investments was already discouraged due to the real bills doctrine's stress on "productive" uses of credit, but other reasons for lending also received the Board's disapproval. For example, in 1926 the Board adopted a policy of discouraging continuous borrowing from the discount window. In 1928, it specifically stated that banks should not borrow from the window for profit. Since then, the Federal Reserve has emphasized nonprice measures along with the discount rate to control borrowing.

Because market rates were well below the discount rate, banks used the discount window sparingly between 1933 and 1951. From 1934 to 1943, daily borrowings averaged $11.8 million, and only $253 million from 1944 to 1951. For the most part, banks held large amounts of excess reserves and were under little pressure to borrow. Even after the business recovery of the early 1940s, borrowing remained at low levels. Banks held large quantities of government securities, and the Federal Reserve's practice of pegging the prices of these securities, instituted in 1942, eliminated the market risk of adjusting reserve positions through sales of governments.

The pegged market for government securities ended in 1947, and the subsequent increased fluctuations of these securities' prices made buying and selling them a riskier way for banks to change reserves. As a result, the discount window began to look more attractive as a source of funds. By mid-1952, borrowings exceeded $1.5 billion, a level not seen since the early 1930s. Given the new importance of the window, Regulation A, the Federal Reserve regulation governing discount window credit, was revised in 1955 to incorporate principles that had developed over the past thirty years. In particular, the General Principles at the beginning of Regulation A stated that borrowing at the discount window is a privilege of member banks, and for all practical purposes enshrined nonprice rationing and the discretion of the discount officer regarding the appropriateness of borrowing as primary elements of lending policy.

The new version of Regulation A notwithstanding, the discount rate was for the most part equal to or greater than the fed funds rate during the late 1950s and early 1960s. As a result, there was not much financial incentive to go to the window. By the mid-1960s, however, the difference between the fed funds rate and the discount rate began to experience large swings, and the resulting fluctuations in incentives to borrow were reflected in discount window credit levels (see Figure 2).

In 1973, the range of permissible discount window lending was expanded by the creation of the seasonal credit program. More significantly, in 1974 the Fed advanced funds to Franklin National Bank, which had been experiencing deteriorating earnings and massive withdrawals. Such an advance was made to avoid potentially serious strains on the financial system if the bank were allowed to fail and to buy time to find a longer term solution. This particular situation was resolved by takeover of the bulk of the bank's assets and deposits by European American Bank, but the significant event here was the lending to a large, failing bank in order to avert what were perceived to be more serious consequences for the banking system. The action set a precedent for lending a decade later to Continental Illinois until a rescue package could be put together.

Reflecting a discount rate substantially below the fed funds rate from 1972 through most of 1974, discount window borrowings grew to levels that were high by historical standards. A recession in late 1974 and early 1975 drove loan demand down, and market rates tended to stay below the discount rate until mid-1977. During the late 1970s, the spread was positive again, and borrowing from the window increased. Borrowing then jumped abruptly upon the adoption of a new operating procedure for day-to-day conduct of monetary policy (described in the following section), which deemphasized direct fed funds rate pegging in favor of targeting certain reserve aggregates. Because this procedure generally requires a positive level of borrowing, the gap between the fed funds rate and the discount rate has frequently remained relatively high during the first half of the 1980s.

The Monetary Control Act of 1980 extended to all banks, savings and loan associations, savings banks, and credit unions holding transactions accounts and nonpersonal time deposits the same borrowing privileges as Federal Reserve member banks. Among other things, the Act directed the Fed to take into consideration "the special needs of savings and other depository institutions for access to discount and borrowing facilities consistent with their long-term asset portfolios and the sensitivity of such institutions to trends in the national money markets." Although the Fed normally expects thrift institutions to first go to their own special industry lenders for help before coming to the window, private savings and loan insurance system failures in 1985 led to increased use of extended credit.

The Role of the Discount Window in Monetary Policy

As a tool of monetary policy, the discount window today is part of a more complex process than one in which discount rate changes automatically lead to increases or decreases in the money supply. In practice, the Federal Reserve's operating procedures for controlling the money supply involve the discount window and open market operations working together.[7] In the procedures, there is an important distinction between borrowed reserves and nonborrowed reserves. Borrowed reserves come from the discount window, while nonborrowed reserves are supplied by Fed open market operations. While nonborrowed reserves can be directly controlled, borrowed reserves are related to the spread between the funds rate and the discount rate.

During the 1970s, the Fed followed a policy of targeting the federal funds rate at a level believed consistent with the level of money stock desired. Open market operations were conducted in order to keep the funds rate within a narrow range, which in turn was selected to realize the money growth objective set by the Federal Open Market Committee. Under this practice of in effect pegging the fed funds rate in the short run, changes in the discount rate only affected the spread between the two rates and therefore the division of total reserves between borrowed and nonborrowed reserves. In other words,

---

[7] These are described in more detail by R. Alton Gilbert (1985) and Alfred Broaddus and Timothy Cook (1983).

if the discount rate were, say, increased while the fed funds rate remained above the discount rate, borrowing reserves from the Fed would become relatively less attractive than going into the fed funds market.[8] This would decrease quantity demanded of borrowed reserves, but would increase demand for their substitute, nonborrowed reserves, thereby tending to put upward pressure on the funds rate. Given the policy of pegging the funds rate, however, the Fed would increase the supply of nonborrowed reserves by purchasing securities through open market operations. The result would be the same fed funds rate as before, but more nonborrowed relative to borrowed reserves.[9]

After October 6, 1979, the Federal Reserve moved from federal funds rate targeting to an operating procedure that involved targeting nonborrowed reserves. Under this procedure, required reserves, since they were at the time determined on the basis of bank deposits held two weeks earlier, were taken as given. The result was that, once the Fed decided on a target for nonborrowed reserves, a level of borrowed reserves was also implied. Again assuming discount rates below the fed funds rate, raising the discount rate would decrease the fed funds-discount rate spread. Since this would decrease the incentive to borrow, demand would increase for nonborrowed reserves in the fed funds market. Under the new procedure the target for nonborrowed reserves was fixed, however, so the Fed would not inject new reserves into the market. Consequently, the demand shift would cause the funds rate to increase until the original spread between it and the discount rate returned. The upshot here is that, since discount rate changes generally affected the fed funds rate, the direct role of discount rate changes in the operating procedures increased after October 1979.

In October 1982, the Federal Reserve moved to a system of targeting borrowed reserves.[10] Under this procedure, when the Federal Open Market Committee issues its directives at its periodic meetings, it specifies a desired degree of "reserve restraint." More restraint generally means a higher level of borrowing, and vice versa. Open market operations are then conducted over the following period to provide the level of nonborrowed reserves consistent with desired borrowed reserves and demand for total reserves. A discount rate increase under this procedure would, as in nonborrowed reserves targeting, shrink the spread between the fed funds and discount rates, and shift demand toward nonborrowed reserves. In order to preserve the targeted borrowing level, the fed funds rate should change by about the same amount as the discount rate so that the original spread is retained. As a result, discount rate changes under borrowed reserves targeting affect the funds rate the same as under nonborrowed reserves targeting.

Discount Window Issues

As is the case with any instrument of public policy, the discount window is the subject of discussions as to its appropriate role. This section will briefly describe three current controversies regarding the discount window, namely, secured versus unsecured lending, lending to institutions outside the banking and thrift industries, and the appropriate relationship between the discount rate and market rates.

The risk faced by the Federal Reserve System when making discount window loans is reduced by requiring that all such loans be secured by collateral. William M. Isaac, who chaired the Federal Deposit Insurance Corporation from 1981 to 1985, has suggested that this aspect of discount window lending be changed to allow unsecured lending to depository institutions.[11] Mr. Isaac's main objection to secured lending is that, as uninsured depositors pull their money out of a troubled bank, secured discount window loans replace deposits on the liability side of the bank's balance sheet. When and if the bank is declared insolvent, the Fed will have a claim to collateral that otherwise may have been liquidated by the FDIC to reduce its losses on payouts to insured depositors. Sensing this possibility, more uninsured depositors have an incentive to leave before the bank is closed.

Mr. Isaac's proposed policy is best understood by considering how risks would shift under alternative policies. Under the current policy of secured lending

---

[8] Broaddus and Cook (1983) analyze the effect of discount rate changes if the discount rate is kept above the fed funds rate.

[9] Although under this procedure discount rate changes did not directly affect the funds rate, many discount rate changes signaled subsequent funds rate changes.

[10] See Henry C. Wallich (1984). In addition, since February 1984 required reserves have been determined on an essentially contemporaneous basis.

[11] **Deposit Insurance Reform and Related Supervisory Issues,** Hearings before the Senate Committee on Banking, Housing, and Urban Affairs, 99th Cong. 1 Sess. (Government Printing Office, 1985), pp. 27-8, 40. As an alternative, Mr. Isaac has suggested that if the policy of making only secured loans at the window is continued, only institutions that have been certified solvent by their primary regulators should be eligible.

at the discount window, if the Fed lends to a bank that fails before the loan is paid back, the fact that the loan is secured makes it unlikely that the Fed will take a loss on the loan. Losses will be borne by the FDIC fund, which is financed by premiums paid by insured banks. Thus, risk in this case is assumed by the stockholders of FDIC-insured banks.[12] Under Mr. Isaac's alternative, the Fed would become a general rather than a fully secured creditor of the failed bank. As a result, losses would be borne by both the Fed and the FDIC fund, depending on the priority given the Fed as a claimant on the failed bank's assets. Since losses borne by the Fed reduce the net revenues available for transfer to the United States Treasury, the taxpaying public would likely end up bearing more of the risk than under current policy. The attractiveness of moving to a policy of unsecured discount window lending thus depends on the degree to which one feels risks should be shifted from bank stockholders to the general public.[13]

A second discount window issue involves the exercise of the Fed's authority to lend to individuals, partnerships, and corporations. Although such lending has not occurred for over half a century, major events such as the failure of Penn Central in the mid-1970s and the problems of farms and the manufacturing sector of the 1980s raise the question of whether or not this authority should be exercised. On the one hand, one might argue that banking is an industry like any other, and that lending to nonfinancial firms threatened by international competition makes just as much sense as lending to forestall or avoid a bank failure. On the other hand, the Federal Reserve's primary responsibility is to the financial system, and decisions regarding lending to assist troubled industries are better left to Congress than to the Board of Governors.[14]

A final issue regarding the discount window is whether to set the discount rate above or below the prevailing fed funds rate.[15] Figure 2 shows that both policies have been followed at different times during the last thirty years. One could make several arguments in favor of a policy of setting the discount rate above the funds rate. First, as mentioned earlier, placing a higher price on discount window credit would ensure that only those placing a high value on a discount window loan would use the credit. Since funds could normally be gotten more cheaply in the fed funds market, institutions would only use the window in emergencies. Second, it would remove the incentive to profit from the spread between the discount rate and the fed funds rate. As a result, the process of allocating discount window credit would be simplified and many of the rules regarding appropriate uses of credit would be unnecessary. Finally, it might simplify the mechanism for controlling the money supply, since borrowed reserves would not likely be a significant element of total reserves. Indeed, setting targets for borrowed or nonborrowed reserves would probably not be feasible under a penalty rate. Targeting total reserves, however, would be possible, and open market operations would be sufficient to keep reserve growth at desired levels.[16]

Despite the possible advantages of keeping the discount rate above the fed funds rate, it is not clear what would be an effective mechanism for setting a discount rate. Should the discount rate be set on the basis of the previous day's funds rate and remain fixed all day or should it change with the funds rate? Letting it stay the same all day would make it easier for banks to keep track of, but incentives to profit from borrowing could result if the funds rate suddenly rose above the discount rate. Further, what is an appropriate markup above the fed funds rate? Too high a markup over the funds rate might discourage borrowing even in emergencies, thus defeating the purpose of a lender of last resort.[17] Finally, some banks that are perceived as risky by the markets can only borrow at a premium over market rates. Even if the discount rate were marked up to a penalty rate over prevailing market rates,

[12] Since Congress has pledged the full faith and credit of the United States government to the fund, it is also possible that the public may bear some of the losses.

[13] Fed Chairman Paul Volcker has characterized the proposal as changing the Fed from a provider of liquidity to a provider of capital to depository institutions. Ibid., pp. 1287-8.

[14] Ibid., pp. 1315-6. For a discussion of the possibility of discount window lending to the Farm Credit System, see **The Problems of Farm Credit**, Hearings before the Subcommittee on Economic Stabilization of the House Committee on Banking, Finance, and Urban Affairs, 99th Cong. 1 Sess. (GPO, 1985), pp. 449-55, 501-4.

[15] For a more complete summary of arguments regarding the appropriate use of the discount rate, see Board of Governors (1971), vol. 2, pp. 25-76.

[16] For further arguments in favor of total reserves targeting, see Goodfriend (1984). For arguments against, see David E. Lindsey et al. (1984).

[17] Lloyd Mints (1945), p. 249, argues that a higher price for discount window credit would discourage borrowing precisely at the time when the central bank should be generous in providing liquidity.

such banks might attempt to borrow at the discount window to finance more risky investments. In such a case, certain administrative measures might be necessary to ensure that, as under present policy, discount window credit is not used to support loan or investment portfolio expansion.

Choosing between policies of keeping the discount rate either consistently above or consistently below the fed funds rate involves a decision not only on how best to manage reserves but also on the relative merits of using prices or administrative means to allocate credit. Administrative limits on borrowing may help to brake depository institutions' incentives to profit from rate differentials, but will not remove them. Pricing would take away such incentives, but there are difficulties with setting an optimal price. As in most policy matters, the choice comes down to two imperfect alternatives.

References

Board of Governors of the Federal Reserve System. *Reappraisal of the Federal Reserve Discount Mechanism*, vol. 2. Washington: Board of Governors, 1971.

Broaddus, Alfred and Timothy Cook. "The Relationship between the Discount Rate and the Federal Funds Rate under the Federal Reserve's Post-October 6, 1979 Operating Procedure." Federal Reserve Bank of Richmond, *Economic Review* 69 (January/February 1983): 12-15.

Gilbert, R. Alton. "Operating Procedures for Conducting Monetary Policy." Federal Reserve Bank of St. Louis, *Review* 67 (February 1985): 13-21.

Goodfriend, Marvin. "Discount Window Borrowing, Monetary Policy, and the Post-October 6, 1979 Federal Reserve Operating Procedure." *Journal of Monetary Economics* 12 (September 1983): 343-56.

──────. "The Promises and Pitfalls of Contemporaneous Reserve Requirements for the Implementation of Monetary Policy." Federal Reserve Bank of Richmond, *Economic Review* 70 (May/June 1984): 3-12.

Gorton, Gary. "Private Clearinghouses and the Origins of Central Banking." Federal Reserve Bank of Philadelphia, *Business Review* (January/February 1984), pp. 3-12.

Humphrey, Thomas M. "The Real Bills Doctrine." Federal Reserve Bank of Richmond, *Economic Review* 68 (September/October 1982): 3-13. Reprinted in Thomas M. Humphrey, *Essays on Inflation*, 5th Edition, Federal Reserve Bank of Richmond, 1986, pp. 80-90.

──────── and Robert E. Keleher. "The Lender of Last Resort: A Historical Perspective." *Cato Journal* 4 (Spring/Summer 1984): 275-318.

Lindsey, David E., Helen T. Farr, Gary P. Gillum, Kenneth J. Kopecky, and Richard D. Porter. "Short-Run Monetary Control: Evidence Under a Non-Borrowed Reserve Operating Procedure." *Journal of Monetary Economics* 13 (January 1984): 87-111.

Mints, Lloyd W. *A History of Banking Theory*. Chicago: University of Chicago Press, 1945.

Wallich, Henry C. "Recent Techniques of Monetary Policy." Federal Reserve Bank of Kansas City, *Economic Review* (May 1984), pp. 21-30.

Article Twenty-Four

"Financial Crises" and the Role of the Lender of Last Resort

The world now appears to be recovering from one of its most severe recessions in 50 years. Prospects for significant and sustainable real output growth for the industrialized nations of the West have substantially improved, though reductions in unemployment rates are expected to lag behind the increased production.

Economic growth in the industrialized countries is particularly important to the less-developed countries. In some of them, heavy debt burdens are imposing severe financial pressure. Such growth would promote export earnings of less-developed countries (LDCs) and, consequently, work to improve the income-generating capacity of these countries. Many investments were undertaken in these countries with the belief that continued commodity price inflation would generate steadily rising export earnings. During the recession in the industrialized countries, however, slumping commodity prices prevented some LDCs from generating anticipated foreign exchange revenue from exports to cover imports and meet debt payments. Since much of the debt carries floating

> *Stable monetary policies and reliable domestic lenders of last resort provide considerable protection against liquidity crises. But does the world also need an international lender of last resort?*

interest rates, rising real interest rates in the industrialized countries further aggravated the balance of payments problems of the less-developed countries. Consequently, commodity price stabilization (world commodity prices have ceased their two-year descent), growth of real income in the industrialized countries and lower real interest rates in the industrialized countries are necessary to reduce the swollen current-account deficits of these less-developed countries. Ultimately, only these circumstances will enable the less-developed countries to better manage their debt burden.

Until these developments take place, however, the immediate problem of how to deal with the existing debt remains. Mexico, Argentina, and Brazil have already rescheduled some of their debt repayments, while many other countries are doing the same.[1] While most analysts agree that these countries' debt problems may have an

---

[1] Even the East European countries of Poland and Romania, whose loans were assumed to be guaranteed by the Soviet Union, have postponed some debt repayments.

impact on the industrialized nations, opinions vary widely as to the role of a lender of the last resort in easing this burden. The role of the International Monetary Fund (IMF) in particular is scrutinized in this light. Some analysts consider that even rescheduling efforts may be insufficient to prevent massive loan defaults, and therefore they advocate increased financial assistance by the IMF.[2]

Without such assistance, some proponents argue, an international financial crisis might ensue. Debt-ridden LDCs might be forced to default, sending shock waves throughout industrialized countries as large commercial banks write off the defaulted loans, making the banks technically insolvent. If their fears were realized, shareholders and uninsured depositors would face the prospect of sizable losses. Because of the potential threat posed by the current debt problems of less-developed countries, industrialized nations are seeking solutions to help ease the burden of indebted countries while keeping their own banks solvent.

Other analysts, however, dispute this rationale for assisting debt-ridden countries. While they agree that some countries may default on their obligations if further financial assistance is not forthcoming, they contend that this is natural in free market lending relations—some loans do indeed turn sour. That is why lenders are rewarded for assuming risk in free capital markets. Providing financial assistance to less-developed countries constitutes support to the large lending banks, they argue. Increased assistance would make existing private loans more secure, as well as provide greater latitude to the less-developed countries in dealing with their balance of payments difficulties. According to this view, foreign defaults should not pose serious threats to the U.S. economy because one role of the Federal Reserve (as the U.S. "lender of last resort") is to prevent external shocks from disrupting the domestic financial system.

This article will analyze the nature of financial crises, their relationship to central bank policy, and the lender of last resort function of the central bank as well as the role of the IMF. The emphasis is less on the current international debt

situation than on the general problem of financial crises and the role of lenders of last resort in curtailing their destructive effects on the domestic economy. The question is important because intervention is likely to change the way future international financial transactions are conducted and will establish precedents for government involvement in future crises.

The article is organized as follows: The next section briefly describes the nature of domestic financial crises. The relationship of domestic to international financial crises is then delineated, followed by an analysis of the role of the domestic

---

"Industrialized nations are seeking solutions to help ease the burden of indebted countries while keeping their own banks solvent."

---

lender of last resort. Finally, we present some alternative views regarding an international lender of last resort.

What Causes Domestic Financial Crises?

The reason financial crises can develop out of stable economic circumstances is found in the nature of portfolio investment itself. Investors base portfolio decisions on expectations of future earnings. Because potential earnings will be determined by future events that can be predicted only with varying degrees of uncertainty, there is an element of risk inherent in all investment decisions.

In allocating wealth, a rational investor will compare the relative expected returns on various assets, incorporating perceptions of the assets' relative susceptibility to decreases in value. The riskier the asset, the greater he will expect its return to be to compensate for the additional risk. Perceptions of potential risk versus potential return of any given asset are based on expectations of future events that will affect that asset's value. Changes in potential returns on assets versus their potential risks will induce the investor to alter the portfolio of assets he wishes to hold. Concern about both expected return and risk necessarily implies attention to future events, such as possible government actions, which

---

[2]Also involved in the efforts to provide additional financial assistance to the Third World countries are the World Bank, the Swiss-based Bank for International Settlements, individual central banks, and some large and already involved private commercial banks.

might affect the return relative to the risk of those assets. A rational individual will then alter portfolio decisions based on his expectations of future events. Of course, expectations are based on incomplete and costly information and thus are not always correct. Individual **perceptions** of risk therefore become an important determinant of future financial events.

Historically, most domestic financial crises have occurred when investors shifted asset preferences due to a perceived increase in risk. Such a shift has normally taken the form of a preference for lower risk, higher quality, more liquid assets such as cash (legal tender), gold, or high quality deposits. Bank runs have occurred when many depositors attempted to withdraw their funds from a commercial bank simultaneously because they feared that the bank might be unable to honor their deposits. When individuals have anticipated that this might be the case, they have tried to convert their deposits into currency. Given fractional reserve banking, however, commercial banks could not honor all such requests immediately because only a small portion of their assets is in the form of currency; the remaining portion is in (longer-maturity) loans and securities.[3] Banks scrambling to sell off loans and securities to obtain the currency demanded by depositors often were forced to sell such assets at a substantial loss. When these losses were big enough to cause insolvency, some banks were forced to close their doors.

If the banks had been mismanaged, closure might have been appropriate. A widespread run, however, has forced even well-managed banks into ruin. In other words, a bank's assets might have exceeded its liabilities, but yet it might have been unable to convert all of its deposit liabilities into currency on demand. Bank runs thus have created liquidity problems too enormous for even well-managed banks to handle successfully. Again, this may have been because individuals decided that the risk of not being able to convert $1 in deposits into $1 in currency on demand had increased sufficiently for them to attempt to make the conversion immediately. Thus, when individuals have believed banks have limited capability to honor their commitments, they

have attempted to be first to remove their deposits.[4]

Thus, in a world of uncertainty, individuals base investment decisions on expected returns versus perceived risk. As perceptions of risk relative to expected returns change, individuals modify asset holdings accordingly, perhaps abruptly and substantially. A financial crisis or bank run may result from such behavior, but the behavior itself is not irrational. It is the natural consequence of making decisions under conditions of uncertainty, that is, with less than complete and perfect information.

A rational individual action, however, may affect the behavior of others. In the 1930s, individual bank runs helped to trigger a chain

---

"A financial crisis is the natural consequence of making decisions under conditions of uncertainty, that is, with less than complete and perfect information."

---

reaction of bank closings throughout the economy. Such a reaction has several important results. First, the intermediation function of bringing together savers and investors may be severely hampered, resulting in higher real interest rates and/or credit rationing and thus less overall investment.[5] Second, the attempted conversion of demand deposits into currency, given a fractional reserve banking system, may result in a sharp contraction of the money supply.[6] Finally, during periods of bank runs and consequent bank failures, transactors sometimes refuse to accept checks, causing a breakdown of the payments system. This breakdown causes financial loss and disruption to businesses and individuals not directly related to the

---

[4]An important attraction of currency relative to demand deposits is that it alone is legal tender, making it the most liquid of all assets. Also, it may readily be exchanged abroad for purchases of goods or foreign currency.
[5]For a recent and informative analysis of the importance of this particular factor, see Ben S. Bernanke, "Nonmonetary Effects of the Financial Crisis in the Propagation of the Great Depression," **American Economic Review**, June 1983, pp. 257-276.
[6]See, among others, Barry L. Anderson and James L. Butkiewicz, "Money, Spending, and the Great Depression," **Southern Economic Journal**, October 1980, pp. 388-403.

---

[3]Actually, banks today hold reserves in cash or on deposit at Federal Reserve Banks. The reserves or deposits at Federal Reserve Banks, however, can be exchanged for currency at any time.

affected institutions,[7] providing a rationale for government involvement as the lender of last resort.

What Is the Relationship between International and Domestic Financial Crises?

Financial crises are not exclusively domestic in nature; current international financial problems pervade newspapers and business and economics literature. Frequently this literature contains references to an "international lender of last resort."[8] To assess the validity of these

---

"After all, one country's balance of payments deficit is another country's balance of payments surplus."

---

proposals, it is important to examine the function of the lender of last resort. First, however, a brief description of international financial crises and their relationship to domestic financial crises is in order.

Not all interpretations of the term "international financial crisis" coincide. An extreme hypothetical example of an international crisis is one in which, given widespread fractional reserve banking, increased world demand for international reserves under a fixed exchange rate reduces the supply of world money, causing a severe liquidity crisis and associated bank failures, as in the domestic case. Such a monetary

contraction and financial breakdown would severely disrupt trade and the domestic economy.

More frequently, however, the term "international financial crisis" is applied to balance of payments (or exchange rate) adjustments. Yet such adjustments are part of the equilibration process between countries and, as such, do not in themselves qualify as an "international crisis." After all, one country's balance of payments deficit (or exchange rate depreciation) is another country's balance of payments surplus (or exchange rate appreciation). This is particularly true on a limited basis; even severe balance of payments problems in small countries do not constitute "an international crisis."

Currently, the phrase "international financial crisis" is loosely associated with the large debt burdens of several less-developed countries. Concern that these countries may default on their debt obligations, many of which are owed to large U. S. commercial banks, is widespread. If default were to occur, these banks would incur immediate losses on these loans and could face the prospect of insolvency. Since federal deposit insurance covers only about 62 percent of all deposits, with the deposits at the large banks most heavily exposed, depositors also are concerned.[9] In addition, federal deposit insurance guarantees deposits only up to $100,000 per account, aggravating large depositors' concerns about the solvency of their banks, and increasing the perception of risk on deposits relative to returns.[10] One way to avoid such a crisis in confidence, some observers contend, is to provide "extraordinary" financial assistance quickly to the affected less-developed countries.

Others question the necessity of extra assistance, even temporarily. This group contends that loan defaults and a few bank failures may even be desirable.[11] These analysts recognize

---

[7]See, for example, O.M.W. Sprague, **History of Crises Under the National Banking System**, 1910, p. 75; and Vera Smith, **The Rationale of Central Banking**, p. 155.

[8]See, for example, Charles P. Kindleberger, **Manias, Panics, and Crashes**, Basic Books, N.Y. 1978, Chapter 10, pp. 182-209; D.E. Moggridge, "Financial Crises and Lenders of Last Resort: Policy in the Crises of 1920 and 1929," **Journal of European History**, Volume 10, No. 1 Spring 1981; Franklin Edwards, "Financial Institutions and Regulations in the 21st Century: After the Crash," Mimeograph, Columbia University (1980); and Jack Guttentag and Richard Herring, "The Lender-of-Last-Resort Function in an International Context," **Essays in International Finance**, No. 151, May 1983, International Finance Section, Princeton University.

[9]"Commercial banks have many deposit accounts that are not insured in full, with uninsured deposits accounting for about 38 percent of total bank deposits. Further, commercial banks have a sizable amount of nondeposit liabilities that are not insured." See **Agenda for Reform**. Federal Home Loan Bank Board, Washington, D.C., March 1983, p. 92.

[10]This is especially true since Penn Square National Bank was permitted to fail in 1982. Prior to this, the general practice of the FDIC was to arrange mergers or liquidations so that no depositor lost any funds. In effect, all deposits were guaranteed. There is currently greater uncertainty about the status of deposits. Interestingly, interest rates paid on large CDs now vary across banks, reflecting concern about the shaky foreign loans made by some banks. As of this writing, however, risk spreads have narrowed substantially since the summer of 1982.

[11]See, for example, A. Dale Tussing, "The Case for Bank Failures," **Journal of Law and Economics** 1965, Volume X; and Thomas Mayer, "Should Large Banks Be Allowed to Fail?" **Journal of Financial and Quantitative Analysis**, November 1975.

that the risks of international lending may exceed the risks associated with domestic lending because (a) the costs of acquiring information on borrowers are higher,(b) borrowers may have trouble converting local currencies into loan transaction currencies, (c) there is international political uncertainty, and (d) there is exposure to foreign exchange risk.[12] These factors need to to be incorporated in commercial bank loan evaluation and risk assessment procedures. Since banks are rewarded for successful lending ventures, according to this point of view, they must accept responsibility for bad lending decisions as well.

Since these analysts are less likely to consider the current situation an "international financial crisis," they do not consider these problems threats to international financial stability. They, therefore, are skeptical of the need for an international lender of last resort. In evaluating these alternative arguments regarding assistance, a discussion of the role of the lender of last resort becomes especially pertinent.

The Role of the Domestic Lender of Last Resort

The call for a domestic lender of last resort arises because of two institutional characteristics, namely, fractional reserve banking and the government monopoly of legal tender issuance.[13] As discussed earlier, fractional reserve banking implies that banks do not keep enough currency. to meet all depositor demands simultaneously. Government monopoly of legal tender issuance prevents banks and others from creating currency to satisfy these demands. The role of the lender of last resort was established to guarantee banks' ability to meet currency demand, thus precluding a panic-induced collapse of the banking system. By ensuring banks' ability to meet depositor demands, the lender of last resort can help prevent (a) the disruption of

financial intermediation, (b) disruptions of the payments system, and (c) contractions of the money stock, all which may occur in times of financial panic.

Some analysts argue that a domestic lender of last resort is unnecessary because federal deposit insurance removes the incentives for bank runs.[14] Insured depositors feel confident that no matter how badly managed a bank is, they will eventually receive their deposits. Minor runs on financial institutions sometimes do occur, such as the run on the Abilene National Bank in 1982, but these episodes pale in comparison to those experienced during the 1930s. As noted earlier, however, de jure federal deposit insurance currently insures only about 62 percent of all deposits. Furthermore, the Federal Deposit Insurance Corporation pricing

---

> "The role of the lender of last resort was established to guarantee banks' ability to meet currency demands."

---

scheme may be altered in the near future to shift some of the risk burden back to large depositors. Finally, in the event of widespread bank failures that deplete the funds of federal deposit insurance, a lender of last resort must ultimately function as a backup for federal deposit insurance itself.

In the early 1900s, prior to the establishment of the Federal Reserve, some of the functions of a lender of last resort were supplied by private institutions. Currency substitutes (script), clearing house certificates, and "bank holidays" were mechanisms for dealing with financial crises.[15] If a bank run began to develop, many banks would refuse to convert deposits into currency on demand. Sometimes banks declared a "bank holiday," closing for business. This

---

[12]See Jack Guttentag and Richard Hering, "The Lender of Last Resort Function in an International Context," **Essays in International Finance.** No. 151, May 1983. p. 2.

[13]100 percent reserve banking would eliminate bank runs. The fact that other banks cannot issue legal tender means that only the issuer of legal tender can meet an abnormal increase in the demand for legal tender. Moreover, because of the government (central bank) monopoly of legal tender issuance, the central bank naturally becomes the central store of bank reserves, the ultimate source of domestic liquidity, and, consequently, the "bankers' bank."

[14]For an extremely insightful analysis of the relationship between deposit insurance and bank runs, see Douglas W. Diamond and Philip H. Dybvig. "Bank Runs, Deposit Insurance, and Liquidity," **Journal of Political Economy**, June 1983, pp. 401-419.

[15]See, for example, Milton Friedman and Anna Schwartz. **A Monetary History of the United States** (Princeton, Princeton University Press. 1963).

enabled banks to avoid selling off massive amounts of assets at reduced prices, thereby avoiding large losses and possible insolvency. The lender of last resort was created to provide sufficient emergency liquidity in times of massive deposit withdrawals to keep the banking system open. Because the lender of last resort guarantees deposit-to-currency convertibility, individuals have confidence that they can *always* convert their deposits into currency on demand, and therefore do not "run" to withdraw deposits when a bank might appear in danger of insolvency. Even after the institution of federal deposit insurance, the ultimate deposit protection rested with the Federal Reserve Bank in its role as lender of last resort.

Having the power to issue legal tender implies that central banks never exhaust their (domestic)

> "In 1971, the Board of Governors affirmed its commitment to assist the financial system, but not individual banks."

---

financial liquidity and are therefore able to lend when other institutions are illiquid. Because the lender of last resort is concerned with the health of the overall domestic economy, it should assume this role only when bank insolvency problems threaten the economy; the classical position is that it should *not* act in the interest of a particular bank or banks.[16] The effective exercise of this liquidity responsibility will prevent a rapid, widespread call-in of loans and a dramatic fall (or collapse) of asset prices. Thus, by supporting the market in liquidity emergencies, the lender of last resort ensures that banks will not be forced to sell liquid assets at losses that might otherwise result in insolvency and its consequent adverse effects.

Ostensibly, the market will handle individual bank crises. In a competitive financial system,

if a bank is fundamentally solvent but temporarily illiquid, others can profit by lending to it. If a particular bank is insolvent, however, its real resources are released to flow into more productive uses. Neither the case of a solvent nor of an insolvent bank involves the lender of last resort. In 1971, the Board of Governors of the Federal Reserve System affirmed its commitment to assist the financial *system*, but not *individual* banks. A special report reappraising the discount mechanism stated:

"The (Federal Reserve) System should not act to prevent losses and impairment of capital of particular financial institutions. If pressures develop against and impair the profitability of institutions whose operations have become unstable, inappropriate to changing economic conditions, or competitively disadvantaged in the marketplace, it is not the Federal Reserve's responsibility to use its broad monetary powers in a bail-out operation... The System should intervene in its capacity as lender of last resort only when liquidity pressures threaten to engulf whole classes of financial institutions whose structures are sound and whose operational impairment would be seriously disruptive to the economy."[17]

Moreover, the function of the lender of last resort is not to prevent shocks that frequently affect the financial system or to stabilize the business cycle but rather to minimize the secondary repercussions of those shocks. In essence, the purpose is to maintain confidence in the financial system so that there will be no need to exercise the lender of last resort function.

One of the most important functions of the lender of last resort is to assure the market that support will be forthcoming if needed. Credible assurance of the central bank's willingness to act in a crisis relieves uncertainty and stabilizes expectations that might otherwise generate depositor panics.[18] To prevent excessive risk-taking by banks confident of assistance, however, the lender of last resort must be certain to specify that in financial crises assistance will be available to the market, not to particular banks.

---

[16]See Thomas M. Humphrey, "The Classical Concept of the Lender of Last Resort." **Economic Review**, Federal Reserve Bank of Richmond, January/February 1975.

[17]Steering Committee, "Report of a System Committee," **Reappraisal of the Federal Reserve Discount Mechanism,** Board of Governors of the Federal Reserve System, Volume 1, August 1971, p.19.
[18]See Humphrey, *op. cit.*

How the Domestic Lender of Last Resort Operates

There are two main ways the lender of last resort supplies liquidity. The most familiar way is to lend funds through the discount window to commercial banks and other institutions if conditions so warrant and if sufficient sound collateral is available. The lender of last resort must be careful, however, to ensure that loans assist institutions coping with liquidity problems, not solvency problems. The rate of interest or discount rate charged on such loans should be a penalty rate high enough to ensure that other market sources of funds have been exhausted and that banks borrow from the Federal Reserve only as a "last resort." In the words of Walter Bagehot in 1873: "Lend freely at a high rate." When the lender of last resort function was developed, discount lending was the primary monetary policy tool and thus was also the primary tool for making last resort loans. Today, many economists still view discount window lending as the only mechanism by which the lender of last resort can provide liquidity.

The second, more efficient, but lesser known way that the lender of last resort can provide liquidity to the market is by engaging in open market operations. By purchasing government securities in the marketplace, the Federal Reserve injects reserves into the marketplace, almost immediately increasing the reserves available to all institutions but without allocating them among particular users. Federal Reserve open market purchases provide a market for individuals, firms, and financial institutions selling securities to meet their currency demands. With open market purchases to stabilize the stock of bank deposits, bank runs should not develop since depositors know that the banking system will not have to sell off its assets at a capital loss. The discount window and open market operations are the means by which the Fed provides liquidity in crisis periods to ensure that banks can readily convert assets into cash to meet currency drains. Consequently, both methods prevent bank runs and the problems associated with such runs.

Provision of liquidity during a crisis via open market purchases is consistent with and a crucial element of longer-run monetary control. Prompt and vigorous lender of last resort action will stop panics long before the money supply strays far off course. The "lender of last resort" function is essentially a very short-run function of a central bank that is activated only during temporary periods of emergency; the "monetary control" function of a central bank is a continuous and longer-run function. The lender of last resort acts to prevent sudden decreases (shocks) in the money stock, and thus works to reinforce stable monetary control. Thus, monetary control and last resort lending are complementary, not conflicting.

A Role for an International Lender of Last Resort?

Traditionally, discussions of the lender of last resort have related almost entirely to the domestic economy with little regard for international concerns. Current international financial problems, however, have elicited calls to extend the lender of last resort function to the international realm. Indeed, several economists

> "The discount window and open market purchases are the means by which the Fed provides liquidity in crisis periods to ensure that banks can readily convert assets into cash to meet currency drains."

contend that the IMF is already assuming this role.[19] Several proposals have been made to create an international lending entity.[20]

While the concept of a *domestic* lender of last resort is well established, the role of a similar *international* lender remains unclear. Localized international liquidity problems related to balance of payments (or exchange rate) adjustments are common but do not require intervention of a last resort lender. Balance of payments adjustments are inherent elements of a country's trade equilibrating process and do not necessarily relate to banking crises. Moreover, when one country loses, another must gain. These

---

[19] See; for example, James W. Dean and Ian H. Giddy, "Averting International Banking Crises," Monograph 1981-1, New York University, The Monograph Series in Finance and Economics, 1981.
[20] See, for example, Charles Kindleberger, *op. cit.*; and Franklin Edwards, *op. cit.*

adjustments, then, pertain only to particular countries, and therefore do not merit the intervention of an international lender of last resort.

As on the domestic level, the need for an international lender of last resort arises in part from fractional reserve banking and governments' exclusive control of legal tender issuance. While no government issues international legal tender, there are international mediums of exchange, particularly when exchange rates are fixed. Many less-developed countries peg their currencies to key currencies such as the dollar. The role of an international lender of last resort would be to prevent severe disruptions (especially monetary contractions) of the world monetary system. Under a fixed exchange rate regime, a financial crisis may result from an increase in the perceived risk of a country's currency relative to its value. If foreign depositors simultaneously attempt to withdraw their money, denominated in an international medium of exchange, from the country's banks, a run on

---

"In its current form, however, the IMF cannot function as a lender of last resort, as it cannot create money or international reserves."

---

the central bank's international reserves may result. If this central bank wishes to maintain a fixed exchange rate, it may ultimately have to borrow an international medium of exchange from other central banks or from an international lender of last resort. Under these particular circumstances an international lender of last resort may have a valid role.[21]

If the central bank cannot borrow in an international medium of exchange, it may go off the fixed exchange rate system and allow its currency to depreciate. In the domestic market, banks are *always* expected to redeem their liabilities at par. In the international arena, however, a country can depreciate its currency instead of

---

[21]See Ralph Hawtrey, **The Art of Central Banking**, p. 228 and Robert Aliber, "Bagehot, the Lender of Last Resort, and the International Financial System," unpublished manuscript, p. 26.

maintaining a fixed exchange value with an international medium of exchange. The ability to allow currency to fluctuate to accommodate crises provides LDCs with a remedy not available to the domestic market. This difference between domestic and international currency standards suggests that a lender of last resort may be less necessary in the international than in the domestic context.[22]

By these standards, current international debt problems do not require the assistance of an international lender of last resort. Current data indicate that world money and reserves continue to increase at moderate rates.[23] Developed-country banks are liquid and able to continue lending, implying that no serious *general* liquidity crisis exists.[24]

In spite of the lack of a general liquidity crisis, some analysts nevertheless contend that an international lender of last resort is essential.[25] To function as a lender of last resort, however, an international organization must have authority to create money, i.e., provide unlimited liquidity on demand. Unlike other institutions, for example, a domestic lender of last resort never faces illiquidity or insolvency since it is the ultimate source of legal tender or currency. An

---

[22]See, for example, Hawtrey, *op. cit.*, p. 228; Aliber, *op. cit.*, p. 27; and D. E. Moggridge, "Financial Crises and Lender of Last Resort: Policy in the Crises of 1920 and 1929," **Journal of European History**, Volume 10, No. 1, Spring 1981, p. 50. The above scenario describes a situation in which demand increases for the conversion of deposits into international media of exchange. The current international debt situation is quite different. There is another important difference between domestic and international financial crises. Since the volume of international debt is often contracted in terms of a foreign currency, exchange rate movements add risk to international debt not associated with the domestic counterpart. Exchange rate risk translates into risk of governmental policy. That is, with debt denominated in domestic currency, governmental policy makers can prevent or forestall default by inflation or taxation. When debt is denominated in foreign currency, however, this option is closed. The servicing of foreign debt requires conversion of domestic money into foreign money at exchange rates that reflect governmental policies. Policies to prevent default, such as taxation or inflation, will merely raise the cost of conversions into foreign currency. See Karl Brunner, et. al., "The International Debt Problem, Insolvency and Illiquidity: A Policy Proposal," Statement prepared by the Ad Hoc Committee on International Debt and U.S. Financial Policies. Distributed by The Center for Research in Government Policy and Business Graduate School of Management, University of Rochester, January 14, 1983, p. 6. Furthermore, actions to prevent exchange rates from adjusting to reflect these governmental policies will alter individuals' expectations of future developments and thus their current portfolio decisions, which will only exacerbate the situation, especially as the debt burden rises and the sustainability of the existing policies weakens.

[23]**International Financial Statistics**, supplement No. 5, **Supplement on Money** and latest data in **International Financial Statistics**, November 1983.

[24]This is not to say that no problem exists. As some point out, in attempting to deal with their debt burden, many developing countries are cutting back on their imports. This, or course, adversely affects the exports of the U.S. and other industrialized countries. However, bigger IMF quotas cannot be justified on the grounds of a **general** liquidity crisis.

[25]See, for example, Edwards, *op. cit.* (1980).

international lender of last resort likewise would have to be the ultimate source of international reserves. For if an international lender of last resort had to borrow the funds it lent, it would not be the *last* resort.[26] Additionally, an international lender of last resort must be able to make loans to solvent, credible borrowers who otherwise could not borrow money in the marketplace during a general liquidity crisis. Such "last resort" lending might occur during a liquidity crisis and likely could manifest itself in increased demand for (international transactions) money.

Many who advocate an international lender of last resort contend that the IMF currently performs this role and should expand its responsibility.[27] Some authors argue that the IMF is in possession of substantial unused financial resources, the power to raise additional funds, a large unpledged gold stock, and the power to issue Special Drawing Rights (SDRs) representing "a formidable package of 'last resort' financial resources and powers."[28]

The IMF was created to promote world trade and assist member countries with short-term balance of payments deficits through extensions of *short-term* loans. Because the IMF lends to some countries that cannot get enough loans in the marketplace, it may superficially resemble a lender of last resort. In its current form, however, the IMF cannot function as a lender of last resort, as it cannot create money or international reserves. Instead, the IMF must depend on limited contributions from member countries for funds to lend. Once the IMF reaches this quota, its funds are exhausted; it cannot create either world currency or the currencies of its members.[29] Since the ability to create money is the chief feature distinguishing a lender of last resort, the IMF does not qualify fully for that role.

In spite of the fact that the IMF is not a true lender of last resort, support has been obtained for increasing IMF quotas to avert an international crisis in confidence. The IMF recently has been providing further financial assistance to selected debt-burdened countries on the condition that the recipient countries implement agreed-upon austerity measures. These measures include reducing government budget deficits and slowing monetary growth to lower inflation and to reduce nominal interest rates, which in turn should increase debtor countries' exports and decrease their imports, thereby improving their balance of payment positions. U. S. commercial banks, among others, also are agreeing to make additional loans, continue existing loans and reschedule repayments on outstanding loans.

A crucial question is whether IMF actions, which ultimately are funded by the U. S. and other member countries, represent support for

---

"Some analysts contend that an international lender of last resort is essential."

---

large U. S. and international commercial banks. Clearly, U. S. banks, which had implicitly accepted the risks of foreign lending, benefit at least temporarily from such financial assistance. Their actual losses and potential insolvency problems are postponed, if not eliminated, provided no defaults are legally declared.[30] Currently, the IMF makes loans to countries suffering liquidity problems, in part because private lenders have assessed these countries to be too risky to increase lending to them. As discussed, the purpose of a lender of last resort is to provide liquidity to prevent the default of well-managed and otherwise sound institutions. Making loans to high-risk debtor countries does not fit that definition.

---

[26]Dean and Giddy, p. 41. See also R. G. Hawtrey, **The Art of Central Banking**, p. 274.

[27]See, for example, Dean and Giddy (1981), p. 33.

[28]Weintraub, Robert, pp. 43-44.

[29]The IMF may borrow from any source and in the currency of any member country, but it must first obtain the consent of the government of the member country in whose currency it proposes to borrow. Thus far it has borrowed limited funds from member countries but never from the markets. In January 1982, the IMF's Executive Board confirmed that quotas should continue to be the main source of funds. See Group of Thirty, **The International Monetary Fund and the Private Markets**, New York 1983, p. 2.

[30]A loan is not legally in default until the lender declares that the borrower has failed to honor the terms of the loan. Also, banks carry loans at book, not market value. However, the FDIC may close a bank based upon a comparison of the market value of assets to insured deposits. There is currently a move to disclose more information about a bank's balance sheet so that depositors may more fully discern the risk attached to dealing with any particular bank.

Some Concluding Thoughts

Under current circumstances, then, no additional powers need be given to the IMF to enable it to assume the role of an international lender of last resort for the global banking system. No "world liquidity crisis" has emerged. Even should such a crisis occur, it could be alleviated by the national monetary authorities of the industrialized countries acting as lenders of last resort for domestic commercial banks and their foreign subsidiaries and by pursuing stable, predictable, non-inflationary and thus credible monetary policies.[31] Central banks must have well-established and recognized policies to avoid allowing bank failures to affect their national money supplies. In sum, stable monetary policies and reliable domestic lenders of last resort provide adequate defense against liquidity crises. Thus the mechanism is already established for preventing international debt problems from triggering a domestic financial crisis.

So long as these policies are pursued consistently, one does not need to be concerned about the financial system's vulnerability to a monetary collapse.

Still, the severity of the current international debt situation highlights the need for a thorough assessment of the IMF's role in an increasingly interdependent world economy and of the financial resources required to support that role. The issue certainly is a complex one. Making temporary short-term loans to ease pressure during time-consuming loan rescheduling negotiations indeed may be a valid role for central banks and international agencies . An assessment of the IMF's role remains crucial even though the recent debate over our nation's IMF funding has ended, with Congress authorizing the increase that everyone hopes can help resolve the debt problem.

—James R. Barth
and Robert E. Keleher

This paper was written while James R. Barth was a Visiting Scholar with the Federal Reserve Bank of Atlanta. He is currently visiting the Congressional Budget Office while on leave from the George Washington University. The authors are grateful for helpful comments and suggestions from Bryan Boulier, R. Dan Brumbaugh, Jerry Dwyer, Padma Gotur, Jim Hauver, John Hilley, George Iden, Jorge Laumas, Neela Manage, Lisa Rockoff, Steve Sheffrin, Lee Slutz, Stephen Thurman, and Joe Whitt.

[31]There is currently some ambiguity about who legally bears the lender of last resort responsibility for a subsidiary of a foreign bank. However, "most U.S. loans through the Eurocurrency market are handled through London branches of U.S. banks, not subsidiaries." Even so, "subsidiaries do play a significant role in some cases, such as subsidiaries of German banks operating in Luxembourg." Despite this loophole in lender of last resort coverage, "the events of 1982-83 illustrate a willingness of central banks to work together in crisis, suggesting that, if necessary, they could agree on the division of lender of last resort responsibility for currently ambiguous cases." See William R. Cline, **International Debt and the Stability of the World Economy**, Institute for International Economics, September 1983, pp. 103-105.

BIBLIOGRAPHY

Agenda for Reform. Federal Home Loan Bank Board, Washington, D.C., March 1983.

Aliber, Robert. "Bagehot, The Lender of Last Resort, and The International Financial System," unpublished manuscript (no date).

Anderson, Barry L. and James L. Butkiewicz. "Money, Spending, and the Great Depression." **Southern Economic Journal**, October 1980.

Bagehot, Walter. **Lombard Street** (1873), Arno Press, New York, 1978.

Barth, James R. and Joseph Pelzman. "International Debt: Conflict and Resolution," International Debt Series Monograph No. 3, Dept. of Economics, George Mason University, January 1984.

Bernanke, Ben S. "Nonmonetary Effects of the Financial Crisis in the Propagation of the Great Depression," **American Economic Review**, June 1983.

Brunner, Karl, et al. "The International Debt Problem, Insolvency and Illiquidity: A Policy Proposal," Statement prepared by the Ad Hoc Committee on International Debt and U. S. Financial Policies, Distributed by The Center for Research in Government Policy and Business, Graduate School of Management, University of Rochester, January 14, 1983.

Dean, James W. and Ian H. Giddy. **Averting International Banking Crises**, Monograph 1981-1, New York University, The Monograph Series in Finance and Economics, 1981.

Diamond, Douglas W. and Philip H. Dybvig. "Bank Runs, Deposit Insurance, and Liquidity," **Journal of Political Economy**, June 1983.

Edwards, Franklin. "Financial Institutions and Regulations in the 21st Century: After the Crash," Mimeograph, Columbia University, 1980.

Friedman, Milton and Anna Schwartz. **A Monetary History of the United States**, Princeton University Press, Princeton, New Jersey, 1963.

Group of Thirty. **The International Monetary Fund and the Private Markets**, New York, 1983, p. 2.

Guttentag, Jack and Richard Herring. **The Lender of Last Resort Function in an International Context**, Essays in International Finance, No. 151, May 1983. International Finance Section, Princeton University.

Hawtrey, Ralph. **The Art of Central Banking**, Frank Cass and Co. Ltd., London, 1962.

Humphrey, Thomas M. "The Classical Concept of the Lender of Last Resort," **Economic Review**, Federal Reserve Bank of Richmond, January/ February 1975.

Kindleberger, Charles P. **Manias, Panics, and Crashes**, Basic Books, New York, 1978.

Mayer, Thomas. "Should Large Banks Be Allowed to Fail?", **Journal of Financial and Quantitative Analysis**, November 1975.

Moggridge, D. E. "Financial Crises and Lenders of Last Resort: Policy in the Crises of 1920 and 1929," **Journal of European History**, Volume 10, No. 1, Spring 1981.

Smith, Vera. **The Rationale of Central Banking**, London, P. S. King & Son Ltd., Westminster, 1936.

Sprague, O. M. W. **History of Crises Under the National Banking System**, Washington, D. C., U. S. Government Printing Office, 1910.

Steering Committee. "Report of a System Committee." **Reappraisal of the Federal Reserve Discount Mechanism**, Board of Governors of the Federal Reserve System, Volume 1, August 1971.

Tussig, A. Dale. "The Case for Bank Failure," **Journal of Law and Economics**, Volume X, October 1967.

Weintraub, Robert E. **International Debt: Crisis and Challenge**. Department of Economics, George Mason University, Fairfax, Virginia, April 1983.

Article Twenty-Five

Why Does Velocity Matter?

DANIEL L. THORNTON

THE significant decline in the income velocity of money during 1982 and in the first quarter of 1983 has engendered confusion and controversy.[1] Amid this controversy, little attention has been paid to the more fundamental role velocity plays in macroeconomics and, hence, about its potential and actual importance in the conduct of monetary policy. This article sets forth the concept of income velocity and illustrates the potential effects of a change in velocity for monetary policy.

INCOME VELOCITY: A BRIEF OVERVIEW

Irving Fisher's famous "equation of exchange" primarily was responsible for the prominent role of income velocity in macroeconomic analysis.[2] In its most rudimentary form, the equation of exchange can be written as the identity given by equation 1 in table 1. Here, M and Y denote the nominal money stock (however defined) and nominal GNP, respectively, and V represents income velocity, the average number of times each unit of nominal money is used to support nominal GNP. Nominal GNP, in turn, can be represented by the average level of prices, P, times real

GNP, X. In this form, the equation of exchange is an accounting identity equating the nominal money stock multiplied by the number of times each unit turns over to nominal output, that is, $V = Y/M$. In this form, the equation is of little practical use since there is one equation and four unknown quantities, M, V, P and X.

Making the Equation of Exchange Useful

Fisher argued, however, that the level of velocity is determined by a number of social and economic factors.[3] He argued further that these factors tend to be relatively stable so that velocity could be treated as a constant, $\overline{V}$.[4] Under this assumption, equation 1 ceases to be an identity and becomes Fisher's useful equation of exchange (equation 2, table 1).[5] If V is constant and M is controlled exogenously by the monetary authority, nominal GNP can be determined — indeed, con-

Daniel L. Thornton is a senior economist at the Federal Reserve Bank of St. Louis. John G. Schulte provided research assistance.

[1]The decline in velocity was a persistent concern of the Federal Open Market Committee (FOMC) in the conduct of monetary policy during 1982 and contributed to the Committee's decision to suspend the use of M1 as an intermediate policy target in October 1982. See Daniel L. Thornton, "The FOMC in 1982: Deemphasizing M1," this *Review* (June/July 1983), pp. 26–35.

[2]Irving Fisher (assisted by Harry G. Brown): *The Publishing Power of Money: Its Determination and Relation to Credit, Interest and Crises* (MacMillan, 1911).

[3]Money was viewed primarily as a medium of exchange necessitated by the lack of synchronization between the sale of one good and the purchase of another. Thus, the proportion of income held (on average) in the form of money balances was determined by institutional factors that determined the pattern of payments and receipts. A discussion of this can be found in most macroeconomics textbooks.

[4]Actually, the classical economists never considered V to be a constant in the sense of unchangeable. Indeed, they recognized the effects of interest rates and price expectations on velocity; however, they generally believed that such factors would be relatively unimportant over the long run. For a good discussion of these issues, see Laurence Harris, *Monetary Theory* (McGraw-Hill, 1981), chapter 6.

[5]Although they stem from different theoretical approaches, Fisher's equation of exchange is similar to the "Cambridge cash balance equation" of Marshall and Pigou. See Alfred Marshall, *Money, Credit and Commerce* (MacMillan, 1923); and A. C. Pigou, "The Value of Money," *Quarterly Journal of Economics* (November 1917), pp. 38–65.

Table 1

Various Forms of the Equation of Exchange

$$
\begin{aligned}
&(1) && MV \equiv PX \\
&(2) && M\overline{V} = Y \\
&(3) && M\overline{V} = P\overline{X} \\
&(4) && \dot{M} + \dot{\overline{V}} = \dot{Y} = \dot{P} + \dot{\overline{X}} \\
&(5) && \dot{P} = \dot{M} + (\dot{\overline{V}} - \dot{\overline{X}})
\end{aligned}
$$

Table 2

Growth Rates of Real Output and Velocity: II/1954–IV/1981

Country	$\dot{M}1$	$\dot{P}$	$\dot{V}$	$\dot{X}$
United States	4.5%	4.5%	3.4%	3.4%
Germany[1]	7.9	4.4	0.5	3.7
Japan[2]	15.3	5.6	−0.5	8.2
United Kingdom[3]	8.8	10.3	4.0	2.1
Canada	6.9	5.2	3.4	4.6

[1]Data covers period II/1960–IV/1981.

[2]Data covers period II/1957–IV/1981.

[3]Data covers period III/1963–IV/1981.

trolled — through monetary policy.[6] That is, for any $\overline{V}$, the monetary authority can obtain any Y it desires simply by setting M at the appropriate level. If a primary goal of policy is to stabilize nominal income growth, a constant velocity would give the monetary authority the means to achieve this goal by controlling money growth.[7] Of course, it is impossible from this relationship to determine the separate effects of changes in M on real output and prices.

The Quantity Theory of Money

If real output is determined independently of the stock of nominal money in the long run, selecting the money stock is tantamount to determining the price level. This is essentially the position of the classical economists, who argued that the amount of real output is determined by the "real" side of the market (e.g., factors of production, technology and relative prices). In the most elementary form of the equation, output is fixed at the full-employment level, $\overline{X}$. With this added assumption, Fisher's equation of exchange becomes the so-called crude quantity theory of money, given by equation 3 of table 1. With V and X constant, there is a direct, proportional link between money and the price

level: if the money stock doubles, the price level will double.[8]

This version of the quantity theory, while appealing because of its simplicity, is of limited use because real output is not constant at the full-employment level; instead it varies over business cycles.

Thus, a more sophisticated quantity theory of money is a long-run (secular) theory of the relationship between money and prices. Under this more general theory, changes in the money stock may result in changes in real output or prices (or both) in the short run, but result primarily in price level changes in the long run (i.e., over business cycles).[9] Within this expanded framework, the quantity theory conclusion of the close correspondence of money growth and price level movements holds in the long run.

Velocity Is Not a Numerical Constant

Frequently, velocity is treated erroneously as a numerical constant; however, this restriction is both unnecessary and incorrect. Equation 1 can be written in the useful growth rate form as equation 4 of table 1. The dots over the variables denote compounded annual growth rates. Velocity need not be constant for

---

[6]Money is assumed to be largely exogenous. Both classical and neoclassical writers acknowledged the feedback of prices to money. Modern writers like Friedman and Schwartz consider money to be "for all practical purposes" exogenous in the sense that it can be controlled by the monetary authority. See Milton Friedman and Anna J. Schwartz, *Monetary Statistics of the United States* (National Bureau of Economic Research, 1970), p. 124.

[7]The goals of economic policy as set forth in the Full-Employment Act of 1946 are (1) full employment, (2) price level stability, (3) equilibrium in the balance of payments and (4) a high rate of economic growth. The first two of these are reiterated in the Humphrey-Hawkins Act. Since Y = P · X, the first two objectives amount to stabilizing nominal GNP.

[8]This is the "neutrality of money." Also, there was the closely related "classical dichotomy" between money and output. For a discussion of these points, see Harris, *Monetary Theory*, chapters 4 and 6, and Don Patinkin, *Money, Interest and Prices* (Harper and Row, 1965), chapter 8.

[9]Furthermore, full employment does not necessarily mean zero unemployment, but is merely a level consistent with stable prices given the structural characteristics of the labor and output markets, including market imperfections. See Milton Friedman, "The Role of Monetary Policy," *American Economic Review* (March 1968), pp. 1–17, for his concept of the natural rate of unemployment.

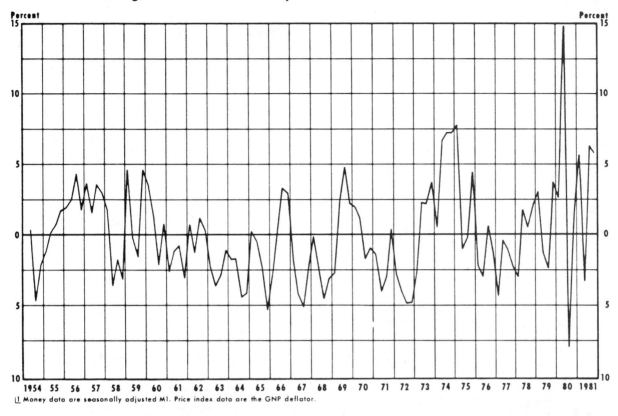

Chart 1
Rate of Price Change minus Rate of Money Growth [1]

Percent   Percent

1954 55 56 57 58 59 60 61 62 63 64 65 66 67 68 69 70 71 72 73 74 75 76 77 78 79 80 1981

[1] Money data are seasonally adjusted M1. Price index data are the GNP deflator.

nominal GNP to be controlled through monetary policy; all that is required is that its growth rate be relatively stable. Equation 4 can be rewritten as equation 5 to show that the rate of increase in prices (inflation) is related to money growth. Thus, in the long run, the relative growth rates between money and prices reflect the relative difference between the growth rates of velocity and real output. The slower velocity growth is relative to real output growth, the faster the growth in nominal money can be consistent with stable prices or a low rate of inflation.

If $\dot{V}$ and $\dot{X}$ are approximately equal on average, then the rate of inflation will equal approximately the growth rate of money. Basically, this situation has existed in the United States for roughly the past three decades. The average quarter-to-quarter compounded annual rates of growth of M1 velocity and real output from II/1954 to IV/1981 were both 3.4 percent. As a result of the equality between $\dot{V}$ and $\dot{X}$, $\dot{M}1$ and $\dot{P}$ were equal over this period. Both the implicit price deflators for GNP and M1 increased at an average compounded annual rate of 4.5 percent over this same period. In the

short run, however, $\dot{X}$ and $\dot{V}$ deviate from each other; thus, so do $\dot{M}1$ and $\dot{P}$. This is illustrated in chart 1, which shows the difference between $\dot{P}$ and $\dot{M}1$ for the period.

This long-run, near-equality between $\dot{P}$ and $\dot{M}1$, however, does not hold for all countries. This is shown in table 2, which shows the average growth of $\dot{V}$, $\dot{X}$, $\dot{P}$ and $\dot{M}1$ for five countries, including the United States.

VELOCITY AND MONETARY POLICY

If one goal of monetary policy is to stabilize nominal GNP growth, policymakers must incorporate velocity considerations into their decisions. There are, however, a variety of ways in which velocity can change. These complicate the analysis of velocity movements for policy decisions.

Permanent Vs. Temporary Changes

If a change in velocity is known and is permanent, the appropriate policy response is a compensatory

Figure 1

Level shift in velocity at t₀ with no change in growth rate

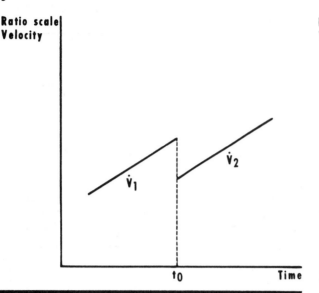

Decrease in the growth rate of velocity at t₀

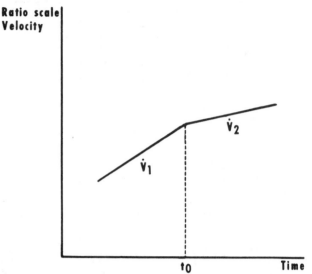

change in money to offset the effects of a velocity change on Y.[10]

If a change is temporary, however, policymakers may decide not to respond to the change because their response may increase rather than reduce the instability of nominal income. For example, suppose that policymakers observe a decline in velocity that they anticipate will reverse itself in the course of a quarter or two. If policymakers want to neutralize the effect of this temporary change on nominal income, they will increase the rate of money growth to keep nominal income growth on course, then reduce money growth later when the velocity change reverses.

Because policymakers are generally uncertain about the timing and extent of such a shift, they may be too aggressive for too long, producing larger swings in nominal income growth than would have occurred otherwise. Such instability need not result inevitably from policy responses to temporary changes in velocity; nevertheless, the danger is there. Thus, if policymakers suspect that the velocity change they observe is temporary, they may choose to ignore it.[11]

Level Vs. Growth Rate Shifts

Policymakers also must distinguish between changes in the levels of velocity and changes in its growth rate; the policy response will be different in the two cases. To illustrate this, consider the cases depicted in figure 1.[12] In both, $\dot{V}_1$ and $\dot{V}_2$ represent the growth rate of velocity before and after the hypothetical change at time t_0.

In the case of a permanent decline in the *level* of velocity that leaves the growth rates unaffected ($\dot{V}_1 = \dot{V}_2$), a policy response that accelerated the growth of money temporarily until the higher desired level is obtained and then returned money growth to its previous rate would produce an unvarying rate of growth in GNP. In the second case ($\dot{V}_2 < \dot{V}_1$), a compensatory and permanent increase in the growth rate of money at time t_0 is necessary to maintain the growth rate of GNP.

If policymakers failed to respond to the velocity changes depicted in figure 1, the consequences would

---

[10]This statement and much of the discussion that follows assumes a long-run neutrality of money; that is, changes in the growth rate of money have no lasting effect on the growth rate of real output. If money is not neutral in the long run, both the policy prescriptions and the effects of a failure to respond to velocity changes would differ accordingly.

[11]For example, at its meeting of November 16, 1982, the Federal Open Market Committee anticipated that M1 might grow due to a

temporary buildup of balances in M1 components for eventual placement in the new money market deposit accounts (MMDAs), which would become effective on December 14, 1982. Thus, the Committee anticipated a short-run decline in velocity resulting from this potential buildup. See "Record of Policy Actions of the FOMC," *Federal Reserve Bulletin* (January 1983), p. 19.

[12]A ratio scale for the natural log of velocity is presented in figure 1 so that the growth rates can be represented by the slopes of straight lines.

Chart 2

Rate of Velocity Change and its Average [1]

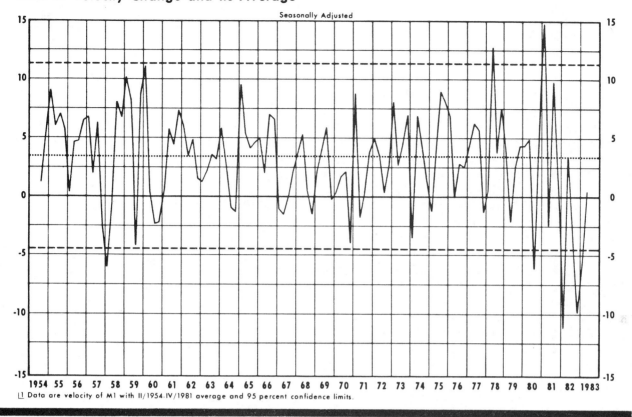

Seasonally Adjusted

[1] Data are velocity of M1 with II/1954–IV/1981 average and 95 percent confidence limits.

be different in the two cases. In the first (level-shift) case, there would be a *temporary* reduction in the rate of change of prices or real output, or both. In the long run, however, velocity would return to its former growth rate and, hence, so would the growth of nominal output. In the second case, the growth rate of prices would be lowered *permanently*; in addition, the growth rate of real output may be lowered temporarily if the monetary authority failed to adjust the growth rate of money in response to a permanent decline in velocity growth.

THE VARIABILITY OF VELOCITY

The timing of the policy response to the velocity change, of course, is very important. Unfortunately, it is difficult to determine whether there has been a significant change in velocity, let alone to foresee such a change. Furthermore, it is difficult to differentiate between level and growth rate shifts, and to differentiate between temporary and permanent changes.

In order to see why this might be the case, consider the historical movements in the growth rate of M1

velocity presented in chart 2. This chart shows the quarter-to-quarter growth rate of M1 velocity, a horizontal line showing the average growth rate of M1 velocity for the period II/1954–IV/1981, and dashed lines representing plus or minus two standard deviations of the quarter-to-quarter growth rate of velocity from its mean over this period.[13]

It is obvious that the quarter-to-quarter growth rate of velocity is highly variable. Nevertheless, it falls outside the range of plus or minus two standard deviations in four of the 111 quarters from II/1954–IV/1981. More recently, there have been three occasions during the last six quarters when the growth rate of velocity has fallen outside of this range. A priori, it is difficult to determine whether these apparent shifts are simply temporary movements in the growth rate associated with a permanent change in the level of velocity, a permanent change in the growth rate, or a temporary change in the growth rate associated with a temporary change in the level. Indeed, it is difficult to know

---

[13]If $\dot{V}$ is normally distributed, then approximately 95 percent of its observed values should fall within ±2 standard deviations.

whether these changes represent a significant change in velocity. It could be that other factors that affect velocity may have caused it to change. Thus, in order to determine whether a policy response is called for, it is necessary to examine the factors that determine velocity.

FACTORS THAT AFFECT VELOCITY

There are a number of factors that can cause velocity to change.[14] Since increased velocity is simply the ratio of nominal GNP to the stock of money, any factor that causes the stock of money to change relative to nominal output, or vice versa, can produce a change in the level of velocity. Likewise, any factor that causes the growth rate of money to change relative to the growth rate of nominal GNP, or vice versa, will cause the growth rate of velocity to change. Furthermore, since the growth rate of velocity is defined as the percentage change in the *level* of velocity per unit of time, factors that affect the level of velocity affect the growth rate if they likewise change through time. Thus, the following discussion will be carried out in terms of the level of velocity, unless otherwise stated.

Many of the factors that affect velocity can be analyzed easily by recognizing that velocity changes whenever people alter their holdings of money relative to their income. Factors that cause people to hold less money relative to their income increase velocity, while factors that cause people to increase their money holdings reduce it. For example, if two households have the same income and monthly expenditure patterns but one receives its income once a month while the other receives it twice a month, the latter, all other things constant, will hold less money on average than the one that receives income once a month. Thus, changes in the pattern of receipts and expenditures can produce changes in society's holdings of money relative to income.

Economizing on Money Balances

Other factors that cause individuals to economize on their holdings of money relative to income increase velocity. For example, the increased use of credit cards could reduce individuals' desires to hold money bal-

ances and, thus, increase velocity. In particular, these and other lines of credit may lessen individuals' desires to hold money as a contingency against uncertainty.[15]

Two of the most commonly cited factors that can cause changes in velocity are changes in real interest rates and expectations of inflation. Increases in the real interest rate tend to cause individuals to hold less money relative to their real income. The same generally will be true of an increase in the expected rate of inflation. Higher expected inflation will cause individuals to economize on their money holdings, raising velocity.

Financial Innovations

Financial innovations also can produce velocity changes. In general, innovations that reduce the implicit or explicit cost, or both, of transferring funds from non-transaction to transaction forms (perhaps by giving transaction characteristics to assets not included in M1) tend to increase the velocity of M1. Therefore, innovations such as money market deposit accounts and money market mutual funds would increase the velocity of M1 to the extent that they lower these costs.

In contrast, innovations that lower the cost of holding M1 relative to non-M1 assets tend to reduce the velocity of M1. This could be the case with automatic transfer of savings, negotiable order of withdrawal (NOW), and Super-NOW accounts.[16] Such innovations, however, may produce a temporary decline in velocity that lasts only until individuals realign their portfolios.

Cyclical Factors

Finally, there are a number of factors that can cause velocity to change with cyclical movements in real income (see appendix). They suggest that velocity tends to rise during periods of rising real income and fall during periods of declining real income.

Furthermore, there is considerable evidence that a change in money growth affects nominal income with a

---

[14]For discussions of some of these, see John A. Tatom, "Was the 1982 Velocity Decline Unusual?" this *Review* (August/September 1983), pp. 5–15; and William T. Gavin, "Velocity and Monetary Targets," *Economic Commentary*, Federal Reserve Bank of Cleveland (June 6, 1983).

[15]For a more detailed discussion, see Mack Ott, "Money, Credit and Velocity," this *Review* (May 1982), pp. 21–34. To date, however, there is little empirical support for this proposition about credit cards.

[16]John A. Tatom, "Recent Financial Innovations: Have They Distorted the Meaning of M1?" this *Review* (April 1982), pp. 23–35; and John A. Tatom, "Money Market Deposit Accounts, Super-NOWs and Monetary Policy," this *Review* (March 1983), pp. 5–16.

lag that is distributed over several quarters. Thus, an acceleration in money growth will produce a temporary decline in velocity as nominal output temporarily grows at a slower rate than does money. Thus, a decline in velocity associated with a recession can be exacerbated if the monetary authority expands money rapidly in order to stimulate a sluggish economy.

Permanent Vs. Temporary Effects

While all the factors mentioned above can affect velocity, they need not produce a lasting effect on its level or on its growth rate. For example, it is commonly recognized that, in a noninflationary environment, interest rates tend to be procyclical — rising during the expansion phase of the business cycle and declining during the contraction phase. Although the level of velocity and its growth rate can be affected by movements in interest rates, neither need change permanently; they, like such cyclical movements in interest rates, simply will average out over the course of a business cycle.

Also, financial innovations can have a permanent effect on the level of velocity but, perhaps, only a temporary effect on its growth rate. An innovation that lowers the cost of holding M1 relative to non-M1 assets induces a shift out of non-M1 into M1 assets, permanently lowering M1 velocity but reducing the growth rate only temporarily. Once the portfolios are realigned, the growth rate of velocity simply may resume its previous path.[17] Nevertheless, financial innovations can affect the extent to which velocity responds to changes in some of the other factors mentioned above.[18]

Forecasting Velocity Changes

Indeed, several economists have suggested recently that the seemingly unusual changes in velocity shown in chart 2 can be accounted for by cyclical movements in velocity and by changes in the inflation rate and interest rates.[19] This section does not attempt to evaluate these claims. Instead, the purpose here is to show that even when these factors are accounted for, it is difficult to forecast short-run changes in velocity.

To illustrate this point, the in-sample standard deviation of a model of velocity growth which recently appeared in this *Review* will be used as an estimate of the true one-quarter-ahead forecast error. The in-sample standard deviation is used to be conservative, and this model was selected because it incorporates many of the factors discussed above and because it performs well in forecasting velocity growth.[20] The in-sample standard deviation is about 2.0 percentage points. Thus, after accounting for factors that significantly influence velocity growth, the approximate 95 percent confidence interval for the forecast of velocity growth, $\dot{V}_f$, will be $\dot{V}_f \pm 2\,(2.0)$ or $\dot{V}_f \pm 4$.[21] This implies a fairly large margin for error. For example, if the forecast for velocity growth is 5 percent, then, loosely interpreted, actual velocity growth can be expected to be between 1 and 9 percent with high probability. This sizable margin for error demonstrates that the monetary authority will generally find it difficult to stabilize nominal output growth in the short run by offsetting short-run changes in velocity.[22]

Furthermore, the sizable error makes it difficult to determine whether a significant change in velocity has taken place. It takes a fairly large change in velocity growth to be significant enough to be considered unusual. Of course, the problems of discriminating between permanent and temporary shifts and between level and growth rate changes remain.

Demand or Inflation?" Federal Reserve Bank of San Francisco *Economic Review* (Spring 1983), pp. 12–19; and Milton Friedman, "Why a Surge of Inflation is Likely Next Year," *Wall Street Journal*, September 1, 1983. Though these economists generally agree on the factors affecting velocity, they disagree on the relative importance of the factors cited.

[20]The Tatom model has a smaller root-mean-squared error than the best univariate time series model recently reported by Hein and Veugelers, as well as a model which explains velocity growth with movements in real interest rates and the expected rate of inflation alone. See Tatom, "Was the 1982 Velocity Decline Unusual?"; and Scott E. Hein and Paul T. W. M. Veugelers, "Velocity Growth Predictability: A Time Series Perspective," this *Review* (October 1983), pp. 34–43.

[21]That is, approximately 95 percent of the intervals so constructed in one quarter would contain the value of velocity in the next. This simplified interpretation of the forecast interval tends to understate the margin of forecast error. See Robert S. Pindyck and Daniel L. Rubinfeld, *Econometric Models and Economic Forecasts* (McGraw-Hill, 1976), chapter 6.

[22]This result implies that recent suggestions that the Federal Reserve use nominal GNP as an intermediate target are ill-advised.

[17]For example, if individuals held expectations of inflation over a long period of time because of, say, excessive money growth, they might attempt to realign their portfolios continually in order to economize on money holdings and, as a result, the growth rate of velocity would be positive over this period.

[18]The availability of more and better substitutes for a commodity tends to increase its own and cross elasticities of demand. Thus, financial innovations affect velocity to the extent that they alter velocity's response to the above factors.

[19]See Tatom, "Was the 1982 Velocity Decline Unusual?"; John P. Judd, "The Recent Decline in Velocity: Instability of Money

SUMMARY AND CONCLUSIONS

This article outlines the meaning of income velocity and reviews its important role as the link between money growth and nominal GNP growth. It demonstrates the problems that the monetary authority faces if it attempts to offset short-run (quarter-to-quarter) changes in velocity growth. Indeed, it appears that, even if a conservative estimate of the one-quarter-ahead forecast standard deviation is used, the forecast errors are large for policy purposes. Thus, while it might seem desirable for the monetary authority to respond to permanent changes in the level or growth rate of velocity, it is difficult to predict such changes; or to verify them quickly *ex post*.

Appendix:
Cyclical Factors That Affect Velocity

The purpose of this appendix is to illustrate four factors that can produce movements in velocity associated with cyclical swings in GNP.

Measured Vs. Theoretical Velocity

Velocity as it is usually measured may differ from its theoretical counterpart. As a result, not all changes in measured velocity indicate true changes in velocity. To illustrate this, consider the common specification of the demand for nominal money,

(A.1) $M^d = f(P, \dot{p}^e, r, r^e, Y_p, Z)$,

where

P = the current price level

$\dot{p}^e$ = the expected future price level

r = the current real interest rate

r^e = the expected future real interest rate

Y_p = current nominal *permanent income*

Z = all other factors that affect money demand.[1]

It is usually assumed that individuals do not suffer from a money illusion (i.e., equation A.1 is homogenous of degree one in P and Y_p) so that equation A.1 can be written as

(A.2) $M^d/P = f(\dot{P}^e, r, r^e, Y_p/P, Z)$

or

(A.3) $m^d = f(\dot{P}^e, r, r^e, y_p, Z)$,

where m^d denotes the demand for *real* money balances and y_p denotes real permanent income. Now assume that A.3 is homogenous of degree s in real permanent income so that A.3 can be written as

(A.4) $m^d/(y_p)^s = f(\dot{P}^e, r, r^e, Z)$.

Further assume that s = 1, so that the theoretical measure of velocity, V*, is

$V^* = Y_p/M = 1/f(\dot{P}^e, r, r^e, Z)$.

Thus, if velocity is measured as Y/M, changes in measured velocity can occur that do not reflect changes in V*. Of course, estimates of Y_p could be used to get a better estimate of V*; however, this problem will continue to the extent that there are estimation errors. Moreover, the most commonly watched measure of velocity is Y/M.

Economies of Scale

Another problem arises when s ≠ 1. It is sometimes argued that the elasticity of the demand for real money balances with respect to real permanent income is less than one. If this is the case, the percentage change in real money balances will be less than the percentage change in real income. An increase in real income will result in a less than proportionate increase in the holding of real money and, hence, an increase in velocity. Thus, if there are cyclical movements in permanent income, velocity would rise during the expansion phase of the cycle and fall during the contraction phase. This would occur even if permanent income

---

[1]See Milton Friedman, "The Quantity Theory of Money: A Restatement," in *Studies in the Quantity Theory of Money* (University of Chicago Press, 1956).

were measured precisely. This factor also could account for a secular rise in velocity as real output expands. For example, if real output is growing at a 4 percent rate and the real income elasticity of the demand for real money is about one-half, then velocity would grow secularly at about a 2 percent rate.

Short-Run Adjustments of Money Demand

Another factor that can account for cyclical movements in velocity is the possibility of short-run adjustments of money demand. A change in one of the factors in f (·) alters an individual's demand for real money while leaving his actual holdings of real money unchanged. As a result, the individual must adjust actual money holdings to his new desired holdings. Such an adjustment is costly, so the adjustment may progress (perhaps slowly) over time. Theoretically, the speed at which this portfolio adjustment takes place depends on the cost of moving to the new equilibrium relative to the cost of being out of equilibrium: the higher the former cost relative to the latter, the slower the speed of adjustment.[2] If these adjustment costs are small, the adjustment will be rapid; however, most empirical estimates suggest a very slow adjustment.[3] In any event, if money demand does not adjust immediately,

an increase in real income can produce a smaller increase in the demand for money in the short run and, hence, a short-run increase in velocity. As the demand for money adjusts towards the new equilibrium, velocity will approach the level implied in A.4.

The above analysis rests in a disequilibrium between actual and desired money holdings. If such disequilibria exist, they also could be caused by real-side shocks, such as natural disasters, oil price shocks and the like.

Lags in the Effect of Money on Nominal Income

Another possibility is a lag effect from money to income.[4] That is, changes in the current money stock produce changes in nominal income with a lag that is distributed over several quarters. If this is the case, a change in the current money stock produces a less than proportional change in current nominal income and, hence, an initial decline in velocity. Thus, periods of relatively rapid money growth tend to be associated initially with declining velocity, while periods of relatively slow money growth tend to be associated initially with rising velocity. Taking this factor and previously mentioned factors into consideration, it could be argued that the decline in velocity during 1982 was precipitated by the decline in real economic activity and exacerbated by the rapid growth of M1 beginning III/1982.

[2]See Zvi Griliches, "Distributed Lags: A Survey," *Econometrica* (January 1967), pp. 16–49.

[3]For a discussion of this problem and some estimates of the speed of adjustment, see Daniel L. Thornton, "Maximum Likelihood Estimates of A Partial Adjustment-Adaptive Expectations Model of the Demand for Money," *Review of Economics and Statistics* (May 1982), pp. 225–29.

[4]If money were exogenous, then this lag would only result from a lagged response of money demand, such as that discussed above. In this instance, this and the previous factor would be identical.

What Has Happened to M1?

Herb Taylor*

During the course of the 1960s and 1970s there seemed to be a strong link between growth in the money supply, as measured by M1, and growth in economic activity, as measured by the gross national product (GNP). Throughout the 1970s, policymakers became more confident in this linkage and the Fed moved toward using M1 growth as an important monetary policy indicator and predictor of future economic performance. This movement culminated in the

Fed's October 1979 decision to switch its operating procedures and focus its efforts on achieving its announced annual money growth targets. But no sooner had the Fed begun to rely more heavily on M1 than the relationship between M1 growth and GNP growth seemed to fall apart. Thus far in the 1980s, growth in the money supply has produced far less growth in nominal GNP than would have been expected on the basis of the previous twenty years' experience. As a result, the Fed has backed away from targeting money growth, at least until the sources of the apparent breakdown in the M1-GNP linkage can be identified.

*Herb Taylor is a Senior Economist in the Research Department of the Federal Reserve Bank of Philadelphia.

Measuring the extent to which the M1-GNP relationship has broken down recently is easy enough to do; explaining the breakdown is more difficult. The many unusual economic and financial circumstances that we have experienced in the last few years provide a variety of potential explanations. But one approach to linking GNP growth to money growth and other key economic variables offers some opportunity to assess the possibilities. Evidence based on this approach is consistent with the view that GNP's responsiveness to money growth has been reduced, at least temporarily, by a combination of declining inflation expectations and recent deposit market deregulation.

THE RELATIONSHIP BETWEEN M1 AND GNP HAS BROKEN DOWN . . .

One of the easiest ways to characterize the relationship that prevailed between M1 and GNP during the 1960s and 1970s—and to document its breakdown in the 1980s—is to look at the performance of what is often called a St. Louis-type equation.[1] The idea behind the St. Louis approach is to link GNP growth directly to a number of key economic variables whose movements reflect changes in domestic stabilization policy and international economic conditions. Empirical estimates of St. Louis equations suggest that for the period of the 1960s and 1970s little is to be gained by expanding the list of these key variables beyond two: growth in the M1 measure of the money stock and growth in cyclically adjusted government expenditures.[2] Between these two variables,

money growth is clearly the dominant influence. Although different statistical procedures suggest different quarter-to-quarter patterns in the response of GNP growth to changes in the policy variables, the end result is almost always found to be the same: a percentage point increase in M1 ultimately produces a percentage point increase in GNP, while the initially positive impact of an increase in government spending ultimately disappears.[3]

When St. Louis equations are applied to the 1980s it is apparent that money growth has not been eliciting the GNP response that it used to. For instance, when a standard St. Louis equation estimated on the basis of our experience during the 1960s and 1970s is fed the money growth and cyclically adjusted government expenditures growth for the 1980s, it predicts GNP growth of about 11½ percent per year between 1980 and 1985. In fact, GNP growth averaged only about 8 percent per year, so money growth has been overpredicting GNP growth by an average 3½ percentage points over the last six years. The pattern of forecast errors that the standard equation produces is shown in Figure 1: GNP responds to money growth about as predicted in 1980; then 1981 begins a three-year period during which money growth substantially overpredicts GNP growth; 1984 marks an apparent return to the historical link between money and GNP growth; then in 1985 money growth again overpredicts GNP growth by a wide margin. The

[1] The St. Louis equation was originally presented in Leonall C. Anderson and Jerry Jordan, "Monetary and Fiscal Policy Actions: A Test of their Relative Importance in Economic Stabilization," Federal Reserve Bank of St. Louis *Review* (November 1968) pp. 11-24. An excellent summary of subsequent developments in the estimation of the St. Louis equation appears in Dallas S. Batten and Daniel L. Thornton, "Polynomial Distributed Lags and the Estimation of the St. Louis Equation," Federal Reserve Bank of St. Louis *Review* (April 1983) pp. 13-25.

[2] The growth of total government expenditures is an inappropriate measure of independent, or exogenous, fiscal policy actions affecting GNP growth because some government

expenditures are affected by GNP growth. Expenditures for unemployment compensation and other income maintenance programs, for example, automatically grow more rapidly when the economy moves into recession and GNP growth slows; then their growth automatically slows as the economy expands and GNP growth picks up. The high employment, or cyclically adjusted, measure of government expenditures attempts to eliminate this automatic response component.

[3] These conclusions about the relative impact of stabilization policies are supported by an exhaustive study of alternative specifications reported in Dallas S. Batten and Daniel L. Thornton, "How Robust Are the Policy Conclusions of the St. Louis Equation? Some Further Evidence," Federal Reserve Bank of St. Louis *Review* (June/July 1984) pp. 26-33.

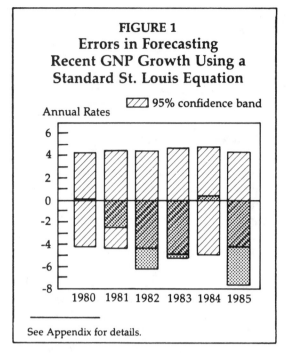

FIGURE 1
Errors in Forecasting Recent GNP Growth Using a Standard St. Louis Equation

Annual Rates   ⬛ 95% confidence band

See Appendix for details.

overpredictions of GNP growth in 1982 and 1985 represent significant breaks with the past M1-GNP relationship by usual statistical standards. As Figure 1 shows, both of these overpredictions exceed estimated 95 percent confidence bands. We would expect to see such large forecasting errors less than 5 percent of the time if the relationship that prevailed in the 1960s and 1970s were still operating.[4]

...AND IT IS DIFFICULT TO SAY JUST WHY...

Unfortunately, while the magnitude and pattern of the apparent breakdown in the M1-GNP relationship is clear, its cause is not. So many unusual economic and financial developments have arisen over the past several years that it is difficult to isolate the impact of each. Deposit market deregulation, particularly the nationwide authorization of NOW accounts in 1981 and Super-NOW accounts in 1983, seems likely to

have altered the M1-GNP relationship, at least temporarily. But the change in the public's inflation outlook since the inflation rate peaked in 1980-81 could be altering the responsiveness of GNP to M1 growth as well. On top of that, back-to-back recessions in 1980 and 1981-82, federal budget deficits hovering around $200 billion since 1982, and a trade deficit that widened to nearly $100 billion in 1985 are all symptomatic of more fundamental changes that could be exerting an unusually strong influence on GNP growth and obscuring its link to the growth of M1. Some further results based on the St. Louis approach can help us assess whether some combination of deregulation and declining inflation expectations have reduced GNP's responsiveness to M1 growth, or whether unusual economic conditions have simply made that responsiveness more difficult to see.

The Long Recession. While monetary and fiscal policies influence the overall level of demand for goods and services, producers' response to that demand varies over the business cycle. During economic expansions, output tends to increase by more than sales, and inventories of goods accumulate. When the economy goes into recession, output tends to decline by more than sales as producers work off the accumulated inventories. Since GNP includes both final sales and producers' additions to inventories, GNP figures tend to overstate the growth in demand during expansions and to understate it during recessions. As a result, money growth usually underpredicts GNP growth during expansions and overpredicts it during recessions. So money's large overpredictions of GNP growth in the 1980s may simply reflect the fact that, for whatever reason, the economy spent a larger proportion of time in recession during the 1980s than it did during the the 1960s and 1970s.[5]

---

[4]The Appendix provides a detailed description of the statistical analysis that produced the results shown in Figure 1 and in subsequent figures in this article.

[5]This business cycle explanation for the recent breakdown in the M1-GNP relationship is analyzed extensively in Lawrence J. Radecki and John Wenninger, "Recent Instability in M1's Velocity," Federal Reserve Bank of New York *Quarterly Review* (Autumn 1985) pp.16-22.

One way to assess whether an unusual business cycle pattern helps account for the apparent breakdown in the M1-GNP linkage is to subtract inventories from GNP and examine the behavior of final sales. If the business cycle explanation is correct, then money growth and government spending ought to continue to predict final sales reliably during the 1980s even though their GNP predictions go awry. But when a St. Louis-type equation linking growth in the money supply and cyclically adjusted government expenditures to growth in final sales is used to forecast into the 1980s, it turns out that this relationship has broken down as well (see Figure 2). The pattern of the errors in predicting final sales growth was somewhat different from the pattern in predicting GNP growth, but the average amount by which money growth overpredicted growth in final sales over the period was about the same as it was for GNP. So it seems that the prolonged

period of recession in the early 1980s does little to explain the diminished response of GNP to M1 growth that we have experienced thus far in the decade.

Taxes. Fiscal policymakers have two tools at their disposal, spending and taxation, and theoretically both could affect the level of GNP. St. Louis-type equations typically include only changes in cyclically adjusted government spending, because changes in cyclically adjusted tax revenues did not seem to contribute much statistically to the determination of GNP growth during the 1960s and 1970s. But under the Reagan Administration, tax policy has been subject to more substantive changes than in the recent past and now may be exerting a stronger independent influence on GNP.

On balance, tax law changes enacted in 1981 and 1982 have sharply reduced tax revenues relative to government spending—as the size of recent federal budget deficits attests. Some have claimed that these large deficits tend to raise interest rates and "crowd out" private credit demands, thus reducing the overall level of spending and GNP. A more conventional analysis suggests that the tax cuts' most important effect is to increase disposable income and hence boost overall spending and GNP. In either case, failing to take account of the impact of taxes could distort our picture of the observed M1-GNP relationship in the 1980s. To investigate this possibility, a St. Louis-type equation incorporating the impact of cyclically adjusted government tax revenues was used to forecast GNP growth over the 1980s. As Figure 3 shows, including tax revenues reduces the equation's average errors somewhat, but it does not alter the basic pattern of the breakdown in the linkage between M1 and GNP. Clearly, taxes are not the whole story.[6]

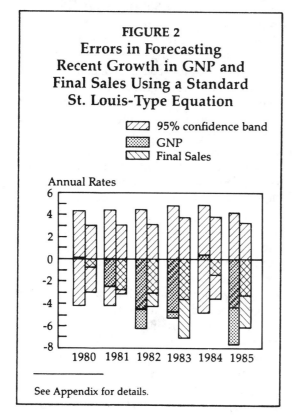

FIGURE 2
Errors in Forecasting Recent Growth in GNP and Final Sales Using a Standard St. Louis-Type Equation

ZZZ 95% confidence band
GNP
Final Sales

Annual Rates

See Appendix for details.

---

[6]Changes in the tax code could have altered GNP not only by changing the overall level of tax revenues but also by changing individuals' and businesses' economic incentives and hence the structure of the economy. The St. Louis approach used here, like most macroeconometric models, cannot provide much help in assessing this possibility. It

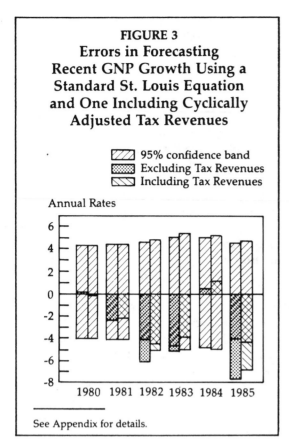

FIGURE 3
Errors in Forecasting
Recent GNP Growth Using a
Standard St. Louis Equation
and One Including Cyclically
Adjusted Tax Revenues

◰ 95% confidence band
▦ Excluding Tax Revenues
◨ Including Tax Revenues

Annual Rates

See Appendix for details.

Trade. In principle the nation's GNP is affected not only by domestic monetary and fiscal policies, but by economic developments abroad as well. Some of the goods and services produced in the U.S. are exported to foreigners whose demands for them depend primarily on economic conditions in their own countries. In order to take this into account, St. Louis equations sometimes include growth in exports as an inde-

would seem, however, that the tax breaks for investment spending and the lower marginal tax rates on personal income that the tax law changes included would contribute to unusually strong, rather than unusually weak, GNP growth. A good discussion of the relevant tax law changes and their implications for individuals and businesses can be found in two recent articles by Stephen A. Meyer in this *Business Review:* "Tax Cuts: Reality or Illusion?" (July/August 1983) pp. 3-16 and "Tax Policy Effects on Investment: The 1981 and 1982 Tax Acts," (November/December 1984) pp. 3-14.

pendent determinant of GNP growth along with growth in the money supply and government expenditures. When they do, fluctuations in export demand seem to contribute little to fluctuations in GNP growth over the 1960s and 1970s. But, as with taxes, this situation may have reversed itself in the 1980s. The relatively slow economic recoveries in other industrialized countries and the well-publicized debt problems of some of the less industrialized countries have depressed the demand for U.S. exports over the past several years. The drag on GNP growth created by this unusually weak export demand may explain the apparent weakness in the response of GNP to recent money growth. To test this possibility, a St. Louis-type equation that includes growth in exports was used to forecast GNP growth for the 1980s. The results, presented in Figure 4a, indicate that taking account of foreign economic conditions, as reflected in U.S. export growth, does little to explain the unexpectedly slow growth in GNP in the 1980s.

Of course, some recent international developments—those affecting exchange rates and the value of the dollar—could have contributed to unusually low GNP growth by boosting our imports as well as reducing our exports. After declining steadily in value during the 1970s, the dollar rose sharply against other major currencies between 1980 and early 1985. This dollar appreciation made U.S.-produced goods expensive relative to foreign-produced goods, and thus not only reduced foreign demand for U.S. exports but also increased U.S. demand for foreign imports—a combination that has produced record trade deficits in the U.S. To the extent that the dollar's strength has come from an independent increase in foreign demand for dollar-denominated assets—perhaps occasioned by renewed confidence in the American economy or increased uncertainty about those of other nations—it would have done more than usual to increase our demand for imports, and hence more than usual to depress GNP growth.

If recent international developments have contributed to the apparent M1-GNP breakdown by creating an extraordinary U.S. demand for imports, then we would expect U.S. import expenditures to grow more rapidly than domestic monetary and fiscal policies would dictate. But when a St. Louis-type equation linking growth in the money supply and cyclically adjusted government expenditures to growth in import expenditures is used to predict into the 1980s, the results do not indicate that the growth in import expenditures has been unusually strong in the 1980s. In fact, the forecast errors, shown in Figure 4b, indicate that, if anything, U.S. import expenditures have been growing more slowly than expected over the last six years.[7] In short, international trade developments do not seem to be responsible for the apparent breakdown in the relationship between money growth and GNP growth.[8]

... BUT IT SEEMS THAT DISINFLATION AND DEREGULATION HAVE BROKEN THE M1-GNP LINK

We have explored the possibility that the historical relationship between GNP growth and M1 growth has been obscured lately by the unusually strong impact of other economic developments and we have come up empty. So it seems that

---

[7]Perhaps the most prominent feature on the international economic landscape over the past several years has been OPEC and its impact on the relative price of oil. In theory, it is not obvious that changing oil prices should have any impact on the relationship between money and GNP growth. Empirically, when growth in the relative price of energy was included in a St. Louis-type equation, it produced no significant improvement in the equation's forecasting performance. This is consistent with the findings in John A. Tatom, "Energy Prices and Short-Run Economic Performance," Federal Reserve Bank of St. Louis *Review* (January 1981) pp. 3-17. Tatom found that increases in the relative price of energy had only a small and transitory effect on GNP growth.

[8]In principle, it is possible that all of the factors we have discussed thus far, when taken together, explain the apparent breakdown in the M1-GNP relationship. To evaluate this possibility, equations linking GNP and final sales growth to growth in M1, cyclically adjusted government expenditures and revenues, and exports, were used to forecast into the 1980s. This produced no substantive change in the pattern of the errors or their statistical significance.

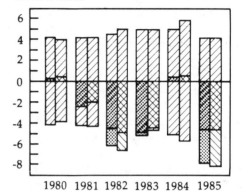

FIGURE 4a

Errors in Forecasting Recent GNP Growth Using a Standard St. Louis Equation and One Including Growth in Exports

95% confidence band
Excluding Exports
Including Exports

Annual Rates

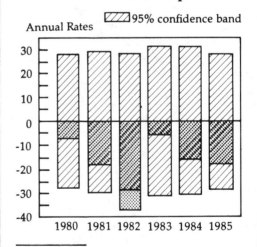

FIGURE 4b

Errors in Forecasting Import Growth Using a Standard St. Louis Equation

95% confidence band

Annual Rates

See Appendix for details.

GNP growth has indeed become less responsive to growth in M1 than it used to be. Two recent phenomena offer plausible explanations for the change: a new inflation outlook and deposit market deregulation. Both would reduce the responsiveness of GNP to increases in the supply of money essentially by increasing the public's demand for money at the same time. Money supply increases that simply accommodate such increases in money demand do nothing to stimulate spending and raise GNP in the usual way. And while direct evidence is difficult to accumulate, the indirect evidence we have suggests that recent declines in GNP's responsiveness to M1 growth represent some combination of these two influences.

Inflation Expectations. The amount of money that people want to hold in their portfolios depends partly on the volume of transactions that they intend to carry out and partly on the rate of return that it pays relative to other financial assets. The more transactions people plan to undertake, the more money they want to have available. On the other hand, the wider the spread between the rates of interest on various financial instruments and any return that money might offer, the smaller the proportion of their portfolio people want to devote to money. One important determinant of market interest rates is the expected rate of inflation. The higher the rate of inflation people expect down the road, the higher market interest rates go, as lenders attempt to preserve the purchasing power of the funds in which they will be repaid.[9] So, in short, high rates of expected inflation, by putting upward pressure on market interest rates, tend to reduce the public's demand for money. Low expected inflation rates, on the other hand, by allowing market interest rates to fall, help raise the public's demand for money. There is some evidence that

during the 1960s and 1970s the public took higher current money growth as an indicator of higher future money growth, and hence higher future inflation.[10] This direct effect of money growth on inflation expectations would have amplified its impact on GNP growth by tending to raise market interest rates and thus reducing growth in money demand. In recent years, however, the public's inflation outlook seems to have changed. After the Fed's intense battle against inflation beginning in 1979 and the prolonged period of recession during which inflation was wrung from the economy in the early 1980s, people became less likely to interpret more rapid current money growth as indicative of an inflationary trend. Without its boost to inflation expectations, and hence market interest rates, more rapid money growth would do less to slow growth in money demand, and hence less to stimulate spending and increase GNP growth than in more inflationary times.

Attempts to accumulate evidence on the impact of changing inflation expectations on the M1-GNP relationship are handicapped by data problems. While the rate of inflation people actually experience can be measured simply by collecting information about the prices of available goods and services, the rate of inflation people expect to experience cannot be observed so directly. Therefore, analysts often rely on survey-based measures of inflation expectations, despite surveys' widely recognized imperfections. But at least one measure, which is based on the semiannual Livingston Survey, offers some support for the role of changing inflation expectations in the M1-GNP breakdown.

Every June and December since 1946, Joseph Livingston, business columnist with *The Philadelphia Inquirer*, has been polling economists on their outlook for the economy six months to a

---

[9]A more detailed discussion of how market interest rates respond to changes in the expected rate of inflation can be found in Herbert Taylor, "Interest Rates: How Much Does Expected Inflation Matter?" this *Business Review* (July/August 1982) pp. 3-12.

[10]Empirical support for the role of money growth in the formation of inflation expectations can be found in Donald J. Mullineaux, "Inflation Expectations and Money Growth in the United States," *American Economic Review* (March 1980) pp. 149-161.

year down the road. The average of their forecasts for changes in the Consumer Price Index is a widely used measure of inflation expectations in the economy. An analysis of this series' behavior indicates a significant positive relationship between inflation expectations and money growth during the 1960s and 1970s. When that relationship is used to predict into the 1980s, however, we find that the expected rate of inflation has been persistently lower than money growth during the 1980s would imply. As shown in Figure 5, money growth most substantially overpredicted the changes in expected inflation during a three-year period beginning in 1980. Considering the lags in money's impact on GNP, this period of uncharacteristic decline in inflation expectations could be particularly helpful in explaining the substantial decline in GNP's responsiveness to M1 growth during the three-year period beginning in 1981. On the other hand, declining inflation expectations do not seem to have played such a major role in the 1985 M1-GNP breakdown. It seems that dereg-

ulation figured more prominently in this more recent episode.

Deregulation. While declining inflation expectations seem to have boosted the public's demand for money one way—by reducing rates of interest on other financial assets—deposit market deregulation has been doing it the other way—by raising rates of return on money itself. Prior to 1980, most people had to hold their money either in currency or in regular checking accounts on which banks are prohibited from paying any interest. But with the nationwide authorization of NOW and Super-NOW accounts, banks and thrift institutions can now offer individuals interest on their checkable deposits.[11] Thus deregulation has effectively raised the return on money relative to other assets and, consequently, increased the amount of money people want to keep on hand. Increases in the money supply that simply accommodate this increase in money demand would do nothing to stimulate additional spending and raise GNP in the usual way. As a result, forecasts based on the historical relationship between money growth and GNP—such as those from the St. Louis equations—would tend to overpredict GNP growth during the period of adjustment to the deregulated environment.

To some extent, the St. Louis equations' overpredictions of GNP growth that we found may reflect the initial impact of changes in deposit market regulations. NOW accounts were authorized nationwide in December 1980, Super-NOW accounts were introduced with a $2,500 minimum balance restriction in January 1983, and the regulatory minimum balance on Super-NOWs was reduced to $1,000 in January 1985. Each

---

FIGURE 5
Errors in Forecasting the Change in Inflation Expectations on the Basis of Recent Monetary Growth

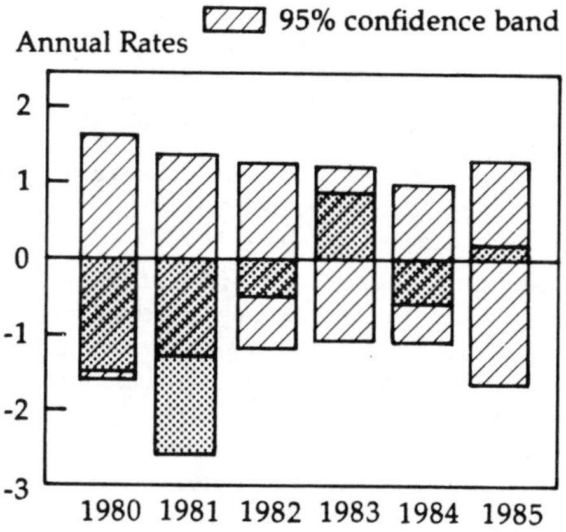

See Appendix for details.

---

[11]NOW accounts became available in New England as early as 1972. The authorization to offer NOWs was extended to depository institutions in New York in 1978 and in New Jersey in 1979. ATS accounts also were authorized in 1978. The Monetary Control Act of 1980 not only allowed all commercial banks, mutual savings banks, and savings and loans to offer NOWs, but also allowed credit unions to offer interest-bearing checking accounts, called share drafts.

step expanded individuals' opportunity to earn a rate of return on their checking account balances that is closer to the rate of return on other financial assets. This narrowing spread not only encouraged people to switch from their old regular checking accounts to the newer accounts, but encouraged them to keep larger balances in those new accounts as well. Thus, the new accounts boosted the public's overall demand for money and the amount of money that the Fed would need to supply to maintain GNP.

In addition to the initial impact of their introduction, the new accounts may have further diminished the response of GNP to money growth by increasing the sensitivity of the public's demand for money to declines in market interest rates. With NOWs and Super-NOWs paying a relatively high rate of interest, recent declines in market rates have made the spread between the return on money and the return on other assets much narrower than in the past, and hence created an unusually strong incentive for individuals to hold additional money balances. For instance, between 1984 and 1985 market interest rates on short-term securities declined from roughly 11 percent to about 7 percent. This decline leaves the spread between market rates and the rate on regular checking accounts, which pay no interest, at 7 percent, but it reduces the spread on Super-NOW accounts paying 6 percent interest to a single percentage point. With the cost of holding money rather than short-term financial assets so low, Super-NOW depositors find that there is little payoff to actively managing their accounts so as to minimize the share of money in their portfolios. So they are much more inclined to let their average money balances rise than they would be if they still held regular checking accounts. As a result, the Fed would have to create a larger increase in the money supply than it did previously in order to bring market interest rates down and stimulate new spending.[12]

The complexity of the deregulation process makes it difficult to pinpoint the timing and the magnitude of its impact on the public's demand for money.[13] But the idea that deregulation has thus altered the M1-GNP relationship is supported by the recent behavior of the broader monetary aggregates. Presumably, a portion of the funds households choose to shift into NOW and Super-NOW accounts are funds that they previously would have held in small time and savings deposits or other relatively liquid assets. But the public's holdings of many of these "near money" assets are already included in the broader money measures, M2 and M3. Consequently the shifts of funds induced by the introduction of NOWs and Super-NOWs should not affect M2 or M3 and their relationship to GNP by as much as they affect M1 and its relationship to GNP.

To evaluate whether it is, in fact, primarily M1's relationship to GNP that has broken down recently, St. Louis-type equations estimated with M2 and M3 growth in place of M1 growth were used to forecast GNP growth over the 1980s. The results, shown in Figure 6, indicate that in general the broader aggregates, particularly M3, do a better job of predicting GNP growth than does M1 over the last six years. So it seems that the breakdown in the relationship between money and GNP has centered on M1, as the deregulation explanation implies. The relative performances of the three aggregates during 1985 in particular, are consistent with the idea

statement in Thomas D. Simpson, "Changes in the Financial System:Implications for Monetary Policy," *Brookings Papers on Economic Activity* 1 (1984) pp. 249-265.

[13]Simpson's *Brookings* paper offers estimates of the magnitude of recent changes in the public's demand for M1. For a presentation of similar evidence and a discussion of some of the difficulties in linking the changes to deregulation, see Rik W. Hafer, "Monetary Stabilization Policy: Evidence from the Money Demand Forecasts," Federal Reserve Bank of St. Louis *Review* (May 1985) pp. 21-26. A thorough review of recent money demand behavior is provided by Robert J. Gordon, "The Short-Run Demand for Money: A Reconsideration," *Journal of Money, Credit, and Banking* (November 1984, Part I) pp. 403-434.

[12]This rationale for the heightened sensitivity of money demand to interest rate movements is given a more formal

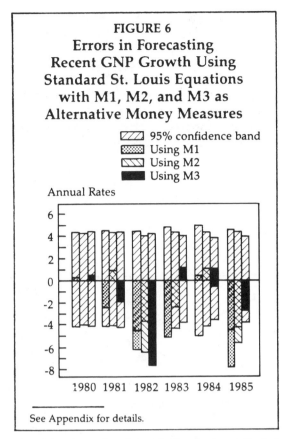

FIGURE 6
Errors in Forecasting Recent GNP Growth Using Standard St. Louis Equations with M1, M2, and M3 as Alternative Money Measures

95% confidence band
Using M1
Using M2
Using M3

Annual Rates

See Appendix for details.

that deposit market deregulation has contributed significantly to the breakdown in the M1-GNP link by increasing the sensitivity of the public's demand for money to interest rate declines. Figure 6 also shows one noteworthy exception to the overall superior performance of M2 and M3. In 1982 all of the aggregates overpredicted GNP growth by a significant margin and the broader aggregates did worse than M1. This reinforces the view that changing inflation expectations contributed significantly to the M1-GNP breakdown around that time.[14]

---

[14]In principle, deposit market deregulation and the changes in the public's demand for money that it creates could affect GNP's response not only to changes in the supply of money but to changes in fiscal policy or international economic developments as well. The test results presented in previous sections did not allow for this possi-

WHAT WILL HAPPEN TO M1?

A significant change in the observed relationship between GNP growth and growth in M1 has occurred during the 1980s, and conclusive evidence as to its cause eludes us. But the St. Louis approach illustrates the magnitude of the breakdown in the M1-GNP linkage and provides some avenues for assessing the possible explanations for it. The evidence based on this approach is consistent with the view that money's impact on GNP is not being obscured by an unusually strong influence from some other economic forces—such as fiscal policy or the international economic situation. Rather it seems that the responsiveness of GNP growth to M1 growth has actually declined, and that the decline has been the result of deposit market deregulation combined with changing inflation expectations. Optimism about the inflation outlook, by helping to bring market interest rates down, and deregulation, by helping to bring interest rates on checkable deposits up, have worked to boost the public's demand for M1. As a result, increases in the supply of M1 have stimulated less of a spending increase than they would have in the past.

Indications are that 1986 will mark another year in which GNP's response to money growth will fall short of predictions based on the experience of the 1960s and 1970s. But if we have put our finger on the right combination of factors behind the recent breakdown, then a predictable link between M1 and GNP growth may soon re-emerge. The deregulation process itself is over; remaining regulations limiting individuals' opportunities to earn competitive interest on their deposits were eliminated this year. Changes in the public's money management practices engendered by deregulation should begin winding down as well. The spread between the interest

---

bility. However, when the forecast errors from the standard St. Louis equation were correlated with recent growth in the money supply, cyclically adjusted government expenditures and taxes, and exports, only the correlations with money growth were statistically significant. This suggests that it is GNP's response to money growth that has changed over the past six years.

rates on the new checking accounts and the interest rates on other financial assets has already been substantially narrowed and, in the future, competition should induce depository institutions to adjust the rates they pay on these accounts as other market rates change. As for inflation expectations, while it is difficult to foresee how money growth will influence the public's inflation outlook in the future, the big changes seem to have occurred in the early 1980s and are now behind us. Of course, the linkage between M1 growth and GNP growth that ultimately emerges may not correspond exactly to the one that we observed in the 1960s and 1970s. But the key long-run link between money growth and GNP growth—that each percentage point increase in the money supply ultimately produces a percentage point increase in GNP—should reemerge.

APPENDIX

A standard St. Louis equation specification might be written:

$$GNP_t = \alpha + \beta(d,q)M1_t + \gamma(d,q)G_t + e_t$$

where GNP_t = seasonally adjusted quarterly GNP growth

$M1_t$ = seasonally adjusted quarterly M1 growth

G_t = cyclically adjusted government expenditures growth

e_t = random error

α represents a constant; $\beta(d,q)$ and $\gamma(d,q)$ are polynomial distributed lags of q quarters and degree d.

In order to quantify the relationship between GNP and M1 during the 1960s and 1970s, St. Louis equations were estimated for the sample period 1963:II through 1979:IV (excluding lags), using ordinary least squares (OLS) regression. Precise specifications were chosen with a grid search procedure. First, the maximum number of quarters to be included in the distributed lags was set at 5 quarters and the specification with the combination of lag length and polynomial degree which minimized the estimated standard error of the regression was selected. Then the maximum number of lags was set at 9 quarters and the process was repeated—similarly with maximum lags of 13 and 17 quarters. The four equations thus selected were then used to construct annual GNP forecasts for the period 1980 through 1985. Because the annual forecasting properties of the four equations were so similar, only the results for equations estimated using up to 9 quarters are reported in this article.

NOTES TO FIGURES

Figure 1. The equation used to construct these forecasts had the following estimated constant and sums of the distributed lag coefficients (standard errors appear in parentheses):

α = 2.16 $\Sigma\beta(6,7)$ = .953 $\Sigma\gamma(7,7)$ = .122
 (1.86)   (.291)   (.121)

Along with the R^2, the standard error of the regression (σ_e) and the Durbin-Watson statistic (DW) for the equation were:

R^2 = .42 σ_e = 3.62   DW = 2.10

Figure 2. In the final sales equation, growth of final sales, measured by GNP less additions to inventories, replaced growth in GNP as the dependent variable in a St. Louis-type equation. Estimating the equation over the 1963:II through 1979:IV sample period produced the following results:

$$\alpha = 2.26 \qquad \Sigma\beta(6,7) = .952 \qquad \Sigma\gamma(7,7) = .150$$
$$(1.39) \qquad\qquad (.210) \qquad\qquad (.087)$$
$$R^2 = .51 \qquad \sigma_e = 2.62 \qquad DW = 2.08$$

Figure 3. The estimated equation used to generate these forecasts was of the form:

$$GNP = \alpha + \beta(d,q)M1_t + \gamma(d,q)G_t + \delta(d,q)R_t + e_t$$

where R_t = cyclically adjusted government tax revenue growth.
The results of OLS regression over the sample period 1963:II through 1979:IV are:

$$\alpha = 3.01 \qquad \Sigma\beta(6,7) = .788 \qquad \Sigma\gamma(7,7) = .070 \qquad \Sigma\delta(2,2) = .083$$
$$(1.53) \qquad\qquad (.308) \qquad\qquad (.127) \qquad\qquad (.063)$$
$$R^2 = .45 \qquad \sigma_e = 3.60 \qquad DW = 2.10$$

Figure 4a. The estimated equation used to generate the forecasts was of the form:

$$GNP = \alpha + \beta(d,q)M1_t + \gamma(d,q)G_t + \xi(d,q)XP_t + e_t$$

where XP = growth in dollar expenditures on U.S. exports of goods and services.
The OLS regression results for the period 1963:II through 1979:IV were:

$$\alpha = 2.57 \qquad \Sigma\beta(6,7) = 1.031 \qquad \Sigma\gamma(7,7) = .069 \qquad \Sigma\xi(9,9) = .019$$
$$(1.89) \qquad\qquad (.335) \qquad\qquad (.127) \qquad\qquad (.065)$$
$$R^2 = .59 \qquad \sigma_e = 3.36 \qquad DW = 1.89$$

Figure 4b. A standard St. Louis-type equation was used to link M1 and cyclically adjusted government expenditure growth to growth in U.S. expenditures on imported goods and services. The estimated relationship based on OLS regression over the period 1963:II through 1979:IV was:

$$\alpha = -4.54 \qquad \Sigma\beta(2,7) = 3.98 \qquad \Sigma\dot\gamma(3,7) = -.037$$
$$(11.70) \qquad\qquad (1.76) \qquad\qquad (.737)$$
$$R^2 = .13 \qquad \sigma_e = 22.17 \qquad DW = 2.40$$

Figure 5. An inflation expectations formation model of the form:

$$\mathit{\Pi}_t^e - \mathit{\Pi}_{t-1}^e = \phi + \theta(d,q)M1_t + n_t$$

where $\mathit{\Pi}_t^e$ is the 6-month-ahead Livingston survey inflation forecast and n_t represents a random error, was estimated for the period 1963:II through 1979:IV. The OLS results were:

$$\phi = -.503 \qquad \Sigma\theta(4,5) = .207$$
$$(.490) \qquad\qquad (.112)$$
$$R^2 = .33 \qquad \sigma_n = .641 \qquad DW = n/a \qquad obs = 34$$

Figure 6. Standard St. Louis equations in which M2 and M3 replaced M1 as the money measure were estimated over the period 1963:II through 1979:IV using OLS. The results were:

M2

$$\alpha = -.37 \qquad \beta(9,9) = 1.028 \qquad \gamma(6,6) = .061$$
$$(2.36) \qquad\qquad (.250) \qquad\qquad (.115)$$
$$R^2 = .45 \qquad \sigma_e = 3.61 \qquad DW = 2.11$$

M3

$$\alpha = 1.40 \qquad \beta(4,6) = .593 \qquad \gamma(7,8) = .209$$
$$(2.11) \qquad\qquad (.179) \qquad\qquad (.132)$$
$$R^2 = .37 \qquad \sigma_e = 3.71 \qquad DW = 2.04$$

Section Five

Monetary Theory

The readings in this section focus on the long run: what eventual effects monetary and fiscal policies have on the economy, why policy evolves over time in the way it does, and how the current institutional arrangements can be improved.

Milton Friedman opens this section with "The Case for Overhauling the Federal Reserve." He begins by offering suggestions for improving the short-run conduct of monetary policy. These modifications preserve the basic institutional features of monetary policy, seeking only to fine-tune Fed operations. More drastic proposals follow. Among them are to legally require the Fed to increase the money supply by some amount each year and to end the Fed's independence by converting it into a bureau of Treasury. These suggestions culminate in the proposal to freeze the amount of high-powered money.

Robert E. Lucas, Jr., and Thomas J. Sargent indict the Keynesian approach to macroeconomic policy and offer an alternative equilibrium approach in "After Keynesian Macroeconomics." They argue forcefully that conventional macroeconometric models are fatally flawed: Not only have these models been spectacular failures, but their lack of a sound theoretical or econometric foundation precludes their ever being of any value in guiding policy. The authors then outline the principles that more satisfactory models should embody. Among them are rational behavior and allowing the private sector to respond optimally to changes in the policy environment. One implication of this approach is that it regards policy as being the choice of stable rules of the economic game, as opposed to the choice of particular numerical values for monetary and fiscal policy tools from period to period.

In "Can Policy Activism Succeed? A Public Choice Perspective," current Nobel Laureate James M. Buchanan suggests that the political economy of macroeconomic policy must be changed in order to achieve success. Attitudinal, educational, and statistical improvements are unlikely to help much. Without institutional or constitutional reform, policy is likely to continue to reflect short-run pressures at the expense of long-run success. Buchanan's argument leads him to propose that monetary and fiscal authorities be governed by constitutional constraints like a fixed growth rate rule for the money supply and a balanced budget amendment.

Alex Cukierman surveys the two main categories of models that explain how monetary policies are arrived at in his article "Central Bank Behavior and

Credibility: Some Recent Theoretical Developments." Both the political approach and the social welfare function approach incorporate the motives, constraints, and information of the central bank and the public. Each approach implies that the central bank is likely to be biased toward inflation.

The last selection on the longer-run aspects of economic policy is Preston J. Miller's "Higher Deficit Policies Lead to Higher Inflation." The article points to three avenues through which higher cyclically adjusted government deficits lead to inflation. The first possibility is that higher deficits may lead to faster money growth, either because the Fed chooses to accommodate deficits or because it is effectively forced to print money to prevent the government from becoming insolvent. The second avenue is through crowding out. Higher deficits raise real interest rates and thereby lower real output growth. Given money growth, this produces higher inflation. Finally, by raising interest rates, deficits lead to private sector innovations that make bonds more like money. The recent development of money market mutual funds and money market deposit accounts are examples of this adaptation. Miller contends that the relevance of his approach is supported by the empirical evidence that countries with higher deficit policies (including the United States) have higher inflation rates.

Article Twenty-Seven

MILTON FRIEDMAN

The Case for Overhauling the Federal Reserve

Changing the Fed's monetary tactics may help, but the System needs basic reform. We should end its money-creating powers, make it a bureau of the Treasury, and freeze the quantity of high-powered money.

Monetary policy can be discussed on two very different levels: the tactics of policy—the specific actions that the monetary authorities should take; and the strategy or framework of policy—the ideal monetary institutions and arrangements for the conduct of monetary policy that should be adopted.

Tactics are more tempting. They are immediately relevant, promise direct results, and are in most respects easier to discuss than the thorny problem of the basic framework appropriate for monetary policy. Yet long experience persuades me that, given our present institutions, a discussion of tactics is unlikely to be rewarding.

The temptation to concentrate on tactics derives in considerable part from a tendency to personalize policy: to speak of the Eisenhower, Kennedy, or Reagan economic policy and the Martin, Burns, or Volcker monetary policy. Sometimes that approach is correct.

The particular person in charge may make a major difference to the course of events. For example, in *Monetary History of the United States, 1867-1960*, Anna Schwartz and I attributed considerable importance to the early death of Benjamin Strong, first governor of the Federal Reserve Bank of New York, in explaining monetary policy from 1929 to 1933. More frequently, perhaps, the personalized approach is misleading. The person ostensibly in charge is like the rooster crowing at dawn. The course of events is decided by deeper and less visible forces that determine both the character of those nominally in charge and the pressures on them.

Monetary developments during the past few decades have, I believe, been determined far more by the institutional structure of the Federal Reserve and by external pressures than by the intentions, knowledge, or personal characteristics of the persons who appeared

MILTON FRIEDMAN, a 1976 Nobel laureate, is a senior research fellow at the Hoover Institution, Stanford University, and Paul Snowden Russell Distinguished Service Professor of Economics at the University of Chicago. This article is adapted from ''Monetary Policy for the 1980s'' in *To Promote Prosperity*, edited by John H. Moore and published by the Hoover Institution Press. © 1984 by the Board of Trustees of the Leland Stanford Jr. University.

to be in charge. Knowing the name, the background, and the personal qualities of the chairman of the Fed, for example, is of little use in judging what happened to monetary growth during his term of office.

If the present monetary structure were producing satisfactory results, we would be well advised to leave it alone. Tactics would then be the only topic. However, the present monetary structure is not producing satisfactory results. Indeed, in my opinion, no major institution in the United States has so poor a record of performance over so long a period yet so high a public reputation as the Federal Reserve.

The conduct of monetary policy is of major importance; monetary instability breeds economic instability. A monetary structure that fosters steadiness and predictability in the general price level is an essential precondition for healthy noninflationary growth. That is why it is important to consider fundamental changes in our monetary institutions. Such changes may be neither feasible nor urgent now. But unless we consider them now, we shall not be prepared to adopt them when and if the need is urgent.

The tactics for avoiding a crisis

Three issues are involved in the tactics of monetary policy: adopting a variable or variables as an intermediate target or targets; choosing the desired path of the target variables; and devising procedures for achieving that path as closely as possible.

• *The intermediate targets.* The Fed has vacillated between using one or more interest rates or one or more monetary aggregates as its intermediate targets. In the past decade, however, it joined monetary authorities in other countries in stressing monetary growth. Since 1975, it has been required by Congress to specify explicit numerical targets for the growth of monetary aggregates. Although many proposals have recently surfaced for the substitution of other targets—from real interest rates to sensitive commodity prices to the price of gold to nominal GNP—I shall assume that one or more monetary aggregates remains the intermediate target.

In my opinion, the selection of a target or of a target path is not and has not been the problem. If the Fed had consistently achieved the targets it specified to Congress, monetary growth would have been highly stable instead of highly variable, inflation would never have become the menace it did, and the United States would have been spared the worst parts of the punishing re-

cession (or recessions) from 1979 to 1982.

The Fed has specified targets for several aggregates primarily, as I have argued elsewhere, to obfuscate the issue and reduce accountability. In general, the different aggregates move together. The exceptions have essentially all been due to the interest-rate restrictions imposed by the Fed under Regulation Q and the associated development of new forms of deposit liabilities. And they would not have arisen if the Fed had achieved its targets for any one of the aggregates.

The use of multiple intermediate targets is undesirable. The Fed has one major instrument of monetary control: control over the quantity of high-powered money. With one instrument, it cannot independently control several aggregates. Its other instruments—primarily the discount rate and reserve requirements—are highly defective as instruments for monetary control and of questionable effectiveness in enabling it to control separately more than one aggregate.

It makes far less difference which aggregate the Fed selects than that it selects one and only one. For simplicity of exposition, I shall assume that the target aggregate is M_1 as currently designed. Selection of another aggregate would alter the desirable numerical targets but not their temporal pattern.

• *The target path.* A long-run growth rate of about 1 to 3 percent per year for M_1 would be roughly consistent with zero inflation. That should be our objective. Actual growth in M_1 was 10.4 percent from fourth quarter 1982 to fourth quarter 1983; 5.2 percent from fourth quarter 1983 to fourth quarter 1984. A crucial question is how rapidly to go from such levels to the 1 to 3 percent range. In my opinion, it is desirable to proceed gradually, over something like a three- to five-year period, which means that the rate of growth should be reduced by about 1 to 1.5 percentage points a year—a very different pattern from the erratic ups and downs of recent years.

The Fed has consistently stated its targets in terms of a range of growth rates. For example, its initial target for M_1 for 1983 was a growth rate of 4 to 8 percent from the fourth quarter of 1982 to the fourth quarter of 1983. That method of stating targets is seriously defective: it provides a widening cone of limits on the absolute money supply as the year proceeds and fosters a shift in base from year to year, thereby frustrating accountability over long periods. This is indeed what happened. In July 1983, Chairman Volcker announced a new target of 5 to 9 percent for the second quarter of 1983 to the second quarter of 1984 but from the second-quarter 1983 base, which is 3 percent (6 percent at an annual rate) above the top of the earlier range.

A better way to state the targets is in terms of a central target for the absolute money supply plus or minus a band of, say, 1.5 percent on either side—about the range the Fed has specified for annual growth rates. [Since this was written and initially published, the Council of Economic Advisers has made the same suggestion, and Chairman Volcker has expressed support for such a change.]

• *Procedures for hitting the target.* There is widespread agreement both inside and outside the Federal Reserve System that current procedures and reserve regulations make accurate control of monetary growth over short periods difficult or impossible. These procedures and regulations do not explain such long sustained departures from the targets as the monetary explosions from April 1980 to April 1981 or July 1982 to July 1983 or the monetary retardations from April 1981 to October 1981 or January 1982 to July 1982. However, they do explain the wide volatility in monetary growth from week to week and month to month, which introduces undesirable uncertainty into the economy and financial markets and reduces Fed accountability for not hitting its targets.

There is also widespread agreement about the changes in procedures and regulations that would enable the Fed to come very much closer to hitting its targets over fairly short periods. The most important such change was the replacement of lagged reserve accounting, introduced in 1968, by contemporaneous reserve accounting comparable to that prevailing from 1914 to 1968. The obstacle to controlling monetary growth posed by lagged reserve accounting has been recognized since 1970 at the latest. Unfortunately, the Fed did not act until 1982, when it finally decided to replace lagged by contemporary reserve requirements. However, it delayed implementation until February 1984—the longest delay in implementing a changed regulation in the history of the Fed. There was no insuperable technical obstacle to implementing the change more promptly.

The other major procedural changes needed are:

1. Selection by the Fed of a single monetary target to end the Fed's juggling between targets;

2. Imposition of the same percentage reserve requirements on all deposit components of the selected target;

3. The use of total rather than nonborrowed reserves as the short-term operating instrument;

4. Linking of the discount rate to a market rate and making it a penalty rate (neither this change nor the preceding was feasible for technical reasons under lagged reserve accounting; they are now feasible, but neither has been adopted);

5. Reduction of the churning in which the Fed engages in the course of its so-called defensive open-market operations.

Even without most of these changes, it would be possible for the Fed to put into effect almost instantaneously a policy that would provide a far stabler monetary environment than we have at present, even though it would by no means be ideal. The obstacle is not feasibility but bureaucratic inertia and the preservation of bureaucratic power and status.

A simple example will illustrate. Let the Fed continue to state targets for M_1 growth. Let it estimate the change in its total holdings of U.S. government securities that would be required in the next six months, say, to produce the targeted growth in M_1. Divide that amount by 26. Let the Fed purchase the resulting amount every week on the open market, in addition to any amount needed to replace maturing securities, and make no other purchases or sales. Finally, let it announce this schedule of purchases in advance and in full detail and stick to it.

Such a policy would assure control over the monetary aggregates, not from day to day, but over the longer period that the Fed insists is all that matters. It would enable the market to know precisely what the Fed would do and adjust its own actions accordingly. It would end the weekly guessing game that currently follows each Thursday's release of figures on the money supply. The financial markets have certainly demonstrated that they have ample flexibility to handle whatever day-to-day or seasonal adjustments might be needed. It is hard to envisage any significant adverse effects from such a policy.

A few numbers will show how much difference such a policy would make to the Fed's open-market activities. In 1982, it added an average of $176 million a week to its total holdings of government securities— an unusually high amount. In the process of acquiring $176 million, it purchased each week an average of $13 *billion* of securities and sold nearly as much. About half of these transactions were on behalf of foreign central banks. But that still leaves roughly $40 of purchases or $80 of transactions for every one dollar added to its portfolio—a degree of churning of a customer's account that would send a private stockbroker to jail, or at least to limbo.

Increased predictability, reduced churning, the loss of inscrutability—these are at the same time the major reasons for making so drastic a change and the major obstacles to its achievement. It would simply upset too many comfortable dovecotes.

A framework for basic reform

The chief problem in discussing the framework of monetary policy is to set limits. The subject is old, yet immediately pertinent; numerous proposals have been made, and few, however ancient, do not have contemporary proponents. In view of my own belief that the important desiderata of structural reform are to reduce the variability of monetary growth, to limit the discretion of the monetary authorities, and to provide a stable monetary framework, I shall limit myself to proposals directed at those objectives, proceeding from the least to the most radical.

• *Imposing a monetary rule on the Fed.* I have long argued that a major improvement in monetary policy could be achieved without any significant change in monetary institutions simply by imposing a monetary rule on the Fed. From an economic point of view, it would be desirable to state the rule in terms of a monetary aggregate such as M_1 that has a close and consistent relation to subsequent changes in national income. However, recent years have demonstrated that the Fed has been unable or unwilling to achieve such a target, even when it sets it itself, and that it has been able to plead inability and thereby avoid accountability. Accordingly, I have reluctantly decided that it is preferable to state the rule in terms of a magnitude that has a somewhat less close relation to national income but that unquestionably can be controlled within very narrow limits within very brief time periods, namely, the Fed's own non-interest-bearing obligations, the monetary base.

In *Free to Choose*, my wife, Rose, and I proposed a specific form of rule as a constitutional amendment: "*Congress shall have the power to authorize non-interest-bearing obligations of the government in the form of currency or book entries, provided that the total dollar amount outstanding increases by no more than 5 percent per year and no less than 3 percent.*

"It might be desirable to include a provision that two-thirds of each House of Congress, or some similar qualified majority, can waive the requirement in case of a declaration of war, the suspension to terminate annually unless renewed."

A constitutional amendment would be the most effective way to establish confidence in the stability of the rule. However, it is clearly not the only way to impose the rule. Congress could equally well legislate it, and, indeed, proposals for a legislated monetary rule have been introduced in Congress.

I remain persuaded that a monetary rule that leads to a predictable long-run path of a specified monetary aggregate is a highly desirable goal—superior either to discretionary control of the quantity of money by a set of monetary authorities or to a commodity standard. However, I am no longer so optimistic as I once was that it can be effected by either persuading the monetary authorities to follow it or legislating its adoption. Congressional attempts in the past decade to push the Fed in that direction have repeatedly failed. The Fed has rhetorically accepted monetary targets but never a firm monetary rule. Moreover, the Fed has not been willing even to match its performance to a rhetorical acceptance of monetary targets. All this suggests that a change in our monetary institutions is required in order to make such a rule effective.

• *Separating regulatory from monetary functions.* A modest institutional reform that promises considerable benefits is to separate the regulatory from the monetary functions of the Fed. Currently, regulatory functions absorb most of the Fed's attention. Moreover, they obscure accountability for monetary control by confusing the two very separate and to some extent inconsistent functions.

As has recently been proposed in a study of the Federal Deposit Insurance Corporation, the Fed should be stripped of its regulatory functions, which would be combined with the largely overlapping functions of the FDIC, the Federal Savings and Loan Insurance Corporation, and the comptroller of the currency. Such a combined agency should have no monetary powers. It also might well include the operating functions of the Federal Reserve Banks—the monitoring of reserve requirements, issuance of currency, clearing of checks, reporting of data, and so forth.

A separate monetary-control agency could be a very small body, charged solely with determining the total quantity of high-powered money through open-market operations. Its function would be clear, highly visible, and subject to effective accountability.

• *Ending the independence of the Fed.* An approach that need involve relatively little institutional change—

although it is far more drastic than the preceding—and that could be implemented by legislation would be to end the independence of the Fed by converting it into a bureau of the Treasury Department. That would end the present division of responsibilities for monetary and fiscal policy that leads to the spectacle of chairmen of the Fed blaming all the nation's ills on the defects of fiscal policy and secretaries of the Treasury blaming them on the defects of monetary policy—a phenomenon that has prevailed for decades. There would be a single locus of authority that could be held responsible.

The immediate objection that arises is that it would make monetary policy a plaything of politics. My own examination of monetary history indicates that this judgment is correct, but that it is an argument for, not against, eliminating the central bank's independence.

I examined this issue at length in an article published more than two decades ago entitled "Should There Be an Independent Monetary Authority?" I concluded that it is "highly dubious that the United States, or for that matter any other country, has in practice ever had an independent central bank in [the] fullest sense of the term. . . . To judge by experience, even those central banks that have been nominally independent in the fullest sense of the term have in fact been closely linked to the executive authority.

"But of course this does not dispose of the matter. The ideal is seldom fully realized. Suppose we could have an independent central bank in the sense of a coordinate constitutionally established, separate organization. Would it be desirable to do so? I think not, for both political and economic reasons.

"The political objections are perhaps more obvious than the economic ones. Is it really tolerable in a democracy to have so much power concentrated in a body free from any kind of direct effective political control? . . .

"One [economic] defect of an independent central bank . . . is that it almost inevitably involves dispersal of responsibility. . . .

"Another defect . . . is the extent to which policy is . . . made highly dependent on personalities. . . .

"A third technical defect is that an independent central bank will almost inevitably give undue emphasis to the point of view of bankers.

"The three defects I have outlined constitute a strong technical argument against an independent central bank."

The experience of the past two decades has led me to alter my views in one respect only—about the importance of personalities. They have on occasion made a great deal of difference, but additional experience and study has impressed me with the continuity of Fed policy, despite the wide differences in the personalities and backgrounds of the persons supposedly in charge.

For the rest, experience has reinforced my views. Anna Schwartz and I pointed out in *Monetary History* that subservience to congressional pressure in 1930 and 1931 would have prevented the disastrous monetary policy followed by the Fed. That is equally true for the past fifteen years. The relevant committees of Congress have generally, though by no means invariably, urged policies on the Fed that would have produced a stabler rate of monetary growth and much less inflation. Excessively rapid and volatile monetary growth from, say, 1971 to 1979 was not the result of political pressure—certainly not from Congress, although in some of these years there clearly was pressure for more rapid growth from the Administration. Nonetheless, no political pressures would have prevented the Fed from increasing M_1 over this period at, say, an average annual rate of 5 percent—the rate of increase during the prior eight years—instead of 6.7 percent.

Subordinating the Fed to the Treasury is by no means ideal. Yet it would be a great improvement over the existing situation, even with no other changes.

• *Competitive issue of money.* Increasing interest has been expressed in recent years in proposals to replace governmental issuance of money and control of its quality by private market arrangements. One set of proposals would end the government monopoly on the issuance of currency and permit its competitive issue. Another would eliminate entirely any issuance of money by government and, instead, restrict the role of government to defining a monetary unit.

The former set of proposals derives largely from a pamphlet by F. A. Hayek entitled *Choice in Currency: A Way to Stop Inflation.* Hayek proposed that all special privileges (such as "legal tender" quality) attached to government-issued currency be removed, and that financial institutions be permitted to issue currency or deposit obligations on whatever terms were mutually acceptable to the issuer and the holder of the liabilities. He envisaged a system in which institutions would in fact issue obligations expressed in terms of purchasing power either of specific commodities, such as gold or silver, or of commodities in general through linkage to a price index. In his opinion, constant-purchasing-power moneys would come to dominate the market and largely replace obligations denominated in dollars or pounds or other similar units and in specific commodities.

The idea of a currency unit linked to a price index is an ancient one—proposed in the nineteenth century by W. Stanley Jevons and Alfred Marshall, who named it a "tabular" standard—and repeatedly rediscovered. It is part of the theoretically highly attractive idea of widespread indexation. Experience, however, has demonstrated that the theoretical attractiveness of the idea is not matched by practice.

I approve of Professor Hayek's proposal to remove restrictions on the issuance of private moneys to compete with government moneys. But I do not share his belief about the outcome. Private moneys now exist—traveler's checks and cashier's checks, bank deposits, money orders, and various forms of bank drafts and negotiable instruments. But these are almost all claims on a specified number of units of government currency (of dollars or pounds or francs or marks). Currently, they are subject to government regulation and control. But even if such regulations and controls were entirely eliminated, the advantage of a single national currency unit buttressed by long tradition will, I suspect, serve to prevent any other type of private currency unit from seriously challenging the dominant government currency, and this despite the high degree of monetary variability many countries have experienced over recent decades.

The recent explosion in financial futures markets offers a possible new road to the achievement, through private market actions, of the equivalent of a tabular standard. This possibility is highly speculative—little more than a gleam in one economist's eye. It involves the establishment of futures markets in one or more price indexes—strictly parallel to the markets that have developed in stock-price indexes. (The Commodities Futures Trading Commission has authorized the Coffee, Sugar, and Cocoa Exchange to begin futures trading in the Consumer Price Index as of June 21, 1985.) Such markets, if active and covering a considerable range of future dates, would provide a relatively costless means of hedging long-term contracts against risks of changes in the price level. A combination of an orthodox dollar contract plus a properly timed set of futures in a price level would be the precise equivalent of a tabular standard, but would have the advantage that any one party to a contract, with the help of speculators and other hedgers in the futures market, could have the benefit of a tabular standard without the agreement of the other party or parties.

Recent changes in banking regulations have opened another route to a partial tabular standard on a substantial scale. The Federal Home Loan Bank has finally authorized federally chartered savings and loan associations to offer price-level-adjusted mortgage (PLAM) loans. Concurrently, the restrictions on the interest rate that can be paid on deposits by a wide range of financial institutions have been eased and removed entirely for deposits of longer maturities.

This would permit financial institutions simultaneously to lend and borrow on a price-level-adjusted basis: to lend on a PLAM and borrow on a price-level-adjusted deposit (PLAD), both at an interest rate specified in real rather than nominal terms. By matching PLAM loans against PLAD deposits, a bank would be fully hedged against changes in inflation, covering its costs by the difference between the interest rate it charges and pays. Similarly, both borrowers and lenders would be safeguarded against changes in inflation with respect to a particular liability and asset.

As yet, I know of no financial institutions that have proceeded along these lines. I conjecture that no major development will occur unless and until inflation once again accelerates. When and if that occurs, PLAMs and PLADs may well become household words and not simply mysterious acronyms.

• *Freezing high-powered money.* The final proposal combines features from most of the preceding. It is radical and far-reaching, yet simple.

The proposal is that, after a transition period, the quantity of high-powered money—non-interest-bearing obligations of the U.S. government—be frozen at a fixed amount. These non-interest-bearing obligations now take two forms: currency and deposits at the Federal Reserve System. The simplest way to envisage the change is to suppose that Federal Reserve deposit liabilities were replaced dollar for dollar by currency notes, which were turned over to the owners of those deposits. Thereafter, the government's monetary role would be limited to keeping the amount constant by replacing worn-out currency. In effect, a monetary rule of zero growth in high-powered money would be adopted. (In practice, it would not be necessary to replace deposits at the Federal Reserve with currency; they could be retained as book entries, so long as the total of such book entries plus currency notes was kept constant.)

This proposal would be consistent with, indeed require, the continued existence of private institutions issuing claims to government currency. These could be regulated as now, with the whole paraphernalia of required reserves, bank examinations, limitations on lending, and the like. However, they could also be freed from all or most such regulations. In particular, the need for reserve requirements to enable the Fed to control the quantity of money would disappear.

Reserve requirements might still be desirable for a different though related reason. The new monetary economists argue that only the existence of such government regulations as reserve requirements and prohibition of the private issuance of currency explains the relatively stable demand for high-powered money. In the absence of such regulations, they contend, non-interest-bearing money would be completely dominated by interest-bearing assets, or, at the very least, the demand for such money would be rendered highly unstable.

I am far from persuaded by this contention. It supposes a closer approach to a frictionless world with minimal transaction costs than seems to me a useful approximation to the actual world. Nonetheless, it is arguable that the elimination of reserve requirements would introduce an unpredictable and erratic element into the demand for high-powered money. For that reason, although personally I would favor the deregulation of financial institutions, thereby incorporating a major element of Hayek's proposed competitive financial system, it would seem prudent to proceed in stages: first, freeze high-powered money; then, after a period, eliminate reserve requirements and other remaining regulations, including the prohibition on the issuance of hand-to-hand currency by private institutions.

Why zero growth? Zero has a special appeal on political grounds that is not shared by any other number. If 3 percent, why not 4 percent? It is hard, as it were, to go to the political barricades to defend 3 rather than 4, or 4 rather than 5. But zero is—as a psychological matter—qualitatively different. It is what has come to be called a Schelling point—a natural point at which people tend to agree, like "splitting the difference" in a dispute over a monetary sum. Moreover, by removing any power to create money it eliminates institutional arrangements lending themselves to discretionary changes in monetary growth.

Would zero growth in high-powered money be consistent with a healthy economy? In the hypothetical long-long-run stationary economy, when the whole economy had become adjusted to the situation, and population, real output, and so on were all stationary, zero growth in high-powered money would imply zero growth in other monetary aggregates and mean stable

velocities for the aggregates. In consequence, the price level would be stable. In a somewhat less than stationary state in which output was rising, if financial innovations kept pace, the money multiplier would tend to rise at the same rate as output, and again prices would be stable. If financial innovations ceased but total output continued to rise, prices would decline. If output rose at about 3 percent per year, prices would tend to fall at 3 percent per year. So long as that was known and relatively stable, all contracts could be adjusted to it, and it would cause no problems and indeed would have some advantages.

However, any such outcome is many decades away. The more interesting and important question is not the final stationary-state result but the intermediate dynamic process.

Once the policy was in effect, the actual behavior of nominal income and the price level would depend on what happened to a monetary aggregate like M_1 relative to high-powered money and what happened to nominal income relative to M_1—that is, on the behavior of the money multiplier (the ratio of M_1 to high-powered money) and on the income velocity of M_1 (the ratio of nominal income to M_1).

Given a loosening of the financial structure through continued deregulation, there would be every reason to expect a continued flow of innovations raising the money multiplier. This process has in fact occurred throughout the past several centuries. For example, in the century from 1870 to 1970, the ratio of the quantity of money, as defined by Anna Schwartz and me in *Monetary History*, to high-powered money rose at the average rate of 1 percent per year. In the post-World War II period, the velocity of M_1 has risen at about 3 percent per year, and at a relatively steady rate. This trend cannot, of course, continue indefinitely. Above, in specifying a desirable target for the Fed, I estimated that the rise in velocity would slow to about 1 or 2 percent per year. However, a complete end to the rapid trend in velocity is not in sight.

There is no way to make precise numerical estimates, but there is every reason to anticipate that for decades after the introduction of a freeze on high-powered money, both the money multiplier and velocity would tend to rise at rates in the range of historical experience. Under these circumstances, a zero rate of growth of high-powered money would imply roughly stable prices, though ultimately, perhaps, slightly declining prices.

What of the transition? Over the three years from 1979 to 1982, high-powered money grew an average of 7.0

percent a year. It would be desirable to bring that rate to zero gradually. As for M_1 growth, about a five-year period seems appropriate—or a transition that reduces the rate of growth of high-powered money by about 1.5 percentage points a year. The only other transitional problem would be to phase out the Fed's powers to create and destroy high-powered money by open-market operations and discounting. Neither transition offers any special problem. The Fed, or its successor agency, could still use part of the existing stock of high-powered money for similar purposes, particularly for lender-of-last-resort purposes, if that function were retained.

The great advantage of this proposal is that it would end the arbitrary power of the Federal Reserve System to determine the quantity of money, and would do so without establishing any comparable locus of power and without introducing any major disturbances into other existing economic and financial institutions.

I have found that few things are harder even for knowledgeable nonexperts to accept than the proposition that twelve (or nineteen) people sitting around a table in Washington, subject to neither election nor dismissal, nor close administrative or political control, have the power to determine the quantity of money—to permit a reduction by one-third during the Great Depression or a near-doubling from 1970 to 1980. That power is too important, too pervasive, to be exercised by a few people, however public-spirited, if there is any feasible alternative.

There is no need for such arbitrary power. In the system I have just described, the total quantity of any monetary aggregate would be determined by the market interactions of many financial institutions and millions of holders of monetary assets. It would be limited by the constant quantity of high-powered money available as ultimate reserves. The ratios of various aggregates to high-powered money would doubtless change from time to time, but in the absence of rigid government controls—such as those exemplified by Regulation Q, fortunately being phased out—the ratios would change gradually and only as financial innovations or changes in business and industry altered the proportions in which the public chose to hold various monetary assets. No small number of individuals would be in a position to introduce major changes in the ratios or in the rates of growth of various monetary aggregates—to move, for example, from a 3 percent per year rate of growth in M_1 for one six-month period (January to July 1982) to a 13 percent rate of growth for the next six months (July 1982 to January 1983).

Conclusion

Major institutional change occurs only at times of crisis. For the rest, the tyranny of the status quo limits changes in institutions to marginal tinkering—we muddle through. It took the Great Depression to produce the FDIC, the most important structural change in our monetary institutions since at least 1914, when the Federal Reserve System began operations, and to shift power over monetary policy from the Federal Reserve Banks, especially that in New York, to the Board in Washington. Since then, our monetary institutions have been remarkably stable. It took the severe inflation of the 1970s and accompanying double-digit interest rates—combined with the enforcement of Regulation Q—to produce money-market mutual funds and thereby force a considerable measure of deregulation of banking.

Nonetheless, it is worth discussing radical changes, not in the expectation that they will be adopted promptly but for two other reasons. One is to construct an ideal goal, so that incremental changes can be judged by whether they move the institutional structure toward or away from that ideal.

The other reason is very different. It is so that if a crisis requiring or facilitating radical change does arise, alternatives will be available that have been carefully developed and fully explored. International monetary arrangements provide an excellent example. For decades, economists had been exploring alternatives to the system of fixed exchange rates—in particular, floating exchange rates among national currencies. The practical men of affairs derided proposals for floating rates as unrealistic, impractical, ivory-tower. Yet when crisis came, when the Bretton Woods fixed-rate system had to be scrapped, the theorists' impractical proposal became highly practical and formed the basis for the new system of international monetary arrangements.

Needless to say, I hope that no crises will occur that will necessitate a drastic change in domestic monetary institutions. The most likely such crisis is continued monetary instability, a return to a roller coaster of inflation about an upward trend, with inflation accelerating to levels of 20, 30, or more percent per year. That would shake the social and political framework of the nation and would produce results none of us would like to witness. Yet, it would be burying one's head in the sand to fail to recognize that such a development is a real possibility. It has occurred elsewhere, and it could occur here. If it does, the best way to cut it short, to minimize the harm it would do, is to be ready not with Band-Aids but with a real cure for the basic illness.

As of now, I believe the best real cure would be the reform outlined above: abolish the money-creating powers of the Federal Reserve, freeze the quantity of high-powered money, and deregulate the financial system.

The less radical changes in policy and procedures suggested in the section on tactics seem to me to offer the best chance of avoiding a crisis. These tactical changes are feasible technically. However, I am not optimistic that they will be adopted. The obstacle is political: as with any bureaucratic organization, it is not in the self-interest of the Fed to adopt policies that would render it accountable. The Fed has persistently avoided doing so over a long period. None of the tactics that I have proposed is new. The proposed changes would have made just as much sense five or ten years ago—indeed, if adopted then, the inflation and volatility of the past ten years would never have occurred. The proposals have had the support of a large fraction of monetary experts outside the Fed. The Fed has resisted them for bureaucratic and political, not technical, reasons. And resistance has been in the Fed's interest. By keeping monetary policy an arcane subject that must be entrusted to "experts" and kept out of politics, incapable of being judged by non-experts, the Fed has been able to maintain the high public reputation of which I spoke at the outset of this article, despite its poor record of performance.

One chairman after another, in testimony to Congress, has emphasized the mystery and difficulty of the Fed's task and the need for discretion, judgment, and the balancing of many considerations. Each has stressed how well the Fed has done and proclaimed its dedication to pursuing a noninflationary policy and has attributed any undesirable outcome to forces outside the Fed's control or to deficiencies in other components of government policy—particularly fiscal policy. The testimony of the four most recent chairmen of the Fed documents their pervasive concern with avoiding accountability—a concern with which it is easy to sympathize in view of the purely coincidental relation between their announced intentions and the actual outcome.

Clearly the problem is not the person who happens to be chairman, but the system.

Article Twenty-Eight

After Keynesian Macroeconomics*

Robert E. Lucas, Jr.
Professor of Economics
University of Chicago

Thomas J. Sargent
Adviser, Research Department
Federal Reserve Bank of Minneapolis
and
Professor of Economics
University of Minnesota

For the applied economist, the confident and apparently successful application of Keynesian principles to economic policy which occurred in the United States in the 1960s was an event of incomparable significance and satisfaction. These principles led to a set of simple, quantitative relationships between fiscal policy and economic activity generally, the basic logic of which could be (and was) explained to the general public and which could be applied to yield improvements in economic performance benefitting everyone. It seemed an economics as free of ideological difficulties as, say, applied chemistry or physics, promising a straightforward expansion in economic possibilities. One might argue as to how this windfall should be distributed, but it seemed a simple lapse of logic to oppose the windfall itself. Understandably and correctly, noneconomists met this promise with skepticism at first; the smoothly growing prosperity of the Kennedy-Johnson years did much to diminish these doubts.

We dwell on these halcyon days of Keynesian economics because without conscious effort they are difficult to recall today. In the present decade, the U.S. economy has undergone its first major depression since the 1930s, to the accompaniment of inflation rates in excess of 10 percent per annum. These events

*A paper presented at a June 1978 conference sponsored by the Federal Reserve Bank of Boston and published in its *After the Phillips Curve: Persistence of High Inflation and High Unemployment.* Conference Series No. 19. Edited for publication in this *Quarterly Review.*

The authors acknowledge helpful criticism from William Poole and Benjamin Friedman.

have been transmitted (by consent of the governments involved) to other advanced countries and in many cases have been amplified. These events did not arise from a reactionary reversion to outmoded, "classical" principles of tight money and balanced budgets. On the contrary, they were accompanied by massive government budget deficits and high rates of monetary expansion, policies which, although bearing an admitted risk of inflation, promised according to modern Keynesian doctrine rapid real growth and low rates of unemployment.

That these predictions were wildly incorrect and that the doctrine on which they were based is fundamentally flawed are now simple matters of fact, involving no novelties in economic theory. The task now facing contemporary students of the business cycle is to sort through the wreckage, determining which features of that remarkable intellectual event called the Keynesian Revolution can be salvaged and put to good use and which others must be discarded. Though it is far from clear what the outcome of this process will be, it is already evident that it will necessarily involve the reopening of basic issues in monetary economics which have been viewed since the thirties as "closed" and the reevaluation of every aspect of the institutional framework within which monetary and fiscal policy is formulated in the advanced countries.

This paper is an early progress report on this process of reevaluation and reconstruction. We begin by reviewing the econometric framework by means of which Keynesian theory evolved from disconnected, qualitative talk about economic activity into a system of equations which can be compared to data in a systematic way and which provide an operational guide in the necessarily quantitative task of formulating monetary and fiscal policy. Next, we identify those aspects of this framework which were central to its failure in the seventies. In so doing, our intent is to establish that the difficulties are *fatal*: that modern macroeconomic models are of *no* value in guiding policy and that this condition will not be remedied by modifications along any line which is currently being pursued. This diagnosis suggests certain principles which a useful theory of business cycles must have. We conclude by reviewing some recent research consistent with these principles.

Macroeconometric Models

The Keynesian Revolution was, in the form in which it succeeded in the United States, a revolution in method. This was not Keynes' (1936)[1] intent, nor is it the view of all of his most eminent followers. Yet if one does not view the revolution in this way, it is impossible to account for some of its most important features: the evolution of macroeconomics into a quantitative, *scientific* discipline, the development of explicit statistical descriptions of economic behavior, the increasing reliance of government officials on technical economic expertise, and the introduction of the use of mathematical control theory to manage an economy. It is the fact that Keynesian theory lent itself so readily to the formulation of explicit econometric models which accounts for the dominant scientific position it attained by the 1960s.

Because of this, neither the success of the Keynesian Revolution nor its eventual failure can be understood at the purely verbal level at which Keynes himself wrote. It is necessary to know something of the way macroeconometric models are constructed and the features they must have in order to "work" as aids in forecasting and policy evaluation. To discuss these issues, we introduce some notation.

An econometric model is a system of equations involving a number of endogenous variables (variables determined by the model), exogenous variables (variables which affect the system but are not affected by it), and stochastic or random shocks. The idea is to use historical data to estimate the model and then to utilize the estimated version to obtain estimates of the consequences of alternative policies. For practical reasons, it is usual to use a standard linear model, taking the structural form[2]

$$A_0y_t + A_1y_{t-1} + \ldots + A_my_{t-m} = B_0x_t + B_1x_{t-1} \quad (1)$$
$$+ \ldots + B_nx_{t-n} + \varepsilon_t$$

$$R_0\varepsilon_t + R_1\varepsilon_{t-1} + \ldots + R_r\varepsilon_{t-r} = u_t, R_0 \equiv I. \quad (2)$$

Here y_t is an $(L \times 1)$ vector of endogenous variables, x_t is a $(K \times 1)$ vector of exogenous variables, and ε_t and u_t are each $(L \times 1)$ vectors of random disturbances. The matrices A_j are each $(L \times L)$; the B_j's are $(L \times K)$, and the R_j's are each $(L \times L)$. The $(L \times L)$ disturbance process u_t is assumed to be a serially uncorrelated process with $Eu_t = 0$ and with contemporaneous covariance matrix $Eu_tu_t' = \Sigma$ and $Eu_tu_s' = 0$ for all $t \neq s$. The defining characteristics of the exogenous variables x_t is that they are uncorrelated with the ε's at all lags so that Eu_tx_s' is an $(L \times K)$ matrix of zeroes for all t and s.

Equations (1) are L equations in the L current values y_t of the endogenous variables. Each of these structural equations is a behavioral relationship, identity, or market clearing condition, and each in principle can involve a number of endogenous variables. The structural equations are usually not regression equations[3] because the ε_t's are in general, by the logic of the model, supposed to be correlated with more than one component of the vector y_t and very possibly one or more components of the vectors $y_{t-1}, \ldots y_{t-m}$.

The structural model (1) and (2) can be solved for y_t in terms of past y's and x's and past shocks. This reduced form system is

$$y_t = -P_1y_{t-1} - \ldots - P_{r+m}y_{t-r-m} + Q_0x_t + \ldots \quad (3)$$
$$+ Q_{r+n}x_{t-n-r} + A_0^{-1}u_t$$

where[4]

$$P_s = A_0^{-1} \sum_{j=-\infty}^{\infty} R_jA_{s-j}$$

---

[1] Author names and years refer to the works listed at the end of this paper.

[2] Linearity is a matter of convenience, not principle. See *Linearity* section below.

[3] A regression equation is an equation to which the application of ordinary least squares will yield consistent estimates.

[4] In these expressions for P_s and Q_s, take matrices not previously defined (for example, any with negative subscripts) to be zero.

$$Q_s = A_0^{-1} \sum_{j=-\infty}^{\infty} R_j B_{s-j}.$$

The reduced form equations are regression equations. that is. the disturbance vector $A_0^{-1}u_t$ is orthogonal to $y_{t-1}, \ldots, y_{t-r-m}, x_t, \ldots, x_{t-n-r}$. This follows from the assumptions that the x's are exogenous and that the u's are serially uncorrelated. Therefore. under general conditions the reduced form can be estimated consistently by the method of least squares. The population parameters of the reduced form (3) together with the parameters of a vector autoregression for x_t

$$x_t = C_1 x_{t-1} + \ldots + C_p x_{t-p} + a_t \qquad (4)$$

where $Ea_t = 0$ and $Ea_t \cdot x_{t-j} = 0$ for $j \geq 1$ completely describe all of the first and second moments of the (y_t, x_t) process. Given long enough time series, good estimates of the reduced form parameters—the P_j's and Q_j's—can be obtained by the method of least squares. All that examination of the data by themselves can deliver is reliable estimates of those parameters.

It is not generally possible to work backward from estimates of the P's and Q's alone to derive unique estimates of the structural parameters, the A_j's, B_j's, and R_j's. In general. infinite numbers of A's, B's, and R's are compatible with a single set of P's and Q's. This is the identification problem of econometrics. In order to derive a set of estimated structural parameters, it is necessary to know a great deal about them in advance. If enough prior information is imposed, it is possible to extract estimates of the A_j's, B_j's. R_j's implied by the data in combination with the prior information.

For purposes of *ex ante* forecasting, or the unconditional prediction of the vector $y_{t+1}, y_{t+2}, \ldots$ given observation of y_s and x_s, $s \leq t$, the estimated reduced form (3). together with (4), is sufficient. This is simply an exercise in a sophisticated kind of extrapolation. requiring no understanding of the structural parameters, that is, the *economics* of the model.

For purposes of *conditional* forecasting, or the prediction of the future behavior of some components of y_t and x_t *conditional* on particular values of other components, selected by policy, one needs to know the structural parameters. This is so because a change in policy necessarily alters some of the structural parameters (for example, those describing the past behavior of the policy variables themselves) and therefore affects the reduced form parameters in a highly complex way (see the equations defining P_s and Q_s above). Unless one knows which structural parameters remain invariant as policy changes and which change (and how), an econometric model is of no value in assessing alternative policies. It should be clear that this is true regardless of how well (3) and (4) fit historical data or how well they perform in unconditional forecasting.

Our discussion to this point has been highly general. and the formal considerations we have reviewed are not in any way specific to *Keynesian* models. The problem of identifying a structural model from a collection of economic time series is one that must be solved by anyone who claims the ability to give quantitative economic advice. The simplest Keynesian models are attempted solutions to this problem. as are the large-scale versions currently in use. So. too, are the monetarist models which imply the desirability of fixed monetary growth rules. So. for that matter, is the armchair advice given by economists who claim to be outside the econometric tradition, though in this case the implicit. underlying structure is not exposed to professional criticism. Any procedure which leads from the study of observed economic behavior to the quantitative assessment of alternative economic policies involves the steps, executed poorly or well, explicitly or implicitly, which we have outlined.

Keynesian Macroeconometrics

In Keynesian macroeconometric models structural parameters are identified by the imposition of several types of a priori restrictions on the A_j's. B_j's. and R_j's. These restrictions usually fall into one of the following three categories:[5]

(a) A priori setting of many of the elements of the A_j's and B_j's to zero.

---

[5]These three categories certainly do not exhaust the set of possible identifying restrictions. but they're the ones most identifying restrictions in Keynesian macroeconometric models fall into. Other possible sorts of identifying restrictions include. for example. a priori knowledge about components of Σ and cross-equation restrictions across elements of the A_j's. B_j's. and C_j's. neither of which is extensively used in Keynesian macroeconometrics.

(b) Restrictions on the orders of serial correlation and the extent of cross-serial correlation of the disturbance vector ε_t, restrictions which amount to a priori setting of many elements of the R_j's to zero.

(c) A priori classifying of variables as exogenous and endogenous. A relative abundance of exogenous variables aids identification.

Existing large Keynesian macroeconometric models are open to serious challenge for the way they have introduced each type of restriction.

Keynes' *General Theory* was rich in suggestions for restrictions of type (a). In it he proposed a theory of national income determination built up from several simple relationships, each involving a few variables only. One of these, for example, was the "fundamental law" relating consumption expenditures to income. This suggested one "row" in equations (1) involving current consumption, current income, and *no other* variables, thereby imposing many zero-restrictions on the A_i's and B_j's. Similarly, the liquidity preference relation expressed the demand for money as a function of only income and an interest rate. By translating the building blocks of the Keynesian theoretical system into explicit equations, models of the form (1) and (2) were constructed with many theoretical restrictions of type (a).

Restrictions on the coefficients R_i governing the behavior of the error terms in (1) are harder to motivate theoretically because the errors are by definition movements in the variables which the *economic* theory cannot account for. The early econometricians took standard assumptions from statistical textbooks, restrictions which had proven useful in the agricultural experimenting which provided the main impetus to the development of modern statistics. Again, these restrictions, well-motivated or not, involve setting many elements in the R_i's equal to zero, thus aiding identification of the model's structure.

The classification of variables into exogenous and endogenous was also done on the basis of prior considerations. In general, variables were classed as endogenous which were, as a matter of institutional fact, determined largely by the actions of private agents (like consumption or private investment expenditures). Exogenous variables were those under governmental control (like tax rates or the supply of money). This division was intended to reflect the ordinary meanings of the words *endogenous*— "determined by the [economic] system"—and *exogenous*—"affecting the [economic] system but not affected by it."

By the mid-1950s, econometric models had been constructed which fit time series data well, in the sense that their reduced forms (3) tracked past data closely and proved useful in short-term forecasting. Moreover, by means of restrictions of the three types reviewed above, their structural parameters A_i, B_j, R_k could be identified. Using this estimated structure, the models could be simulated to obtain estimates of the consequences of different government economic policies, such as tax rates, expenditures, or monetary policy.

This Keynesian solution to the problem of identifying a structural model has become increasingly suspect as a result of both theoretical and statistical developments. Many of these developments are due to efforts of researchers sympathetic to the Keynesian tradition, and many were advanced well before the spectacular failure of the Keynesian models in the 1970s.[6]

Since its inception, macroeconomics has been criticized for its lack of foundations in microeconomic and general equilibrium theory. As was recognized early on by astute commentators like Leontief (1965, disapprovingly) and Tobin (1965, approvingly), the creation of a distinct branch of theory with its own distinct postulates was Keynes' conscious aim. Yet a main theme of theoretical work since the *General Theory* has been the attempt to use microeconomic theory based on the classical postulate that agents act in their own interests to suggest a list of variables that belong on the right side of a given behavioral schedule, say, a demand schedule for a factor of production or a consumption schedule.[7] But

---

[6]Criticisms of the Keynesian solutions of the identification problem along much the following lines have been made in Lucas 1976, Sims forthcoming, and Sargent and Sims 1977.

[7]Much of this work was done by economists operating well within the Keynesian tradition, often within the context of some Keynesian macroeconometric model. Sometimes a theory with optimizing agents was resorted to in order to resolve empirical paradoxes by finding variables omitted from some of the earlier Keynesian econometric formulations. The works of Modigliani and Friedman on consumption are good examples of this line of work; its econometric implications

Continued on next page

from the point of view of identification of a given structural equation by means of restrictions of type (a), one needs reliable prior information that certain variables should be excluded from the right-hand side. Modern probabilistic microeconomic theory almost never implies either the exclusion restrictions suggested by Keynes or those imposed by macroeconometric models.

Let us consider one example with extremely dire implications for the identification of existing macro models. Expectations about the future prices, tax rates, and income levels play a critical role in many demand and supply schedules. In the best models, for example, investment demand typically is supposed to respond to businesses' expectations of future tax credits, tax rates, and factor costs, and the supply of labor typically is supposed to depend on the rate of inflation that workers expect in the future. Such structural equations are usually identified by the assumption that the expectation about, say, factor prices or the rate of inflation attribute to agents is a function only of a few lagged values of the variable which the agent is supposed to be forecasting. However, the macro models themselves contain complicated dynamic interactions among endogenous variables, including factor prices and the rate of inflation, and they generally imply that a wise agent would use current and many lagged values of many and usually most endogenous and exogenous variables in the model in order to form expectations about any one variable. Thus, virtually any version of the hypothesis that agents act in their own interests will contradict the identification restrictions imposed on expectations formation. Further, the restrictions on expecta-

tions that have been used to achieve identification are entirely arbitrary and have not been derived from any deeper assumption reflecting first principles about economic behavior. No general first principle has ever been set down which would imply that, say, the expected rate of inflation should be modeled as a linear function of lagged rates of inflation alone with weights that add up to unity, yet this hypothesis is used as an identifying restriction in almost all existing models. The casual treatment of expectations is not a peripheral problem in these models, for the role of expectations is pervasive in them and exerts a massive influence on their dynamic properties (a point Keynes himself insisted on). The failure of existing models to derive restrictions on expectations from any first principles grounded in economic theory is a symptom of a deeper and more general failure to derive behavioral relationships from any consistently posed dynamic optimization problems.

As for the second category, restrictions of type (b), existing Keynesian macro models make severe a priori restrictions on the R_j's. Typically, the R_j's are supposed to be diagonal so that cross-equation lagged serial correlation is ignored, and also the order of the ε_t process is assumed to be short so that only low-order serial correlation is allowed. There are at present no theoretical grounds for introducing these restrictions, and for good reasons there is little prospect that economic theory will soon provide any such grounds. In principle, identification can be achieved without imposing any such restrictions. Foregoing the use of category (b) restrictions would increase the category (a) and (c) restrictions needed. In any event, existing macro models do heavily restrict the R_j's.

Turning to the third category, all existing large models adopt an a priori classification of variables as either strictly endogenous variables, the y_t's, or strictly exogenous variables, the x_t's. Increasingly it is being recognized that the classification of a variable as exogenous on the basis of the observation that it could be set without reference to the current and past values of other variables has nothing to do with the econometrically relevant question of how this variable has *in fact* been related to others over a given historical period. Moreover, in light of recent developments in time series econometrics, we know that this arbitrary classification procedure is not necessary. Christopher Sims (1972) has shown that in a time series context the hypothesis of econometric

---

have been extended in important work by Robert Merton. The works of Tobin and Baumol on portfolio balance and of Jorgenson on investment are also in the tradition of applying optimizing microeconomic theories for generating macroeconomic behavior relations. In the last 30 years, Keynesian econometric models have to a large extent developed along the line of trying to model agents' behavior as stemming from more and more sophisticated optimum problems.

Our point here is certainly not to assert that Keynesian economists have completely foregone any use of optimizing microeconomic theory as a guide. Rather, it is that, especially when explicitly stochastic and dynamic problems have been studied, it has become increasingly apparent that microeconomic theory has very damaging implications for the restrictions conventionally used to identify Keynesian macroeconometric models. Furthermore, as emphasized long ago by Tobin (1965), there is a point beyond which Keynesian models must suspend the hypothesis either of cleared markets or of optimizing agents if they are to possess the operating characteristics and policy implications that are the hallmarks of Keynesian economics.

exogeneity can be tested. That is, Sims showed that the hypothesis that x_t is strictly econometrically exogenous in (1) necessarily implies certain restrictions that can be tested given time series on the y's and x's. Tests along the lines of Sims' ought to be used routinely to check classifications into exogenous and endogenous sets of variables. To date they have not been. Prominent builders of large econometric models have even denied the usefulness of such tests. (See, for example, Ando 1977, pp. 209-10, and L. R. Klein in Okun and Perry 1973, p. 644.)

Failure of Keynesian Macroeconometrics

There are, therefore, a number of theoretical reasons for believing that the parameters identified as structural by current macroeconomic methods are not in fact structural. That is, we see no reason to believe that these models have isolated structures which will remain invariant across the class of interventions that figure in contemporary discussions of economic policy. Yet the question of whether a particular model is structural is an empirical, not a theoretical, one. If the macroeconometric models had compiled a record of parameter stability, particularly in the face of breaks in the stochastic behavior of the exogenous variables and disturbances, one would be skeptical as to the importance of prior theoretical objections of the sort we have raised.

In fact, however, the track record of the major econometric models is, on any dimension other than very short-term unconditional forecasting, very poor. Formal statistical tests for parameter instability, conducted by subdividing past series into periods and checking for parameter stability across time, invariably reveal major shifts. (For one example, see Muench et. al. 1974.) Moreover, this difficulty is implicitly acknowledged by model builders themselves, who routinely employ an elaborate system of add-factors in forecasting, in an attempt to offset the continuing drift of the model away from the actual series.

Though not, of course, designed as such by anyone, macroeconometric models were subjected to a decisive test in the 1970s. A key element in all Keynesian models is a trade-off between inflation and real output: the higher is the inflation rate, the higher is output (or equivalently, the lower is the rate of unemployment). For example, the models of the late 1960s predicted a sustained U.S. unemployment rate of 4 percent as consistent with a 4 percent annual rate of inflation. Based on this prediction, many economists at that time urged a deliberate policy of inflation. Certainly the erratic "fits and starts" character of actual U.S. policy in the 1970s cannot be attributed to recommendations based on Keynesian models, but the inflationary bias on average of monetary and fiscal policy in this period should, according to all of these models, have produced the lowest average unemployment rates for any decade since the 1940s. In fact, as we know, they produced the highest unemployment rates since the 1930s. This was econometric failure on a grand scale.

This failure has not led to widespread conversions of Keynesian economists to other faiths, nor should it have been expected to. In economics as in other sciences, a theoretical framework is always broader and more flexible than any particular set of equations, and there is always the hope that if a particular specific model fails one can find a more successful model based on roughly the same ideas. The failure has, however, already had some important consequences, with serious implications for both economic policymaking and the practice of economic science.

For policy, the central fact is that Keynesian policy recommendations have no sounder basis, in a scientific sense, than recommendations of non-Keynesian economists or, for that matter, noneconomists. To note one consequence of the wide recognition of this, the current wave of protectionist sentiment directed at "saving jobs" would have been answered ten years ago with the Keynesian counterargument that fiscal policy can achieve the same end, but more efficiently. Today, of course, no one would take this response seriously, so it is not offered. Indeed, economists who ten years ago championed Keynesian fiscal policy as an alternative to inefficient direct controls increasingly favor such controls as supplements to Keynesian policy. The idea seems to be that if people refuse to obey the equations we have fit to their past behavior, we can pass laws to make them do so.

Scientifically, the Keynesian failure of the 1970s has resulted in a new openness. Fewer and fewer economists are involved in monitoring and refining the major econometric models; more and more are developing alternative theories of the business cycle, based on different theoretical principles. In addition, more attention and respect is accorded to the theoretical casualties of the Keynesian Revolution, to the ideas of Keynes' contemporaries and of earlier economists whose thinking has been regarded for years as outmoded.

No one can foresee where these developments will lead. Some, of course, continue to believe that the problems of existing Keynesian models can be resolved within the existing framework, that these models can be adequately refined by changing a few structural equations, by adding or subtracting a few variables here and there, or perhaps by disaggregating various blocks of equations. We have couched our criticisms in such general terms precisely to emphasize their generic character and hence the futility of pursuing minor variations within this general framework. A second response to the failure of Keynesian analytical methods is to renounce analytical methods entirely, returning to judgmental methods.

The first of these responses identifies the quantitative, scientific goals of the Keynesian Revolution with the details of the particular models developed so far. The second renounces both these models and the objectives they were designed to attain. There is, we believe, an intermediate course, to which we now turn.

Equilibrium Business Cycle Theory

Before the 1930s, economists did not recognize a need for a special branch of economics, with its own special postulates, designed to explain the business cycle. Keynes founded that subdiscipline, called *macroeconomics*, because he thought explaining the characteristics of business cycles was impossible within the discipline imposed by classical economic theory, a discipline imposed by its insistence on adherence to the two postulates (a) that markets clear and (b) that agents act in their own self-interest. The outstanding facts that seemed impossible to reconcile with these two postulates were the length and severity of business depressions and the large-scale unemployment they entailed. A related observation was that measures of aggregate demand and prices were positively correlated with measures of real output and employment, in apparent contradiction to the classical result that changes in a purely nominal magnitude like the general price level were pure unit changes which should not alter real behavior.

After freeing himself of the straightjacket (or discipline) imposed by the classical postulates, Keynes described a model in which rules of thumb, such as the consumption function and liquidity preference schedule, took the place of decision functions that a classical economist would insist be derived from the theory of choice. And rather than require that wages and prices be determined by the postulate that markets clear—which for the labor market seemed patently contradicted by the severity of business depressions—Keynes took as an unexamined postulate that money wages are sticky, meaning that they are set at a level or by a process that could be taken as uninfluenced by the macroeconomic forces he proposed to analyze.

When Keynes wrote, the terms *equilibrium* and *classical* carried certain positive and normative connotations which seemed to rule out either modifier being applied to business cycle theory. The term *equilibrium* was thought to refer to a system at rest, and some used both *equilibrium* and *classical* interchangeably with *ideal*. Thus an economy in classical equilibrium would be both unchanging and unimprovable by policy interventions. With terms used in this way, it is no wonder that few economists regarded equilibrium theory as a promising starting point to understand business cycles and design policies to mitigate or eliminate them.

In recent years, the meaning of the term *equilibrium* has changed so dramatically that a theorist of the 1930s would not recognize it. An economy following a multivariate stochastic process is now routinely described as being in equilibrium, by which is meant nothing more than that at each point in time, postulates (a) and (b) above are satisfied. This development, which stemmed mainly from work by K. J. Arrow (1964) and G. Debreu (1959), implies that simply to look at any economic time series and conclude that it is a disequilibrium phenomenon is a meaningless observation. Indeed, a more likely conjecture, on the basis of recent work by Hugo Sonnenschein (1973), is that the general hypothesis that a collection of time series describes an economy in competitive equilibrium is *without content.*[*]

The research line being pursued by some of us

---

[*]For an example that illustrates the emptiness at a general level of the statement that employers are always operating along dynamic stochastic demands for factors, see the remarks on econometric identi-
Continued on next page

involves the attempt to discover a particular, econometrically testable equilibrium theory of the business cycle, one that can serve as the foundation for quantitative analysis of macroeconomic policy. There is no denying that this approach is counterrevolutionary, for it presupposes that Keynes and his followers were wrong to give up on the possibility that an equilibrium theory could account for the business cycle. As of now, no successful equilibrium macroeconometric model at the level of detail of, say, the Federal Reserve-MIT-Penn model has been constructed. But small theoretical equilibrium models have been constructed that show potential for explaining some key features of the business cycle long thought inexplicable within the confines of classical postulates. The equilibrium models also provide reasons for understanding why estimated Keynesian models fail to hold up outside the sample over which they have been estimated. We now turn to describing some of the key facts about business cycles and the way the *new classical* models confront them.

For a long time most of the economics profession has, with some reason, followed Keynes in rejecting classical macroeconomic models because they seemed incapable of explaining some important characteristics of time series measuring important economic aggregates. Perhaps the most important failure of the classical model was its apparent inability to explain the positive correlation in the time series between prices and/or wages, on the one hand, and measures of aggregate output or employment, on the other. A second and related failure was its inability to explain the positive correlations between measures of aggregate demand, like the money stock, and aggregate output or employment. Static analysis of classical macroeconomic models typically implied that the levels of output and employment were determined

independently of both the absolute level of prices and of aggregate demand. But the pervasive presence of positive correlations in the time series seems consistent with causal connections flowing from aggregate demand and inflation to output and employment, contrary to the classical neutrality propositions. Keynesian macroeconometric models do imply such causal connections.

We now have rigorous theoretical models which illustrate how these correlations can emerge while retaining the classical postulates that markets clear and agents optimize (Phelps 1970 and Lucas 1972, 1975). The key step in obtaining such models has been to relax the ancillary postulate used in much classical economic analysis that agents have perfect information. The new classical models still assume that markets clear and that agents optimize; agents make their supply and demand decisions based on real variables, including perceived relative prices. However, each agent is assumed to have limited information and to receive information about some prices more often than other prices. On the basis of their limited information—the lists that they have of current and past absolute prices of various goods—agents are assumed to make the best possible estimate of all of the relative prices that influence their supply and demand decisions.

Because they do not have all of the information necessary to compute perfectly the relative prices they care about, agents make errors in estimating the pertinent relative prices, errors that are unavoidable given their limited information. In particular, under certain conditions, agents tend temporarily to mistake a general increase in all absolute prices as an increase in the relative price of the good they are selling, leading them to increase their supply of that good over what they had previously planned. Since on average everyone is making the same mistake, aggregate output rises above what it would have been. This increase of output above what it would have been occurs whenever this period's average economy-wide price level is above what agents had expected it to be on the basis of previous information. Symmetrically, aggregate output decreases whenever the aggregate price turns out to be lower than agents had expected. The hypothesis of *rational expectations* is being imposed here: agents are assumed to make the best possible use of the limited information they have and to know the pertinent objective probability distri-

---

fication in Sargent 1978. In applied problems that involve modeling agents' optimum decision rules, one is impressed at how generalizing the specification of agents' objective functions in plausible ways quickly leads to econometric underidentification.

A somewhat different class of examples comes from the difficulties in using time series observations to refute the view that agents only respond to unexpected changes in the money supply. In the equilibrium macroeconometric models we will describe, predictable changes in the money supply do not affect real GNP or total employment. In Keynesian models, they do. At a general level, it is impossible to discriminate between these two views by observing time series drawn from an economy described by a stationary vector random process (Sargent 1976b).

butions. This hypothesis is imposed by way of adhering to the tenets of equilibrium theory.

In the new classical theory, disturbances to aggregate demand lead to a positive correlation between unexpected changes in the aggregate price level and revisions in aggregate output from its previously planned level. Further, it is easy to show that the theory implies correlations between revisions in aggregate output and unexpected changes in any variables that help determine aggregate demand. In most macroeconomic models, the money supply is one determinant of aggregate demand. The new theory can easily account for positive correlations between revisions to aggregate output and unexpected increases in the money supply.

While such a theory predicts positive correlations between the inflation rate or money supply, on the one hand, and the level of output, on the other, it also asserts that those correlations do not depict trade-offs that can be exploited by a policy authority. That is, the theory predicts that there is no way that the monetary authority can follow a systematic activist policy and achieve a rate of output that is on average higher over the business cycle than what would occur if it simply adopted a no-feedback, X-percent rule of the kind Friedman (1948) and Simons (1936) recommended. For the theory predicts that aggregate output is a function of current and past unexpected changes in the money supply. Output will be high only when the money supply is and has been higher than it had been expected to be, that is, higher than average. There is simply no way that on average over the whole business cycle the money supply can be higher than average. Thus, while the theory can explain some of the correlations long thought to invalidate classical macroeconomic theory, it is classical both in its adherence to the classical theoretical postulates and in the nonactivist flavor of its implications for monetary policy.

Small-scale econometric models in the standard sense have been constructed which capture some of the main features of the new classical theory. (See, for example, Sargent 1976a.)[9] In particular, these models incorporate the hypothesis that expectations are rational or that agents use all available information. To some degree, these models achieve econometric identification by invoking restrictions in each of the three categories (a), (b), and (c). However, a distinguishing feature of these "classical" models is

that they also rely heavily on an important fourth category of identifying restrictions. This category (d) consists of a set of restrictions that are derived from probabilistic economic theory but play no role in the Keynesian framework. These restrictions in general do not take the form of zero restrictions of the type (a). Instead they typically take the form of cross-equation restrictions among the A_j, B_j, C_j parameters. The source of these restrictions is the implication from economic theory that current decisions depend on agents' forecasts of future variables, combined with the implication that these forecasts are formed optimally, given the behavior of past variables. The restrictions do not have as simple a mathematical expression as simply setting a number of parameters equal to zero, but their economic motivation is easy to understand. Ways of utilizing these restrictions in econometric estimation and testing are rapidly being developed.

Another key characteristic of recent work on equilibrium macroeconometric models is that the reliance on entirely a priori categorizations (c) of variables as strictly exogenous and endogenous has been markedly reduced, although not entirely eliminated. This development stems jointly from the fact that the models assign important roles to agents' optimal forecasts of future variables and from Christopher Sims' (1972) demonstration that there is a close connection between the concept of strict econometric exogeneity and the forms of the optimal predictors for a vector of time series. Building a model with rational expectations necessarily forces one to consider which set of other variables helps forecast a given variable, say, income or the inflation rate. If variable y helps predict variable x, the Sims' theorems imply that x cannot be regarded as exogenous with respect to y.

---

[9]Dissatisfaction with the Keynesian methods of achieving identification has also led to other lines of macroeconometric work. One line is the index models described by Sargent and Sims (1977) and Geweke (1977). These models amount to a statistically precise way of implementing Wesley Mitchell's notion that a small number of common influences explain the covariation of a large number of economic aggregates over the business cycle. This low dimensionality hypothesis is a potential device for restricting the number of parameters to be estimated in vector time series models. This line of work is not entirely atheoretical (but see the comments of Ando and Klein in Sims 1977), though it is distinctly un-Keynesian. As it happens, certain equilibrium models of the business cycle do seem to lead to low dimensional index models with an interesting pattern of variables' loadings on indexes. In general, modern Keynesian models do not so easily assume a low-index form. See the discussion in Sargent and Sims 1977.

The result of this connection between predictability and exogeneity has been that in equilibrium macroeconometric models the distinction between endogenous and exogenous variables has not been drawn on an entirely a priori basis. Furthermore, special cases of the theoretical models, which often involve side restrictions on the R_j's not themselves drawn from economic theory, have strong testable predictions as to exogeneity relations among variables.

A key characteristic of equilibrium macroeconometric models is that as a result of the restrictions across the A_j's, B_j's, and C_j's, the models predict that in general the parameters in many of the equations will change if there is a policy intervention that takes the form of a change in one equation that describes how some policy variable is being set. Since they ignore these cross-equation restrictions, Keynesian models in general assume that all other equations remain unchanged when an equation describing a policy variable is changed. We think this is one important reason Keynesian models have broken down when the equations governing policy variables or exogenous variables have changed significantly. We hope that the new methods we have described will give us the capability to predict the consequences for all of the equations of changes in the rules governing policy variables. Having that capability is necessary before we can claim to have a scientific basis for making quantitative statements about macroeconomic policy.

So far, these new theoretical and econometric developments have not been fully integrated, although clearly they are very close, both conceptually and operationally. We consider the best currently existing equilibrium models as prototypes of better, future models which will, we hope, prove of practical use in the formulation of policy.

But we should not understate the econometric success already attained by equilibrium models. Early versions of these models have been estimated and subjected to some stringent econometric tests by McCallum (1976), Barro (1977, forthcoming), and Sargent (1976a), with the result that they do seem able to explain some broad features of the business cycle. New and more sophisticated models involving more complicated cross-equation restrictions are in the works (Sargent 1978). Work to date has already shown that equilibrium models can attain within-sample fits about as good as those obtained by

Keynesian models, thereby making concrete the point that the good fits of the Keynesian models provide no good reason for trusting policy recommendations derived from them.

Criticism of Equilibrium Theory

The central idea of the equilibrium explanations of business cycles sketched above is that economic fluctuations arise as agents react to unanticipated changes in variables which impinge on their decisions. Clearly, any explanation of this general type must imply severe limitations on the ability of government policy to offset these initiating changes. First, governments must somehow be able to foresee shocks invisible to private agents but at the same time be unable to reveal this advance information (hence, defusing the shocks). Though it is not hard to design theoretical models in which these two conditions are assumed to hold, it is difficult to imagine actual situations in which such models would apply. Second, the governmental countercyclical policy must itself be unforeseeable by private agents (certainly a frequently realized condition historically) while at the same time be systematically related to the state of the economy. Effectiveness, then, rests on the inability of private agents to recognize systematic patterns in monetary and fiscal policy.

To a large extent, criticism of equilibrium models is simply a reaction to these implications for policy. So wide is (or was) the consensus that *the* task of macroeconomics is the discovery of the particular monetary and fiscal policies which can eliminate fluctuations by reacting to private sector instability that the assertion that this task either should not or cannot be performed is regarded as frivolous, regardless of whatever reasoning and evidence may support it. Certainly one must have some sympathy with this reaction: an unfounded faith in the curability of a particular ill has served often enough as a stimulus to the finding of genuine cures. Yet to confuse a possibly functional faith in the existence of efficacious, reactive monetary and fiscal policies with scientific evidence that such policies are known is clearly dangerous, and to use such faith as a criterion for judging the extent to which particular theories fit the facts is worse still.

There are, of course, legitimate questions about how well equilibrium theories can fit the facts of the business cycle. Indeed, this is the reason for our insistence on the preliminary and tentative character of the particular models we now have. Yet these tentative models share certain features which can be regarded as essential, so it is not unreasonable to speculate as to the likelihood that *any* model of this type can be successful or to ask what equilibrium business cycle theorists will have in ten years if we get lucky.

Four general reasons for pessimism have been prominently advanced:

(a) Equilibrium models unrealistically postulate cleared markets.
(b) These models cannot account for "persistence" (serial correlation) of cyclical movements.
(c) Econometrically implemented models are linear (in logarithms).
(d) Learning behavior has not been incorporated in these models.

Cleared Markets

One essential feature of equilibrium models is that all markets clear, or that all observed prices and quantities are viewed as outcomes of decisions taken by individual firms and households. In practice, this has meant a conventional, competitive supply-equals-demand assumption, though other kinds of equilibria can easily be imagined (if not so easily analyzed). If, therefore, one takes as a basic "fact" that labor markets do not clear, one arrives immediately at a contradiction between theory and fact. The facts we actually have, however, are simply the available time series on employment and wage rates plus the responses to our unemployment surveys. Cleared markets is simply a principle, not verifiable by direct observation, which may or may not be useful in constructing successful hypotheses about the behavior of these series. Alternative principles, such as the postulate of the existence of a third-party auctioneer inducing wage rigidity and uncleared markets, are similarly "unrealistic," in the not especially important sense of not offering a good description of observed labor market institutions.

A refinement of the unexplained postulate of an uncleared labor market has been suggested by the indisputable fact that long-term labor contracts with horizons of two or three years exist. Yet the length per se over which contracts run does not bear on the issue, for we know from Arrow and Debreu that if *infinitely* long-term contracts are determined so that prices and wages are contingent on the same informa-

tion that is available under the assumption of period-by-period market clearing, then precisely the same price-quantity process will result with the long-term contract as would occur under period-by-period market clearing. Thus equilibrium theorizing provides a way, probably the only way we have, to construct a *model* of a long-term contract. The fact that long-term contracts exist, then, has *no* implications about the applicability of equilibrium theorizing.

Rather, the real issue here is whether actual contracts can be adequately accounted for within an equilibrium model, that is, a model in which agents are proceeding in their own best interests. Stanley Fischer (1977), Edmund Phelps and John Taylor (1977), and Robert Hall (1978) have shown that some of the nonactivist conclusions of the equilibrium models are modified if one substitutes for period-by-period market clearing the imposition of long-term contracts drawn contingent on restricted information sets that are exogenously imposed and that are assumed to be independent of monetary and fiscal regimes. Economic theory leads us to predict that the costs of collecting and processing information will make it optimal for contracts to be made contingent on a small subset of the information that could possibly be collected at any date. But theory also suggests that the particular set of information upon which contracts will be made contingent is not immutable but depends on the structure of costs and benefits of collecting various kinds of information. This structure of costs and benefits will change with every change in the exogenous stochastic processes facing agents. This theoretical presumption is supported by an examination of the way labor contracts differ across high-inflation and low-inflation countries and the way they have evolved in the U.S. over the last 25 years.

So the issue here is really the same fundamental one involved in the dispute between Keynes and the classical economists: Should we regard certain superficial characteristics of existing wage contracts as given when analyzing the consequences of alternative monetary and fiscal regimes? Classical economic theory says no. To understand the implications of long-term contracts for monetary policy, we need a model of the way those contracts are likely to respond to alternative monetary policy regimes. An extension of existing equilibrium models in this direction might well lead to interesting variations, but it seems to us unlikely that major modifications of the implications of these models for monetary and fiscal policy will follow from this.

Persistence

A second line of criticism stems from the correct observation that if agents' expectations are rational and if their information sets include lagged values of the variable being forecast, then agents' forecast errors must be a serially uncorrelated random process. That is, on average there must be no detectable relationships between a period's forecast error and any previous period's. This feature has led several critics to conclude that equilibrium models cannot account for more than an insignificant part of the highly serially correlated movements we observe in real output, employment, unemployment, and other series. Tobin (1977, p. 461) has put the argument succinctly:

> One currently popular explanation of variations in employment is temporary confusion of relative and absolute prices. Employers and workers are fooled into too many jobs by unexpected inflation, but only until they learn it affects other prices, not just the prices of what they sell. The reverse happens temporarily when inflation falls short of expectation. This model can scarcely explain more than transient disequilibrium in labor markets.
>
> So how can the faithful explain the slow cycles of unemployment we actually observe? Only by arguing that the natural rate itself fluctuates, that variations in unemployment rates are substantially changes in voluntary, frictional, or structural unemployment rather than in involuntary joblessness due to generally deficient demand.

The critics typically conclude that the theory only attributes a very minor role to aggregate demand fluctuations and necessarily depends on disturbances to aggregate supply to account for most of the fluctuations in real output over the business cycle. "In other words," as Modigliani (1977) has said, "what happened to the United States in the 1930's was a severe attack of contagious laziness."

This criticism is fallacious because it fails to distinguish properly between *sources of impulses* and *propagation mechanisms*, a distinction stressed by Ragnar Frisch in a classic 1933 paper that provided many of the technical foundations for Keynesian macroeconometric models. Even though the new classical theory implies that the forecast errors which are the aggregate demand impulses are serially uncorrelated, it is certainly logically possible that propagation mechanisms are at work that convert these impulses into serially correlated movements in real variables like output and employment. Indeed, detailed theoretical work has already shown that two concrete propagation mechanisms do precisely that.

One mechanism stems from the presence of costs to firms of adjusting their stocks of capital and labor rapidly. The presence of these costs is known to make it optimal for firms to spread out over time their response to the relative price signals they receive. That is, such a mechanism causes a firm to convert the serially uncorrelated forecast errors in predicting relative prices into serially correlated movements in factor demands and output.

A second propagation mechanism is already present in the most classical of economic growth models. Households' optimal accumulation plans for claims on physical capital and other assets convert serially uncorrelated impulses into serially correlated demands for the accumulation of real assets. This happens because agents typically want to divide any unexpected changes in income partly between consuming and accumulating assets. Thus, the demand for assets next period depends on initial stocks and on unexpected changes in the prices or income facing agents. This dependence makes serially uncorrelated surprises lead to serially correlated movements in demands for physical assets. Lucas (1975) showed how this propagation mechanism readily accepts errors in forecasting aggregate demand as an impulse source.

A third likely propagation mechanism has been identified by recent work in search theory. (See, for example, McCall 1965, Mortensen 1970, and Lucas and Prescott 1974.) Search theory tries to explain why workers who for some reason are without jobs find it rational not necessarily to take the first job offer that comes along but instead to remain unemployed for awhile until a better offer materializes. Similarly, the theory explains why a firm may find it optimal to wait until a more suitable job applicant appears so that vacancies persist for some time. Mainly for technical reasons, consistent theoretical models that permit this propagation mechanism to accept errors in forecasting aggregate demand as an impulse have not yet been worked out, but the mechanism seems likely eventually to play an important role in a successful model of the time series behavior of the unemployment rate.

In models where agents have imperfect information, either of the first two mechanisms and probably the third can make serially correlated movements in real variables stem from the introduction of a serially uncorrelated sequence of forecasting errors. Thus theoretical and econometric models have been constructed in which in principle the serially uncorrelated process of forecasting errors can account for any proportion between zero and one of the steady-state variance of real output or employment. The argument that such models must necessarily attribute most of the variance in real output and employment to variations in aggregate supply is simply wrong logically.

Linearity

Most of the econometric work implementing equilibrium models has involved fitting statistical models that are linear in the variables (but often highly nonlinear in the parameters). This feature is subject to criticism on the basis of the indisputable principle that there generally exist nonlinear models that provide better approximations than linear models. More specifically, models that are linear in the variables provide no way to detect and analyze systematic effects of higher than first-order moments of the shocks and the exogenous variables on the first-order moments of the endogenous variables. Such systematic effects are generally present where the endogenous variables are set by risk-averse agents.

There are no *theoretical* reasons that most applied work has used linear models, only compelling technical reasons given today's computer technology. The predominant technical requirement of econometric work which imposes rational expectations is the ability to write down analytical expressions giving agents' decision rules as functions of the parameters of their objective functions and as functions of the parameters governing the exogenous random processes they face. Dynamic stochastic maximum problems with quadratic objectives, which produce linear decision rules, do meet this essential requirement—that is their virtue. Only a few other functional forms for agents' objective functions in dynamic stochastic optimum problems have this same necessary analytical tractability. Computer

technology in the foreseeable future seems to require working with such a class of functions, and the class of linear decision rules has just semed most convenient for most purposes. No issue of principle is involved in selecting one out of the very restricted class of functions available. Theoretically, we know how to calculate, with expensive recursive methods, the nonlinear decision rules that would stem from a very wide class of objective functions; no new econometric principles would be involved in estimating their parameters, only a much higher computer bill. Further, as Frisch and Slutsky emphasized, linear stochastic difference equations are a very flexible device for studying business cycles. It is an open question whether for explaining the central features of the business cycle there will be a big reward to fitting nonlinear models.

Stationary Models and the Neglect of Learning

Benjamin Friedman and others have criticized rational expectations models apparently on the grounds that much theoretical and almost all empirical work has assumed that agents have been operating for a long time in a stochastically stationary environment. Therefore, agents are typically assumed to have discovered the probability laws of the variables they want to forecast. Modigliani (1977, p. 6) put the argument this way:

> At the logical level, Benjamin Friedman has called attention to the omission from [equilibrium macroeconomic models] of an explicit learning model, and has suggested that, as a result, it can only be interpreted as a description not of short-run but of long-run equilibrium in which no agent would wish to recontract. But then the implications of [equilibrium macroeconomic models] are clearly far from startling, and their policy relevance is almost nil.

But it has been only a matter of analytical convenience and not of necessity that equilibrium models have used the assumption of stochastically stationary shocks and the assumption that agents have already learned the probability distributions they face. Both of these assumptions can be abandoned, albeit at a cost in terms of the simplicity of the model. (For example, see Crawford 1971 and Grossman 1975.) In fact, within the framework of quadratic objective functions, in which the "separation principle" applies, one can apply the Kalman filtering formula to derive optimum linear decision rules with time dependent coefficients. In this framework, the Kalman filter permits a neat application of Bayesian learning to updating optimal forecasting rules from period to period as new information becomes available. The Kalman filter also permits the derivation of optimum decision rules for an interesting class of nonstationary exogenous processes assumed to face agents. Equilibrium theorizing in this context thus readily leads to a *model* of how process nonstationarity and Bayesian learning applied by agents to the exogenous variables leads to time-dependent coefficients in agents' decision rules.

While models incorporating Bayesian learning and stochastic nonstationarity are both technically feasible and consistent with the equilibrium modeling strategy, we know of almost no successful applied work along these lines. One probable reason for this is that nonstationary time series models are cumbersome and come in so many varieties. Another is that the hypothesis of Bayesian learning is vacuous until one either arbitrarily imputes a prior distribution to agents or develops a method of estimating parameters of the prior from time series data. Determining a prior distribution from the data would involve estimating initial conditions and would proliferate nuisance parameters in a very unpleasant way. Whether these techniques will pay off in terms of explaining macroeconomic time series is an empirical matter: it is not a matter distinguishing equilibrium from Keynesian macroeconometric models. In fact, no existing Keynesian macroeconometric model incorporates either an economic model of learning or an economic model in any way restricting the pattern of coefficient nonstationarities across equations.

The macroeconometric models criticized by Friedman and Modigliani, which assume agents have caught on to the stationary random processes they face, give rise to systems of linear stochastic difference equations of the form (1), (2), and (4). As has been known for a long time, such stochastic difference equations generate series that "look like" economic time series. Further, if viewed as structural (that is, invariant with respect to policy interventions), the models have some of the implications for countercyclical policy that we have described above. Whether or not these policy implications are correct depends on whether or not the models are structural

and not at all on whether the models can successfully be caricatured by terms such as "long-run" or "short-run."

It is worth reemphasizing that we do not wish our responses to these criticisms to be mistaken for a claim that existing equilibrium models can satisfactorily account for all the main features of the observed business cycle. Rather, we have simply argued that no sound reasons have yet been advanced which even suggest that these models are, as a class, *incapable* of providing a satisfactory business cycle theory.

Summary and Conclusions

Let us attempt to set out in compact form the main arguments advanced in this paper. We will then comment briefly on the main implications of these arguments for the way we can usefully think about economic policy.

Our first and most important point is that existing Keynesian macroeconometric models cannot provide reliable guidance in the formulation of monetary, fiscal, or other types of policy. This conclusion is based in part on the spectacular recent failures of these models and in part on their lack of a sound theoretical or econometric basis. Second, on the latter ground, there is no hope that minor or even major modification of these models will lead to significant improvement in their reliability.

Third, *equilibrium* models can be formulated which are free of these difficulties and which offer a different set of principles to identify structural econometric models. The key elements of these models are that agents are rational, reacting to policy changes in a way which is in their best interests privately, and that the impulses which trigger business fluctuations are mainly unanticipated shocks.

Fourth, equilibrium models already developed account for the main qualitative features of the business cycle. These models are being subjected to continued criticism, especially by those engaged in developing them, but arguments to the effect that equilibrium theories are in principle unable to account for a substantial part of observed fluctuations appear due mainly to simple misunderstandings.

The policy implications of equilibrium theories are sometimes caricatured, by friendly as well as unfriendly commentators, as the assertion that "economic policy does not matter" or "has no effect."[10] This implication would certainly startle neoclassical economists who have successfully applied equilibrium theory to the study of innumerable problems involving important effects of fiscal policies on resource allocation and income distribution. Our intent is not to reject these accomplishments but rather to try to *imitate* them or to extend the equilibrium methods which have been applied to many economic problems to cover a phenomenon which has so far resisted their application: the business cycle.

Should this intellectual arbitrage prove successful, it will suggest important changes in the way we think about policy. Most fundamentally, it will focus attention on the need to think of policy as the choice of stable rules of the game, well understood by economic agents. Only in such a setting will economic theory help predict the actions agents will choose to take. This approach will also suggest that policies which affect behavior mainly because their consequences cannot be correctly diagnosed, such as monetary instability and deficit financing, have the capacity only to disrupt. The deliberate provision of misinformation cannot be used in a systematic way to improve the economic environment.

The *objectives* of equilibrium business cycle theory are taken, without modification, from the goal which motivated the construction of the Keynesian macroeconometric models: to provide a scientifically based means of assessing, quantitatively, the likely effects of alternative economic policies. Without the econometric successes achieved by the Keynesian models, this goal would be simply inconceivable. However, unless the now evident limits of these models are also frankly acknowledged and radically different new directions taken, the real accomplishments of the Keynesian Revolution will be lost as surely as those we now know to be illusory.

---

[10] A main source of this belief is probably Sargent and Wallace 1975, which showed that in the context of a fairly standard macroeconomic model, but with agents' expectations assumed rational, the choice of a reactive monetary rule is of no consequence for the behavior of real variables. The point of this example was to show that within precisely that model used to rationalize reactive monetary policies, such policies could be shown to be of no value. It hardly follows that all policy is ineffective in all contexts.

References

Aigner, D., and Goldberger, A., eds. 1977. *Latent Variables in Socio-Economic Models.* Amsterdam: North Holland.

Ando, Albert. 1977. A Comment. In *New Methods in Business Cycle Research: Proceedings from a Conference.* ed. C. A. Sims, pp. 209-12. Federal Reserve Bank of Minneapolis, Minnesota.

Arrow, Kenneth J. 1964. The Role of Securities in the Optimal Allocation of Risk-bearing. *Review of Economic Studies* 31 (April): 91-96.

Barro, Robert J. 1977. Unanticipated Money Growth and Unemployment in the United States. *American Economic Review* 67 (March): 101-15.

———. Forthcoming. Unanticipated Money, Output and the Price Level in the United States. *Journal of Political Economy.*

Brunner, K., and Meltzer, A. H., eds. 1976. *The Phillips Curve and Labor Markets.* Carnegie-Rochester Conference Series on Public Policy, vol. 1. Amsterdam: North Holland.

Crawford, Robert. 1971. Implications of Learning for Economic Models of Uncertainty. Manuscript. Pittsburgh: Carnegie-Mellon University.

Debreu, Gerard. 1959. *The Theory of Value.* New York: Wiley.

Fischer, Stanley. 1977. Long-Term Contracts, Rational Expectations, and the Optimal Money Supply Rule. *Journal of Political Economy* 85 (February): 191-205.

Friedman, Milton. 1948. A Monetary and Fiscal Framework for Economic Stability. *American Economic Review* 38 (June): 245-64.

Frisch, Ragnar. 1933. Propagation Problems and Impulse Problems in Dynamic Economics. Reprinted in 1965. *Readings in Business Cycles.* ed. R. A. Gordon and L. R. Klein. American Economic Association, 10: 155-85. Homewood, Ill.: Irwin.

Geweke, John. 1977. The Dynamic Factor Analysis of Economic Time Series. In *Latent Variables in Socio-Economic Models.* ed. D. Aigner and A. Goldberger, pp. 365-83. Amsterdam: North Holland.

Gordon, R. A., and Klein, L. R., eds. 1965. *Readings in Business Cycles.* American Economic Association, vol. 10. Homewood, Ill.: Irwin.

Grossman, Sanford. 1975. Rational Expectations and the Econometric Modeling of Markets Subject to Uncertainty: A Bayesian Approach. *Journal of Econometrics* 3 (August): 255-72.

Hall, Robert E. 1978. The Macroeconomic Impact of Changes in Income Taxes in the Short and Medium Runs. *Journal of Political Economy* 86 (April): S71-S85.

Harris, S., ed. 1965. *The New Economics: Keynes' Influence on Theory and Public Policy.* Clifton, N. J.: Kelley.

Keynes, J. M. 1936. *The General Theory of Employment, Interest, and Money.* London: Macmillan.

Leontief, W. 1965. Postulates: Keynes' General Theory and the Classicists. In *The New Economics: Keynes' Influence on Theory and Public Policy.* ed. S. Harris. Clifton, N. J.: Kelley.

Lucas, R. E., Jr. 1972. Expectations and the Neutrality of Money. *Journal of Economic Theory* 4 (April): 103-24.

———. 1975. An Equilibrium Model of the Business Cycle. *Journal of Political Economy* 83 (December): 1113-44.

———. 1976. Econometric Policy Evaluation: A Critique. In *The Phillips Curve and Labor Markets*, ed. K. Brunner and A. H. Meltzer. Carnegie-Rochester Conference Series on Public Policy 1: 19-46. Amsterdam: North Holland.

Lucas, R. E., Jr., and Prescott, Edward C. 1974. Equilibrium Search and Unemployment. *Journal of Economic Theory* 7 (February): 188-209.

McCall. John J. 1965. The Economics of Information and Optimal Stopping Rules. *Journal of Business* 38 (July): 300-317.

McCallum, B. T. 1976. Rational Expectations and the Natural Rate Hypothesis: Some Consistent Estimates. *Econometrica* 44 (January): 43-52.

Modigliani, Franco. 1977. The Monetarist Controversy, or Should We Forsake Stabilization Policies? *American Economic Review* 67 (March): 1-19.

Mortensen, Dale T. 1970. A Theory of Wage and Employment Dynamics. In *Microeconomic Foundations of Employment and Inflation Theory*, ed. E. S. Phelps, pp. 167-211. New York: Norton.

Muench, T.; Rolnick, A.; Wallace, N.; and Weiler, W. 1974. Tests for Structural Change and Prediction Intervals for the Reduced Forms of Two Structural Models of the U.S.: The FRB-MIT and Michigan Quarterly Models. *Annals of Economic and Social Measurement* 3 (July): 491-519.

Okun, Arthur, and Perry, George L., eds. 1973. *Brookings Papers on Economic Activity*, vol. 3. Washington, D. C.: Brookings Institution.

Phelps, E. S., ed. 1970. *Microeconomic Foundations of Employment and Inflation Theory*. New York: Norton.

Phelps, E. S., and Taylor, John B. 1977. Stabilizing Powers of Monetary Policy under Rational Expectations. *Journal of Political Economy* 85 (February): 163-90.

Sargent, T. J. 1976a. A Classical Macroeconometric Model for the United States. *Journal of Political Economy* 84 (April): 207-37.

———. 1976b. The Observational Equivalence of Natural and Unnatural Rate Theories of Macroeconomics. *Journal of Political Economy* 84 (June): 631-40.

———. 1978. Estimation of Dynamic Labor Demand Schedules under Rational Expectations. *Journal of Political Economy* 86 (December): 1009-44.

Sargent, T. J., and Wallace, Neil. 1975. "Rational" Expectations, the Optimal Monetary Instrument, and the Optimal Money Supply Rule. *Journal of Political Economy* 83 (April): 241-54.

Sargent, T. J., and Sims, C. A. 1977. Business Cycle Modeling Without Pretending to Have Too Much A Priori Economic Theory. In *New Methods in Business Cycle Research: Proceedings from a Conference*, ed. C. A. Sims, pp. 45-109. Federal Reserve Bank of Minneapolis, Minnesota.

Simons, Henry C. 1936. Rules Versus Authorities in Monetary Policy. *Journal of Political Economy* 44 (February): 1-30.

Sims, C. A. 1972. Money, Income, and Causality *American Economic Review* 62 (September): 540-52.

———. Forthcoming. Macroeconomics and Reality. *Econometrica*.

———, ed. 1977. *New Methods in Business Cycle Research: Proceedings from a Conference*. Federal Reserve Bank of Minneapolis, Minnesota.

Sonnenschein, Hugo. 1973. Do Walras' Identity and Continuity Characterize the Class of Community Excess Demand Functions? *Journal of Economic Theory* 6 (August): 345-54.

Tobin, James. 1965. Money Wage Rates and Employment. In *The New Economics: Keynes' Influence on Theory and Public Policy*, ed. S. Harris. Clifton, N. J.: Kelly.

———. 1977. How Dead is Keynes? *Economic Inquiry* 15 (October): 459-68.

Article Twenty-Nine

Can Policy Activism Succeed?
A Public Choice Perspective

James M. Buchanan
CENTER FOR STUDY OF PUBLIC CHOICE
GEORGE MASON UNIVERSITY

1. Introduction

The question posed in the title assigned to me presupposes the existence of an ordering of options along some scale of presumably agreed-on preferredness or desirability. Only if this presupposition is made does it become appropriate to ask whether or not politics, as it operates, can be expected to select the most preferred option on the ordering, or, less ambitiously, to select, on average, options that would allow the pattern or sequence of "choices" to be adjudged "successful." The generalized public-choice answer to the question, given the required presupposition, is reasonably straightforward, and it is essentially that of classical political economy. Those who make political decisions can be expected to choose in accordance with agreed-on or "public interest" norms only if the institutional structure is such as to make these norms coincident with those of "private interest." The public chooser, whether voter, aspiring or elected politician, or bureaucrat, is no different in this role than in other roles, and if incentives are such that the coincidence of interest is absent, there will be no "successful" political ordering over the feasible options. I shall return to the possible coincidence of interest following Section 2.

The more fundamental question to be asked, however, involves the appropriateness of the required presupposition—that concerning the possibility of any meaningful ordering of policy options, quite independently of any problems of implementation. This question has been obscured rather than clarified by those economists who resort to "social welfare functions." These functions impose a totally artificial and meaningless ordering on "social states" without offering any assistance toward facilitating choice from among the set of options feasibly available to the public chooser. Section 2 examines this fundamental question in the context of the issues that prompted the assigned title.

2. Is It Possible to Define an Ordering of Policy Options Along an Agreed-on "Success" Scalar?

In this section I propose to ignore totally all problems of policy implementation—all public choice problems, if you will. For simplicity, assume the existence of a genuinely benevolent despot, who sincerely seeks to do that which is "best" for all of those who are members of the political–economic–social community. How can we describe the utility function of this despot? It is easy, of course, to list several desired end-states. Full employment, stable and predictable value in the monetary unit, high and sustainable rates of economic growth, stable international order—these may be mutually agreed-on objectives for policy action. But there may be conflict among the separate objectives (to raise a topic of much debate–discussion of the 1950s that has been relatively neglected in the 1980s). How are we to model the trade-offs among the objectives within the utility function of the benevolent despot, if indeed such conflicts should arise?

I presume that the despot can act so as to influence macroeconomic variables in the economy; I leave possible rational expectations feedbacks to the other paper in this session. But how "should" the despot act, and, in this model, how "will" he act? There is no definitive answer to these questions until and unless the utility function is defined more fully.

There is, of course, an empty response to the question posed in the title to this section. Clearly, if the despot can, by our presumption, influence macroeconomic variables by policy action, then, by some criterion of his own, he can be "successful." But presumably we seek to employ a more objective criterion for success, one that can at least conceptually be observed by others than the despot himself.

For simplicity, let us assume that the despot is concerned only about domestic employment and monetary stability; we ignore all nondomestic considerations, and we put aside problems of growth. Further, let us restrict attention to standard macropolicy tools. The despot here is assumed to be unable, at least in the time frame of the policy under consideration, to modify the structural features of the economy. With these simplifications, we can go further and specify the objective function more precisely. Let us assume that the despot seeks to guarantee that level of employment that is consistent with stability in the value of the monetary unit, given the institutional structure of the economy. The objective reduces to a single price level target.

Even in this highly restricted setting, which is by no means that which might command consensus as a normative posture, the despot cannot simply "choose" the ultimate end objective from an available set of options. That is to say, "stability in the value of the monetary unit" cannot be selected as if from off a policy shelf. The despot is further restricted by the tools of policy available, which in this setting are those of the familiar fiscal (budgetary) and monetary instruments. Nominal demand can be increased, directly or indirectly, or reduced, directly or indirectly, by the use of fiscal–monetary tools, either separately or in some mix. Even if we ignore, as indicated, the expectational-induced feedbacks generated by resort to any instrument, there remains the task of predicting accurately the relationship between the instrument, economic structure, and ultimate objective. The structural features of the economy are not invariant over time, and a policy thrust that might be successful under one set of conditions, say in t_0, may fail, say, in t_1, because of structural shifts. At best, therefore, the truly benevolent despot can only be partially successful, even given the most clearly defined target for policy.

3. Monolithic and Nonbenevolent Despot

The presumption of benevolence on the part of political agents is not, of course, acceptable within a public-choice perspective. It is precisely this presumption that has been a central focus of the overall public-choice critique of the theory of economic policy. Political agents must be presumed to maximize personal utilities in a behavioral model that is invariant, as between public and private roles or capacities. The structure of decision making may, however, affect utility-maximizing behavior through shifts in the effective constraints on choice.

In this section, I shall discuss briefly the simplest possible decision structure, one in which political decisions are lodged within a single monolithic authority (in the limit in one person) which (who) is not directly accountable to or subject to constituency pressures, whether or not these be explicitly "democratic" (electoral) in nature. In this model, it is evident, quite apart from any historical record, that the despot will find if advantageous to resort to money creation over and beyond any amount that might characterize the "ideal" behavior of the benevolent counterpart considered above. This result emerges, quite simply, because incentive effects must be taken into account, and the despot, even if totally immune from constituency pressures, must reckon with individual adjustments to alternative revenue-generating instruments. Through a policy of revenue-maximizing inflation, defined in a dynamic sense, the despot can extract the full value of monetary structure (that is, the value differential between a monetary structure and a barter structure).[1]

The amount of revenue that may be potentially raised through money creation is, of course, finite. And the totally uncontrolled despot may seek to utilize the taxing and debt-issue power over and beyond the inflationary revenue limits. The precise features of the despot's policy mix will depend, in part, on his time horizon in relation to the behavioral reactions of the population. These features need not be examined in detail here. It is sufficient, for my purposes, to conclude that the monolithic despot will be successful only in terms of his own criteria, and that by any of the more familiar criteria for policy success, the failure would be manifest.

4. Monolithic and Nonbenevolent Agent Subject to Electoral Constraints

The analysis becomes more complex once we introduce electoral feedback constraints on the behavior of the monolithic political agent. Assume now that decision authority remains concentrated, but that the holder of this authority is subject to potential electoral replacement at designated periodic intervals. In this model the "governor" cannot expect to use his authority for personal enrichment for any extended period. Under some conditions, simple wealth-maximizing strategy might involve revenue-maximizing exploitation during the period of office, with no attention to possible reelection. In other conditions, the wealth-maximizing strategy might involve the effort to remain in office, in which case, short-run revenue maximization via inflation, debt creation, and taxation will be mitigated. If the agent is modeled as a simple revenue maximizer, it seems unlikely that his pattern of behavior would be adjudged "successful" by external criteria under either of these circumstances.

The more interesting model is one in which the agent is motivated by other considerations than wealth, the simplest model being that in which political position is itself the single maximand. The agent's behavior will, in this case, be constrained by expectations of electoral support. The question then becomes one of determining to what extent voters, generally, or in a required winning coalition, will support or oppose patterns of policy outcomes that might be deemed "successful" by external criteria. Given the postulated motivation here, the agent will base behavior strictly on constituency response.

Consider this question in the terms introduced earlier, that of a unique objective of monetary stability. Will a sufficiently large voting constituency support a regime that seeks only this policy objective? This question may be examined in the calculus of the individual voter or potential voter.

Two separate difficulties arise. The first involves the absence of individual voter responsibility for electoral outcomes in large-number constituencies. Even if the individual knows that the agent elected is fully responsive to the electoral process, because he knows that his own voting choice will rarely, if ever, be decisive, the individual may not vote. And if he does vote, he has little or no incentive to become informed about the alternatives. And if he votes, and even if he is reasonably well informed, there is little or no incentive for him to vote his "interests" rather than his "whims." Hence, there is only a remote linkage between what might be defined by the observing external "expert" as the "interest" of the voters and the support that is given to a prospective political agent who promises these externally defined "interests." This difficulty alone suggests that political agents cannot be "held responsible" by the electoral process nearly to the extent that is suggested by naive models of electoral feedback.

A second difficulty emerges even when the first is totally ignored. Even if all individuals are somehow motivated to vote and to do so in terms of their well-considered interests, these interests will not be identical for all voters. There are differentials among persons in the relative benefits and costs of any macropolicy action. Even the ideally responsive political agent will meet only the demands of the relevant coalition of voters, as determined by the precise voting rules.

Consider a single political agent who must satisfy a simple majority of constituency voters. If voters' interests in the employment–inflation trade-off can be presumed to be single peaked, the political agent's optimal strategy requires satisfying the median voter. It seems likely that this median voter will tend to be *myopic* in his behavior in the electoral process. He will place an unduly high value on the short-term benefits of enhancing employment relative to the long-term, and possibly permanent, costs of inflation. He will do so because, as a currently decisive voter, he can insure the capture of *some* benefits in the immediate future. By foregoing such short-term benefits in a "rational" consideration of the long-term costs, the currently decisive voter *cannot* guarantee against the incurrence of such long-term costs in future periods. This asymmetrical result follows from the potential shiftability of majority voting coalitions. A subsequent period may allow a different median voter or coalition of voters to emerge as dominant—a decisive voter or group that may choose to inflate from strictly short-term considerations. To the extent that this takes place, all of the initial benefits of policy prudence may be offset. In the recognition of this prospect, why should the decisive voter or coalition of voters in the initial period exhibit nonmyopic "rationality" in the sense indicated?[2]

The ultimate answer to the assigned question is clear in this highly simplified model for "democratic" politics. Policy activism cannot be successful if the criterion of success is long-term monetary stability, a criterion that seems most likely to emerge consensually in a constitutional process of deliberation.[3]

5. Nonmonolithic and Nonbenevolent Agents in a Political Structure Subject to Varying Electoral Constraints

The political models examined in sections 3 and 4 were oversimplified in the assumption that authority was placed in a single agent or agency. As we approach reality, it is necessary to recognize that policy-making authority is likely to be divided among several agents or agencies, who (which) may be subjected to quite different electoral controls or constraints and, hence, potentially affected by differing electoral pressures. For example, fiscal or budgetary policies may be made in a wholly different process, institutionally, from monetary policy, and, even within the institutional structure of budgetary policy, authority may be divided between executive and legislative branches of government, subjected to varying electoral constraints, as defined by such things as breadth of constituencies, length of terms of office, voting structure within agency (in legislatures and committees), legally defined responsibilities, and so on.

The direction of difference in effects between this more realistic political model and the monolithic model previously examined seems evident. To the extent that policy-making authority is divided, the proclivity toward response to short-term pressures is increased. Any array of results along the success criterion indicated would indicate that the divided-authority model ranks well below its monolithic counterpart.

6. Nonbenevolent but Monolithic Agent Divorced from Direct Electoral Constraints but Subject to Legal–Constitutional Rules against Personal Enrichment

If there is little or no basis for expecting political agents to express benevolence in their policy behavior, and if, as suggested, the standard "democratic" controls will not themselves insure patterns of outcomes that meet reasonable criteria of success, alternative institutional structures must be analyzed. Consider, first, a model in which decision-making authority is lodged in a single agent or agency and one that is specifically divorced from the electoral process—an agent or agency that does not face continual electoral checks. To prevent that potential for excess under the model discussed in section 3, however, suppose that the agent or members of the agency are placed within enforcible legal–constitutional limits with reference to his or their personal or private enrichment, either directly or indirectiy. That is to say, the agent or members of the agency cannot use the money creation and/or taxing power to finance their own private consumption needs or accumulation (e.g., Swiss bank accounts) desires. Beyond this restriction, however, we shall assume that the agent or members of the agency is (are) not limited in behavior except in the overall and general mandate to carry out "good" macroeconomic policy.

This model can, of course, be recognized as one that is closely analogous to the monetary authority of the Federal Reserve Board in the United States. Some elements of the model discussed in section 3—that of the nonconstrained despot—describe the existing structure, and, more importantly, some political controls are exercised; but, for my purposes, the existing monetary authority fits the model reasonably well.

The problem becomes one of predicting the behavior of such an agent and of assessing this behavior in terms of the success criterion introduced. Neither economic nor public-choice analysis is capable of being of much assistance in this respect. To make a prediction, one must get inside the utility function of the agent (or of those who participate in agency decisions). In particular, it would be necessary to know something about the internal rate of time preference that will characterize behavior. If, as we have assumed, demand-enhancing action is known to generate short-term benefits at the expense of long-term costs, the behavior of the monopolistic and discretionary agent in making this trade-off will depend strictly on his own, private, rate of time preference, as expressed "for" the community. That is to say, under the conditions indicated, the agent will not, personally, secure the benefits or suffer the costs. By definition, the agent is not *responsible*, in the sense of a reward–penalty calculus.

This absence of responsibility itself suggests that the behavior of the discretionary agent is likely to be less carefully considered, to be based on less information, and hence to be more erratic than would be the case under some alternative reward–penalty structure. The model further suggests that the agent here is more likely to be responsive to the passing whims of intellectual-media "fashion" than might be the case in the presence of some residual claimancy status. To the extent that the agent is at all responsive to interest-group pressures, such response seems likely to be biased toward those groups seeking near-term benefits and biased against those groups that might be concerned about long-term costs, if for no other reason than the difference in temporal dimension itself. Organized pressures for the promotion of short-term benefits exist while there may be no offsetting organization of long-term interests. This bias might well be exaggerated if the agent or agency is assigned functions that cause the development of relationships with particular functional groups in the policy (e.g., banking and finance). In sum, although there is really no satisfactory predictive model for behavior of the genuinely discretionary agent or agency, there are plausibly acceptable reasons to suggest that policy failures will tend to take the directions indicated in the discussion here.

Viewed in this perspective, and in application to the Federal Reserve agency in the United States, and perhaps notably after the removal of international monetary constraints, there should have been no surprise that the behavior exhibited has been highly erratic. Any other pattern would indeed have required more explanation than that which has been observed. From both analysis and observation the ultimate answer to the question concerning "successful" policy activism in this model, as in the others examined, must be negative.

7. Nonbenevolent and Monolithic Agent Divorced from Electoral Constraints but Subject to Legal-Constitutional Rules Against Personal Enrichment but Also to Constitutional Rules That Direct Policy Action

The generally negative answer to the question posed in the title prompts examination of still other institutional structures that do not involve attempts at "policy activism," as such, but which, instead, embody sets of predictable and directed policy actions in accordance with constitutionally specified rules. In familiar terminology, if "policy activism," when applied in a setting of *discretionary authority*, must fail to meet the success criterion, can a setting of *rules* do better? It would be inappropriate to discuss at length the relative advantages of alternative regimes or sets of rules. But it is clear that almost any well-defined set of rules would eliminate most of the incentive and motivational sources for the failure of discretionary agency models as previously discussed.

In a very real sense there is no agency problem in an effectively operating rule-ordered regime. A fiscal–monetary authority, charged with the actual implementation of policy, but only in the carrying out of specified rules, defined either in terms of means or objectives, cannot itself be judged on other than purely administrative criteria of success or failure. More ultimate criteria must now be applied to the alternative sets of rules, with success or failure accordingly assigned. And working models of such alternative sets might be analyzed, just as the models of a discretionary agency have been analyzed here. But there seems to be a closer relationship between the rules that might be selected and the success criterion adopted than there is between the latter and the pronounced goals of a discretionary agency.

The potential for success of rule-guided macropolicy depends, in large part, on the *absence* of policy activism, not only for the removal of the potential for self-interested behavior on the part of discretionary agents, but also for the built-in predictability of such action that is inherent in the notion of rules, as such. The relative advantages of rule-guided policy over agency discretion could be treated at length, but this effort would carry me well beyond my assignment in this paper.

8. Fiscal Policy and Monetary Policy

There are two distinct policy instruments, or sets of instruments, in both the familiar textbook terminology and, indeed, in the overall subject of this conference: fiscal policy instruments and monetary policy instruments. To this point I have made no distinction between these two sets, and I have avoided altogether any discussion of relative efficacy as well as relative vulnerability to the sorts of influences on behavior that are emphasized in a public-choice approach. It is time to explore some of the differences that are directly relevant to the arguments that I have advanced.

Fiscal policy involves budgetary manipulation and, hence, a necessary linkage between any macropolicy objectives and the whole process of public-sector allocation. Given this necessary linkage, and given the institutional–political history, it seems totally unreal to suggest that any shift of authority over fiscal policy would be delegated to either discretionary or even to rule-bound authority. It seems highly unlikely that fiscal policy, in any sense, would be removed from the ordinary procedures of democratic decision making, with divided legislative and executive responsibilities and roles in its overall formulation. It becomes unrealistic in the extreme to presume that we, in the United States, would transfer to an agency immune from electoral constraints any authority to manipulate either side of the budget in accordance with rules or intentions to improve macroeconomic performance. Decisions on tax rates, spending rates, and, in consequence, deficits and borrowing requirements, are likely to remain within the responsibility of "democratic" determination, with the predicted result that any meaningful success criterion will fail to be satisfied. There will be a bias toward "easy budgets," with higher-than-desired deficits, to the extent that any considerations of macroeconomic policy enter the policy argument.[4]

Given this predicted bias, and quite apart from any consideration as to the independent efficacy of budgetary policy in effectuating desired results, any genuine hope for "success" in macroeconomic policy must involve a reduction or removal of budgetary manipulation from the potentially usable kit of tools.[5] If "fiscal policy" can be isolated so as to insure that its operation does not make the task of monetary management more difficult, a major step toward genuine reform will have been made. It is in this context that the argument for a constitutional rule requiring budget balance becomes important in macroeconomic policy discussion.

If fiscal policy is so isolated, the task of policy action is left to the monetary agency or regime. A monetary agency can be made effective if the discretion of the agent is limited by the imposition of legally binding and enforcible rules for policy actions. These rules may take on any one of several forms, and it would be out of place to discuss these alternatives in detail here. The monetary agency can be directed to act on the defined monetary aggregates so as to insure prespecified quantity targets (as in some Friedman-like growth rule). Or the authority might be directed to act so as to achieve a specifically defined outcome target, such as the maintenance of stability in the value of the monetary unit. In either case the structure of the rules must be such as to invoke penalties for the failure of the authorities to act in accordance with the declared norms. Some allowance for within-threshold departures from targeted objectives would, of course, be necessary.

But only with some such feedbacks in place can the persons in positions of responsibility as monetary agents be expected to perform so as to further the success criterion that is implicit in the imposition of the rules. It seems at least conceptually possible to build in a workable reward–penalty structure for the compensation and employment of rule-bound monetary agents. And, in the limiting case, such a reward–penalty structure, appropriately related to the achievement of the desired policy target, may obviate the need for explicit definition of a rule for policy action. For example, if the compensations of all employees of the monetary authority should be indexed so as to insure personal penalty from any departures from monetary stability, perhaps nothing more need be required by way of rules. (Such a scheme might involve the maintenance of fixed nominal salary levels against inflation, and double indexing of salaries against deflation, or some more sophisticated formulae.)

If no incentive–motivational structure is deemed to be institutionally and politically feasible, under the operation of any fiat money regime, the argument for more basic regime shift in the direction of an automatic or self-correcting system based on some commodity base is substantially strengthened. The relative advantage of all such systems lies in their incorporation of market-like incentives to generate behavior that will tend to generate at least long-term stability in the value of the monetary unit.

9. Conclusion

In this discussion, as elsewhere, the primary implication of public-choice theory is that institutional–constitutional change or reform is required to achieve ultimate success in macroeconomic policy. There is relatively little to be gained by advancing arguments for "better informed" and "more public-spirited" agents, to be instructed by increasingly sophisticated "economic consultants" who are abreast of the frontiers of the "new science." All such effort will do little more than provide employment for those who are involved. It is the *political economy of policy* that must be reformed. Until and unless this step is taken, observed patterns of policy outcomes will continue to reflect accurately the existing political economy within which these outcomes are produced. And we shall continue to have conferences and discussions about the failures of "policy activism."

Notes

1. For further elaboration and analysis, see Geoffrey Brennan and James Buchanan (1980) Chap. 6; and (1981).
2. For further elaboration of the analysis, see Geoffrey Brennan and James Buchanan (forthcoming), Chaps. 5 and 6.
3. I shall not develop the argument in support of the contractarian–constitutional criterion for measuring policy success or failure. Let me say only that such a criterion must be used unless we are willing to introduce external and nonindividualistic standards of evaluation.

A more controversial position is the one that suggests that the monetary stability criterion would, indeed, be the one that would emerge from the ideally constructed constitutional setting. I shall not develop the argument in support of this position, although I think it can be plausibly made.
4. For an early statement of this point, see Buchanan (1962). For a more extended discussion, see James M. Buchanan and Richard E. Wagner (1977, 1978).
5. Keynes and the Keynesians must bear a heavy responsibility for destroying the set of classical precepts for fiscal prudence that had operated to keep the natural proclivities of politicians in bounds. By offering what could be interpreted as plausible excuses for fiscal profligacy, modern politicians have, for several decades, been able to act out their natural urges, with the results that we now observe. For further discussion see Buchanan (1984).

References

Brennan, Geoffrey, and James M. Buchanan. 1980. *The Power to Tax*. Cambridge: Cambridge University Press.

_____. 1981. *Monopoly in Money and Inflation*. London: Institute of Economic Affairs.

_____. n.d. *The Reason of Rules*. Cambridge: Cambridge University Press, forthcoming.

Buchanan, James M. 1962. Easy Budgets and Tight Money. *Lloyds Bank Review*. 64: 17–30.

_____. Victorian Budgetary Norms, Keynesian Advocacy and Modern Fiscal Politics. Prepared for Nobel Symposium on Governmental Growth, Stockholm, Sweden, August 1984. Center for Study of Public Choice Working Paper No. 4–02.

Buchanan, James M., and Richard E. Wagner. 1977. *Democracy in Deficit*. New York: Academic Press.

_____, eds. 1978. *Fiscal Responsibility in Constitutional Democracy*. Boston: Martinus Nijhoff.

Central Bank Behavior and Credibility: Some Recent Theoretical Developments

Alex Cukierman

ONE of the most widely accepted tenets of monetary theory is that persistent inflation is a monetary phenomenon. A deeper understanding of persistent inflation, therefore, must uncover the reasons for persistent increases in the money stock. This leads naturally to an investigation of the motives and constraints facing central bankers who decide the course of monetary policy.

Recent theoretical literature on the behavior of monetary policymakers may be divided into two broad categories — positive and normative. The *positive* literature formulates hypotheses about the objectives and constraints facing central bankers and derives implications for the behavior of both observable variables (e.g., the rate of monetary growth and the rate of inflation) and unobservable variables (e.g., policy credibility). The *normative* literature focuses on the issue of how, given the behavior of central bankers, monetary institutions can be redesigned to improve social welfare. Both approaches use the same general analytic framework to model central bank behavior.

This paper, the first in a two-part survey, focuses on the positive aspects of central bank behavior, with particular emphasis on the characterization and the determinants of policy credibility.

POSITIVE APPROACHES TO CENTRAL BANK BEHAVIOR AND THE IMPORTANCE OF CREDIBILITY: AN OVERVIEW

Positive (and normative) theories of central bank behavior rely heavily on the notion that unanticipated money growth has temporary, positive effects on output and employment as a result either of the Lucas (1973) effect[1] or the existence of long-term contracts in conjunction with ex post determination of employment by labor demand.[2] They also rely on the view that central bankers have a well-defined objective function (preferences) for economic stimulation and inflation within each period as well as intertemporal preferences over combinations of those variables in the present and in the future.

The notion of policy credibility is a fundamental one because the ability of monetary policymakers to achieve their future objectives depends on the inflationary expectations of the public. These inflationary expectations depend, in turn, on the public's evaluation of the credibility of the monetary policymakers. For example, Fellner (1976) and Haberler (1980), who coined the term "Credibility Hypothesis," have stressed that the less credible disinflationary policies are, the longer and the more severe their interim adverse economic effects will be.

Alex Cukierman is a professor of economics at Tel-Aviv University and a former visiting scholar at the Federal Reserve Bank of St. Louis. David J. Flanagan provided research assistance.

[1]A recent exposition appears in chapter 3 of Cukierman (1984).

[2]Fischer (1977), Taylor (1980).

The theoretical literature defines credibility as the extent to which the public believes that a shift in policy has taken place when, indeed, such a shift has actually occurred.[3] More important, to be credible, a policy must be consistent, at each stage, with the public's information about the objectives and constraints facing the central bank. The public will not believe an announced policy if it knows the policy is incompatible with the current objectives of policymakers.

Part of the theoretical literature interprets the central bank's objective function as a social welfare function. In this approach, the policymaker is cast as a benevolent planner whose sole concern is to maximize a well-defined social welfare function. Another part of the literature interprets the objective function of the policymaker in terms of political objectives. In this approach, the importance assigned to preventing inflation relative to stimulating the economy depends on the relative influence on the central bank of the pro-stimulation and anti-inflation advocates within government and the private sector. Formal models based on the social welfare and political approaches are similar at times; however, interpretations of their results are quite different depending on which approach is used. Therefore, the two approaches are discussed separately.

THE SOCIAL WELFARE APPROACH AS A POSITIVE THEORY OF CENTRAL BANK BEHAVIOR

The social welfare approach is based on three key relationships. First, the economy is one in which deviations of employment from its natural level are positively related to unanticipated inflation; this can result from either the existence of a Lucas (1973)-type short-run Phillips curve or a Fischer (1977)-Taylor (1980) contract framework. Second, the monetary authority has a social welfare function that gives a negative weight to inflation and a positive weight to employment even beyond the natural rate.[4] It chooses the rate of money growth and, hence, inflation, over which it has perfect control, that maximizes the social

Table 1
The Monetary Policy Game: Basic Model

I. Output Relationship

(1) $y = y_n + (m - m^e)$

II. Social Welfare Function = Policymaker's Objective Function

(2) $W = -m^2 + 2(y - y_n)$

III. Policymaker's Objective Function in terms of m

(3) $W = -m^2 + 2(m - m^e)$

IV. Public's Utility Function

(4) $U = -(m - m^e)^2$

welfare function.[5] Finally, the public understands the central bank's behavior and forms its inflationary expectations accordingly. Since inflation is "bad," the best rate of monetary expansion must be zero. Therefore, social welfare is maximized when both the actual and expected inflation are zero and employment is at its natural level.

Yet, the relatively simple model just described is sufficient to generate an inflationary bias; as a result, social welfare is lower than it would have been had the monetary authority been credibly committed to a zero money growth (zero inflation) rule.[6] In essence, the monetary authorities and the public are caught up in a kind of "prisoners' dilemma."

The Prisoners'-Dilemma Aspect of Monetary Policy

The dilemma is illustrated simply in the following model.[7] The monetary authority and the public can be viewed as engaged in a game to determine what the level of output and the rate of inflation will be. The economy's output is determined by a Lucas-Sargent aggregate supply function as shown in equation 1 in table 1, where y is the actual level of output, y_n is its

---

[3]Under this definition, a new policy is credible if it is promptly believed, whether or not the new policy is more or less inflationary than the old one. This point is made in a related survey by McCallum (1984).

[4]The natural rate is the level of employment that would be obtained in the absence of monetary disturbances. Employment or output beyond this level contributes to social welfare if distortionary taxes or other constraints hold employment below its optimal level. An elaboration appears at the end of this section.

[5]Short-run discrepancies between the rate of inflation and the rate of monetary growth are abstracted from, in this discussion, by assuming that those two rates are equal at all times.

[6]This scenario originated in a well-known example by Kydland and Prescott (1977) and was elaborated and formulated within an explicitly dynamic framework by Barro and Gordon (1983b).

[7]This model is based on a static reformulation by Backus and Driffill (1985a).

Table 2

Payoff Tables for Basic Monetary Policy Game

I. Policymaker's Payoff Table (from equation 3)

Policymaker chooses (m)	Public expects (m^e)	
	0	1
0	0	- 2
1	1	- 1

II. Public's Payoff Table (from equation 4)

Policymaker chooses (m)	Public expects (m^e)	
	0	1
0	0	- 1
1	- 1	0

natural level, and m and m^e are the actual and expected inflation rates, respectively.[8] The policymaker's objective function (taken to be identical to the social welfare function) is shown in equation 2 (table 1).[9]

When equation 1 is substituted into 2, the policymaker's objective function now takes the form shown in equation 3 in table 1. Taking m^e as given, the value of m that maximizes social welfare is m = 1, resulting in a positive inflation rate. This outcome can easily be seen in the monetary policymaker's payoff matrix shown in table 2 (I). If the monetary authority chooses zero inflation, m = 0, its payoff is either 0 or - 2, depending on whether m^e equals 0 or 1. If it chooses m = 1, however, its payoff is either 1 or - 1, depending on whether m^e equals 0 or 1. Inflation is clearly the dominant strategy from the point of view of the monetary authority; the payoffs for m = 1 are higher *regardless of what inflation rate the public expects*.

So far the analysis has focused solely on the monetary policymaker's objective function. However, the public also has an objective function; it is assumed to resist being fooled by policymakers. The public is assumed to maximize a utility function similar to equation 4 in table 1, taking m as given. Because the public knows the monetary authority's incentive

structure, it expects the monetary authority to choose m = 1; consequently, it chooses m^e = 1.[10] The resultant outcome is an inferior solution, with payoffs of - 1 to the monetary authority and 0 to the public.

The inflationary bias occurs because the monetary authority has the incentive to inflate in order to increase employment once the public's inflationary expectations have been set. This incentive is present regardless of whether the public expects a zero or a positive rate of inflation. Because the public recognizes this incentive, it rationally expects a positive rate of inflation; this forces the monetary authority actually to inflate in order to maintain employment at its natural level. As a result, the economy ends up with the same employment level as under a zero money growth rule, but with excessive inflation and lower welfare.

Barro and Gordon (1983b) characterize this solution as "discretionary" because the monetary authority can choose whatever rate of monetary growth (and, hence, inflation) it desires. If the monetary authority had been credibly committed to zero money growth (by a constitutional amendment, for example), the superior solution, m = m^e = 0, could have been achieved. But, in the absence of credible commitments on the part of the policymaker, the (Nash) equilibrium to the policy game involves positive and suboptimal inflation.[11]

A Dynamic Extension of the Model

As pointed out by Barro and Gordon (1983b), the prisoners'-dilemma aspect of the policy game carries over to the case in which the policymaker cares about social welfare in both the present and future periods. This can be illustrated by generalizing the objective function of the policymaker as shown in equation 5:

$$(5) \quad W = \sum_{i=0}^{\infty} \beta^i \left[A(m_i - m_i^e) - \frac{m_i^2}{2} \right].$$

β is the discount factor applied to future welfare in the policymaker's social welfare function. The term in brackets is the level of social welfare attained in the ith period.[12] The constant, A, is the marginal rate of substitution between economic stimulation and inflation prevention; the larger A is, the more the policy-

---

[8]Since output and employment are positively related, y can also be viewed as a proxy for employment.

[9]The various constants in equations 1 and 2 have been chosen for simplicity of exposition. The main qualitative point does not depend on the values of those constants.

[10]This is obtained by differentiating equation 4 with respect to m^e, equating to zero and solving for m^e.

[11]A Nash equilibrium is defined as a situation in which each of two sides chooses his best strategy, taking as given the optimal response of the other side.

[12]This term is a slightly more general form of equation 3.

maker cares about employment relative to inflation prevention at the margin.

As before, the policymaker chooses m_i to maximize the social welfare function in equation 5, taking m_i^e as given. Since there is nothing that links the periods, maximization of equation 5 is equivalent to maximization of welfare within each period separately. More formally, the policymaker maximizes equation 6 for all i:

$$(6)\quad W_i = A(m_i - m_i^e) - \frac{m_i^2}{2}.$$

As shown in the monetary policymaker's pay-off matrix in table 3, the best choice is $m_i = A$ in all periods.[13]

As before, the public resists being fooled. Because it understands the structure of incentives facing the policymaker, it rationally sets $m_i^e = A$ in all periods. Again, the economy ends up with a positive rate of inflation. As before, the discretionary solution is not optimal; zero money growth yields a value of zero to the policymaker (if the public expects money growth to be zero), while the discretionary result yields a social welfare of $-A^2/2$.

It is tempting to argue that a sophisticated policymaker would eliminate this suboptimality by simply consistently setting $m_i = 0$, thus convincing the public that m_i^e should equal zero as well. The public, however, knows that, as soon as they expect inflation to be zero, the policymaker can increase welfare (to $A^2/2$) by reverting to the discretionary inflation solution. Because the policymaker will revert to discretion in this case, the public will rationally expect that inflation will equal A. As a result, the best solution, $m_i = m_i^e = 0$ is unstable, whereas the discretionary (Nash) solution $m_i = m_i^e = A$ is stable.[14]

The Impact of Asymmetric Information

To this point, the public and the policymaker were assumed to have the same information. Suppose, however, that this is not the case. Backus and Driffill (1985a, 1985b) consider a model in which the policymaker is one of two types: "weak" or "strong." If the policymaker is weak, his payoff matrix is the one shown in table 2(I) or 3(I); he, therefore, has an incentive to generate inflation. If the policymaker is strong, however, he always prefers zero inflation.

---

[13]It is obtained from the first-order condition for the maximization of (6).

[14]The dynamic inconsistency of the first best solution was originally noted by Kydland and Prescott (1977).

Table 3

Payoff Tables for a Typical Period in the Dynamic Monetary Policy Game

I. Policymaker's Payoff Table (from equation 6)

Policymaker chooses (m_i)	Public expects (m_i^e)	
	0	A
0	0	$-3A^2/2$
A	$A^2/2$	$-A^2/2$

II. Public's Payoff Table (from equation 4)

Policymaker chooses (m_i)	Public expects (m_i^e)	
	0	A
0	0	$-A^2$
A	$-A^2$	0

In the beginning, the public assigns some probability to the condition that the policymaker is strong and, therefore, will not inflate. Weak policymakers are tempted to inflate. However, since they maximize welfare over several periods, they have an incentive to appear strong, at least initially, to discourage inflationary expectations. The public watches the actions of the policymaker and adjusts its probability accordingly that the policymaker is strong. This probability is considered to be a measure of credibility.

As long as the policymaker does not inflate, the public assigns some positive probability to the event that the policymaker is strong. If the policymaker inflates *even one time*, however, he immediately reveals himself to be weak. Because strong policymakers never inflate, there is no way that a policymaker can reestablish his lost reputation. Consequently, once inflation starts, it continues forever.

Backus and Driffill formulate this problem as a dynamic, mixed-strategies Bayesian game using Kreps and Wilson's (1982a, 1982b) notion of sequential equilibrium.[15] This formulation captures the incentive of the weak policymaker to act temporarily as if he were strong in order to maintain future inflationary expectations at a lower level. It also provides the public with a rationale for watching the actions of the policymaker, at least until it is known that he is weak. This analysis is restricted, however, by the fact that the policymaker can be one of only two unchanging types. As

---

[15]A similar analysis appears in Barro (1985).

a consequence, once a reputation is destroyed, it cannot be rebuilt. Those features of the analysis are inconsistent with the observed frequent reversals in the rate of monetary growth in the United States, England and other democracies.

Criticism of the Social Welfare Approach

Because equation 2, or its multi-period variant, equation 5, is used frequently as a social welfare function in the theoretical literature on central bank behavior, it is important to examine why it takes this specific form.[16] The negative effect of inflation on social welfare results from the familiar loss of consumer surplus that inflation produces through the decrease in the public's real money balances. The positive association between deviations of employment from its natural level and social welfare can be explained by the existence of various labor market distortions (like taxes and unemployment benefits) that make the natural level of employment too low (Barro and Gordon, 1983b). Another explanation, offered by Canzoneri (1985), is that the presence of large unions keeps real wages too high and the natural employment level too low.

The view that the existence of distortionary taxes necessarily induces an inflationary bias on the part of a socially minded central bank raises several questions. First, this notion relies only on the distortionary effect of taxes on the allocation of time between labor and leisure, neglecting the utility from the public good that is financed by these taxes. Since individuals take the level of the public good provided by government as being independent from their individual labor-leisure decisions, while the central bank takes into consideration that this level depends on total tax collections — which depend in turn on total employment — there is also an externality. If the socially optimal level of the public good is higher than the amount that can be financed through the taxes collected in the absence of central bank intervention, the bank has an incentive to increase total tax collections. Whether this implies that it has an incentive to increase employment or decrease it depends on the tax structure and the elasticity of labor demand. In the latter case, the tax distortion and the public good externality have conflicting effects on the socially optimal level of employment in relation to its general equilibrium level in the absence of central bank intervention. Cukierman and

Drazen (1986) show within a nominal contracts framework of the Fischer (1977) type that, if the demand for labor is sufficiently inelastic, the last effect dominates, producing an incentive to decrease employment via unanticipated deflation. Furthermore, the range of cases in which the central bank turns out not to have an inflationary bias is by no means negligible.[17] The upshot is that a socially minded policymaker facing distortionary labor taxes should not be automatically presumed to possess an inflationary bias.

Second, if the level of employment is too low because of distortionary taxes, a full analysis of the behavior of policymakers should be able to determine simultaneously both inflation and other taxes, taking into consideration the tax revenues from inflation. Such an extension is considered by Alesina and Tabellini (1985) within a framework in which fiscal and monetary policies are determined by two independent authorities. An important implication of this framework is that the resulting equilibrium rate of inflation is not necessarily suboptimal. This will be discussed more fully in the second installment of this survey.

Finally, the social welfare function interpretation of the policymaker's objectives does not fit very well with the notion that there are two alternative types of policymakers. One possibility might be that there are two alternative welfare functions that characterize the economy. If that is the case, however, it seems peculiar that the relevant one is known only to the policymaker. Indeed, this possibility seems untenable. Another possibility is that, while the objective function of the weak policymaker is identical to the social welfare function, the strong policymaker's objective function is different from it. Once it is recognized that the objectives of the policymaker may differ from the social welfare function, however, there is no reason to restrict the analysis to only a single alternative formulation. Consideration of a variety of alternatives is handled by a political interpretation of the policymaker's objective function.

THE POLITICAL APPROACH AS A POSITIVE THEORY OF CENTRAL BANK BEHAVIOR

Recent work in both economics and political science suggests that monetary policy is not totally divorced from the general political process. For exam-

---

[17]For example, when there is too much of the public good in the no-intervention equilibrium, the central bank has a deflationary bias, provided labor demand is sufficiently elastic.

[16]In addition to the papers quoted above, those include Barro and Gordon (1983a), Backus and Driffill (1983b), Rogoff (1985) and, to some extent, Canzoneri (1985).

ple, in spite of the Federal Reserve's statutory independence from other branches of government, monetary policy is partly responsive to the desires of the President, Congress, the financial community and periodically some other less visible institutions or groups.[18]

Discretionary Policy, Changing Objectives and Asymmetric Information

The central bank knows both the extent of the political pressure focused on it to change monetary policy at any given moment and how likely it is to accommodate this pressure. Further, the formation of effective coalitions determined to change the course of monetary policy is subject to large stochastic elements. Cukierman and Meltzer (1986a) formalize this notion with an objective function similar to equation 5 in which the monetary authority's marginal prefer-

ence for economic stimulation vs. inflation prevention shifts randomly through time. In this formulation, the constant marginal rate of substitution A is replaced by a random variable x_i which reflects the current compromise that the central bank strikes between advocates of economic stimulation and advocates of price stability.[19]

The crucial element in this formulation is that x_i is in a continuous state of flux and is not known by the general public. However, the public can rationally and gradually detect *changes* in x_i by observing changes in the rate of growth of the money supply; this detection activity provides an explanation for "Fed watching." Since the public is unaware, at any given moment, of the precise value of the central bank's current x_i, the central bank is able to affect output through surprise money creation.

There are both similarities and differences between the social welfare and the political interpretation of the policymaker's objective function adopted in this section.[20] The political approach views the policymaker as choosing money growth to maximize the expected value of

$$(7) \quad \sum_{i=0}^{\infty} \beta_i [x_i (m_i - m_i^e) - \frac{m_i^2}{2}],$$

where x_i is a stochastic variable with some persistence.[21]

Equation 7 is formally equivalent to equation 5 with the sole exception that A is replaced by x_i; however, its interpretation is quite different. Equation 7 reflects the current political compromise between competing objectives preferred by the policymaker; it is not a social welfare function. Similarly, the discount factor β reflects the time preference of the policymaker as an

---

[18] The precise channels through which these responses are elicited are subtle and, at times, elude precise formulation because the President, Congress and the Federal Reserve all have a common interest in preserving an image of the Central Bank as an independent, apolitical institution.

Kane (1980, 1982) has argued that the Federal Reserve performs a scapegoat function for the President and Congress. In return, the Fed gets a fair degree of independence which is necessary in order to credibly perform the scapegoat function. A general discussion of the political approach in the context of monetary reform appears in Willet and McArthur (1985).

Weintraub (1978, p. 356) concludes after summarizing the history of the post-accord monetary policy that much of this policy ". . . can be explained just by noting who the President was when the policy under review was in effect." In a study of Presidential influence on monetary policy, Beck (1982) concludes that presidential political demands are somehow transmitted to the Fed. Beck notes that the transmission mechanism requires further study but that it seems clear that presidential preferences are an important determinant of Fed policymaking (Beck, 1982, p. 443). Woolley (1984) holds a similar view. Hetzel (1985) argues that current institutional arrangements allow Congressmen to pass on political pressures of various constituent groups to the Fed while avoiding association with the consequences that adversely affect the welfare of other groups. This explains Congress' consistent preference (noted by Woolley, 1984, chapter 7) for attempting to influence monetary policy through a variety of threats to limit the Fed's institutional autonomy rather than through an explicit mandate to guide monetary policy (Hetzel, 1985, p. 7). Since the autonomy of the Fed depends on Congress, it must be at least somewhat sensitive to the wishes of Congress provided the Fed values autonomy.

Both Congress and the Presidency are institutions largely concerned with various redistributional considerations. As a consequence the Fed is, possibly to a lesser degree, also sensitive to redistributional considerations. In addition, the Fed is not indifferent to the interests of groups with which it deals on a daily basis, e.g., banks and the financial community in general (Woolley, chapter 4). Arthur Burns (1979) appears to share the view that the Fed is not a totally free agent. He believes that the Fed can work to achieve price stability only if the policy does not adversely affect production and employment and does not irritate Congress. In Burns' words, the role of the Fed is to continue "probing the limits of its freedom to undernourish . . . inflation" (Burns 1979, p. 16).

[19] The motivation of either group of advocates may be mostly distributional. Some people are relatively more adversely affected by unemployment than by inflation. Changes in x_i reflect changes in (a) the relative sizes of those groups, (b) the degree to which they are adversely affected by inflation and unemployment and, (c) the perceptions of the central bank about those changes and the degree of urgency in accommodating them. In some long-run sense, the central bank may be responding to the desires of voters. However, the public does not know the extent to which the central bank currently responds to voters.

[20] The following discussion draws heavily on Cukierman and Meltzer (1986a).

[21] The precise stochastic structure is:

(a) $x_i = A + p_i$ $\quad\quad$ $A > 0$

(b) $p_i = \rho p_{i-1} + v_i$ $\quad\quad$ $0 < \rho < 1$

(c) $v_i \sim N(0, \sigma_v^2)$.

A is a positive, publicly known, constant and p_i a first-order Markoff process whose realization is known only to the policymaker.

institution with its own priorities rather than the social rate of discount.[22]

The political interpretation avoids some of the criticisms directed toward the social welfare interpretation for the policymaker's objective function. Thus, while it is difficult to explain why the monetary authority should be better informed about the social welfare function than the public, it is easy to believe that the policymaker is better informed about x_i, which simply reflects the policymaker's currently preferred compromise between conflicting objectives.[23]

The policymaker acts in a discretionary manner in planning the rate of money growth (and inflation), taking into account the tradeoffs he faces between current stimulation and the public's future inflationary expectations. In particular, the policymaker knows that current actions which raise future inflation expectations make it more costly (in terms of inflation) to further stimulate the economy in the future. The policymaker chooses both the current money growth and plans for future money growth to achieve a maximum for the expected value of the objective function in equation 7.

The Effects of Imperfect Control and Uncertain Future Objectives

The decision pattern just described is complicated by two additional conditions. First, the policymaker is assumed to have imperfect control of the money supply — actual money growth deviates randomly from the growth planned by the monetary authority as shown in equation 8,

(8) $m_i = m_i^p + \eta_i$,

where m_i^p is the rate of monetary growth planned by the policymaker for period i and η_i is period i's realization of a white noise process, the variance of which is determined by the precision of existing monetary control procedures.[24]

Second, the policymaker is assumed to be uncertain about his own future objectives. He knows, however, their current values and uses their persistent structure (see footnote 21) to derive optimal predictors of future values of x_i. These predictions are necessary, even though no commitment to any particular future money growth is required, because he knows that the current rate of monetary growth will affect future inflationary expectations. If he expects to care more about employment in the future than he does now, he will increase his ability to create surprises at relatively low inflation in future periods by choosing a relatively low current monetary growth. If he expects to care less about employment in the future than he does at present, he will choose faster current monetary growth (and faster inflation).

The important point is that the policymaker must predict his own uncertain objectives in the future when choosing the current rate of money growth. This uncertainty arises because he does not currently know for certain what the future optimal (for him) balance will be between pressures exerted by various groups and institutions. The more stable the underlying socio-political environment, the smaller this uncertainty will be. The uncertainty can be measured by the variance of the policymaker's objectives; this is denoted as σ_v^2 (see footnote 21).

Cukierman and Meltzer (1986a) (CM hereafter) show that the solution to the policymaker's decision problem in equation 7 is

(9) $m_i^p = B_o A + B p_i$,

where B_o and B are positive constants that depend on the parameters of the policymaker's objective function and the precision of monetary control, and where p_i is the random part of x_i (see footnote 21). When equation 9 is substituted into equation 8, actual money growth can be expressed as

(10) $m_i = B_o A + B p_i + \eta_i$.

This model assumes that the public does not know the current state of the policymaker's objectives — x_i or p_i is known only by the policymaker.[25] The public, however, knows the policymaker's decision rule in equation 10 and has observed m in each period up to and including the previous one. Since m_i has some degree of persistence, past values of money growth convey noisy, but meaningful, information about future money growth to the public. The noise is induced by the control error, η_i.

---

[22] This formulation is consistent with the views of long-time students of the Fed like Lombra and Moran (1980), Lombra (1984) and Kane (1982) concerning the Federal Reserve System. In particular, Kane (1982, p. 207) writes:

"Inherent in the utopian view of the Fed is the presumption that the Fed can somehow evaluate the public interest on its own. In the contemporary United States, it is hard to conceive of the public interest except as a delicate balance of conflicting private interests."

[23] In addition, the political approach does not rely on the notion that distortionary taxes necessarily induce policies biased toward inflation.

[24] The case in which the level of precision in monetary control is a choice variable is considered later in this paper.

[25] Since A is public information, knowledge of x_i is equivalent to knowledge of p_i.

The optimal predictor of future money growth adjusts slowly to actual changes in observed money growth; specifically,

(11) $m_i^e = (\rho - \lambda) m_{i-1} + \lambda m_{i-1}^e + (1 - \rho) B_o A.$[26]

The parameter λ is determined by the degree of persistence in the policymaker's objectives, the precision of monetary control and the degree of instability in the political environment of the policymaker as measured by σ_τ^2. Because λ is bounded between 0 and ρ, the value of $\rho - \lambda$ is positive.

Equation 11 specifies that expected money growth is a weighted average of last period's money growth, m_{i-1}, the last period's expectation, m_{i-1}^e and B_o A.[27] Inflationary expectations partially adjust to changes in actual and planned money growth because, as implied by equation 10, actual money growth is influenced both by persistent changes in the objectives of the policymaker and by transitory control errors. The public, therefore, rationally attributes only part of the fluctuations in m to persistent changes in the objectives of the policymaker.

When choosing the rate of money growth, the policymaker takes into consideration its effect on future inflation expectations (equation 11). In fact, the policymaker's decision rule (equation 9) is the solution to maximization of the expected value of his objective function (equation 7), given how the public's inflation expectations are formed (equation 11).

The equilibrium formed from these equations is self-fulfilling. Given the decision rule of the policymaker (equation 9) and the money growth equation (equation 10), the best predictor of future inflation is given by equation 11. Conversely, given this predictor, the best strategy for the policymaker is shown by equation 9, which induces the money growth shown by equation 10.

Monetary Surprises and Credibility

The self-fulfilling nature of equilibrium does not mean that there are no monetary surprises. In fact, monetary surprises occur frequently; their expected value, however, is zero. The reason for frequent monetary surprises is that the objectives of the policymaker are continually changing; the public, however, becomes aware of those changes only gradually by observing past rates of inflation. Thus, when the policymaker becomes relatively less concerned about inflation prevention, the public recognizes this policy change only gradually. In the interim, actual inflation is higher than expected and employment is above its natural level. Conversely, when the policymaker becomes relatively more concerned about inflation prevention, inflation is lower than expected and output is below its natural level until the public recognizes this policy change.

The public monitors changes in monetary growth because these figures provide additional information about future inflation. This incentive to monitor money growth explains why resources are devoted to Fed watching (Bull, 1982; Hardouvelis, 1984). In the absence of asymmetric information, there would be no reason for this activity.

Recently Fischer (1984) has stressed the importance of the speed with which the public's expectations adjust for determining the costs of disinflation policy actions. The faster expectations adjust, the lower the output costs of disinflation will be. CM show that the speed with which expectations adjust is systematically related to the precision of monetary control. In particular, the less precise monetary control is, the larger is λ in equation 11 and the longer it takes for the public to recognize that the policymaker's objectives have changed.[28]

CM conceive of credibility as the speed with which the public recognizes that a change in the policymaker's objectives has actually occurred. This concept of credibility seems appropriate when policy is discretionary and the policymaker's objectives (known only to him) are in constant flux. The parameter λ from equation 11 is a natural and convenient measure of credibility.[29] Using this measure, credibility is higher, the more precise monetary control is (the lower the variance of η).

It has been observed that short-run considerations often are given relatively large weight in the actual conduct of monetary policy.[30] In terms of the frame-

---

[26]In statistical terms m_i^e is the expected value of m_i conditioned on $m_{i-1}, m_{i-2}, \ldots$

[27]Taking unconditional expected values on both sides of equation 10, B_o A can be recognized as the unconditional mean money growth.

[28]With a higher λ, less weight is given to the last observed inflation, m_{i-1}, and more weight is given to the last inflation expectation, m_{i-1}^e.

[29]As shown in equation (10b) of CM, λ is a known function of σ_τ^2 and ρ as well so that credibility is also influenced by the instability of objectives and their persistence.

[30]For example, see Brunner and Meltzer (1964), Kane (1977, 1980), Pierce (1980), and Mayer (1982).

work presented here, this observation means that the policymaker has a high time preference (β in equation 7 is low). CM show that the higher the policymaker's time preference, ceteris paribus, the higher the variability and the uncertainty in the rate of monetary growth.

The characterization of credibility differs somewhat among various models of monetary policy behavior. As explained above, in the CM formulation, credibility is a parameter. It measures the speed with which the public detects the actual changes in the policymaker's objectives. CM characterize credibility under discretion and asymmetric information. In models with two types of policymakers, credibility or reputation is a state variable.[31] It is the current subjective probability assigned by the public to the event that the policymaker is strong.

Barro and Gordon (1983b), on the other hand, focus on the credibility of the first-best, non-inflationary policy and point out that this policy is "incredible" under discretion and symmetric information.

The Credibility of Publicly Announced Monetary Targets

Cukierman and Meltzer (1986b) extend the politically based model to the case in which the policymaker makes noisy (e.g., announcements of target ranges rather than a specific level) but unbiased announcements about his future plans.[32] In this case, the public finds it optimal to use the information from past announcements in addition to past monetary growth to form its expectations. In comparison to the case in which no announcements are made, noisy announcements *never* increase (and usually decrease) the public's uncertainty about future monetary growth. In the case in which announcements are made, credibility is naturally defined as the deviation between the current announcement and the public's expectation. This deviation depends on the relative amounts of noise in both the control of the money supply and the announcements, as well as on the

magnitude of recent changes in the policymaker's objectives.

THE ROLE OF AMBIGUITY AND SECRECY IN THE CONDUCT OF MONETARY POLICY

Various students of central bank behavior have suggested that the low credibility and ambiguity in the specification of objectives by central banks may be, to some extent, deliberate.[33] The political approach presented in the previous section provides an explanation for this inclination for policy ambiguity. Consider the case in which the level of noise in monetary control is a choice variable rather than a technological datum. The policymaker will choose, once and for all, the variance of the monetary control error that maximizes the unconditional expected value of his objective function, which, for this discussion, is equation 7.[34]

For any given level of control precision, the planned and actual money growth are determined by equations 9 and 10, respectively, and the public's inflationary expectations are determined by equation 11. By choosing more noisy control procedures, the policymaker increases λ in equation 11; this, in turn, increases the length of time it takes the public to recognize a change in the policymaker's objectives.

Whether a longer recognition period is desirable, however, depends upon the change in policymaker objectives. It is advantageous when the policymaker becomes relatively more concerned about economic stimulation; in this case, he can produce positive surprises for a longer time period. When the policymaker becomes relatively more concerned about inflation, however, a higher λ is detrimental; it lengthens the period of recession and negative surprises necessary to decrease inflation. Thus, the policymaker would like to have lower credibility (in the CM sense)

---

[31]Backus and Driffill (1985a, 1985b); Barro (1985).

[32]House Concurrent Resolution 133, and later the Humphrey-Hawkins Act, require the Federal Reserve to announce planned rates of growth for principal monetary aggregates. The purpose of this legislation is to provide the public and Congress with more precise information about the particular monetary actions contemplated by the monetary authority. Announcements are (or have been) made in Germany, Japan, U.K., France, Canada, Australia and Switzerland.

[33]In recent hearings before the Joint Economic Committee, Lombra argues that the observed incompleteness in the specification of quantitative goals for monetary policy is deliberate (Lombra, 1984 p. 113). Similar views are expressed in Brunner and Meltzer (1964) and Lombra and Moran (1980). The penchant of the Central Bank for secrecy has recently been revealed in the legal record of a case in which the Federal Open Market Committee (FOMC) was sued under the Freedom of Information Act of 1966. The suit required the FOMC to make public immediately after each FOMC meeting the policy directives and minutes for that meeting (Goodfriend, 1986). The Federal Reserve argued the case for secrecy on a number of different grounds. The important issue from the point of view of this section is that the Federal Reserve attempted to preserve its information advantage.

[34]The following discussion is based on section VI of Cukierman and Meltzer (1986a).

when he becomes more interested in stimulating employment and higher credibility when he becomes more interested in preventing inflation.[35]

Although positive and negative surprises cancel each other out on average, the policymaker may still find it advantageous to choose control procedures that slow down public recognition of changes in his objectives. Greater ambiguity provides the policymaker with greater control in timing monetary surprises. When there is more ambiguity about policy, he can create larger positive surprises when he cares more about stimulation and leave the inevitable negative surprises for periods in which he is relatively more concerned about inflation.

Thus the policymaker makes a once-and-for-all (politically) optimal choice of control procedures that also determines his public credibility. This choice is systematically related to the degree of time preference of the policymaker; in particular, policymakers with a stronger time preference will choose less precise control procedures.[36]

Moreover, the higher the degree of uncertainty in the policymaker's objectives, the more likely he is to choose less precise control procedures and lower credibility. When the policymaker's objectives are relatively unstable, a rational public will give more weight to recent developments in forecasting the future rate of growth of money. Consequently, for a given precision in monetary control, it is more difficult to exploit the benefits of monetary surprises. By decreasing the precision of monetary control, a policymaker with relatively unstable objectives can partially offset this effect by increasing the length of time it takes the public to detect a given shift in its objectives.

ESTABLISHING CREDIBILITY BY DETERRENCE

Ever since Kydland and Prescott (1977) pointed out that the monetary authority and the public are caught in a prisoners' dilemma resulting in excessive inflation, it has become natural to look for mechanisms that would eliminate or reduce this inefficient result. Obviously, a first-best solution would be to effectively commit the policymaker to a zero inflation policy.[37] If such commitments are impossible, second-best solutions may be sought.

One second-best solution that relies on deterrence within a symmetric information environment has been suggested in Barro and Gordon (1983a). It can be illustrated using the relationships previously described. The basic idea is that the public must determine its inflation expectation in a way that deters the policymaker from choosing its optimal discretionary rate of inflation, for example, A in equation 6. Suppose that the policymaker announces a rate of inflation, m*, that is *lower* than A. The public then sets its inflationary expectation for the current period as follows: If actual inflation in the previous period accords with expectations, they expect that inflation will continue at m*. If the previous period's inflation does not accord with expectations, they expect instead that the monetary authority will inflate at the higher discretionary rate, A. Thus, whenever the monetary authority inflates at rate A rather than at its announced rate m*, the public "punishes" it for one period by believing that it will continue to do so in the next period as well.[38]

The monetary authority maximizes its objective function (equation 5) subject to the public's behavior.[39] In considering whether to inflate at rate A today, it compares the difference between the current value of social welfare when it inflates at rate A rather than at rate m* (given that the public expects m*) with the discounted value of the loss in next period's welfare because the public's inflation expectations increase from m* to A.[40] As long as the latter term (which acts as a deterrent) is larger than the former term (which

[35]This may explain why public concern about lack of credibility is aroused mostly when disinflation is considered. Not much concern was expressed at the end of the '60s and the '70s complaining about the lack of credibility of the *increased* inflationary policies of those times.

[36]Long-time students of the Fed like Brunner and Meltzer (1964), Kane (1977, 1980), Mayer (1982) and Pierce (1980) suggest that the Federal Reserve engages primarily in "fire fighting." In terms of the model, this would imply a high rate of time preference (low β in equation 7). In conjunction with the result obtained by CM, this implies that the Fed is likely to have a preference for incomplete control procedures and imperfect credibility.

[37]Or to whatever the optimal rate of inflation happens to be.

[38]In spite of its popularity, this term does not quite catch the function of this strategy. The idea is not to *punish* the monetary authority but rather to *deter* it from inflating at the discretionary rate A. This observation is due to Edward Green.

[39]The example here is within the social welfare framework in which the policymaker's objectives are identical to the social welfare function.

[40]The calculation of this loss is based on the understanding that the monetary authority chooses A also in the next period. The reason is that this choice yields a better value to its objective function than the choice m*. Given that, in the next period, expectations are at A, inflation at A yields $-A^2/2$ to the policymaker whereas inflating at m* yields $A(m^* - A) - (m^*)^2/2$ which is smaller for any $m^* < A$.

represents the temptation to inflate at rate A), the policymaker picks m*, the lower inflation rate.

Formally (from equation 5), the condition for effective deterrence of the higher inflation A is

$$(12) \quad \frac{\beta}{2} [(A^2 - (m^*)^2] > A (A - m^*) + \frac{(m^*)^2 - A^2}{2}$$

The left-hand term is the discounted value of the loss in next period's welfare due to the increase in expectations. The right-hand term is the gain in current welfare induced by higher current employment.[41]

The lowest credibly sustainable rate of inflation can be found by equating the two sides of equation 12 and solving for m*.[42] The solution is shown in equation 13:

$$(13) \quad m^* = \frac{1 - \beta}{1 + \beta} A.$$

This rate is higher than the first-best zero inflation, but lower than the rate of inflation, A, that would occur in the absence of deterrence. Equation 13 expresses the best enforceable rule as a function of the discount factor β. The higher the degree of time preference, the higher the minimum sustainable rate of inflation will be.[43] Once this mechanism is in place, it is self-fulfilling: the public believes that the policymaker will inflate at rate m* and, indeed, the policymaker does so. In the absence of commitments, therefore, a second-best lower rate of inflation can be credibly sustained by an appropriate deterrence mechanism.

Criticism of the Deterrence Approach to Central Bank Credibility

The deterrence approach to enhancing central bank credibility has been interpreted by some (e.g., Barro and Gordon, 1983a) as a positive theory of inflation.[44] Taylor (1983), however, raises doubts about its usefulness as a positive theory of inflation on the grounds

that, in other similar dynamic inconsistency situations, society has found ways to circumvent the problem. He cites patents as a device for eliminating the dynamic inconsistency problems faced by inventors as an example.

In addition, the deterrence equilibrium implies that the rate of inflation remains constant (Canzoneri, 1985). This implication is clearly at odds with observations that both inflation and monetary growth fluctuate substantially over time. Further, the deterrence equilibrium depends critically on the punishment strategy assumed in the analysis. Consequently, the infinite-horizon monetary policy game has multiple Nash equilibria with no mechanism for choosing among them (Backus and Driffill, 1985a). Therefore, any specific link between the current actions of the policymaker and the future expectations of the public is strictly arbitrary.

Finally the deterrence strategy may be subject to a free rider problem.[45] Individuals may simply find that it is not worthwhile to achieve a lower rate of inflation via the deterrence mechanism if the private costs of monitoring the policymaker's actions are higher than the marginal private benefits. This problem, while of lesser importance in the context of oligopoly theory from which the formal structure of the deterrence equilibrium above has originated, may be serious if the public is composed of many individuals.[46] Each individual may rely on the others to deter the policymaker from acting in a discretionary manner, thus eliminating the deterrence mechanism that made the lower inflation policy credible in the first place.

CONCLUDING REMARKS

Traditional economic analysis generally has treated policymakers' behavior as determined exogenously. In contrast, recent literature on central bank behavior focuses explicitly on how the motives, constraints and information of policymakers and the public determine monetary policy outcomes.

Some analysts use a political explanation of the policymaker's objectives; others identify the policymaker's objectives with a social welfare function. Both approaches show how an inflationary bias is created by interactions between the policymaker and the

---

[41]Note that the ideal inflation expectation, m* = 0, cannot be sustained if there is positive time preference. It would require the inequality

$$\beta \frac{A^2}{2} > \frac{A^2}{2}$$

to hold; however, this condition cannot be satisfied when $\beta < 1$. A somewhat higher rate of inflation can be sustained by this mechanism even for $\beta < 1$.

[42]Since this is a quadratic equation there are two roots, the smallest of which corresponds to the minimum credibly sustainable inflation.

[43]Obviously other deterrence mechanisms will yield different sustainable ranges for the rate of inflation.

[44]It also can be considered from a normative point of view, in which it represents a mechanism that improves welfare in comparison to a situation in which this mechanism is absent.

[45]Suggested by Edward Green in conversation.

[46]J. Friedman (1971, 1977) contains an early discussion of the deterrence strategy in the context of oligopoly.

public. Models utilizing the political approach, however, seem to be better able to explain two widely observed phenomena: the preference of monetary authorities for ambiguity in public policy pronouncements and the large swings in actual rates of money growth and inflation. Unfortunately, existing political models have not identified explicitly how various groups and political institutions combine to shape the objectives of the monetary authority.[47]

More recently, models have appeared that combine explicitly some interaction between political behavior, institutions, and economic policymaking. Some of these models rely on the existence of long-term contracts to induce a tradeoff between lower inflation and stimulation. A central theme of this literature is the optimal design of monetary institutions. Those developments will be described in the second part of this survey.

REFERENCES

Alesina, Alberto, and Guido Tabellini. "Rules and Discretion with Non Coordinated Monetary and Fiscal Policies," manuscript (September 1985).

Backus, David, and John Driffill. "Inflation and Reputation," *American Economic Review* (June 1985a), pp. 530–38.

————. "Rational Expectations and Policy Credibility Following a Change in Regime," *Review of Economic Studies* (1985b), pp. 211–21.

Barro, Robert J. "Reputation in a Model of Monetary Policy with Incomplete Information," manuscript, University of Rochester (February 1985). Forthcoming *Journal of Monetary Economics.*

Barro, Robert J., and David B. Gordon. "Rules, Discretion and Reputation in a Model of Monetary Policy," *Journal of Monetary Economics* (July 1983a), pp. 101–22.

————. "A Positive Theory of Monetary Policy in a Natural Rate Model," *Journal of Political Economy* (August 1983b), pp. 589–610.

Beck, Nathaniel. "Presidential Influence on the Federal Reserve in the 1970s," *American Journal of Political Science* (August 1982), pp. 415–45.

Brunner, Karl, and Allan H. Meltzer. *The Federal Reserve Attachment to Free Reserves,* House Committee on Banking and Currency, Washington, D.C. (1964).

Bull, Clive. "Rational Expectations, Monetary Data and Central Bank Watching," *Giornale degli Economisti e Annali di Economia* (January/February 1982), pp. 31–40.

Burns, Arthur F. *The Anguish of Central Banking,* per Jacobsson Foundation, Belgrade, Yugoslavia (1979).

Canzoneri, Matthew B. "Monetary Policy Games and the Role of Private Information," *American Economic Review* (December 1985), pp. 1056–70.

Cukierman, Alex. *Inflation, Stagflation, Relative Prices, and Imperfect Information,* Cambridge University Press, Cambridge, London, New York (1984), pp. 1056–70.

Cukierman, Alex, and Allan Drazen. "Do Distortionary Taxes Induce Policies Biased Towards Inflation?: A Microeconomic Analysis," Tel-Aviv University (August 1986).

Cukierman, Alex, and Allan H. Meltzer. "A Theory of Ambiguity, Credibility and Inflation Under Discretion and Asymmetric Information," manuscript, Carnegie-Mellon University (February 1986a). Forthcoming *Econometrica.*

————. "The Credibility of Monetary Announcements," forthcoming in Manfred J.M. Neumann, ed., *Monetary Policy and Uncertainty* (Nomos Verlagsgesellschaft, Baden-Baden, Germany, 1986b).

Fellner, William. *Towards a Reconstruction of Macroeconomics: Problems of Theory and Policy* (American Enterprise Institute, 1976).

Fischer, Stanley. "Long Term Contracts, Rational Expectations and the Optimal Money Supply Rule," *Journal of Political Economy* (April 1977), pp. 191–206.

————. "Contracts, Credibility and Disinflation," Working Paper No. 1339 NBER (April 1984).

Friedman, James. "A Non Cooperative Equilibrium for Supergames," *Review of Economic Studies* (January 1971), pp. 861–74.

————. *Oligopoly and the Theory of Games* (North Holland Publishing Company, Amsterdam, New York, Oxford, 1977).

Goodfriend, Marvin. "Monetary Mystique: Secrecy and Central Banking," *Journal of Monetary Economics* (January 1986), pp. 63–92.

Haberler, Gottfried. "Notes on Rational and Irrational Expectations," Reprint No. 111, American Enterprise Institute (March 1980).

Hardouvelis, Gikas A. "Market Perceptions of Federal Reserve Policy and the Weekly Monetary Announcements," *Journal of Monetary Economics* (September 1984), pp. 225–40.

Hetzel, Robert L. "The Formulation of Monetary Policy," manuscript, Federal Reserve Bank of Richmond (August 1985).

Kane, Edward J. "Good Intentions and Unintended Evil: The Case Against Selective Credit Allocation," *Journal of Money, Credit and Banking,* Part 1 (February 1977), pp. 55–69.

————. "Politics and Fed Policymaking: The More Things Change the More they Remain the Same," *Journal of Monetary Economics* (April 1980), pp. 199–212.

————. "External Pressure and the Operation of the Fed," in R.E. Lombra and W.E. Witte, *Political Economy of International and Domestic Monetary Relations* (Iowa State University Press, 1982), pp. 211–32.

Kreps, David M., and Robert Wilson. "Sequential Equilibria," *Econometrica* (1982a), pp. 863–94.

————. "Reputation and Imperfect Information," *Journal of Economic Theory,* 27 (1982b), pp. 253–79.

Kydland, Finn E., and Prescott, Edward C. "Rules Rather than Discretion: The Inconsistency of Optimal Plans," *Journal of Political Economy* (June 1977), pp. 473–91.

Lombra, Raymond E. "Monetary Policy: The Rhetoric Versus the Record," in *Monetary Reform and Economic Stability,* Hearings before the Joint Economic Committee, 98th Cong., 2nd Sess. (U.S. Government Printing Office, May 16 and June 5, 1984), pp. 101–35.

---

[47]While there is a substantial amount of descriptive narration (e.g., Woolley, 1964; and Hetzel, 1985), there is very little analytical discussion of these issues.

_____ , and Michael Moran. "Policy Advice and Policymaking at the Federal Reserve," *Carnegie Rochester Conference Series on Public Policy* (1980), pp. 9–68.

Lucas, Robert E., Jr. "Some International Evidence on Output-Inflation Tradeoffs," *American Economic Review* (June 1973), pp. 326–35.

Mayer, Thomas. "A Case Study of Federal Reserve Policymaking: Regulation Q in 1966," *Journal of Monetary Economics* (September 1982), pp. 259–72.

McCallum, Bennett T. "Credibility and Monetary Policy," in *Price Stability and Public Policy* — A Symposium Sponsored by the Federal Reserve Bank of Kansas City, Jackson Hole, Wyoming (August 2 and 3, 1984).

Pierce, James L. "Making Reserve Targets Work," in Controlling Monetary Aggregates III, *Federal Reserve Bank of Boston Conference Series* (1980), No. 23.

Rogoff, Kenneth. "The Optimal Degree of Commitment to an Intermediate Monetary Target," manuscript, University of Wisconsin (1985), forthcoming, *Quarterly Journal of Economics*.

Taylor, John B. "Aggregate Dynamics and Staggered Contracts," *Journal of Political Economy* (February 1980), pp. 1–23.

_____ . "Comments on 'Rules, Discretion and Reputation in a Model of Monetary Policy' by Barro and Gordon," *Journal of Monetary Economics* (July 1983), pp. 123–25.

Weintraub, Robert E. "Congressional Supervision of Monetary Policy," *Journal of Monetary Economics* (April 1978), pp. 341–62.

Willet, Thomas D., and John McArthur. "Theories of Central Bank Behavior and Implications for Monetary Reform: A Constitutional Perspective," paper presented at the meeting of the Western Economic Association, June 30–July 4, 1985, Anaheim, California.

Woolley, John T. *Monetary Politics — The Federal Reserve and the Politics of Monetary Policy* (Cambridge University Press, Cambridge, London, New York, 1984).

Article Thirty-One

Higher Deficit Policies Lead to Higher Inflation*

Preston J. Miller

Monetary Adviser
Research Department
Federal Reserve Bank of Minneapolis

If Congress does not act, the U.S. federal budget deficit could easily exceed $200 billion in each of the three fiscal years 1983–85.[1] This budget hemorrhage would come on top of deficits averaging $76.5 billion per year over the last three fiscal years and would make sixteen straight years the budget has been in the red. Deficits have been persistent and have been getting larger.

The divergence of the government's expenditures and revenues perhaps has been no larger than the divergence of economists' views on that policy's likely economic effects. And nowhere has the divergence of views seemed wider than on its inflationary effects.

Many economists argue that persistently higher deficits do not necessarily lead to higher inflation. (See, for example, Blinder 1982, Friedman 1981a, Grossman 1982, Hamburger and Zwick 1981, Hein 1981, Sprinkel 1981, and Weintraub 1981.) They argue that inflation results when the supply of money grows faster than the supply of goods, which in turn results when the Federal Reserve purchases too many government bonds. These economists (whom I label *monetarists*) thus conclude that the Federal Reserve can prevent higher deficits from causing more inflation by refusing to buy the extra government bonds that result from those deficits (that is, by refusing to *monetize the deficits*). As support for this view that higher deficits are not necessarily inflationary, monetarists cite numerous empirical studies which indicate weak, if any, correlation between deficits and inflation in the United States.

In this paper, I take the opposing view: Persistently higher deficits—changes in budget policy that for any given economic conditions imply higher deficits than would have occurred under previous budget policy—do indeed lead to more inflation. A theory which admits the possibility of such policy changes suggests that the changes affect inflation in three ways.

One way is by necessary monetary accommodation. Contrary to what monetarists believe, the Federal Reserve may have to monetize some of the extra debt; that may be the only way to prevent the government from becoming insolvent.

Even to the extent that the Federal Reserve does not monetize the debt, however, adjustments in the private economy to the higher deficit policy lead to more inflation, in two other ways: by crowding out and by private monetization of debt. When additional government debt is not monetized by the Federal Reserve, the debt adds to net credit demands and raises interest rates. Higher interest rates crowd out investment in plant and equipment, which reduces the rate of real growth in the economy. With the same amount of money chasing fewer goods, prices are driven up. In the financial sector, meanwhile, higher interest rates make profitable the development of new financial instruments that make government bonds more like money. These instruments allow people to hold interest-bearing

---

*This is a substantially revised version of a paper presented at The Economic Consequences of Government Deficits: An Economic Policy Conference, cosponsored by the Center for the Study of American Business and the Institute of Banking and Financial Markets and held at Washington University, St. Louis, Missouri, in October 1982. That paper is forthcoming in a volume of the conference proceedings.

[1] The Congressional Budget Office's (CBO's) baseline budget projections for fiscal years 1983–85, which are based on assumptions of no change in current laws and no change in real discretionary spending, are $194 billion, $197 billion, and $214 billion, respectively. These large baseline deficits are based on the CBO's assumption of a weak economic recovery. However, even assuming a strong economic recovery over the next three years, the CBO estimates that deficits would still be $178 billion, $155 billion, and $162 billion, respectively. (See U.S., Congress, CBO 1983).

assets that are as risk-free and as useful in transactions as money is. In this way, the private sector effectively monetizes government debt that the Federal Reserve doesn't, so the inflationary effects of higher deficit policies increase.

Despite monetarists' claims, this view that higher deficit policies lead to higher inflation is supported by empirical work. Studies properly designed to capture the effects of budget policy changes show that both U.S. and international experiences are consistent with this view: a change in budget policy which results in higher deficits year-in and year-out leads to higher average inflation. Studies that do not support this view mistakenly relate isolated deficits and inflation rates instead of properly relating deficit policies and average inflation experience.

How Governments Can Run Persistent Deficits

A budget deficit occurs when spending exceeds taxes, user fees, and other explicit revenues. The simplest form of a higher deficit policy—a permanent increase in deficits—requires that spending permanently exceed revenues, but this would seem to violate the simple accounting constraint that what goes out must not exceed what comes in. That it doesn't is due to the existence of *fiat debt*, those government liabilities for which there are no offsetting assets. When fiat debt has value in an economy, the government can finance permanently higher deficits by implicitly taxing (depreciating the value of) its outstanding stock of that debt.

The Budget Constraint

The concepts of deficit policies, fiat debt, and implicit taxation and the proposition that higher deficit policies lead to higher inflation can be explained more precisely by referring to a formal representation (in equation form) of the limits faced by a federal government and a central bank (like the Federal Reserve) trying to finance a budget deficit. I will derive the consolidated federal government–central bank *budget constraint* assuming that the government borrows by selling fiat bonds which are discounts issued for one period. The government sells the bonds in an open market at a price below their face value (par) and retires all outstanding privately held bonds at par. The difference between par and market price (the discount) represents interest. The bonds which are not purchased by the private sector are purchased by the central bank by creating money: currency and bank reserves. Because the money is backed only by fiat bonds, it too is a form of fiat debt.

First I will derive separate period-by-period budget constraints for the federal government and the central bank and

consolidate them. Then I will generate the consolidated budget constraint that must hold over time when the economy grows at a constant rate (so-called steady-state growth). This last step provides a shorthand way of examining long-run relationships.[2]

In current-dollar terms, the *federal government's period-by-period budget constraint* states that each period it must raise enough revenue from new bond sales to finance both debt service—the principal and interest payments on its privately held debt—and the deficit net of debt service. In algebraic form, the constraint says

Deficit = Net bond sales

where

Net bond sales = Total sales of new bonds

— Principal and interest payments to retire bonds previously sold to the private sector.

Introducing symbols that distinguish prices and quantities lets me write this constraint as

$$(1) \quad P(G - T) = P^B B^* - B_{-1}$$

where

P = general price level

G = real government expenditures (net of debt service)

T = real government tax receipts

$G - T$ = real government deficit

$P(G - T)$ = current-dollar government deficit

B^* = total stock of government bonds sold in the current period

B_{-1} = stock of privately held government bonds sold in the previous period

P^B = price of government bonds when issued, defined to be $1/(1 + R)$, where R is the nominal one-period interest rate.

---

[2] In general, a persistent deficit policy is feasible when the present value of real government expenditures does not exceed the present value of real government revenues defined to include both explicit and implicit taxes. The steady-state assumptions provide a way of looking at these present-value relationships for a smoothly growing economy.

According to (1), the federal government sells B^* bonds on the open market but retires only its bonds purchased by the private sector B_{-1}. The difference between total bonds sold and bonds sold to the private sector consists of bonds sold to the central bank. Again, the central bank pays for its bond purchases by creating money which ends up in the private sector. Because the central bank simply accumulates bonds in its portfolio rather than presenting the maturing bonds for payment, the *central bank's period-by-period budget constraint* is simply

> Central bank bond purchases = Money created

or, in the symbolic notation just introduced,

$$(2) \qquad P^B(B^* - B) = M - M_{-1}$$

where

$$M = \text{stock of money}$$

$P^B(B^* - B)$ = value of bonds purchased by the central bank (total less value purchased by the private sector)

$M - M_{-1}$ = increase in the money stock.

The *consolidated federal government–central bank period-by-period budget constraint* is found by combining the two institutions' budget constraints to get

> Deficit = Money created + Net private bond sales

or

$$(3) \qquad P(G - T) = (M - M_{-1}) + (P^B B - B_{-1}).$$

This constraint states that the government's current-dollar deficit is financed by the increase in values of its money and bonds held in the private sector.

To examine how the federal government can finance a permanent deficit, we cannot just look at the period-by-period budget constraint. Instead we must examine all current and future deficits and their means of finance to determine if the government will be able to finance the permanent deficits without ever becoming insolvent. For my purposes, which abstract from the cyclical fluctuations of the economy and focus on the effects of persistent or permanent shifts in budget policy, it is enough to consider a representative fiscal period in an economy growing smoothly over time, a steady-state economy, and derive the consolidated budget constraint assuming perfectly smooth, or constant, growth in real output.

To derive this constraint from the period-by-period version, I first divide all terms in (3) by PX, where X is the rate of real output. Then I impose the steady-state real growth conditions—that for all time periods

$G_t/X_t = \tilde{G}$	Real government expenditures are a constant proportion of real output.
$T_t/X_t = \tilde{T}$	Real government tax receipts are a constant proportion of real output.
$X_t/X_{t-1} = 1 + \nu$	Real output grows at the constant rate ν.
$P_t/P_{t-1} = 1 + \Pi$	Prices grow at the constant rate Π.
$P^B = 1/(1 + R)$	The nominal interest rate is constant.
$\dot{M}/PX = \tilde{M}^d(R,\Pi)$	The real, per unit of output, money stock each period is equal to its demand, the latter being a time invariant function of the interest rate and inflation rate.
$P^B B/PX = \tilde{B}^d(R,\Pi)$	The real, per unit of output, value of privately held government bonds each period is equal to its demand, the latter being a time invariant function of the interest rate and inflation rate.

Making these substitutions in (3) divided by PX yields, finally, the *consolidated federal government–central bank steady-state budget constraint* for a representative fiscal period:

$$(4) \qquad \tilde{G} - \tilde{T} = \left\{1 - [1/(1 + \Pi)(1 + \nu)]\right\} \tilde{M}^d(R,\Pi)$$
$$+ \left\{1 - [(1 + R)/(1 + \Pi)(1 + \nu)]\right\} \tilde{B}^d(R,\Pi).$$

The budget constraint in this form demonstrates the importance of fiat debt to a government that wants to persistently run deficits. According to (4), a persistent deficit policy ($\tilde{G} - \tilde{T} > 0$) is feasible if the real deficit does not exceed the real revenue the government can extract from its money and bond issue (that is, from depreciating the value of its fiat debt). The terms in braces determine the government's tax take from money and bond issue. The tax bases for the two taxes are real private holdings of money and bonds, M/P and $P^B B/P$, respectively. The tax bases both grow smoothly at the rate ν. With no growth in the tax base, $\nu = 0$, the terms in the braces can be considered the *implicit tax rates* on real money and real bond holdings.

Some insights are gained about those tax rates by setting $\nu = 0$ and applying a little algebra. The implicit tax rate on money, $\{1 - [1/(1 + \Pi)]\}$, is positive as long as the rate of inflation is positive ($\Pi > 0$). The implicit tax rate on bonds, $\{1 - [(1 + R)/(1 + \Pi)]\}$, is positive as long as the real rate of interest is negative ($R - \Pi < 0$). Money and bond issue provide the government with positive tax takes as long as the terms in braces are positive, and that requires for each that the sum of the implicit tax rate and the growth in the tax base is positive.[3] Only when the demands for fiat money and bonds and the implicit tax takes on them are positive can a permanent deficit be financed.

Clarifications

The proposition that higher deficit policies lead to higher inflation can be stated more precisely now as "a permanent increase in $\tilde{G} - \tilde{T}$ requires an increase in Π in order for budget constraint (4) to be satisfied." In order to properly interpret "a permanent increase in $\tilde{G} - \tilde{T}$" when testing the proposition with actual data, it is helpful to recall the definitions and assumptions used in the construction of (4). Two points are worth emphasizing.

One is that a sustained increase in $\tilde{G} - \tilde{T}$ must be interpreted as a policy-induced increase in the deficit, that is, as a change in expenditure programs or tax rates which raises the deficit permanently for a given path of the economy. It does not refer to an increase in deficits caused by a cyclical downturn in the economy. Cyclical deficits are by definition temporary; they diminish as the economy recovers. To be consistent with this interpretation, the budget constraint (4) is derived under the assumption of steady real growth, not cycles of ups and downs.

This distinction between policy-induced and cyclical deficits is crucial because my argument does not claim that cyclical deficits are inflationary. An increase in the reported deficit could well be associated with lower inflation when both changes are caused by a weakening in economic conditions. Thus, the measure $\tilde{G} - \tilde{T}$ that I am considering is not the reported deficit, relative to reported real GNP, but

is instead the real deficit net of debt service which would occur assuming trend real GNP, relative to trend real GNP.

The other point worth emphasizing is that a sustained increase in $\tilde{G} - \tilde{T}$ must be interpreted as a policy change for a government that can issue fiat debt, debt not backed by anything. If debt issued today were assumed to be backed, for example, by higher explicit taxes in the future, then an increase in $\tilde{G} - \tilde{T}$ could not be sustained over time; a higher $\tilde{G} - \tilde{T}$ today would imply a lower $\tilde{G} - \tilde{T}$ in the future. Nor can the debt be backed by real goods. If the government issued bonds to purchase capital goods, its period-by-period budget constraint would be different from (1). Since the government then could always sell its capital to finance expenditures, the change in the current value of its capital stock would have to be included in (1). Or, if money were backed by a commodity like gold, the central bank's period-by-period budget constraint would be different from (2). The central bank could not always issue money to buy unbacked government bonds; its money issue would be constrained by its holdings of gold, and the value of gold would show up in its budget constraint. The consolidated federal government–central bank budget constraints (3) and (4), then, are based on the assumption that the consolidated balance sheet has privately held money and bonds on the liability side but no capital goods on the asset side, which makes both money and bonds forms of fiat debt.

Why Higher Deficit Policies Increase Inflation

While the government's budget constraint is useful in showing how a permanent deficit might be financed and in clarifying what is meant by "higher deficit policies lead to higher inflation," it cannot determine whether that proposition is true. In order to determine whether a higher deficit policy can, in fact, be financed and, if it can, whether it will lead to higher inflation, a theory of the economy and monetary system is required.

The Legal Restrictions Theory

When the government issues fiat debt, budget policy determines the total amount of debt [by (1)], while monetary policy determines its distribution between fiat money and fiat bonds [by (2)]. The supplies of these assets together with the aggregate demands $\tilde{M}^d$ and $\tilde{B}^d$ determine the rate of inflation Π and the nominal interest rate R. In order

---

[3] The condition for money is $\Pi + \nu > 0$, or simply $\Pi > -\nu$. The condition for bonds is $\Pi - R + \nu > 0$, or simply $R - \Pi < \nu$. Both of these conditions for positive taxes are approximations found by setting $\Pi\nu = 0$. The approximations would be exact in continuous time.

to determine the relative roles of monetary and budget policies in affecting inflation and interest rates, however, we need a theory of the economy and monetary system to describe the nature of $\bar{M}^d$ and $\bar{B}^d$.

The budget constraint indicates that at least one of the demands $\bar{M}^d$ or $\bar{B}^d$ must be positive if higher deficits are to be feasible. So the theory of the demands for money and government bonds should include an explanation of why people would value either of them. Valued fiat debt is by no means assured. When private markets exist for making all possible types of trades (when markets are *complete*), fiat money and bonds are of no use either as goods (they are not physically consumed or used in production) or as assets (they do not expand the trades that can be made), and the private sector has no demand for them. Or, in an unrestricted economy, when assets exist which have rates of return in all states of the economy that exceed the rates of return on fiat debt, the demands for fiat debt will be zero. In these cases, according to (4), persistent deficit policies simply cannot be financed.

Although positive demands for fiat debt are not assured, governments can enact laws and regulations to assure them. And they do. In the United States, for example, fiat debt has value in part because of such government rules as legal tender laws and reserve requirements. These laws and regulations force individuals and depository institutions to demand government fiat debt even when it is being taxed, and this allows persistent deficits to be financed.

The laws and regulations a government enacts not only assure the demands for its fiat debt; they also separate the demands for money and bonds. U.S. depository institutions, for instance, are not only required to hold in reserve a proportion of their deposits in the form of fiat debt (which increases the total demand for such debt). That fiat debt is further specified to be in the form of money, not bonds (which separates the demands for money and bonds). Institutions also are prevented by law from issuing bearer notes backed by government bonds (which, along with the large denominations of bonds, also separates the demands for money and bonds).[4]

Without laws and regulations, if fiat money and bonds were held at all, they would become perfect substitutes; the distinction between them would disappear (Wallace 1979). To see why that is so, suppose that money and bonds were issued in the same denominations and that the government in no way restricted or regulated the use of either instrument. Both assets would then be held only if they paid the same rate of return. If an n-period bond paid a positive interest rate while money didn't, for instance, a trader could profit by breaking the bond into n one-period bonds, each paying a positive rate of return. Everyone would then prefer one-period bonds to money, and no one would hold money. Thus, without legal restrictions, the demand for fiat debt could fall to zero, and if it didn't, bonds and money would become perfect substitutes, leaving the government with only one implicit tax rate.

If money and bonds were perfect substitutes, deficits would be directly inflationary, and monetary policy would be irrelevant. That is because budget policy would determine the growth of total fiat debt, while monetary policy would determine the distribution of fiat debt between two perfect substitutes. So without the laws and regulations that enhance and separate the demands for fiat debt, the government would have an unassured base for its implicit taxes—one or both of the types of debt might not be demanded—and its steady-state implicit tax rates on money and bonds would be equal.

A purpose behind these laws and regulations, then, may be to allow the government to raise its implicit taxes more efficiently. By increasing the demands for fiat debt, they increase the tax base for implicit taxes and so allow a given amount of revenue to be raised at lower implicit tax rates. By assuring two distinct debt instruments yielding different returns, they allow the government to tax-discriminate in financing deficits.[5] [This occurs whenever nominal interest rates on government bonds are positive, for then, according to (4), the implicit tax rate on money is higher than the implicit tax rate on bonds.]

Three Channels for Inflation

This *legal restrictions theory* of fiat money and fiat bonds can generate a model which has some properties common to monetarist models which deny the influence of deficits on inflation: money growth as the immediate cause of inflation, a one-for-one relationship between changes in inflation and changes in nominal interest rates, and expansiveness of open market purchases (Miller 1982a,b). These properties result when the restrictions cause money to cir-

---

[4] For a discussion of how this last restriction works, see Neil Wallace's paper, "A Legal Restrictions Theory of the Demand for 'Money' and the Role of Monetary Policy," in this *Quarterly Review*.

[5] It might also be argued that restrictions having the effect of separating demands for money and bonds were imposed so that the government could control the stock of money to pursue a price stabilization goal and control the stock of bonds to smooth tax rates over time. This tax discrimination rationale for legal restrictions was first worked out in Bryant and Wallace 1980 and was employed in Miller 1982a,b,c.

culate as a medium of exchange, while bonds compete with capital as a store of value. However, when the separation of demands for money and bonds is due to government restrictions, higher deficits lead to more inflation, in three ways: monetary accommodation, crowding out, and private monetization of government debt.[6]

Monetarists commonly acknowledge that higher deficits lead to more inflation when the Federal Reserve *accommodates* by monetizing the deficits. But these economists tend to view the Fed's accommodation either as a lack of resolve or as shortsightedness (Friedman 1981a, Hein 1981, Weintraub 1981). This view implies that more inflation is avoidable if the Fed acts responsibly. The restrictions theory, however, suggests that the Fed may have little choice.

A key implication of the theory of financial restrictions is that federal budget and monetary policies must be coordinated (Sargent and Wallace 1981; Miller 1982a,b). In fact, if deficits are financed efficiently (that is, with minimal distortion of private sector incentives and behavior), it is not feasible to finance larger deficits—even temporary ones— by bond issue alone (Miller 1982c). Larger deficits require accommodation by the monetary authority; if it is not forthcoming, the increase in bonds will cause real interest payments on bonds to grow without limit, thereby forcing the government into insolvency. Central bank monetization of deficits—and more inflation—is, then, necessary at some point to prevent the insolvency.[7]

The need to monetize deficits in order to prevent insolvency can be viewed another way. If the central bank ignores budget policy and sticks to a predetermined path of money—say, a no-growth path—then the federal government is denied the option of creating money to finance deficits. Additional bond issue becomes like that of state and local governments: it must be backed by higher revenue in the future. Trying to service the bonds by issuing new bonds only causes the interest on the debt and, thus, total debt to snowball.

Crowding out is another way that, under the legal restrictions theory, higher deficits lead to more inflation. Different degrees of monetary accommodation are feasible for a given increase in deficits. Less monetary accommodation requires more bonds to be sold on the open market to private investors, and in general this drives more private capital out of the market. That is because bonds compete with private capital in individual portfolios. When there are decreasing returns to capital, the substitution of government current expenditures for private capital expenditures raises the real rate of interest and lowers the path of real output (Friedman 1981b, Miller 1982c). A given money path combined with a lower output path produces a higher price path.

Finally, the legal restrictions theory implies that higher deficits lead to more inflation by encouraging the private sector to circumvent the restrictions on bonds and so, in effect, to *privately monetize* government debt. A plausible explanation of how this happens is the following. Suppose the legal restrictions can be circumvented by private intermediaries in successive steps only at successively higher costs. The profit from finding ways around the restrictions is the difference between those increasing costs and the revenue that can be earned by substituting bond holdings for money holdings. This profit, then, is related directly to the difference in returns on bonds and money: the nominal interest rate.

When a policy of higher deficits raises interest rates, therefore, the private sector responds by pursuing more ways to circumvent the restrictions on substituting bonds for money. Private intermediaries find it profitable, for example, to develop financial instruments backed by government bonds, which the private sector can use in lieu of money and which earn interest at something less than the government bond rate. As a result, bonds become easier to use for spending, and that implies more inflation for given deficits and money growth. In terms of the budget constraint, as the private sector finds ways to shift its fiat debt holdings from highly taxed money to less highly taxed bonds, total implicit taxes fall. For a given increase in deficits, the government can only offset these losses if inflation increases and so raises the implicit tax rates on money and bonds.

Casual observation suggests that this third way higher

---

[6] Strictly speaking, more inflation will result through these channels provided the private sector's demands for fiat money and bonds do not increase. It is assumed in what follows that the government does not raise these demands by tightening restrictions (for example, by raising reserve requirements). It seems reasonable that, if an increase in implicit taxes on fiat debt were required, the increase could be levied by some combination of tighter regulations (an increase in the base) and higher inflation (an increase in the tax rate).

Under a transaction cost theory of separate demands for money and bonds, higher deficits do not lead to higher inflation through monetary accommodation or crowding out. According to this theory, private monetization causes bonds to be almost perfect substitutes for money, so deficits are directly inflationary. (See Bryant and Wallace 1979.)

[7] Deficits also can be so large that insolvency will not be avoided even with monetary accommodation. Higher inflation drives the implicit tax rates on fiat debt toward one (as the budget constraint makes clear) but lowers the demand for fiat debt. Hence, the implicit taxes that can be raised through monetary accommodation and its resulting inflation are bounded.

deficits lead to inflation under the legal restrictions theory is more than a theoretical possibility. In recent years in the United States there have developed, at money market mutual funds, demand deposit accounts that are backed by Treasury securities and, at banks, deep-discount insured certificates of deposit that are backed by Treasury securities, issued in denominations of as little as $250, and assured of purchase by a broker (Sloane 1982). In Brazil, which has run high deficits for years, Treasury bills have become very liquid: their average turnover is now less than two days.

What Has Actually Happened

Despite many claims to the contrary, evidence does suggest that higher inflation results from higher deficit policies. Both U.S. and international experiences suggest it. The reason that many studies fail to detect any relationship is that they fail to distinguish between deficit policies and deficit realizations.

Proper and Improper Tests

In order to clarify the statistical issue, I posit a simple time series model to serve as a frame of reference. The model is motivated by the theory described in the previous section and can be easily generalized to allow, for example, longer lags. The main difference between this and the earlier discussion is that here I do not construct the model for the steady state. Its long-run properties thus are not immediately apparent but instead must be derived.

The *state* of the economy at time t is described by the rate of real output X_t, the aggregate price level P_t, and the nominal interest rate on one-period bonds R_t. Policy *instruments* include total unbacked federal debt B_t^* and unbacked money—the value of B^* purchased by the monetary authority—M_t. *Budget policy* (5) and *monetary policy* (6) are rules for determining current values of those instruments as linear functions (feedback rules) of the state of the economy and the policy instruments in the previous period:

(5) $\quad B_t^* = a_1 + b_1 t + c_{11}X_{t-1} + c_{12}P_{t-1} + c_{13}R_{t-1}$
$$+ d_{11}B_{t-1}^* + d_{12}M_{t-1} + \epsilon_{1t}$$

(6) $\quad M_t = a_2 + b_2 t + c_{21}X_{t-1} + c_{22}P_{t-1} + c_{23}R_{t-1}$
$$+ d_{21}B_{t-1}^* + d_{22}M_{t-1} + \epsilon_{2t}$$

where the a's, b's, c's, and d's are coefficients and the ϵ's are serially uncorrelated random disturbances. Policies are thus associated with numerical values of the coefficients in

these feedback rules. The debt level B_t^* and the money supply M_t that actually occur in any period depend on the policy rules, the state of the economy and the policy instruments in the previous period, and the random disturbances.

The *economic process* describes how the current state of the economy is determined by its own past values and the past and previously expected current values of the policy instruments:

(7) $\quad X_t = f_1 + g_1 t + h_{11}X_{t-1} + h_{12}P_{t-1} + h_{13}R_{t-1}$
$$+ i_{11}B_{t-1}^* + i_{12}M_{t-1} + j_{11}E_tB_t^*$$
$$+ j_{12}E_tM_t + \mu_{1t}$$

(8) $\quad P_t = f_2 + g_2 t + h_{21}X_{t-1} + h_{22}P_{t-1} + h_{23}R_{t-1}$
$$+ i_{21}B_{t-1}^* + i_{22}M_{t-1} + j_{21}E_tB_t^*$$
$$+ j_{22}E_tM_t + \mu_{2t}$$

(9) $\quad R_t = f_3 + g_3 t + h_{31}X_{t-1} + h_{32}P_{t-1} + h_{33}R_{t-1}$
$$+ i_{31}B_{t-1}^* + i_{32}M_{t-1} + j_{31}E_tB_t^*$$
$$+ j_{32}E_tM_t + \mu_{3t}$$

where the f's, g's, h's, i's, and j's are coefficients; the μ's are serially uncorrelated random disturbances; and $E_tB_t^*$ and E_tM_t are people's expectations of the current levels of debt and money, respectively, conditional on known values of the state of the economy and the policy instruments at time $t - 1$. The j coefficients play the important role of representing how the current state of the economy is affected by people's expectations of policy instrument values. I assume that those expectations are rational, that is, consistent with the forecasts that would be generated by the model—here, the policy rules (5) and (6).

Because the expectations terms cannot be directly observed, the coefficients of the economic process (7)–(9) cannot be statistically estimated. Replacing the unobserved expectations with the objective forecasts based on the policy rules (5) and (6) produces an estimable system with each equation analogous to the following one for the price level:

(10) $\quad P_t = \alpha + \beta t + \gamma_1 X_{t-1} + \gamma_2 P_{t-1} + \gamma_3 R_{t-1}$
$$+ \delta_1 B_{t-1}^* + \delta_2 M_{t-1} + \mu_{2t}$$

where

$$\alpha = f_2 + j_{21}a_1 + j_{22}a_2$$

$$\beta = g_2 + j_{21}b_1 + j_{22}b_2$$

$$\gamma_1 = h_{21} + j_{21}c_{11} + j_{22}c_{21}$$

$$\gamma_2 = h_{22} + j_{21}c_{12} + j_{22}c_{22}$$

$$\gamma_3 = h_{23} + j_{21}c_{13} + j_{22}c_{23}$$

$$\delta_1 = i_{21} + j_{21}d_{11} + j_{22}d_{21}$$

$$\delta_2 = i_{22} + j_{21}d_{12} + j_{22}d_{22}.$$

The coefficients of the estimable system, of which (10) is an example, are combinations of the coefficients of policies (5) and (6) and coefficients of the economic process (7), (8), and (9). The coefficients of the policies—the a's, b's, c's, and d's—appear in the estimable system because of the assumptions that the current state of the economy depends on people's expectations of policy (not all the j's are zero) and that those expectations incorporate information about the policies actually in place.

The empirical counterpart of the proposition that higher deficit policies lead to higher inflation now can be restated in terms of (5) and (10) as "an increase in a_1 or b_1—a constant or growing increase in deficits—leads to an increase in α or β—a constant or growing increase in the price level P_t."[8] If the model (5)–(9) is correct, the proposition is true when people's expectations of deficits incorporate information about the actual policy rule (5) (expectations are rational) and when those expectations are positively related to inflation ($j_{21} > 0$). Since economists who argue that deficits are not inflationary generally accept the rational expectations assumption, the controversial part of the proposition is the required relationship between expectations and inflation, that $j_{21} > 0$.

In order to determine whether or not j_{21} is positive, it is necessary to empirically estimate the coefficients of a system of equations which includes at least (5) and (10). A shift in budget policy (5) must be detected, and estimates of the coefficients of (10) must be made before and after the policy shift. In order to have reliable estimates, there should be many such policy shifts.

Examining studies which find no inflationary effects of deficit policies in the context of system (5)–(10) reveals why those studies are flawed. They attempt to estimate the coefficient on deficits in a price equation $\left[\delta_1 \text{ in } (10)\right]$ and test the proposition that higher deficits increase inflation by examining whether that coefficient is significantly positive.

(See, for example, Blinder 1982, Hein 1981, Perry 1978, Stein 1976, and Weintraub 1981.) In order for this estimation technique to be valid, the relationship of prices to the other variables must not change over the period of estimation, but according to the model (5)–(9), that assumption is valid only if the deficit policy (5) doesn't change.

Thus, studies done in the standard way offer little evidence about whether higher deficit *policies* lead to higher inflation. If the assumptions underlying their estimation technique are valid, then deficit policy did not change during the estimation period and these studies can offer no evidence about the effects of such a change. They at best can detect the relationship between deficit *realizations* and inflation under a given policy (δ_1), and as my model (5)–(9) suggests, this relationship can be of any sign or magnitude. In more intuitive terms, the standard studies pick up how deficits and inflation were related over the business cycle under a given policy, and that relationship can be anything. However, if policy did change during the estimation period, then the assumptions underlying the estimation technique in standard studies are violated and their estimates are not valid. The coefficients in (10) cannot be expected to remain invariant under different policies.

Evidence From Studies of Deficit Policy Changes

Persuasive evidence that higher deficit policies lead to more inflation comes from studies of dramatic budget policy changes in countries around the world. For example, Sargent's (1981) study strongly suggests that the European hyperinflations of the 1920s were fueled by policies of high deficits and unbacked debt and were abruptly halted when policies of balanced budgets and backed debt were reinstated. Harberger (1982) and McKinnon (1982), in their separate studies of Chile and of Argentina and Chile, respectively, document the pivotal role played by budget policies in determining those countries' inflation outcomes. Patinkin (1979) describes a similar experience for Israel.

The evidence for the modern U.S. economy cannot be as strong. This is because, in post–World War II history through 1981, there seems to have been only one major shift in federal budget policy—a shift in the late 1960s from nearly balanced budgets to persistent deficits—and that shift

---

[8]An increase in a_1 or b_1 implies an increase in deficits for given economic conditions, the type of increase considered in the previous sections. In a strict sense, an increase in a_1 or b_1 implies, respectively, a constant or growing increase in deficits only when $d_{11} = 1$. A change in any of the c's need not change the average size of deficits; it might only change the responsiveness of deficits to changes in economic conditions.

does not seem to have been large compared to the examples cited above. To determine whether that apparent shift to a policy of higher deficits was statistically significant and to examine the shift's impact on inflation, I estimate over the period 1948–81 a vector autoregressive model (VAR) [a version of (5), (6), and equations like (10)], test for a significant change in budget policy (5), and estimate separate models for the period before and the period after the change (Miller 1982d).

Because there is only one shift in U.S. budget policy to examine, a finding of higher inflation in the period of higher deficits would be very weak evidence for the proposition: many other changes (besides policy changes) in the two periods could account for inflation being higher when deficits were. So, in an attempt to judge the proposition more conclusively, I also test some other implications of the legal restrictions theory which generates the proposition. The theory suggests that, in the period of higher deficits, along with inflation being higher, fiat bonds should be more like fiat money and less fiat money should be held for any given level of GNP. If the legal restrictions theory is correct,

bonds become more like money as people develop ways to circumvent the restrictions separating the demands for money and bonds, and less fiat money is held for a given level of GNP (its velocity, GNP/M, rises) as fiat bonds take on some functions formerly served by money. If these other implications are supported by the U.S. data, then that corroborates, and strengthens, any direct evidence supporting the proposition.

The VARs I examine contain five quarterly time series: a measure of real output, real GNP (RGNP); a measure of the price level, the GNP deflator (GNPD); a representative market interest rate, the 90-day Treasury bill rate (RTB); a measure of fiat money, total bank reserves (TR); and a measure of total fiat debt, federal debt (DEBT). The measure of fiat money is the St. Louis Federal Reserve Bank's "total reserves" series, adjusted for seasonal factors and changes in reserve requirements. It is intended as a measure of the unbacked money that the private sector would have held if there had been no changes in financial restrictions. The measure of fiat debt is constructed by adding the accumulated, quarterly national income account deficit (not annualized) to the total public debt net of government account holdings in 1948. In the VARs, all series except the bill rate are logged.

This limited set of variables is intended to be the smallest system able to capture major channels of policy influence: monetary and budget policies together determine the inflation rate and the interest rate, which in turn affect real output by their impact on the rate of investment. Monetary policies and budget policies are represented as rules which determine the current levels of bank reserves and federal debt, respectively, as functions of lagged values of all the variables in the system.

Each variable in the system is regressed on a constant and on m lags of all five variables. Thus, the system can be written as

$$(11) \quad Y_t = C + \sum_{i=1}^{m} A_i Y_{t-i} + \lambda_t$$

where

$$(12) \quad Y \equiv \begin{bmatrix} \ln (RGNP) \\ \ln (GNPD) \\ RTB \\ \ln (DEBT) \\ \ln (TR) \end{bmatrix}$$

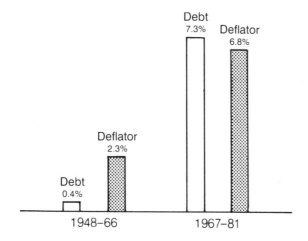

Chart 1

Along with a higher deficit policy came higher inflation.

Average Annual Rates of Growth in Federal Debt and the GNP Deflator During 1948–66 and 1967–81

Debt 7.3%
Deflator 6.8%
Deflator 2.3%
Debt 0.4%

1948–66   1967–81

Source: U.S. Department of Commerce

Charts 2 and 3

**After the shift to a higher deficit policy, bonds seemed to explain
at least as much of inflation's changes as money did. . .**

Percentages of the Forecast Variance of the GNP Deflator Caused by
Unexpected Changes (Innovations) in Federal Debt (Bonds) and Total Reserves (Money)
According to Models Based on Data for 1948–66 and 1967–81

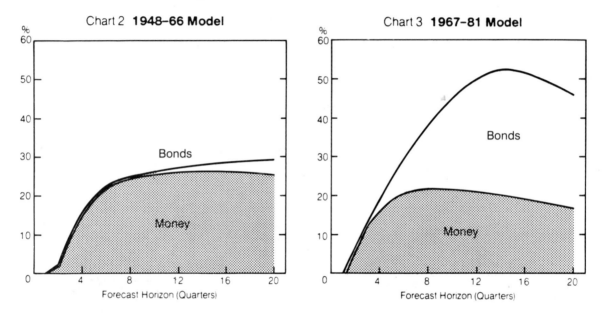

Chart 2 **1948–66 Model**

Chart 3 **1967–81 Model**

Sources of basic data U S Department of Commerce Federal Reserve Bank of St Louis

$$(13) \quad \lambda \equiv \begin{bmatrix} \lambda_1 \\ \cdot \\ \cdot \\ \cdot \\ \lambda_5 \end{bmatrix}$$

C and A, are 5×1 and 5×5 matrices of coefficients, respectively, and m = lag length. The coefficients in the matrices C and A, are estimated by ordinary least squares, and $E \lambda \lambda' = \Lambda$ is estimated by the variance-covariance matrix of residuals.

For the test for a change in budget policy, I divide the entire postwar period into two subperiods: from 1948:1 to 1966:4, when budgets were nearly balanced, and from 1967:1 to 1981:4, when budgets were almost constantly in deficit. To test whether the change in budget policy is

statistically significant, I determine the probability that the residuals from the two subperiod DEBT regressions were drawn from the same distribution. The probabilities are determined for lag lengths $m = 1$ through 8. For all lag lengths except 8, the probability that the residuals were drawn from the same distribution is less than 5 percent (and for lag length 8 it is only 7 percent). Since the DEBT equation reflects the budget policy, this result means that one can state with a high degree of confidence that deficit policies were different in the two subperiods.

The proposition that higher deficits lead to higher inflation can be directly examined without employing other equations of the VARs. And the data do support it. (See Chart 1.) Between the two subperiods, the average annual growth rate of federal debt shot up from only about half a percent to nearly 7.5 percent. At the same time, inflation clearly increased: The average annual growth rate of the GNP deflator roughly tripled between the two subperiods.

We can also easily examine one of the possibly corroborating implications of the legal restrictions theory—that the velocity of fiat money should grow faster when deficits are higher. And this too is supported by the data. The average annual growth rate of total reserve velocity increased between the two subperiods, from 3.1 percent in the first to 3.9 percent in the second.

Testing the other corroborating implication of the restrictions theory, that bonds should become more like money in the period of higher deficits, does require the use of all equations in the VARs. Again, if the theory is correct, then in the second subperiod the response of the economic process, especially inflation, to an increase in total federal debt should have changed and changed in a way to make it close to the response to a comparable increase in money. In order to examine this implication, I estimate VARs of lag length 3 over each subperiod and then study the effects of money and bonds on inflation from two different perspectives.

Charts 2 and 3 show that bonds did indeed become more like money in their contribution to the forecast variance of the GNP deflator. The charts show cumulated parts of the decomposition of variance of the GNP deflator according to the VARs estimated over each subperiod. The parts are the proportions of the forecast variance in the GNP deflator which are attributable to innovations in bonds and money (DEBT and TR). Loosely speaking, the charts show how much of the parts of the GNP deflator which could not be predicted ahead is due to DEBT and TR being different from expected. In the first subperiod, for forecasts of ten quarters and more ahead, TR accounted for about 25 percent of the forecast variance of the GNP deflator, while DEBT accounted for almost none (Chart 2). However, for those forecasts in the second subperiod—when deficits and inflation both increased—TR and DEBT accounted for similar percentages of the GNP deflator's forecast variance, with DEBT actually accounting for slightly more than TR (Chart 3).

Charts 4 and 5 illustrate a similar result for the response over time of the GNP deflator to standardized shocks in bonds and money, according to the VARs estimated over each subperiod. In the first subperiod, the two shocks produced quite different reactions in the deflator: an unexpected increase in DEBT was correlated with a decline in the deflator from its expected level for about eight quarters, followed by increases thereafter; an unexpected increase in

Charts 4 and 5

. . .and bonds' impact on inflation over time closely resembled money's.

Responses of the GNP Deflator to Unexpected Increases in Federal Debt (Bonds) and Total Reserves (Money)* According to Models Based on Data for 1948–66 and 1967–81

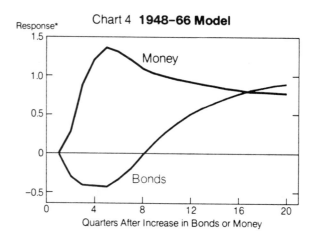

Chart 4 **1948–66 Model**

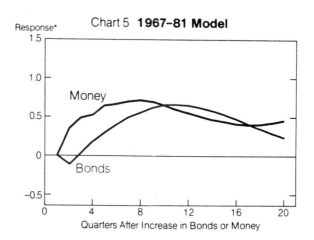

Chart 5 **1967–81 Model**

*The response of the GNP deflator to standardized positive shocks in DEBT and TR is measured in terms of the standard error of the forecast of GNPD.

Sources of basic data: U.S. Department of Commerce; Federal Reserve Bank of St. Louis

TR was correlated with an immediate and sustained increase in the deflator (Chart 4). In the second, higher deficit subperiod, though, the dynamic responses of the deflator to positive shocks in DEBT and TR were very similar: after both shocks, the deflator increased almost immediately, the effect grew for two or three years, and then it dissipated (Chart 5).

Summary

Theory suggests that deficits matter for inflation if *deficits* is interpreted to mean deficit policy. A persistently higher deficit policy can be financed in an economy with valued fiat debt, money and privately held unbacked bonds. In such an economy, deficits determine the growth of total fiat debt. If the demands for the two types of debt are separate, then persistently higher deficits lead to higher inflation through necessary monetary accommodation and crowding out.

Separateness of demands for the two types of debt is not natural. Government restrictions on the use of bonds cause them to be imperfect substitutes for money. Larger deficits increase interest rates, and, thus, private incentives to circumvent the restrictions. As the private sector breaks down the restrictions, bonds become easier to use in transactions, so more inflation results from the same monetary and budget policies.

Empirical evidence supports the proposition that higher deficit policies increase inflation. Studies of many countries document the inflationary effects of deficit policies, including my study of the United States. The evidence for this country may not yet be as persuasive as that for others because of the minimal number and size of budget policy changes that have occurred. Unfortunately, we may have another and a larger change to investigate if current budget projections are realized.

References

Blinder, Alan S. 1982. On the monetization of deficits. Paper prepared for The Economic Consequences of Government Deficits: An Economic Policy Conference, cosponsored by the Center for the Study of American Business and the Institute of Banking and Financial Markets, held at Washington University, St. Louis, Missouri, October. Also forthcoming, in conference proceedings volume.

Bryant, John, and Wallace, Neil. 1979. The inefficiency of interest-bearing national debt. *Journal of Political Economy* 87 (April): 365-81.

_____. 1980. A suggestion for further simplifying the theory of money. Research Department Staff Report 62. Federal Reserve Bank of Minneapolis.

Friedman, Milton. 1981a. A memorandum to the Fed. *Wall Street Journal* (January 30).

_____. 1981b. Deficits and inflation. *Newsweek* (February 23): 70.

Grossman, Herschel I. 1982. The American fiscal deficit: Facts and effects. Working Paper 934. National Bureau of Economic Research.

Hamburger, Michael J., and Zwick, Burton. 1981. Deficits, money and inflation. *Journal of Monetary Economics* 7 (January): 141-50.

Harberger, Arnold C. 1982. The Chilean economy in the 1970s: Crisis, stabilization, liberalization, reform. In *Economic policy in a world of change*, ed. Karl Brunner and Allan H. Meltzer. Carnegie-Rochester Conference Series on Public Policy 17: 115-52. Amsterdam: North-Holland.

Hein, Scott E. 1981. Deficits and inflation. *Review* 63 (March): 3-10. Federal Reserve Bank of St. Louis.

McKinnon, Ronald I. 1982. The order of economic liberalization: Lessons from Chile and Argentina. In *Economic policy in a world of change*, ed. Karl Brunner and Allan H. Meltzer. Carnegie-Rochester Conference Series on Public Policy 17: 159-86. Amsterdam: North-Holland.

Miller, Preston J. 1982a. Fiscal policy in a monetarist model. Research Department Staff Report 67. Federal Reserve Bank of Minneapolis.

_____. 1982b. A monetarist approach to federal budget control. Research Department Working Paper 210. Federal Reserve Bank of Minneapolis.

_____. 1982c. Optimal crowding out in a monetarist model. Research Department Working Paper 212. Federal Reserve Bank of Minneapolis.

_____. 1982d. A time series analysis of federal budget policy. Research Department Working Paper 213. Federal Reserve Bank of Minneapolis.

Patinkin, Don. 1979. The inflationary experience: Some lessons from Israel. In *Essays in post-Keynesian inflation*, ed. James H. Gapinski and Charles E. Rockwood, pp. 125-34. Cambridge, Mass.: Ballinger.

Perry, George L. 1978. Slowing the wage-price spiral: The macroeconomic view. In *Brookings Papers on Economic Activity*, ed. Arthur M. Okun and George L. Perry, 2: 259-91. Washington, D.C.: Brookings Institution.

Sargent, Thomas J. 1981. The ends of four big inflations. Research Department Working Paper 158. Federal Reserve Bank of Minneapolis. Also 1982, in *Inflation: Causes and effects*, ed. Robert E. Hall, pp. 41-97. National Bureau of Economic Research Project Report. Chicago: University of Chicago Press.

Sargent, Thomas J., and Wallace, Neil. 1981. Some unpleasant monetarist arithmetic. *Federal Reserve Bank of Minneapolis Quarterly Review* 5 (Fall): 1-17.

Sloane, Leonard. 1982. Your money: Zero coupon, insured C.D.'s. *New York Times* (September 4): 20.

Sprinkel, Beryl. 1981. Testimony. In Conduct of monetary policy: Hearings before the Committee on Banking, Finance and Urban Affairs, House of Representatives, U.S. Congress, July 23, pp. 428-92. 97th Cong., 1st sess. Serial 97-17.

Stein, Jerome L. 1976. Inside the monetarist black box. In *Monetarism*, ed. Jerome L. Stein. Studies in Monetary Economics 1: 183-232. Amsterdam: North-Holland.

U.S. Congress. Congressional Budget Office (CBO). 1983. Baseline budget projections for fiscal years 1984-1988. Report to the Senate and House committees on the budget, February.

Wallace, Neil. 1979. Significant rate-of-return dominance: A proposed explanation in terms of legal restrictions. Unpublished paper, October.

Weintraub, Robert E. 1981. Deficits: Their impact on inflation and growth. Staff study prepared for the Subcommittee on Monetary and Fiscal Policy of the Joint Economic Committee, U.S. Congress. 97th Cong., 1st sess., July.

International Finance

The increasingly open world economy, the shifts in income and wealth across countries due to changes in prices of raw materials like oil, the large changes in individual countries' current account positions, and differential regulations across countries have each contributed to the dramatic increase in activity in international financial markets. The readings in this section describe various aspects of these markets.

The first article in this section, "A Guide to Foreign Exchange Markets" by K. Alec Chrystal, identifies who deals in the markets for foreign currencies and why. It also explains how trading in these markets takes place, noting the sizable differences between the large-bank-dominated wholesale market and the much-smaller-scale retail market for foreign exchange. The use of futures and options contracts to hedge exchange rate risk is then outlined. Finally, Chrystal discusses the central role that the U.S. dollar plays in foreign exchange trading.

In "Current Illusions about the International Debt Crisis," Lawrence J. Brainard counsels against misconstruing recent improvements in the liquidity position of foreign borrowers as improvements in their solvency. The major change in the international economic landscape has been the large recent decline in U.S. nominal interest rates. The author contends that to solve the debt problem significant structural reforms are required in many less-developed countries. What is distressing is that even the crucible of the recent crisis has produced few fundamental changes. Now that the immediate crisis has been staved off, a longer-term approach to continuing problems is called for.

Marvin Goodfriend examines the tremendous growth of the overseas markets for deposits and loans that are denominated in U.S. dollars in "Eurodollars." These markets are relatively free of the reserve requirements and other regulations that banks located in the United States face, and in fact it is just this advantage that spawned activity in Eurodollars not just in Europe but all over the world. The similarity of the features of onshore and offshore deposits explains why their interest rates are nearly identical. There are no obvious effects of the differential risks of these deposits on their relative yields. The persistence of the relative regulatory advantages of Eurodollars suggests that their share of dollar-denominated market is likely to continue to rise.

The final article, "Country Risk, Portfolio Decisions, and Regulation in International Bank Lending" by Ingo Walter, advances the prescient argument that banks should more consistently apply the basic principles of portfolio theory when considering international lending. Walter concedes that the task is difficult; neither the returns nor the risks associated with loans to an individual country are easy to identify, let alone to measure. Calculation of the extent to which returns are correlated across countries is also crucial but is even more problematic. Nonetheless, banks are well advised to put their assessments of the returns and risks of loans to various countries on a common footing and to make some allowance for the correlation of these returns across countries.

Article Thirty-Two

A Guide to Foreign Exchange Markets

K. Alec Chrystal

THE economies of the free world are becoming increasingly interdependent. U.S. exports now amount to almost 10 percent of Gross National Product. For both Britain and Canada, the figure currently exceeds 25 percent. Imports are about the same size. Trade of this magnitude would not be possible without the ability to buy and sell currencies. Currencies must be bought and sold because the acceptable means of payment in other countries is not the U.S. dollar. As a result, importers, exporters, travel agents, tourists and many others with overseas business must change dollars into foreign currency and/or the reverse.

The trading of currencies takes place in foreign exchange markets whose major function is to facilitate international trade and investment. Foreign exchange markets, however, are shrouded in mystery. One reason for this is that a considerable amount of foreign exchange market activity does not appear to be related directly to the needs of international trade and investment.

The purpose of this paper is to explain how these markets work.[1] The basics of foreign exchange will first

---

K. Alec Chrystal, professor of economics-elect, University of Sheffield, England, is a visiting scholar at the Federal Reserve Bank of St. Louis. Leslie Bailis Koppel provided research assistance. The author wishes to thank Joseph Hempen, Centerre Bank, St. Louis, for his advice on this paper.

[1]For further discussion of foreign exchange markets in the United States, see Kubarych (1983). See also Dufey and Giddy (1978) and McKinnon (1979).

be described. This will be followed by a discussion of some of the more important activities of market participants. Finally, there will be an introduction to the analysis of a new feature of exchange markets — currency options. The concern of this paper is with the structure and mechanics of foreign exchange markets, not with the determinants of exchange rates themselves.

THE BASICS OF FOREIGN EXCHANGE MARKETS

There is an almost bewildering variety of foreign exchange markets. Spot markets and forward markets abound in a number of currencies. In addition, there are diverse prices quoted for these currencies. This section attempts to bring order to this seeming disarray.

Spot, Forward, Bid, Ask

Virtually every major newspaper, such as the *Wall Street Journal* or the *London Financial Times*, prints a daily list of exchange rates. These are expressed either as the number of units of a particular currency that exchange for one U.S. dollar or as the number of U.S. dollars that exchange for one unit of a particular currency. Sometimes both are listed side by side (see table 1).

For major currencies, up to four different prices typically will be quoted. One is the "spot" price. The others may be "30 days forward," "90 days forward,"

Table 1

Foreign Exchange Rate Quotations

Foreign Exchange

Wednesday, September 7, 1983

The New York foreign exchange selling rates below apply to trading among banks in amounts of $1 million and more, as quoted at 3 p.m. Eastern time by Bankers Trust Co. Retail transactions provide fewer units of foreign currency per dollar.

Country	U.S. $ equiv. Wed.	U.S. $ equiv. Tues.	Currency per U.S. $ Wed.	Currency per U.S. $ Tues.
Argentina (Peso)	.09652	.09652	10.36	10.36
Australia (Dollar)	.8772	.8777	1.1340	1.1393
Austria (Schilling)	.05296	.0560	18.88	17.84
Belgium (Franc)				
Commercial rate	.01851	.01855	54.01	53.90
Financial rate	.01844	.01846	54.21	54.15
Brazil (Cruzeiro)	.001459	.00149	685.	671.00
Britain (Pound)	1.4910	1.5000	.6707	.6666
30-Day Forward	1.4915	1.5004	.6704	.6664
90-Day Forward	1.4930	1.5010	.6697	.6662
180-Day Forward	1.4952	1.5028	.6688	.6654
Canada (Dollar)	.8120	.8123	1.2315	1.2310
30-Day Forward	.8125	.8128	1.2307	1.2303
90-Day Forward	.8134	.8137	1.2293	1.2289
180-Day Forward	.8145	.8147	1.2277	1.2274
Chile (Official rate)	.01246	.01246	80.21	80.21
China (Yuan)	.50499	.50489	1.9802	1.9806
Colombia (Peso)	.01228	.01228	81.4	81.40
Denmark (Krone)	.10362	.10405	9.65	9.6100
Ecuador (Sucre)				
Official rate	.02082	.02082	48.03	48.03
Floating rate	.010917	.010917	91.60	91.60
Finland (Markka)	.17424	.17485	5.7390	5.7190
France (Franc)	.1238	.1238	8.0750	8.0750
30-Day Forward	.1235	.1230	8.0955	8.1300
90-Day Forward	.1224	.1223	8.1695	8.1725
180-Day Forward	.1203	.1202	8.3100	8.3150
Greece (Drachma)	.01075	.01078	93.	92.70
Hong Kong (Dollar)	.1297	.13089	7.71	7.6400
India (Rupee)	.0980	.0980	10.20	10.20
Indonesia (Rupiah)	.001015	.001015	985.	985.
Ireland (Punt)	1.1715	1.1775	.8536	.8493
Israel (Shekel)	.0173	.0173	57.80	57.80
Italy (Lira)	.000624	.0006255	1602.	1598.50
Japan (Yen)	.004072	.004067	245.55	245.85
30-Day Forward	.004083	.004079	244.88	245.15
90-Day Forward	.004107	.004102	243.48	243.75
180-Day Forward	.004147	.004142	241.10	241.39
Lebanon (Pound)	.20618	.20618	4.85	4.85
Malaysia (Ringgit)	.42462	.42489	2.3550	2.3535
Mexico (Peso)				
Floating rate	.00665	.00666	150.25	150.00
Netherlands (Guilder)	.33288	.3333	3.0040	3.000
New Zealand (Dollar)	.6497	.6505	1.5397	1.5327
Norway (Krone)	.13368	.1340	7.48	7.4625
Pakistan (Rupee)	.07518	.07518	13.30	13.30
Peru (Sol)	.0005105	.0005105	1958.89	1958.89
Philippines (Peso)	.09085	.09085	11.007	11.007
Portugal (Escudo)	.00804	.00807	124.35	123.90
Saudi Arabia (Riyal)	.28735	.28735	3.48	3.48
Singapore (Dollar)	.46609	.4664	2.1455	2.1440
South Africa (Rand)	.8870	.8900	1.1273	1.1236
South Korea (Won)	.001285	.001285	778.20	778.20
Spain (Peseta)	.00655	.00658	152.60	151.90
Sweden (Krona)	.12635	.12666	7.9140	7.8950
Switzerland (Franc)	.4596	.4591	2.1755	2.1780
30-Day Forward	.4619	.4615	216.46	2.1666
90-Day Forward	.4662	.4657	2.1449	2.1470
180-Day Forward	.4728	.4723	2.1150	2.1172
Taiwan (Dollar)	.02489	.02489	40.17	40.17
Thailand (Baht)	.043459	.043459	23.01	23.01
Uruguay (New Peso)				
Financial	.02798	.02798	35.73	35.73
Venezuela (Bolivar)				
Official rate	.23256	.23256	4.30	4.30
Floating rate	.07194	.07272	13.90	13.75
W. Germany (Mark)	.3726	.3726	2.6835	2.6835
30-Day Forward	.3740	.3741	2.6731	2.6728
90-Day Forward	.3767	.3768	2.6540	2.6538
180-Day Forward	.3808	.3808	2.6260	2.6259
SDR	1.04637	1.04903	.955685	.953625

Special Drawing Rights are based on exchange rates for the U.S., West German, British, French and Japanese currencies. Source: International Monetary Fund.
z-Not quoted.

The Dollar Spot and Forward

Sept 7	Day's spread	Close	One month	% p.a.	Three months	% p.a.
UK†	1.4860-1.4975	1.4910-1.4920	0.02-0.07c dis	−0.36	0.17-0.22dis	−0.52
Ireland†	1.1665-1.1720	1.1710-1.1720	0.36-0.30c pm	3.39	0.88-0.78 pm	2.84
Canada	1.2305-1.2320	1.2310-1.2315	0.09-0.06c pm	0.73	0.24-0.21 pm	0.73
Nethlnd.	3.0050-3.0150	3.0050-3.0070	1.12-1.02c pm	4.26	3.00-2.90 pm	3.92
Belgium	54.06-54.20	54.06-54.08	7-6c pm	1.44	14-11 pm	0.92
Denmark	9.6400-9.6800	9.6400-9.6450	2-2¹₂ore dis	−2.79	par-1¹₂ dis	−0.10
W. Ger	2.6850-2.6980	2.6865-2.6875	1.07-1.02pf pm	4.66	3.00-2.95 pm	4.42
Portugal	124.20-125.00	124.40-124.70	115-290c dis	−19.51	330-790dis	−17.98
Spain	152.40-152.70	152.50-152.60	170-220c dis	−15.33	675-775dis	−18.99
Italy	1604-1608	1605-1606	10-10¹₂lire dis	−7.65	29¹₂-31 dis	−7.53
Norway	7.4730-7.4940	7.4730-7.4780	1.90-2.20ore dis	−3.29	5.90-6.20ds	−3.23
France	8.0775-8.1225	8.0825-8.0875	2.02-2.12c dis	−3.07	9.85-9.85ds	−4.81
Sweden	7.9120-7.9265	7.9120-7.9170	0.90-1.10ore dis	−1.51	2.25-2.45ds	−1.19
Japan	245.50-246.50	245.65-245.75	0.69-0.64y pm	3.24	2.11-2.03 pm	3.36
Austria	18.89-18.95¹₂	18.89-18.90	7.50-6.70gro pm	4.50	21.00-18.50 pm	4.17
Switz	2.1770-2.1875	2.1800-2.1810	1.10-1.05c pm	5.91	3.10-3.05 pm	5.63

†UK and Ireland are quoted in U.S. currency. Forward premiums and discounts apply to the U.S. dollar and not to the individual currency.

Belgian rate is for convertible francs. Financial franc 54.40-54.45.

London Financial Times, September 8, 1983

Wall Street Journal, September 8, 1983

and "180 days forward." These may be expressed either in "European Terms" (such as number of $ per £) or in "American Terms" (such as number of £ per $). (See the glossary for further explanation.)

The spot price is what you must pay to buy currencies for immediate delivery (two working days in the interbank market; over the counter, if you buy bank notes or travelers checks). The forward prices for each currency are what you will have to pay if you sign a contract today to buy that currency on a specific future date (30 days from now, etc.). In this market, you pay for the currency when the contract matures.

Why would anyone buy and sell foreign currency forward? There are some major advantages from having such opportunities available. For example, an exporter who has receipts of foreign currency due at some future date can sell those funds forward now, thereby avoiding all risks associated with subsequent adverse exchange rate changes. Similarly, an importer who will have to pay for a shipment of goods in foreign currency in, say, three months can buy the foreign exchange forward and, again, avoid having to bear the exchange rate risk.

The exchange rates quoted in the financial press (for example, those in table 1) are not the ones individuals would get at a local bank. Unless otherwise specified, the published prices refer to those quoted by banks to other banks for currency deals in excess of $1 million. Even these prices will vary somewhat depending upon whether the bank buys or sells. The difference between the buying and selling price is sometimes known as the "bid-ask spread." The spread partly reflects the banks' costs and profit margins in transactions; however, major banks make their profits more from capital gains than from the spread.[2]

The market for bank notes and travelers checks is quite separate from the interbank foreign exchange market. For smaller currency exchanges, such as an individual going on vacation abroad might make, the spread is greater than in the interbank market. This presumably reflects the larger average costs — including the exchange rate risks that banks face by holding bank notes in denominations too small to be sold in the interbank market — associated with these smaller exchanges. As a result, individuals generally pay a higher price for foreign exchange than those quoted in the newspapers.

Table 2
Dollar Price of Deutschemarks and Sterling at Various Banks

	Deutschemark		Sterling	
	Buy	Sell	Buy	Sell
Retail				
Local (St. Louis) banks (avg.)	.3572	–.3844	1.4225	–1.5025
Wholesale				
New York banks	.3681	–.3683	1.4570	–1.4580
European banks (high)	.3694	–.3696	1.4573	–1.4583
European banks (low)	.3677	–.3678	1.4610	–1.4620
Bankers trust	.3681		1.4588	

Note: These prices were all quoted on November 28, 1983, between 2:00 p.m. and 2:45 p.m. (Central Standard Time). Prices for local banks were acquired by telephoning for their price on a $10,000 transaction. The prices quoted were reference rates and not the final price they would offer on a firm transaction. Figure for Bankers Trust is that given in the *Wall Street Journal*, November 29, 1983, as priced at 2:00 p.m. (Central Standard Time) on November 28, 1983. Other prices were taken from the Telerate information system at 2:35 p.m. New York prices were the latest available (Morgan and Citibank, respectively). European prices were the last prices quoted before close of trading in Europe by various banks. Deutschemark prices were actually quoted in American terms. The sell prices above have been rounded up. The difference between buy and sell prices for DM in the interbank market actually worked out at $0.00015.

An example of the range of spot exchange rates available is presented in table 2, which shows prices for deutschemarks and sterling quoted within a one-hour period on November 28, 1983. There are two important points to notice. First, all except those in the first line are prices quoted in the interbank, or wholesale, market for transactions in excess of $1 million. The sterling prices have a bid-ask spread of only 0.1 cent (which is only about 0.07 percent of the price, or $7 on $10,000). On DM, the spread per dollars worth works out to be about half that on sterling ($4 on $10,000).[3]

Second, the prices quoted by local banks for small, or retail, transactions, which serve only as a guide and do not necessarily represent prices on actual deals, involve a much larger bid-ask spread. These retail spreads vary from bank to bank, but are related to (and larger than) the interbank rates. In some cases, they

---

[2]Notice the *Wall Street Journal* quotes only a bank selling price at a particular time. The *Financial Times* quotes the bid-ask spread and the range over the day.

[3]In practice, the spread will vary during the day, depending upon market conditions. For example, the sterling spread may be as little as 0.01 cents at times and on average is about 0.05 cents. Spreads generally will be larger on less widely traded currencies.

may be of the order of 4 cents or less on sterling, though the prices quoted in St. Louis involved average spreads of 8 cents on sterling. The latter represents a spread of about 5½ percent (about $550 per $10,000 transaction). The equivalent spread for DM was 7 percent ($700 per $10,000 transaction).

The spread on forward transactions will usually be wider than on spot, especially for longer maturities. For interbank trade, the closing spread on one and three months forward sterling on September 8, 1983, was .15 cents, while the spot spread was .10 cents. This is shown in the top line of the *Financial Times* report in table 1. Of course, like the spot spread, the forward spread varies with time of day and market conditions. At times it may be as low as .02 cents. No information is available for the size of spread on the forward prices typically offered on small transactions, since the retail market on forward transactions is very small.

HOW DOES "THE" FOREIGN EXCHANGE MARKET OPERATE?

It is generally not possible to go to a specific building and "see" the market where prices of foreign exchange are determined. With few exceptions, the vast bulk of foreign exchange business is done over the telephone between specialist divisions of major banks. Foreign exchange dealers in each bank usually operate from one room; each dealer has several telephones and is surrounded by video screens and news tapes. Typically, each dealer specializes in one or a small number of markets (such as sterling/dollar or deutschemark/dollar). Trades are conducted with other dealers who represent banks around the world. These dealers typically deal regularly with one another and are thus able to make firm commitments by word of mouth.

Only the head or regional offices of the larger banks actively deal in foreign exchange. The largest of these banks are known as "market makers" since they stand ready to buy or sell any of the major currencies on a more or less continuous basis. Unusually large transactions, however, will only be accommodated by market makers on more favorable terms. In such cases, foreign exchange brokers may be used as middlemen to find a taker or takers for the deal. Brokers (of which there are four major firms and a handful of smaller ones) do not trade on their own account, but specialize in setting up large foreign exchange transactions in return for a commission (typically 0.03 cents or less on the sterling spread). In April 1983, 56 percent of spot transactions by value involving banks in the United States were channeled through brokers.[4] If all interbank transactions are included, the figure rises to 59 percent.

Most small banks and local offices of major banks do not deal directly in the interbank foreign exchange market. Rather they typically will have a credit line with a large bank or their head office. Transactions will thus involve an extra step (see figure 1). The customer deals with a local bank, which in turn deals with a major bank or head office. The interbank foreign exchange market exists between the major banks either directly or indirectly via a broker.

FUTURES AND OPTION MARKETS FOR FOREIGN EXCHANGE

Until very recently, the interbank market was the only channel through which foreign exchange transactions took place. The past decade has produced major innovations in foreign exchange trading. On May 16, 1972, the International Money Market (IMM) opened under the auspices of the Chicago Mercantile Exchange. One novel feature of the IMM is that it provides a trading floor on which deals are struck by brokers face to face, rather than over telephone lines. The most significant difference between the IMM and the interbank market, however, is that trading on the IMM is in futures contracts for foreign exchange, the typical business being contracts for delivery on the third Wednesday of March, June, September or December. Activity at the IMM has expanded greatly since its opening. For example, during 1972, 144,336 contracts were traded; the figure for 1981 was 6,121,932.

There is an important distinction between "forward" transactions and "futures" contracts. The former are individual agreements between two parties, say, a bank and customer. The latter is a contract traded on an organized market of a standard size and settlement date, which is resalable at the market price up to the close of trading in the contract. These organized markets are discussed more fully below.

While the major banks conduct foreign exchange deals in large denominations, the IMM trading is done in contracts of standard size which are fairly small. Examples of the standard contracts at present are £25,000; DM125,000; Canadian $100,000. These are actually smaller today than in the early days of the IMM.

Further, unlike prices on the interbank market, price movements in any single day are subject to specific

---

[4]See Federal Reserve Bank of New York (1983).

Figure 1
Structure of Foreign Exchange Markets

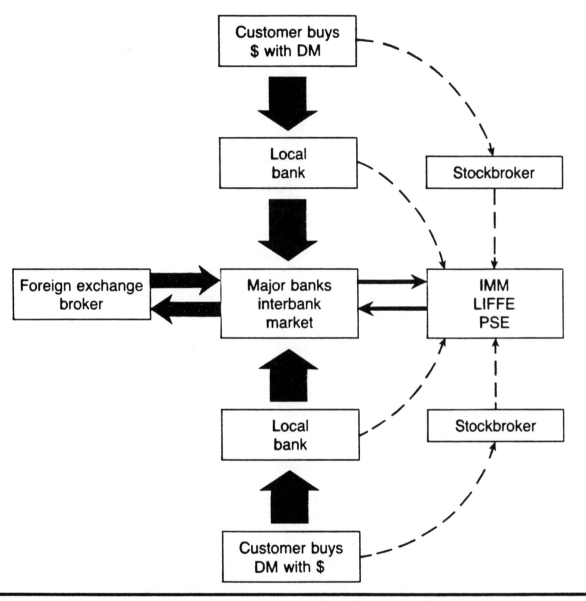

NOTE: The International Money Market (IMM) Chicago trades foreign exchange futures and DM futures options.
The London International Financial Futures Exchange (LIFFE) trades foreign exchange futures.
The Philadelphia Stock Exchange (PSE) trades foreign currency options.

limits at the IMM. For example, for sterling futures, prices are not allowed to vary more than $.0500 away from the previous day's settlement price; this limit is expanded if it is reached in the same direction for two successive days. The limit does not apply on the last day a contract is traded.

Unlike the interbank market, parties to a foreign exchange contract at the IMM typically do not know each other. Default risk, however, is minor because contracts are guaranteed by the exchange itself. To minimize the cost of this guarantee, the exchange insists upon "margin requirements" to cover fluctuations in the value of a contract. This means that an individual or firm buying a futures contract would, in effect, place a deposit equal to about 4 percent of the value of a contract.[5]

Perhaps the major limitation of the IMM from the point of view of importers or exporters is that contracts cover only eight currencies — those of Britain, Canada, West Germany, Switzerland, Japan, Mexico, France and the Netherlands — and they are specified in standard sizes for particular dates. Only by chance will these conform exactly to the needs of importers and exporters. Large firms and financial institutions will find the market useful, however, if they have a fairly continuous stream of payments and receipts in the traded foreign currencies. Although contracts have a specified standard date, they offer a fairly flexible method of avoiding exchange rate risk because they are marketable continuously.

A major economic advantage of the IMM for non-bank customers is its low transaction cost. Though the brokerage cost of a contract will vary, a "round trip" (that is, one buy and one sell) costs as little as $15. This is only .04 percent of the value of a sterling contract and less for some of the larger contracts. Of course, such costs are high compared with the interbank market, where the brokerage cost on DM 1 million would be about $6.25 (the equivalent-valued eight futures contracts would cost $60 in brokerage, taking $7.50 per single deal). They are low, however, compared with those in the retail market, where the spread may involve a cost of up to 2.5 percent or 3 percent per transaction.

A market similar to the IMM, the London International Financial Futures Exchange (LIFFE), opened in September 1982. On LIFFE, futures are traded in sterling, deutschemarks, Swiss francs and yen in identical bundles to those sold on the IMM. In its first year, the foreign exchange business of LIFFE did not take off in a big way. The major provider of exchange rate risk coverage for business continues to be the bank network. Less than 5 percent of such cover is provided by markets such as IMM and LIFFE at present.

An entirely new feature of foreign exchange markets that has arisen in the 1980s is the existence of option markets.[6] The Philadelphia Exchange was the first to introduce foreign exchange options. These are in five currencies (deutschemark, sterling, Swiss franc, yen and Canadian dollar). Trades are conducted in standard bundles half the size of the IMM futures contracts. The IMM introduced an options market in German marks on January 24, 1984; this market trades options on futures contracts whereas the Philadelphia options are for spot currencies.

Futures and options prices for foreign exchange are published daily in the financial press. Table 3 shows prices for February 14, 1984, as displayed in the *Wall Street Journal* on the following day. Futures prices on the IMM are presented for five currencies (left-hand column). There are five contracts quoted for each currency: March, June, September, December and March 1985. For each contract, opening and last settlement (settle) prices, the range over the day, the change from the previous day, the range over the life of the contract and the number of contracts outstanding with the exchange (open interest) are listed.

Consider the March and June DM futures. March futures opened at $.3653 per mark and closed at $.3706 per mark; June opened at $.3698 per mark and closed at $.3746 per mark. Turn now to the Chicago Mercantile Exchange (IMM) futures options (center column). These are options on the futures contracts just discussed (see inset for explanation of options). Thus, the line labeled "Futures" lists the settle prices of the March and June futures as above.

Let us look at the call options. These are rights to buy DM futures at specified prices — the strike price. For example, take the call option at strike price 35. This means that one can purchase an option to buy DM 125,000 March futures up to the March settlement date for $.3500 per mark. This option will cost 2.05 cents per mark, or $2,562.50, plus brokerage fees. The June option to buy June futures DM at $.3500 per mark will cost 2.46 cents per mark, or $3,075.00, plus brokerage fees.

---

[5]A bank may also insist upon some minimum deposit to cover a forward contract, though there is no firm rule.

[6]For a discussion of options in commodities, see Belongia (1983).

Table 3

Futures and Options Markets

Futures Prices

Tuesday, February 14, 1984
Open Interest Reflects Previous Trading Day.

	Open	High	Low	Settle	Change	Lifetime High	Lifetime Low	Open Interest
BRITISH POUND (IMM)—25,000 pounds; $ per pound								
Mar	1.4150	1.4400	1.4150	1.4370	+ .0170	1.6010	1.3930	17,694
June	1.4175	1.4435	1.4175	1.4395	+ .0170	1.5520	1.3950	3,251
Sept	1.4285	1.4410	1.4220	1.4410	+ .0160	1.5240	1.3980	157
Dec	1.4280	1.4435	1.4245	1.4435	+ .0160	1.4650	1.3990	75
Mar85	1.4280	1.4460	1.4270	1.4470	+ .0170	1.4625	1.4000	65
Est vol 10,651 vol Mon 1,987 open int 21,242, +78.								
CANADIAN DOLLAR (IMM)—100,000 dlrs.; $ per Can $								
Mar	.8010	.8024	.8010	.8020	....	.8169	.7979	4,033
June	.8014	.8029	.8013	.8023	....	.8168	.7983	740
Sept	....	....	....	.8026	....	.8147	.7988	312
Dec	.8021	.8031	.8021	.8029	....	.8040	.8021	152
Mar85	.8035	.8035	.8035	.8032	....	.8035	.8023	50
Est vol 1,087 vol Mon 535; open int 5,287, −103.								
JAPANESE YEN (IMM) 12.5 million yen; $ per yen (.00)								
Mar	.4276	.4297	.4276	.4294	+ .0011	.4396	.4125	25,730
June	.4315	.4337	.4312	.4334	+ .0011	.4435	.4180	3,908
Sept	.4354	.4375	.4354	.4374	+ .0012	.4450	.4354	974
Dec	.4416	.4420	.4400	.4415	+ .0012	.4493	.4395	271
Est vol 9,133; vol Mon 3,306; open int 30,883, +534.								
SWISS FRANC (IMM)—125,000 francs; $ per franc								
Mar	.4495	.4556	.4486	.4549	+ .0047	.5230	.4470	24,164
June	.4564	.4629	.4557	.4622	+ .0051	.5045	.4536	3,165
Sept	.4632	.4692	.4632	.4688	+ .0052	.5020	.4598	153
Dec	.4705	.4780	.4705	.4747	+ .0049	.4880	.4665	71
Mar85	....	....	....	.4830	+ .0050	.4840	.4755	5
Est vol 30,610; vol Mon 8,466; open int 27,558, +296.								
W. GERMAN MARK (IMM)—125,000 marks; $ per mark								
Mar	.3653	.3713	.3650	.3706	− .0036	.4100	.3537	30,974
June	.3698	.3754	.3688	.3746	− .0037	.4002	.3568	4,911
Sept	.3743	.3790	.3743	.3780	− .0034	.4030	.3602	362
Dec	.3780	.3825	.3780	.3825	− .0043	.3825	.3640	204
Mar85	....	....	....	.3838	+ .0035	.3699	.3699	1
Est vol 30,248; vol Mon 9,045; open int 36,452, +680.								

Futures Options

Chicago Mercantile Exchange

W. GERMAN MARK—125,000 marks, cents per mark

Strike Price	Calls—Settle Mar	Calls—Settle Jun	Puts—Settle Mar	Puts—Settle Jun
34	....	....	0.01	0.01
35	2.05	2.46	0.01	0.09
36	1.11	1.66	0.06	0.25
37	0.38	1.00	0.33	0.57
38	0.10	0.54	1.00	1.02
39	0.01	0.27	....	....
Futures	.3706	.3746	....	....

Estimated total vol. 2,187.
Calls: Mon vol. 180; open int. 2,416.
Puts: Mon vol. 73; open int. 1,841.

Foreign Currency Options

Philadelphia Exchange

Option & Strike Underlying Price	Calls—Last Mar	Calls—Last Jun	Calls—Last Sep	Puts—Last Mar	Puts—Last Jun	Puts—Last Sep
12,500 British Pounds-cents per unit.						
BPound 140	3.40	r	5.70	0.40	1.85	r
143.00 .145	0.70	2.40	r	3.40	r	r
50,000 Canadian Dollars-cents per unit.						
CDollar 80	r	r	0.68	r	r	r
62,500 West German Marks-cents per unit.						
DMark 34	2.57	r	r	r	r	r
36.88 .35	1.99	2.18	r	r	r	r
36.88 .36	1.04	1.59	r	0.05	0.35	r
36.88 .37	0.38	1.00	r	0.37	0.56	r
36.88 .38	0.10	0.62	0.85	r	r	r
36.88 .39	r	0.28	s	r	r	s
36.88 .40	0.01	0.11	s	r	r	s
6,250,000 Japanese Yen-100ths of a cent per unit.						
JYen 42	0.95	1.49	2.04	r	r	r
42.75 .43	0.30	0.90	r	0.50	0.60	r
42.75 .44	0.04	0.45	0.99	r	r	r
62,500 Swiss Francs-cents per unit.						
SFranc 44	r	r	3.15	r	0.24	r
45.18 .45	0.65	r	r	0.26	r	r
45.18 .46	0.28	1.09	1.82	r	1.00	r
45.18 .47	0.06	r	r	r	r	r
45.18 .48	0.02	0.28	r	r	r	r
Total call vol.	2,271	Call open int.	37,349			
Total put vol.	799	Put open int.	26,173			

r—Not traded. s—No option offered. o—Old.
Last is premium (purchase price).

Wall Street Journal, February 15, 1984

The March call option at strike price $.3900 per mark costs only 0.01 cents per mark or $12.50. These price differences indicate that the market expects the dollar price of the mark to exceed $.3500, but not to rise substantially above $.3900.

Notice that when you exercise a futures call option you buy the relevant futures contract but only fulfill that futures contract at maturity. In contrast, the Philadelphia foreign currency options (right column) are options to buy foreign exchange (spot) itself rather than futures. So, when a call option is exercised, foreign currency is obtained immediately.

The only difference in presentation of the currency option prices as compared with the futures options is that, in the former, the spot exchange rate is listed for comparison rather than the futures price. Thus, on the Philadelphia exchange, call options on March DM 62,500 at strike price $.3500 per mark cost 1.99 cents per mark or $1,243.75, plus brokerage. Brokerage fees here would be of the same order as on the IMM, about $16 per transaction round trip, per contract.

We have seen that there are several different markets for foreign exchange — spot, forward, futures, options on spot, options on futures. The channels through which these markets are formed are, however, fairly straightforward (see figure 1). The main channel is the interbank network, though for large interbank transactions, foreign exchange brokers may be used as middlemen.

FOREIGN EXCHANGE MARKET ACTIVITIES

Much foreign exchange market trading does not appear to be related to the simple basic purpose of allowing businesses to buy or sell foreign currency in order, say, to sell or purchase goods overseas. It is certainly easy to see the usefulness of the large range of foreign exchange transactions available through the interbank and organized markets (spot, forward, futures, options) to facilitate trade between nations. It is also clear that there is a useful role for foreign exchange brokers in helping to "make" the interbank market. There are several other activities, however, in foreign exchange markets that are less well understood and whose relevance is less obvious to people interested in understanding what these markets accomplish.

Foreign Exchange Options

An option is a contract specifying the right to buy or sell — in this case foreign exchange — within a specific period (American option) or at a specific date (European option). A call option confers the right to buy. A put option confers the right to sell. Since each of these options must have a buyer and a seller, there are four possible ways of trading a single option: buy a call, sell a call, buy a put, sell a put.

The buyer of an option has the right to undertake the contract specified but may choose not to do so if it turns out to be unprofitable. The seller of the option *must* fulfill the contract if the buyer desires. Clearly, the buyer must pay the seller some premium (the option price) for this privilege. An option that would be profitable to exercise at the current exchange rate is said to be "in the money." The price at which it is exercised is the "exercise" or "strike" price.

Consider a call option on £1000 (although options of this size are not presently available on organized exchanges, it is used to present a simple illustration of the principles involved). Suppose this costs $0.03 per pound or $30 and the exercise price is $1.50 per pound. The option expires in three months. This means that the buyer has paid $30 for the right to buy £1000 with dollars at a price of $1.50 per pound any time in the next three months. If the current spot price of sterling is, say, $1.45, the option is "out of the money" because sterling can be bought cheaper on the spot market. However, if the spot price were to rise to, say, $1.55, the option would be in the money. If sold at that time, the option buyer would get a $50 return (1000 × $0.05), which would more than cover the cost of the option ($50 − $30 = $20 profit). In contrast, a put option at the same terms would be in the money at the current spot price of $1.45, but out of the money at $1.55.

Figure 2 presents a diagrammatic illustration of how the profitability of an option depends upon the relationship between the exercise price and the current spot price.[1] Figure 2a illustrates the profit avail-

---

[1]The pricing of options has been the subject of a large theoretical literature with a major contribution being made by Black and Scholes (1973). The Black-Scholes formula has been modified for foreign exchange options by Garman and Kohlhagen (1983) [see also Giddy (1983)], but the Black-Scholes formula is complex and beyond the scope of the present paper.

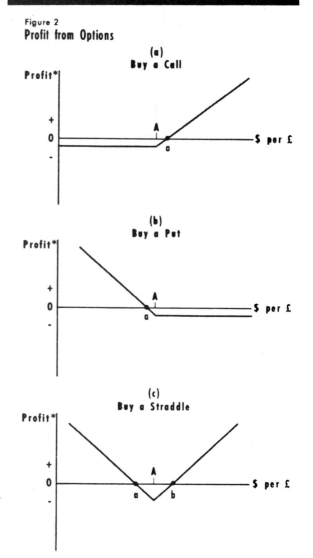

Figure 2
Profit from Options

(a)
Buy a Call

(b)
Buy a Put

(c)
Buy a Straddle

*Profit from exercise of option at current spot exchange rate.

One simple relationship which is of interest may be called "option price parity." This arises because arbitrage will ensure that the difference between a call option price (per unit) and a put option price (per unit) at the same exercise price will be equal to the present value of the difference between the exercise price and the forward exchange rate at maturity of the options (if the options are marketable, it will also hold for any date to maturity). The relationship may be expressed:

$$C - P = \frac{F - E}{1 + r},$$

when C and P are the call and put option prices at exercise price E. F is the forward exchange rate and r is the interest rate per period of the contracts. This arises because the simultaneous buying of a call and selling of a put is equivalent to buying currency forward at price E. The forward contract, however, would be paid for at the end of the period, whereas the options are transacted at the beginning. Hence, the forward contract has to be discounted back to the present.

able from buying a call option at exercise price A. At spot exchange rate A and anything lower, the option will not be exercised so the loss will equal the price of the option. At a spot exchange rate above a, the option is sufficiently in the money to more than cover its cost. Between A and a, the option is in the money but not by enough to cover cost. The profit from *selling* a call could be illustrated by reversing the + and − signs in figure 2a, or by flipping the profit line about the horizontal axis.

Figure 2b illustrates the profit from buying a put option. At spot exchange rates below a, the option with exercise price A will show a profit.

Figure 2c illustrates the profit from a simultaneous purchase of a put and call at the same exercise price. This combination will show a profit at exercise price A if the spot price goes *either* above b or below a. It is known as a "straddle." The straddle is of special interest because it makes clear the role of options as a hedge against risk. The price of a straddle can be regarded as the market valuation of the variability of the exchange rate. That is, the buyer of the straddle will show a profit if the spot price moves from some central value (the exercise price) by more than plus or minus some known percentage. The seller of the straddle accepts that risk for a lump sum. More complicated "multiple strategies" are also possible.[2]

---

[2]See Giddy (1983).

Two major classes of activity will be discussed. First, the existence of a large number of foreign exchange markets in many locations creates opportunities to profit from "arbitrage." Second, there is implicitly a market in (foreign exchange) risk bearing. Those who wish to avoid foreign exchange risk (at a price) may do so. Those who accept the risk in expectation of profits are known as "speculators."

Triangular Arbitrage

Triangular arbitrage is the process that ensures that all exchange rates are mutually consistent. If, for example, one U.S. dollar exchanges for one Canadian dollar, and one Canadian dollar exchanges for one British pound, then the U.S. dollar-pound exchange rate should be one pound for one dollar. If it differs, then there is an opportunity for profit making. To see why this is so, suppose that you could purchase two U.S. dollars with one British pound. By first buying C$1 with U.S.$1, then purchasing £1 with C$1, and finally buying U.S.$2 with £1, you could double your money immediately. Clearly this opportunity will not last for long since it involves making large profits with certainty. The process of triangular arbitrage is exactly that of finding and exploiting profitable opportunities in such exchange rate inconsistencies. As a result of triangular arbitrage, such inconsistencies will be eliminated rapidly. Cross rates, however, will only be roughly consistent given the bid-ask spread associated with transaction costs.

In the past, the possibility of making profits from triangular arbitrage was greater as a result of the practice of expressing exchange rates in American terms in the United States and in European terms elsewhere. The adoption of standard practice has reduced the likelihood of inconsistencies.[7] Also, in recent years, such opportunities for profit making have been greatly reduced by high-speed, computerized information systems and the increased sophistication of the banks operating in the market.

Arbitrage of a slightly different kind results from price differences in different locations. This is "space" arbitrage. For example, if sterling were cheaper in London than in New York, it would be profitable to buy in London and sell in New York. Similarly, if prices in the interbank market differed from those at the IMM, it would be profitable to arbitrage between them. As a result of this activity, prices in different locations will be brought broadly into line.

Interest Arbitrage

Interest arbitrage is slightly different in nature from triangular or space arbitrage; however, the basic motive of finding and exploiting profitable opportunities still applies. There is no reason why interest rates denominated in different currencies should be equal. Interest rates are the cost of borrowing or the return to lending for a specific period of time. The relative price (exchange rate) of money may change over time so that the comparison of, say, a U.S. and a British interest rate requires some allowance for expected exchange rate changes. Thus, it will be not at all unusual to find

---

[7]All except U.K. and Irish exchange rates are expressed in American terms. Futures and options contracts are expressed in European terms.

interest rates denominated in dollars and interest rates denominated in, say, pounds being somewhat different. However, real returns on assets of similar quality should be the same if the exchange rate risk is covered or hedged in the forward market. Were this not true, it would be possible to borrow in one currency and lend in another at a profit with no exchange risk.

Suppose we lend one dollar for a year in the United States at an interest rate of r_{us}. The amount accumulated at the end of the year per dollar lent will be $1 + r_{us}$ (capital plus interest). If, instead of making dollar loans, we converted them into pounds and lent them in the United Kingdom at the rate r_{uk}, the amount of pounds we would have for each original dollar at the end of the year would be $S(1 + r_{uk})$, where S is the spot exchange rate (in pounds per dollar) at the beginning of the period. At the outset, it is not known if $1 + r_{us}$ dollars is going to be worth more than $S(1 + r_{uk})$ pounds in a year's time because the spot exchange rate in a year's time is unknown. This uncertainty can be avoided by selling the pounds forward into dollars. Then the relative value of the two loans would no longer depend on what subsequently happens to the spot exchange rate. By doing this, we end up with $\frac{S}{F}(1 + r_{uk})$ dollars per original dollar invested. This is known as the "covered," or hedged, return on pounds.

Since the covered return in our example is denominated in dollars, it can reasonably be compared with the U.S. interest rate. If these returns are very different, investors will move funds where the return is highest on a covered basis. This process is interest arbitrage. It is assumed that the assets involved are equally safe and, because the returns are covered, all exchange risk is avoided. Of course, if funds do move in large volume between assets or between financial centers, then interest rates and the exchange rates (spot and forward) will change in predictable ways. Funds will continue to flow between countries until there is no extra profit to be made from interest arbitrage. This will occur when the returns on both dollar- and sterling-denominated assets are equal, that is, when

(1) $\quad (1 + r_{us}) = \frac{S}{F}(1 + r_{uk})$.

This result is known as covered interest parity. It holds more or less exactly, subject only to a margin due to transaction costs, so long as the appropriate dollar and sterling interest rates are compared.[8]

Speculation

Arbitrage in the foreign exchange markets involves little or no risk since transactions can be completed rapidly. An alternative source of profit is available from outguessing other market participants as to what future exchange rates will be. This is called speculation. Although any foreign exchange transaction that is not entirely hedged forward has a speculative element, only deliberate speculation for profit is discussed here.

Until recently, the main foreign exchange speculators were the foreign exchange departments of banks, with a lesser role being played by portfolio managers of other financial institutions and international corporations. The IMM, however, has made it much easier for individuals and smaller businesses to speculate. A high proportion of IMM transactions appears to be speculative in the sense that only about 5 percent of contracts lead to ultimate delivery of foreign exchange. This means that most of the activity involves the buying and selling of a contract *at different times* and possibly different prices prior to maturity. It is possible, however, that buying and selling of contracts before maturity would arise out of a strategy to reduce risk. So it is not possible to say that all such activity is speculative.

Speculation is important for the efficient working of foreign exchange markets. It is a form of arbitrage that occurs across time rather than across space or between markets at the same time. Just as arbitrage increases the efficiency of markets by keeping prices consistent, so speculation increases the efficiency of forward, futures and options markets by keeping those markets liquid. Those who wish to avoid foreign exchange risk may thereby do so in a well-developed market. Without speculators, risk avoidance in foreign exchange markets would be more difficult and, in many cases, impossible.[9]

Risk Reduction

Speculation clearly involves a shifting of risk from one party to another. For example, if a bank buys for-

---

[8]Since there are many different interest rates, it obviously cannot hold for all of them. Where (1) does hold is if the interest rates chosen are eurocurrency deposit rates of the same duration. In other words, if for

r_{us} we take, say, the three-month eurodollar deposit rate in Paris and for r_{uk} we take the three-month eurosterling deposit rate in Paris, then (1) will hold just about exactly. Indeed, if we took the interest rate and exchange rate quotes all from the same bank, it would be remarkable if (1) did not hold. Otherwise the bank would be offering to pay you to borrow from it and lend straight back! That is, the price of borrowing would be less than the covered return on lending. A margin between borrowing and lending rates, of course, will make this even less likely so that in reality you would lose.

[9]This is not to say that all speculative activity is necessarily beneficial.

Covered Interest Parity: An Example

The following interest rate and exchange rate quotations are taken from the *London Financial Times* of September 8, 1983 (table 1).

Closing Exchange Rate: dollars per pound	Spot	3-Month Forward
	1.4910–1.4920	.17–.22 discount

Interest Rates: 3-Month Offer Rate	Eurosterling	Eurodollar
	$9^{13}/_{16}$	$10\frac{1}{4}$

The interest rate on the three-month eurodollar deposit is a little higher (.7 percent) than that on an eurosterling deposit. If the exchange rate remains unchanged, it would be better to hold dollars; if the exchange rate falls, the eurosterling deposit would be preferable. Suppose you decide to cover the exchange risk by selling the dollars forward into pounds. Let us compare the return to holding a sterling deposit with the return to holding a dollar deposit sold forward into sterling (assuming that you start with sterling).

Two important points need to be clarified about the above data. First, the interest rates are annualized so they are not what would actually be earned over a three-month period. For example, the three-month rate equivalent to an annual rate of $10\frac{1}{4}$ percent is 2.47 percent.

Second, the forward exchange rates need some explanation. The dollar is at a discount against sterling. This means the forward dollar buys less sterling. So we have to *add* the discount onto the spot price to get the forward price (because the price is the number of dollars per pound, not the reverse). Notice also that the discount is measured in fractions of a cent, not fractions of a dollar! So the bid-ask spread on the forward rate would be 1.4927 − 1.4942.

Now let us see if we would do better to invest in a three-month eurosterling deposit or a three-month eurodollar deposit where the dollars to be received were sold forward into sterling. The return per £100 invested in eurosterling is £2.369 (annual interest rate of $9^{13}/_{16}$), whereas the return on a covered eurodollar deposit is

$$£2.251 = \left(100 \times \frac{1.4910}{1.4942} \, 1.0247\right) - 100.$$

Thus, we could not make a profit out of covered interest arbitrage. Despite the fact that dollar interest rates are higher, the discount on forward dollars in the forward market means they buy fewer forward pounds. As a result, there is no benefit to the operation. Transaction costs for most individuals would be even greater than those above as they would face a larger bid-ask spread than that quoted on the interbank market.

Consequently, there is no benefit for the typical investor from making a covered or hedged eurocurrency deposit. The return will be at least as high on a deposit in the currency in which you start and wish to end up. That is, if you have dollars and wish to end up with dollars, make a eurodollar deposit. If you have sterling and wish to end up with sterling, make a eurosterling deposit. If you have sterling and wish to end up in dollars, there is likely to be little or no difference between holding a eurosterling deposit sold forward into dollars or buying dollars spot and holding a eurodollar deposit. Of course, if you hold an "uncovered" deposit and exchange rates subsequently change, the result will be very different.

---

ward foreign exchange from a customer, it increases its exposure to risk while the customer reduces his. However, there is not a fixed amount of risk that has to be "shared out." Some strategies may involve a net reduction of risk all around.

As a general rule, financial institutions (or other firms), operating in a variety of currencies, will try to minimize the risk of losses due to unexpected exchange rate changes. One simple way to do this is to ensure that assets and liabilities denominated in each operating currency are equal. This is known as "matching." For example, a bank that sells sterling forward to a customer may simultaneously buy sterling forward. In this event, the bank is exposed to zero exchange rate risk.

Why Is the Dollar the "Money" of Foreign Exchange Markets?

One interesting aspect of the organization of the foreign exchange markets is that the "money" used in these markets is generally the U.S. dollar. This is generally true for spot markets and universally true for forward markets. "Cross-markets" between many currencies are very thin, and future cross markets are virtually nonexistent. For example, the bulk of foreign exchange trading between £s and cruzeiro will involve dollar-£ and dollar-cruzeiro transactions instead of direct £-cruzeiro trading. The only exception to this is the transactions involving the major Organization for Economic Cooperation and Development (OECD) currencies, especially within Europe. Of the $702.5 billion turnover in foreign exchange reported by U.S. banks in April 1983, only $1.5 billion did not involve U.S. dollars.

There are two explanations for this special role of the dollar in foreign exchange markets. Both rely upon the fact that transaction costs are likely to be lower if the dollar is used as a medium. Krugman shows that the clearing of foreign exchange markets requires some "intermediary" currency.[1] Even if every country is in payments balance vis a vis the rest of the world, it will not necessarily be in bilateral balance with each other country. Because some currency has to be used to cover this residual finance, it is natural to choose the currency that has the lowest transaction costs. Chrystal shows there are economic reasons why cross-markets between many currencies do not exist.[2] It typically will be easier and cheaper to set up a deal in two steps via the dollar than in a single step (cruzeiro-dollar, dollar-drachma rather than cruzeiro-drachma). This is because these cross-markets, if they existed, would be fairly thin and hence relatively costly for such transactions. The two markets with the dollar, on the other hand, are well developed.

These analyses refer to the role of the dollar in the interbank market. In the development of the trading places such as the IMM in Chicago and LIFFE in London to date, it is also true that all currency futures are traded against the dollar.

[1]See Krugman (1980).

[2]See Chrystal (1982).

Banks often use "swaps" to close gaps in the maturity structure of their assets and liabilities in a currency. This involves the simultaneous purchase and sale of a currency for *different* maturity dates. In April 1983, 33 percent of U.S. banks' foreign exchange turnover involved swaps as compared with 63 percent spot contracts and only 4 percent outright forward contracts.[10]

Suppose a bank has sold DM to a customer three months forward and bought the same amount of DM from a different customer six months forward. There are two ways in which the bank could achieve zero foreign exchange risk exposure. It could either undertake two separate offsetting forward transactions, or it could set up a single swap with another bank that has the opposite mismatch of dollar-DM flows whereby it receives DM in exchange for dollars in three months and receives back dollars in exchange for DM in six months. Once the swap is set up, the bank's net profits are protected against subsequent changes in spot exchange rates during the next six months.

Within the limits imposed by the nature of the contracts, a similar effect can be achieved by an appropriate portfolio of futures contracts on the IMM. Thus, a bank would buy and sell futures contracts so as to match closely its forward commitments to customers. In reality, banks will use a combination of methods to reduce foreign exchange risk.

Markets that permit banks, firms and individuals to hedge foreign exchange risk are essential in times of fluctuating exchange rates. This is especially important for banks if they are to be able to provide efficient foreign exchange services for their customers. In the absence of markets that permit foreign exchange risk hedging, the cost and uncertainty of international transactions would be greatly increased, and international specialization and trade would be greatly reduced.

[10]See Federal Reserve Bank of New York (1983).

CONCLUSION

The foreign exchange markets are complex and, for the outsider, hard to comprehend. The primary function of these markets is straightforward. It is to facilitate international transactions related to trade, travel or investment. Foreign exchange markets can now accommodate a large range of current and forward transactions.

Given the variability of exchange rates, it is important for banks and firms operating in foreign currencies to be able to reduce exchange rate risk whenever possible. Some risk reduction is achieved by interbank swaps, but some is also taken up by speculation. Arbitrage and speculation both increase the efficiency of spot and forward foreign exchange markets and have enabled foreign exchange markets to achieve a high level of efficiency. Without the successful operation of these markets, the obstacles to international trade and investment would be substantial and the world would be a poorer place.

Glossary

American option — an option that can be exercised any time up to maturity.

American terms — an exchange rate expressed as number of currency units per dollar.

arbitrage — the simultaneous purchase and sale of currency in separate markets for a profit arising from a price discrepancy between the markets.

bid-ask spread — the difference between the buying (bid) and selling (ask) price.

covered interest arbitrage — buying a country's currency spot, investing for a period, and selling the proceeds forward in order to make a net profit due to the higher interest rate in that country. This act involves "hedging" because it guarantees a covered return without risk. The opportunities to profit in this way seldom arise because covered interest differentials are normally close to zero.

covered interest parity — the gap between interest rates in foreign and domestic currencies will be matched by the forward exchange rate differential, such that the "covered" interest rate differential will be close to zero.

eurodollar deposits — bank deposits, generally bearing interest and made for a specific time period, that are denominated in dollars but are in banks outside the United States. Similarly, euro-sterling deposits would be denominated in sterling but outside the United Kingdom.

European option — an option that can be exercised only on a specified date.

European terms — an exchange rate expressed as number of dollars per currency unit.

floating exchange rate — an exchange rate that is allowed to adjust freely to the supply of and demand for foreign exchange.

foreign exchange speculation — the act of taking a net position in a foreign currency with the intention of making a profit from exchange rate changes.

forward exchange rate — the price of foreign currency for delivery at a future date agreed to by a contract today.

futures market — a market in which contracts are traded to buy or sell a standard amount of currency in the future at a particular price.

hedging — or covering exchange risk, means that foreign currency is sold forward into local currency so that its value is not affected by subsequent exchange rate changes. Say an exporter knows he will be paid £10,000 in two months. He can wait until he gets the money and convert it into dollars at whatever the spot rate turns out to be. This outcome is uncertain as the spot rate may change. Alternatively, he can sell £10,000 two months forward at today's two-month forward price. Suppose this is $1.5 per £. In two months, he will receive £10,000, fulfill his forward contract and receive $15,000. This export contract has been hedged or covered in the forward market.

matching — equating assets and liabilities denominated in each currency so that losses due to foreign exchange rate changes are minimized.

options market — a market in which contracts are traded that gives a purchaser the right but no obligation to buy (call) or to sell (put) a currency in the future at a given price.

spot exchange rate — the price paid to exchange currencies for immediate delivery (two business days in the interbank market, or over the counter in the retail and travelers check market).

swap — the simultaneous purchase and sale of a currency for different maturity dates that closes the gaps in the maturity structure of assets and liabilities in a currency.

REFERENCES

Belongia, Michael T. "Commodity Options: A New Risk Management Tool for Agricultural Markets," this *Review* (June/July 1983), pp. 5–15.

Black, Fisher, and Myron Scholes. "The Pricing of Options and Corporate Liabilities," *Journal of Political Economy* (May/June 1973), pp. 637–54.

Chrystal, K. Alec. "On the Theory of International Money" (paper presented to U.K. International Economics Study Group Conference, September 1982, Sussex, England). Forthcoming in J. Black and G. S. Dorrance, eds., *Problems of International Finance* (London: Macmillan, 1984).

Dufey, Gunter, and Ian H. Giddy. *The International Money Market* (Prentice-Hall, 1978).

Federal Reserve Bank of New York. "Summary of Results of U.S. Foreign Exchange Market Turnover Survey Conducted in April 1983" (September 8, 1983).

Garman, Mark B., and Steven W. Kohlhagen. "Foreign Currency Option Values," *Journal of International Money and Finance* (December 1983), pp. 231–37.

Giddy, Ian H. "Foreign Exchange Options," *Journal of Futures Markets* (Summer 1983), pp. 143–66.

Krugman, Paul. "Vehicle Currencies and the Structure of International Exchange," *Journal of Money, Credit and Banking* (August 1980), pp. 513–26.

Kubarych, Roger M. *Foreign Exchange Markets in the United States.* (Federal Reserve Bank of New York, 1983).

McKinnon, Ronald I. *Money in International Exchange: The Convertible Currency System* (Oxford University Press, 1979).

Article Thirty-Three

Current Illusions about the
International Debt Crisis

Lawrence J. Brainard

𝕴F RECENT media accounts are to be believed, the international debt crisis is over.[2] In the middle of last year, the newspapers were filled with dire warnings of impending disaster and of a need, if disaster was to be avoided, to 'cap' rates of interest. In the United States, Paul Volcker, Chairman of the Federal Reserve Board, and Anthony Solomon, Chairman of the New York Board of the Federal Reserve, as well as Martin Feldstein, then Chairman of the Council of Economic Advisers in the Executive Office of the President, publicly called for caps as a way to deal with the effects of rising rates of interest.[2] The change in sentiment about the debt crisis in such a short period of time is remarkable. Is there evidence to support this radical change in thinking?

The principal change in the international economic environment since May 1984 has been the decline in rates of interest in the United States. This has relieved pressures on the adjustment process in the heavily-indebted countries and also served to dampen the domestic reactions which were materialising against those programmes. For the time being, then, talk about capping rates of interest has receded. How have the adjustment programmes fared?

Two of the large debtor countries, Brazil and Mexico, achieved impressive balance-of-payments gains during 1984. The Brazilian current account moved from a deficit of $5.5 billion in 1983 to a surplus estimated at $650 million last year. Thanks to the disbursement of new loans and the rescheduling of old ones, Brazil's foreign-exchange cash reserves rose $9 billion, from the minus $1.5 billion reached in 1983 to $7.5 billion at the end of 1984. Mexico was able to maintain an estimated $4.1 billion surplus in 1984, down from the $5.5 billion in 1983, a vast improvement over the $13 billion deficit registered in 1981. Mexico's international reserves rose $3 billion during 1984 to reach a level of $8.1 billion at the end of the year. Neither country expects to need new money from the banks in 1985.

LAWRENCE J. BRAINARD is a Senior Vice President, and Head of International Economic and Political Analysis, at the Bankers Trust Company in New York. Dr Brainard has been an adviser to, among others, the Office of Technology Assessment in the United States Congress (1979) and the National Security Council in the Executive Office of the President of the United States (1982).

Elsewhere, progress has been decidedly mixed. Argentina and the Philippines reached agreement with their creditor banks on debt-rescheduling 'packages' after protracted negotiations. Both agreements, which include substantial commitments of new money, are scheduled to be signed during the first half of this year. Chile and Peru encountered significant economic difficulties during 1984 due to the depressed prices of copper and other minerals. Chile has remained current on her interest payments to banks, but the country appears to require additional new money from the banks in 1985. Peru has been unable to keep her interest payments current and arrears are rising. Colombia has initiated discussions with a committee of her creditor banks to formulate a programme to meet her external financing needs and to reschedule certain external obligations of the private sector.

Although progress is evident in developments over the past year, it is an illusion to believe that the international debt crisis is over. Unlike belief in Santa Claus or the tooth fairy, this illusion is a dangerous one, for it easily leads to complacency about problems which still have the potential to damage seriously the stability of the international financial system and the national security of the United States and other Western countries.

Why does human nature seem to be so bent on reducing complex issues to simple and misleading formulations? As a contribution to a better understanding of the 'fundamentals' of the debt problem, this article discusses six common illusions, which are then used to structure an assessment of current and future prospects.

Illusion No. 1 — One Economic Problem can be Solved
  by Creating Another Economic Problem of
  Even More Massive Proportions

A significant portion of the impressive improvement in the balance-of-payments performance of many Latin American countries in 1984 was directly tied to the high rate of economic growth achieved in the United States. Most econometric studies show a more important role for growth in the member countries of the Organisation for Economic Cooperation and Development (OECD) than for rates of interest in determining the balance-of-payments performance of developing countries. William Cline, of the Institute for International Economics in Washington, has run a trade model under varying assumptions about rates of interest and rates of growth. His conclusions indicate that a solution to the debt crisis requires real growth in the OECD countries of the order of 2.5 per cent per annum for the rest of the 1980s.[3] This is not a particularly daunting target; and it should easily be surpassed in 1985.

The problem with these projections is that no account is taken of the huge trade and budget deficits which are sustaining these relatively rapid rates of economic growth in the United States. The continuation of deficits at current levels, not to mention the probability of even higher deficits, will inevitably act as a brake on economic growth by pushing up rates of interest — if not this year then in 1986 or 1987. Concerted action by Congress and the Administration to reduce these deficits substantially would slow domestic and foreign economic growth (which is also responding to strong demand for imports in the United States) and directly restrain the growth of developing-country exports.

The choice appears to be between (i) faster growth in the short term with future rises in rates of interest and (ii) slower growth in the short term with future declines in rates of interest. It seems that a continuation of relatively rapid growth in the short run is the most likely outcome, not because it is necessarily preferred by policy makers, but because political obstacles prevent anything significant being done about the trade and budget deficits at the present time.

The pattern of reacting to one disequilibrium (balance-of-payments imbalances in the developing countries) by creating another (fiscal stimulation and budget deficits) is already well entrenched in recent economic history. The recycling of the surpluses of the oil-producing countries by the banks was strongly encouraged and supported by the governments of the major industrialised countries during the 1970s. What has changed is that major industrialised countries are avoiding any resort to monetary expansion to achieve the goal of economic recovery. Instead, expansion in the United States, in particular, is seen as the way to promote recovery in the world economy as a whole.

During the 1970s every major sovereign borrower outside the major industrialised countries filled itself with debt. The debt crisis in the developing countries has brought a stop to this trend for the time being. But the unprecedented expansion of debt continues and is now focussed on the American economy and, to a lesser extent, on the Euro-markets. The results of these developments weaken the disciplines of the market-place, amplify the variability of market variables — such as rates of interest, foreign rates of exchange and commodity prices — and place increased stress on financial institutions.[4]

Governments are unlikely to address in the near future the fundamental weaknesses of the international financial system which have accounted for the emergence of these problems. Economic disequilibria, therefore, will tend to persist, contributing to instabilities in financial markets and to recurring crises. It may be that, for the time being, the debt crisis will benefit from these trends. But it should be clear that a lasting solution to the debt problem can only be achieved when the international financial system regains effective disciplines.

Illusion No. 2 — Politicians will Do What has to be Done

Bankers have taken comfort in the apparent willingness of political leaders in developing countries to pursue the harsh economic adjustment measures needed to sustain the servicing of their foreign debts. This is particularly welcome given the sometimes extreme anti-bank rhetoric heard in many of these countries. The willingness of President Alfonsin of Argentina to negotiate an agreement with the International Monetary Fund (IMF) and the banks is a case in point.

It is an illusion, however, to believe that politicians will always know what should be done or that they will always do what is in their country's long-term interest. At present, the balance of costs and benefits by political leaders in the heavily-indebted countries appears to favour cooperation with the IMF and the banks in working out the adjustment process. But these costs and benefits can shift over time for any number of reasons: increased domestic political costs — domestic unrest, loss of electoral support — or reduced benefits due, for example, to a drying up of new credits.

Moreover, bankers cannot assume that foreign policy in the United States will necessarily continue to give the same weight to their concerns, which has so far 'been the case. The Reagan Administration, or a new one some years hence, may wish to impose a different approach to these problems in specific cases. And the debt problems of developing countries are not always the primary concerns of policy makers in developed countries when decisions on trade policy are at stake.

Illusion No. 3 — Multi-year Rescheduling Represents
a Long-term Solution to the Debt Crisis

A multi-year approach to the rescheduling of debt first surfaced in the negotiations with Mexico in mid-1984. The impetus to this approach was provided by Jacques de Larosière, Managing Director of the IMF, and Mr Volcker at the June meeting of the International Monetary Conference, an annual private gathering of senior international bankers. The concept was sold on the basis that it was a way of rewarding those countries which had been successful in their adjustment efforts. In addition to such influential support, the concept was seen as a way of moving from the mode of 'crisis management' of debt problems to a more normalised process, one freed from the pressure of annual negotiations. Monitoring of economic developments was to be performed by the IMF by means of semi-annual consultations with countries in the context of the Fund's Article IV reviews of all member countries ('enhanced Article IV monitoring').

Many specialists on economic development have criticised the current approach to adjustment as being too short term in orientation, ignoring the need for countries to implement structural changes over a three-to-five year time horizon.[5] As currently conceived, multi-year restructuring is not based on any particular model of the development process over the medium term. It is silent on the role of institutions such as the World Bank which would seem best qualified to identify and implement medium-term adjustment programmes. All that happens is a 'block' of maturities coming due over the next five-to-seven years is rescheduled. The final maturities of this debt are being stretched out, some fourteen years in Mexico's case, and interest-rate spreads are being reduced. Although details of the

IMF's 'enhanced Article IV monitoring' have not been worked out, they would presumably follow traditional IMF priorities which emphasise short-term criteria.

Why do the banks seem to be so willing to embrace a process which ignores the policy changes in debtor countries that are essential to the servicing of their debt over the long term? Many banks believe that an active role in policy advice is inappropriate and they look to the IMF to play that part. The acceptance by banks of multi-year rescheduling therefore absolves them from the responsibility to play an active role in the process. By themselves, banks have limited leverage over sovereign borrowers in matters related to economic policy and performance. They view reliance on the IMF to discipline debtor countries as a pragmatic and reasonable response to the present crisis.

This reliance on the IMF may be seen as the fundamental weakness underlying lending to sovereign borrowers by banks. The implicit assumption of such lending is that someone, namely the IMF, will be there to provide the economic disciplines, should they be needed. This begs the question of whether this is an appropriate or feasible role for the IMF. The Fund seems to be ambivalent on the issue, having accepted the concept of enhanced monitoring, while at the same time maintaining that it cannot play the role of 'traffic cop' for the banks; that is, it cannot signal to the banks what to do. For its part, the American government appears to support the Fund's enforcement of economic disciplines in the system — that is, on the debtor countries. This is a necessary condition if the banks are to keep on lending. Continued lending by the banks seems essential because the American government cannot begin to supply the volume of funds which is likely to be demanded.

In summary, multi-year rescheduling, as currently formulated, does not address the key development issues embedded in the current crisis. It does not bring together the relevant participants — the banks, the multilateral development institutions, the IMF and the creditor and debtor governments — to begin working out desirable and feasible adjustment programmes over the medium term. For this reason, multi-year rescheduling cannot be seen as a prelude to the resumption of voluntary lending by the banks.

Illusion No. 4 — the IMF Can Play the Part of Traffic Cop for as Long as Necessary

During the past three years the IMF has performed an indispensable leadership role in holding together many of the debt-rescheduling 'packages'. Intervention by the Fund was instrumental, for example, in securing bank support for new money commitments in Mexico in late 1982. Similar cases followed. Mexico was the first country which was able to secure support from the banks and the IMF for a multi-year rescheduling package. In the negotiations, Mexico asked that a new standby credit, or a similar facility, should not be required on the expiration of the current three-year 'extended Fund facility' at the end of 1985. The unstated reasons were political. A continuation of what were seen in the Mexican political context as unduly restrictive external restraints would have strengthened the hand of those opposed to such adjustment efforts.

In the draft Mexican agreement the concept of 'enhanced Article IV monitoring' emerged as a compromise. In this approach the banks play a passive role in the monitoring process. They receive a specified set of economic data and the Article IV report of the IMF which will be produced on a semi-annual basis after the expiration of the current 'extended Fund facility'. The Article IV report not only substitutes for active monitoring by the banks; it also provides the basis for any action by the banks in response to adverse changes in economic performance and policy.

The banks are clearly looking to the IMF's semi-annual report for appropriate signals. Are such expectations likely to be met? Consider the Fund's predicament. If it gives the banks what they expect, it will run afoul of the Mexicans. If it gives top priority to conditioning its response to the realities of the Mexican political scene, it will disappoint the banks. A choice of priorities by the IMF must be made. Mexico is an important and influential Fund member; the banks are not.

Senior IMF officials have stated their willingness to perform the requested 'enhanced Article IV consultations'. At the same time, however, they have emphasised that they cannot give the banks 'stop-go' signals in the semi-annual reports, for this would jeopardise the Fund's relationship with its member countries. In the circumstances the position of the Fund is pragmatic and realistic.

The banks have avoided, so far, a direct role for themselves in the enhanced monitoring process. Many banks believe that an active role in monitoring is inappropriate. These feelings reflect a perception that past efforts by the banks at monitoring failed. An experience in 1976-77 with a balance-of-payments loan to the Government of Peru is often cited as supporting evidence. A related view is that circumstances necessitate an active role of the IMF in support of the bank agreement, since the banks are the only parties likely to come up with the new financing required over the longer term.

One is left with the impression that, as regards monitoring, the desires of banks and the priorities of the IMF may not turn out to be the same.

Illusion No. 5 — the Resumption of Voluntary New Lending
  by Banks is Just around the Corner

Will recovery in the world economy and adjustment in developing countries restore market relations between bank lenders and these borrowers similar to those that existed before the present crisis? Many studies have addressed this issue by looking at projections of the balance-of-payments and debt positions of the major borrowing countries. Although the results depend critically on the particular assumptions used, a number of the studies conclude that continued progress in the economic situations of the debtor countries is both possible and feasible during the remainder of the 1980s.[6] Can it be concluded that a resumption of voluntary lending by banks to these countries will emerge in response to these trends? An answer to this question must consider the factors which are important in influencing the decision making of banks in the coming years.

One dimension of the answer concerns the future environment in which sovereign lending will take place. For reasons already mentioned (under Illusion No. 1), the international financial system is likely to experience greater rather than lesser instability in future. Governments are unlikely to address the weaknesses of the present financial system. To repeat, economic disequilibria will tend to persist, contributing to instabilities in financial markets and to recurring crises. The continuing reliance on market disciplines in this environment means that greater variability and extreme values of market variables will be observed. It has long been clear, for example, that the sharp upward trend in the dollar would be matched by a similar trend on the downward-side after the peak was reached.

These factors place increasing stress on financial markets and institutions. Banks and regulators will consequently be placing top priority on the preservation and increase of bank capital in the years ahead. Cautious and conservative bank lending policies are to be expected as a response.

A second aspect of the willingness of banks to resume new lending to sovereign borrowers is the extent to which their interests are maintained and protected in the various rescheduling agreements. If banks are happy with such provisions, they will respond sooner than otherwise would be the case. One result of the dependence of the banks on the IMF for economic-performance disciplines in debtor countries (see under Illusion No. 3) is the politicisation of credit decisions — that is, involuntary new money, 'rewards' for countries that have met certain criteria and political pressures from those countries unable or unwilling to meet IMF targets. For many banks these features of the present situation amount to the loss of bank control of lending decisions. This result must be seen as a major deterrent to the recovery of confidence necessary for a revival of sovereign lending.

Perhaps the most direct obstacle to a revival of voluntary bank lending is the fact that levels of debt were, and still are, excessive for most countries. Under the best of external circumstances — continued growth in the world economy, lower rates of interest in the United States and rising commodity prices — debt as a percentage of export earnings in the major debtor countries will remain above desirable levels until after 1990.[7] And even though the trends in debt ratios would be favourable in this 'best' case, many banks would still wish to reduce their levels of exposure. Thus sustained current-account surpluses and/or access to increased official financing would be a necessary pre-condition for most countries to restore normal credit relations with their creditors in the next three-to-four years.

The attitudes of banks towards sovereign lending are changing. The factors noted above are acting to alter future flows of bank credit to developing countries. Banks are rethinking their business strategies. Stimulated by the rapid evolution of domestic financial markets, banks in the United States, for instance, are focussing on new opportunities brought by inter-state banking and investment banking. Lending to sovereign countries will be less of a priority in the future.

Illusion No. 6 — the Debt Crisis is Over

My purpose in discussing current illusions about the international debt crisis is to focus attention on problems and challenges as opposed to imagined solutions. The international community has demonstrated an impressive degree of skill and cooperation in dealing with the initial phase of the international debt crisis. These resources now need to be refocussed on problems of a different nature from those that were addressed in the past two-and-a-half years.

What is missing from current discussions about the debt crisis is an understanding of the process of economic development, an understanding based on the realism of economic and political factors that influence all the actors in this drama — the banks, the international agencies, governments and, above all, the people and institutions in developing countries affected by all the efforts at adjustment and economic recovery. Sustained growth in the world economy is clearly desirable, but growth, by itself, will not ensure the efficiency and rationality of economic-policy management in individual debtor countries. While not losing sight of the external factors influencing the process of development, there is a need to start focussing on the internal conditions in the heavily-indebted countries that are essential for sustained economic growth and development.

The challenge facing the international community is to find ways in which the various IMF programmes and debt-rescheduling agreements can lead to medium-term structural changes essential to increasing a country's productive use of resources over time. New approaches to devising programmes of structural adjustment take time and money and it is unlikely that a given model can be replicated in other countries. A necessary first step is to recognise the problem. A second step is to create a framework within which all the relevant parties — the IMF, the World Bank, the creditor banks and the individual country — may need to define the 'terms of reference'; that is, the ability or willingness of a country to undertake meaningful policy changes and the degree of financial support forthcoming from international agencies or the banks. Where the process goes from here depends on the specific circumstances of each country.

Even if it is desirable, is such an approach at all probable? Many of the countries which wound up in debt trouble pursued policies of heavy state intervention in the economy and discrimination against foreign direct investment and private enterprise. There are few signs that fundamental changes in such policies are in the offing. There also seems to be little recognition by the international agencies, developed-country governments or the banks that a new approach is needed. Recent news reports that Brazil, Mexico and Argentina are having difficulties in meeting targets in their existing IMF programmes, however, should help to bring attention to the need for basic structural reforms as a pre-condition to such adjustment programmes.[8] If this happens, a modest step forward will have been achieved. But a medium-term approach to the present crisis based on structural adjustment still lies ahead.

1. See, for example, Gary Hector, 'The World Debt: the Bomb is Defused', *Fortune*, New York, 18 February 1985, pp. 36-50. The first sentence of the article reads: 'Evidence is building that the international debt crisis is over.'

2. 'Volcker Terms Economy Strong Despite Rates', *Wall Street Journal*, New York, 14 May 1984, p. 3; and Martin Feldstein, 'International Debt Policy: the Next Steps', Remarks before the Council of the Americas, Washington, 8 May 1984, p. 12.

3. William R. Cline, 'International Debt: from Crisis to Recovery', paper presented at the annual meeting of the American Economic Association, Dallas, Texas, 28 December 1984. These projections represent up-dates to his original analysis contained in Cline, *International Debt: Systemic Risk and Policy Response* (Washington: Institute for International Economics, 1984).

4. For a discussion of the debt crisis in the United States, see Henry Kaufman, *Dangers in the Rapid Growth of Debt: the Need for a National Policy Response*, Bond Market Research Report (New York: Salomon Brothers, 1985).

5. For one example, see Gustav Ranis, 'Needed: Commitment to Structural Adjustment', *Challenge*, New York, July-August 1984, pp. 21-26.

6. See Cline, 'International Debt: from Crisis to Recovery', *op. cit.*, and 'The LDC Debt Problem: at the Midpoint?', *World Financial Markets*, Morgan Guaranty Trust Company, New York, October-November 1984.

7. See *ibid*.

8. 'IMF Severs Credits to Brazil until Nation Adheres to Austere Economic Measures', *Wall Street Journal*, 15 February 1985, p. 27; and 'Raging Inflation Imperils Argentina's IMF Pact', *New York Times*, 18 February 1985, p. D3.

Article Thirty-Four

EURODOLLARS

Marvin Goodfriend

THE NATURE OF THE EURODOLLAR

Eurodollars are bank deposit liabilities, denominated in United States dollars, not subject to United States banking regulations.[1] For the most part, banks offering Eurodollar deposits are located outside the United States. However, since late 1981 non-United States residents have been able to conduct business free of United States banking regulations at International Banking Facilities (IBFs) in the United States. Eurodollar deposits may be owned by individuals, corporations, or governments from anywhere in the world, with the exception that only non-United States residents can hold deposits at United States IBFs.

The term Eurodollar dates from an earlier period when the market was located primarily in Europe. Although the bulk of Eurodollar deposits is still held in Europe, today Eurodollar deposits are held in such places as the Bahamas, Bahrain, Canada, the Cayman Islands, Hong Kong, Japan, the Netherlands Antillies, Panama, Singapore, and United States IBFs.[2] Nevertheless, dollar-denominated deposits located in United States IBFs and anywhere in the world outside the United States are still referred to as Eurodollars.

Banks in the Eurodollar market including United States IBFs compete with United States banks to attract dollar-denominated funds. Since the Eurodollar market is relatively free of regulation, banks in the Eurodollar market can operate on narrower margins or spreads between dollar borrowing and lending rates than can banks in the United States. This gives Eurodollar deposits an advantage relative to deposits issued by banks operating under United States regulations. In short, the Eurodollar market has grown up as a means of separating the United States dollar from the country of jurisdiction or responsibility for that currency, the

---

[1] Dollar-denominated deposits at a bank located outside the United States or in a United States IBF are Eurodollars, even if the bank if affiliated with a bank whose home office is a non-IBF United States bank. See Terrell and Mills [1983], Key [1982] and Lichtenstein [1982] for discussions of IBFs.

[2] See Ashby [1978] and [1979] for discussions of Europe's declining share of the global Eurocurrency market. The Eurocurrency market includes, along with Eurodollars, foreign currency-denominated deposits held at banks located outside a currency's home country.

United States. It has done so largely to reduce the regulatory costs involved in dollar-denominated financial intermediation.

THE SIZE OF THE EURODOLLAR MARKET

Measuring the size of the Eurodollar market involves looking at the volume of dollar-denominated loans and deposits on the books of banks located outside the United States. However, dollar-denominated loans and deposits may not match. Consequently, a decision must be made whether to measure the volume of Eurodollars from the asset or liability side of the bank balance sheet.

A liability side measure may be too broad, since it may include foreign currency liabilities incurred to fund loans to domestic residents denominated in domestic currency. Strictly speaking, this is a traditional type of international financial intermediation. Measuring Eurodollar market volume from dollar-deno-minated assets, however, may also overstate the size of Eurodollar volume since these assets may reflect nothing more than traditional foreign lending funded with domestic currency-denominated deposits supplied by domestic residents.

In practice, Eurodollar volume is measured as the dollar-denominated deposit liabilities of banks located outside the United States. For example, the Bank for International Settlements (BIS) defines and measures Eurodollars as dollars that have "been acquired by a bank outside the United States and used directly or after conversion into another currency for lending to a nonbank customer, perhaps after one or more redeposits from one bank to another."[3]

Under a liability side measure such as the one used by the BIS, the sum of all dollar-denominated liabilities of banks outside the United States measures the gross size of the Eurodollar market. For some purposes, it is useful to net part of interbank deposits out of the gross to arrive at an estimate of Eurodollar deposits held by original suppliers to the Eurodollar market. Roughly speaking, to construct the net size measure, deposits owned by banks in the Eurodollar market are netted out. But deposits owned by banks located outside of the Eurodollar market area are not netted out because these banks are considered to be original suppliers of funds to the Eurodollar market. For still other purposes, such as comparing the volume of deposits created in the Eurodollar market with the United States monetary aggregates, it is useful to further net out all bank-owned Eurodollar deposits. Doing so leaves only the nonbank portion of the net size measure, or what might be called the net-net size of the Eurodollar market.

The most readily accessible estimates of the size of the Eurodollar market are compiled by Morgan Guaranty Trust Company of New York and reported in its

---

[3] Bank for International Settlements [1964, p. 127]. In principle, today the definition includes acquisitions of IBFs.

monthly bank letter *World Financial Markets*.[4] Morgan's estimates are based on a liability side measure and include data compiled by the BIS. However, Morgan's estimates are somewhat more comprehensive. Morgan reports estimates of the size of the entire Eurocurrency market based roughly on all foreign-currency liabilities of banks in major European countries, nine other market areas, and United States IBFs.

As of December 1985 Morgan estimated the gross size of the Eurocurrency market at $2,796 billion.[5] The net size was put at $1,668 billion.[6] Morgan also reports that Eurodollars made up 75 percent of gross Eurocurrency liabilities, putting the gross size of the Eurodollar market at $2,097 billion.[7] No net Eurodollar market size is given. However, 75 percent of the net size of the Eurocurrency market yields $1,251 billion as an approximate measure of the net size of the Eurodollar market.

M2 is the narrowest United States monetary aggregate that includes Eurodollar deposits. M2 includes overnight Eurodollar deposits held by United States nonbank non-money market fund residents at branches of Federal Reserve member banks worldwide. As of December 1985, M2 measured $2,567 billion; its Eurodollar component was $17 billion.[8] Eurodollar deposits owned by United States nonbank non-money market fund residents continue to grow, but this comparison shows clearly that such Eurodollar deposits still account for a relatively small portion of United States nonbank non-money market fund resident holdings of monetary assets.

INCENTIVES FOR DEVELOPMENT OF THE EURODOLLAR MARKET[9]

By accepting deposits and making loans denominated in United States dollars outside the United States and in United States IBFs, banks can avoid United States banking regulations. In particular, banks located outside the United

---

[4] See Morgan Guaranty [January 1979, pp. 9-13], for a discussion of Morgan's method of measuring the size of the Eurodollar market. Other informative discussions of issues involved in measuring the Eurodollar market's size are found in Dufey and Giddy [1978, pp. 21-34] and Mayer [1976].

[5] Morgan Guaranty [June/July 1986, p. 11]. Most of the growth of the Eurocurrency market has occurred in the last two decades. For instance, Dufey and Giddy [1978, p. 22] report Morgan's earliest estimate of the gross size of the Eurocurrency market as only $20 billion in 1964. See Dufey and Giddy [1978, Chapter III] for a discussion of the growth of the Eurocurrency market.

[6] Morgan Guaranty [June/July 1986, p. 11].

[7] Ibid.

[8] Board of Governors of the Federal Reserve System [1986, pp. 1, 5]. At present, Eurodollars held by non-United States residents are not included in any of the United States monetary aggregates. As improved data sources become available, the possible inclusion of Eurodollars held by non-United States residents other than banks and official institutions could be reviewed. See Board of Governors of the Federal Reserve System [1980, p. 98].

[9] See Dufey and Giddy [1978, pp. 110-12] for more discussion of the conditions that made large-scale Eurodollar market growth possible.

States and in United States IBFs have no non-interest-bearing reserve requirements against their dollar-denominated deposits. These banks hold balances with United States banks for clearing purposes only. Moreover, there is no required Federal Deposit Insurance Corporation insurance assessment associated with Eurodollar deposits. Virtually no restrictions exist for interest rates payable on Eurodollar deposits or charged on Eurodollar loans, and there are few restrictions on the types of assets allowed in portfolio.

In most Eurodollar financial centers, entry into Eurodollar banking is virtually free of regulatory impediments. In addition, banks intending to do Eurodollar business can set up in locations where tax rates are low. For example, Eurodollar deposits and loans negotiated in London or elsewhere are often booked in locations such as Nassau and the Cayman Islands to obtain more favorable tax treatment. In fact, various states in the United States have amended their tax codes to grant IBFs relief from local taxes.

Foreign monetary authorities are generally reluctant to regulate Eurodollar business because to do so would drive the business away, denying the host country income, tax revenue, and jobs. Even if the United States monetary authorities could induce a group of foreign countries to participate in a plan to regulate their Euromarkets, such a plan would be ineffective unless every country agreed not to host unregulated Eurodollar business. In practice, competition for this business has been fierce, so even if a consensus should develop in the United States to regulate Eurodollar business, it would be extremely difficult to impose regulations on the entire Eurodollar market.

INSTRUMENTS OF THE EURODOLLAR MARKET[10]

The overwhelming majority of money in the Eurodollar market is held in fixed-rate time deposits (TDs). The maturities of Eurodollar TDs range from overnight to several years, although most are from one week to six months. Eurodollar time deposits are intrinsically different from dollar deposits held at banks in the United States only in that the former are liabilities of financial institutions located outside the United States or in United States IBFs. The bulk of Eurodollar time deposits are interbank liabilities. They pay a fixed, competitively determined rate of return.[11]

From their introduction in 1966, the volume of negotiable Eurodollar certificates of deposit (CDs) outstanding reached roughly $50 billion at the beginning

---

[10] Bank for International Settlements [1986, Chapters 1 and 4], Dobbs-Higginson [1980, pp. 55-61], Dufey and Giddy [1978, pp. 228-32], and Stigum [1983, Chapters 15 and 16] contain informative discussions of Eurodollar instruments.

[11] See Stigum [1983, p. 578-80] and Dufey and Giddy [1978, p. 227] for discussions of Eurodollar deposit rate tiering according to perceived issuing bank creditworthiness.

of 1980.[12] By 1985, Eurodollar CD volume was around $100 billion. Essentially, a Eurodollar CD is a negotiable receipt for a dollar deposit at a bank located outside the United States or in a United States IBF.

Recently, fixed-rate three-month Eurodollar CDs have yielded approximately 30 basis points below the three-month time deposit London Interbank Offer Rate (LIBOR).[13] LIBOR is the rate at which major international banks are willing to offer term Eurodollar deposits to each other. An active secondary market allows investors to sell Eurodollar CDs before the deposits mature. Secondary market makers' spreads for short-term fixed-rate CDs have been around 3 basis points.[14]

Eurodollar CDs are issued by banks to "tap" the market for funds. Consequently, they have come to be called Tap CDs. Such Tap CDs are commonly issued in denominations of from $250,000 to $5 million. Some large Eurodollar CD issues are marketed in several portions in order to satisfy investors with preferences for smaller instruments. These are known as Tranche CDs. Tranche CDs are issued in aggregate amounts of $10 million to $30 million and offered by banks to individual investors in $10,000 certificates with each certificate having the same interest rate, issue date, interest payment dates, and maturity.

Since the late 1970s Eurodollar Floating Rate CDs (FRCDs) and Eurodollar Floating Rate Notes (FRNs) have come into use as means of protecting both borrower and lender against interest rate risk. These "floaters" shift the burden of risk from the principal value of the paper to its coupon.

Eurodollar FRCDs and FRNs are both negotiable bearer paper. The coupon or interest rate on these instruments is reset periodically, typically every three or six months, at a small spread above the corresponding LIBOR. Depending on maturity, Eurodollar FRCD yields range from 1/8 percent under the London Interbank Bid Rate (LIBID) up to LIBOR.[15] Eurodollar FRN yields also range from 1/8 percent under LIBID up to LIBOR. To determine LIBOR for Eurodollar FRNs, "the issuer chooses an agent bank who in turn polls three or four Reference Banks—generally, the London offices of major international banks. Rates are those prevailing at 11:00 a.m. London time two business days prior to the commencement of the next coupon period."[16]

Eurodollar FRCDs have been issued in maturities from 1-1/2 to 5 years and are employed as an alternative to short-term money market instruments. Eurodol-

---

[12] Bank of England, Financial Statistics Division, International Banking Group. This data only includes London dollar CDs. But until then, virtually all Eurodollar CDs were issued in London. See *The Economist* [1980, p. 89].

[13] This spread was calculated from data in Salomon Brothers [1986].

[14] Data on interest rate spreads in the Eurodollar market were provided by Robert Smith, First Boston Corporation.

[15] The interbank bid rate is normally 1/8 percent below the interbank offer rate.

[16] Salomon Brothers [1980, p. 7].

lar FRNs have been issued in maturities from 4 to 20 years, with the majority of issues concentrated in the 5- to 7-year range. Eurodollar FRNs tend to be seen as an alternative to straight fixed-interest bonds, but they can in principle be used like FRCDs. Eurodollar FRNs have been issued primarily, but not exclusively, by banks.

A secondary market exists in Eurodollar FRCDs and FRNs. Secondary market makers' spreads for FRCDs are around 5 basis points. The spread quoted on FRNs in the secondary market is generally 10 basis points.

Since 1984, Note Issuance Facilities (NIFs) have become a significant Eurodollar instrument.[17] NIFs are medium-term arrangements between a borrower and a bank, usually 5 to 7 years, under which a borrower can issue short-term paper, usually 3 to 6 months maturity, in its own name. Under this arrangement, underwriting banks are committed either to purchase any notes, known as Euro-notes, which the borrower cannot sell or to provide standby credit at a predetermined spread relative to some reference rate such as LIBOR. Underwriting fees are paid on the full amount of the line of credit, regardless of the amount currently drawn. The fee is 5 basis points for top borrowers and ranges up to 15 basis points for worse credit risks. The notes are generally denominated in United States dollars, with large face amounts of $100,000, $500,000, or more.

Well-regarded borrowers can issue Euro-notes at around LIBID. Top borrowers can issue at yields 1/16 or 1/8 percentage point below LIBID. The latter are comparable investments to Eurodollars CDs.

In 1985, nonbank corporate borrowers accounted for roughly 60 percent of NIFs arranged. Most borrowers were from countries in the Organization of Economic Cooperation and Development. As of April 1986, about $75 billion of NIFs had been arranged, with only an estimated $10 billion to $15 billion having been drawn. Most paper is placed with smaller, non-underwriter, banks. In 1985, about one third or more of placements may have been with nonbank investors, including money market funds, corporations, insurance companies, wealthy individuals, and central banks.

Since mid-1984, some NIFs have been arranged partly or entirely without underwriting commitments. Non-underwritten agreements represented half the total of NIFs arranged in the second half of 1985. Since the middle of 1985, NIFs have become more like United States commercial paper programs. The issuance of notes has been separated from the standby arrangement, notes are issued in shorter odd maturities, and the notes can be marketed quickly. Under this arrangement, the bank is simply a marketing agent. Euro-notes issued under

---

[17] Material on NIFs was taken from Bank for International Settlements [1986, Chapter 1].

such conditions are known as Euro-commercial paper. As of April 1986 about $17 billion of Euro-commercial paper had been issued.

For most United States corporations, the United States commercial paper market probably remains a cheaper source of funds than Euro-commercial paper. Most United States corporate NIFs are maintained for supplementary purposes at present. For some non-United States corporations, however, Euro-commercial paper may be as cheap as U.S commercial paper because of the premium that foreign issuers pay in the United States commercial paper market. The secondary market for Euro-commercial paper is relatively undeveloped compared to the United States commercial paper market. Trading is particularly thin and concentrated in the first few days after notes are issued. The overwhelming majority of notes are apparently held to maturity.

INTEREST RATE RELATIONSHIPS BETWEEN EURODOLLAR DEPOSITS AND DEPOSITS AT BANKS IN THE UNITED STATES

Arbitrage keeps interest rates closely aligned between Eurodollar deposits and deposits with roughly comparable characteristics at banks located in the United States. This is illustrated in Charts 1 and 2. Chart 1 compares yields on Federal funds and overnight Eurodollar deposits. Chart 2 compares yields on Eurodollar CDs and CDs issued by banks located in the United States.[18]

THE RELATIVE RISKINESS OF EURODOLLAR DEPOSITS AND DOLLAR DEPOSITS HELD IN THE UNITED STATES[19]

There are three basic sources of risk associated with holding Eurodollars. The first concerns the chance that authorities where a Eurodollar deposit is held may interfere in the movement or repatriation of interest or principal of the deposit. But this risk factor does not necessarily imply that Eurodollar deposits are riskier than dollar deposits held in the United States. Rather, it can depend on the deposit holder's residence. For United States residents, Eurodollars may appear riskier than domestic deposits because of the possibility that authorities in the foreign country where the deposit is located may interfere in the movement or repatriation of the interest or principal of the deposit. Foreign residents, Iranians for example, may feel that the United States Government is more likely to block their deposits than the British Government. Consequently, they may perceive

---

[18] See Kreicher [1982] for a detailed discussion of Eurodollar arbitrage.

[19] See Dufey and Giddy [1978, pp. 187-90] and Tyson [1980] for more discussion of the riskiness of Eurodollars.

Chart 1

**YIELDS ON FEDERAL FUNDS
AND OVERNIGHT EURODOLLAR DEPOSITS**

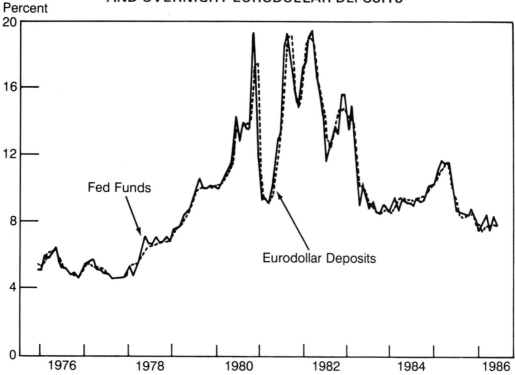

Source: Morgan Guaranty Trust Company of New York, *World Financial Markets.*

greater risk from potential government interference by holding dollar deposits in the United States than by holding Eurodollar deposits in London.

A second element of risk associated with Eurodollars concerns the potential for international jurisdictional legal disputes. For example, uncertainty surrounding interaction between United States and foreign legal systems compounds the difficulty in assessing the likelihood and timing of Eurodollar deposit payment in the event of a Eurodollar issuing bank's failure.

A third type of risk associated with holding Eurodollars concerns the relative soundness per se of foreign banks compared to banks located in the United States. Specifically, it has been argued that Eurodollars are riskier than deposits held in the United States because deposits held in the United States generally carry deposit insurance of some kind while Eurodollar deposits generally do not. In addition, it has been argued that in event of a financial crisis banks located in

Chart 2

YIELDS ON UNITED STATES AND EURODOLLAR
THREE-MONTH CERTIFICATES OF DEPOSIT
(At or Near the First of the Month)

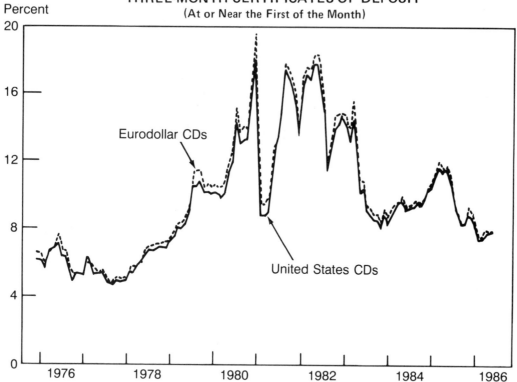

Source: Salomon Brothers, *An Analytical Record of Yields and Yield Spreads.*

the United States are more likely to be supported by the Federal Reserve System, whereas neither Federal Reserve support nor the support of foreign central banks for Eurodollar banking activities in their jurisdictions is certain.

A related factor compounding the three basic risk factors identified above is the greater cost of evaluating foreign investments compared with domestic investments. Acquiring information on the soundness of foreign banks is generally more costly than assessing the soundness of more well-known domestic banks. This means that for a given level of expenditure on research, investors must generally accept more ignorance about the soundness of a foreign bank than a domestic bank.

Two comments on this argument are relevant here. First, the fact that it is more costly to evaluate foreign than domestic investments does not imply that Eurodollar deposits are inherently riskier than deposits held in the United States.

If a depositor resides in the United States, the argument implies that a given expenditure on research will generally yield more information about the safety of deposits located in the United States than in the Eurodollar market. But if the depositor resides outside the United States, the reverse may be true. Having said this, it must be pointed out that the amount of financial disclosure required by regulatory authorities abroad is generally not as great as in the United States. This fact may make it more difficult to evaluate the soundness of non-United States banks than United States banks for any depositor, regardless of his residence.

Second, to a large extent assessing the safety of Eurodollar deposits relative to deposits in banks located in the United States is made easier by the fact that many banks in the Eurodollar market are affiliated with and bear the name of a bank whose home office is in the United States. For example, a London branch of a United States bank is as closely associated with its home office as a branch located in the United States.

However, in many cases foreign offices bearing the name of a United States bank, usually in a slightly altered form, have been set up as subsidiaries rather than branches. Under most legal systems, a branch cannot fail unless its head office fails; but a subsidiary can fail even if its parent institution remains in business. Technically, a foreign office can bear the name of a United States bank in some form, but the parent institution may not be legally bound to stand fully behind the obligations of its foreign office. This suggests that a foreign office named after a parent United States bank may not be as sound as its namesake, although the parent bank unquestionably has great incentive to aid the foreign office in meeting its obligations in order to preserve confidence in the bank's name.[20]

On the whole, it is difficult to assess the relative riskiness of Eurodollar deposits and dollar deposits held in the United States. Some factors affecting relative risk can be identified, but their importance is difficult to measure. What is more, perceived relative riskiness can depend on the residence of the depositor. The extent to which risk-related factors affect the interest rate relationship between Eurodollar deposits and comparable deposits at banks in the United States remains unclear.

SUMMARY

From the depositor's point of view, Eurodollar deposits including those at United States IBFs are relatively close substitutes for dollar deposits at non-IBF

---

[20] See Mendelsohn [1984] and Stoakes [1985] for discussion of a case where a large United States bank refused to make good deposits of its Philippine branch after they were frozen by Philippine exchange controls. Also see Dufey and Giddy [1984] on this issue.

banks located in the United States. Eurodollar deposits are attractive because they are free of reserve requirements and most other regulatory burdens imposed by United States authorities. In fact, the tremendous growth of the Eurodollar market in the last two decades has largely resulted from efforts to move dollar financial intermediation outside the regulatory jurisdiction of the United States.

Host countries have competed eagerly for Eurodollar business by promising relatively few regulations, low taxes, and other incentives to attract a portion of the Eurodollar banking industry. Even the United States, by introducing IBFs in 1981, has begun competing for Eurodollar business. Financial intermediation in United States dollars is likely to continue to move abroad or to IBFs as long as incentives exist for it to do so. Since these incentives are not likely to disappear soon, the Eurodollar market's share of world dollar financial intermediation is likely to continue growing.

References

Ashby, David F. V. "Challenge from the New Euro-Centres." *The Banker*, January 1978, pp. 53-61.

"Changing Patterns in the $800 Billion Super-Dollar Market." *The Banker*, March 1979, pp. 21-23.

Bank of England, Personal correspondence, Financial Statistics Division, International Banking Group, April 28, 1980.

Bank for International Settlements. *1964 Annual Report*. Basle, Switzerland.

Bank for International Settlements. *Recent Innovations in International Banking*. Basle, Switzerland, April 1986.

Board of Governors of the Federal Reserve System. *Federal Reserve Bulletin* (February 1980).

————. H.6 statistical release, "Money Stock Measures and Liquid Assets." September 11, 1986.

Credit Suisse First Boston Limited. "A Description of the London Dollar Negotiable Certificate of Deposit Market." January 1980.

Dobbs-Higginson, M.S. *Investment Manual for Fixed Income Securities in the International and Major Domestic Capital Markets*. London: Credit Suisse First Boston Limited, 1980.

Dufey, Gunter and Ian H. Giddy. "Eurocurrency Deposit Risk." *Journal of Banking and Finance* 8 (December 1984), pp. 567-89.

————. *The International Money Market*. Englewood Cliffs, New Jersey: Prentice-Hall, 1978.

Key, Sydney J. "International Banking Facilities." *Federal Reserve Bulletin* (October 1982), pp. 565-77.

Kreicher, Lawrence. "Eurodollar Arbitrage." Federal Reserve Bank of New York, *Quarterly Review* (Summer 1982), pp. 10-21.

Lichtenstein, Cynthia C. "United States Banks and the Eurocurrency Markets: The Regulatory Structure." *The Banking Law Journal* 99 (June/July 1982), pp. 484-511.

"The London Dollar Certificate of Deposit." *Bank of England Quarterly Bulletin* 13 (December 1973), pp. 446-52.

Mayer, Helmut W. "The BIS Concept of the Eurocurrency Market." *Euromoney*, May 1976, pp. 60-66.

Mendelsohn, M.S. "Wells Suit Revives Jurisdiction Issue." *American Banker*, March 2, 1984, p. 18+.

Morgan Guaranty Trust Company of New York. *World Financial Markets.* Various issues.

"Out-of-Towners." *The Economist*, July 12, 1980, p. 89.

Salomon Brothers. *An Analytical Record of Yields and Yield Spreads.* New York: Salomon Brothers, 1986.

————. *Eurodollar Floating Rate Notes: A Guide to the Market.* New York: Salomon Brothers, 1980.

Stigum, Marcia. *The Money Market: Myth, Reality, and Practice.* Homewood, Illinois: Dow Jones-Irwin, 1983.

Stoakes, Christopher. "Eurodollar Deposits on Trial." *Euromoney*, August 1985, p. 25.

Terrell, Henry S., and Rodney H. Mills. "International Banking Facilities and the Eurodollar Market." Staff Study 124. Washington: Board of Governors of the Federal Reserve System, August 1983.

Tyson, David O. "Fund Managers Wary of Risks in Non-Domestic CDs." *The Money Manager*, July 14, 1980, pp. 3-4.

Article Thirty-Five

COUNTRY RISK, PORTFOLIO DECISIONS AND REGULATION IN INTERNATIONAL BANK LENDING*

Ingo WALTER**

New York University, New York, NY 10006, USA

This paper examines the concept of 'country risk' and relates it to the construction of efficient loan portfolios in international banking. Applicability of conventional portfolio-theoretic concepts to the management of country lending exposure is examined, as are the requisites of country review systems for national exposure management. The issue of international banking regulation is assessed in this context, focusing on the dangers inherent in national and international regulatory initiatives for optimum global capital allocation.

1. Introduction

In the growing literature on 'country risk', one finds relatively little discussion of what is, or ought to be, management's ultimate objective — incorporating country-specific risk characteristics into the design of asset portfolios that are in some sense 'efficient'. We shall attempt to develop in this article some of the issues involved in closing this gap, both within the asset management decision process of individual banks and in the context of bank regulation.

Modern portfolio theory suggests that there are two types of risk facing any asset manager — unsystematic (diversifiable) risk, and systematic (non-diversifiable) risk. Using a stock market analogy, unsystematic risk is associated with factors affecting individual asset (share) returns. This kind of risk can be reduced, and even eliminated, by diversifying a portfolio across shares subject to different return movements in the market. Systematic risk, on the other hand, is associated with factors affecting the stock market as a whole; it influences all shares in a portfolio and is therefore non-diversifiable. The relative riskiness of a particular stock can be measured by its 'beta' coefficient, the ratio of its own return volatility to the overall return volatility

*Based on a more extensive paper presented at a conference on 'Internationalization of Financial Markets and National Economic Policy', held at the Graduate School of Business Administration, New York University on 10–11 April 1980. Helpful comments by Kaj Areskoug, Ernest Bloch, Larry Brainard, Peter Gray, Dennis Logue, Noralyn Marshall, Arturo Porzecanski, Richard Stapleton, and Clas Wihlborg are gratefully acknowledged, as is research support during the summer of 1980 by the Deutsche Forschungsgemeinschaft under a grant to the Universität Mannheim (Forschungsbereich 5).

**Visiting Professor of Economics, Universität Mannheim, D-68 Mannheim, Federal Republic of Germany.

of the stock market as a whole. Its value to the investor depends not only on its expected returns, but also on how it would affect the riskiness of the entire portfolio. Such concepts permit a skilled investor to build an 'efficient' stock portfolio which maximizes returns subject to risk, given his own personal risk preferences.

Instead of stocks, banks involved in international lending have 'portfolios' of cross-border exposures in different politically-sovereign states. In a global context, much of this exposure is in the nature of unsystematic 'country' risk and thus is diversifiable, resulting in reduced riskiness of the entire portfolio. Systematic risk, on the other hand, derives from factors affecting a number of countries simultaneously, and is less readily reduced through diversification of country exposures. Change in cross-border exposure in a particular country must be evaluated in terms of both its implications for returns and its impact on the riskiness of the bank's overall asset portfolio. An 'efficient' international loan portfolio of a given risk might then be constructed once management's degree of risk aversion is known, returns on country exposures have been correctly assessed, and an attempt has been made to identify something similar in concept to individual country 'betas'. The risk premium associated with exposures in a particular country will tend to reflect the implicit 'beta' associated with the country in question.

It is easy (and dangerous) to push this analogy too far in any mechanistic attempt to develop the principles underlying 'efficient' portfolios of international bank exposures. There are a number of factors that limit the applicability of conventional portfolio theory in this particular context. For one thing, unlike the case of the stock market, the measurement of risks and returns relating to country exposures is extraordinarily difficult. It is here that the 'science' of portfolio management shades into the 'art' of international banking.

Still, as with any other portfolio management problem, the task facing managers of international banks is to maximize the real, economic value of their assets subject to various types of risks. One of these is linked to the political and economic fortunes of countries in which they have cross-border exposures. Returns on these assets depend on competitive factors facing a bank in the market-place for its services. What needs to be evaluated is the expected value of these returns in the future, together with elements that may influence their variance (reflecting the degree of risk).

We can express this in the form of a conventional present value equation such as the following:

$$PV_j^0 = \sum_{t=0}^{n} \frac{E(F_t)}{(1 + i_t + \alpha_t)^t},$$

where PV_j^0 is the present value of the future stream of returns to the bank related to exposure in a particular country j, $E(F_t)$ denotes the expected value of that future returns stream at time t, i_t is the risk-free discount factor representing the bank's cost of funds, and α_t represents a country risk premium, which depends on the variance of the expected future returns associated with country j relative to β_j (the beta coefficient associated with the institution involved). Prospective future developments in countries in which a bank has cross-border exposures will be reflected in the means as well as the variances of the probability distributions associated with these returns, and hence will influence both $E(F_t)$ and α_t.

2. Expected returns in international lending

If rational portfolio decisions in international lending depend on defensible assessments of risks and returns, it is important to develop first an accurate picture of the expected returns side $E(F_t)$. One important component is, of course, repayment of principal. A second component covers the interest returns which, in the case of floating-rate syndicated loans (comprising perhaps 40–50% of medium and long-term international financings in recent years), usually involves the spread over the three- or six-month London Interbank Offered Rate (LIBOR), or a similar floating base rate of interest. Changes in LIBOR itself tend to show up as shifts in both $E(F_t)$ and i_t, and thus cancel out, although a bank does face some residual interest-rate risk through negotiated spreads, generally fixed for the life of the loan, which may narrow or widen with future market conditions. A recent innovation, 'floating spreads', eliminates this residual risk as well. But principal and interest returns, properly adjusted in a time context for maturities, drawn-down schedules, and the like, represent only a part of the picture.

First, and most obvious in the case of lead managers, co-managers, agents, and others involved in the process of international loan syndication, there is a share of fees agreed upon with the borrower. These may be quite substantial, perhaps well in excess of the incremental costs involved in providing syndication services and — especially since they represent a relatively certain and immediate 'front-end' payment — may add materially to the overall returns of banks engaged in syndicate management. On occasion, borrowers unwilling to incur higher published spreads for prestige or future market-access reasons may inflate front-end fees in order to compensate international lenders.

Second, banks often lend to a particular borrower at terms that might otherwise be considered unattractive in order to develop or maintain a 'relationship'. This involves existing and past ties, and focuses on the expectation of future earnings from a variety of activities that include continued private and public-sector lending activities, foreign exchange transactions, deposit balances, advisory services, custodial business, and the like. There is ample evidence of the importance of the 'relationship' factor in international lending behavior, with regular scrambles by banks to get 'close to' the borrower within syndicates, and in the tendency for losers of syndication mandates to participate anyway in the loans in order to maintain a relationship with the borrower. Similarly, borrowers can sometimes 'encourage' banks to participate in loans that would not otherwise be attractive by suggesting that failure to do so may lead to a loss of collateral business or pressure on their operations in host countries — thereby requiring the addition to apparent returns, in effect, of an insurance premium against possible future earnings losses elsewhere in the relationship. Particularly where the country relationship has been highly profitable in the past, and/or promises to be so in the future, such anticipated 'indirect' returns can be an important part of the total, characterized by their own profile of expected earnings.

Third, a bank's lending to a particular borrower may generate future returns with third parties that might not otherwise materialize. A major syndication may create opportunities for future trade financing or letter of credit business with home or third-country suppliers, for example. Or a particular loan can cement a relationship with a particular domestic or foreign client ('do-good') in a way that promises additional future earnings. Once again, the ultimate returns from this source to the bank may be quite indirect and their assessment quite speculative.

It is clear, therefore, that return of principal and interest, fees, and the remaining less tangible earnings components form a many-sided, probabilistic picture. Each element has its own time-profile and expected value, so that $E(F_t)$ in our formula is itself a highly complex composite. Each element also has its own measure of variability, so that the associated risk premium α_t is similarly complex. And often there are tradeoffs, as when the terms of loan agreements (legal documentation) are relaxed at the insistence of the borrower, thereby possibly exchanging higher expected returns in some of the aforementioned earnings components for greater risk in others. Partly for such reasons, profit attribution in international banking tends to be extraordinarily difficult, and in most banks is considered quite imperfect. For such reasons as well, the returns facing individual banks that are members of lending syndicates may well differ substantially from one to the other, particularly between banks in the management group and the rest.

3. Value of assets exposed to country risk

What kinds of eventualities associated with conditions in countries where a bank has cross-border exposure would tend to influence the real (economic) value of the exposed assets? First, the borrowing country may ultimately be unwilling or unable to effect debt service in full, the default resulting in realized accounting losses of principal and/or accrued interest which the bank must book against earnings, capital or reserves after recovering what it can through the 'right of offset' or other means. The consequences of default for the borrower's access to international capital markets and normal channels of trade are such that this event tends to be triggered by a unique and relatively rare set of circumstances — consequences that are magnified by cross-default clauses commonly written into international loan agreements.

Second, the borrowing country may be unable to meet its external debt obligations on contractual terms and be forced to stretch-out repayment. By definition, the necessary refinancing or rescheduling under such circumstances cannot be accomplished at market terms and occurs under duress, and so the original lenders are forced to extend further credit in the hope of avoiding accounting losses in the end. This may involve an extension of maturities, a new grace period, negotiation of new facilities, an adjustment in interest spreads, or other modifications. Even if this ultimately results in increased accounting returns, if the lender under free-market conditions would have restructured his portfolio out of the exposed assets in question at any point, but cannot do so because he is locked-in, he has in fact incurred an economic loss. The real value of this particular component of his asset portfolio, in effect, has declined. The difference between *economic* and *accounting* shifts in asset values under such circumstances is not always accepted by bankers, and this may influence their reaction to the causative debt service problems and their portfolio decisions in the future.

Third, the borrowing country may be perfectly able and willing to service its external debt — successfully avoiding both default and problems leading to reschedulings or forced refinancings — yet something happens that raises the riskiness of the exposed assets from the perspective of the foreign lender. Assassination of the head of state, for example, may mean nothing at all from a debt service point of view, or it may mean eventual debt repudiation and default, or any of a number of eventualities in-between. Even though neither of our first two types of losses has been incurred by the lender, he has suffered a decline in the value of his assets insofar as he cannot immediately reallocate them in a manner consistent with his new perception of the constellation or relative risks and returns. Some such reallocation may be possible at the margin by running down exposures beginning with the very short maturities. This process, however, is usually far from the kind of instantaneous adjustment — characteristic of efficient financial markets — that is needed to avoid longer-run downward adjustment in the value of the bank's loan portfolio. Once again, bankers are reluctant to recognize such shifts, and they often ignore them in portfolio valuation and decision-making. Yet international lending to South Korea after the assassination of President Park Chung Hee, Thailand after the Vietnamese invasion of Cambodia, and Eastern Europe after the Soviet invasion of Afghanistan seems to suggest that markets are in fact responsive to shifts in 'risk-classes' of countries. Thus, relative rates of change in (net) new loans in effect become a substitute for market-type portfolio adjustments.

In terms of our formula, a number of events may reduce PV_j^0. Prospective defaults can be viewed as reductions in $E(F_t)$, anticipated rescheduling or refinancing losses as forced introduction of higher-valued t's that are less than compensated for by negotiated increases in $E(F_t)$, and losses from risk-class shifts as increases in α_t. Reschedulings or forced refinancings may additionally have the effect of increasing α_t if, as a result, the country is viewed by the market as being more risky.

4. Diversification and risk

The purpose of 'country risk assessment' is, of course, to get a fix on $E(F_t)$ and α_t — usually (as we have previously argued, mistakenly) focusing exclusively on possible threats to interest and principal. Its application to the construction of international loan portfolios is in part related to the objective of diversification, under the presumption that the α_t values for individual countries are essentially independent. If there is indeed zero correlation among returns on the country exposures in a bank's asset portfolio, it is possible for management through diversification to virtually eliminate variability in returns on international lending. The greater the degree of this correlation, the more difficult it is to do so. Yet even with some correlation in earnings variability, bank managers are in principle free to choose how much unsystematic risk to incorporate into their portfolios through the extent of diversification and the kinds of exposures incurred. Our discussion of risk and returns indicates how difficult it is to apply conventional financial theory to international bank lending. Neither the risks associated with individual country exposures nor the returns are easy to measure or identify, nor are the conventional efficient market assumptions satisfied, although movement toward 'efficient' loan portfolios is at least conceptually possible. There are, moreover, some additional problems as well.

For one thing, risk-aversion and hence portfolio preference may be quite different as viewed by (a) an undiversified bank owner or manager, (b) a diversified stock market investor, and (c) the regulatory authorities. The first of these is well served by conventional measures of the dispersion of expected portfolio returns. The second would also have to worry about the covariance of returns on the bank's international portfolio with returns on other assets in his own portfolio — indeed, some of the affected shareholders might possibly reside outside of the bank's country of domicile. The difference between the two perspectives could be attributed to gaps in management's information about (or response to) the market's valuation of the bank's equities. The regulatory authorities, for their part, would tend to focus on the 'bankruptcy tail' associated with different asset portfolios, given the limits of their own liability. When a bank adds a particular loan to its portfolio, therefore, its impact on the riskiness of that portfolio will depend on which of these three specific perspectives is being applied. We shall return to this point later.

A second problem, already mentioned in our earlier discussion, is that international banks are to a significant extent unable to 'buy' and 'sell' assets exposed to country risk. This important option, as envisaged in conventional portfolio theory, is limited to short-term exposure, which can be 'run down' in a relatively short period of time and the assets deployed elsewhere. But the 'term exposure' that makes up a good deal of total international lending is basically locked-in for the duration, with management unable to react through portfolio adjustment to changes in the variance of expected returns. As a result, the lender is not independent of the factors that generate the ultimate returns, as might be the case if a secondary market existed for such assets.

A third problem is that the principal and interest component of $E(F_t)$ in international loan portfolios, unlike stock or bond portfolios, may be subject to asymmetrical variance. That is, the variance of these returns may be entirely on the down-side. In conventional stock or bond portfolios, the investor can win or lose with changes in prices and interest rates. In international loan portfolios, assuming the borrower bears the interest-rate risk as in LIBOR-based loans, prospects of the bank for up-side variance in returns do not exist. As in the case of mortgage and other types of lending subject to asymmetrical variance, such truncated returns distributions tend to induce among bankers a reluctance to recognize changes in the value of their assets until losses are essentially certain. It encourages lenders to take extra care in the assessment of the down-side risks involved, design of loan documentation, assembly of syndicates, and management of 'problem' situations. It may also give added bargaining leverage to 'problem' borrowers in dealing with the international banks, which can itself ultimately accentuate the downside variance of returns. The idea of asymmetrical variance, however, has to be modified if we go beyond the interest and principal components of $E(F_t)$ to take a broader view of expected returns, the prospects for which can improve significantly with a more favorable country outlook.

A fourth problem is that changes in country exposure may be 'lumpy' in the case of banks faced with large loans representing discrete jumps in cross-border exposure, so that portfolios may be difficult to adjust at the margin. And the fact that American and certain other banks are subject to capital-based or similar lending constraints may give rise to additional limits on building efficient portfolios.

Despite such difficulties, some of the basic lessons of portfolio theory can be applied. One of these is the effects of the ability of banks to diversify· and its impact on the value of their overall international loan portfolios. In one sense, the whole purpose of country risk assessment is to ascertain the covariance of expected returns on a portfolio of loans *within* a particular country. But individual country exposures in a bank's global loan portfolio may also have *in common* certain sources of risk, and this moves us closer to an application of the concept of 'systematic' risk, or limits to the value of diversification in international lending.

One source of non-diversifiable risk relates to conditions in the Euromarkets as a whole. Countries requiring rollover financing may face difficulties under tight market conditions. Similarly, since the interest cost of much of the external debt of countries to international banks is linked to LIBOR, tighter international credit conditions may raise the borrowers' respective debt service (balance of payments) burdens, and thereby increase the risk associated with exposed assets in a number of countries at once. Moreover, the Euromarkets tend to be highly sensitive to the fortunes of individual countries, and serious problems in the case of one borrower may impede the ability of others to secure access to credit.

Other sources of possible covariance in returns on country exposures include conditions facing them in major export markets. This is quite clear in the case of commodity markets, where cyclical price weakness can seriously affect the terms and balances of trade of a number of countries at once — e.g., sugar, coffee, copper, and rubber. It also holds for manufactured exports, where a variety of countries may be adversely affected simultaneously by recessions and declines in import demand in principal markets, and by protectionist pressures affecting particular industry segments. Similarly, on the import side a large number of countries are clearly affected by changes in petroleum supplies and costs, and perhaps somewhat narrower analogies may be drawn for other categories of imports (food, raw materials) as well. Such risks are not totally non-diversifiable, however, since care can be taken in constructing international loan portfolios to incorporate such covariances in banks' exposure decisions.

Finally, there is the matter of the geographic distribution of country exposures. Countries in a particular region, such as Southeast Asia, may be subject to common economic or political threats. Portfolio diversification can still be achieved within such constraints. But the degree of difficulty increases when the commonalities become more prevalent, as in the case of geopolitical shocks, perceived 'domino' effects, and the like.

5. Lending decisions and approaches to country risk assessment

Despite the difficulties in measuring risks and returns, in recognizing and reacting to changes in values of country exposure in international loan portfolios, and in developing and implementing approaches to effective diversification, there is little doubt that the core lessons of portfolio theory are of substantial value in international banking. Yet exposure limits in international bank lending often seem to be set in the absence of such an overriding philosophy, and on the implicit assumption that there is zero correlation among countries, or between country conditions and the various other sources of risk we have identified. The reason may have something to do with the difficulties encountered in the country risk assessment process itself and a natural tendency to focus intensively on country-by-country analysis. A great deal has been written about this problem, and it is not necessary to review that literature once again here. The problem essentially breaks down to a matter of forecasting expected returns $E(F_t)$ and the specific sources of risk that load into our α_t variable, risk that arises out of structural (supply-side) elements, demand-side and monetary elements, external economic and political developments, as well as the quality of the national economic management and the domestic political constraints bearing upon decision-makers.

In the absence of an efficient market whose data can be analyzed, the delivery of effective country risk assessment ideally requires the employment of a true 'renaissance person' — exceedingly intelligent, a holder of doctorates from respectable institutions in economics, political science, sociology, psychology and perhaps a few other fields as well, totally objective, with a great deal of common sense. In addition to being rather well-traveled, he or she is up-to-date on developments in all countries of interest to the bank (and in other countries that might affect them), and personally acquainted with key policymakers. Obviously, there are few such individuals wandering around these days. And so the question is whether international banks, *as institutions*, can in some way put together all of these qualities, using relatively 'ordinary' individuals and traditional organizational linkages to assemble a superior ability to forecast the future of countries, its bearing on the real value of exposed assets, and its implications for portfolio management. Low quality estimates of $E(F_t)$ and α_t yield low quality portfolio decisions and, ultimately, second-rate performance of the bank in the competitive marketplace.

In the design of a country analysis function aiming at high-quality $E(F_t)$ and α_t estimates for use in portfolio decisions, the emphasis clearly must be on the fact that it is the beginning, not the end, of the task. Approaches that try to be overly precise risk triggering arguments among users over irrelevant points. Those that are too general may fail to concentrate on the true sources of risk in country exposure, and on the specific concerns facing a particular bank. Risk to medium- and long-term exposure requires a far more complex analysis than risk in short-term lending, yet one that is still much simpler than risk to any foreign direct investment exposure that a bank may have in a particular country.

The twin temptations of 'quick and dirty' and 'overloaded' country risk assessments constantly seem to confront international banks. The first approach promises mechanical short-cuts and the use of low-priced talent to grind out results at reasonable cost, but often appears to succeed only in producing nonsense — there really is no substitute for high-quality analysis, flexibility, judgement, and familiarity. The second approach may rely on well qualified internal personnel at high cost, yet encounter a dangerous narrowing of country expertise, possibly cause dissention, and create bottlenecks in the decision-making process.

The conflicting demands of country assessment — ranging from high levels of usability, auditability and comparability, and the need to capture exceedingly complex and country-specific qualitative judgments over extended periods of time, to the need to avoid abuse of the results in decision-making — probably means that there is no such thing as an 'ideal' system.

'Appropriate' systems will certainly differ for different banks. The key may reside as much on the 'human resources' side as on the 'technology' side. To train line bankers in using reasonably unsophisticated yet sensible country assessments properly, and in being sensitive to changing country risk profiles and sources of covariance as they go about their business, may in the end contribute more to sound portfolio decisions than comparable resources devoted to the design and implementation of more elegant systems. This would appear to follow from the view of multinational banks' general competitive advantage as 'information factories', to which their global operations and headquarters-affiliate links are ideally suited. Whether in systems-design or in the training function, resources devoted to the assessment of country risk clearly are subject to constraints, and there is some implicit optimum where the incremental costs in country assessment begin to outweigh the economic losses implicit in inefficient international loan portfolios.

To get the best possible fix on the critical $E(F_t)$ and α_t variables that have been the core of our discussion, the exercise of country risk assessment should be an integrated managerial process that focuses the network of information and actively involves individuals with different functions and perspectives. The exercise will thus have intangible portfolio benefits all its own, quite apart from its more visible output in the form of defensible country-by-country evaluations. Mechanization and decentralization of the country review process will tend to cut down and perhaps eliminate this benefit, and may thereby help to stifle an environment conducive to sound portfolio decisions.

Each bank's institutional information-flow and decision-making setup has its own profile, depending on such factors as the organization's size and structure. Some banks incorporate country assessments into portfolio decisions quite flexibly and informally, while others seem to rely on rigid and formalized review procedures. In some cases the review process is closely tied as well to the annual budget cycle and the allocation of lending authority to countries and regions. These again may be quite rigid in some banks, while in others they are relatively easily altered as perceived market and risk conditions change. In some banks, the determination of 'loan loss provisions' is an integral part of the process, and affects the anticipated net profitability of loans by adjusting for risk and presumably permits improved performance evaluation within the bank's organizational framework.

While few international banks fail to maintain adequate cross-border exposure measurement, allocation, and monitoring, there seems to be far greater variability in the state of the country assessment systems themselves. Some are carefully thought through, while others are largely cosmetic or pseudo-scientific. Some are well integrated into the life of the organization, while others seem separate and even isolated. Until fairly recently, smaller U.S. banks, particularly when participating in loan syndications, tended to rely on the country evaluations of the larger money center banks. Besides being unsatisfactory from a regulatory point of view (see below), we have already noted that the appropriate risk-return calculus of lead banks is not necessarily the same as that of the smaller banks. Banks in Europe and Japan so far do not appear to have placed a great deal of emphasis on the design of formal approaches to country assessment or to incorporate them into international lending decisions, preferring instead to rely much more informally on the collective experience and wisdom of senior bank officers.

Whatever the approach, rational portfolio decisions demand that forecasts of country futures be maintained on a comparable basis — and modified in the light of covariances arising out of common export markets or sources of supply, conditions in and access to international financial markets, and regional as well as global political developments. It should also be clear that, in assessing the impact of a particular change in country exposure on the value of a bank's asset portfolio as a whole, it is not only the specific country-related variance of returns that is of importance, but also the intercountry covariance of returns, and this can easily be masked by an exclusive focus on country-specific sources of risk. And so it is possible to envision the application of the portfolio context we have developed — with risk aversion dictated by top management, correctly attributed returns estimated by line bankers, carefully defined risks to these returns estimated by formal or informal approaches to country evaluation, and covariances therein brought into the picture in the setting of exposure limits and term sublimits.

6. Regulatory influence on portfolio decisions

With the growth in international lending during the 1970s came increasing concern on the part of those responsible for bank regulation and supervision that sound banking practice be maintained, including adequate information on exposure, country risk assessment, loan diversification and pricing. In terms of our earlier discussion, the regulatory function focuses exclusively on the expected value of interest and principal recovery and its variance — usually with reference to potential impairment of capital — without regard to the other types of returns relevant to bank portfolio decisions. One might therefore envision a scenario whereby influence of regulators on bank lending decisions could well move them *away from* efficient international loan portfolios, particularly since different banks have different sets of returns, access to information, perceptions of risk, and risk preferences. In the process, certain borrowers could be closed out of international credit markets who would otherwise have continued access. Is this a danger?

For American banks, losses in international lending have consistently been below domestic losses. Yet in the late 1970s, a borrower's market characterized by declining, compressed averaged spreads and lengthening average maturities 'has caused concern among bankers about an erosion of documentation and lending standards. Some borrowers will no longer provide financial accounts that were standard loan documentation a couple of years ago.... Borrowers are demanding less stringent conditions in their loans' legal documentation, including less use of cross-default clauses'.[1] Such implicit concerns about the α_t values in the equation we have been using were instrumental in moving U.S. bank regulators toward a uniform system of segregating country risks from other lending risks, and dealing with them separately in their examination reports. The emphasis has been on diversification of country exposure within a bank's international loan portfolio based on capital ratios, and on an assessment of the bank's own country risk analysis and monitoring capabilities. This new supervisory aspect necessitated agreement in November 1978 on a uniform country risk screening procedure by the U.S. regulatory authorities themselves, undertaken in the form of a joint effort by the Federal Reserve System, the Comptroller of the Currency, and the Federal Deposit Insurance Corporation for use by bank examiners.

In current practice, a nine-member committee of international bank examiners representing the three supervisory authorities meets several times each year to reach a consensus on the riskiness of exposure in selected countries based on a set of 'briefing notes' generated by Federal Reserve economists. These, together with oral supplements, form the basis of 'comments' and of the examiners' discussions with senior bank management. Although the purpose is explicitly *not* to preclude certain countries from additional U.S. bank lending, or to suggest 'superior' international loan portfolios, one would suspect that the inherent 'second guessing' function of the examination process is bound to have an affect on international lending decisions by influencing our α_t variable. There is the undeniable advantage of forcing the less well-managed banks to conduct independent country risk monitoring in order to justify individual exposure positions, and to pay careful attention to risks and returns in international lending. But beyond this, aversion of banks to having particular country exposures subject to 'listing' or 'comment' in examination reports may well drive them away from optimum loan portfolios that still meet acceptable standards of risk from a public-policy point of view by influencing relative risk premiums used in making portfolio decisions. This could involve implicit imposition of the supervisory authorities' own views of risk and diversification on the banks. Whether this consideration — together with possible flaws in the supervisory application of country analyses by bank examiners — leads to significant distortions in the international allocation of credit remains to be seen.

So far, the United States is alone in making country risk assessment an integral part of the bank examination process. Most other countries make no distinction among international lending risks pertaining to different countries, and rely almost entirely on uniform capital-asset ratios. Nor is supervisory pressure on banks to develop defensible, independent country risk

[1] *IMF Survey*, 3 September 1979, p. 277.

assessment and monitoring systems very much in evidence outside the U.S. On the other hand, there may be a good deal of moral suasion present in the informal discussions between banks and their supervisory authorities that is an important part of the regulatory process in a number of countries. Clearly, international differences in the supervisory function, as it embodies elements of country risk, have the potential of influencing both the flow of international credit and competitive relationships in international banking.

The best recent example occurred in October 1979, when the Japanese Ministry of Finance clamped an embargo on further overseas foreign-currency lending by Japanese banks, exempting only export credits and loans for energy imports. The authorities apparently feared the vulnerability of the banks, 80% funded in the interbank market, to a repetition of the 1974 Euromarket credit squeeze. A return of the Japanese banks to the market in June 1980 was accompanied by ceilings on Euroloans, American-type lending limits, and far sharper surveillance even to the point, apparently, of imposing Ministry of Finance judgments on loan size and borrower qualifications.

There is also some movement to achieve a greater degree of international regulatory uniformity with respect to country exposure. The supervisory authorities in the United States have pushed hard to expand and refine data on cross-border exposure of American banks, and to some extent this has been paralleled by similar improvements elsewhere, including international efforts to compile and publish the relevant data. For instance, the Bank for International Settlements has assembled a great deal of information on country debt and provides guidance for national supervisory authorities on how to interpret it. The emerging consensus seems to be that authorities should apply bank supervision on a consolidated balance sheet basis, as is done in the U.S. The view is taking hold that, even though foreign subsidiaries are legally independent entities, in case of debt service problems the liabilities would nevertheless fall due to the parent bank. Both Switzerland and the United Kingdom have moved in this direction. The idea of minimum capital-asset ratios is also catching on. There is, however, no consensus on formal, systematic guidelines for diversification of loan port-folios exposed to country risk.

Besides the supervisory role at the national level, there is the possibility that country evaluations on the part of international organizations may influence the management of loan portfolios by private banks. Among the international institutions concerned with this issue are the BIS Cooke Committee of national bank supervisors, the Berne Union focusing on government export credit guarantees, and the so-called Paris Club involved in rescheduling official debt of countries in trouble. All are concerned in one way or another with assessment of country risk. While no direct links yet exist, attitudes emerging in such forums have the potential of influencing bank regulators at the national level and, through them, bank portfolio decisions.

Of possibly greater importance is the International Monetary Fund, and to a lesser extent the World Bank, which maintain detailed country evaluations used in their respective decisions on balance of payments and project financing. While these assessments are nominally confidential, important elements are available to member governments and there is the possibility that IMF opinion will gradually add a certain degree of uniformity to bank lending decisions via its links to national regulators. A strong argument can of course be made for the widest possible dissemination of data collected and analyzed by international institutions. But this hardly justifies, on either competence or portfolio grounds, undue influence of IMF staff assessments of country risk on the private banks' international lending decisions.

At the same time, in actual or potential problem situations there is great value in coordinated lending by the IMF and the banks — assuming reasonably thoughtful application of IMF conditionality. If the problems are serious enough, the banks are naturally more than anxious to have a country approach the IMF, and have been known to await the outcome of such negotiations before committing themselves to further financing. Indeed, additional bank loans may be dependent on successful discussions with the IMF, and drawdowns under such facilities carefully tied to the borrower's observance of conditions attached to parellel drawings on its IMF standby facility. In this way, added weight can be given to the IMF's influence in pressing for effective adjustment and economic discipline in deficit countries, while the implicit value of the banks' exposed assets is supported. Such parallelism, however, has so far appeared only in serious problem situations. Its extension to ordinary country lending situations could superimpose IMF country assessments upon the private banks, distorting loan portfolios by influencing risk perceptions and affecting the direction and volume of international bank lending.

7. Conclusions

Whereas assessment of country risk is itself an exceedingly difficult task, building country evaluations into the design of international loan portfolios that are in some sense 'efficient' is even more complicated. Neither the risks nor the returns are clearly definable, and the assumptions underlying conventional financial theory are hardly satisfied. Nevertheless, it is important for banks to realize what they ought to be doing when they make international lending decisions, and when they throw scarce human and financial resources into country risk assessment. Portfolio theory can contribute importantly in clarifying the risks. It also helps to identify the dangers inherent in externally-imposed risk evaluations for rational portfolio decisions, particularly when they emanate from the regulatory system. At the same time, the development of informational and interactive networks within banks as part of the country evaluation process can itself lead to improved international lending decisions that implicitly embody some of the elusive portfolio concepts we have tried to focus on here.

Application of the portfolio concepts we have suggested will also help pin down the link between risk and pricing. Portfolio theory says that the riskiness of any single loan is not what is important, but rather the effect of that loan on the riskiness of the overall bank or shareholder portfolio. So, for example, loans by different banks for similar maturities to a single country might well have quite different pricing, dependent on both the nature of the 'indirect' returns accruing to the lending banks and on the covariances with the total market return.

References

Caldwell, J. Alexander and J. Antonio Villamil, 1979, U.S. lenders are learning to discriminate, Euromoney, May.

Donaldson, T.H., 1979, Lending in international commercial banking (Halsted-Wiley, New York).

Eaton, Jonathan and Mark Gersovitz, 1979, Debt with potential repudiation: Theoretical and empirical analysis, Mimeo. (Princeton University, Princeton, NJ).

Kobrin, Steven J., 1979, Political risk: A review and reconsideration, Journal of International Business Studies, Sept.

Kubarych, Roger M., 1980, Portfolio approaches to managing country risk: The view from the Federal Reserve Bank of New York, Federal Reserve Bank of New York, Mimeo., Jan.

Nagy, Panchras, 1979, Quantifying country risk: A system developed by economists at the bank of Montreal, Columbia Journal of World Business, Jan.

Porzecanski, Arturo C., 1980, The assessment of country risk: Lessons from the Latin American experience, in: J.C. Garcia-Zamor and S. Sutin, eds., Financing development in Latin America (Praeger, New York).

Sargen, Nicholas, 1977, Use of economic indicators and country risk appraisal, Federal Reserve Bank of San Francisco, Economic Review, Fall.

Van Agtmael, Antoine, 1976, Evaluating the risks of lending to developing countries, Euromoney, April.

Volcker, Paul A., 1980, The recycling problem revisited, Federal Reserve Board, Mimeo., March.

Walter, Ingo, 1981, International capital allocation, in: R.G. Hawkins, R.M. Levich and C. Wihlborg, eds., Internationalization of financial markets and national economic policy (JAI Press, Greenwich, CT).

407